T0399671

ENTERPRISE CYBERSECURITY IN DIGITAL BUSINESS

Cyber risk is the highest perceived business risk according to risk managers and corporate insurance experts. Cybersecurity typically is viewed as the boogeyman: it strikes fear into the hearts of non-technical employees. *Enterprise Cybersecurity in Digital Business: Building a Cyber Resilient Organization* provides a clear guide for companies to understand cyber from a business perspective rather than a technical perspective, and to build resilience for their business.

Written by a world-renowned expert in the field, the book is based on three years of research with the Fortune 1000 and cyber insurance industry carriers, reinsurers, and brokers. It acts as a roadmap to understand cybersecurity maturity, set goals to increase resiliency, create new roles to fill business gaps related to cybersecurity, and make cyber inclusive for everyone in the business. It is unique since it provides strategies and learnings that have shown to lower risk and demystify cyber for each person. With a clear structure covering the key areas of the Evolution of Cybersecurity, Cybersecurity Basics, Cybersecurity Tools, Cybersecurity Regulation, Cybersecurity Incident Response, Forensics and Audit, GDPR, Cybersecurity Insurance, Cybersecurity Risk Management, Cybersecurity Risk Management Strategy, and Vendor Risk Management Strategy, the book provides a guide for professionals as well as a key text for students studying this field.

The book is essential reading for CEOs, Chief Information Security Officers, Data Protection Officers, Compliance Managers, and other cyber stakeholders, who are looking to get up to speed with the issues surrounding cybersecurity and how they can respond. It is also a strong textbook for postgraduate and executive education students in cybersecurity as it relates to business.

Ariel Evans is the CEO of Cyber Intelligence 4U and a Senior Cyber Security Expert and an Entrepreneur based in Israel. She also is the Enterprise Cybersecurity Chairperson at Rutgers and Pace Universities.

ENTERPRISE CYBERSECURITY IN DIGITAL BUSINESS

Building a Cyber Resilient Organization

Ariel Evans

LONDON AND NEW YORK

Cover image: © Ariel Evans

First published 2022
by Routledge
4 Park Square, Milton Park, Abingdon, Oxon OX14 4RN

and by Routledge
605 Third Avenue, New York, NY 10158

Routledge is an imprint of the Taylor & Francis Group, an informa business

British Library Cataloguing-in-Publication Data
A catalogue record for this book is available from the British Library

Library of Congress Cataloging-in-Publication Data
A catalog record has been requested for this book

ISBN: 978-0-367-51147-0 (hbk)
ISBN: 978-0-367-51149-4 (pbk)
ISBN: 978-1-003-05261-6 (ebk)

DOI: 10.4324/9781003052616

Typeset in Joanna
by KnowledgeWorks Global Ltd.

CONTENTS

FIGURES

IMAGES

NOTICES

Enterprise Cybersecurity in Digital Business is a new science. Domain knowledge and best practices in this field are constantly evolving. As new information and experience broaden these learnings, changes in investigative methods, or research practices may become necessary.

Practitioners should always rely on their own experience and knowledge in evaluating and using any information, methods, or algorithms described in this handbook. In using the preceding, they should be mindful of their own cybersecurity and the cybersecurity of their business partners, including parties for whom they have a professional responsibility.

To the fullest extent of the law, neither the publisher nor the authors, contributors, or editors, assume any liability for any damage to organizations or individuals as a matter of negligence or otherwise, or from any use of any methods, algorithms, information, or ideas contained in the material herein.

ABSTRACT

Gartner reports that "Executive leaders face a large challenge in staying up to date on all fast-moving risks facing their organization and to ensure risk management activities are appropriate and create value. Risks, especially digital risks, evolve constantly and so do the tools and options for managing risk."[1]

CYBER RISK IS DIGITAL. Cybercriminals steal your **data**, interrupt your **business processes** with denial-of-service or ransomware attacks, and cause your fines and penalty based on the type of data that you process and store in your **systems** and **technologies**. The increase in cybercrime is parallel to the increase in the **digitalization of a company's business assets**, the exponential growth of the internet, regulation, and technology innovation. Current estimates show that 85% of an organization's assets are now in digital form.[2] The average cost of a data breach in the United States today is US$3.86M[3] and the annual cost of cybercrime will top US$8.8T by 2022.[4]

Digital business is creating pressure for organizations to restructure and more formally address privacy, digital trust, and risk in response to regulatory mandates. Recommendations are to invest in people, process, and organizational change to address the expanding role of security into risk, privacy, and digital trust that arise from the digitalization of business. Businesses today more than ever need a firm grasp of cybersecurity from a business perspective to meet these challenges.

Over the past several years, cybersecurity has become a boardroom initiative. The board and senior executives have the fiduciary duty to protect the business assets. However, most boards and executives are mystified by cyber. Recently, Aon announced that cyber events now rank among the top three triggers for director and officers (D&O) derivative actions.[5] This is game-changing information that drives home the need for boards and executives to understand cyber risk and it's impacts on their business as a means to rebut these claims.

Through 2022, 80% of organizations (up from 30% in 2018) will undergo some change in their security organization structure as a direct result of digitalization.[6] Organizations often struggle with the coexistence of separate functions: security, privacy, compliance, and risk management. New positions are needed to address the different skillsets for risk and security with a focus on integrating cyber risk management into the organization from a business perspective. Cyber risk is an evolving science that is merging into the enterprise security and risk management functions. It requires an education in digital asset risk quantification and scoring. A digital risk officer role will be needed that addresses operational, legal, privacy, security, compliance, and other cyber risk domain knowledge to manage the firm's overall cyber risk.[7]

Consolidating the scope of cyber risk with enterprise risk will allow for a number of security, privacy, and risk processes to be integrated and more easily managed. Processes that prioritize incident response, threat management, security assessments, vulnerability management, risk assessments, and budgeting can be unified across functional domains, eliminating redundancies, and bridging the domain knowledge differences.

Cyber risk is a complex topic that has been misunderstood and mislabeled as vulnerabilities, incidents, and threats by various vendors in the cybersecurity market. Digital asset cyber risk is financially quantifiable. Financial exposures allow an organization to understand how to prioritize the protection of the business from data loss, business interruption and regulatory fines, pinpoint hidden exposures, and ensure the adequate amount of cyber insurance is in place to transfer risk.

Cyber risk can be scored based on the digital asset characteristics and usage in terms of impact and likelihood metrics which identify areas that can be tightened up to reduce the risk inherent cyber risk. Security assessments can be used to measure the effectiveness of mitigating controls. These mitigating cyber risk scores can identify the gaps in the organization's cybersecurity controls and prioritize scarce resources, determine budget needs, and be used to measure increase cyber resiliency.

We will examine a variety of cybersecurity, privacy, compliance, and cyber risk variables and explain their unique characteristics, how they are used, how to bridge the gap between the organizational roles, processes, and technologies that will be required to optimize cyber resilience. Cyber risk is part of a larger picture of enterprise integrated risk management; however, it must be understood in its true context. We will examine these factors, actors, technologies, programs, and cyber risk strategies from a digital asset perspective that lead to increased cybersecurity maturity and to optimal cyber resilience.

In this book, we provide a topology for an integrated security, privacy, compliance, and cyber risk management strategy that aligns to the organizational maturity and awareness that exists within the company, a maturity mapping methodology that aligns to a summary of roles and responsibilities and use cases to roadmap an organization's journey to increase cyber resilience. Case studies will be presented that coincide with the use cases presented. We will delve into cyber insurance uses cases for limits adequacy using the digital asset methodology which aligns exactly to how a cyber insurance claim would be paid. We will explore how this evolving science is now ready for mainstream companies to implement and take advantage of.

Integrated cyber risk management is a strategic imperative. The future of effective cybersecurity, privacy, compliance, and risk programs must be measured using a digital asset approach to provide meaningful metrics to Boards, Directors and Officers, CISOs, DPOs, Compliance Managers, Auditors, Vendor, and Regulators to benchmark progress and roadmap strategies that lead to optimal cyber resilience. This approach will not only prioritize the mitigation of cyber risks but transform the risks into opportunities for better competitive positions, better products, better processes, better services, better culture, and from the merger and acquisitions (M&A) perspective.

Enterprise Cybersecurity in Digital Business—How to Build a Cyber Resilient Organization Across Risk, Privacy, and Security will provide transparency into metrics for all cyber stakeholders including:

Integrated cyber risk

- Identification of the most valuable digital assets
- Utilization of a crown jewel asset strategy
- Quantifying how much financial exposure the organization has related to a data breach, ransomware, business interruption, and regulatory loss
- How to discover hidden exposures in the billions
- Quantifying privacy exposures, cloud exposures, IoT exposures
- The relationship between inherent cyber risk, security assessments, and residual cyber risk and the use of AI to reduce cyber risk in the near future
- The use of cyber risk thresholds based on digital asset classifications
- How to measure the effectiveness of the cyber program
- How to find gaps in the cyber program controls
- Best practices to prioritize cyber, privacy, compliance, and risk initiatives
- How to measure cyber maturity and cyber resiliency
- Cost-based business unit cyber budgeting for cyber, risk, privacy, and compliance programs
- Resource prioritization based on cyber risk reduction

Cyber risk transference

- Quantifying the adequate amount of the cyber insurance aggregate limit
- Quantifying the adequate amounts of sublimits for ransomware, business interruption, and regulatory loss for both dependent and nondependent use cases
- Defining an effective ransomware strategy

Vendor cyber risk

- Understanding the relationships of vendors associated with the digital assets in their proper context
- Quantifying how much financial exposure and cyber risk the organization has with third parties
- Determining the effectiveness of the vendors' cyber controls in context to the risk that they pose
- Demonstrating how to continuously monitor a risky vendor

M&A cyber risk

- Determining how cyber resiliency would impact an acquisition price
- Understanding the financial exposures and gaps in controls that will be inherited in an acquisition

This Textbook will provide the means to know this information and utilize it with confidence.

Notes

1. Gartner, "Executive Leadership: Strategic Risk Management Primer for 2020", 23 July 2020, ID G00726446, Malcolm Murray.
2. Allianz Global Corporate & Specialty, 2018, "Allianz Risk Barometer 2018 – Preview" January 3, 2018, https://www.youtube.com/watch?time_continue=9&v=3NbtFQw3AGYhttp://www.agcs.allianz.com/insights/white-papers-and-case-studies/allianz-risk-barometer-2018/.
3. IBM Cost of a Data Breach Report 2020, https://www.ibm.com/security/data-breach.
4. Nick Eubanks, "The True Cost of Cyber Crime for Businesses," Forbes, July 13, 2017, www.forbes.com/sites/theyec/2017/07/13/the-true-cost-of-cybercrime-for-businesses/#380e0f694947.
5. Erin Myers, "Cyber risk management truly go enterprise-side in 2018, predicts Aon report," Advisen, January 12, 2018, http://www.advisen.com/tools/fpnproc/fpns/articles_new_35/P/300792105.html?rid=300792105&list_id=35.
6. Kevin Kalinich, Jacqueline Waters, Chris Rafferty, Ethical Boardroom 2019, "Is cyber risk a D&O risk?", https://ethicalboardroom.com/is-cyber-risk-a-do-risk/.
7. Gartner, "Security Organization Dynamics", Research ID: G00381600, October 8, 2020, Sam Olyaei, Tom Scholtz.

ABOUT THE AUTHOR

M. (Maryellen) Ariel Evans is a cyber risk pioneer. She is an educator, author, and serial entrepreneur. Ariel is the visionary behind the digital asset approach for cyber risk quantification and scoring. She has over two decades of senior executive experience leading governance, legal, cyber, compliance, risk, and internal audit teams.

She is the Founder of Cyber Intelligence 4U, Inc. (CIU), a cybersecurity workforce accelerator with over 4,000 graduates of their cybersecurity in business certificate programs since 2018. Courses include "Enterprise Cybersecurity in Digital Business," "Cyber Risk Management," "Executive Cybersecurity," "Vendor Cyber Risk Management," and "Cyber Sales." Her programs are taught at leading universities, including Rutgers, and Pace, and several others in the United States, Europe, the Middle East, and Canada. CIU is partnered with ISACA Chapters to provide Continuing Professional Education (CPE) hours based on her content. In 2021, new programs will provide training in "Cloud Security," "Mobile Security," "Vendor Risk Management," "Privacy," "CMMC," "New York State Department of Financial Services Part 500," and "Control Assessments."

All Evans' cybersecurity programs are driven from the business perspective. Her programs allow companies to understand cybersecurity in context using the language of metrics. The courses allow firms to invest correctly in people, process, tools, and the organizational changes that are needed to address the expanding role of cybersecurity into privacy, digital trust, and risk. All these requirements arise from the digitalization of business.

Additionally, her courses are unique since they utilize a hands-on approach with the VRisk® Cybersecurity Platform to provide students real-world experience when learning how to conduct privacy impact assessments, maturity assessments, model cyber risk modeling, and plan strategic initiatives, among others. Evans has orchestrated an advisory board of over 200 top-flight CIOs, CISOs, CTOs, DPOs, and other leading executives who work together to create market-driven content for her programs.

Evans is also the CEO of Cyber Innovative Technologies (CIT), a leading cyber risk management software company whose platform is utilized by leading companies worldwide and whose VRisk product is the application used for the hands-on learning in the Cyber Intelligence 4U courses.

After moving to Israel in 2014, she worked with innovative companies where she created and sold a cybersecurity value-added distribution company for 20× revenues.

This led to three years of research with the Fortune 1000 and cyber insurance industry to understand the gap between the technology and the business. The result was the creation of both CIU, CIT, and her first book "Managing Cyber Risk."

Formerly, she was a founder of two software companies in the United States that successfully exited to BMC and elance.com. Additionally, she was the acting chief information security officer (CISO) for a Telco subsidiary in the United States and the primary author of the PCI e-commerce guideline issued in January 2013 and a consultant on cyber risk to Fortune 1000 companies on Wall Street. Ariel acts as the cyber expert on the board to several companies.

Ariel has an MBA from the Stern School of Business at New York University in Finance and Entrepreneurship with her undergraduate work in Nuclear Physics. She is a frequent guest lecturer and keynote speaker at many universities, organizations, and venues worldwide. Ariel is also a frequent guest on i24 news, tech republic, The Jim Bohannon Show, and Cheddar TV. She can be reached at ariel@cyberintelu.com.

ACKNOWLEDGMENT

No book writes itself and no author can share knowledge without standing on the shoulder of giants. I want to express my heartfelt thanks and appreciation to my colleagues, friends, researchers, and mentors who have helped me to frame my thoughts and complete this book.

A special thank you to all 200 members of the Pace Seidenberg Cybersecurity Advisory Board, whose amazing collaboration has helped to make this book possible. There are too many of you to thank individually. Much thanks to Meredith Schnur, my cyber insurance mentor and friend who is a Managing Director for the US Cyber Brokerage Team at Marsh USA, Inc. for her insight into cyber insurance. I would also like to thank Paul Ferrillo, Partner at McDermott Will & Emery, whose collaboration with Advisen, AIG, and K2 Intelligence provided visionary thought leadership. A thanks also to Alexander Schlager, Kathy Smith, and Diana Preis at Verizon who championed my cyber program and made it a part of the Verizon culture.

Additionally, I would like to thank my Board of Directors. Former Rear Admiral Danelle Barrett, who was the Cybersecurity Division Director and Deputy Chief Information Officer of the US Navy, Randal Milch, who is the Faculty Director, Master of Science in Cybersecurity Risk and Strategy at New York University/Professor of Practice, NYU School of Law and Former General Counsel at Verizon, Thomas Manning, the former Chairman of Dun and Bradstreet and currently a Senior Fellow at Harvard Advanced Leadership Initiative, Ursuline Foley, the former CIO of XL Capital, Dr. Yoav Intrator, the former Managing Director of JPMorgan Chase and the CEO of JPMorgan Chase Israel, Michael Madon, the former Deputy Assistant Secretary, Intelligence for the Department of the Treasury and cyber entrepreneur who sold his company Attata to Mimecast, and David Kimmel, the Founder of Summit Capital.

A hearty thanks to Dean Jonathan Hill from Pace University's Seidenberg School of Computer Science and Information Systems. Also, a special thank you to Alex Tosheff, CSO of VMware for his review and support of my books.

A special thanks to the many book reviewers, including Les Correia, Global Head of Application Security at The Estée Lauder Companies, Sean O'Rourke, Cyber Liability Consultant at Combs & Company, Pasqualle Cirullo, the Head of Information Technology at Paramount Assets, Ahmed Mousa, the Manager—Utility of the Future—Electric & Gas Asset Strategy at PSEG, Vito Sardanopoli, CISO at US Imaging, Anna Ransley, CIO at Heineken, Scott Aurnou, Cybersecurity Attorney at The Cyber Advocate, Alex Golbin, the Global Head of Risk Assessments at IHS Markit, Tali Tollman, Cyber Insurance Advisor, Yoav Intrator, CEO at JPMorgan Chase Israel, Doug Shin, CISO at Agricultural Bank of China, Stefan Natu, Principal Machine Learning Architect at AWS, Patricia Lee, the Vice President of Professional Services at Spruce Technology, and David Berger, CISO at SDG Corporation.

Finally, I cannot forget to triple thank my husband again and again. Dr. Yoav Intrator, who is bar none an expert in technology innovation, AI, and blockchain and whose example propels me to excel, for his support, wisdom, and his unconditional belief and love in me. You are my rock.

PREFACE

This book is about thought leadership and critical thinking. Build on concepts from cybersecurity, privacy, the cyber insurance industry, and digital asset cyber risk methodologies—primarily quantification and digital asset scoring analysis. The cyber risk today is digital. Many authors and companies are using methodologies that do not allow for the ability to assign defensible values to digital assets. This is being frowned upon by the industry, academic, and the analyst community. Not using standard language and definitions is misleading. Many are mislabeling threats as risk, vulnerabilities as risk, and incidents as risk. This has to stop.

Specifically, there are those that use deep and dark web data to create analytic scores which are using external data, such as botnets, spam propagation, and executive reconnaissance. These are threats, not risks. Additionally, the cyber insurance advisor sees your risk posture as a function of loss events. Loss events have a 100% probability. They are incidents, not risks. Lastly, the Factor Analysis of Information Risk (FAIR) model is myopic and is seeing risk only through the lens of vulnerabilities. Vulnerabilities are weaknesses in systems and address only one of the three aspects of residual risk. Furthermore, the model is not defensible.

Today 85% of your business is a digital asset. In 2001, we were still pushing paper and only 10% of the business was digital. This explosion in digitization must be the basis of any cyber risk program. *Cybercriminals attack the digital assets.* They steal your data using malware. They interrupt your business processes through denial-of-service and ransomware attacks. They also cause regulatory penalties and fines based on the type of data your company processes in systems and stores in technologies.

Furthermore, the digital asset methodology is the only university-recognized approach to quantify financial exposures associated with cyber risk. It paves the road to measure resiliency, identify gaps in the cybersecurity program, and integrate security, risk, privacy, and compliance into a digital-based effective strategy ending the struggle between the redundancy and inefficiency across the security, privacy, governance, compliance, and risk management teams.

Digital business is creating pressure for organizations to restructure and more formally address privacy, digital risk, and compliance, in response to regulatory mandates. This book provides a roadmap for understanding cyber maturity and moving toward an integrated cyber risk management approach that will reduce costs and risks allowing companies to have meaningful metrics and KPIs. The data is not based on statistics from taxonomies or other nondynamic methods. It is based on digital asset relationships, values, and the interplay of cybersecurity controls that make cyber risk such a fascinating topic. It is written in a practical manner and uses solid business impact analysis and cyber tool information to derive data.

The digital asset approach allows cyber to function as its own line of business—charging back business units to protect the digital assets. We are on the verge of revolutionary and dynamic changes that are needed to get ahead of the cybercriminals. Without these changes, we will perish. As was been attributed to Einstein, "The definition of insanity is doing the same thing over and over again and expecting different results."

Our focus is to put cyber into a business perspective and holistically understand the enterprise's needs. Throughout this book, we provide benchmarks to use to set goals for cyber resiliency that we can measure against. There is a saying in Buddhism, "start where you are." Beginning mediators use this as motivation and as their path unfolds in practice and they understand the journey is the destination. Cyber is a journey without a destination. We will always have cyber risk. It is a journey of managing it with the best chances of success. May your journey be one of wonder, growth, and resilience.

INTRODUCTION

Abstract

A new report from the World Economic Forum (WEF), in partnership with Zurich Insurance Group and Marsh & McLennan Companies, spotlights that for North American and European business leaders, cybersecurity is their biggest risk for the second consecutive year.[1] It eclipsed environmental issues and M&A in 2018 to take the distinguished title. It is the conversation that everyone is having because it is now on everyone's board agenda, it is on everyone's risk registry, and it is now overshadowing everything else that is out there.

It is also the fifth domain of warfare joining land, sea, air, and space. Instead of tanks, ships, planes, and bombs, we have hackers, malware, and economic disruption. Nation-states, criminal organizations, terrorist groups, and cybercriminals are targeting civilian populations and corporate infrastructure. We have seen this since the 1980s with the uncorroborated malware attack on Russia's Trans-Siberia pipeline,[2] and Marcus Hess' arrest for selling US government intellectual property to the KGB. However, the stakes have gotten much higher. Between 2014 and 2016, we saw the Justice Department's claim that Iran had attacked US infrastructure online by infiltrating the computerized controls of a small dam 25 miles north of New York City,[3] China's breach of the Office of Personnel Management; Russian meddling with US elections; and the North Korea's shocking attack on Sony pictures, heralding a new way of war on American soil.

What does this mean for you and why are you reading this book? Eighty-five percent of our world is controlled by digital technology.[4] The water we drink, the government we elect, and the information that we consume are all at the behest of computer (information technology) systems. In the last 25 years, we have made almost everything dependent upon computers and their ability to communicate across networks. McKinsey estimates that 98% of the economy is being impacted by digitization. This has prompted the need for cyber resiliency. The only way to create and maintain cyber resiliency is to address it from an enterprise perspective as it relates to the digital business.

In order to protect our way of life, we have to effectively face and deal with these cyber threats and protect our digital infrastructure by bringing everyone together to be cyber resilient. **You** are the stakeholders here regardless of what sector or industry you are in—public or private, civilian or military, and domestic or international. It is your privacy, your financial, and political stability. The good guys need to come together for a holistic understanding of cybersecurity, its challenges, and solutions.

This book is written as a Textbook for those that want to reorganize their cyber-related roles and implement enterprise digital cyber risk programs using integrated technologies. It provides clear direction into how best to work with digital assets to optimize people, process, and tools. Most importantly, it provides a line of sight into how an organization can benchmark and increase cyber resilience. It is for anyone in the organization, including all stakeholders whether they be executives, or managers, in roles as diverse as CEOs, COOs, CFOs, Chief Digital Officers, CISOs, DPOs, General Counsel, Business Unit Owners, Auditors, Vendors, Regulators, Compliance Managers, Data Stewards, Human Resources, and Governance Teams. It is useful regardless of the type of organization you work for or with and speaks to every industry audience. It focuses on strategic and tactical use cases that lead to decreasing cyber risk regardless of the size or maturity of your organization. **Nondigital risk management practices are a roadblock to achieving strategic business outcomes**. Using the digital asset approach can benchmark and lead toward obtaining the needed results and move the meter on the cyber resiliency of the business.

Purpose and organization of the Textbook

Digital asset cyber risk is an evolving science. Cyber risk touches many aspects of the business. Cyber risk grew out of information technology. This has led to a disconnect between the risk owners and the front-line risk mitigators. Security managers and Chief Information Security Officers (CISOs) are not providing meaningful metrics and KPIs that can be digested by boards into a business context. Typically, a CISO will walk into a room with a list of 300 vulnerabilities and announce that this is his or her cyber plan. That is not a cyber plan, it is a list of 300 vulnerabilities. Historically, it has been not uncommon for a CISO to attempt to mesmerize their board with cyber and technical jargon. However, the mystification of the board with cyber jargon impairs the board from its fiduciary duty to protect the digital assets. This Textbook is about providing corporate cyber stakeholders—managers, executives, and directors—with context and tools to accomplish several strategic objectives: understanding and managing cyber risk from a digital perspective; applying these digital principles across privacy, cybersecurity, and regulation; organizing the company to provide adequate oversight and leadership; and ensuring that improved understanding leads to better cyber resilience.

We will delve into cyber maturity and organizational roles. Keeping in mind that there is no such thing as a flawless, universally suitable model for an organization's risk, security, and privacy teams. Leaders in every enterprise must measure their maturity and develop an appropriate model, taking into consideration the skills, tools, and processes needed to manage digital asset cyber risk.

Combining privacy and regulatory standards, guidelines, requirements, and best practices, we explore the interconnectedness of security, privacy, compliance, and risk. Each from a perspective of the individual role and responsibilities.

Pivoting later to incident response, forensics, and auditing and then onward to cyber insurance needs and ransomware strategies. Again, providing the digital asset context to calculate adequate cyber insurance limits and to implement effective ransomware strategies.

We move into the quantification and scoring of cyber risk tying back financial exposures to attack vectors and use cases. The scoring of inherent cyber risk provides an understanding of which assets have more intrinsic risk due to how they are constructed and how they are used and protected. We tie in the security control assessments, which allow companies to measure the effectiveness of their cybersecurity controls and demonstrate how they mitigate inherent cyber risk. We then look at event data from cybersecurity tools which increases cyber risk. This data is used in remediation prioritization and budgeting.

Cyber risk is a multifaceted topic. It is complex due to the relationships of the digital assets, their use by third parties, the adoption of cloud-first strategies, and the technologies that support them. Digital asset cyber risk allows us to measure cloud exposure, IoT exposure, privacy exposure, and tie them to our cybersecurity program. KPIs for cyber risk thresholds and other measurable metrics are easy to digest and action on using this method.

Cybersecurity is dynamic. Although the inherent cyber characteristics of digital asset components (system, process, technology, or data) are primarily static, the interactions with security teams performing control assessments, and the cyber tools providing vulnerability, incident, or threat data are not. Understanding the interconnectivity of digital assets can prevent the next Equifax where the impact of not patching a relatively simple system impacted the crown jewel assets of the business—the customer's privacy information and credit scores. This book is about keeping pace with the dynamic and interconnected nature of cyber risk using an integrated digital asset approach to understand and manage it in perspective.

This Textbook focuses on businesses, our review, and treatment of cyber risk applies to all types of entities, including large corporations, joint ventures, partnerships, associations, nonprofit, large, small, and medium enterprises, government whether regional, national, or international, and all industries. Cyber is like COVID-19, it knows no bounds. All organizations regardless of size, industry, and geography are impacted by cyber.

The Textbook is written by a cyber risk, governance, compliance, and privacy expert for cyber stakeholders, based on decades of cyber risk management experience, in the front lines as a CISO, and Risk Manager in diverse roles, including governance, audit, risk, incident management, business continuity, information security, across numerous global companies on Wall Street, the Defense Industry, Technology, Retail, and Manufacturing; as a cyber expert on the board and/or chair to multiple boards of directors and committees, as a member or leader of several global organizations and associations as a speaker, teacher, panelist, and author, and most recently as the CEO of a cyber risk management software firm and the founder of a cyber workforce accelerator. As an Israeli American, I have been at the forefront of cyber and seen the full radius of cyber risk from multiple dimensions.

Cyber risk is the number one business issue. It is now recognized as an enterprise risk and not an information technology risk. Like other risk domains, it has reputational, operational, legal, and financial impacts. Digital cyber risk is a multifaceted subject that requires skills across several domains—not just IT. In essence, everyone in an organization—from the board member and CEO, CISO, Compliance Manager,

Data Privacy Officer, Remediator, Vendor, and Auditor has a role and must understand digital cyber risk in their specific context.

Furthermore, digital assets are what a cybercriminal wants to steal, alter, or interrupt. Data breaches cause fines and have reputational, legal, and operational losses. Cybercriminals typically attack the digital asset by inserting malware on a system usually from phishing emails. This can result in stolen data or cause interruption of the business process due to a denial-of-service or ransomware attack. Both result losses and fines from regulators. Fines can also now be for the misuse of data as well as for a breach or business interruption. Regulations are evolving and poised to impact your firm based on the specific types of data processed and stored in systems and technologies. Digital asset risk modeling is the foundation on which to build a strong cybersecurity program with defensible metrics that can measure cyber resiliency. Cyber resiliency is the measure of an entity's ability to continuously deliver the intended business outcome despite adverse cyber events. It can have vast implications including sustainability. Many companies are unaware that they have billions of dollars in hidden exposures waiting to be stolen.

Cyber risk scoring use cases include the identification of asset-based risks, recognizing gaps in the firm's cybersecurity controls, and the integration of cyber tool data to prioritize remediation work. Future work will pave the road for the insertion of AI technologies for virtual patching and a host of other nonhuman actions to reduce cyber risk.

Digital asset cyber risk programs can measure cyber tool return on investment (ROI), align cyber budgeting to cost-based budgeting, and work across the cybersecurity, privacy, and risk functions to ensure teams communicate and work together effectively. Cyber risk benchmarks and measures program effectiveness across the controls, tools, and processes.

Companies must pivot their mindset and understand this from a business perspective. At this stage of cyber evolution, it is changed or die.[5] In this book, I deconstruct and debunk age-old myths about cybersecurity and empower the reader with information across three critical areas to ensure a cyber risk mindset—relate, repeat, and reframe to enable important positive changes in enterprise cybersecurity in digital businesses.

Notes

1. Heather A. Turner, NU Property Casualty 360, "The top business risks of 2019", October 1, 2019, https://www.propertycasualty360.com/2019/10/01/the-top-business-risks-of-2019/?slreturn=20201121064253.
2. Thomas C. Reed, "At the Abyss: An Insider's History of the Cold War", ISBN 0-89141-821-0, March 5, 2005.
3. Mark Thomson, Time, "Iranian cyber attack on New York Dam shows future of war", March 24, 2016, https://time.com/4270728/iran-cyber-attack-dam-fbi/.
4. Nick Eubanks, "The True Cost of Cyber Crime for Businesses," Forbes, July 13, 2017, www.forbes.com/sites/theyec/2017/07/13/the-true-cost-of-cybercrime-for-businesses/#380e0f694947.
5. Alan Deutschman, "Change or Die: The Three Keys to Change at Work and in Life", SBN-13: 9780061373671, HarperCollins Publishers, December 26, 2007.

OVERVIEW

This book has ten parts—The Evolution of Cybersecurity, Cybersecurity Basics, Cybersecurity Tools, Cybersecurity Regulation, Cybersecurity Incident Response, Forensics and Audit, Cybersecurity Risk Management, GDPR and Privacy, Cybersecurity Risk Management Strategy, Cybersecurity Insurance, and Introduction to Vendor Risk Management Strategy in 35 chapters as follows:

Part 1 – The Evolution of Cybersecurity. Provides context and introduces the foundational elements of cybersecurity, how it evolved out of information technology into a business issue in six chapters:

Chapter 1 – "Cyber—A business Issue" offers context on how cybersecurity has evolved from an information technology (IT) issue into a business issue, in today's interconnected, dynamic high-risk cyber world. It offers statistics and introduces the concept of digital assets that are now 85% of the business value.

Chapter 2 – "Cyber risk" breaks down the components of cyberattack surfaces, terminology, enterprise risks of today and links them to regulation and compliance risks and explores some of the most important cyber events of the last few years and the components of an enterprise cybersecurity program.

Chapter 3 – "The history of cybersecurity" provides background on its origins in academia and profiles cybercrime through the decades and explores at a high level some of the most important cyber events of the last few years.

Chapter 4 – "Cyber consequences" provides a deep dive into several landmark cybersecurity case studies, including data breaches, ransomware, and other cyberattacks.

Chapter 5 – "Cyber trends and spending" focuses on cyber spending across industries and geographies, and merger and acquisition issues.

Chapter 6 – "Cyber roles" reviews the roles and responsibilities of each business and technical stakeholder and focuses on their interdependencies.

Part 2 – Cybersecurity Basics. Part 2 focuses on normalizing the language of cybersecurity, statistics, the relationship between enterprise risk and compliance, and programs and maps an organizations maturity across over 20 attributes in six chapters:

Chapter 7 – "Cyber-attack surfaces and digital asset inventories" reviews attack surfaces and the increases over the past decades in relationships to digital assets and demonstrates how to do a digital asset inventory.

Chapter 8 – "Cyber terminology and statistics" provides a glossary of terms that are required to understand the basics of cybersecurity and explains recent statistics that ties back to case studies.

Chapter 9 – "Enterprise threats of today and cybercriminals" looks at the most recent attack types and deep dives into each cause with case studies.

Chapter 10 – "Cybersecurity regulations, standards, and frameworks" outlines the relationship between regulation and compliance and the control testing frameworks utilized.

Chapter 11 – "Enterprise cybersecurity programs" looks at the components of oversight, encryption, audit, secure software design lifecycle, policies, and other categories in an enterprise cybersecurity program.

Chapter 12 – "Organizational cyber maturities" maps organizational characteristics to five maturity categories for companies to benchmark their maturity.

Part 3 – Cybersecurity Tools. Part 3 focuses on the policy mechanisms of a cybersecurity program and the use of cybersecurity tools in two chapters:

Chapter 13 – "Cyber policies" discusses policy types and best practices for their creation, including incorporating the following sections into all cybersecurity policies: overview, scope, policy purpose, roles/responsibilities, monitoring/reporting, enforcement, exceptions, and definitions.

Chapter 14 – "Cybersecurity tools" outlines the purposes of cyber tools and their alignment to the National Institute of Standards in Technology (NIST) core functions. We explore basic, intermediate, and advanced tool maturities and the principles behind them, and how they are used by the different teams in the firm.

Part 4 – Cybersecurity Regulation. Part 4 focuses on cybersecurity regulations and guidelines by breaking them down by geography, data types, and industry while addressing the frameworks that can be used to measure cybersecurity control effectiveness in four chapters:

Chapter 15 – "US Federal Regulations" explores cyber regulation that is administered by a department or agency of the US government.

Chapter 16 – "US State Regulations" explores cyber regulation that is administered by the state Attorney Generals.

Chapter 17 – "New York State Department of Financial Services Part 500" explores the new cyber regulation that is required for financial services firms working in New York State.

Chapter 18 – "Global, industry, or other types of cybersecurity regulations" explores cyber regulation that is administered by an industry governing body, and cyber regulation does not fall into any of the above categories.

Part 5 – Incident Response, Forensics, and Audit. Part 5 integrates incident response, forensics, and audit with a focus on how to work with these teams from the business perspective in three chapters:

Chapter 19 – "Incident response plans" reviews incident response plans and procedures.
Chapter 20 – "Forensic methods" is a deep dive into digital investigative techniques and methods.
Chapter 21 – "IT audit" summarizes the phases of an IT audit and expectations from the audit committee.

Part 6 – Cybersecurity Risk Management. Part 6 provides the method for cyber risk quantification and calculating cyber risk exposures based on the digital asset method from an inherent perspective, mitigating control perspective, and residual perspective in three chapters:

Chapter 22 – "Cybersecurity financial exposures" focuses on algorithms to calculate risk exposures based on the digital asset approach.
Chapter 23 – "Digital asset cyber risk modeling and scoring" focuses on algorithms to calculate inherent cyber risk scores based on the digital asset approach.
Chapter 24 – "Mitigating cybersecurity scores and residual cyber risk scores" focuses on algorithms to calculate risk mitigation using cybersecurity controls and residual cyber risk scores based on data from cybersecurity tools.

Part 7 – GDPR and Privacy. Part 7 provides an overview of the GDPR and ties organizational and system requirements into layperson language for privacy practitioners in four chapters:

Chapter 25 – "GDPR overview" delves into the who, what, why, and how of GDPR regulation.
Chapter 26 – "GDPR articles" deconstructs each GDPR article, translating them into layperson language with suggestions of how to meet each requirement.
Chapter 27 – "GDRP evidence" outlines the evidence requirements for each article.
Chapter 28 – "GDPR Privacy Impact Assessment (PIA)" outlines the requirements to perform a privacy impact assessment.

Part 8 – Cybersecurity Risk Management Strategy. Part 8 focuses on the use cases of digital asset cyber risk exposures and scores in two chapters:

Chapter 29 – "CISO strategies" focuses on crown jewel strategies, the prioritization of risk reduction based on exposures and cyber risk scores, cyber budgeting, and cyber tool ROI and road mapping.

Chapter 30 – "Cyber in the Boardroom" outlines the four major initiatives for boards and how to achieve them, including Protecting the Digital Assets, Vendor Risk Management, Cyber Insurance, and Cyber M&A.

Part 9 – Cybersecurity Insurance. Part 9 focuses on cyber insurance, its use, gaps, and how to determine how much to buy or sell to an organization based on defining adequate limits for the aggregate and sublimit categories in three chapters:

Chapter 31 – "Cyber insurance overview" explores the use of cases for cyber insurance, first- and third-party insurance, gaps in property and casualty, and D&O insurance policies related to cybersecurity.

Chapter 32 – "Calculating limits adequacy" is a deep dive into calculating the aggregate limit and sublimits based on the financial exposure of the organization.

Chapter 33 – "Ransomware strategies" provides a comprehensive approach to understand when ransomware should be paid versus restoring all the systems.

Part 10 – Introduction to Cybersecurity Vendor Risk Management. The concluding chapters introduce the concept of cyber vendor risk and regulations in two chapters:

Chapter 34 – "Vendor risk overview" defines the different cyber risks associated with each type of vendor.

Chapter 35 – "Vendor cybersecurity regulations" reviews the gaps and overlaps between regulations that require a cyber vendor risk management program.

The Way Forward
Abbreviations
Glossary
Notes at the end of each chapter

PART I

THE EVOLUTION OF CYBER RISK

1 CYBER

A business issue

I know not with what weapons World War III will be fought, but World War IV will be fought with sticks and stones.

Albert Einstein

The internet—welcome to my nightmare

Alice Cooper's debut album featured the title song "Welcome to my Nightmare." For you millennials, I will save you the google; here are the beginning lyrics: "Welcome to my Nightmare, I think you're gonna like it, I think you are going to feel like you belong." The internet makes us feel like we all belong. It provides us with technological superiority that gives us a terrific way of life. We don't have to go to the bank and wait in line or trudge to the store when we have a headache or drive 60 miles to visit Mom. We can learn, work, talk, and buy things almost all at the same time. We multitask our little hearts out. We are entertained, maintained, and optimized for life.

But what happens when the computer gets a virus, or we get hacked? Computer viruses began to become a serious threat in the late 1980s. Increasing network connectivity meant that viruses could nearly wipe out networks. This spurred the creation of the first commercially available antivirus software, and the cybersecurity industry was born.

Real cyber trouble began to brew in the mid-90s when the internet allowed us to innovate exponentially and optimize the way computers could help companies communicate with each other and with consumers. It changed the fundamental way we manage inventories, supply chains, customer relationships, and the financial world.

Internet users grew from 0.5B to over 4.7B users over the past two decades.[1] That's over 900% more attack surface. Cybersecurity Ventures predicts there will be 6 billion internet users by 2022—and more than 7.5 billion internet users by 2030.[2]

The internet can be our cyber nightmare, or we can take an offensive advantage by utilizing people, processes, and tools to make it more costly for cybercriminals to attack us, thwarting their evil plans. The more we connect and have at stake, the more we need to identify, detect, protect, respond, recover, and be resilient.

DOI: 10.4324/9781003052616-2

In his book, *The Fifth Domain*, Richard A. Clarke describes cyber resiliency. "Cyber resilience must be built upon, rather than be seen as a replacement for sound security fundamentals. When confidentiality, integrity, and availability are compromised, resilience is about the ability to respond rapidly, return to a good state, manage bad outcomes, and learn from the incident so that future incidents are less likely. Here, it is important to note that thinking of "resilience" as the ability to recover to a previous state or bounce back is too limiting. For resilience to be a useful concept in the field of cybersecurity, it requires that the concept fully embody the idea of returning stronger or better than before."[3]

This is where the business comes in to provide the right amount of budget to hire the right people, have the right cyber tools and processes needed to obtain the right amount of resiliency. We will be providing a framework to benchmark and measure cyber resiliency in this book.

Cyber gets real for businesses

Regulators put their money where their mouth is

The first big shot across the bow for American companies was felt in 2013 when Target was breached by cyber attackers who gained access to Target's computer gateway with credentials stolen from a third-party vendor. Using the credentials to exploit weaknesses in Target's system, the attackers gained access to a customer service database, installed malware on the system, and captured full names, phone numbers, email addresses, payment card numbers, credit card verification codes, and other sensitive data.[4] As of early 2019, Target has settled over US$206 million in lawsuits in relationship to over US$457 million in damages filed by Visa, Mastercard, the State of Minnesota, and several banks, according to Advisen. Additionally, seven out of the ten board members were ousted, and the Chief Executive Officer (CEO) was fired.

At the same time this was happening, other nation-states were redefining how their data would be used, collected, and secured. The European Union crafted new regulations after five years of thoughtful consideration and implemented a rigorous privacy law. The General Data Protection Regulation (GDPR) went into effect on May 25, 2018. The first enforcement action was enacted against Hospital do Barreiro in Portugal for 400,000 EUR. The fine was due to insufficient access policies, which allowed technicians and physicians to consult patients' clinical files without proper authorization.[5] Coming full circle to 2019, the largest fine to date was levied for 183 million GBP to British Airways for the use of poor security controls that resulted in a 2018 Web skimming attack affecting 500,000 consumers.[6] The 183 million GBP is equivalent approximately to 200 million EUR and US$225 million. As of May 2020, the British Airways fine is almost 55% of all the fines levied to date by the European Union for privacy data breaches and misuse of data, which is total approximately 350 million EUR.

The European Union's stepped-up privacy laws can be compared with the unprecedented move by the United States Federal Trade Commission (FTC) to fine Facebook US$5 billion. Facebook failed to protect the business assets of their customers. The FTC's bold move fined Facebook for its role in the Cambridge Analytica data breach.

Specifically, the FTC fined Facebook because it violated the law by failing to protect data from third parties, serving ads through the use of phone numbers provided for security, and lying to users that its facial recognition software was turned off by default.[7]

The US enforcement landscape for data privacy and data security changed as a result of the US$5 billion FTC Facebook settlement, coming on the heels of the US$575 million FTC Equifax settlement and the fines by the UK Information Commissioner's Office (ICO) on British Airways and Marriott following significant data breaches. These actions indicate a new era of aggressive data privacy and data security enforcement on both sides of the pond.

Highest Penalties in Privacy Enforcement Actions

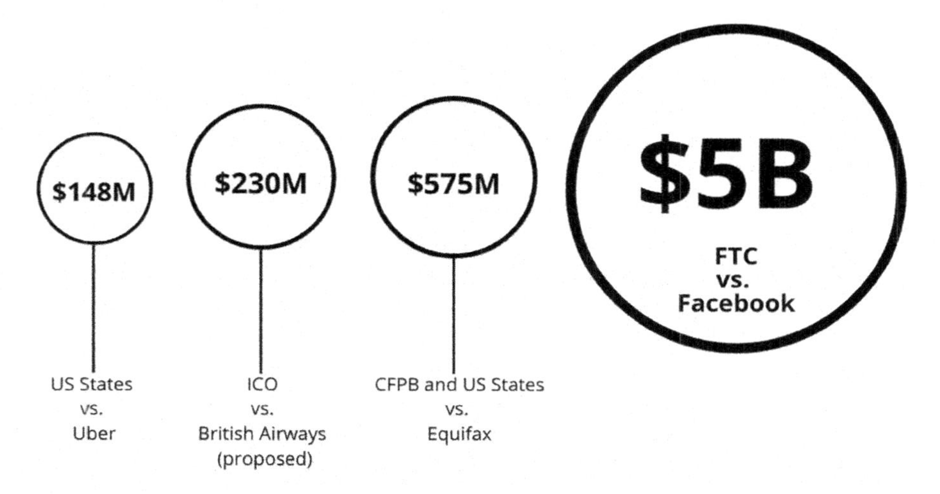

Figure 1.1 Highest Penalties in Privacy Enforcement Actions

In addition to the fines, the FTC has mandated a privacy program for Facebook.[8] The order lays out provisions for a privacy program which Facebook must implement within 180 days, including requirements but not limited to the following:

- **Document the program.** Document the "content, implementation, and maintenance of the Privacy Program" and provide that description to the Principal Executive Officer (Mark Zuckerberg) and an Independent Privacy Committee that reports to the board at least once a year.
- **Hire an independent privacy chief.** Designate an employee as a "Chief Privacy Officer for Product" (CPO) to run the program. The CPO's hiring and removal must be approved by the Independent Privacy Committee.
- **Conduct risk assessments.** Assess and document, at least annually, both internal and external risks in each area of operations, including, within 30 days, risks relating to a Covered Incident. A Covered Incident is a verified incident where data from 500 or more users was accessed, collected, used, or shared by a third party in violation of Facebook's terms.

- **Implement safeguards which include the following**:
  - —Annual third-party certifications, monitoring, and enforcement against third parties that violate contract terms.
  - —Privacy review of new products, services, or practices, with documentation and a detailed written report about any privacy risks and safeguards, and a quarterly report from the CPO to the Principal Executive Officer (Mark Zuckerberg) of these reviews and all privacy decisions, in advance of meetings of the Independent Privacy Commission.
  - —Controls that limit employee access to information and that protect information shared with affiliates.
  - —Disclosure and consent for facial recognition.
- **Test safeguards.** Safeguards must be tested, assessed, and monitored annually and within 30 days after a cyber incident.
- **Implement training.** Establish regular privacy training programs.
- **Ensure the performance of service providers.** Retain providers capable of safeguarding information and contractually require them to safeguard it.
- **Use outside experts.** Seek guidance from independent third parties on implementing, maintaining, and updating the program.
- **Evaluate the program.** Evaluate the program at least annually, taking into account cyber incidents.

The cost of this effort will be substantial. In February of 2019, Mark Zuckerberg vowed to spend more than US$3.7 billion on safety and security on the company's platform that year.[9]

Although Facebook is making substantial investments to improve its data security and privacy practices, the long-term cost of those investments and impact on the bottom-line spooked investors after the breach, leading to a US$120 billion loss in market value at the end of July 2019. This was the largest one-day loss of value for a US publicly traded company.[10] This loss is an example of a reputational amplification that we will discuss in detail in a later chapter.

As of August 2019, Mark Zuckerberg's net worth is about US$68.2 billion, making him the fifth-richest person in the world. After news of Facebook's FTC fine broke in July, Zuckerberg's 410 million shares of Facebook stock appreciated by more than US$1 billion. When grilled by the Senate Commerce and Judiciary Committees on privacy, data mining, and regulations about his cyber program, Zuckerberg said, "One of my greatest regrets in running the company is that we were slow in identifying the Russian information operations in 2016. As long as there are people sitting in Russia whose job is to try to interfere in elections around the world, this will be an ongoing conflict."[11]

The FTC's message is clear—it is time for adequate investment in cybersecurity and data privacy. Directors and officers have the fiduciary duty to protect the assets of the business. Most data breaches result in mass firings of CEOs and Chief Information Security Officers (CISOs). Good cyber equals job security. Just ask Yahoo's former CEO Marissa Mayer, Uber's former CEO Travis Kalanick, SONY's former CEO Amy

Pascal, Equifax's former CEO Richard Smith, and CIO David Webb and Target's former CEO Gregg Steinhafel. All were dismissed after data breaches.

On top of that, in 2018, Aon reported: "Cyber events are now among the top three triggers of Directors and Officers (D&O) derivative actions."[12] This indicates that Directors and Officers are now personally liable for data breaches. In addition, 32% of data breaches lead to C-level executives being fired and 31% of global data breaches led to employees getting laid off.[13]

Digitization—the explosion in cybercrime

Digitization is the process of converting information into a digital (i.e., computer-readable) format, in which the information is organized into bits.[14] For our purposes, digitization produces digital data, which in computer science is the discrete, discontinuous representation of information seen on your computer as characters (letters, numbers, spaces, punctuation marks, or symbols). Digitization results is the representation of an object, image, sound, document, or signal (typically an analog signal) by generating a series of numbers that describe a discrete set of points.[15] The result is called digital representation or, more specifically, a digital image for the object and a digital form for the signal. In computer science, the digitized data is in the form of binary numbers, which facilitate computer processing and other operations, but, strictly speaking, digitizing simply means the conversion of analog source material into a numerical format; the decimal or any other number system that can be used instead.

Why all the fuss? According to Forbes, today, 85% of a business is a digital asset. In 2001, 10% of your business was a digital asset.[16] Cybercrime cost businesses US$178,000,000 in 2001 and US$3,500,000,000 in 2019.[17] The explosion in digitization is parallel to the explosion in cybercrime.

Cloud first—you better believe it

In addition to regulatory impacts, the technology impacts are just lurking behind the curtain. The use of a Cloud First Strategy has many companies unable to manage vendor risk properly. A cloud service is a vendor that provides you with either software, a platform, or infrastructure to run your business applications. The security and risk are shared by the Cloud Service Provider (CSP) and the organization. More and more attention is being paid to cloud security and risk, and more enforcement measures will be put in place as the amount of infrastructure being outsourced continues to grow. The average cloud to on-premise ratio is approximately 60:40 based on our research. According to Virgil David Dafinoiu, Cloud CISO and Next-Gen Leader at AT&T, "Cloud security will be the #1 cyber risk in 2021 as businesses increasingly rely on cloud services in the wake of the pandemic and the accompanying move to telework."

Today we see companies spinning up Cloud CISO roles to focus solely on cloud security and risk. These companies are proactively changing their organizational structure to meet the current needs. Many companies send sensitive data into the cloud or files to business partners. This data is the responsibility of the organization to protect. If the third party suffers a data breach, it is the first party that has to notify the customer and incur the lion's share of the costs.

The Internet of Things—friend or foe

The Internet of Things (IoT) puts a new spin on an old issue—interconnectivity. We are all connected, and those endpoints are a point of ingress and egress for cybercriminals to damage an organization. IoT has increased the attack surface exponentially. This increase in the attack surface related to IoT usage is very concerning. Most IoT devices have no security baked in. Adoption of IoT at the current rate with security as an afterthought will have us coping with the impacts for generations to come. Simultaneously, most of the business assets are now digital. Couple all this with the popular strategy of outsourcing not only people but also infrastructure and you have the perfect storm for cyber attackers—a ginormous attack surface, business strategies that promote an "assumed" risk transference to vendors with businesses reliant on their digital security.

There is a global lack of guidance and regulation regarding IoT technology. Some governments are looking to add IoT into their regulations. They include:

In the United Kingdom (U.K.), there are regulatory proposals for consumer IoT security that would set out clear guidelines that must be complied with and includes an obligation to encrypt security-sensitive data, including remote management and control. The standard of encryption should be "appropriate to the properties of the technology and usage," meaning there is no one-size-fits-all approach.[18] That is rather vague but better than nothing.

In the UK, US, Canada, Australia, and New Zealand, there are statements of intent that acknowledge that compromised IoT devices could have serious consequences for individuals, economies, and national security. More rigor is required to define what controls need to be in place.

In California, the IoT Device Security Act[19] has been put into law, which demands that companies building connected products ensure these are implemented with "reasonable security features." This creates a whole new digital asset paradigm that is being explored by many working committees. How to know which technologies make up our systems will become front and center and not an afterthought. Many companies will scramble to know if they are in scope for this act. The digital asset cyber risk methodology is the only approach that will stave off these types of fine in the future.

The good news is that globally, there is a clear recognition that we are not doing enough to ensure the security of data processed by IoT devices. There is a move that manufacturers should provide a clear framework through which security teams can submit any vulnerabilities found in their IoT devices to the manufacturer.

Working groups that are focusing on software component transparency such as the US Department of Commerce National Telecommunications and Information Administration (NITA) Software Component Transparency working group[20] are working to address the significant challenge to all industry verticals to secure digital assets that incorporate software components from complex supply chains. There is no clear line of sight for buyers to know where the technology components in software have originated from.

The inherent cyber risk must be understood in context to mitigate it down to acceptable levels. In 2017, I received a call from the Israel Security Agency, better known by the acronym Shabak (Hebrew: שב"כ) seeking advice. The question was "Should we buy Lenovo laptops?" I told them that it would be risky for an intelligence agency to buy any laptops from a Chinese technology company.

In 2015, FireEye released an important report "REDLINE DRAWN," which in their conclusion stated, "In 2013, when we released the APT1 report exposing a PLA cyber-espionage operation, it seemed like a quixotic effort to impede a persistent, well-resourced military operation targeting global corporations. Three years later, we see a less voluminous threat but more focused, calculated, and still successful in compromising corporate networks. Yet China is not the only actor in transition: we've observed multiple state-backed, and other well-resourced groups develop and hone their operations against corporate and government networks. The landscape we confront today is far more complex and diverse, less dominated by Chinese activity, and increasingly populated by a range of other criminal and state actors."[21]

Evolving cyber roles—change or die

The purpose of IT is to keep things up and running, ensuring operations, and delivering new digital products to market. It is in direct opposition to cybersecurity agendas, which ask for more controls and to slow things down. This is an organizational structural issue. Today we have the majority of organizations with ineffective reporting structures where the CISO reports to the Chief Information Officer (CIO) who runs IT, not the business risk owners at the C-Level, such as the board, CEO, Chief Financial Officer (CFO), or Chief Risk Officer (CRO). These diametrically opposing agendas are not the best approach to maximize cyber resilience. The need to reorganize to a commonsense approach is woefully lacking in most companies.

Coming full circle, cyber must be understood by everyone in the organization to increase resiliency in the context of their role. Most security awareness programs lack the support to enable long-term behavioral change. The need to upskill the organization into diverse roles that address privacy, compliance, risk, and cyber are clearly needed to enable effective reductions in cyber risk.

As cyber continues to evolve, we are seeing new roles emerge. Gartner states that "Through 2022, 80% of organizations (up from 30% in 2018) will undergo some change in their security organization structure as a direct result of digitalization."[22]

The emerging Digital Asset Risk Officer position is useful for organizations of all sizes who struggle with understanding the relationships between privacy, security, risk, and compliance management functions. In the age of the digital revolution and the continuously evolving threat landscape, a single established digital asset risk management function is better positioned to address the needs holistically of the organization. A Chief Digital Asset Risk Officer can also be held accountable for the organization's overall digital risk. Integrated digital asset cyber risk management supports these new functions and addresses the issues of meaningful metrics for each member of the cyber ecosystem. New university cybersecurity certificate programs at Pace, UConn, Rutgers, and others are springing up to address this most urgent business need. Certification bodies like ISACA are also recognizing this need.

Digital business transformation is driving the way organizations are designed. The increase in the rates of change and complexity in digital technology adoption require a constant change in security roles, processes, and capabilities. We see the appearance of new business-driven security roles and integrated cyber risk management platforms. These new roles include security champions, security architects, cloud auditors, and digital asset risk officers to name a few.

Managing all the moving parts that are required cannot be done in spreadsheets. Using an integrated cyber risk management platform can orchestrate a digital asset cybersecurity program that provides security, privacy, technology, and risk management leaders to communicate holistically and reduce risk in a coordinated fashion. It also bridges the gap between the CISO and the board, ensuring that meaningful and digestible metrics can be used to properly de-risk, budget, and ensure cybersecurity risk reduction. Companies like Cyber Innovative Technologies provide this type of platform.

New roles require investment. Large banks, such as Citi, Bank of America, and JPMorgan Chase, view cybersecurity as a competitive differentiator for both consumer and commercial clients.[23] Each invests close to a billion dollars a year in their cybersecurity programs.

Digital asset cyber—turning threat into opportunity

Cyber thugs attack your digital assets. They steal your data. They interrupt your business processes with ransomware or denial-of-service attacks. They cause regulatory fines and penalties from regulators including but not limited to the European Union Supervisory Authority for GDPR, US Department of Health and Human Services for Healthcare, the Payment Card Industry Security Council for credit card data, etc., based on the type of data that they store and process in systems and technologies, the industry and geography that your firm is doing business in.

A common mistake companies make when trying to understand cybersecurity metrics is to present technical data to nontechnical decision makers. When a CISO walks into the boardroom and provides a list of 300 vulnerabilities to the board, stating, "This is our cyber program," the board is mystified. First, it is not a cyber program. It is a list of 300 vulnerabilities, which are 300 weaknesses in systems that hackers can exploit to access your digital assets. These include items with consuming terms, such as SQL injections, Cross-Site Scripting, or man-in-the-middle attacks, etc. Second, these technical issues are not correlated back to the digital assets that they are impacting. Is it the trading system or is it a less critical system? Third, if you do not correlate data back to the digital asset, you cannot see the financial impact and understand how to prioritize risk remediation. This leaves the board and other stakeholders at a serious disadvantage.

As I said, vulnerabilities are weaknesses in systems and are not a cyber program. You will learn about these more in a few chapters. A cyber program consists of people, processes, tools, and insurance that reduce financial exposure and risk associated with digital assets. Boards have no idea what a man-in-the-middle attack is exactly and, nor should they.

Digital assets can be used to quantify financial exposures, aligned exactly to how a cyber insurance claim is paid. They are the only defensible metrics that quantify exposures and measure the inherent risk of the digital asset. They can be scored to baseline cyber resilience by measuring inherent (cyber risk without controls) cyber risk and demonstrate the effectiveness of security controls in reducing risk (mitigating controls) and pinpointing when cyber risk rises above the desired thresholds from detected vulnerabilities, threats, and incidents (residual cyber risk).

In his book, *The Fifth Domain*, Richard Clarke says, "Cyber resilience must be built upon, rather than be seen as a replacement for sound security fundamentals."[24] In order to do that, you have to be able to benchmark it and then set goals to increase it.

Throughout the book, we will try to show you that you do have a choice to make about the cybersecurity of your enterprise. In the chapters that follow, we will build a foundation for the nontechies that will help define strategies and lay out a plan for how companies can build their cyber resilience.

Notes

1. Internet World Stats, "Internet growth stats", December 2017, www.internetworldstats.com/emarketing.htm.
2. Steven Morgan, Cybercrime Magazine, "Humans on the internet will triple from 2015 to 2022 and hit 6 billion", July 18, 2019, https://cybersecurityventures.com/how-many-internet-users-will-the-world-have-in-2022-and-in-2030.
3. Richard A. Clarke, Robert K Knake, "The fifth domain: Defending our country, our companies, and ourselves in the age of cyber threats", July 16, 2019, Penguin Press, Kindle Edition, Page 14.
4. Kevin McCoy, USA Today, "Target to pay $18.5 million for 2013 data breach that affected 41 Million consumers", May 23, 2017, https://www.usatoday.com/story/money/2017/05/23/target-pay-185m-2013-data-breach-affected-consumers/102063932/.
5. Sonia Queriroz Vaz, Cuatrecasas, "Hospital Do Barreiro fined by Comissao Nacional de Proteccao de Dados in 400,000 euro for allowing improper access to clinical files", October 30, 2018, https://blog.cuatrecasas.com/propiedad-intelectual/hospital-do-barreiro-fined-by-comissao-nacional-proteccao-dados-in-400000-euro-for-allowing-improper-access-to-clinical-files/?lang=en.
6. Ingrid Lunden, TechCrunch, "UKs ICO fines British Airways a record £183M over GDPR breach that leaked data from 500,000 users", July 8, 2019, https://techcrunch.com/2019/07/08/uks-ico-fines-british-airways-a-record-183m-over-gdpr-breach-that-leaked-data-from-500000-users/.
7. Makena Kelly, The Verge, "FTC hits Facebook with $5 billion fine and new privacy checks", July 24, 2019, https://www.theverge.com/2019/7/24/20707013/ftc-facebook-settlement-data-cambridge-analytica-penalty-privacy-punishment-5-billion.
8. Federal Trade Commission, "FTC imposes $5 billion Penalty and sweeping new privacy restrictions on Facebook", July 24, 2019, https://www.ftc.gov/news-events/press-releases/2019/07/ftc-imposes-5-billion-penalty-sweeping-new-privacy-restrictions.

9. Janko Roettgers, Variety, "Mark Zuckerberg says Facebook will spend more than $3.7 billion on safety, security in 2019", February 5, 2019, https://variety.com/2019/digital/news/facebook-2019-safety-speding-1203128797/.
10. MarketWatch, "Facebook stock drops roughly 20% loses $120 billion in value after warning that revenue growth will take a hit", July 26, 2018, https://www.marketwatch.com/story/facebook-stock-crushed-after-revenue-user-growth-miss-2018-07-25#:~:text=On%20Thursday%2C%20Facebook%20FB%2C%20%2D,and%20showed%20slowing%20user%20growth.&text=Its%20market%20capitalization%20as%20of%20Wednesday%3A%20%24630%20billion.
11. Transcript courtesy of Bloomberg Government, The Washington Post, "Transcripts of Mark Zuckerberg's Senate hearing", April 10, 2018, https://www.washingtonpost.com/news/the-switch/wp/2018/04/10/transcript-of-mark-zuckerbergs-senate-hearing/.
12. Lucy Hook, Insurance Business, "Cyber claims against directors and officers to rise in 2018, says Aon firm Stroz Friedberg", January 16, 2018, https://www.insurancebusinessmag.com/uk/news/cyber/cyber-claims-against-directors-and-officers-to-rise-in-2018-says-aon-firm-stroz-friedberg-89465.aspx.
13. Burns & Levinson LLP, "The likelihood of company executives being fired post-data breach-it isn't pretty", October 18, 2018, https://www.jdsupra.com/legalnews/the-likelihood-of-company-executives-31966/.
14. WhatIs.com, "definition of digitization", 2020, https://whatis.techtarget.com/search/query?q=digitization.
15. Thomas Wiiberniet, Customer Think, "Digitization, digitalization, digital transformation—A stake in the ground", January 2, 2021, https://customerthink.com/digitization-digitalization-digital-transformation-a-stake-in-the-ground/.
16. Nick Eubanks, Forbes, "The true cost of cyber crime for businesses", July 13, 2017, www.forbes.com/sites/theyec/2017/07/13/the-true-cost-of-cybercrime-for-businesses/#380e0f694947.
17. Statista, "Amount of monetary damage caused by reported cyber crime to the IC3 from 2001 to 2019", March 27, 2020, https://www.statista.com/statistics/267132/total-damage-caused-by-by-cyber-crime-in-the-us/.
18. Wombie Bond Dickinson, Lexology, "The Internet of Things (IoT) and cybersecurity: key challenges and new regulation", March 5, 2020, https://www.lexology.com/library/detail.aspx?g=04d2c471-b6c7-4917-be13-8348aa8d94f8.
19. The National Law Review, "IoT manufacturers—What you need to know about California's IoT law", September 10, 2020, https://www.natlawreview.com/article/iot-manufacturers-what-you-need-to-know-about-california-s-iot-law.
20. National Telecommunications and Information Administration, "NTIA software component transparency," October 19, 2020, https://www.ntia.doc.gov/SoftwareTransparency.
21. Fireeye, "Redline dawn: China recalculates its use of cyber espionage," 2016, https://www.fireeye.com/content/dam/fireeye-www/current-threats/pdfs/rpt-china-espionage.pdf.
22. Gartner, "Security organization dynamics", Research ID: G00381600, 8 October 2020, Sam Olyaei, Tom Scholtz.
23. Dr. Yoav Intrator, Head of Israel Innovation & Technology Center, Managing Director, JPMorgan Chase & Co.
24. Richard A. Clarke, Robert K Knake, "The fifth domain: Defending our country, our companies, and ourselves in the age of cyber threats", July 16, 2019, Penguin Press, Kindle Edition, Page 14.

2 CYBER RISK

Cyber risk has emerged as a significant threat to the financial system. Financial institutions worldwide face potential losses from cyber-attacks ranging from 9% of net income based on experiences so far up to half of the profits in a worst-case scenario.

Christine Lagarde, President, European Central Bank

Digital assets—the keys to the kingdom

What are digital assets? They are the assets attacked by cyber-criminals. They include systems, business processes, data, and technologies.

A system is a consolidated set of technologies that provides the basis for collecting, creating, storing, processing, and distributing information. Systems can be purchased from vendors or developed internally (homegrown) by the organization. This is an important point that relates to which organization has cybersecurity responsibilities. The business unit that purchases or pays for the development of the system is the system owner.

Examples of typical business system categories include transactional processing, decision support, executive information, management information, workflow, enterprise resource planning systems, and cyber risk management systems. A transaction processing system's primary purpose is record keeping, which is required in any organization to conduct business. These may include sales, supply chain, order entry, payroll, and specific transactional functional systems. A decision support system uses sophisticated data analysis tools for problem-specific decision-making. An executive information system can be used for trend analysis, exception reporting, and has drill-down capabilities. A management information system provides the management with day-to-day summaries of its operations and provides information to managers and decision-makers to increase operational efficiency. A workflow system uses business rules to direct, coordinate, and monitor the sets of interrelated tasks that form a business process. An enterprise resource planning system is a business process management software that allows an organization to use a set of integrated programs managing the company from an enterprise perspective. A cyber risk system or platform is a cyber risk management application that orchestrates the cybersecurity information across privacy, risk, compliance, regulation, audit, vulnerability management, incident management, and threat management.

The relative importance of digital assets can comparatively be categorized by classifying them as crown jewels, business-critical, and business crucial systems based on their value to the business. These categorizations are useful in setting cyber risk thresholds.

DOI: 10.4324/9781003052616-3

Systems are owned by business units. The business unit is an organizational subset that is a logical element or segment of a company (such as accounting, production, marketing, etc.) representing a specific business function. The organization may be a subsidiary that is owned by a parent company, and a holding company may own an organization. These business relationships demonstrate the hierarchical associations that exist between organizations and digital assets. We will discuss this further and explain how these relate to more effective cybersecurity budgeting methods in future chapters.

Systems exist either on-premise or in a cloud service. If on-premise, then the firm is responsible for 100% of the cybersecurity of that system. The cybersecurity responsibility can be outsourced to another company if the firm is short on cybersecurity resources; however, the firm is still responsible for it. It is the firm's data, and the company will have to report any data breaches. It may have to also report operational disruptions (business interruptions due to cyber-attacks) depending on the regulatory oversight required by the firm.

Cloud service providers provide companies with software, infrastructure, or platforms delivered as a service that the firm will develop and use to process and store its data. The environment for these cloud services is off-premise. Depending upon the relationship type Software as a Service (SaaS), Infrastructure as a Service (IaaS), or Platform as a Service (PaaS), the responsibility for the cybersecurity controls will vary and has to be explicitly written into the contracts with the service provider. We will explore this shared responsibility model in detail in further chapters. Identifying on-premise versus cloud systems in a digital asset inventory is a critical part of cybersecurity risk management.

Technologies are the components of a system and they may include, but are not limited to, the hardware, software, data communication lines, devices, network and telecommunications equipment, internet-related information

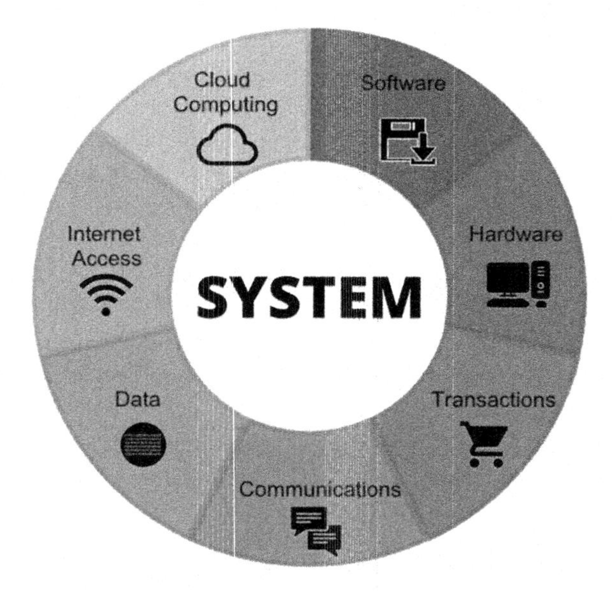

Figure 2.1 Systems and Their Components

technology infrastructure, wide area network and other information technology equipment, owned, licensed to, or controlled by the company or any of its subsidiaries.[1]

And let us not forget endpoints. They are technology devices that allow communication back and forth with a network to which they are connected. Examples of endpoints include desktops, laptops, smartphones, tablets, servers, workstations, and IoT devices. Endpoints are one of the key areas that, when vulnerable, provide points of entry for cyber-criminals to do nefarious activities. Endpoints are where attackers can execute malware that can exploit vulnerabilities, exfiltrate data, or make systems unavailable.

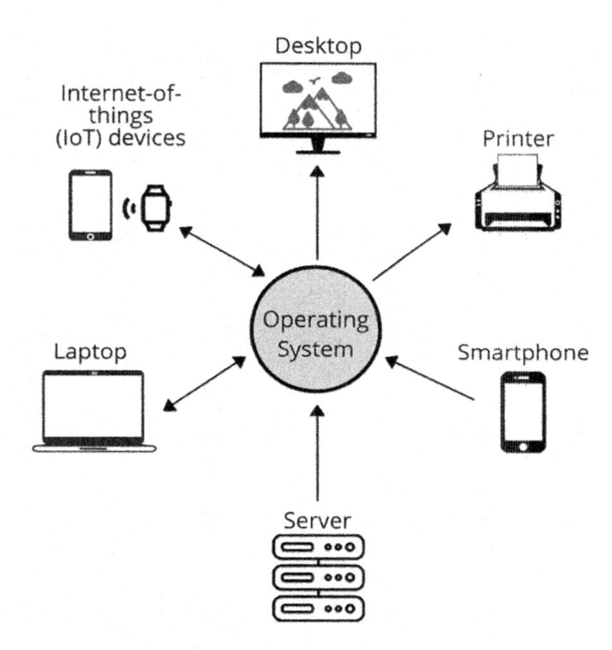

Figure 2.2 Endpoints

Because systems are made up of technologies, they will inherit any risk that the technology has, regardless of cybersecurity controls. As an example, if my system uses IoT technology, then my system inherits that risk. This is important since technologies are shared across the company's infrastructure and will increase exposures and risk due to the fact that they are touching more than one system. Technology attributes are also important since they influence the likelihood a cybercriminal can breach it. In the case of IoT, it has a higher likelihood that a cybercriminal can breach it since it does not typically have any abilities for the organization's system administrators or security personnel to manage access to the device. We call that inherent access risk since it is the risk to access the digital asset which is baked into it.

Business processes are a set of digital rules utilized by one or more systems to take inputs, transform them, and produce outputs that are reported or utilized by other systems. When a business process cannot complete transactions, the business loses revenue. Denial of service and ransomware attacks interrupt the business processes and make the systems unavailable. Business processes are owned or used by a system. When business processes are developed, they may interact with more than one system. However, one business unit created that business process, and that identifies who owns it.

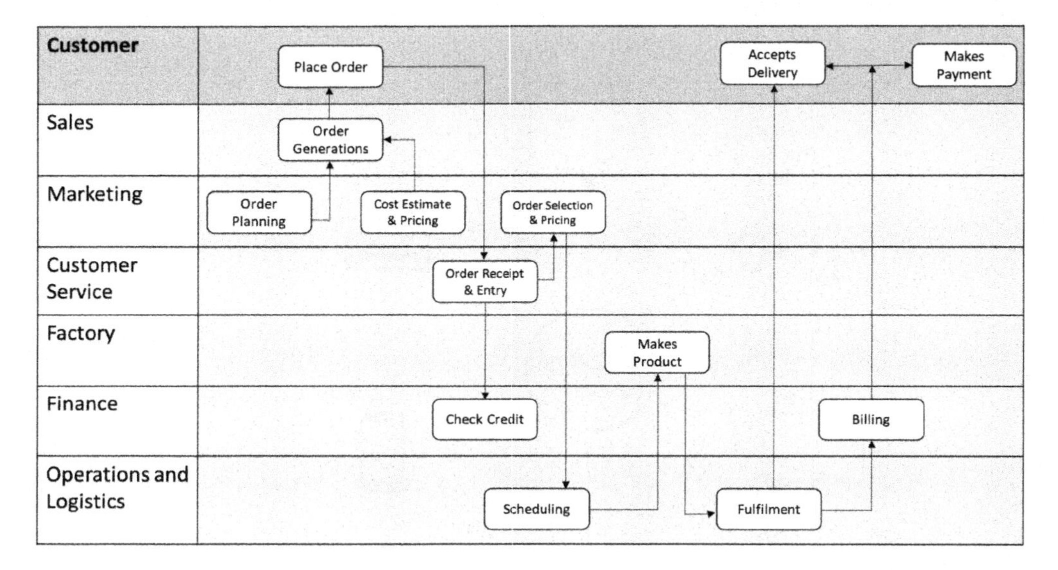

Figure 2.3 Example of a Business Process

Data is distinct pieces of information that use characters or symbols on which operations are performed by a computer. They are stored and transmitted in the form of electrical signals, which are recorded on magnetic, optical, or mechanical recording media. Data can be categorized in terms of types processed or stored. These categorizations are important to tie the digital assets back to regulations. Databases store our data, and business processes transform that data. Cloud service providers can also store and process data on our behalf.

A record is a basic data structure. Data is displayed in records in a database and are referred to as rows. A record is a collection of fields, possibly different data types, typically in fixed numbers and sequence. Unique records are records that are not duplicated. They are used in our cyber exposure calculations further in this book.

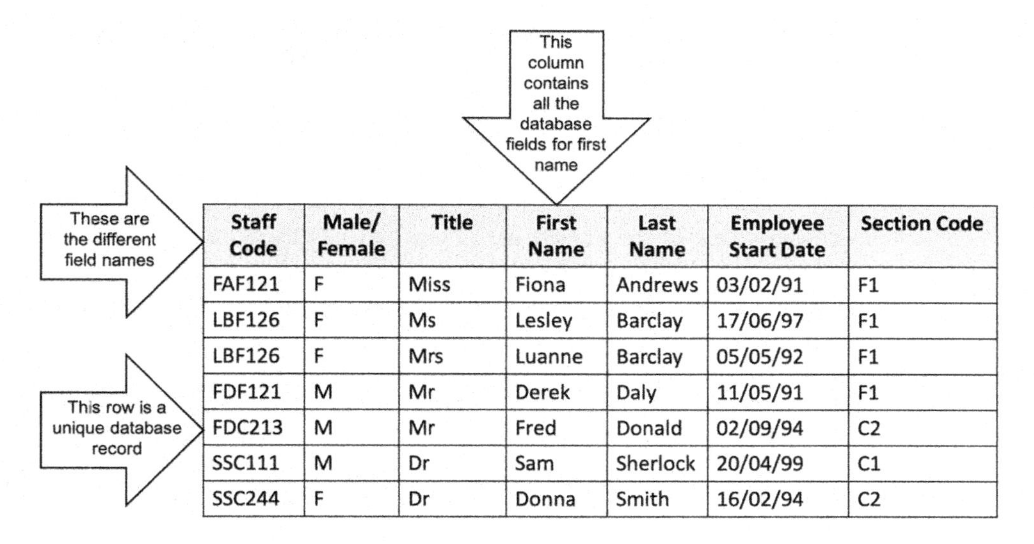

Staff Code	Male/ Female	Title	First Name	Last Name	Employee Start Date	Section Code
FAF121	F	Miss	Fiona	Andrews	03/02/91	F1
LBF126	F	Ms	Lesley	Barclay	17/06/97	F1
LBF126	F	Mrs	Luanne	Barclay	05/05/92	F1
FDF121	M	Mr	Derek	Daly	11/05/91	F1
FDC213	M	Mr	Fred	Donald	02/09/94	C2
SSC111	M	Dr	Sam	Sherlock	20/04/99	C1
SSC244	F	Dr	Donna	Smith	16/02/94	C2

Figure 2.4 Example of a Record

As I referenced earlier, digital assets have hierarchical and relational relationships. The digital asset model is organized into a tree-like structure where attributes and characteristics are inherited. The data is stored as records, typically in a database. Databases are technologies which are a component of a system that utilizes business processes owned by a business unit that reports to the organization. Business processes are relational since they are owned by one business unit but used by many business units. The business units purchase or pay for the development of the systems and processes. Systems are owned by one business unit but may be used by many. Technologies are typically used by many systems.

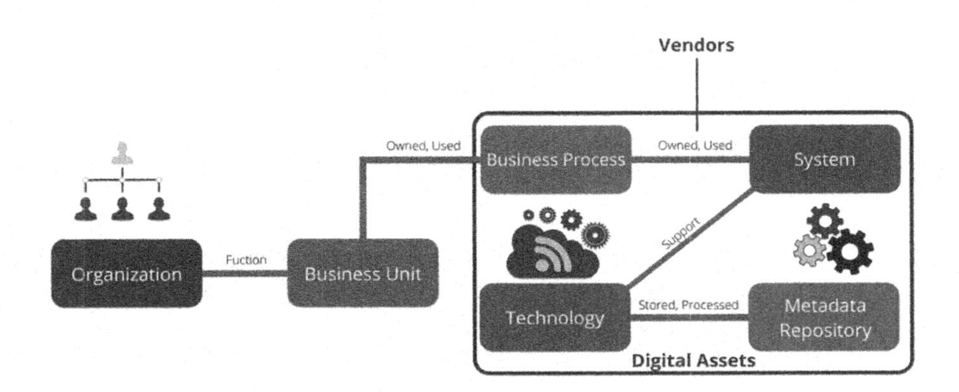

Figure 2.5 Digital Asset Relationships[2]

Why is this important? When you have a vulnerability, such as a SQL injection that impacts Oracle MySQL version 8.0, it will impact all the systems that use Oracle MySQL version 8.0. In many cases, companies standardize on technologies, and it would be most likely to have Oracle MySQL version 8.0 running across their entire infrastructure if they are an Oracle shop. Two hundred systems using Oracle MySQL Version 8.0 may mean 200 more systems likely to have cyber exposure. One of the biggest pain points a CISO has is that they cannot equate cyber events (vulnerabilities, incidents, and threats) back to the business since they don't know which systems are impacted by that cyber incident. This leaves the board and senior executives at a serious disadvantage. The digital asset approach fixes that issue.

Digital assets are used to quantify cyber exposures and manage cyber risk across the entire cybersecurity lifecycle. We will be deep diving into this in the Parts 8 and 9.

Digital asset link to the CIA triad

The CIA triad is a model intended to guide policies for information security within an organization. Confidentiality is the ability to ensure that only authorized and approved users have access to the data. Integrity ensures that the data is unaltered and is consistent, accurate, and trustworthy over its entire life cycle. Availability is the ability to ensure the data is available to users.

Figure 2.6 The CIA Triad

Digital asset cyber risk metrics

Cybersecurity exposures

Cybersecurity exposures are the financial amounts of potential loss that an organization stands to lose should the digital assets' security fail or not be effective. They are directly related to the damage a cybercriminal may cause to an organization from various attack vectors. They are also directly related to how a cyber insurance company pays a claim. Cyber Insurance is a risk transference mechanism to reduce risk in terms of business interruption, data exfiltration, and regulatory losses due to cyber-attacks. There are three categories of cyber exposures: data exfiltration, business interruption, and regulatory loss.

Data exfiltration

Data exfiltration happens when data is stolen by insiders or external actors resulting in a data breach. This can be due to many causes, including, and not limited too, misconfigured systems, or poor access controls. Specifically, it is the unauthorized copying, transfer, or retrieval of data from a computer or server. Data exfiltration is a malicious activity performed through various techniques, typically by cybercriminals. As an example, an employee clicks on a phishing email, malware is inserted, the payload is delivered, and data is exfiltrated—stolen by the attacker. Phishing is the deceptive practice of sending emails purporting to be from reputable individuals in companies to induce users to reveal personal information, such as passwords and credit card numbers.

Data exfiltration when related to personal identifiable information (PII) is also a privacy violation. As an example, the GDPR is a privacy regulation that protects the rights of data subjects. Article 33 of the GDPR requires companies in scope for GDPR to notify the supervisory authority in the event of a data breach. Data breaches always impact confidentiality and may also impact integrity.

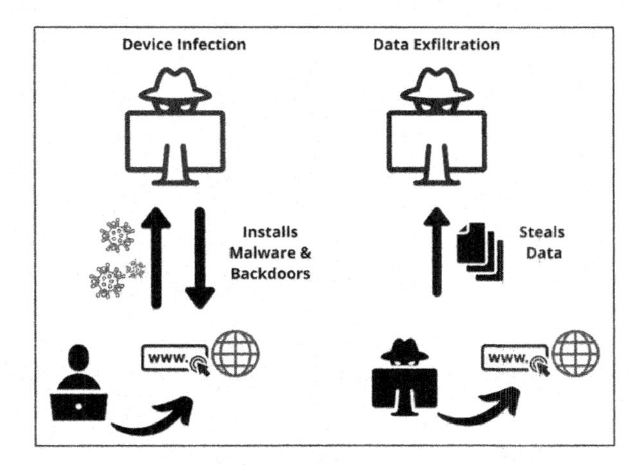

Figure 2.7 Cybercriminal Stealing Data

The financial exposure of data exfiltration is related to the cost of the record stolen multiplied by the number of records stolen. The average cost of a data breach in the U.S. showed a 1.6% increase in costs in 2018 and a 12% rise over the last five years.[3]

The three types of data most at risk are: customer financial, internal employee, and intellectual property information. Other types of sensitive data that are highly attractive to cybercriminals include information associated with access to usernames and associated passwords, system authentication-related information, and cryptographic keys.

It is not surprising that, for hackers and malicious insiders, the vast amounts of customer financial information held by financial services, payment processors, and merchants is the number one target. A hacker is an unauthorized user who attempts to gain access to a digital asset. A finding is a failure of a cybersecurity control to perform properly.

The fraudulent acquisition and use of a person's private identifying information, usually for financial gain, is very profitable. Financial fraud using stolen credit, debit card, and bank account numbers demands a high price for large quantities of data.

Identity theft can be anything from a minor inconvenience to a major setback for an individual consumer. The Pomemon Cost of a Data Breach study[4] sponsored by IBM interviewed over 500 organizations that had a data breach to get an industry average of the record cost. While the global average cost of a data breach is US$3.92 million, the US average cost is $8.19 million. The cost of a record for financial data is US$220 per record. The other primary favorite target of cybercriminals is medical data, whose theft will result in the use of another's identity to obtain medical care or drugs. The cost of a record for medical data is US$429 per record, which is almost twice as much as financial data.

All 50 states and the European Union now have mandatory public breach notification laws and employ heavy fines for noncompliant security policies and infrastructure.

Internal employee documentation that is processed and stored by HR, payroll and the benefits departments often keep the employees' bank account information in order to direct deposit their pay into their bank accounts. They also have confidential personal information, including the full names, current addresses, and employment history, with which identity thieves can impersonate victims. Like the theft of consumer financial information, data exfiltration involving employee documentation can be disastrous for the company attacked. Data breach notifications also apply to this type of data.

Intellectual property and confidential corporate data must be secured to maintain a competitive advantage. Hardware, software, pharmaceutical, universities, manufacturers, and critical infrastructure companies that design products must protect their research and development activities, processes, and data.

Critical Infrastructure represents the digital assets that are instrumental for society to function without a debilitating impact on the security, economy, health, safety, or environment.

Unauthorized leaks of confidential corporate data, such as the profit and loss statement, 10-Q filings, and other mandatory financial reporting, can damage a company's brand, strategy, and profit. Corporate espionage is particularly sinister because of the malicious intent toward the organization.

Business interruption

Business Interruption is when business processes are interrupted by a cyber-attack, and authorized users cannot access systems typically due to a denial of service or ransomware attack. This is an availability issue. In a denial-of-service attack, an attacker floods the Web application servicer with traffic shutting it down. In a ransomware attack, they typically send a phishing email, the user clicks on it, and malware is inserted that encrypts the entire infrastructure.

Business interruption exposures are related to the amounts of revenue the company will lose when their business processes are interrupted. Ransomware attacks impact the entire organization's revenue, while denial of service attacks occur at the system level.

Attributes used to calculate business interruption are revenues, recovery time objectives, ransomware recovery time objectives, and the percentage of on-premise systems versus the cloud.

Regulatory loss

Regulatory loss happens when a regulator fines an organization for a cyber-breach. The regulations are based on types of data processed, and/or geography and/or type of business. These include, but are not limited to, the GDPR, HIPAA, PCI, CCPA, 23 NYCRR Part 500, U.S. Privacy Laws, Insurance Data Security Act, and many others. This is a confidentiality violation and may also be an integrity issue.

Regulatory exposures vary depending on the law. They can be percentages of revenue, fixed amounts, based on records exfiltrated, and so on. We cover this in the cyber risk quantification chapter in detail.

Cyber exposure use cases

Use cases for cybersecurity exposures include:

- Identifying the riskiest assets to prevent data loss. This is a key requirement that enables the board of directors to protect the business assets.
- Setting up a crown jewel risk strategy that identifies and focuses on the preservation of the crown jewel assets. Many firms adopt a crown jewel strategy.
- Determining the adequate amount of cyber insurance limits and sublimits. This includes the aggregate limit and sublimits for cyber extortion, business interruption, and regulatory sublimits. Cyber insurance is a key strategic requirement of the CFO, and the CRO.
- Identification of hidden exposures. In many cases, there are billions of dollars of hidden exposures in an organization due to undiscovered misuse of data retention and disposal policies. Not understanding this can put a firm out of business.
- Understanding the exposures allows for quick and accurate prioritization of cybersecurity controls to efficiently utilize scarce resources and reduce the maximum amount of cyber risk. This is a key requirement of the CRO and CISO.
- Calculation of the return on investment (ROI) of cybersecurity tools. This helps the CISO build a business case for risk reduction and value.
- Cybersecurity tool road maps based on risk reduction.

- Business-based cyber risk reporting to senior executives and the board that benchmark resiliency and identify the cyber program effectiveness lending to correct budgeting and resourcing.

The calculations and use cases will be explored in detail in the risk management and strategy chapters.

Cyber risk scores

Digital asset cyber risk is measured in terms of an empirical score related to the behavioral and user characteristics of the digital asset, and how the organization uses and protects it. An empirical score relies on a comprehensive and diverse set of impact and likelihood risk data related to the digital asset. Aggregated, it is used to determine the cyber risk profile of any organization as a benchmark to measure cyber resilience and set goals to increase cyber resiliency.

Inherent cyber risk

Inherent cyber risk is the cyber risk score without cybersecurity controls in place that is measured for each digital asset. It is as if there is zero percent effectiveness of the cybersecurity controls. It is the worst-case scenario and what I call "Cybergeddon risk." This score is static and is based on the characteristics of the digital asset alone, which typically do not change over time unless the system is replaced or re-architected. It can be used to benchmark cyber resiliency.

Inherent risk uses impact and likelihood attributes to calculate the score. Impact is the degree to which a cyber-issue may have an adverse outcome on the organization. There are several factors that can influence impact in cybersecurity. Likelihood is a probability a cyber-attack will cause damage. Each can be measured at the level of the digital asset.

Inherent Cyber Risk can be calculated differently for each organization or system based on data types, technology types, and other intrinsic attributes. Most organizations use one score; however, digital asset metrics allow for multiple scores. As an example, the Israeli Prime Minister's Cyber Defense Methodology uses three times the impact plus likelihood.[5] We will discuss the impact and likelihood attributes in the cyber risk and strategy chapters in detail.

Mitigating risk scores

Security Assessments play an important part in the cybersecurity lifecycle. They are done to analyze the effectiveness of the mitigating cybersecurity controls that are in place. All the different security frameworks are a set of cybersecurity control tests. Control tests are specific to some aspect of the cybersecurity program to measure specific goals for access control, or encryption, etc. All control tests can be mapped across frameworks. As an example, NIST CSF cybersecurity control PR.AC-1 (Access control policies and procedures) can be mapped to the control tests of COBIT 2019 managed security category. This is important to understand to reduce redundancy in testing when a system processes different types of regulated data, such as credit card and healthcare. Most often, the two teams doing the assessments are siloed and do not speak to each other. Understanding digital asset relationships can eliminate this duplicate effort.

Security assessments have a relationship to inherent cyber risk. They decrease inherent cyber risk based on how well the controls are in place. If the control has four objectives, and only two are met, then the control is only 50% effective if all the objectives are weighted equally. The image below shows the first level of cyber risk relationships. We explore this in detail in the framework chapters.

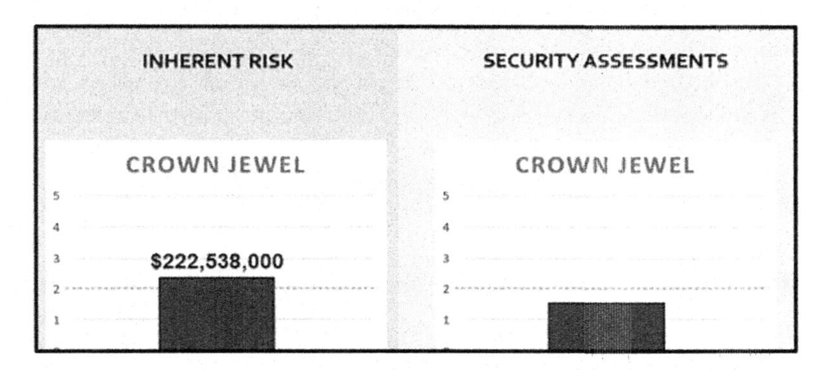

Figure 2.8 The Relationship Between Inherent Cyber Risk and Security Assessments[6]

Residual cyber risk

Residual Cyber Risk is the digital asset cyber risk score with cybersecurity controls in place. It is the best-case scenario. It incorporates data from cybersecurity tools to demonstrate the dynamic nature of cyber. Cyber risk rises when incidents, threats, and vulnerabilities happen. We can get this data from cyber tools. The image below shows the cyber risk relationships between inherent, mitigating controls, and residual risk. We explore this in detail in cyber risk management and strategy. It is the cornerstone of continuous monitoring and goal setting to increase cyber resiliency.

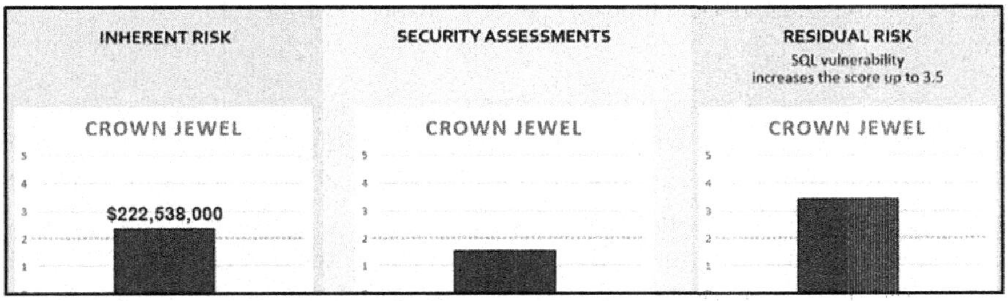

Figure 2.9 The Relationship Between Security Assessments and Residual Cyber Risk[7]

Cyber scoring use cases

Use cases of cybersecurity scores include:

- The ability to benchmark and continuously monitor cybersecurity resiliency.
- The ability to identify weak areas in the digital asset and tighten them.
- The identification of trends and gaps in an organization's cybersecurity program.
- The evaluation of gaps in a vendor's cybersecurity program.
- The prioritization of remediation activities for vulnerability, incident, threats, and findings.
- Dynamic resource planning to efficiently utilize scarce resources and reduce the maximum amount of cyber risk.
- Consolidated business-based risk reporting to senior executives and the board that demonstrate resiliency, and the cyber program effectiveness lending to correct budgeting and resourcing.

The risk management chapter explains how to calculate these scores.

Risk amplifiers

Cyber risk amplifiers represent the potential financial loss or harm related to digital assets that can amplify the financial exposures from reputational, organizational, and legal impacts.

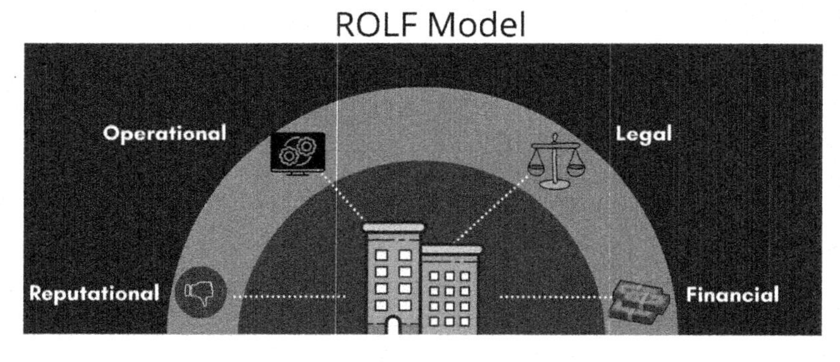

Figure 2.10 Reputational, Operational, Legal, and Financial Risk (ROLF)

Reputational risk is a matter of corporate trust. The loss can be demonstrated in lost revenue due to increased operating, capital, or regulatory costs or destruction of shareholder value. As an example, Equifax had a reputational amplifier when their stock price decreased 30% after their data breach.

Operational loss involves losing key employees. After a data breach, 31% of C-Level executives and employees are fired or let go. Operational loss also includes the costs related to the remediation of the cyber event. In the United States, the average is over US$9 million after a cyber-attack.

Legal risk amplification is the result of class actions, D&O derivative actions and other lawsuits that result from a data breach. The cyber insurance industry tracks these and has many statistics to understand the potential financial impacts.

What is not cyber risk

Most companies are confused about what cyber risk really is. Many cyber risk product vendors label vulnerabilities, threats, or incidents as risk. These are not risks. They are factors that will increase cyber risk.

As an example, the Factor Analysis of Information Risk (FAIR) looks at vulnerabilities only. As you just read, vulnerabilities are weaknesses in systems that attackers exploit. It is a component of residual risk. The FAIR Risk Model touches only one part of cyber risk and sees it only through the lens of vulnerabilities and is very myopic. FAIR cannot assign defensible values.

The features that are needed for a defensible security program must include tools that support risk-based decisions. A defensible security program is one that substantiates if the enterprise is doing enough to reasonably protect its information resources.

Some vendors look at "cyber risk" by using Deep and Dark Web Analytics scores. There are botnets, spam propagation, and data about executive reconnaissance. These are threats, not risk. A cyber threat is a malicious attempt to damage or disrupt a computer network or system. A botnet is a number of internet-connected devices, each of which is running one or more bots. Botnets can be used to perform Distributed Denial-of-Service attacks, steal data, send spam, and allow the attacker to access the device and its connection. Spam is a popular means of virus propagation and is a serious security threat. Threats influence risk, they are not risk in and of themselves.[8]

The Cyber Insurance Advisor measures incidents in terms of loss events. Loss events are incidents; they have a 100% probability and are not risk.

Defensible Cyber Risk programs are digital. They use quantified exposures and digital asset scores based on how the cyber-criminal damages your business and is associated to the effectiveness of cyber controls and the events (threats, incidents, and vulnerabilities) in the cybersecurity lifecycle.

Notes

1. EX-2.1—SEC.gov | HOME. https://www.sec.gov/Archives/edgar/data/726513/000119312517163312/d394159dex21.htm.
2. Maryellen Evans, Digital Asset Based Cyber Risk Algorithmic Engine, Integrated Cyber Risk Methodology and Automated Cyber Risk Management System. US 2020/0106801 Al United States Patent and Trademark Office, April 2, 2020.
3. Dan Swinhoe, CSO United States, "What is the cost of a data breach?", August 13, 2020, https://www.csoonline.com/article/3434601/what-is-the-cost-of-a-data-breach.html.

4. IBM Security, “Cost of a Data Breach Study”. July 2020. https://www.ibm.com/security/services?p1=Search&p4=43700056097600130&p5=b&cm_mmc=Search_Google-_-1S_1S-_-WW_NA-_-%2Bibm%20%2Bdata%20%2Bbreach%20%2Bcost_b&cm_mmca7=71700000061027108&cm_mmca8=kwd-417449383408&cm_mmca9=CjwKCAiA8ov_BRAoEiwAOZogwQwPjW7hL228U2n1z_-d7HDWvYupcZHnoluLaJcrwLZmN4ebFPiUuRoCN8gQAvD_BwE&cm_mmca10=454725094964&cm_mmca11=b&gclid=CjwKCAiA8ov_BRAoEiwAOZogwQwPjW7hL228U2n1z_-d7HDWvYupcZHnoluLaJcrwLZmN4ebFPiUuRoCN8gQAvD_BwE&gclsrc=aw.ds.
5. Prime Minister’s office National Cyber Security Directorate, National cyber security authority, “Cyber defense methodology for an organization,” June 2017, https://www.gov.il/BlobFolder/policy/cyber_security_methodology_for_organizations/he/Cyber1.0_english_617_A4.pdf.
6. Maryellen Evans, Digital Asset Based Cyber Risk Algorithmic Engine, Integrated Cyber Risk Methodology and Automated Cyber Risk Management System. US 2020/0106801 Al United States Patent and Trademark Office, April 2, 2020.
7. Maryellen Evans, Digital Asset Based Cyber Risk Algorithmic Engine, Integrated Cyber Risk Methodology and Automated Cyber Risk Management System. US 2020/0106801 Al United States Patent and Trademark Office, April 2, 2020.
8. GitHub – BOT-CODER/SniperMan: This Tool is used to make …. https://github.com/BOT-CODER/SniperMan/.

3 THE HISTORY OF CYBERSECURITY

The Stellar Evolution of Cybersecurity. The evolutionary processes of stars depend upon their initial mass. The evolutionary processes of cybersecurity depend upon the hyperconvergence of Cyber Dependencies, People, Processes, and Technology.

Ludmila Morozova-Buss, International Cybersecurity
Woman Influencer of the Year

The 60s—feds, tech, and computers

The only ones focused on computers in the 1960s were the federal government. The Advanced Research Projects Agency (ARPA) of the United States Department of Defense funded research into time-sharing of computers in the 1960s, and this led to the creation of the internet. No—Al Gore did not invent it.

Packet sharing research led to packet switching that led to the ARPANET. In telecommunications, packet switching is a method of grouping data transmitted over a digital network into packets. The ARPANET is the precursor to what we know as the internet today. Work on the ARPANET project consisted of several international working groups which contributed to the creation of different protocols and standards through which multiple separate networks could become one single network, aka "a network of networks".

The 70s—hippie cyber

Cybersecurity began as a research project in the 70s. An experimental program written in 1971 by Bob Thomas at Bolt, Beranek and Newman Inc., created a computer program to move across a network, leaving breadcrumbs wherever it traveled. He called this program Creeper. It traveled between Tenex terminals on the early ARPANET, printing the message "I'M THE CREEPER: CATCH ME IF YOU CAN."

In response to Creeper, the inventor of email, Ray Tomlinson, made the virus self-replicating, creating the first computer worm. Tomlinson also wrote the first antivirus software, Reaper, that could track Creeper and delete it.

Modern computers were born in the 70s when the world's first general microprocessor, the Intel 4004, came out in November of 1971. C, the first computer programming language, was developed early in the 70s. The UNIX operating system used the C programming language in 1973. The beginning phases of integration became possible when microchips in simple personal computers began to be

DOI: 10.4324/9781003052616-4

produced along with pocket calculators from Texas Instruments and others. The first home computers came to the United States with the introduction of Apple II. These devices at the time were very expensive and not affordable to the average consumer.

In 1974, the term "internet" was first used as an abbreviation for internetwork, leading to important influences on TCP/IP design. Moore's Law kicked in, and the availability of affordable personal computers was the beginning of the first bulletin board systems. Moore's Law refers to Moore's perception that the number of transistors on a microchip doubles every two years, though the cost of computer is halved. Moore's Law states that we can expect the speed and capability of our computers to increase every couple of years, and we will pay less for them.[1]

In 1976, the first supercomputer was introduced that could perform hundreds of millions of calculations per second. The 1970s also saw the beginning of the video game era. Another 70s milestone was the start of fiber optics. Corning Glass created a glass fiber so clear that it could be used to communicate pulses of light. This led to adoption by GTE and AT&T to transmit sound and image data using fiber optics. The industry was revolutionized, and Telcos were now in the data business. Japan led the world with the integration of the computer and robots. The stage was set for the integration of data at the consumer and business levels.

The 80s—tech, crime, and DoS

In 1981, the National Science Foundation (NSF) sponsored the Computer Science Network (CSNET) and access to ARPANET was extended. The Internet Protocol Suite (TCP/IP) was standardized in 1982, which enabled the proliferation of interconnected networks worldwide. In 1986, TCP/IP network connectivity grew again when the National Science Foundation Network (NSFNet) provided researchers with access to supercomputer sites in the United States. The NSFNet has expanded globally into university and research organizations. As an intercontinental network, this landmark was the beginning of the internet. In 1989, in the United States and Australia, commercial internet service providers (ISPs) appeared. In 1990, the ARPANET was decommissioned.

In 1982, Russia was still a part of the Soviet Union. The first nation-state cyberattack involving a SCADA system was allegedly masterminded by the Central Intelligence Agency to disrupt a portion of Russia's Trans-Siberia pipeline by implanting malware in pirated Canadian software. In his book, At the Abyss: An Insider's History of the Çold War (ISBN 0-89141-821-0) Thomas C. Reed, former Secretary of the United States Air Force under both Gerald Ford and Jimmy Carter, said the United States had added a Trojan horse to the control program for the gas pipeline that the Soviet Union purchased from a Canadian firm. According to Reed, the Trojan horse contributed to a major explosion when the components were deployed on a Trans-Siberian gas pipeline. He wrote: "The pipeline software that was to run the pumps, turbines, and valves was programmed to go haywire, to reset pump speeds and valve settings to produce pressures far beyond those acceptable to the pipeline joints and welds. The result was the most monumental non-nuclear explosion and fire ever seen from space."[2] Reed's account has not been corroborated by intelligence agencies in the United States.

The first convicted cyber-criminal was Markus Hess.[3] In the 1980's, Hess, a German national, hacked into the networks of military and industrial computers based in the United States, Europe, and East Asia. He was convicted of selling the information to the Soviet KGB for US$54,000. During his time with the KGB, Hess broke into an estimated 400 U.S. military computers. These systems included sensitive semiconductor, satellite, space, and aircraft technology information. Hess's activities were discovered in 1986, and he was prosecuted for espionage and received a 20 months suspended jail sentence.

Hess' initial activities started at the University of Bremen in Germany via a satellite link to a gateway service that routed him to any one of several computer systems that also used the service. Hess was able to exploit this packet-switching technology. Once connected, Hess laterally moved to steal the data.

Computer viruses began to become a serious threat in the late 80s. Increasing network connectivity meant that viruses could nearly wipe out networks. This spurred the creation of the first commercially available antivirus software.

In 1983, the first cyber-related U.S. patent was awarded for cryptography. The patent introduced the RSA (Rivest–Shamir–Adleman) algorithm, which was one of the first public-key cryptosystems. Cryptography is one of the bedrocks of modern cybersecurity.[4]

In 1988, Robert Morris wrote a program called the Morris Worm. It was designed to propagate across networks, infiltrate UNIX terminals using a known bug, and then replicate itself. The replication was so aggressive that the early internet availability was seriously damaged due to the large scale of the Denial of Service (DoS) attacks. Morris was the first person convicted under the Computer Fraud and Abuse Act and led to the formation of the Computer Emergency Response Team (the precursor to US-CERT).[5]

Novel advances in semiconductor technology and optical networking created new economic opportunities for commercial involvement in expanding the internet. Email was created in 1989 when MCI Mail and Compuserve generated internet connections, providing email and public access items to the internet's first half a million consumer users.

Meantime, the Air Force was surprised when it discovered that they were using weak passwords on their space division systems. The first known weak password was used by the Air Force Space division was simply SERVICE!

The 90s—internet, business, and viruses

In 1990, an alternate internet backbone for commercial use was launched. This was one of the networks that added to the core of the commercial internet. In March 1990, the first high-speed T1 line was used, allowing much more robust communications than with satellites. In the late 1990's, Tim Berners-Lee began writing the first Web browser, and by Christmas had built all the tools necessary for a working Web: including the HyperText Transfer Protocol (HTTP) 0.9, the HyperText Markup Language (HTML), the first Web browser, the first HTTP server software, and the first Web server.

In June 1993, the first DEFCON conference was held and is now one of the world's most popular cybersecurity technical conferences. It conference started in 1993 in Los Vegas with around 100 people and is now one of the world's most famous technical conferences on cybersecurity with around 20,000 cybersecurity experts from around the globe in attendance.

In 1994, Stanford Federal Credit Union was the first financial institution to offer online internet banking services to its members.[6] In 2005, 16% of the world used the internet, in 2010 30%, in 2017 48%, and in 2019 54%. That is unprecedented in terms of the growth of the attack surface.

Businesses started to see vast commercial opportunities with technology advancement and the potential of the internet's traffic volume. Internet-based technology creation began to explode with new transistor technology.

In 1994, The Health Insurance Portability and Accountability Act (HIPAA) was enacted by the 104th United States Congress and signed into law by President Bill Clinton in 1996. It was created primarily to modernize healthcare information flow, stipulate how the healthcare and health insurance industries can protect Personally Identifiable Information (PII) from fraud and theft, and resolve health insurance coverage limitations.

Since 1995, the internet was revolutionizing business by impacting culture, finance, and commerce. The near-real-time instant communication facilitated by email, instant messaging, telephony, Voice over Internet Protocol (VoIP), two-way interactive video calls, and the World Wide Web expanded the attack surface by over 600% since 1995. The internet is like a self-replicating cell, the data creates more need, and more need creates more data. This is evidenced in areas such as online learning, e-commerce, and social networking, to name a few.

In the late 1990s, the number of internet users was estimated to have risen between 20% and 50%. The estimated total number of internet users as of March 31, 2011, was 2.095 billion (30.2% of the world population). It is reported that only 1 percent of the information flowing through two-way telecommunications was carried by the internet in 1993, that figure had risen to 51% by 2000, and more than 97% of all telecommunicated information was carried over the internet by 2007.[7]

Antivirus and firewalls were created in the late 90s. This followed with more network-centric security tools, including Intrusion Protection Systems (IPS). We cover cybersecurity tools in another section of this book and will not delve into detail here.

In 1995, internet computing security rules were born with the introduction of the secure socket layer internet protocol.

Brave new world the 00s—internet, innovation, and security

In Aldous Huxley's *A Brave New World*, the book warns of the dangers of giving government control over new and powerful technologies. Today I wonder if it is the other way around. Are we unleashing technologies that are so powerful that we are unmindful of what the results will be?

Today, big business is innovating and creating new powerful technologies—most without considering the security and unsettling unintended consequences. Technology innovation, including the Internet of things (IoT) and quantum computing, are edging the world in this direction. Couple that with the fact that cyber is now the fifth domain of warfare alongside land, sea, air, and space. Nation-states are training hackers with offensive cyber tactics. In 2002, George W. Bush created the Department of Homeland Security. This department took on IT infrastructure duties and created a division specifically to address cybersecurity head on.

In 2003, the first universally known hacker group "Anonymous"[8] was established. Anonymous sees themselves as anarchists and is a decentralized online community acting anonymously in a coordinated manner, usually toward a loosely self-agreed upon goal. Beginning in 2008 they gained attention when the group hacked the Church of Scientology website with a series of distributed denial of service (DDoS) attacks. Anonymous has kept its notoriety with a series of high-profile incidents with one major theme-protecting citizens' privacy. Most recently, the Anonymous group has been increasingly associated with collaborative hacktivism. Protests and other acts against companies, such as PayPal, MasterCard, Visa, and Sony were perpetrated by individuals claiming to be with Anonymous. Julian Assange's WikiLeaks and the Occupy movement are openly endorsed by their members.[9]

As we moved into the new century, cyber-attacks became more targeted. Several data breaches targeted consumer's credit card data. In 2004, the first version of the Payment Card Industry Data Security Standard was introduced to protect cardholder data. That did not stop cybercriminals like Albert Gonzalez and his associates from stealing more than 45 million payment cards used by customers of the U.S. retailer TJX, which owns TJ Maxx, and the U.K. outlet TK Maxx. This was the first big data breach that was masterminded on a grand scale. Protegrity estimates that the breach cost over US$1.7 billion.[10]

In this decade, disclosures of security breaches were rare. On January 12, 2010, Google announced a major breach in China. Operation Aurora was a series of cyber-attacks using advanced persistent threats by groups with ties to the People's Liberation Army. First publicly disclosed by Google on January 12, 2010, Google reported that the attacks began in mid-2009 and continued through December 2009. The attack was aimed at dozens of organizations, including confirmed attacks on Adobe Systems, Akamai Technologies, Juniper Networks, and Rackspace. According to media sources, unconfirmed attacks occurred at Yahoo, Symantec, Northrop Grumman, Morgan Stanley, Dow Chemical, and BlackBerry. McAfee disclosed that the primary objective of the attack was to gain access to these high tech, security and defense contractors, and potentially change source code repositories. According to McAfee, Security Configuration Management was wide open. McAfee's Vice President of Threat Research Dimitri Alperovitch stated, "No one ever thought about securing them, yet these were the crown jewels of most of these companies in many ways—much more valuable than any financial or personally identifiable data that they may have and spend so much time and effort protecting."[11] Any potential attacks on cyber tools and technologies needs to be included in the cyber risk program. This is painfully obvious that we did not learn from a decade ago with the same basic idea being used in the SolarWinds attack.

This was a huge wake-up call to the security community that it was lax and that proper measures are still not understood and applied to digital asset technologies. In March 2010, Symantec, which was involved in investigating the attack for Google, identified China as the source of 21.3% of all (12 billion) malicious emails sent throughout the world.[12] Amitai Etzioni of the Center for Communitarian Policy Studies proposed that the United States and China commit to a policy of mutually assured restraint with regard to cyberspace in order to deter possible cyberattacks like Operation Aurora. This policy would encourage both states to take the steps they consider necessary for their self-defense while promising to refrain from taking aggressive actions at the same time; it would also involve vetting certain commitments. We all see how well that is working today.

The preteens and teens—the breach, the bad, and the ugly

This is where things became more serious. We saw breach, after breach after breach, on the heels of Operation Aurora. In 2013, starting with Target, followed by Home Depot, Anthem, Equifax, Yahoo, Capital One, and Facebook have paved the road for companies that will be remembered for compromising the data of billions of consumers. From 2014, the European Union started work on stringent regulations to protect citizen privacy. After the Facebook data breach, California followed suit.

What is remarkable about these breaches from a historical perspective? Target was the first time the board of directors was brought to task for a data breach. Seven out of 10 members were ousted.[13] It was also the first third party related data breach with far-reaching implications, hoisting vendor security into the cyber spotlight.

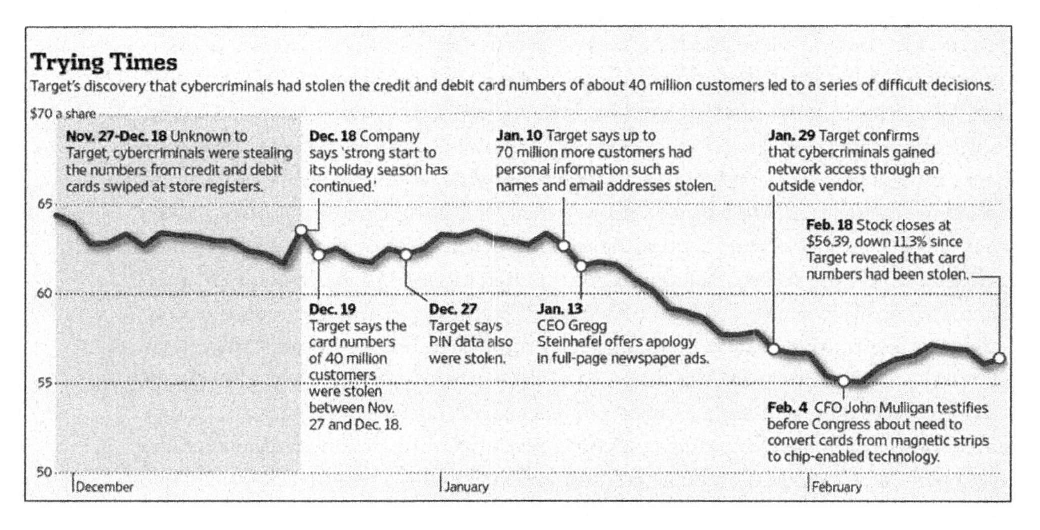

Image 3.1 Target Data Breach Timeline

In 2014, Home Depot suffered a data breach when hackers obtained a total of 56 million credit card numbers as a result of the breach using the same methods as the Target data breach.[14] The use of stolen third-party vendor credentials and RAM scraping malware were instrumental in both data breaches' success. Consumers start to get angry. We stated to see lawsuits in double digit millions.

In 2015, Anthem was the biggest healthcare breach. Anthem was not required by law to encrypt the data.[15] Anthem had a US$100 million insurance policy from American International Group (AIG) for cyber specific issues. One report suggested that all of this money would be consumed by the process of notifying customers of the breach alone. This case was the beginning of understanding healthcare data is a subset of privacy data, and strong encryption should be required by law.

Figure 3.1 Home Depot: The Largest Retail Data Breach Involving a Point of Sale System to Date

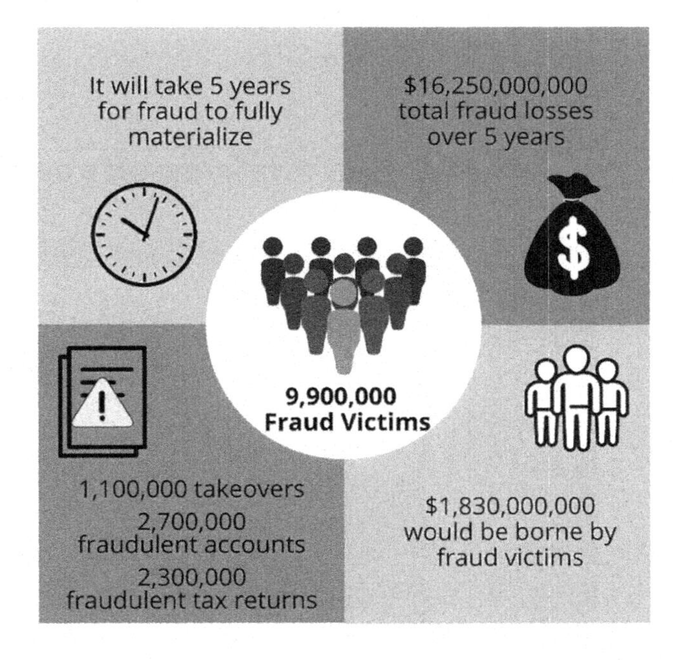

Image 3.2 Anthem Data Breach

Equifax is the poster child for cyber negligence. In 2017, Equifax's crown jewels assets were breached when it failed to patch a simple system interconnected to the credit of over one-third of the American consumers. According to Advisen, Equifax's security was so scant that the "settled" lawsuits totaled over US$1.8 billion in early 2020.

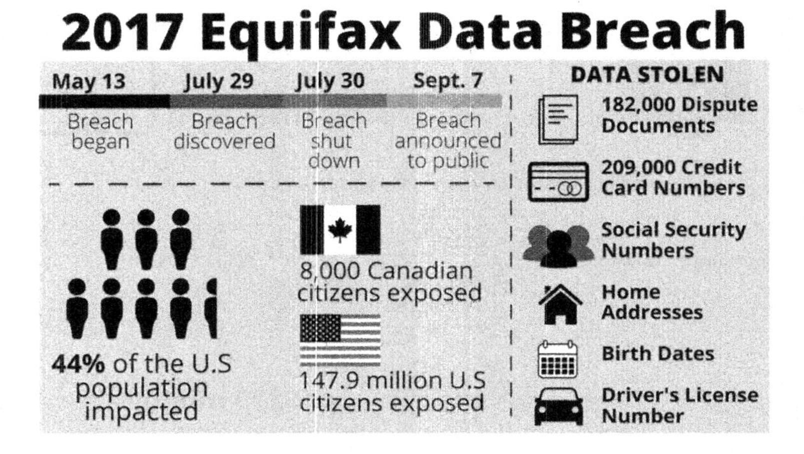

Image 3.3 Equifax Loses the Trust of Nation

Yahoo was significant in terms of the first time that a data breach impacted an acquisition. In 2016, Yahoo revealed the biggest breach of all time. Three billion records were compromised in two data breaches between 2013 and 2016. The acquisition price was slashed by a mere 7.5%, and Yahoo's Marissa Mayer resigned shortly afterward.[16]

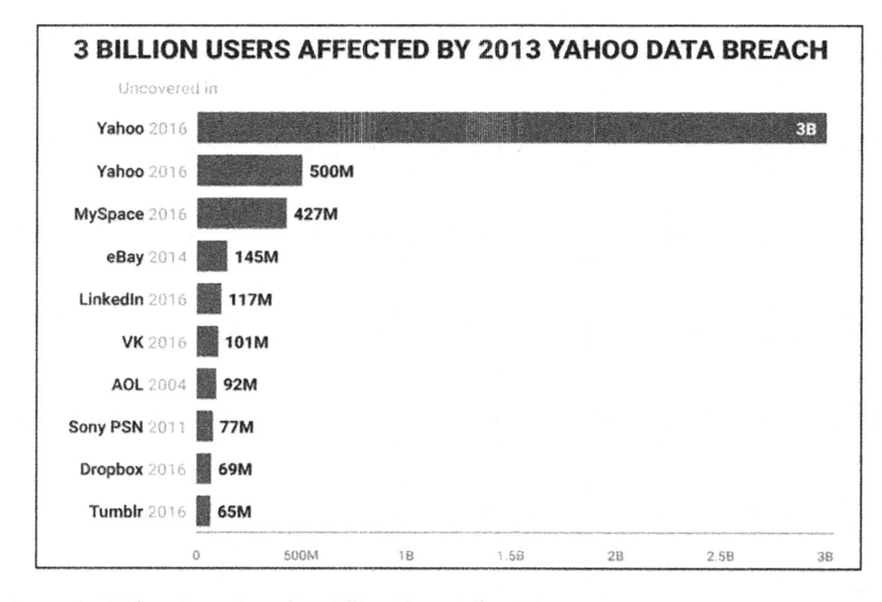

Image 3.4 Yahoo Data Breach: 3 Billion Users Affected

Capital One was interesting because the breach involved a third-party consultant and AWS.[17] According to several sources with direct knowledge of the breach investigation, the problem occurred partially due to a misconfigured open-source Web Application Firewall (WAF). Capital One was using Amazon Web Services (AWS) as part of its operations environment in the cloud to support banking customers. A settlement has been reached with Capital One and the government to pay US$80 million to the Office of the Comptroller of the Currency (OCC) without admitting or denying the allegations. It has moved ahead with its cloud migration efforts in the wake of last year's data breach. The OCC charters, regulates, and supervises all national banks and federal savings associations as well as federal branches and agencies of foreign banks. The OCC is an independent bureau of the U.S. Department of the Treasury. The moral of this story is: make sure your third- and fourth-party vendors are being monitored.

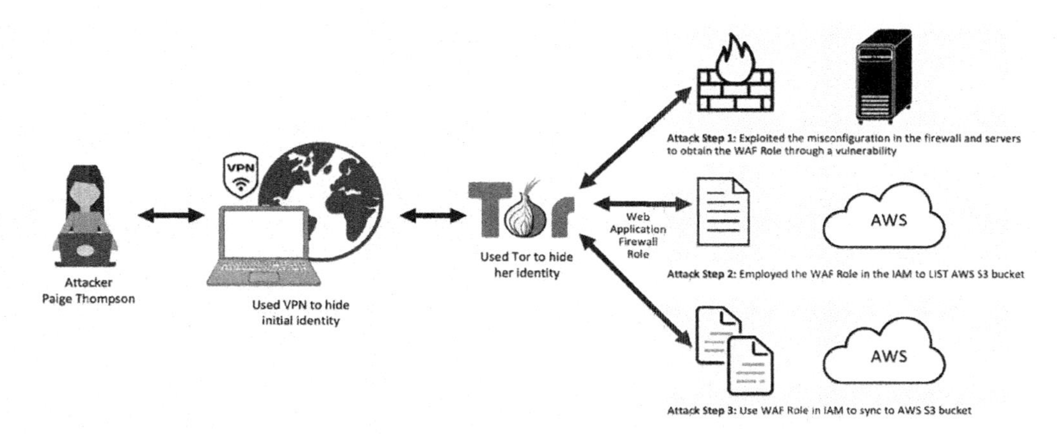

Image 3.5 Captial One Data Breach

In 2019, Facebook was made a privacy example by the United States Top Cyber Cop – The Federal Trade Commission.[18] A whopping US$5 billion fine and stringent privacy and security requirements were levied against Facebook for their negligent cyber posture, disregard for consumers' privacy, and deceptive use of consumer data. It is a thundering wake up call for companies to take privacy seriously or suffer the consequences.

Image 3.6 Facebook Data Breach

The data relating to the Facebook breaches was regulated and, thus, required notification to the authorities. In addition, Facebook had to set aside funds to compensate the victims. Companies like Facebook have become case studies that highlight the lack of proper cybersecurity programs and are now being forced to equip themselves with more enterprise cybersecurity programs. We will be referring to this case study again and again to highlight the importance of treating cybersecurity as a business issue.

Cyberspace is the new battleground for nation-states and hacktivists. To keep up with digitization, the cybersecurity industry is constantly innovating and using advanced machine learning and Artificial Intelligence (AI) driven approaches, i.e., to analyze digital asset, systems and network behavior, and prevent adversaries from winning. It is an exciting time for cyber firms to be in the market; hindsight allows us to learn from the example of others mistakes and foresee how to not become a statistic.

Notes

1. Investopedia, "Moore's Law", August 27, 2020, https://www.investopedia.com/terms/m/mooreslaw.asp.
2. "Hardware - Is it possible to turn a computer into a bomb..." https://security.stackexchange.com/questions/13105/is-it-possible-to-turn-a-computer-into-a-bomb.
3. Goodchild, Joan. "10 infamous hacks and hackers", CIO. February 20, 2018.
4. Tim Matthews, Cybersecurity Insiders, "A brief history of cybersecurity", 2020, https://www.cybersecurity-insiders.com/a-brief-history-of-cybersecurity/#:~:text=The%20first%20U.S.%20patent%20for%20cybersecurity%20came%20in%20September%20of,the%20first%20p.
5. Kehoe, Brendan P. (2007). "The Robert Morris Internet worm", Computer Science and Artificial Intelligence Laboratory (CSAIL). Massachusetts Institute of Technology. Retrieved August 23, 2008
6. PR Newswire, "Leading Credit Union launches PassMark authentication system", February 3, 2005.
7. Statista, "Number of internet users worldwide from 2005 to 2019", January 7, 2020, https://www.statista.com/statistics/273018/number-of-internet-users-worldwide/#:~:text=Global%20number%20of%20internet%20users%202005%2D2019&text=In%202019%2C%20the%20number%20of,billion%20in%20the%20previous%20year.
8. Wikipedia, "Anonymous (group)", November 3, 2020, https://en.wikipedia.org/wiki/Anonymous_(group).
9. Edvard Pettersson/Bloomberg, Time, "Wikileaks founder Julian Assange accused of conspiring with LulzSec and anonymous hackers", June 24, 2020, https://time.com/5859079/julian-assange-hackers-anonymous-indictment/.
10. Ryan Singel, Wired, "Data breach will cost TJX $1.7B, security firm estimates", March 30, 2007, https://www.wired.com/2007/03/data-breach-wil/.
11. Council of foreign relations, "Operation aurora", January 2010, https://www.cfr.org/cyber-operations/operation-aurora.
12. Sheridan, Michael, "Chinese city is world's hacker hub", London Sunday Times, March 28, 2010.
13. Law360, "7 Target board members in ISS' crosshairs over data breach", May 28, 2014, https://www.law360.com/articles/542228/7-target-board-members-in-iss-crosshairs-over-data-breach.

14. Brian Krebs, Krebs on Security, "Home depot: Hackers stole 53M email addresses", November 14, 2020, https://krebsonsecurity.com/tag/home-depot-breach/#:~:text=Home%20Depot%20said%20today%20that,retail%20card%20breach%20on%20record.
15. Lance Whitney, CNET, "Anthem's stolen customer data not encrypted", February 6, 2015, https://www.cnet.com/news/anthems-hacked-customer-data-was-not-encrypted/#:~:text=But%20under%20federal%20law%2C%20health,have%20to%20encrypt%20user%20data.&text=Health%20insurer%20Anthem%20says%20the,not%20required%20to%20do%20so.
16. Ingrid Lunden, TechCrunch, "After data breaches, Verizon knocks $350M off Yahoo sale, now valued at $4.48B", February 21, 2017, https://techcrunch.com/2017/02/21/verizon-knocks-350m-off-yahoo-sale-after-data-breaches-now-valued-at-4-48b/?guccounter=1#:~:text=After%20the%20disclosure%20of%20two,%244.48%20billion%20to%20acquire%20Yahoo.
17. Brian Krebs, Krebs on security, "What we can learn from the Capital One hack", August 19, 2020, https://krebsonsecurity.com/2019/08/what-we-can-learn-from-the-capital-one-hack/.
18. Federal Trade Commission, "FTC imposes $5 billion penalty and sweeping new privacy restrictions on Facebook", July 24, 2019, https://www.ftc.gov/news-events/press-releases/2019/07/ftc-imposes-5-billion-penalty-sweeping-new-privacy-restrictions.

4 CYBERSECURITY CONSEQUENCES

Sixty percent of small and midsized businesses that are hacked go out of businesses within six months.
National Cyber Security Alliance

Yahoo—the bigger they are, the harder they fall

The largest data breach to date is Yahoo, which had over three billion records stolen. Yahoo was the eighth largest Web services provider in the world before its acquisition by Verizon Media. Yahoo was one of the initial leaders of the earlier internet era. In the 1990s, Yahoo had revenues of US$5.17 billion[1] and almost 9,000 employees.

In 2014, Yahoo announced an attack that affected 500 million accounts. In 2016, they announced that a previous attack in 2013 impacted one billion customer accounts. The impact was to crown jewel assets that included user identities and passwords that were encrypted poorly and easy to crack. The attackers also obtained the security questions and backup email addresses used to reset passwords.

It began when Russian hackers sent spear-phishing emails to Yahoo employees, and employees clicked on the link, and the malware was downloaded and installed on the Yahoo network. Once on the network, the hackers began reconnaissance for the crown jewel digital assets that included Yahoo's user database and the account management tool used to manage it. Hackers then established a backdoor on a Yahoo server to come and go as they liked. The database contained the customer names, phone numbers, password challenge questions/answers, password recovery emails, and a unique cryptographic value for each account. Cryptographic values were then used to generate cookies to access accounts via a software program installed on a Yahoo server. Those cookies generated gave the hackers free access to users' email accounts without a password.

As you will see in the case of Equifax where TransUnion and Experian patched the vulnerability, Yahoo also ignored the warning signs. Critical Web service providers, including Yahoo and Google, were penetrated in 2010 by the same hackers. Google responded immediately and hired more security analysts, architects, and managers and invested heavily in its security infrastructure.

Yahoo made some minimal cybersecurity additions. Yahoo's business focus was to develop and grow new products and update Yahoo's email features. Yahoo focused on adding infrastructure for product growth and all but ignored the threat.

DOI: 10.4324/9781003052616-5

They used poor encryption with passwords that were hashed with MD5 (a cipher deprecated by most companies) and did not encrypt the security questions.

Yahoo was fined US$35 million by the SEC for failing to disclose their known data breaches.[2]

Another first! Yahoo stock dropped by 3%, and it lost US$1.3 billion in the market cap after it disclosed the 2014 breach. Yahoo settled lawsuit for US$117.5 million in regards to nearly 200 million people who had sensitive information stolen due to the data breach.[3] This is an example of how the loss of trust can reduce the stock price that result in a reputational amplification.

Days before the ink was to be dry on the Verizon acquisition, Yahoo disclosed the data breach to Verizon in 2014, and the brakes were put on momemtarily. Yahoo agreed to reduce the purchase price by US$350 million (a 7.25% reduction in the acquision price), and to share liabilities and expenses relating to the breaches going forward. Yahoo has disclosed security incident expenses of US$16 million (US$5 million for forensics and US$11 million for lawyers) associated with the breach.[4]

Several class action lawsuits and shareholder legal actions are still active in state courts. The SEC officials noted that Yahoo left "its investors totally in the dark about a massive data breach" for two years, and that "public companies should have controls and procedures in place to properly evaluate cyber incidents and disclose material information to investors."[5] Regulators are now laying the foundation for ramped-up enforcement actions with real penalties.

Lessons learned include (1) having meaningful commitment at the top to cybersecurity and not ignoring when there is a pink elephant in the living room; (2) ensuirng that there are disclosure processes and procedures that uphold the law and don't scoff at it; and (3) making sure that basic security is in place. Not only were they negligent in protecting their shareholders' digital assets, they didn't even have basic security controls in place (i.e., automatic reset of all user passwords).

Reputationally, Yahoo has lost consumer and corporate trust. Yahoo's CEO didn't receive an annual bonus, and Yahoo's general counsel resigned after the SEC found Yahoo's legal team had sufficient information for a further investigation but did nothing. The SEC has called out Yahoo senior executives who knew about the breaches well before disclosure. Yahoo did not have cybersecurity liability insurance and, therefore, paid US$16 million for security incident expenses.[6] On November 23, 2016, lawsuits related to the 2014 breach were filed, including case amendments that included the August, 2013 breach. Shareholder derivative actions remain pending in state courts. Consumer data breach class actions, including a class-action lawsuit, were filed against Yahoo in N.Y. state on behalf of all affected U.S. residents, stating that Yahoo failed to provide adequate protection of its users' personal and confidential information. In total, the financial impact was over US$12B.[7]

Equifax—cybersecurity's poster child

I don't have to tell you things are bad. Everybody knows things are bad. It's the cyber-criminals. Everybody's working three jobs or scared of losing their job. Big business keeps paying CEOs millions of dollars and cyber budgets buy a nickel's worth of tools. Companies are being ransomed left and right.

Hackers are running wild on the dark web and there's nobody anywhere who seems to know what to do, and there's no end to it. We know we don't have enough resources, enough tools and we sit watching our screens while some cyber podcaster tells us that today we had fifteen data breaches and sixty-three ransomware attacks, as if that's the way it's supposed to be.

We know things are bad—worse than bad. They're crazy. It's like everything everywhere is going crazy. We sit behind our desks, and slowly the world we are living in is getting harder, and all we say is: "Please, at least leave us alone in our cubes. Let me have my computer and my Diet Coke and I won't say anything. Just leave us alone."

Well, I'm not gonna leave you alone. I want you to get MAD! I don't want you to protest. I don't want you to riot—I don't want you to write to your congressman, because I wouldn't know what to tell you to write. All I know is that first you've got to get mad. (shouting) You've got to say: "I'm a human being, god-dammit! My data and life have value!"

So, I want you to get up now. I want all of you to get up out of your chairs. I want you to get up right now and go to the window. Open it, and stick your head out, and yell: 'I'm as mad as hell, and I'm not gonna take this anymore!'

I want you to get up right now. Sit up. Go to your windows. Open them and stick your head out and yell—"I'm as mad as hell and I'm not gonna take this anymore!" Things have got to change. But first, you've gotta get mad! ... You've got to say, "I'm as mad as hell, and I'm not gonna take this anymore!" Then we'll figure out what to do about inadequate cybersecurity, your personal data and GDPR. But first, get up out of your chairs, open the window, stick your head out, and yell, and say it: "I'm as mad as hell, and I'm not gonna take this anymore!"—Adapted from the Network Script[8]

Equifax is a global data, analytics, and technology company (one of the three large credit reporting companies in the USA). They blend unique data, analytics, and technology to create insights that power decisions to move people forward. Headquartered in Atlanta, Equifax operates or has investments in 24 countries in North America, Central and South America, Europe, and the Asia Pacific region. It is a member of Standard & Poor's (S&P) 500® Index, and its common stock is traded on the New York Stock Exchange (NYSE) under the symbol EFX. Equifax employs approximately 11,000 employees worldwide.[9]

Equifax lost the trust of a nation. Equifax failed to protect the crown jewel assets—the customer privacy data and credit scores. The breach was due to not patching a relatively simple system connected to the crown jewel assets. This shows a complete non-understanding of the relationship between digital assets.

Equifax was aware of the issue and chose to ignore it. They have paid over US$1.4B in remediation costs and US$1.8B in settled lawsuits as of January, 2020. More are still pending. They had a reputational amplication of financial loss due to the decrease in their stock price of over 33% that has never recovered. The giant cybersecurity breach compromised personal information of almost ½ of the U.S. population -as many as 143 million Americans.[10]

The breach occurred between mid-May and July, 2017. The company said it discovered the hack on July 29, 2017 and was only notified of the breach in early September, 2017.[11] The time between the detection and notice was six weeks. This is one of the key reasons that breach notification laws have been put in place to prevent this type of behavior. Competitors Experian and Transunion were also alerted and they immediately patched the vulnerability.

Lessons learned include:

1 Ensure that you have a culture of security—Equifax had no effective tone at the top resulting in a culture of insecurity, furthermore, the CISO had a music degree.
2 Ensure that you are not willfully negligent—competitors understood that they had to patch the vulnerability as soon as possible.
3 Understand your digital asset relationships—Equifax did not understand that a relatively simple unpatched system was connected to the crown jewels.
4 Ensure you have automated monitoring in place—Equifax's Web application environment was not optimized to monitor suspicious behavior.

Target—tone at the top

Target was the first data breach that moved cyber from the control room to the board room. Secondly, the highly publicized breach was due to a third-party HVAC vendor with lax security controls. At the time, there was little insight into the interplay between third parties and organizations regarding cyber risk. As a result, 7 out of 10 board members were ousted, and cyber was thrown front and center on all public companies' radar.

Target is a component of the S&P 500 Index. At the time of the breach, the company was ranked No. 39 on the 2018 Fortune 500 list of the largest United States corporations by total revenue. As of November, 2019, Target had 1806 stores in the United States.[12]

Forty million credit card numbers were stolen from 2000 Target stores in December 2013 by criminals accessing data on the point-of-sale systems (POS). On January 10, 2014, Target went on to reveal that PII data (names, addresses, phone numbers, and email addresses) of up to 70 million customers was also stolen. In total, 98 million people were affected due to an overlap of data stolen. This data was then sold online in black market forums known as card shops. In March, 2014, the Senate Committee on Commerce decided that Target had opportunities to prevent the breach and did nothing. Target said the total cost of the data breach had been US$202 million.[13]

Phishing emails were sent to employees at Fazio Mechanical (which was a third-party HVAC vendor for Target) that delivered malware named the "Citadel" Trojan. Fazio Mechanical's vendor credentials were stolen by attackers and used to access Target's network. Attackers then exploited a Web application vulnerability with an SQL injection method of attack.

Once the backdoor was created, the attackers took their time conducting reconnaissance to locate the servers they wanted to steal data from. After the servers were located, the attackers probably used a "pass-the-hash" attack to steal an Admin access token to create a new Admin account. Next, 70 million customers' PII was stolen, but these servers did not store credit card numbers or associated info, so attackers had to go after point-of-sale (POS) machines. Attackers next installed malware onto

POS machines to copy all credit and debit card data used for purchases. After copying the POS data, the data was then forwarded to servers in America and Brazil to wait for the attackers to retrieve it at their convenience.

Within one week, Verizon security consultants reported that they were able to crack 472,308 of Target's 547,470 passwords (86%) that allowed access to various internal networks, including; target.com, corp.target.com; email.target.com; stores.target.com; hq.target.com; labs.target.com; and olk.target.com.[14]

Lessons learned include:

1 Make sure that the firm has reliable audits—the audits from Trustwave were flawed. It missed important PCI controls were not in place.
2 Ensure there is an automated response in place—there was no automated response to the FireEye security system flagged hacker activity as of November 30, 2013.
3 Ensure you have team integration—the security team personnel in Bangalore sent notification of attack to HQ in Minnesota on November 30, 2013, without any action being taken by HQ.
4 Use a Crown Jewel Strategy—Target did not limit the number of people who had access to more sensitive network areas (Crown Jewels). Target should limit the access to portions of the network containing business-critical systems to only the employees who directly manage those systems. In the end, the result is a high "likelihood" of an attack due to ignoring confidentiality of data.
5 Implement multi-factor authentication—Target should have implemented multi-factor authentication for the vendor portals.
6 Follow your policies—Target had a password policy, but it was discovered it was not being followed.
7 Segement your networks—Target should have properly segregated networks so the portion of the network third-party vendors access would not allow attackers access to other critical networks (Crown Jewels), which maps to the accessibility portion of CIA triad.
8 Ensure you are auditing—Target should have had internal IT audits to capture this problem.
9 Perfrom penetrtaion testing—Target should have hired White Hat Hackers to perform penetration testing on its network. Target should have had PCI audits periodically by external audit companies.
10 Proper techniques—Target's Security Operation Center (SOC) should have set the FireEye security system to enact corrective intervention techniques and actions when suspicious activity is detected, and not just send notifications.
11 Overreliance on others—Target SOC should have taken into account notifications from Bangalore team. Security notifications should be treated with the severity it deserves when received.
12 Invest in updating security tools—there were multiple layers of safety defenses at Target. They had firewalls, applications for malware detection, intrusion detection, and prevention capabilities, and tools for preventing data loss. But they needed to invest in updating the effectiveness of these tools.

British Airways

To fly, to serve, to pay the largest GDPR-related fine

British Airways was handed a record fine for their 2018 data breach. It was the first major breach under the new GDPR laws and was 367 times larger than the previous recorded fine. The fine amounted to 1.5% of British Airways' global turnover (maximum penalty 4%).[15]

British Airwarys is the second largest U.K. airline and is the third-largest airline group globally by revenue. It is listed on the London Stock Exchange (LSE) and in the FTSE 100 Index. They had 291 aircraft on the balance sheet, plus 282 aircraft leased (2018), 268 destinations served globally at the time of the data breach. Revenue in 2018 was €14.5B/£13B/US$16B, and the number of employees was ~40,000.[16]

The attack lasted over two weeks and began on August 21, 2018, and ended on September 5, 2018. The data at risk included personal and financial details of customers making or changing bookings at BA.com. On September 6, 2018 British Airways publicly disclosed the data breach. On September 7, 2018, an email from CEO Alex Kruz, was sent to potentially affected customers, disclosing that their full name, billing address, email address, credit card number, and CVV value was disclosed in the breach with a promise to reimburse any losses. On September 11, 2018, it was revealed that the threat actor was Magecart. On July 8, 2019, the Information Commissioner's Office (ICO) fined British Airways £183.39m (~US$230m), equal to 1.5% of Turnover, for infringements of the General Data Protection Regulation, citing "poor security arrangements".[17]

Between August 21 and September 5, 2018, 380,000 transactions were compromised on both the BA.com Web and mobile app platforms during credit card purchases and booking changes. In October of 2018, this scope was revealed to be potentially 429,000 transactions.[18] Exfiltration of PII and credit card information was done using Web skimming techniques, under which the website payments page was compromised by malware, allowing a script to capture and communicate CVV information during the payments verification cycle and before the CVV data was discarded by British Airways' post verification, as required by the PCI Standards.

The breach impacted revenue & profit negatively, and resulted in decrease in the stock price. Both their cost of capital increased, and their corporate insurance costs increased due to weak controls. They had to offer a ProtectMyID subscription to customers for 12 months and address multiple customer claims related to the breach, including Web and mobile remediation costs.[19]

The damning GDPR verdict by the ICO was a record-breaking fine. Rowenna Fielding, the Protecture of the ICO stated, "for payment info on a public-facing website, one would expect robust security measures to be in place, which would need to include auditing of the site, security testing, and risk assessments."[20]

This fine issued by the ICO was the largest issued under GDPR violations to date, although still less than the 4% global turnover allowed for under the GDPR, Article 83(5). The fine closest to this is the £500k fine against Facebook and Equifax.[21]

The ICO criticized the "poor security arrangements". The GDPR Security Principle requires organizations to implement appropriate technical and organizational measures to protect the integrity and confidentiality of personal data, and this will largely be ascertained by the 'nature, scope and context of processing' (Article 32).[22]

Lessons learned include to:

1. Prioritize cybersecurity—British Airways executives' focus was on cost-cutting measures since the early 2000's in response to budget airline transformation of the market. Regular and very public union unrest, and in 2017 an IT power issue took flight operations down completely for a day; possibly a toxic mix of 'eyes off the ball' and signaling to the outside world that affairs are not in order. ICO stated BA had "poor security arrangements".
2. Improve audit quality— British Airways had flawed IT audits. Their Modernizr JavaScript library was six years out of date at the time of the breach.[23] British Airways should have recurrent software application and library audits, and a register for identification of aging or unpatched code (software life cycle management); include redundancy in the audit process by checking Web pages for redundant scripts libraries and remove the script completely to reduce the attack surface; provide periodic external PCI Audits and independent testing of payments Web and mobile applications.
3. Ensure an adequate automated response—British Airways was PCI complaint in not storing CVV data but had a blind spot in the Web facing application for payments, unable to detect script manipulation where customers entered PII and financial data. Traffic monitoring may have detected outbound traffic to 'baways.com'.
4. Increase the maturity of the security profile—there was a lack of a SOC Analyst function to detect system vulnerabilities or attacks in theatre (the breach lasted for 15 days).
5. Institute a formal risk review—for risk tolerance and categorizing critical assets/crown jewels (repeat customers being a KPI for airline passenger load factors).
6. Ensure internet-facing application priority for testing—using regular penetration testing/white hat attacks to test for cyber resiliency.
7. Utilize Advanced Threat Prevention (ATP)—technology for automated malware quarantine and examination.

Maersk—Russia, ransomware, and insurance

The largest operating unit in A.P. Moller–Maersk Group by revenue and staff (around 25,000 employees in 2012) is the Maersk Line. In 2013, the company described itself as the world's largest overseas cargo carrier with over 600 vessels and a 3.8 million twenty-foot equivalent unit (TEU) container capacity. As of September 2015, Maersk was the largest container fleet and held 15.1% of the global TEU. Maersk's revenue in 2019 was US$35B, and had 88,000 employees.[24]

A June 2017 cyberattack snarled Maersk's shipping terminal operations worldwide and briefly shut down the Port of Los Angeles' largest cargo terminal, which had cost the Danish shipping giant US$300 million.[25] The worm, dubbed NotPetya,[26] casued a business interruption which locked access to Maersk systems that operate the shipping terminals all over the world and took two weeks to fix. In late June, a few weeks later, a similar ransomware attack called WannaCry seized computers in British health clinics. NotPetya has been traced to corrupted tax-accounting software commonly used in Ukraine. NotPetya, like WannaCry, exploited a vulnerability in unpatched Mircrosoft Windows utilizing a break-in tool that was rumored to have been stolen from the U.S. National Security Agency (NSA).

The malware NotPetya appeared to be ransomware.[27] However, its true purpose was to merely wreak havoc. The Ukraine was particularly hard hit in the attack; however, the worm also targeted the operations of a large British advertising agency, a skin care device firm, a German broadcaster, and the U.S. pharmaceutical giant Merck. Maersk was only one of around 7,000 businesses attacked globally in this attack.[28]

For the most part, NotPetya victims have been tight-lipped, but Maersk decided to publicly air some of its struggles, signaling a shift to foster more collaboration as businesses grapple with their dependence on vulnerable technologies.

NotPetya made all the firm's applications and data unavailable. No data was lost, no workers were endangered, and ships normally operated throughout the ordeal, however, the affected terminals could not move freight for up to two days. Thanks to work-arounds created by Maersk workers, products began to flow normally bit by bit again. The company was back to normal two weeks after the attack. Maersk's APM Terminal at Pier 400 was closed from June 27 to July 1 at the Port of Los Angeles, leaving at least one anchored vessel waiting in the harbor. In subsequent days, freight operations ramped up again.

Three of Maersk's global enterprises were affected by NotPetya: Maersk Line, Damco, and APM Terminals. During the shutdown and subsequent slow period, the company not only lost business, it also lost money as it cobbled together ways of working without the digital systems on which it typically relies. Additional costs were incurred by the mission of restoring IT. Maersk had to reroute ships and was unable to dock or unload cargo ships in dozens of ports and needed to rebuild their IT infrastructure, re-installing 4000 servers. Operationally, over 50,000 endpoints and thousands of applications were infected. There was two weeks of major operations disruptions across 600 sites in 130 countries. Maersk had up to US$300m in losses due to business interruption and their stock price lost value.[29]

Lessons learned include:[30]

1 Establish and enforce patch management discipline—Maersk failed to install the patch for the EternalBlue exploit, released by Microsoft earlier that year, which spread across the network. Maersk is still running Windows 2000—an operating system so old Microsoft no longer supported it in 2016.
2 Better auditing was needed—Maersk had flawed audits and teams that were lax in reporting issues.

3 Implement automated detection and response for malware—following detection, the remediation process was improvised and required significant manual intervention over two weeks.
4 Ensure an adequate response strategy—there was limited operational and strategic direction in responding to the attack.
5 Rotate online backup on a regular (weekly) basis.
6 Enforce "right-to-work" policies—such that employees must raise a change control request and given admin rights for a limited period.
7 Establish and test a BCM plan.

Notes

1. Wikipedia, "Yahoo!", October 31, 2020, https://en.wikipedia.org/wiki/Yahoo!.
2. Jacob Kastrenakes, The Verge, "SEC issues $35 million fine over Yahoo failing to disclose data breach", April 24, 2018, https://www.theverge.com/2018/4/24/17275994/yahoo-sec-fine-2014-data-breach-35-million.
3. Kelly Tyko, USA Today, "Yahoo data breach settlement 2019: How to get up to $358 or free credit monitoroing", October 15, 2019, https://www.usatoday.com/story/money/2019/10/14/yahoo-data-breach-117-5-million-settlement-get-cash-monitoring/3976582002/.
4. Jeremy Kirk, Bank Info Security, "Yahoo takes $350 million hit in Verizon deal", February 22, 2017, https://www.bankinfosecurity.com/yahoo-takes-350-million-hit-in-verizon-deal-a-9736.
5. U.S. Securities and Exchange Commission, "Altaba, formally known as Yahoo! Charged with failing to disclose massive cybersecurity breach; Agrees to pay $35 million", April 24, 2018, https://www.sec.gov/news/press-release/2018-71.
6. Edward J. McAndrew, Ballard Spahr, "The hacked & the hacker-for-hire: Lessons from the Yahoo data breaches (So far)", May 11, 2018, https://www.ballardspahr.com/alertspublications/articles/2018-05-11-yahoo-data-breach.
7. Robert McMillian, Ryan Knutson, Deepa Seetharaman,/WSJ, Daily Newsflash, "Yahoo discloses new breach of 1 billion user accounts", December 15, 2016, https://www.programbusiness.com/news/Yahoo-Discloses-New-Breach-of-1-Billion-User-Accounts.
8. Neil Hughes, "I'm mad as hell speech from Network (1976)", July 15, 2014, https://neilchughes.com/2014/07/15/im-mad-as-hell-speech-from-network-1976/.
9. Wikipedia, "Equifax", October 10, 2020, https://en.wikipedia.org/wiki/Equifax.
10. Alfred Ng, Steven Musil, CNET, "Equifax data breach may affect nearly half the US population", September 7, 2017, https://www.cnet.com/news/equifax-data-leak-hits-nearly-half-of-the-us-population/#:~:text=Equifax%20said%20Thursday%20that%20thieves,US%20population%20of%20323%20million.
11. Wikipedia, "Equifax", October 10, 2020, https://en.wikipedia.org/wiki/Equifax.
12. Wikipedia, "Target Corporation", October 31, 2020, https://en.wikipedia.org/wiki/Target_Corporation.
13. Reuters, NBC News, "Target settles 2013 hacked customer data breach for $18.5 million", May 24, 2017, https://www.nbcnews.com/business/business-news/target-settles-2013-hacked-customer-data-breach-18-5-million-n764031.
14. Brian Krebs, Krebs on Security, "Credit card issuer TCM bank leaked applicant data for 16 months", August 18, 2020, https://krebsonsecurity.com/tag/target-breach/.
15. Enforcement tracker, "GDPR enforcement tracker", 2020, https://www.enforcementtracker.com/.
16. Wikipedia BA, "British Airways", September 6, 2020, https://en.wikipedia.org/wiki/British_Airways#cite_note-IAG_Annual_2018-2.

17. BBC News, "British Airways faces record £183m fine for data breach", July 8, 2019, https://www.bbc.com/news/business-48905907.
18. John Bosnell, ORX News, "British Airways suffer data breach comprimising information on over 429,000 customer cards", 2019, https://managingrisktogether.orx.org/sites/default/files/public/downloads/2019/01/british-airways-suffers-data-breach-compromising-information-over-429-000-customer-cards.pdf.
19. Business Traveller, "BA data theft," October 5, 2019, https://www.businesstraveller.com/forums/topic/ba-data-theft/page/4/.
20. David Bisson, CNET, "British Airways faces $230M GDPR fine for 2018 data breach", July 8, 2019, https://www.cnet.com/news/british-airways-faces-record-breaking-230m-gdpr-fine-for-201 Tripwire, "NotPetya: Timeline of a Ransomworm", June 28, 2017, https://www.tripwire.com/state-of-security/security-data-protection/cyber-security/notpetya-timeline-of-a-ransomworm/.
21. Aljazeera, "British Airways share price hit after record data theft fine", July 8, 2019, https://www.aljazeera.com/economy/2019/7/8/british-airways-share-price-hit-after-record-data-theft-fine.
22. Emma Hughes, Engage Hogan Lovells, "Time to take notice: ICO to impose record fine for data security breach", July 8, 2019, https://www.engage.hoganlovells.com/knowledgeservices/news/time-to-take-notice-ico-to-impose-record-fine-for-data-security-breach.
23. Guard Script, "How to avoid a $200 million hack," July 8, 2019, https://www.guardscript.com/blog/2019/07/08/how-to-avoid-a-200-million-hack/.
24. Maersk, "A.P. Moller- Maersk shows improved performance and strategic process," February 20, 2020, https://www.maersk.com/news/articles/2020/02/20/ap-moller-maersk-shows-improved-performance-and-strategic-progress.
25. Nate Lord, Digital Guardian, "The cost of a malware infection? For Maersk, $300 million", August 7, 2020, https://digitalguardian.com/blog/cost-malware-infection-maersk-300-million#:~:text=For%20Maersk%2C%20%24300%20Million,-Nate%20Lord&text=The%20NotPetya%20fallout%20continues%2C%20with,following%20a%20June%20cyber%20attack.
26. David Bisson, The Sgtate of Security, Tripwire, "NotPetya: Timeline of a Ransomworm", June 28, 2017, https://www.tripwire.com/state-of-security/security-data-protection/cyber-security/notpetya-timeline-of-a-ransomworm/.
27. Andy Greenberg, Wired, "The untold story of NotPetya, the most devastating cyberattack in history", August 22, 2018, https://www.wired.com/story/notpetya-cyberattack-ukraine-russia-code-crashed-the-world.
28. Jill Leovy, Los Angeles Times, "Cyberattack cost Maersk as much as $300 million and disrupted operation for 2 weeks", August 17, 2017, https://www.latimes.com/business/la-fi-maersk-cyberattack-20170817-story.html.
29. Matthew J. Schwartz, Bank Info Security, "Maersk previews NotPetya impact: up to $300 million", August 17, 2017, https://www.bankinfosecurity.com/maersk-previews-notpetya-impact-up-to-300-million-a-10203.
30. Warwick Ashford, ComputerWeekly.com, "NotPetya offers industry-wide lessons, says Maersk's tech chief", June 7, 2019, https://www.computerweekly.com/news/252464773/NotPetya-offers-industry-wide-lessons-says-Maersks-tech-chief.

5 CYBERSECURITY TRENDS AND SPENDING

If you spend more on coffee than on IT security, you will be hacked. What's more, you deserve to be hacked.

Richard A. Clarke, National Coordinator for Security,
Infrastructure Protection, and Counter-terrorism
for the United States between 1998 and 2003

Cyber as a business issue—breach me not

In 2013, Cybersecurity moved into the boardroom. The Target breach was the first wakeup call that directors and officers were being taken to task to protect the digital assets. The Privacy Rights Clearinghouse (PRC) is a non-profit corporation whose mission is to help protect consumer information and provide consumer advocacy services. It has been tracking privacy breaches since 2005 and have reported over 9000 data breaches to date.[1]

Most reported data breaches occur in North America. This correlates to the fact that the United States now has data breach notification laws in every state. The average cost of a data breach is expected to be over US$150 million by 2020, with an annual global cost projection of US$2.1 trillion.[2] In 2019, a collection of 2.7 billion identity records, consisting of 774 million unique email addresses and 21 million unique passwords, was posted on the Web for sale.[3] *That is almost half of the world's adult population.*

In 2018, global GDP amounted to about US$84.93 trillion. The prediction above related to the annual global cost of cybersecurity breaches of US$2.1 trillion would be the equivalent of 2.5% of GDP.[4] In 2018, natural disasters caused US$160 billion in economic damage worldwide.[5] *Comparatively cyber is 13 times more destructive than mother nature.* These numbers will just continue to rise. Attackers are smarter, faster, and today we are not spending enough to be able to outpace them and move towards cyber resiliency.

One strategy to get in front of the attackers is to make it so expensive to target you that they move on to another victim. This is your best offense.

Technology trends—cloud first strategies and cloud security

Cloud-first strategies continue to dominate the technology landscape. The use of cloud technology allows companies to gain a competitive advantage by driving lower total costs of ownership, transform their business, and differentiate themselves from the competition.

DOI: 10.4324/9781003052616-6

According to a recent Gartner report, 40% of companies in North America plan to spend the majority of new or additional financing on the cloud. The global demand for cloud services is expected to rise 80%, from US$182 billion to US$331 billion by 2022, according to the most recent Gartner report. A large portion of that growth is reflected by Software as a Service (SaaS), with sales growth also on track to increase by 80% in that same period. More than a third of companies regard cloud investments as being a top-three priority. By the end of the year, Gartner expects more than 30% of the latest software investments made by technology providers will move from cloud-first to cloud-only models.[6]

That means the demand for cloud security and cloud auditing will be ginormous. The myth that everything in the cloud is 100% protected is ridiculous. The cloud is a shared responsibility model. Cybersecurity teams need to understand which controls they are responsible for and which the CSP is responsible for and ensure they are in place.

Cloud security requires adopting a new set of skills, including:

- expertise in the shared responsibilities between CSP and organizations
- deep knowledge of cloud architectures and their deployment models
- expertise in cloud technologies, such as hypervisors
- experience with Internet-of-Things (IoT) applications, including sensors
- experience with different cloud deployment models including SaaS, PaaS, and IaaS

Cloud auditors will need to verify that effective cybersecurity is in place. They are the last line of defense in cloud-first strategies.

Innovation trends—design now secure later

In 2022, it is predicted that we will have over 20 billion interconnected devices. Most connected devices have little or no built-in security. That makes them vulnerable to malware and the firm open to data exfiltration, ransomware, denial of service, and regulatory fines. Security isn't a top priority for IoT device makers. Device makers compete on price and embedding security increases the cost of their offering significantly.

The IoT includes devices that connect to the internet, and to each other on your home or business network. Each connection point is an attack surface. This exponentially increases how cybercriminals can attack you and your company. In 2017, Xiongmai Technology, an IoT camera manufacturer from Hangzhou, admitted its cameras had been exploited by the Mirai malware to form part of a botnet which launched a distributed-denial-of-service (DDoS) attack targeting websites, including Twitter, PayPal, and Spotify.

In this case, hundreds of thousands of infected wired computers were drawn into the Mirai botnet in 2016. A botnet is a group of internet-connected devices that can combine the processing power of small devices to launch a large-scale cyberattack. Botnets run one or more bots. A bot is a software application that runs automated repetitive tasks over the internet much faster than a person could. Botnets can be used to perform Distributed-Denial-of-Service attacks, steal data, send spam, and allow the attacker to access the device and its connection.

The Mirai assault was one of the worst in U.S. history.[7] The disruptive Distributed-Denial-of-Service (DDoS) attack caused intermittent service interruption for millions of internet users. The affected IoT devices typically do not support firmware updates, making it is nearly impossible to mitigate this risk.

Smart devices including TVs, surveillance cameras, locks, meters, thermostats, etc. will add a degree of comfort to your life, courtesy of the IoT. However, they will make your home vulnerable to cybercriminals as well. Having a protection plan for securing smart home devices will be critical in the next few years.

Where is your safety most at risk? In your home IoT environment, you might have a smart alarm or a smart thermostat. What if a hacker accesses information you've shared with your digital assistant, whose voice-activated speakers use Amazon Echo or Google Home? Maybe you shared passwords or financial information with your executive admin. According to the 2017 Internet Security Threat Survey, released by Symantec, the average IoT computer was targeted once every 2 minutes during peak activity hours.

Cybercriminals may access your home network through your router. For example, in 2018, VPNFilter malware infected over half a million routers in more than 50 countries.[8]

VPNFilter can install malware onto devices and systems connected to your router. A router is hardware that allows communication between your connected devices and the internet. A router can be made inoperable. Cybercriminals can also collect information passing through a router, block network traffic and steal passwords.

Your Wi-Fi router is the "front door" to your smart home. Like any front door, it should be solid and equipped with strong locks. Building a more secure smart home starts with your Wi-Fi router. It's the foundational item that connects all your connected devices and makes them operable. Most people simply use the router provided by their internet service provider. Security cameras and home routers are top IoT targets for hackers because they have little or no built-in security, making them vulnerable to malware.

Security is usually not first and foremost to IoT device manufacturers because they have to charge more for it and many firms use price as their key criteria to purchase IoT technology. This leads to poor IoT cyber hygiene. Manufacturers' poor security practices include no system hardening (which gives a computer system inherent protection mechanisms that makes it more secure), no ability to update software, (which open the IoT up to the exploitation of vulnerabilities), not changing the default password or using hardcoded passwords.

For your personal home connectivity devices, the company should provide you access to their privacy policies if they store your data and how they protect it, if they sell it to a third party without your permission and how often they do updates to patch vulnerabilities to their routers.

Threat trends—survival of the fittest or cyber Darwinism

The average ransom payment increased by 104% in Q4 2019 to US$84,116 and was US$780,000 for a large enterprise. The cost of ransomware attacks surpassed US$7.5 billion in the first three quarters of 2020. This is an increase from estimated damages of US$11.5 billion in 2019 and US$8 billion in 2018.[9] Ransomware costs businesses more than US$75 billion a year, according to PurpleSec. The Coronavirus pandemic has pushed the world's healthcare systems to their limits. Ransomware attackers are taking advantage of this crisis by extorting healthcare organizations or face downtime that would cripple the industry. The cost of a record for healthcare is the highest per industry. Medical and insurance fraud is a favorite for cybercriminals. These cybercriminals' actions are brutal. Many attackers have installed back doors and lie dormant doing reconnaissance on a firm, timing their attacks when the organizations are the most vulnerable and more apt to pay. The global median dwell time in 2018 is 78 days, down from 101 days in 2017. The average attacker is going undetected on a network or system for less than three months.[10] However, in small to medium enterprises, the average dwell time is much longer, up to 895 days. Small and midsized firms typically lack the cybersecurity tools to detect malware quickly. The average dwell time for confirmed persistent malware was 798 days.[11]

Cybercriminals gain access to a victim's network, wait for a particularly opportune moment to deliver the ransomware payload, and infect the organization. Attackers typically gain access by exploiting unpatched vulnerabilities in the company's Web application servers. Most recently associated with the WFH environments, attackers exploited a widely publicized flaw in the Pulse Secure VPN. Attackers can use brute force methods of guessing passwords of organizations using Remote Desktop Protocol without multifactor authentication. Another way into the organization is to exploit known bugs in infrastructure that firms have failed to patch.

Attackers are in stealth mode waiting for the correct time to execute a ransomware attack or steal data from their victims. The motives of attackers vary considerably. Nation states are usually intent on disruption, criminals on making profits, and others are a combination of the two.

"That dwell time can vary between days, weeks, or even months," says Jérôme Segura, head of threat intelligence at the monitoring firm Malwarebytes. "When the time has come for ransomware deployment, threat actors will typically choose weekends, and preferably the wee hours of Sunday morning. This made sense prepandemic as staff would typically return to work on Mondays to witness the damage. Now many businesses have their resources stretched far more than before and as a result, may be in a tougher position to respond to a compromise."[12]

Resource trends—do not be caught short

Competition for cybersecurity talent is fierce. Millions of cybersecurity jobs are unfilled as the industry struggles with a shortage of properly trained professionals. According to New York Times, there will be 3.5 million unfilled cybersecurity jobs by 2021.[13]

Not only is the technical talent an issue, but the business talent is also a greater issue. Over the past decade, the increase in cyberattacks moved cyber into the boardroom, as highlighted earlier in our discussions regarding Target. Executives realized cybersecurity was a business issue and understood the need to hire qualified talent. According to the Bureau of Labor Statistics, the rate of growth for jobs in information security is projected at 37% between 2012 and 2022—that's much faster than the average growth rate for all other occupations.[14] For many professionals currently in the cybersecurity field, the only way to learn necessary skills fast and keep current is through cybersecurity certificate programs. Cybersecurity is not always taught at the university level. The need for certificate programs exists for moving people into this complex field from existing IT and business areas. Many companies are now starting to put more budget behind cybersecurity hiring and training. The issue is that everyone is trying to hire, all at the same time, creating intense competition for talent. One report says it takes up to six months to find qualified security and business personnel.[15]

The fundamental problem facing the technical skills gap is that there are not enough people coming into the field to begin with. It starts and ends with cyber education. We need more interest beginning at the middle school and high school levels in Science, Technology, Engineering, and Math (STEM). This will lead to more graduates in disciplines like cybersecurity. Cybersecurity should have been incorporated into university programs as a Bachelor of Science degree 15 years ago.[16]

Pivoting IT staff into cybersecurity is a good approach to train your staff up. IT teams already have a solid foundational set of skills needed to understand digital assets and how they are related. One drawback is that they typically do not have a "security first" mindset. IT works for the CIO who has an innovation mindset and wants to keep things up 24/7.

Many companies buy layered cybersecurity tool after layered cybersecurity tool. The average enterprise uses over 45 security-specific tools. Tools are like cars. They have to be maintained; you have to tune them to be effective. The average firewall loses 50% of its effectiveness over a two-year period if it is not tuned. This takes skilled staff and management that is skilled in understanding the business ramifications of not maintaining these tools. Cyber teams have to be experts in terms of what these tools do and how to maintain them. IT support teams (usually not security teams) are installing, managing, and monitoring security tools without the background to make them effective. This is one area to start to train up right away and achieve benefits.

Cybersecurity training for end-users is not simply about phishing. It is identifying cyber-related business roles that fill gaps in leadership, specifically around risk and privacy. Traditional cybersecurity teams are not trained to manage digital asset cybersecurity risk. Digital asset cyber risk is opening up the doors for more business-focused roles that are desperately needed to meet the challenges evident when cyber took the #1 business risk spot in 2018. We explore ideas for business roles in great detail in Chapter 6: Cyber Roles. According to Gartner, 68% of digital organizations have a cybersecurity expert on staff but remain incapable of managing digital risk, and ninety percent of CEOs are prioritizing digital initiatives.[17] Without adequate business resources to address digital risk, cyber events will overshadow digital initiatives.

The cybersecurity job market will continue to explode as IoT, and new technologies open up novel means for attackers to exploit your organization. Companies have to invest more money in people, processes, and tools in order to make it too expensive for the cybercriminal to attack you and move on to a more likely target. Companies should validate if their existing business and security teams can adequately address the emerging challenges resulting from IoT and digitization. Once understood in context, it is wise to create a list of new competencies and skills needed, map them to existing or new roles and prioritize them. Incorporating this formally into your human resources staffing framework and outlining these responsibilities will fill the gaps between existing roles and new roles.

Regulatory trends—comply or bust

Cybersecurity regulation has increased by sector, geography, and data type by over 4000% between 2010 and 2020. Prior to 2010, we had the PCI and HIPAA. PCI is for banks, merchants and data processors and applies only to credit card data and HIPAA is for medical data in the United States.

Over the past three years, several new cybersecurity regulations have been enacted. They include in 2018, the General Data Protection Regulation (GDPR), the New York State Department of Financial Services Part 500 (NYCRR Part 500), the Insurance Data Security Act, and the new SEC guidance. In 2019, the FTC stepped up enforcement and the California Consumer Protection Act (CCPA) was enacted. In 2020, the Department of Defense enacted the Cybersecurity Maturity Model Capability audits for government contractors by third-party auditors.

These new regulations put in scope E.U. privacy data (regardless of physical location), California resident privacy data, insurance companies in states where they adopted the law (which is expected to be all 50 in three years), U.S. financial services companies, NYS financial services companies, and defense contractors.

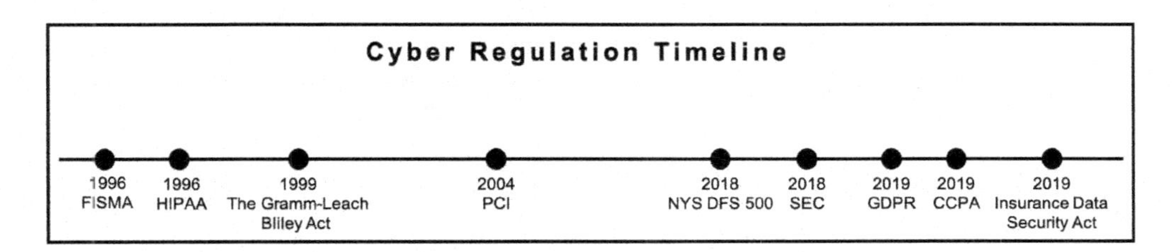

Figure 5.1 Cybersecurity Regulation Timeline (US Focus)

Integration trends—integrate or die

Risk, security, privacy, and compliance are inter-related. In Buddhism, this type of relationship is called the principle of interbeing. One cannot exist without the other, and they are important to each other's health. Cyber risk prioritizes security needs; privacy is a specific type of cyber risk related to the data type and is now heavily regulated by compliance. Effective cybersecurity uses people, process, tools, and insurance to reduce cyber risk and simultaneously maintain privacy.

Looking at these functions with a siloed mindset is a serious disadvantage for firms. I would even go so far as to say it is disastrous. Using dozens of excel spreadsheets to try and manage these functions is an exercise in futility. There are no metrics that are sharable and easy to communicate to each set of stakeholders. There is no way in an increasingly digital and interconnected world that security, privacy, and risk management can understand this from a holistic perspective and thrive.

Digitalization and interconnectivity have morphed cybersecurity. A decade ago, you could get away with a siloed approach to cybersecurity. The complexity introduced by regulation and technology since 2010 has altered the ability to be able to have proper oversight and effective risk, compliance, privacy, and security programs unless you are using a digital asset holistic approach.

Dirty deeds done dirt cheap—cybercriminal marketplaces

Cybercriminals operate on the dark web, which uses encrypted online content that is not indexed by conventional search engines like Google or Firefox. The dark web is also known as the darknet. The dark web is a component of the deep web. According to FireCompas, only 4% of internet pages are indexed by search engines.[18]

Private medical, research, and financial forums and databases in the deep web are accessible by search engines. Additionally, the deep web contains specialized platforms and forums of a highly unlawful nature, collectively these are known as the dark web. These dark web resources trade in illegal products and services. This market is also called the shadow market.

Specific browsers like Tor are required to access dark websites, which contain anonymous message boards for criminals to communicate, online marketplaces for drugs, market exchanges for stolen data, and other illegal activities and content. Transactions in the dark web are typically paid for using bitcoin, and physical goods are routinely shipped in ways that shroud the buyers and sellers from the FBI and other law enforcement agencies.

The dark web has become the "Amazon" of online illegal goods. Many of the legitimate types of innovation from online sellers like Amazon and eBay, such as seller ratings and customer reviews, have been repurposed to sell black-market items on the dark web.

The dark web attracts those that need anonymity when conducting business, including drugdealers, hackers, weapons dealers, and traffickers of child pornography. More troubling is the growing service economy within the dark web that includes hitmen, mercenaries, and other illegal operatives who anonymously advertise their services.

In 2016, The Economist reported that drug activity fueled by the dark web grew from about US$17 million in 2012 to approximately US$180 million in 2015.[19]

However, these are mere estimations, as the very nature of the dark web makes it difficult to accurately gauge the illegal economy it supports.

Law enforcement has struggled to curb dark web activity. After the FBI took down the popular dark web drug market known as Silk Road in 2013, Silk Road 2 popped up and immediately thrived, until the FBI and Europol shut it down in 2014. However, it is like "whack a mole", and Silk Road 3 emerged soon after that. In addition to the difficulty in shutting down dark web marketplaces, the technology has evolved to the point where open-source code allows for decentralized marketplaces, to work in a decentralized manner. Consequently, the dark web economy continues to grow, in spite of law enforcement's best efforts.

Cyber spending

Estimates put worldwide cybersecurity spending at US$114 billion in 2018 with a growth rate of 12.4%. Venture capital investment in cybersecurity technology is up, topping US$5 billion in 2018 alone.[20] In Israel alone, there are 300 cybersecurity companies, while globally there are tens of thousands. Spending on cybersecurity is nearing US$1 billion a year for banks like JPMorgan Chase and Bank of America.

Cyber insurance solutions are finally starting to differentiate themselves from the property and casualty market. The digital asset approach provides actuaries, reinsurance, and cyber insurance brokers with the tools that they need for stand-alone offerings that offer adequacy and allow for risk diversification.

The cyber insurance market is starting to grow; however, Covid-19 has put a monkey wrench into the market with the explosion in ransomware attacks. The cyber insurance market is on fire—between the proliferation of ransomware and claims, and reinsurers pivoting on their risk transfer strategies, companies are working day and night just to get their towers built. Rates are skyrocketing, budgets are being blown out of the water and insurers are scaling back on ransomware coverage and contingent business interruption insurance due to the massive vendor/supplier risk issues.

Mergers and acquisitions (M&A) topped US$2.5 trillion in 2018.[21] Cyber M&A has come under direct scrutiny after the Yahoo data breach that impacted their acquisition by Verizon. The industry is now advocating the use of digital asset exposures in M&A transactions. This underserved market has been using a compliance checklist mentality that does not consider cyber exposures in their due diligence process. Inadequate data will provide inadequate information. M&A transactions in 2018 were 3% of worldwide GDP. There is a huge gap in proper M&A due diligence that needs to be amended.

As indicated earlier, cloud security is a key area of concern due to high growth levels. Cloud security is just coming into view on a company's risk registers. Most thought that the CSP does it all and the company has no responsibility. That is not the case. The organization owns the data and will be the one reporting the data breach to regulators and consumers. Cloud auditors are needed to bridge the gap between the CSP and the company and ensure the right controls are in place to reduce risk to acceptable levels.

By 2025, 60% of global IT risk management (ITRM) buyers will depend on risk management solutions to aggregate digital risks in their business ecosystem, up from 15% in 2019. By 2025, 50% of ITRM solutions will evolve to support digital risk management capabilities, including cloud, operational technology (OT), IoT, and the social media environments of digital businesses, up from less than 30% in 2019. By 2021, 30% of security programs will incorporate at least two new roles due to new risks in digital ecosystems.[22]

Digital asset cyber risk management will bridge the gaps between the board and the technology teams, allow for holistic data to be used by privacy, security, risk, and compliance teams and is the next level of assurance in cybersecurity.

Notes

1. Privacy Rights Clearinghouse, https://privacyrights.org/data-breaches.
2. Experian, "Data breach industry forecast," 2015, https://www.experian.com/assets/data-breach/white-papers/2015-industry-forecast-experian.pdf.
3. Victoria Song, Gizmodo, "Mother of all breaches exposes 773 million emails, 21 million passwords", Janua18, 2019, https://www.gizmodo.com.au/2019/01/mother-of-all-breaches-exposes-773-million-emails-21-million-passwords/.
4. Chris Udemans, Technode, "China's IoT manufacturers are reducing costs at the expense of our privacy and security", July 2, 2018, https://technode.com/2018/07/02/iot-security-privacy/.
5. Security, "Cybercrime will cost businesses $2 trillion by 2019," May 12, 2015, https://www.securitymagazine.com/articles/86352-cybercrime-will-cost-businesses-2-trillion-by-2019.
6. Gleen Hicks, Ioffice, "Why you need to adopt a cloud first strategy now", October 8, 2019, https://www.iofficecorp.com/blog/cloud-first-strategy-2020#:~:text=The%20Market%20For%20Cloud%20Services,the%20most%20recent%20Gartner%20research.
7. Purplesec.us, "The ultimate list of cybersecurity statistics or 2019," 2019, https://purplesec.us/resources/cyber-security-statistics/.
8. Norton, "VPNfilter malware now targeting even more router brands. How to check if you're affected," 2020, https://us.norton.com/internetsecurity-emerging-threats-vpnfilter-malware-targets-over-500000-routers.html.
9. Purplesec, "2020 cybersecurity statistics. The ultimate list of stats, data, & trends," 2020, https://purplesec.us/resources/cyber-security-statistics/.
10. Alison DeNisco Rayome, TechRepublic, "Cybersecurity: Malware lingers in SMBs for an average of 800 days before discovery", July 11, 2019, https://www.techrepublic.com/article/cybersecurity-malware-lingers-in-smbs-for-an-average-of-800-days-before-discovery/.
11. Paulette Perhach, The New York Times, "The mad dash to find a cybersecurity force", November 7, 2018, https://www.nytimes.com/2018/11/07/business/the-mad-dash-to-find-a-cybersecurity-force.html.
12. Lily Hay Newman, Wired, "The Covid-19 pandemic reveals ransomware's long game", April 28, 2020, https://www.wired.com/story/covid-19-pandemic-ransomware-long-game/.
13. Kelly O'Hara, Monster, "The future of cybersecurity jobs", 2020, https://www.monster.com/career-advice/article/future-of-cybersecurity-jobs.
14. David Barton, Security, "The cybersecurity talent gap = an industry crisis", April 30, 2019, https://www.securitymagazine.com/articles/90182-the-cybersecurity-talent-gap-an-industry-crisis.

15. Kelly Jackson Higgins, Dark Reading, "It takes an average of 3 to 6 months to fill a cybersecurity job", March 12, 2019, https://www.darkreading.com/cloud/it-takes-an-average-of-3-to-6-months-to-fill-a-cybersecurity-job/d/d-id/1334135.
16. Can STEM qualifications hold the key to the future of https://www.forbes.com/sites/forbestechcouncil/2019/09/11/can-stem-qualifications-hold-the-key-to-the-future-of-cybersecurity/
17. Gartner, "Gartner survey finds only 65 percent of organizations have a cybersecurity expert", July 17, 2018, https://www.gartner.com/en/newsroom/press-releases/2018-07-17-gartner-survey-finds-only-65-percent-of-organizations-have-a-cybersecurity-expert.
18. Positive Technologies, "The criminal cyberservices market", July 25, 2018, https://www.ptsecurity.com/ww-en/analytics/darkweb-2018/#:~:text=According%20to%20FireCompas%2C%20only%204,are%20indexed%20by%20search%20engines.&text=Private%20forums%20and%20databases%20(medical,web%2C%20or%20the%20deep%20Internet.
19. The Economist, "Shedding light on the dark web", July 16, 2016, https://www.economist.com/international/2016/07/16/shedding-light-on-the-dark-web.
20. Stephen Grocer, New York Times, "A record $2.5 trillion in mergers were announced in the first half of 2018", June 30, 2018, https://www.nytimes.com/2018/07/03/business/dealbook/mergers-record-levels.html.
21. Gartner, "Gartner forecasts worldwide information security spending to exceed $124 billion in 2019", August 15, 2018, https://www.gartner.com/en/newsroom/press-releases/2018-08-15-gartner-forecasts-worldwide-information-security-spending-to-exceed-124-billion-in-2019.
22. LogicManager is recognized for ability to execute in the https://www.logicmanager.com/2019-gartner-mq-itrm/

6 CYBER ROLES

It's a full-on war for cyber talent.

Matt Comyns, Managing Partner Caldwell Partners

The cyber ecosystem

There are many stakeholders in the cyber ecosystem. These include C-Level executive responsibilities that touch the CEO, CIO, CRO, CFO, CISO, CPO, Chief Communications Officer, Director of HR, and Lead General Counsel. Public companies are required to have audit subcommittees. Other roles are more functional, such as compliance managers, system owners, and IT teams. We will also explore the external roles of regulators and vendors in cybersecurity, risk, privacy, and compliance.

Cyber risk management depends on the support of cross-functional partners. C-Level executives, CISOs, and CROs must work together to identify key stakeholders to target areas of responsibility that can shift based on the organizational maturity. Responsibilities must be crafted to demonstrate how different stakeholders are involved in enterprise cyber risk management, how they play different roles, and work together to manage strategy, incidents, and day-to-day needs. To improve transparency and increase accountability, HR should formally document these roles and their cyber responsibilities and have it approved by senior leadership.

The (RACI) charts below suggest the different types of needs that are assigned to roles in cybersecurity in terms of Responsibility, Accountability, Consulted, and Informed actives. This example is for a very mature organization. The first chart looks at strategic activities and the second chart at tactical activities.

Responsibility	CEO	CIO	CISO	CPO	CFO	BOD	CRO	Chief HR	Chief Communications	Chief GC	Third-party risk management
Cyber Resiliency Strategy	R	I	R	I	I	R	A	I	I	I	I
Cyber Insurance Limits	R	C	I	I	A	R	R	I	I	I	I
Vendor Risk Management	I	C	C	I	I	R	C	I	I	C	A
Cyber Communications - External	R	I	C	I	I	I	I	I	A	C	I
Cyber Tools Roadmap	I	I	A	I	I	I	I	I	I	I	I
Operational Cyber	I	I	A	I	C	I	I	I	I	I	I
Digital Risk Reduction	R	I	R	I	I	R	A	I	I	I	R
Incident Response	I	I	A	I	I	I	C	I	I	C	I
Vulnerability Management	I	I	A	I	I	I	C	I	I	I	I
Ransomware Strategy	R	C	R	I	R	R	R	I	I	A	I
Policy Management	R	C	C	C	I	R	A	I	C	C	I

R= Responsible for achieving the project; multiple people can be responsible.
A= Accountable for ensuring the project is completed (e.g. the project "owner"); only one person can be accountable.
C= Consulted throughout the project- typically two-way communication.
I= Informed of project progress and completion- typically one-way communication.

Figure 6.1 Typical Strategic Roles and Responsibilities

DOI: 10.4324/9781003052616-7

Responsibility	CEO	CIO	CISO	CPO	CFO	BOD	CRO	Chief HR	Chief Communications	Chief GC	Third-party risk management
Managing Exposure Reduction	I	C	C	I	I	R	A	I	I	I	I
Managing Gaps in the Cyber Program	I	R	R	R	C	I	A	I	I	I	I
Cyber Communications - Internal	C	I	C	I	I	I	I	A	I	R	I
Privacy Impact Assessment	I	I	I	A	I	R	R	I	I	I	I
Trigger Cyber Crisis Response	C	C	A	C		I		R	R	C	
Conduct Initial Investigation	I	R	A	R		I		C	C	R	
Contain and Remediate the Crisis	I	R	A	I		I		I	I	I	
Manage Vendor Relationships	I	R	A	R		I		I	R	R	
Maintain and Manage Business Continuity	I	A	R	I		I		C	R	I	
Manage Internal Communications to Employees	C	C	C	C		I		A	R	C	
Conduct Post- Crisis Analysis	R	R	R	R		C		R	R	A	

R= Responsible for achieving the project; multiple people can be responsible.
A= Accountable for ensuring the project is completed (e.g. the project "owner"); only one person can be accountable.
C= Consulted throughout the project- typically two-way communication.
I= Informed of project progress and completion- typically one-way communication.

Figure 6.2 Typical Tactical Roles and Responsibilities

The Board of Directors

The Board of Directors is a group of individuals elected to represent the shareholders. A board's mandate is to establish corporate management policies and oversight and make decisions on major company issues, including cybersecurity. They have the fiduciary duty to protect the business assets, 85% of which are digital. The Board also needs to look at cyber from a self-preservation angle. Aon's announcement that cyber events are now among the top three triggers for Director and Officer (D&O) derivative actions should get their attention. D&O derivative claims are those brought by shareholders in the name of a company, against the company and certain of its executives, to enforce a right against these individuals, which the company itself has declined to pursue. Ensuring that the Board understands the cyber program and is actively engaged should suffice to rebut those claims.

After the Target breach, the board of directors' role to provide organizational oversight and leadership on cybersecurity is indisputable. Federal regulators require that financial institutions, critical infrastructure, and publicly traded corporations be regularly updated on cybersecurity risks and understand the cybersecurity defenses the company has in place. Many regulators are going even further with legislation that requires the board of directors to approve the company's cybersecurity plan, be regularly updated on cybersecurity events, and direct the firm's significant cybersecurity initiatives. At the state level, we see that New York State's Department of Financial Services requires the board of directors to endorse its cybersecurity compliance initiative. Some companies have cyber experts that sit on the board and counsel the Board on their program. This is an interesting idea, however, impossible to scale. Boards need to be able to understand cyber from a business perspective.

The issue that the board faces is that they need metrics and KPIs that allow them to understand cyber risk, ransomware strategies, cyber insurance needs, regulatory needs, resource, and budgeting needs. The Board Officers and Directors typically do not have information technology or security backgrounds. The Board is responsible for organizational oversight which includes having a strong governance program that addresses the cybersecurity requirements and oversees how those requirements will be implemented and maintained over time. This scope contains a considerable amount of requirements. Metrics and KPIs must be easy to understand and useful for the Board.

The Board is responsible for ensuring that adequate cybersecurity protections are in place and that directors are sufficiently knowledgeable about their company's cybersecurity protections and that they align with best practices. Boards must receive regular reports about the company's digital asset risk and its cybersecurity issues in layman's terms. Boards are expected to understand the company's cyber exposures and how they should be prioritized and mitigated. Boards need to ensure that the CISO liaisons with the Risk Officer, Data Privacy Officer, and Compliance Manager relating to incidents, vulnerabilities, and threats as well as cybersecurity risk assessments; privacy impact assessments, security control decisions; vendor agreements; results of security testing; data breaches, denial-of-service attacks, ransomware attacks, and policy violations.

In the case of a confirmed and serious cyber incident like a data breach, the Board must be informed immediately, updated on the status of the initial investigation and the remediation of the crisis. Additionally, they must be informed if a vendor is involved, and on the external communications and be consulted on the post crisis analysis.

Boards should also consider the organization structure. New roles like the Chief Digital Asset Risk Officer and Data Privacy Officer are being implemented worldwide to bridge the CISO and digital risk and privacy risk gaps. Another factor that the board should appreciate is the reporting of the CISO to the Chief Information Officer (CIO). These roles have diametrically opposing agendas and need to be reconsidered. A CIO has to innovate and keep things up 24/7. A CISO wants to put controls on things and slow things down. The CIO may be rewarded when the new system is deployed on time and under budget, while the CISO is biting his or her nails and will not be sleeping at night because of the CIO's possible security short-cuts.

A large part of Board engagement is to ensure that there is thought leadership and critical thinking. This requires the Board is knowledgeable about cybersecurity and that Directors know how to ask probing questions. Metrics should easily highlight cyber shortcomings, and Directors should hold management accountable and ask about risk acceptance or remediation plans.

Boards must review and approve cybersecurity policies and procedures. Companies should have a set of documented privacy, data and information security policies, and plans. The policies should be written by subject matter experts, reviewed by legal and then go to the Board for approval. The subject matter experts should present the goal, scope, and requirements of the policy and enforcement guidelines. Policies should be considered living documents and should be updated, at a minimum, annually. It is best that the policies are enterprise wide and not business unit driven. This ensures that they are consistent and easy to monitor.

Companies should establish a regular cadence of effectively communicating cybersecurity risks to the Board. Cyber risks are digital and need to be communicated in metrics and KPIs that the board understands. A key requirement of effective Board oversight is to require the use of quantitative, digital risk metrics. This does not mean the NIST CSF Framework. That is a set of cybersecurity control tests. It is not risk data. It has a relationship to risk in respect that it measures the effectiveness of controls that mitigate risk. Do not make this mistake please.

Consistent with assessing digital risk, the Board also should ensure that the company's auditing procedures take into account cybersecurity issues. Regulators will review whether companies have developed sufficient cyber risk auditing procedures and whether the board is reviewing these audit results. The Board's audit committee typically does this.

The Board has to understand third-party risks. This is both the internal risk that we see with a service provider with access to a firm's network and with external cloud service providers and data processors who are provided data by the firm. All the new regulations require third-party risk assessments. This includes the GDPR, the Insurance Data Security Act, New York State Department of Financial Service Part 500, the CCPA, and many more. Vendor cyber risk should be assessed and monitored. Companies should have a cyber due diligence process before engaging third-party vendors to ensure that the vendor is contractually committed to fulfilling cybersecurity obligations.

Companies that grow through acquisition should be sure to integrate cybersecurity due diligence into their processes. As in the case of Verizon and Yahoo, too often corporate deals close without an adequate cybersecurity due diligence that looks at the acquisition in context. The firm is either migrating data and/or ingesting new digital asset infrastructures into their organization. If you already have a CRM system, you are most likely only going to migrate the data. In this case you inherit the additional data exposures. If you are buying the firm because of their technology, you are going to inherit their inherent cyber risk and financial exposures. There should be a cyber risk assessment that looks at exposures, and inherent risk that demonstrates program gaps.

Chief Exceutive Officer (CEO)

Organizations with cyber-minded CEOs can better manage cyber risk, better protect against cyberattacks, and better leverage cybersecurity for strategic opportunities.

CEOs must make a much-needed shift from a technology and operations focused mindset to a more strategic mindset that is business focused on protecting the digital assets of the business, including capturing the strategic picture of cybersecurity in the business, speaking the language of business impact in all cybersecurity communications, and building "muscle memory" for threat response at the CEO and Board level.

Many CEOs fail their companies by relying on the CISO or CIO and not truly understanding their cybersecurity risks. The CEO must ensure that their organizations have adequate funding to manage all those risks. CEOs must benchmark cyber resilience and set goals with the CISO and CRO to increase it, moving from a compliance mindset to a risk mindset.

Cybersecurity begins and ends at the highest level of management. The CEO must understand the cyber risks and spearhead the organization's cybersecurity activities. It is he or she that has the ultimate personal accountability. The CEO must ensure strong leadership for cybersecurity by hiring a Chief Information Security Officer or, if resources are too scarce, outsource the role.

The CEO is responsible for working with the CISO to establish and maintain a cybersecurity strategy. They must ensure that the CISO has the proper budget to meet the risk objectives of the firm. This includes people, processes, and tools. The CEO must know the organization's crown jewel digital assets and their various levels of importance, exposure, inherent risks, and risk reduction programs. They must understand the organization's cyber maturity and collaborate to set goals to increase maturity. The CEO must ensure that the firm has an effective ransomware strategy and an adequate amount of cyber insurance. The CEO must understand the results of the cyber risk assessment to provide executive oversight.

The CEO sets the tone at the top. The cybersecurity culture should be collaborative. Cybersecurity should be one of the top three business concerns, and everyone should be aware of it. Understanding cybersecurity needs to be done at all levels of the business. Cybersecurity training should be part of employee onboarding. Cybersecurity training should include continuous awareness training for phishing and other important areas to which employees are vulnerable.

Many companies send employees to cybersecurity certificate training. Employee training should be role specific and include annual policy review, enterprise cybersecurity best practices, data safety, and regulatory requirements. According to Dean Jonathan Hill at Pace University's Seidenberg School of Computer Science and Information Systems, "Pace helps companies understand cyber from the business perspective with our cybersecurity certificate program. The program drives increases in enterprise cyber resilience by providing market-driven cybersecurity content from over 200 advisory board members."

Chief Financial Officer (CFO)

CFOs are responsible for corporate finances and are focused on saving money and delivering returns to investors. CFOs must make a much-needed shift from a spreadsheet mentality to a more strategic mindset that is investor relevant and focused on protecting the digital assets of the business. This includes understanding the huge financial risks of cybersecurity in terms of exposures, reporting breaches costs to investors, and work to build trust using business-based cyber budgeting techniques.

Many companies utilize a crown jewel approach for cyber risk management. In many cases, finance owns the majority of the data generated and used in the business. In some cases, the CISO may report to the CFO. Protecting financial data requires that it is mapped and classified properly. This is also critical to understand how your organization's digital supply chain functions and how the data flows across your entire organization, and its relative importance. Companies must have a digital asset inventory that includes their data and prioritize crown jewel and business critical information in need of most protection since it is impossible to protect everything.

General Counsel (GC)

In terms of cybersecurity, legal teams are responsible for corporate legal responses and strategy. They require a deep understanding of the cybersecurity regulations. They are part of incident response teams and craft and/or review regulatory policies and press statements. They are responsible for attribution, determining the responsibility for harmful conduct.

General Counsel is typically consulted when there is a data breach and has responsibility in the initial investigation, vendor management, and external communications. They are accountable for the legal post crisis analysis and communication with regulators.

Many times, when I walk into an organization and interview the legal team, they are incredulous when I tell them that they are in scope for HIPAA or PCI. Despite over twenty years of cyber laws on the books related to healthcare and credit card data, most legal teams are not aware that they are processing cardholder or healthcare data. The digital asset approach clarifies this for them very quickly.

Data Privacy or Protection Officer (DPO)

The DPO is responsible for ensuring that the company or organization correctly protects individuals' personal data according to current legislation. They manage the GDPR and privacy programs addressing privacy risks. They communicate to the board on privacy issues and with regulators like the European Union Supervisory Authority or State Attorneys General. They offer advice on privacy matters, monitor GDPR, and privacy compliance, and liaise with the authorities.

The DPO informs and advises the company of its obligations under data protection law. They monitor compliance of the organization with all legislation in relation to data protection, including audits. They conduct awareness raising activities as well as training of staff involved in processing activities.

They oversee the Privacy Impact Assessment (PIA). This is not a set of questionnaires. It is a measurement of the confidentiality and integrity of the privacy data. They act as the contact point for requests from individuals regarding the processing of their personal data and the exercise of their rights.

The DPO is typically consulted when there is a privacy data breach and has responsibility in the initial investigation and vendor management and external communications related to a privacy breach. Additionally, in the case of a data breach, they are responsible for the post crisis analysis and communication with the European Union Supervisory Authority or State Attorneys General.

Chief Risk Officer (CRO)

Cyber risk innovation is transforming and disrupting cybersecurity. As a result, the Chief Risk Officer role is also changing dramatically, with most organizations treating cyber as an enterprise risk. As a vital member of the C-suite, today's truly effective CRO must be central in establishing, leading, and monitoring the organization's cybersecurity risk management program. Treating cyber risk as an enterprise risk requires incorporating digital asset risk metrics, defining cyber risk tolerances, and managing the cyber risk program.

We see that based on the industry, there is more embracing of this as a business tenet. For example, in the banking sector, the Federal Financial Institutions Examination Council (FFIEC) has required companies to conduct a sophisticated cyber risk appetite analysis with over 20 high-level sophisticated requirements.

The cybersecurity domain traditionally has fallen to the Chief Information Officer. As we discussed earlier, this has significant drawbacks. The CIO is too focused on the development and keeping the lights on and has little to no cyber risk understanding. Cybersecurity risk is the number one business risk and has to be managed holistically and not just from an IT perspective. The CRO has a much deeper view of cyber risk and can communicate across the entire business. This aggregated view of cyber risk is critical to have an effective risk reduction program.

Today's cyber risk innovations allow the CRO to have digital asset cybersecurity and risk analytics, with real-time dashboards, reports, and workflows. There is a wide disparity among organizations as to the sophistication of these analytics. As we discussed, financial services firms have largely figured out the need for integrated cyber risk management. As companies mature, we will see the CROs taking on the cyber risk portfolio's responsibility as their industry regulation requires this level of information.

The digital CRO is tasked with establishing a dynamic cyber risk program that is holistic and provides information to each role in the cyber ecosystem in the context of how they need to see the data.

Chief Information Officer (CIO)

Cybersecurity is a company-wide issue—and it's everyone's responsibility to manage it appropriately—but today, many companies may not have a CRO, CISO or cybersecurity function; therefore, the CIO must act as a steward for the data and ensure that the proper controls and processes are in place for data security.

- The CIO must be aware of the regulations that govern their industry or their business. With this information, they must communicate their cybersecurity posture and any risk to the necessary parties both internally and externally.

- The CIO must focus on both the training and overall awareness of cybersecurity. For example, the CIO may need to facilitate the cybersecurity awareness of end-users or those managing applications or analytics.
- The CIO must enforce and manage cybersecurity controls for vendors.

Chief Information Security Officer (CISO)

There are two types of Chief Information Security Officers: operational and governance. The operational CISO is technical. They establish and maintain the enterprise vision, strategy, and program to ensure information assets and technologies are adequately protected. They manage cybersecurity tools and roadmap. They are in charge of the cybersecurity remediation program resources and projects. A governance CISO is a risk manager with a solid business background. They establish policies for cybersecurity and communicates cyber risk to the board. They align cybersecurity strategies to risk and work with the operational CISO to reduce risks to acceptable levels.

The technical CISO manages several cybersecurity initiatives, including access control, encryption, security tool management and roadmap, incident response, monitoring, and a host of other functions.

Compliance manager

A compliance manager is a specialist who, through policy enforcement and program preparation, creates and maintains a company's legal and ethical credibility to protect the digital asset of the firm. They ensure that all departments of an organization comply with the cybersecurity laws and regulations that the company upholds. Compliance managers manage all the compliance programs, work with the security teams to align program goals. They should be framework experts based on their regulation needs in PCI, ISO, NIST, NYS DFS Part 500, and others in terms of cybersecurity. They ensure the company complies with its outside regulatory requirements and internal policies.

IT auditor

An IT auditor examines and evaluates an organization's information technology infrastructure, policies, and operations. IT auditors examine administrative, technical and physical cybersecurity controls, and overall business and financial controls that involve information technology systems. They are experts in understanding cybersecurity controls and the verification of controls.

New positions in cloud auditing are on the rise. This requires a strong understanding of cloud security controls.

System owners

System owners make the decisions to develop a system or to purchase systems. They are responsible for the maintenance of the system and to ensure that their data is secure. They own the system and processes, and they are the risk acceptors, and define risk thresholds for their systems.

Information technology (IT) personnel

Information technology personnel may act as remediators of findings, incidents, or vulnerabilities. They participate in cybersecurity control assessments and identify issues and may help to remediate them. They may be part of a team for incident response or vulnerability remediation.

Regulators

Regulators can be industry, data-driven, geography, and/or government focused. Credit card data is regulated by an industry body—the PCI Security Council. The Payment Card Industry Data Security Standard (PCI-DSS) is the only framework that can be used. This perspective framework has over 250 control tests and is pass/fail.

EU privacy data is regulated with the GDPR by the European Union Supervisory Authority. The GDPR has over 100 articles and sub-articles and does not mandate a perspective framework. Regulators investigate data breaches and complaints about the misuse of data. They update and enforce regulations and deploy fines.

Healthcare data in the U.S. is regulated by the Department of Health and Human Services. Insurance companies are regulated by the National Association of Insurance Commissioners. New York State Department of Financial Services regulates finance and insurance companies operating in NY state. There are no prescribed frameworks for any of these regulations.

Each regulatory body may have a perspective framework or not. Frameworks are specific control tests that measure the effectiveness of the cyber controls related to confidentiality, integrity, and availability of data. Many regulations describe the requirement for control tests as a risk assessment. It is not a risk assessment. It is a security control test assessment. They look at categories of security and describe the test's goal and require the security team to measure the effectiveness of the control. In some cases, it is pass-fail, and in others, it is degrees of maturity. We will cover these in detail in later chapters.

Vendors (third parties)

Vendors include supply chain and partners that are contracted to work with your firm. They may or may not process your data. However, all vendors have some relationship to your digital assets.

Vendors are the cause of 63% of reported data breaches. This third-party vendor risk is inherited by the first Party. The average third-party breach costs over US$10 million.

Vendors can be service providers, such as attorneys, management consulting firms, and IT consulting firms that work with your digital assets. They can be cloud service providers that provide your firm infrastructure, platform or software as a service solution. They can be providers of technologies or systems, such as Microsoft or Oracle. Each have different types of cyber risks and should be treated differently. We will discuss this in more detail in later chapters.

Vendor cybersecurity risk management is required by almost all the new regulations and some pre-existing ones like HIPAA and PCI.

Security manager

Security Managers can also be called an SOC Manager, Security Director, or SecOps Lead. This person typically manages the security operations center (SOC) and is in charge of overseeing the security team. This position includes resourcing, building the operational cyber processes, and designing the technology stack. A security manager should have a background in running a security team and should be able to provide technical advice as well as administrative oversight.

Security engineer

Security Engineers can also be called Security Architects, Security Incident Event Manager (SIEM) Engineers, and other titles that relate to the security role. Each company will be organized differently and depending on the number of people on the team and the needs of an organization, there will be a variety of positions. If it is a large organization, it is likely to see people on the team who specialize in incidents, endpoint security, and other specific areas of security engineering. Team members in this role are typically responsible for building out security architectures, managing events or incidents, and engineering security systems and working closely with the DevOps teams to ensure continuity and speed of releases. Security architects also document the requirements, procedures, and protocols of the architecture and systems that they create.

Security analyst

A Security Analyst can analyze threats, events, incidents, or vulnerabilities. They may also be referred to more specially as a Threat Analyst, Incident Responder, or other related name. Security analysts are the front line in the organization's cybersecurity. Their job is to identify, investigate, and respond to threats, vulnerabilities, and/or incidents. They are also usually involved in creating the disaster recovery (DR) plans.

Notes

1. Gartner, Top Security and Risk Management Trends, Research ID G00466211, 27 February 2020, Peter Firstbrook, Neil MacDonald, Lawrence Orans, Mario de Boer, Katell Thielemann, Bart Willemsen, Akif Khan, Michael Kranawetter.
2. Steve Morgan, Cybercrime Magazine, "Cybersecurity talent crunch to create 3.5 million unfilled jobs globally by 2021", October 24, 2019, https://cybersecurityventures.com/jobs/.
3. Cerius Executives, "Interim executives vs. management consultants – What's the difference & costs?", 2020, https://ceriusexecutives.com/management-consultants-whats-the-difference-costs/.

PART II
CYBER BASICS

7 ATTACK SURFACES AND DIGITAL ASSET INVENTORY

Threat is a mirror of security gaps. Cyber-threat is mainly a reflection of our weaknesses. An accurate vision of digital and behavior gaps is crucial for a consistent cyber-resilience.

Stephane Nappo, CISO Société Générale

Attack surfaces

There are two categories of attack surfaces, an enterprise attack surface and a global attack surface. The internet is a global attack surface. Within the enterprise, the attack surfaces are the physical and digital assets that include systems, business processes, data, and technologies.

The explosion in the use of the internet, the percentage of the business that is now a digital asset, the cloud first strategies of most organizations and the mass proliferation of IoT devices has catapulted cybersecurity into the #1 business risk.

Attack Surface Drivers

- **Internet Usage** –Up over 1000 percent over two decades
- **Digitization** –Increase of 600% over two decades
- **Cloud Service Providers**–Market size of $383 million predicted for 2026 with a CAGR of almost 30%
- **IoT Devices Increase** of 400% increase over the past five 5 years

Figure 7.1 Attack Surface Drivers

The internet

The global attack surface is the internet. The internet is a global computer network consisting of interconnected networks using standardized communication protocols, providing a variety of information and communication facilities. In 2001, there were half a billion internet users. In 2014, there were 3 billion and in 2020 there were 4.7 billion. This has been over a 1000% of the internet increase over two decades, expanding the threat surface exponentially. Cybersecurity Ventures predicts there will be 6 billion internet users by 2022—and more than 7.5 billion internet users by 2030.[1]

DOI: 10.4324/9781003052616-9

The global attack surface provides a means that an attacker can utilize to reach our digital assets.

Enterprise assets

The attack surface of an enterprise's digital asset environment is the sum of the different points of ingress or egress where an unauthorized user can try to exfiltrate data, interrupt a business process, or alter the integrity of the data from a company's digital infrastructure. Keeping the attack surface as small as possible is a basic security concept. Enterprise attack surfaces are both physical and digital. The term attack surface is often confused with the term attack vector. What is being attacked is the attack surface; the vector is the means by which an intruder gets access to the digital assets.

Physical computer related assets—endpoints

Physical attack surfaces are things you can physically touch. In information technology, a physical asset is often called an endpoint device. This endpoint can connect you to the digital assets. These include desktops, laptops, mobile phones, USB drives and ports, and hard drives that have been removed from any device. The attacker may steal a laptop on the bus, a USB drive on someone's desk, or a mobile phone on a train. They now have physical possession of the device. They do not have to use a covert method like a phishing attack to do damage. They do need to gain access to the device with the users' credentials. Inside the organization, the physical attack surface can be exploited by disgruntled employees, and by contractors who work inside the firewall. Credentials can be obtained from carelessly discarded hardware, and passwords left on sticky notes on people's desk or phone. Data disposal and password policies should be in place to ensure everyone in the organization understands the requirements that aid in reducing these types of issues.

Physical access to buildings, server rooms, and sensitive departments are not attack surfaces, however, they are security issues. Badging, visitor policies, electronic key cards for entry, security guards, and cameras are all important aspects of keeping individuals with cybercrime on their minds one step away from your physical and digital assets. Other security hardening measures include fencing, locks, biometric access control systems, and fire suppression systems. Physical locations should be monitored using security cameras that use notification systems, such as intrusion detection sensors, heat sensors, and smoke detectors. Lastly, disaster recovery policies and procedures should be in place and should be regularly tested to ensure that they work and to lessen the time it takes to recover from a cyber event, man-made, or natural disaster.

Digital assets

The attack surface includes the digital assets—systems, processes, data, and the technologies that support them (i.e., networks, software, hardware, databases,

Web application servers, IoT devices, messaging, etc.). They are used by individuals, customers, vendors, government entities, regulators—in essence, everyone. The value of our businesses is directly related to these digital assets and our cyber resilience is a direct measure of how well we have protected them. Let's explore this.

Digital assets are systems, technologies, business processes, and data. Access to digital assets can happen directly from the physical device or indirectly using the internet.

Both physical and digital attack surfaces should be limited in size to reduce the probability of unauthorized access. Organizations are required to do digital and physical asset inventories for most regulatory requirements, including PCI, NYS DFS Part 500, HIPAA, etc. Inventorying physical and digital assets is the first step in compliance, cyber risk, and privacy management.

Systems

A system is a consolidated set of technologies that provides the basis for collecting, creating, storing, processing, and distributing information and is owned by a business unit. As an example, the Customer Relationship Management (CRM) system is owned by the sales team, SAP financials is owned by the finance team. Systems can be purchased from vendors. As an example, Salesforce.com is a CRM system that is provided in a SaaS cloud from Salesforce.com. Many companies develop their own home-grown systems. In this case, the firm is responsible for the security patches of the technologies that are part of the system.

Business processes

A business process is a set of digital rules that are utilized by one or more systems to take inputs, transform them, and produce outputs that are reported or utilized by other systems. With the CRM system, there are different processes, such as customer registration lead registration opportunity analysis. The process is what generates the revenue.

Technologies

Technologies are computer-related components that typically consist of hardware and software, databases, messaging, and devices. Oracle sells databases, Microsoft provides the .Net framework, VMWare sells virtualization software. It is important to understand the role of technologies in cybersecurity.

Systems are made up of technologies. In the case of Salesforce.com, it consists of a Web application server, database, etc. Salesforce is responsible to update the security patches of these technologies. However, it is the case of a homegrown system, the firm is responsible for the security patches of the technologies that are the part of the system.

In the CRM example, you might use salesforce.com, you might use Microsoft CRM Dynamics, you might have your own homegrown system. Each has different layers of technologies within it, it might be sitting in a cloud, it might be using middleware to communicate, each has a database, a Web application server, etc.

Data

Data is the information that is processed and stored. Data can be classified into different types, including privacy, credit card, intellectual property, customer data, supply chain data, etc. These types tie back to compliance and regulatory requirements.

Each system has business processes that process different types of data. Examples are personal identifiable information (PII), privacy, healthcare data, credit card data, employee data, financial data, etc. The data types have relationships to the systems, regulations and sometime even to the assessment framework. When scoping a security assessment, we must first identify what digital assets you have and what data types are associated to them to scope the compliance requirements and regulations. Furthermore, each regulation requires an inventory of all the digital assets. The inventory must be documented and maintained. You cannot protect what you cannot see. Inventories are used not only in the scoping exercise but also for the risk quantification, scoring, and other very useful information.

Asset classifications

Digital assets can be classified based on their value to the business and may be related to the type of data they process or store, and the revenue that they generate. Crown jewel digital assets are an organization's most prized or valuable systems assets, in terms of profitability and future prospects. The crown jewels of an organization should be heavily guarded, allowing only certain individuals access to trade secrets and proprietary information. Negative impact on the crown jewels can result in business unsustainability. Some types of crown jewel digital assets can further be classified as safety, mission critical, and transactional.

Business critical assets are those that are required in order to achieve a positive outcome and may result in loss, although not in unsustainability. They may include patents/copyrights, corporate financial data, customer sales information, human resource information, proprietary software, scientific research, schematics, and internal manufacturing processes. Disruption due to a cyber-attack will not cause the organization to become unsustainable; however, it will have a significant financial impact in terms of loss of revenue or fines. For example, an e-commerce business might identify its business-critical assets as its website, inventory system, sales and accounts receivable system, any proprietary products it produces, and its interfaces with delivery systems, either electronic or physical.

Business crucial assets are less important to the company than business critical. These levels of importance are used for setting risk thresholds.

Vendors and digital assets

Vendors have a relationship to digital assets. They implement systems, process your data, maintain security, provide you technology, and may provide cloud services, including software, platform, or infrastructure as a service offering. Vendors are untrusted and much attention has been paid recently to reported data breaches attributable to vendors. There are different types of vendors and they include cloud service providers, system vendors, service vendors, and technology vendors. Having clear written agreements and incident response plans between the organization and the vendor is required to meet many vendor risk requirements, including NYS DFS Part 500, GDPR, CCPA, and a host of other regulations.

Cloud Service Providers are a third party that provides either infrastructure, platform, or software as a service in an off-premise deployment to the organization. The cybersecurity model is a shared responsibility model between the CSP and the organization. Some cybersecurity controls are maintained by the organization and some by the CSP.

A system vendor is a third party that provides a set of end-to-end technology components that allows the organization to implement specific functions. There are tens of thousands of examples. A few examples include Guidewire which provides Guidewire ClaimsCenter, SAP which provides SAP Financials, SolarWinds which provides Orion, and Peoplesoft which provides Peoplesoft HR. The system vendor is responsible to provide patches for any vulnerabilities that impact the security of their offering.

IT service vendors are a third party that designs, develops, tests, deploys, or maintains a system, business process, technology, or data. Examples include McKinsey implementing SAP, Deloitte doing an audit, or E&Y providing accounting services. Many service vendors work with your data directly. As an example, lawyers perform legal work, including mergers and acquisitions, lawsuits, etc. Accountants manage and maintain the general ledger. Data is often provided to the service vendor and there can be a high risk of data exfiltration.

A technology vendor provides a computer-based component to store, retrieve, transmit, and manipulate data or information. Examples include Oracle that provides databases (i.e., Oracle MySQL), Microsoft that provides technology infrastructure (i.e., .Net framework), etc.

Vendor risk is also called third-party risk. The organization is the first party. The organization owns the data, and they are responsible to protect it. The organization will be fined the most and has the most to lose if their third party has a cyber issue. The first party inherits the cyber risk of the third party. If you get breached the regulator will come knocking on your door and they're going to demand to see the vendor risk management program you have in place. The level of fines in this area will depend on how well you have documented and implemented a third-party cyber risk management program. Vendor issues are the most well-known because they have gotten the most press.

Cloud service providers—rocking our world

Back at the beginning of this millennium, most people did not realize that cloud services existed. Starting with Software as a Service (SaaS), the industry was brand spanking new. The concept of cloud computing can be traced back to the 1960s, however from a usage perspective, the origin of modern cloud computing started in 1999 with Salesforce.com. This was the first successful public Software-as-a-Service (SaaS) offering. I am proud to say I was one of the first users back in the day.

In 2019, 90% of companies were running some type of cloud.[2] There are several types of cloud services. Cloud services can be deployed as Infrastructure as a service (IaaS), Platform as a Service (PaaS), or Software as a Service (SaaS). Most companies today opt for a cloud first strategy and put their non-core applications in the cloud. This shift over the past two decades has made the cloud industry one of the most importance aspects of business today.

SaaS is when software is accessed via an online network and paid via a subscription rather than licensed perpetually and installed on individual computers. This model provides users with access to software running on the provider's infrastructure, and users manage the application's settings only and create their own content on top. There are many examples, including Dropbox, Cisco WebEx, and Salesforce.

PaaS is when a business develops and runs an application over the internet without having to build the infrastructure and manage it themselves-saving the company time and money. Users typically consume and manage a collection of software or development components in this model through the use of programming language, libraries, or resources provided by the provider.

IaaS is when the businesses can access storage, networking, and servers in the cloud on a pay as you use basis. This model enables users to deploy and manage computing, networking, and storage servers. From the operating system and up, the users handle everything.

Additionally, the market is also segmented by the type of deployment model used. They can be delivered as either public, private, community or hybrid cloud—or recently multi-cloud. Private clouds have only one customer (tenant) on an instance. This is also referred to as single tenant. These include vendors such as OpenStack, Cloudstack, and VMware. Hybrid cloud is a cloud infrastructure environment that uses a mix of public and private cloud solutions where applications can communicate and pass data between the clouds. In a public cloud, the computing infrastructure is hosted by the cloud vendor at the vendor's premises. These are the offerings from Azure, AWS, Google, Salesforce, etc. Clouds that are built for specific purposes (government, medical, etc.) are called Community Clouds. For example: Azure Government, AWS GovCloud, Salesforce Government Cloud, and the AWS China region.

The customer has minimal visibility and no control over where the computing infrastructure is hosted. As of 2020, the largest SaaS public cloud providers are Amazon Web Services (AWS), IBM Cloud, Google Cloud, and Microsoft Azure.

Cloud security is not well understood. Couple all cloud strategies with the popular approach of outsourcing not only people, but infrastructure and you have the perfect storm for cyber attackers – a ginormous attack surface, business strategies that promote an 'assumed' risk transference to vendors with businesses reliant on their digital security.

IoT – the Internet of Things

The Internet of Things is a network of physical objects embedded in sensors, software, and other technologies to connect and share data over the internet with other devices and systems. Most IoT devices have no security baked in. Adoption of IoT at the current rate with security as an afterthought will have us coping with impacts for generations to come.

Despite the ongoing pandemic, the Internet of Things industry continues to expand. For the first time in history starting in 2020, there are more IoT connections (e.g., connected vehicles, smart home devices, connected industrial equipment) available than non-IoT connections (smartphones, laptops, and computers). At the end of 2020, 11.7 billion (or 54%) of the 21.7 billion active linked devices worldwide are IoT system connections. More than 30 billion IoT connections, approximately four IoT devices per person on average, are expected to exist by 2025.[3]

This is a competitive market and to drive down the costs the manufacturers may opt to have no embedded access controls. This creates a dangerous precedent. As we have seen with the Hangzhou IoT camera maker, which confirmed in 2017 that its cameras had been exploited as part of a botnet by the Mirai malware that led to an unprecedented, distributed denial-of-service (DDoS) attack targeting websites such as Twitter, PayPal, and Spotify.

Digital asset inventories

Digital asset inventories are required to comply with the GDPR, CCPA, HIPAA, PCI, and other data-driven regulations that necessitate the ability to scope the security control assessments and ensure adequate controls area applied on the systems and technologies that are storing and processing that data.

Digital asset inventories can be done in an excel spreadsheet for immature companies that have a limited number of digital assets and in an asset management system for more mature companies.

A digital asset inventory includes all systems, technologies, and business processes with a map of the data that they store and process. You will need additional attributes for cyber risk management.

We are going to cover the excel approach in this chapter. This manual method is to collect data business unit by business unit. Some may want to start with crown jewel assets only and then add business critical and business crucial. It could be a combination of the two. There is no one right way. Here is an example to get started with.

Step	Instructions
Step 1	Identify what data does your firm process and stores. Types may include credit card data, healthcare data, insurance related data (policy and claims), financial data, PII, EU privacy data, etc.
Step 2	Identify the business units and departments in your firm. Create an organizational chart with a hierarchy
Step 3	Identify the people in your company that own the systems. A system owner is the person who made the decision to buy the system or develop the system. They are responsible to have the system maintained.
Step 4	Using the system owners have them provide the following data about each system: Unique ID number: The system number or random generated unique number. System Name: The legal name of the system. System Description: Briefly describe what the primary purpose of the system is. Data processed: Based on your answers in step one, identify all types of data that system processes. Technologies: Identify all the technologies used by that system. Vendor Name: If vendor supported, identify the vendor. If Vendor Supported and a Cloud Service identify the deployment model and service model. Processes: Identify any business process that generates revenue. Asset Classification: Define the asset classification. System Type: Cloud or On-premise.
Step 5	Complete this for the scope of the exercise.

Figure 7.2 Digital Asset Inventory Process[4]

Notes

1. Steve Morgan, Cybercrime Magazine, "Humans on the internet will triple from 2015 to 2022 and hit 6 billion", July 18, 2019, https://cybersecurityventures.com/how-many-internet-users-will-the-world-have-in-2022-and-in-2030/#:~:text=Looking%20ahead%2C%20Cybersecurity%20Ventures%20predicts,years%20of%20age%20and%20older).
2. Nick Galov, Hosting Tribunal.com, "25 must-know cloud computing statistics in 2020", 2020, https://hostingtribunal.com/blog/cloud-computing-statistics/#gref.
3. IoT Analytics, "State of the IoT 2020: 12 billion IoT connections, surpassing non-IoT for the first time", November 19, 2020, https://iot-analytics.com/state-of-the-iot-2020-12-billion-iot-connections-surpassing-non-iot-for-the-first-time/.
4. Maryellen Evans. Digital Asset Based Cyber Risk Algorithmic Engine, Integrated Cyber Risk Methodology and Automated Cyber Risk Management System. US 2020/0106801 Al United States Patent and Trademark Office, April 2, 2020.

8 KEY CYBERSECURITY TERMINOLOGY AND STATISTICS

We don't have a cyber problem, we have an English problem.

Paul Ferrillo, Partner, McDermott, Will, and Emory

Cyber risk and the CIA triad

A **cyber-attack** is an assault perpetrated by a threat source that attempts to exfiltrate data, interrupt business processes, and/or alter data. Exfiltrating data is a confidentiality issue, the interrupting of business processes is an availability issue and altering data is an integrity issue.

The **CIA (Confidentiality, Integrity, and Availability) Triad** does not have a single inventor and emerged from the collective wisdom of many cybersecurity experts. The notion of confidentiality was first mentioned in a 1976 US Air Force study. Integrity came from a 1987 paper that identified the financial industry's need for data accuracy. Availability became a topic after the first denial-of-service attack in 1988, as we talked about in earlier chapters with the creation of the Morris Worm.

Confidentiality is the ability to ensure that only authorized and approved users have access to the data. Confidentiality is violated when there is a data breach or access is incorrectly provided to a user as in the case of using someone else's user ID and password. Confidentiality is a component of privacy metrics. Privacy has become sacrosanct today with the advent of the GDPR and CCPA and we will continue to see new regulations evolve at a state and nation state level.

Integrity is the ability to ensure that the data is unaltered and is consistent, accurate, and trustworthy over its entire life cycle. When an organization has unauthorized access to their digital assets, integrity can be altered. When someone has access that they should not have, integrity can be compromised. Integrity is a component of privacy measurements.

Availability is the ability to ensure the data is available to authorized users. Availability is violated when there is a business interruption. Business interruption is when business as usual is interrupted when the authorized users cannot access an application. It results in a loss of revenue. In cybersecurity, it is typically a result of a denial-of-service or ransomware attack.

In the GDPR, article 5f requires the organization to ensure that the confidentiality and integrity of the digital assets are adequate. Both confidentiality and integrity are privacy metrics that require measurement. There is no way to ensure adequacy

DOI: 10.4324/9781003052616-10

without a clear understanding of what digital asset attributes influence confidentiality and integrity and to measure them. There are many inherent digital asset attributes that can be used to measure the likelihood that there will be a cyber event. We will discuss this in the GDPR and Cyber Risk Scoring chapters in detail.

Thus, the CIA triad provides a meaningful way to measure cyber risk, privacy, and resiliency. It can be linked to the digital assets inherent risk when measuring the likelihood of a data breach or business interruption. The three elements of the CIA triad are measurable and can be compared across the wide array of digital assets to identify gaps and prioritize remediation work.

Cyber risk and resiliency

Cyber Risk is a measure of impact and likelihood at the digital asset level. There are two categories of cyber risk metrics: Cyber Financial Exposures and Cyber Risk Scores. They are the cornerstone of measuring cyber resiliency.

Cyber Financial Exposure

Cyber Financial Exposures are financial impacts that negatively impact the firm and are due to a compromise of confidentiality, integrity, or availability related to costs associated to record loss, revenue loss, and regulatory fines and penalties.

Cyber exposures are due to data exfiltration, business interruption, and regulatory fines.

Data exfiltration

Data exfiltration exposures are calculated based on the number of records that can be taken multiplied by the cost of the records. Data exfiltration happens when attackers (individual cyber criminals, organized criminals, nation-states) steal the organization's information. Data is exfiltrated by cyber criminals to sell on the dark web and commit financial, insurance or healthcare fraud.

The costs associated with this type of cyber incident include public relations assistance, auditing, consulting, investigation costs, communication costs, legal costs, credit monitoring, forensic costs, notification costs, call center costs, and other activities that are related to ensuring the individuals whose data has been taken are being cared for and for the cyber forensics to understand why the breach happened in the first place.

IBM and the Ponemon Institute have teamed up to provide the Cost of a Data Breach Report[1] for over ten years by conducting surveys of over 400 companies and 2200 individuals across over 100 countries to determine the industry average of the cost per record. Healthcare has almost twice the cost of any other record type. This is due to the amount of insurance fraud.

Now in its 11th year, the report has a high level of confidence in the data and provides insights into the detailed costs of data breaches and their financial impact on and organization. In 2020, the Annual Cost of a Data Breach Study showed that the cost of a data breach was US$3.86 million globally and US$8.64 million in the

United States. The 2020 report shows that the cost of healthcare breaches is more than double the average.

In the United States, data breaches are more expensive to fix. The average cost was US$7.91 million. The cost of a data breach differs greatly across sectors of industry as well. For healthcare data breaches, they hold the highest cost which is an average of US$429 per record in 2019. This is substantially higher than data breaches associated with PII, which cost an average of US$150 per record in 2020.

According to the IBM report, the mean time to identify a breach was 207 days. The mean time to contain a breach was 73 days.

In 2019, IBM determined that organizations that have experienced a data breach have almost a 30% chance of experiencing a second material breach within two years. There are several factors that can have an impact on the cost of data breaches. Companies that have good incident response can contain a breach within 30 days. These companies save approximately US$1 million in breach resolution costs. The use of encryption will also reduce the cost of a data breach. Other factors include business continuity management and security awareness training. Another factor that adds to this cost is employee churn. Having a Data Privacy Officer (DPO) or Chief Information Security Officer (CISO) goes a long way to helping to demonstrate a commitment to customer trust and responsibility. Credit monitoring also lessens the churn impact. *My research shows that integrated Cybersecurity automation lowers the cost of a data breach by over 25%.*

Third parties have higher likelihoods of causing malicious data breaches. Third-party vulnerabilities were responsible for 16% of malicious breaches and cloud misconfigurations constituted 19%. In 2019, companies that are compliant with regulation have more than 13% less costs.

Cyber insurance policies typically will show this cost of a breach erroneously labeled as "network interruption". It is more appropriate to refer to it as a data breach and not a network interruption. The loss associated with a data breach can be financially calculated based on the maximum number of records stolen and is usually related to the aggregate cyber insurance limit. We will discuss cyber insurance in detail in Part 6.

Business interruption

Business interruption exposures can be due to either ransomware or denial-of-service attacks. Denial of service happens at the system level and ransomware happens at the organizational level. Business interruption can be dependent or non-dependent. Dependent will look at revenue loss over time due to interruption of the on-premise applications and non-dependent looks a revenue loss from cloud-based systems.

Understanding which digital assets are on-premise or in the cloud is a misunderstood concept in terms of cyber risk. There is no cut and dry approach to knowing who owns the responsibility to ensure which cybersecurity controls they are responsible to manage and maintain. We will review this in Part 10 when we start to speak about vendor cyber risk management.

Cyber insurance policies typically will business interruptions as two separate sublimits "cyber extortion" sublimits related to ransomware and "business interruption" sublimits related to DoS attacks.

Regulatory exposures

Regulatory exposures are dependent on the fines prescribed by the regulatory body. Their costs may be related to the number of records lost, willful neglect, organizational revenue, and operational downtime and noncompliance with specific compliance requirements or a combination of these.

Cyber risk scores

Cyber Risk Scores are empirical values that are associated to the impacts and likelihoods of a cyber event. There are three types of Cyber Risk Scores that are relational and are measured throughout the cybersecurity lifecycle. Each score is at the digital asset level. These scores are: Inherent Cyber Risk, Mitigating Control Risk, and Residual Cyber Risk.

Inherent Cyber Risk Scores: These scores are the cyber risk looking at the risk existing in the digital asset itself, how it behaves and how it is used. This is what I have defined as raw cyber risk, "cybergeddon risk" and the risk as if there was zero percent effectiveness of cyber controls. It contains specific asset and user behavioral attributes that increase or decrease likelihood and impact of cyber events. Inherent cyber risk is a static metric based on the digital asset behavioral and user analytics. Inherent cyber risk is the worst-case scenario. This will be explained in great detail in Part 8.

Mitigating Control Cyber Risk Score: These scores consider the inherent cyber risk and ingest information related to the cybersecurity control assessment to demonstrate cyber risk reduction. Cybersecurity control assessments, such as the NIST Cyber Security Framework (CSF) or ISO 27001 measure the effectiveness of mitigation controls. Mitigating controls always reduce inherent cyber risk by their very nature.

Security control assessments will reduce the inherent cyber risk in relationship to their effectiveness. Security control assessments measure the effectiveness of the cybersecurity controls across several domains (e.g., access control, encryption, etc.). Control assessments can be done at the level of the organization, system, data, or technology.

Residual Cyber Risk Score: These scores are always in flux. They have a relationship to the inherent cyber risk and the control assessment cyber risk (assuming one was actually done as prescribed by regulation on an annual basis). They ingest the threat, vulnerability, and incident information that increase cyber risk by their nature. Here, decisions are made to accept risk or mitigate it.

Integrated cyber risk management

Cyber risk scores are measured across the cybersecurity lifecycle. An integrated cyber risk approach will utilize data from cybersecurity tools, such as a Vulnerability Management Scanner (VMS), Security Incident Event Management (SIEM), and/or Advance Threat Prevention (ATP) system to demonstrate how the risk score will rise in context of which digital asset(s) are impacted.

Cyber Resiliency is a measure of an entity's ability to continuously deliver the intended outcome despite adverse cyber events. Inherent Cyber Risk scores are used to benchmark Cyber Resiliency and to define the organization's goals in terms of cybersecurity. Inherent cyber risk scores benchmark cyber resiliency. Goals are achieved by enhancing the effectiveness of the mitigating controls.

Risk influencers: events, incidents, threats

Events and incidents

A cyber event is a suspicious occurrence that may be an indication that an incident is occurring. The event will be investigated by the cybersecurity team to determine if it is a false positive or a real incident. Security Incident and Event Monitoring systems are a sophisticated cyber tool that the security team uses to detect suspicious behavior on the network. However, this system has to be fine-tuned or companies can get a lot of noise that becomes unmanageable to shift through. It is not possible to go through thousands of events a day with one or two security operations analysts.

Once it is determined to not be a false positive, it is classified as an incident. A cyber incident is an occurrence that may result in a loss or adverse consequence to the digital asset. An incident is not necessarily a data breach. A data breach is the unauthorized movement or disclosure of information. An incident can be a denial-of-service or ransomware attack which is a business interruption and not a data breach.

Has data been altered if it was breached? Not necessarily. The team must verify if the data has been changed before it was exfiltrated. Forensic investigations must be done to ascertain what the event means and if there is an impact to confidentiality, integrity or availably.

Vulnerabilities

Vulnerabilities are weaknesses in systems that can be exploited by cyber criminals to gain access to the firm to exfiltrate data, or interrupt business. They are updated using patches to fix the weakness.

Threats

A threat is a malicious attempt to damage or disrupt a computer network or system.

Threat actors and attack vectors

Cyber criminals attack the digital assets. Actors can be employees, cyber terrorists, hackers, customers, suppliers, third-parties, or consultants. Data can be stolen either at rest (inactive data that is physically stored in databases, spreadsheets, tapes, etc.) or in transit (data that is active and flows over untrusted or trusted networks) or in use (which opened in a program for creating or editing). Data exfiltration is associated to systems either in house (on-premise), in the cloud or on a device such as mobile apps or tablets.

A threat actor, also called a malicious or nefarious actor, is a group or individual that is associated with an incident that has or may impact an organization's cybersecurity. The incident can be intentional or accidental.

Actors can be categorized as external, internal, or partner. There is no trust or privilege with external threat actors. Internal threat actors or partners have some level of trust or privilege that exists or has previously existed.

External actors are responsible for 70% of incidents.[2] They are also associated with the most severe impacts. These threat actors can be categorized as commodity or advanced. A commodity threat actor launches a broad-based attack planning to impact as many targets as possible. An advanced threat actor targets a specific organization with the goal of implanting some type of advanced persistent threat (APT) to gain network access. Most APT actors have a dwell time of 56 days.[3] The dwell time is the time between when they infiltrated the network and when they delivered their payload to steal the data. In computer security, the payload is the part of data transmitted in as private user text which could contain malware, such as worms or viruses. Worms and viruses can perform malicious actions, including deleting data, sending spam, or encrypting data. The payload is the part of the malware that performs the malicious action.

Another type of external threat actor is the hacktivist. A hacktivist is a socially or politically motivated hacker who gains unauthorized access to a computer environment in order to further social or political ends. One famous group of hacktivists is Anonymous. They are famous for their acts of civil disobedience without revealing their identities. Anonymous' beginnings were less nefarious. They originated in 2003 as an imageboard to promote the concept of an online global brain of community users. Anonymous is legendary for its widespread and rebellious hacking activities.

Hacktivists use several of the same techniques used to identify website vulnerabilities and obtain unauthorized access or carry out distributed-denial-of-service (DDoS) attacks by financially motivated cybercriminals. Most hacktivists want to gain access to confidential information that can adversely affect the credibility of an individual, a brand, a business, or a government.

Cyber terrorists are those that are politically or ideologically motivated; possibly for financial gain, espionage, or as propaganda and use computers and information technology to cause severe disruption or widespread fear in society. These terrorist organizations are designated by the US Department of State and are on the US Treasury Department's Office of Foreign Asset Control (OFAC) list.[4] Their limited offensive cyber activity is usually disruptive or involves harassing in some sort. Terrorist organizations primarily use social media for communications and recruitment. They can be individuals, organizations, or nation-states. Their most common attacks are website defacements and claimed leaks. Be advised that when paying a ransomware demand you do not want to be paying it to anyone on the OFAC list. That would put you in violation of the Patriot Act.

Nation state actors are usually highly organized and well-funded cybercriminals. They are affiliated with nation states or political organizations with nation state ties that aggressively target public and private networks to steal, compromise, change, or destroy data. Their favorite motive is espionage, due to political, economic, or military ideations. Many are part of a state apparatus. They typically receive direction, funding, or technical assistance from a nation-state. Nation-state has been used interchangeably with Advanced Persistent Threats. This is not accurate. APT refers to a type of activity conducted by a range of actor types, not just nation state directed. Common nation state tactics include social engineering, direct compromise, data exfiltration, remote access trojans, spear-phishing password attacks, and destructive malware.[5]

Data breach statistics

The Verizon Data Breach Investigations Report[2]—also known as DBIR—is an excellent source of cyber statistics. The majority of breaches are done by outsiders. According to the most recent Report, 70% of breaches are done by external actors and 55% by organized criminal groups and 30% involved internal actors.

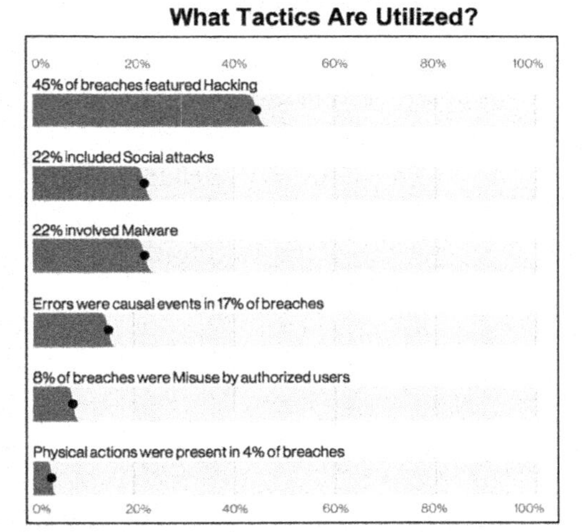

Image 8.1 Data Breach Actors and Tactics[2]

What tactics are used, who are the breach victims and what do they have in common? Forty-four percent of breaches featured hacking and 22% of breaches involved social media and malware.

Attack vectors are a path that a hacker uses to gain access to a computer environment in order to deliver a malicious payload. Attack vectors are mechanisms that enable hackers to exploit weaknesses in system and people. All of these methods involve computer programming except deception. Deception is when a person is hoodwinked into removing or weakening system defenses. In the case of SolarWinds, the vendor misled the customer into disabling the firewall that monitored Orion and the attackers knew that and took advantage of this human error. Email is the most common delivery method and office documents the most common file types.

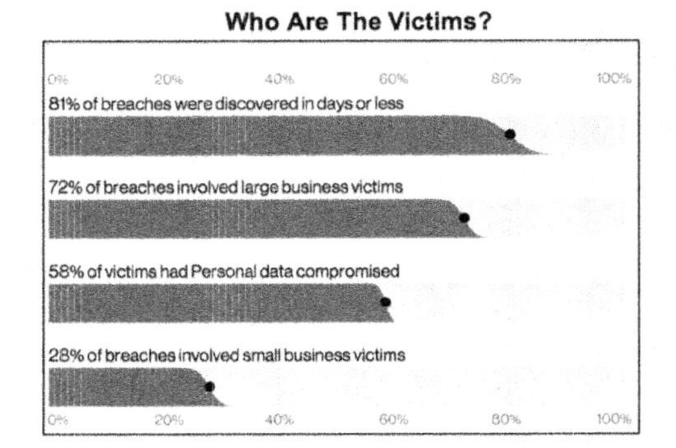

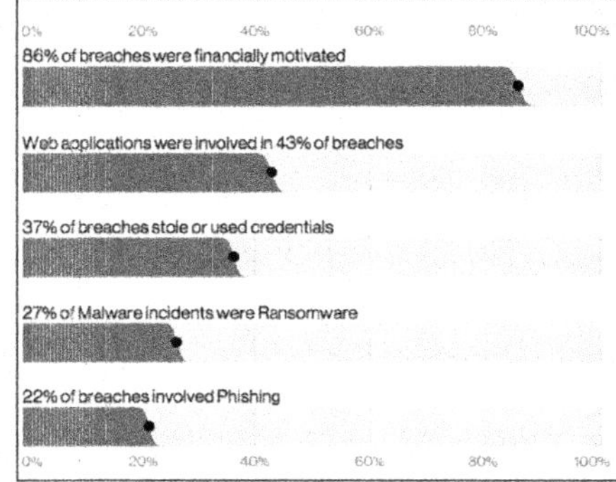

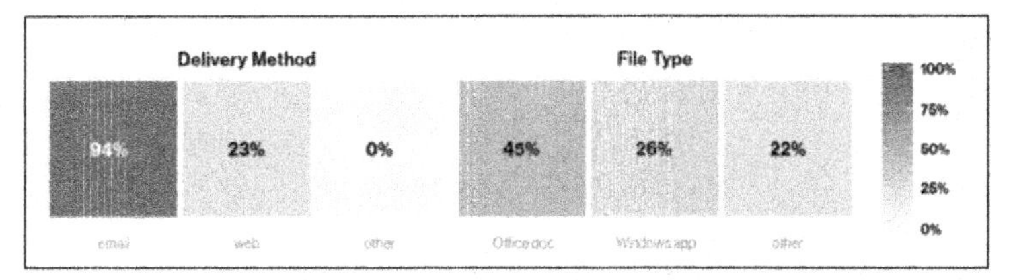

Image 8.2 Data Breach Victims and Commonalities[2]

Seventy-two percent of the breaches involved large enterprises and 28% were focused on small medium enterprises. Eighty-six percent of the attacks were financially motivated. Twenty-seven percent were ransomware attacks. Phishing accounted for 22% of the data breaches. The majority of breaches are financially motivated and have long dwell times.

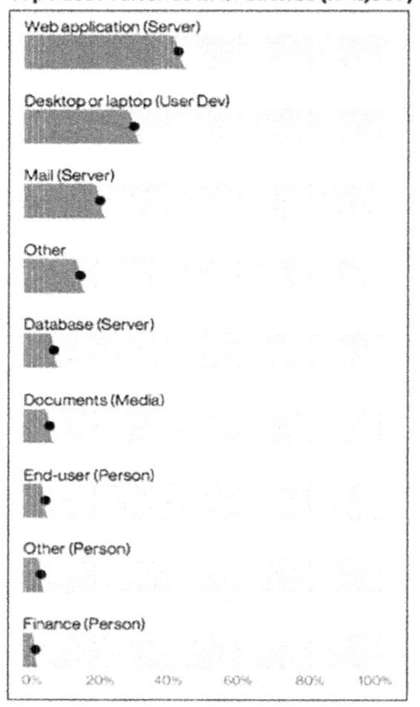

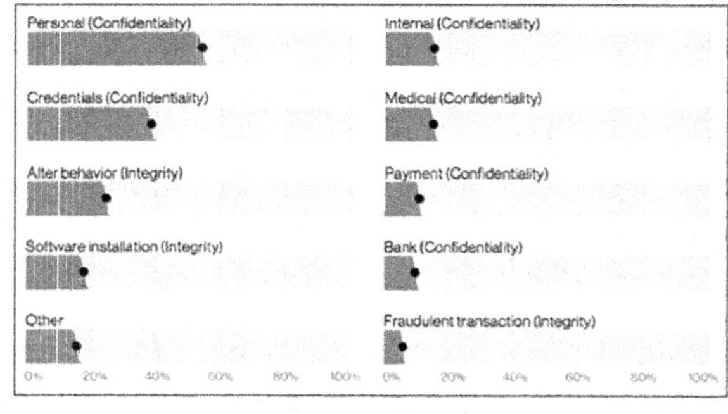

Other Malware Filetypes (n=13.6million)

shell script
Java
browser app
link
PDF
Flash
archive
Linux app
OSX app
Android app
DLL

Image 8.3 Data Breach Assets, Attributes and Malware Filetypes[2]

The majority of assets attacked are Web application servers. This is mainly due to cloud first strategies, where there is a shift of non-core systems from an on-premise environment to a cloud environment.

Office documents and Windows applications are still the malware filetype of choice. Most malware is distributed via email, with a smaller amount coming from Web services, and almost none through other means (at least when detected).

Notes

1. IBM Security, "Cost of a data breach report 2020", July 2020, https://www.ibm.com/account/reg/us-en/signup?formid=urx-46542.
2. Verizon, "2020 Data Breach Investigations Report", 2020, https://enterprise.verizon.com/resources/reports/2020-data-breach-investigations-report.pdf.
3. Fireeye, "FireEye Mandiant M-trends 2020 report reveals cyber criminals are increasingly turning to ransomware as a secondary source of income", February 20, 2020, https://investors.fireeye.com/news-releases/news-release-details/fireeye-mandiant-m-trends-2020-report-reveals-cyber-criminals#:~:text=In%20the%202020%20M%2DTrends,observed%20in%20the%20previous%20year.
4. William & Mary, "Treasury department's office of foreign asset control (OFAC)", 2020, https://www.wm.edu/offices/techtransfer/ExportControls/Regulations/OFAC/index.php#:~:text=Currently%2C%20sanctioned%20countries%20include%20the,periodically%20and%20is%20available%20here.
5. Cybersecurity Spotlight – Cyber Threat Actors. https://www.cisecurity.org/spotlight/cybersecurity-spotlight-cyber-threat-actors/

9 ENTERPRISE THREATS OF TODAY AND CYBERCRIMINALS

The dark web, once the virtual province of small-time hackers, has matured into a full-blown e-commerce hub for the exchange of illicitly obtained data, malicious code and cyber mercenary services.

Richard Davis, Director Compliance and Risk Management at Merck

Ransomware

Cybercrime is the new mafia. Ransomware is a form of malware that a cybercriminal uses to hold a firm's computer systems hostage until a "ransom" is paid. Either the firm pays the ransom, or the organization has to restore all of their computer systems. The firm has to have a high level of confidence in their disaster recovery program to entertain not paying.

Ransomware often infiltrates a computer as a computer worm or trojan horse that takes advantage of open security vulnerabilities. A vulnerability is a weakness in a system that has to be patched (fixed) in order not to allow an attacker to gain access. The cyber insurance industry is now seeing double digit ransomware demands. AIG announced that they had a US$16 million demand at the Advisen Cyber Risk conference in October of 2019.

Over US$8 billion was paid in ransom in 2018 and the average costs were between US$133,000 and US$250,000 depending on the industry. The cost of ransomware attacks surpassed US$7.5 billion in 2019.[1] Ransomware Costs Forecast to Reach US$20 billion by 2021.

- There will be ransomware attack every 11 seconds by 2021. By that time, the global cost will be $20 billion yearly. (CyberSecurity Ventures)
- Today, businesses suffer ransomware attacks every 40 seconds. (Kaspersky)
- Phishing emails are the cause of two-thirds of ransomware infections. (Statista)
- Every year, ransomware generates an estimated $1 billion in revenue for cybercriminals. (Bromium)
- About 9% of the American population has been a victim of a ransomware attack at some point. (Stanford University)

Figure 9.1 Ransomware Statistics[2]

High profile ransomware attacks include Maersk, Merck, and the city of Baltimore. Baltimore's budget office has estimated that the ransomware attack on city computers

DOI: 10.4324/9781003052616-11

will cost at least US$18.2 million—a combination of lost or delayed revenue and direct costs to restore systems. It is estimated the city's information technology will spend about US$10 million on recovery efforts.[3]

Ransomware is typically demanded in bitcoin. Bitcoin is a digital currency that can be transferred from one person to another without the use of a bank. Cybercriminals use bitcoin because of its anonymity. Converting your money to bitcoin, sending, and receiving it doesn't even require the use of a legal name or address. Here is what a ransom demand may look like.

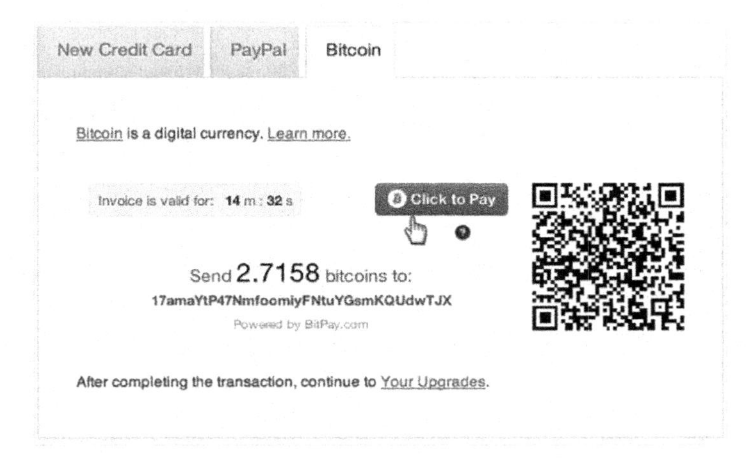

Image 9.1 Bitcoin Ransomware Demand[4]

Some industries are targeted more than others. Finance is one of the worst hit industries.

Crimeware

Crimeware is a class of malware designed specifically to automate cybercriminal activities. Crimeware malware (as opposed to spyware and adware) uses social engineering to perpetrate identity theft in order to gain access to the victim's financial and retail online accounts. Once access is provided via the malware, the cybercriminal will have access to the funds from those accounts and can make unauthorized transactions. Verizon's Data Breach Report reports on incidents and breaches across industry sectors.

	Incidents									Breaches								
	Accommodation (72)	Education (61)	Finance (52)	Healthcare (62)	Information (51)	Manufacturing (31-33)	Professional (54)	Public (92)	Retail (44-45)	Accommodation (72)	Education (61)	Finance (52)	Healthcare (62)	Information (51)	Manufacturing (31-33)	Professional (54)	Public (92)	Retail (44-45)
Crimeware	17	31	52	76	206	58	60	4,758	21	3	3	7	1	3	5	8	8	3

Image 9.2 Industry Statistics[5]

Other data that interests cybercriminals is confidential or sensitive corporate information. Crimeware uses malicious code to steal confidential and sensitive data. The following data from Verizon's Data Breach Report profiles incidents. DoS attacks lead the pack.

Incidents

Pattern	Accommodation (72)	Administrative (56)	Construction (23)	Education (61)	Entertainment (71)	Finance (52)	Healthcare (62)	Information (51)	Manufacturing (31-33)	Mining + Utilities (21 + 22)	Other Services (81)	Professional (54)	Public (92)	Real Estate (53)	Retail (44-45)	Transportation (48-49)
Everything Else	18	6	15	86	23	166	161	154	81	119	34	358	392	11	39	35
Crimeware	34	5	10	179	35	63	192	403	393	21	15	135	4,289	1	55	24
Web Applications	18	10	10	65	30	152	140	162	107	16	30	139	149	14	66	22
Privilege Misuse	6		2	7	11	36	74	10	54	11	2	14	25	3	16	7
Denial of Service	17	1		403	61	924	1	4,611	150	14	2	6,712	313		67	2
Miscellaneous Errors	15	2		62	22	128	163	115	47	6	20	63	112	6	21	15
Cyber-Espionage	1	3		2		3	1	11	75	6	1	40	26	2	1	2
Lost and Stolen Assets	1	1		15	8	22	66	11	27	3	4	25	1,540	2	8	5
Point of Sale	17				4				2			1	1		8	
Payment Card Skimmers						16			1				1		9	

0% 25% 50% 75% 100%

Image 9.3 Crimeware Incident Statistics[6]

The following information from Verizon's Data Breach Report profiles data breaches and their patterns.

Breaches

Pattern	Accommodation (72)	Administrative (56)	Construction (23)	Education (61)	Entertainment (71)	Finance (52)	Healthcare (62)	Information (51)	Manufacturing (31-33)	Mining + Utilities (21+22)	Other Services (81)	Professional (54)	Public (92)	Real Estate (53)	Retail (44-45)	Transportation (48-49)
Web Applications	18	9	9	59	28	142	116	149	80	9	26	109	80	13	59	15
Everything Else	15	5	13	63	17	95	97	52	32	12	9	90	59	10	25	16
Privilege Misuse	5		2	7	9	35	73	8	49	5	2	14	22	2	13	6
Crimeware	23	1	1	24	14	19	26	27	113	4	5	29	30		14	9
Miscellaneous Errors	15	2		62	22	126	162	114	47	6	20	59	112	6	21	15
Cyber-Espionage	1	3		2		3	1	9	34	6	1	9	25			2
Lost and Stolen Assets	1	1		10	4	13	46	5	24	3	4	17	18	2	4	4
Point of Sale	16				4				2			1	1		4	
Payment Card Skimmers						16			1				1		7	
Denial of Service				1				2					1			

0% 25% 50% 75% 100%

Image 9.4 Crimeware Data Breach Statistics[7]

Espionage

Cyber spying, or cyber espionage, is the act of obtaining unauthorized classified or secret information from individuals, competitors, rivals, groups, governments and enemies for personal, economic, political, or military advantage. It uses methods on the internet, networks, or individual computers through the use of proxy servers, cracking techniques, and malicious software, including Trojan horses and spyware.

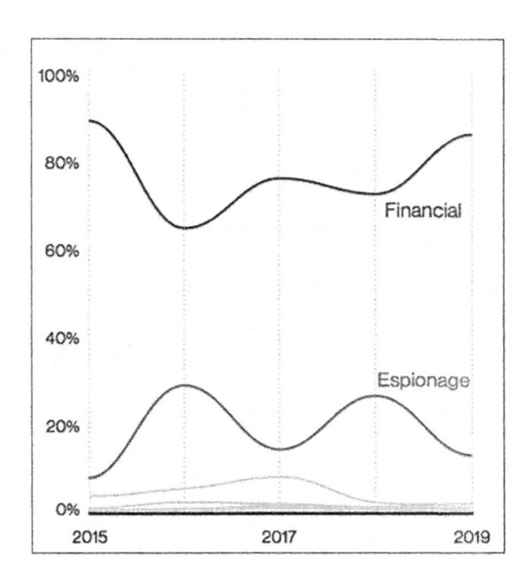

Image 9.5 Threat Actor Motivations[8]

Although cyber espionage makes great TV, it accounts for less than 30% of data breaches.[9] Over 100 countries have dedicated cyber-attack capabilities. It is the main source of revenue for Eastern Bloc gangs. Russian and Sicilian mafias are actively recruiting "hacking" experts.

Intellectual property (IP) theft

Cyber theft of IP is the stealing of copyrights, trade secrets, patents, etc., using the internet and computers. Russia, China, and other countries are actively stealing valuable corporate and government data. IP can also be stolen by hacking into the target company's computer environment. Taking advantage of a third parties poor cybersecurity hygiene is one of the easier ways for a cybercriminal to steal IP.

Some of the ways through which one can protect IP from cyber theft is to frequently update the list of IP that are needed to be secured. This will enhance the security related to accessing trade secrets and reduce the number of people who can access trade secrets. Updating all software systems regularly and constantly monitoring for unusual cyber activities is also a best practice. Security awareness training reduces phishing attack success and installing up-to date anti-virus software will prevent some malware from being installed.

Willful neglect means conscious, intentional failure, or reckless indifference to the obligation to comply with cybersecurity measures. Data breaches via negligence include incidents, such as leaving a laptop or a smart phone in a coffee shop or on a bus. Negligence is responsible for about 42% of all breaches.[10] Equifax as an example, chose not to patch a system whose breach was not isolated to a crown jewel system. From a negligence perspective, regulators will look to see what the competitors did to respond to an event. In the case of Equifax, both TransUnion LLC and Experian patched the Apache Struts vulnerability that led to the Equifax breach. The Senate found that Equifax willfully neglected its cyber obligations. This is an important term when we talk about HIPAA and other regulators that increase fines based on willful neglect.

Social media

There are almost 3 billion active Facebook uses. Many times, the lines are blurred between person and corporate use. Many employers allow their employees to engage in social media posts and most have a corporate blog. The most prevalent social media platforms that cross these blurred boundaries are Facebook, Twitter, and LinkedIn.

Inappropriate employee use of social media can lead to liability in the form of defamation, trade libel, trademark, and copyright infringement claims. Research from Cyber Intelligence 4U, Inc. has shown that only 39% of corporate directors and general counsel at public companies believe their company has a good handle on social media cybersecurity related risks. Less than 40% of companies have a social media policy.[11] When properly tied to a robust internet and email policy, a comprehensive social media policy can help to reduce defamation, trade libel, trademark, and copyright infringement claims.

Vendors

Vendors represent the majority of reported actors involved in data breaches. Most companies send vendors the majority of their data to be processed or stored. When data leaves the organization, the security of that data is now completely in the hands of the third-party. All third-party breach costs are borne by the first party. It is the organization's data and it is their duty to secure it, regardless of who it was given to. Facebook, Target, and Home Depot are only a few of the high-profile data breaches that involved third parties.

Cyber-criminals and the dark web

In general

The dark web consists of encrypted online information which is not indexed by conventional web search engines like Google. It uses special browsers (i.e., Tor) to access dark websites. This paves the road for creating sites dedicated as online marketplaces for drugs, market exchanges for stolen financial and private data, and other illegal activities. Most transactions in this hidden economy are paid anonymously using bitcoin. Illegal goods are shipped in ways that shelter both the buyers and sellers from the watchful eyes of law enforcement. According to FireCompass, less than 5% of internet pages are indexed by search engines.[12]

Most dark web users require anonymity when doing business. Usually they are nefarious individuals, or groups, such as drug-dealers, financial criminals, insurance identity thieves, weapon dealers, hitmen, and child pornography peddlers.[13]

The terms "dark web" and the "deep web" are often mistakenly used interchangeably. Like the dark web, the deep web pages don't pop up when you run a web search. They are related to sites that require a login, such as personal email, online banking, or other such sites. The deep web includes private (medical, research, financial, etc.) databases and forums. The dark web uses encryption to keep illegal content anonymous.

In 2016, The Economist reported that drug activity fueled by the dark web grew from about US$17 million in 2012 to approximately US$180 million in 2015.[14] There is not more recent data related to the size of the dark web market. The deep web is 500 times the size of the publicly facing internet. The nature of the dark web precludes this information from being readily available.

Regulators have fought valiantly to restrict dark web criminal activity. In 2013, the FBI took down the popular dark web drug market known as Silk Road. However, Silk Road 2 popped up and immediately thrived, until the FBI and Europol shut it down in 2014. However, Silk Road 3 emerged soon thereafter. The fight goes on.

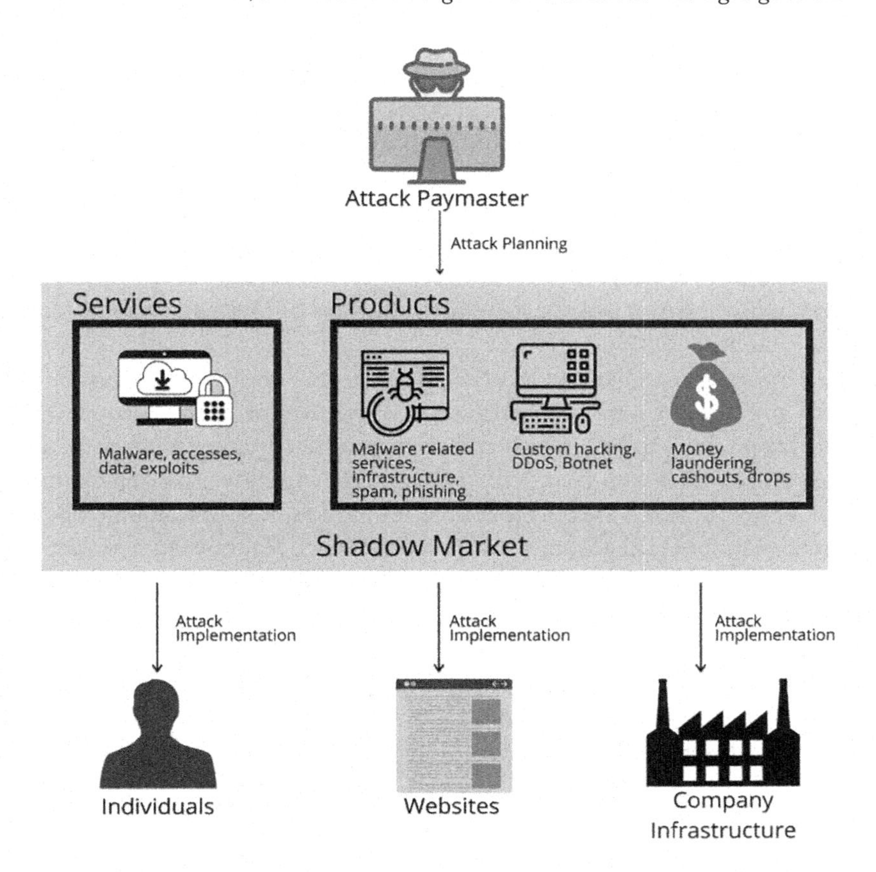

Image 9.6 The Shadow Market Relationships in Cyberattacks[15]

How it works

The diagram is a schematic representation of the position occupied by the shadow market in the planning and implementation of cyberattacks.[16]

Dark web market products fall into the following categories: malware designed as ransomware, miners, etc., exploits for zero-day vulnerabilities, data related markets (personal, accounting, payment, etc.), and access methods, including web shells, passwords for sites, or servers.

Malware is the main element in almost every cybercriminal's arsenal. Malware handles tasks related to automation, speed of execution, and attack invisibility. Malware can be divided into several types based on its purpose. These include cryptominers, data-stealing Trojans (stealers), hacking tools, malware for DDoS, ransomware, Random Access Trojans (RATs), trojan loaders, botnet malware, and ATM malware.

Sellers hawking ready-made Trojans or recruiting their services for malware developers are plentiful. The demand for these goods and services in the dark web completely overshadows the supply. Custom jobs are not uncommon; when a solution is required that is not off the shelf, cybercriminals can design and develop it quickly and inexpensively.

Cryptocurrency valuations caused an explosion in the demand for hidden mining software. In 2018, hidden mining software was over 20% of malware for sale on the dark web.[17] The growing cryptocurrency market spurred the need for data-stealing malware (stealers, spyware) aimed primarily at taking funds from cryptocurrency accounts.

Almost 20% of software on the dark web for sale was hacking tools for website attacks, mass mailings, address and password generators, and packers and encryptors of executable files. The average prices for tools in the cybercrime world are dirt cheap. The most expensive malware is for stealing money out of ATMs.

Stealers are also popular with cybercriminals. They steal passwords from data you cut and paste, capture keystrokes while saving the title of the window where the keys were pressed. They can bypass or disable antivirus software easily. They can send stolen files to the attacker's email. Stealers in 2018, cost approximately US$10. Prices for stolen data range from a few dollars to several hundred dollars for credentials for email accounts, and social networks. Malware is a very lucrative business that enables the theft of user data for payment systems or passwords for cryptocurrency wallets.

Like with the SolarWinds attack, hackers are not simply just after a certain set of data. They want to establish a long-term latent presence in the system and execute commands remotely at will. Typically, cybercriminals use a remote access Trojan (RAT) to do this. RATs are a type of malware that allows the cybercriminal to track user actions, run files and execute commands, capture screenshots, turn on the webcam and microphone, scan the local network, and download files from the internet. RATs sell for an average of approximately US$500 on the dark web. Forensic teams must ensure that after a ransom is paid that the cybercriminal has not left a RAT lurking in their system.

Seizing control of multiple devices may be on the cybercrime menu. This requires special software called a botnet. A botnet is a set of infected devices under the single control of the cybercriminal. It is designed to coordinate the control of the infected devices, such as a command-and-control (C&C) center.

Prices for malware to create a botnet start at US$200. A complete package that includes C&C server software, software for creating Trojans configured to work with a particular server (builder), and additional Trojan modules can cost around US$1,500. The ROI on a botnet will pay for itself in less than a month when used solely to conduct DDoS attacks.[18]

Next on our cybercrime menu are Trojans for ATMs. This is another kind of malware which is the most expensive class of ready-made malware, with prices starting from US$1,500. Criminals need to have good programming skills, and knowledge of the internal workings of ATMs made by various manufacturers like Diebold. A single ATM Trojan can be used to attack identical ATMs simultaneously.

Ransomware Trojans—According to an IBM study, up to 70% of US companies polled have paid a ransom to recover data.[19] The biggest ransomware attacks in 2017 were the WannaCry and NotPetya. The total damage caused by ransomware attacks exceeds US$1.5 billion in 2017. The average cost of acquiring a Ransomware Trojan is around US$300. Ransomware demands have risen over 100% from 2019 to 2020. In 2018, the demand as between US$200 to US$500 per record. Global Ransomware Damage Costs Predicted To Reach US$20 billion by 2021.[20]

The dark web marketplace is sophisticated. Data for sale ends up on the shadow market from cybercriminals who obtain personal information and user credentials for various sites. Popular data bought and sold on the dark web market includes logins and passwords for various social networks, online banks, etc., credit card data, personal data, such as scanned copies of passports, identity cards, driving licenses, etc., financial statements of companies prior to public release, and other sensitive information.

The most common items for sale on the dark web are user credentials. Passwords for online stores are also in high demand. The personal account details often have bank cards linked to them. This enables criminals to make purchases with other people's money (OPM) or use these platforms to cash out money from stolen bank cards by buying goods in someone else's name for subsequent resale. Most credentials sell for up to US$10. Most criminals sell social network credentials in batches numbering several thousand to several million. In 2018, credentials for access to online banking personal accounts are sold per piece at an average price of US$22, for accounts that had balances ranging from a few tens of dollars to tens of thousands.[21]

Credit card data is another popular item for sale on the dark web. Criminals can buy and sell goods on the internet, cash out funds through payment systems or make duplicate bank cards to be used for withdrawing cash from ATMs. Nine US dollars is the cost of details for one bank card.[22]

Even multifactor authentication is no problem. This can be overcome by purchasing details of calls and text messages of the victim's mobile phone number on the dark web. A text message containing a one-time payment code can be obtained for less than US$300.

Scanned copies of sensitive documents, such as passports, driving licenses, identity cards, corporate, or personal financial documents and credit details are commonly available on the dark web. Two US dollars is the average cost of a scanned copy of a passport.[23]

Stolen log in user IDs and passwords are used by cybercriminals to register on various online services. They buy various data that allows them to bypass the multifactor authentication mechanisms that is needed. These can be combinations of bank account details or credit/debit card information or an identification number. Each of these identifying elements are available on the dark web.

On the dark web, cybercriminals can obtain credentials to gain control over news sites adding to the proliferation of fake news. They can infect visitors with malware when visiting the news pages online. The most common business interruption is a denial-of-service attack which is often aimed at Government sites.

There is an entire segment of the shadow market that is dedicated to creating new solutions when there is not an off the shelf one available. Marketplaces that allow buyers to place ads for programmers are common. These types of malware development service pricing starts on average from US$500.[24]

One approach to create a new malware program is to reverse engineer existing ones from sites where the code is not available. These custom jobs start at US$1,000 per project.

Distribution services

Distributing malware is the process of delivering the target malware to a victim's computer. This can be done using phishing that embeds the malware in email attachments. The malware is downloaded from a link in phishing emails in this case. In the recent SolarWinds attack, cybercriminals embedded the malware in the file containing the software update.

Cybercriminals often use a website to distribute malware, steal user credentials or payment data. This costs US$50 to US$200 on the dark web. Twenty-seven percent of attacks use a phishing email with a link to a web resource requesting user credentials.[25] In 2017, Initial Coin Offerings (ICOs) were targeted by cloning sites, where afterward the attackers used phishing mailshots that victimized users who visited the sites and transferred cryptocurrency to the wallets of the criminals. In 2018, the Bee Token ICO had over US$1,000,000 worth of Ethereum stolen.

Botnets are usually deployed using DDoS attacks. There are a large amount of automated services and offers for hacker teams to conduct DDoS attacks. These attacks are relatively cheap—less than US$100 for a 24-hour attack. DDoS attacks are used by competitors to take their competitor's websites offline. Neustar estimates the damage caused by every hour of attack for a third of US companies at US$250,000.[26]

Notes

1. Purplesec, "2020 Ransomware statistics, data, &/trends", 2020, https://purplesec.us/resources/cyber-security-statistics/ransomware/#:~:text=costing%20businesses%20an%20estimated%20%248,Reach%20%2420%20Billion%20by%202021.
2. Luke Azezina, DataProt, "Ransomware statistics in 2020: From random barrages to targeted hits", November 13, 2019, https://dataprot.net/statistics/ransomware-statistics/.
3. Luke Broadwater, The Baltimore Sun, "Baltimore transfers $6 million to pay for ransomware attack; city considers insurance against hacks", August 28, 2019, https://www.baltimoresun.com/politics/bs-md-ci-ransomware-expenses-20190828-njgznd7dsfaxbbaglnvnbkgjhe-story.html.
4. Andy Skelton, Wordpress.com, "Pay another way: Bitcoin", November 15, 2012, https://wordpress.com/blog/2012/11/15/pay-another-way-bitcoin/.
5. Verizon, "2020 data breach investigations report, Verizon business", July 2020, https://enterprise.verizon.com/resources/reports/dbir/.
6. Verizon, "2020 data breach investigations report, Verizon business", July 2020, https://enterprise.verizon.com/resources/reports/dbir/.
7. Verizon, "2020 data breach investigations report, Verizon business", July 2020, https://enterprise.verizon.com/resources/reports/dbir/.
8. Verizon, "2020 data breach investigations report, Verizon business", July 2020, https://enterprise.verizon.com/resources/reports/dbir/.
9. Verizon, "Money still makes the cyber-crime world go round-Verizon business 2020 data breach investigations report is live", May 19, 2020, https://www.globenewswire.com/news-release/2020/05/19/2035340/0/en/Money-still-makes-the-cyber-crime-world-go-round-Verizon-Business-2020-Data-Breach-Investigations-Report-is-live.html.
10. Rutrell Yasin, Dark Reading, "Employee negligence the cause of many data breaches", May 24, 2016, https://www.darkreading.com/vulnerabilities—threats/employee-negligence-the-cause-of-many-data-breaches-/d/d-id/1325656.
11. Alicia Russell, Onalytica, "Why every CEO should have a social media presence", March 1, 2017, https://onalytica.com/blog/posts/why-every-ceo-should-have-a-social-media-presence/.
12. Positive Technologies, "The criminal cyberservices market", July 25, 2018, https://www.ptsecurity.com/ww-en/analytics/darkweb-2018/.
13. M3 Marketing, "What is the Dark Web?", 2020, https://www.mv3marketing.com/glossary/dark-web/.
14. Stefano Siggia, Pideeco, "How do criminals launder their money using the dark web?", February 7, 2020, https://pideeco.be/articles/dark-web-and-money-laundering/.
15. Positive Technologies, "The criminal cyberservices market", July 25, 2018, https://www.ptsecurity.com/ww-en/analytics/darkweb-2018/.
16. Positive Technologies, "The criminal cyberservices market", July 25, 2018, https://www.ptsecurity.com/ww-en/analytics/darkweb-2018/.
17. Positive Technologies, "Cybersecurity threatscape 2018: trends and forecasts", March 18, 2019, https://www.ptsecurity.com/ww-en/analytics/cybersecurity-threatscape-2018/.
18. Rob Sobers, Varonis, "110 must-know cybersecurity statistics for 2020", October 26, 2020, https://www.varonis.com/blog/cybersecurity-statistics/.
19. Charlie Osborne, ZD Net, "The average DDoS attack for businesses rises to over $2.5 million", May 2, 2017, https://www.zdnet.com/article/the-average-ddos-attack-cost-for-businesses-rises-to-over-2-5m/.
20. Steve Morgan, Cybercrime magazine, "Global ransomware damage costs predicted to reach $20 billion (USD) by 2021", October 21, 2019, https://cybersecurityventures.com/global-ransomware-damage-costs-predicted-to-reach-20-billion-usd-by-2021/.

21. Positive Technologies, "The criminal cyberservices market", July 25, 2018, https://www.ptsecurity.com/ww-en/analytics/darkweb-2018/.
22. Positive Technologies, "The criminal cyberservices market", July 25, 2018, https://www.ptsecurity.com/ww-en/analytics/darkweb-2018/.
23. Positive Technologies, "The criminal cyberservices market", July 25, 2018, https://www.ptsecurity.com/ww-en/analytics/darkweb-2018/.
24. Positive Technologies, "The criminal cyberservices market", July 25, 2018, https://www.ptsecurity.com/ww-en/analytics/darkweb-2018/.
25. Positive Technologies, "The criminal cyberservices market", July 25, 2018, https://www.ptsecurity.com/ww-en/analytics/darkweb-2018/.
26. Positive Technologies, "The criminal cyberservices market", July 25, 2018, https://www.ptsecurity.com/ww-en/analytics/darkweb-2018/.

10 CYBERSECURITY REGULATIONS, STANDARDS, AND FRAMEWORKS

As our country increasingly relies on digital commerce and digital assets, it will be important for Government to strengthen our security laws accordingly.

Ursuline Foley, Board Director and Former CIO Axa XL

General

A cybersecurity regulation is a legal directive that establishes mechanisms that should be in place to safeguard digital assets. Cyber regulations force companies to spend money on cybersecurity programs that protect their systems and data.

As an example, The General Data Protection Regulation, also known formally as (EU) 2016/697 (GDPR) is an EU law that focuses on data protection of EU citizen privacy. It is a set of requirements that provides for the rights of the data subjects and the mechanisms to protect those rights. The GDPR seeks to reduce cyber fraud in the billions and provide a level of control to individuals over their personal data. GDPR also centralizes cyber regulation, thereby streamlining the regulatory environment for both EU and non-EU businesses.[1] GDPR is a set of over 100 articles and sub-articles with no specific security control framework prescribed.

Cybersecurity guidelines or standards may use perspective cybersecurity control assessment frameworks for various required assessments across industries. Frameworks are a set of standard techniques that are published by governance bodies whose goal is to standardize the protection mechanisms used by companies. The principal objective is to reduce the probability of cyber risks, including prevention, or mitigation of cyber-attacks.

Some regulations or industry guidelines use prescriptive frameworks. As an example, the Payment Card Industry Data Security Standard (PCI-DSS) is a global guideline with an inflexible framework for banks, merchants, and data processors that process credit card data. "The PCI Security Standards Council's mission is to enhance global payment account data security by developing standards and supporting services that drive education, awareness, and effective implementation by stakeholders."[2] It is enforced by the PCI security council and their acquiring banks. The PCI-DSS framework must be used for security control assessments to obtain PCI compliance. Non-compliance may result in fines and possible loss of credit card privileges.

DOI: 10.4324/9781003052616-12

An information security framework is a mature set of documented, agreed upon and understood policies, procedures, and testing requirements that define how information is protected in a business, with the goal to lower risk and vulnerability, and therefore increase cyber resiliency in an ever-connected world.

As an example, the National Institute of Standards and Technology (NIST) is laboratory that creates best practices and frameworks that are prescribed for federal agencies. It is a non-regulatory agency of the United States Department of Commerce. The NIST cybersecurity framework is a very popular framework used by many companies worldwide. The NIST special publication 800–53 for organization cyber controls are used by companies for organizational IT-related controls. "The NIST Cybersecurity Framework was created as a policy framework of computer security guidance for how private sector organizations in the United States can assess and improve their ability to prevent, detect, and respond to cyberattacks."[3]

The International Organization of Standardization (ISO) publishes the ISO/IEC 27000 family of standards that address how a management system that is intended to bring information security under management control measures specific requirements to manage that system from a cyber perspective.[4] Accreditation certification bodies may certify companies that met the standard after the successful completion of a successful audit.

Framework components

Cybersecurity Control Frameworks are a set of standards used for cybersecurity control assessments. Their requirements have several components. There is a policy component, a test component, and a results component. Each framework's test components are made up of a series of categories of control tests. It is the job of the security team to perform these tests in conjunction with compliance, audit, and business teams. Controls are applied to the digital assets and can be system, technology, data, or organizational focused. The results of the tests are called *security control assessment findings*.

The policy component relates to cybersecurity goals that are defined in policies. Cybersecurity policies are enforceable legal documents that outline the specific goals for specific types of controls related to cybersecurity categories. Examples of cybersecurity categories are access control, encryption, audit, business continuity, organizational oversight and leadership, etc. They form the foundation for controls tests in a cybersecurity assessment and are part of the governance of the organization. In a mature organization, a governance CISO would most likely be responsible to create these policies with the approval of the legal team and input from the business and the operational CISO. In less mature organizations where there is only one CISO or security manager then that would most likely fall on their shoulders.

As an example, the Firewall Policy states management's expectations for how the firewall should function and may be a component of the overall security policy. This policy must set expectations for the configuration of firewalls. The policy must also specify the rules for the placement of firewalls within internal network infrastructures as well as how to manage their interface to the internet. The firewall policy must be updated by management as the firm's security, availability, confidentiality, or risks change, and ensure that any service provider managing its firewall is aware of its firewall policy.

Security control tests are the specific criteria to perform the test and the requirements to pass the test. Keeping with our example of the Firewall Policy—it states that it must address the company's security, availability, and confidentiality. Policies should state management's expectations for how the firewall should function, its placement in the operating environment, and ensure it is a component of the overall security, availability, and confidentiality policies and require all 3rd party service providers, with firewall management responsibilities to align to the policies. Regular reviews of the firewall and updates to the firewall policy should be performed by management to ensure its alignment with any changes in security, availability, confidentiality, or risk needs and ensure that all IT controls are kept current and reflect changes and development to security policies.

The third leg of the assessment is the results. Continuing with the firewall policy example, the firewalls must be aligned to the policy and tested to ensure that it is fulfilling the expectations and that regular reviews and updates to the firewalls are made as prescribed. The assessment results are what is used in the mitigating risk calculations as a finding.

Each framework has a set of control tests that can be classified as Administrative, Physical, & Technical Safeguards to ensure the confidentiality, integrity, and availability of all personal and/or sensitive data created, received, maintained, or transmitted is adequate. These controls that are tested are used to identify and protect against reasonably anticipated threats to the integrity of the data, protect against reasonably anticipated, unauthorized uses or disclosures, ensure compliance by the workforce and provide a means for managing risk in an ongoing fashion.

Administrative controls at a minimum, should include having a Security Manager or Officer, implementation of workforce security measures, incident response mechanisms, disaster recovery plans, and provide for the evaluations of these controls.

Physical controls include facilities access, workstation use and security, device, and media controls.

Technical controls at a minimum, should include access and audit controls that measure integrity, confidentiality, and availability, including authentication mechanisms and transmission security.

Cybersecurity control tests

The foundations of the control tests for an effective information security program should include both organization and system controls. These control tests require an inventory of digital assets, a vulnerability assessment of the system, measuring of the effectiveness of cybersecurity program controls (people, process, and tools) administrative access and role-based privileges, secure configurations, audit log analysis. They also measure email and Web browser protections, malware defenses, control of access points, data recovery capabilities, network and data protection capabilities, monitoring of accounts, security awareness, application security, and incident response typically at a minimum.

The most frequently used frameworks in the U.S. are:[5]

1 PCI-DSS (47%)
2 ISO 27001/27002 (35%)
3 CIS Critical Security Controls (32%)
4 NIST Framework for Improving Critical Infrastructure Security (29%)

Most companies utilize more than one framework. The frameworks have mapping control tests but different objectives in terms of the data that they are focusing on. In general, companies with more than 10,000 employees are slightly more likely to have adopted a security framework (90%) but even smaller companies with fewer than 1,000 employees report significant rates of adoption (77%).[6] Control frameworks can be a requirement based on the type of data the company processes or the type of business.

NIST

"The NIST 800 Series is a set of documents that describe United States federal government computer security policies, procedures, and guidelines".[7] There are 178 Special Publications in the 800 series. The NIST cybersecurity framework for critical infrastructure is the best-known framework for technical control testing and the NIST 800–53 Rev. 4 is the best-known for testing organizational controls.

The NIST Cybersecurity Framework (CSF) is voluntary guidance, based on existing standards, guidelines, and practices for organizations to better manage and reduce cybersecurity risk.[8] NIST is designed to help organizations manage and reduce risks by enabling communications between both internal and external organizational stakeholders. There are now 108 control tests in version 1.1.[9] Version 1.0 had 98. The cybersecurity framework is used by all federal agencies and leading companies like JP Morgan Chase, NTT, Siemens, AT&T, and Intel as well as nation states including Israel and Japan.

The NIST CSF is understandable for all levels of cyber sophistication and uses language that can be easily comprehended for everyone. There are 5 levels of the framework—identify, protect, detect, respond, and recover that has control tests that align to each area.[10] It is adaptable to many technologies, industries, lifecycle phases and is meant to be customized. Best yet it is risk based! It uses categories of cybersecurity outcomes. It provides how much security is appropriate and is a living framework with a set of best practices that are updated to reflect threat landscape and evolve faster than regulation. The NIST CSF consists of three main components: Core, Implementation Tiers, and Profiles.

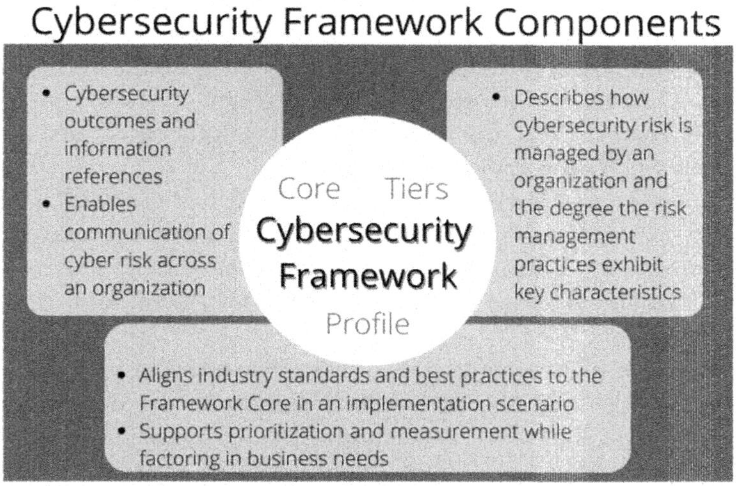

Cybersecurity Framework Components

- Cybersecurity outcomes and information references
- Enables communication of cyber risk across an organization

Core Tiers
Cybersecurity Framework
Profile

- Describes how cybersecurity risk is managed by an organization and the degree the risk management practices exhibit key characteristics

- Aligns industry standards and best practices to the Framework Core in an implementation scenario
- Supports prioritization and measurement while factoring in business needs

Image 10.1 NIST Cybersecurity Framework Components[11]

NIST core

The Framework Core defines a set of cybersecurity activities and desired outcomes that use an easily understood common language. The Core acts as a guide for organizations to manage and reduce cybersecurity risks. The framework is meant as a complement to the firms' existing cybersecurity and risk management processes.

Each cybersecurity activity and desired outcome is organized into Categories that align to Informative References. The Framework is intuitive and acts as a translation layer by enabling communication between multidisciplinary teams. NIST is framed in nontechnical language. The three parts of the Core are: Functions, Categories, and Subcategories. The Core has five high level functions that are ubiquitously referred to in cybersecurity. They are Identify, Protect, Detect, Respond, and Recover.

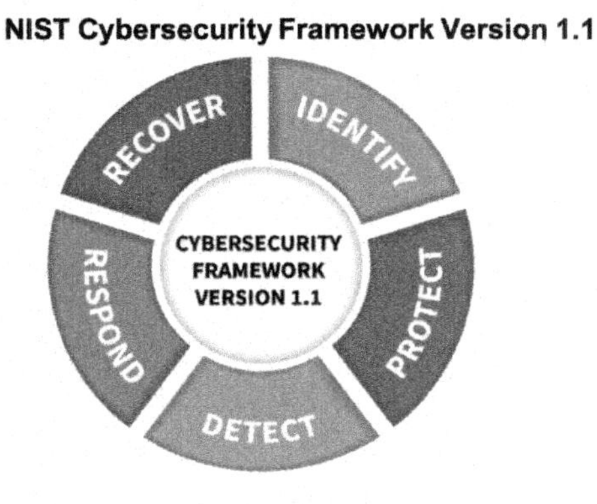

Image 10.2 NICE Core Functions[12]

Within the 5 functions are 23 Categories. The image depicts the Framework Core's Functions and Categories.

The Categories cover cybersecurity objectives for an organization. They are purposefully not being overly detailed as to allow flexibility in how they are applied. They cover required topics that address physical, administrative, and technical requirements with a focus on business outcomes.

There are 108 Subcategories which are the deepest part of the core. They are outcome-driven statements that form the basis of creating a cybersecurity program. The Framework does not mandate how an organization must achieve the desired outcomes. It enables risk-based implementations that are customized to the organization's needs.

As an example, we have outlined five subcategories pictured from the Business Environment Category (ID.BE). These represent outcome focused statements. The column to the right is used to outline broad references that are more technical to meet the desired outcome. Companies should use a cafeteria style to choose and customize reference activities they will undertake to achieve the desired risk management outcome.

Function	Category	ID
Identify	Asset Management	ID.AM
	Business Environment	ID.BE
	Governance	ID.GV
	Risk Assessment	ID.RA
	Risk Management Strategy	ID.RM
	Supply Chain Risk Management	ID.SC
Protect	Identity Management and Access Control	PR.AC
	Awareness and Training	PR.AT
	Data Security	PR.DS
	Information Protection Processes & Procedures	PR.IP
	Maintenance	PR.MA
	Protective Technology	PR.PT
Detect	Anomalies and Events	DE.AE
	Security Continuous Monitoring	DE.CM
	Detection Processes	DE.DP
Respond	Response Planning	RS.RP
	Communications	RS.CO
	Analysis	RS.AN
	Mitigation	RS.MI
	Improvements	RS.IM
Recover	Recovery Planning	RC.RP
	Improvements	RC.IM
	Communications	RC.CO

Subcategory	Informative References
ID.BE-1: The organization's role in the supply chain is identified and communicated	**COBIT 5** APO08.01, APO08.04, APO08.05, APO10.03, APO10.04, APO10.05 **ISO/IEC 27001:2013** A.15.1.1, A.15.1.2, A.15.1.3, A.15.2.1, A.15.2.2 **NIST SP 800-53 Rev. 4** CP-2, SA-12
ID.BE-2: The organization's place in critical infrastructure and its industry sector is identified and communicated	**COBIT 5** APO02.06, APO03.01 **ISO/IEC 27001:2013** Clause 4.1 **NIST SP 800-53 Rev. 4** PM-8
ID.BE-3: Priorities for organizational mission, objectives, and activities are established and communicated	**COBIT 5** APO02.01, APO02.06, APO03.01 **ISA 62443-2-1:2009** 4.2.2.1, 4.2.3.6 **NIST SP 800-53 Rev. 4** PM-11, SA-14
ID.BE-4: Dependencies and critical functions for delivery of critical services are established	**COBIT 5** APO10.01, BAI04.02, BAI09.02 **ISO/IEC 27001:2013** A.11.2.2, A.11.2.3, A.12.1.3 **NIST SP 800-53 Rev. 4** CP-8, PE-9, PE-11, PM-8, SA-14
ID.BE-5: Resilience requirements to support delivery of critical services are established for all operating states (e.g. under duress/attack, during recovery, normal operations)	**COBIT 5** DSS04.02 **ISO/IEC 27001:2013** A.11.1.4, A.17.1.1, A.17.1.2, A.17.2.1 **NIST SP 800-53 Rev. 4** CP-2, CP-11, SA-14

Image 10.3 NIST Framework Component Categories[13]

Implementation tier

The Framework Implementation Tiers are used to provide context on how a firm views cybersecurity risk management. The Tiers are used to set the appropriate level of rigor for the cybersecurity program. They are associated back to risk tolerance, resourcing, and budget.

Framework profiles

Profiles represent the company's unique alignment of their cyber requirements and objectives, risk appetite, resources, and budget to obtain the desired outcomes of the Framework Core.[14] Profiles are used to identify opportunities for improving the cybersecurity posture by doing a scenario analysis of a "Current" Profile with a "Target" Profile.

Profiles are used to optimize the Cybersecurity Framework to each organization's desired outcome. The Framework is flexible. There are many many ways organizations use it to map their cybersecurity requirements, people, process, and tools against the subcategories of the Framework Core to create a Current-State Profile. These requirements are used to provide a gap analysis between the current operating state of the firm and the ideal operating state.

The profile of each requirement and the gap analysis allows organizations to prioritize remediation plans. Prioritization can be based on the size of gap, and budget needed for the corrective actions.

"Tiers describe the degree to which an organization's cybersecurity risk management program aligns to the characteristics defined in the Framework. The Tiers range from Partial (Tier 1) to Adaptive (Tier 4) and describe an increasing degree of rigor, and how well integrated cybersecurity risk decisions are into broader risk decisions, and the degree to which the organization shares and receives cybersecurity info from external parties."[15]

Tiers may align to maturity levels. Organizations should determine the desired cybersecurity maturity. This should align to the acceptable level of cyber risk.

Tiers should be customized to the language of each firm to make them meaningful. We have adapted the maturity tiers to unaware, tactical, focused, strategic, and pervasive in this course and in our risk management and strategy modules.

Preform once, apply to many—eliminating redundancy

The NIST Cybersecurity Framework is a subset of NIST 800–53 and also shares controls found in ISO 27002.

Let us take an example of how the NIST maps to other well-known control tests. Supply change risk management has 2 subcategories. The first one is ensuring that processes are identified, accessed, managed, and agreed upon by stakeholders. It is mapped across CIS Controls, COBIT 5, ISA 62443, ISO 27001, and NIST SP 800–53. The idea is to ensure that only one test is done across areas that require multiple compliance requirements.

Function	Category	ID
Identify	Asset Management	ID.AM
	Business Environment	ID.BE
	Governance	ID.GV
	Risk Assessment	ID.RA
	Risk Management Strategy	ID.RM
	Supply Chain Risk Management	ID.SC
Protect	Identity Management and Access Control	PR.AC
	Awareness and Training	PR.AT
	Data Security	PR.DS
	Information Protection Processes & Procedures	PR.IP
	Maintenance	PR.MA
	Protective Technology	PR.PT
Detect	Anomalies and Events	DE.AE
	Security Continuous Monitoring	DE.CM
	Detection Processes	DE.DP
Respond	Response Planning	RS.RP
	Communications	RS.CO
	Analysis	RS.AN
	Mitigation	RS.MI
	Improvements	RS.IM
Recover	Recovery Planning	RC.RP
	Improvements	RC.IM
	Communications	RC.CO

Image 10.4 NIST Categories[16]

Mapping control frameworks is essential to reduce redundancy between testing teams. Many systems will process different types of data and will require compliance with a specific regulation whose framework may or may not be perspective. As an example, if the system processes credit card and privacy data then the firm must use the PCI–DSS for systems that process credit card data and can use ISO 27001 systems that only have privacy data. Mapping ensures that disparate teams are not testing controls of the same system twice or three times.

Core Example 1.1- Cybersecurity Framework Component

Function	Category	Subcategory	Informative References
IDENTIFY (ID)	**Supply Chain Risk Management (ID.SC):** The organization's priorities, constraints, risk tolerances, and assumptions are established and used to support risk decisions associated with managing supply chain risk. The organization has established and implemented the processes to identify, assess and manage supply chain risks.	**ID.SC-1:** Cyber supply chain risk management processes are identified, established, assessed, managed, and agreed to by organizational stakeholders	**CIS CSC** 4 **COBIT 5** APO10.01, APO10.04, APO12.04, APO12.05, APO13.02, BAI01.03, BAI02.03, BAI04.02 **ISA 62443-2-1:2009** 4.3.4.2 **ISO/IEC 27001:2013** A.15.1.1, A.15.1.2, A.15.1.3, A.15.2.1, A.15.2.2 **NIST SP 800-53 Rev. 4** SA-9, SA-12, PM-9
		ID.SC-2: Suppliers and third party partners of information systems, components, and services are identified, prioritized, and assessed using a cyber supply chain risk assessment process	**COBIT 5** APO10.01, APO10.02, APO10.04, APO10.05, APO12.01, APO12.02, APO12.03, APO12.04, APO12.05, APO12.06, APO13.02, BAI02.03 **ISA 62443-2-1:2009** 4.2.3.1, 4.2.3.2, 4.2.3.3, 4.2.3.4, 4.2.3.6, 4.2.3.8, 4.2.3.9, 4.2.3.10, 4.2.3.12 4.2.3.13, 4.2.3.14 **ISO/IEC 27001:2013** A.15.2.1, A.15.2.2 **NIST SP 800-53 Rev. 4** RA-2, RA-3, SA-12, SA-14, SA-15, PM-9

Image 10.5 NIST Framework Mappings[17]

International Organization for Standardization—ISO family

The ISO 27001 and 27002 are frameworks from the International Organization for Standardization. ISO is an independent organization of 161 national standards bodies.[18] It is a voluntary, consensus-based organization that provides knowledge sharing, and supports the development of market relevant international standards.

The ISO/IEC 27000-series is a family of standards and is aka ISO27K. It comprises information security standards that are created together by the International Organization for Standardization (ISO) and the International Electrotechnical Commission (IEC). The standards provide best practice recommendations on information security management. This includes the management of information risks using information security controls. The scope is related to an Information Security Management System (ISMS).

The ISO 27000 family addresses information assets security. ISO 27001 has 114 controls in 14 clauses and 35 control categories.

The ISO series covers more than just privacy, confidentiality, IT, technical, and cybersecurity issues. It is used by firms of all shapes and sizes to assess their information risks and remediate them using cybersecurity controls. "Given the dynamic nature of information risk and security, the ISMS concept incorporates continuous feedback and improvement activities to respond to changes in the threats, vulnerabilities or impacts of incidents."[19]

The standards are the product of ISO/IEC JTC1 (Joint Technical Committee 1) SC27 (Subcommittee 27). This international body meets in person twice a year.

ISO 27002 is much more detailed and precise than ISO 27001. ISO 27002 is not a management standard, therefore you cannot get certified against. A management standard defines how to run a system. ISO 27001 defines how to run an information security management system (ISMS). Certification of the ISMS demonstrates that information security is planned, implemented, monitored, reviewed, and improved. It defines management's distinct responsibilities and objectives with details on how they are measured, reviewed, and audited.

The difference between ISO 27002 and ISO 27001 is the level of detail. ISO 27002 explains one control on a whole page, while ISO 27001 dedicates only one sentence to each control.[20] Appendix A contains the high-level overview of the security controls needed to build an Information Security Management System (ISMS). ISO 27002 provides those specific controls that are necessary to actually implement ISO 27001. Therefore, you cannot meet ISO 27001 without implementing ISO 27002.

ISO's 27001 has been around since the 2005. This first in the game advantage has led to a misaligned de facto IT security framework outside of the United States. ISO 27002 is extensively used by multinational corporations and for companies that do not have to specifically comply only with US federal regulations.[21]

ISO 27002 does not make a distinction between controls that are applicable to an organization. ISO 27001 is a prescriptive risk assessment that identifies each control required to decrease the risks, and if it is, to which extent it should be applied.[22]

The ISO 27000 series are designed with a certain focus. ISO 27001 is used to build the foundations of information security in your organization and devise its framework. ISO 27002 is used to implement controls. ISO 27005 is a framework for a risk assessment and treatment plan.

CIS Critical Security Controls

The CIS Critical Security Controls[23] is a guideline from the Center for Internet Security that are a recommended set of actions for cyber defense that provide specific means to stop the top pervasive and dangerous cyberattacks. A principal benefit of the controls is that they prioritize and focus a smaller number of actions with high pay-off results. This framework is great for lower maturity companies that need to understand how to prioritize the control testing and are resource deficient.

The CIS controls are internationally recognized for bringing together expert insight about threats, business technologies, and defensive options into an effective, coherent, and simple way to manage an organization's security program. CIS uses a horizontal approach to identify a core set of sub controls based on an organization's level of maturity.

Implementational groups based on resources are defined and controls are mapped based on available resources. Group 1 has 43 control tests; group 2 has 140 control tests; and group 3 has 171 control tests. This method optimizes scarce security resources.

CIS controls are categorized as basic, foundational, and organizational.[24] It begins as all control frameworks with an inventory of digital assets.

The following CIS controls can be downloaded at https://learn.cisecurity.org/cis-controls-download.[25]

Control set 1: Inventory and Control of Hardware Assets—It uses 8 control tests to ascertain how well the organization is actively managing all hardware devices on the network so that only authorized devices are given access, and unauthorized and unmanaged devices are found and prevented from gaining access. This includes inventory, tracking, and correction activities.

Control set 2: Inventory and Control of Software Assets—It uses 10 control tests to ascertain how well the organization is actively managing all software on the network so that only authorized software is installed. It is used to ensure that unauthorized users are not found, and unmanaged software is prevented from installation or execution. This includes inventory, tracking, and correction activities.

Control set 3: Continuous Vulnerability Management—It uses 7 control tests to ascertain how well the organization is continuously acquiring, assessing, and acting on new information related to cybersecurity activities that identify vulnerabilities, remediate them, and minimize vulnerability risk.

Control set 4: Controlled Use of Administrative Privileges—It uses 9 control tests to ascertain how well the organization is using processes and tools related to the use, assignment, and configuration of administrative privileges on computers, networks, and applications. This includes activities that track, control, prevent, and correct administrative privileges.

Control set 5: Secure Configuration for Hardware and Software on Mobile Devices, Laptops, Workstations, and Servers—It uses 5 control tests to ascertain how well the organization is establishing, implementing, and actively managing the security configuration of mobile devices, laptops, servers, and workstations using best practices for configuration management and change control process in order to prevent attackers from exploiting vulnerable services and settings. This includes activities to track, report, and correct misconfigurations.

Control set 6: Maintenance, Monitoring and Analysis of Audit Logs—It uses 8 control tests to ascertain how well the organization is collecting, managing, and analyzing audit logs of events that could help detect, understand, or recover from an attack.

Control set 7: Email and Web Browser Protections—It uses 10 control tests to ascertain how well the organization is minimizing the attack surface. This includes identifying opportunities for attackers to social engineer interactions with Web browsers and email systems.

Control set 8: Malware Defenses—It uses 8 control tests to ascertain how well the organization is controlling the installation, spread, and execution of malicious code. This must be done at multiple points in the organization, while optimizing the use of automation to enable rapid updating of defense, data gathering, and corrective action.

Control set 9: Limitation and Control of Network Ports, Protocols, and Services—It uses 5 control tests to ascertain how well the organization is managing the ongoing operational use of ports, protocols, and services on networked devices in order to minimize windows of vulnerability available to attackers. This includes activities for tracking, controlling, and correcting.

Control set 10: Data Recovery Capabilities—It uses 5 control tests to ascertain how well the organization is using the processes and tools to properly back up critical information with a proven methodology for timely recovery of it.

Control set 11: Secure Configuration for Network Devices, such as Firewalls, Routers, and Switches—It uses 7 control tests to ascertain how well the organization is establishing, implementing, and actively managing the security configuration of network infrastructure devices using best practices for configuration management and change control process in order to prevent attackers from exploiting vulnerable services and settings. This includes activities for tracking, controlling, and correcting.

Control set 12: Boundary Defense—It uses 12 control tests to ascertain how well the organization is detecting, preventing, and correcting the flow of information transferring networks of different trust levels with a focus on security-damaging data.

Control set 13: Data Protection—It uses 9 control tests to ascertain how well the organization is using the processes and tools to prevent data exfiltration, the mitigation of the effects of exfiltrated data, and to ensure the privacy and integrity of sensitive information.

Control set 14: Controlled Access Based on the Need to Know—It uses 9 control tests to ascertain how well the organization is using processes and tools to track/control/prevent/correct secure access to critical assets (e.g., information, resources, and systems) according to the formal determination of which persons, computers, and applications have a need and right to access these critical assets based on an approved classification.

Control set 15: Wireless Access Control—It uses 10 control tests to ascertain how well the organization is using processes and tools that track, control, prevent, and correct the security use of Wireless Local Area Networks (WLANs), access points, and wireless client systems.

Control set 16: Account Monitoring and Control—It uses 13 control tests to ascertain how well the organization is actively managing the system and application life cycle of user accounts. This includes their creation, use, dormancy, deletion—in order to minimize opportunities for attackers to leverage them.

Control set 17: Implement a Security Awareness and Training Program—It uses 9 control tests to ascertain how well the organization is for all functional roles in the organization (prioritizing those mission-critical to the business and its security). This includes identifying the required knowledge, skills and abilities needed to support defense of the enterprise, developing a corporate wide plan to assess, identify gaps, and remediate through policy, organizational planning, training, and awareness programs.

Control set 18: Application Software Security—It uses 11 control tests to ascertain how well the organization is managing the cybersecurity life cycle of both home grown and purchased software in order to prevent, detect, and correct security weaknesses.

Control set 19: Incident Response and Management—It uses 8 control tests to ascertain how well the organization is protecting the company's data, and the firm's reputation, by developing an incident response program which includes plans, roles and responsibilities, training, communications, and management oversight) for quickly discovering an attack and then effectively containing the damage, eradicating the attacker's presence, and restoring the integrity of the network and systems.

Control set 20: Penetration Tests and Red Team Exercises—It uses 8 control tests to ascertain how well the organization is testing the strength of an organization's defense in terms of people, process, and tools by simulating the objectives and actions of an attacker.

PCI-DSS

The Payment Card Industry Data Security Standard (PCI-DSS)[26] is an information security standard for organizations that handle branded credit cards from the major card brands. These include Mastercard, Visa, American Express, JBC, and Discover. The standard was first released in 2004 and is updated every two years.

The PCI Standard is a mandated guideline created by the card brands and administered by the Payment Card Industry Security Standards Council. The standard was created to reduce credit card fraud. It requires an annual or quarterly report to be created to validate compliance. This report is done by either an external Qualified Security Assessor (QSA) or by a firm specific Internal Security Assessor (ISA). The report is titled the "Report on Compliance" (RoC) and is required for organizations handling large volumes of transactions. Otherwise, a Self-Assessment Questionnaire (SAQ) is required for companies handling smaller volumes.[27] The latest version is 3.2.1, which was released in May 2018. The standard can be downloaded at https://www.pcisecuritystandards.org/document_library#agreement.[28] Version 4 is expected to be released in mid-2021.

PCI-DSS is required for banks, merchants, and data processors. PCI-DSS has 6 major control objectives:

- Build and maintain a secure network and systems
- Protect cardholder data
- Maintain a vulnerability management program
- Implement strong access control measures

- Regularly monitor and test networks
- Maintain an information security policy

There are 12 sets of requirements within the 6 control objectives.[29] These include:

- "Installing and maintaining a firewall configuration to protect cardholder data. The purpose of a firewall is to scan all network traffic, block untrusted networks from accessing the system.
- Changing vendor-supplied defaults for system passwords and other security parameters. These passwords are easily discovered through public information and can be used by malicious individuals to gain unauthorized access to systems.
- Protecting stored cardholder data. Encryption, hashing, masking, and truncation are methods used to protect card holder data.
- Encrypting transmission of cardholder data over open, public networks. Strong encryption, including using only trusted keys and certifications reduces risk of being targeted by malicious individuals through hacking.
- Protecting all systems against malware and performing regular updates of anti-virus software. Malware can enter a network through numerous ways, including internet use, employee email, mobile devices, or storage devices. Up-to-date anti-virus software or supplemental anti-malware software will reduce the risk of exploitation via malware.
- Developing and maintaining secure systems and applications. Vulnerabilities in systems and applications allow unscrupulous individuals to gain privileged access. Security patches should be immediately installed to fix vulnerability and prevent exploitation and compromise of cardholder data.
- Restricting access to cardholder data to only authorized personnel. Systems and processes must be used to restrict access to cardholder data on a "need to know" basis.
- Identifying and authenticating access to system components. Each person with access to system components should be assigned a unique identification (ID) that allows accountability of access to critical data systems.
- Restricting physical access to cardholder data. Physical access to cardholder data or systems that hold this data must be secure to prevent the unauthorized access or removal of data.
- Tracking and monitoring all access to cardholder data and network resources. Logging mechanisms should be in place to track user activities that are critical to prevent, detect or minimize impact of data compromises.
- Testing security systems and processes regularly. New vulnerabilities are continuously discovered. Systems, processes, and software need to be tested frequently to uncover vulnerabilities that could be used by malicious individuals
- Maintaining an information security policy for all personnel. A strong security policy includes making personnel understand the sensitivity of data and their responsibility to protect it."

PCI has several supplemental guidelines regarding the use of technologies, approaches, and special testing requirements. These include:

- Information Supplement: Requirement 11.3 Penetration Testing
- Information Supplement: Requirement 6.6 Code Reviews and Application Firewalls Clarified
- PCI DSS Applicability in an EMV Environment
- Prioritized Approach for PCI DSS
- Prioritized Approach Tool
- PCI DSS Quick Reference Guide
- PCI DSS Virtualization Guidelines
- PCI DSS Tokenization Guidelines
- PCI DSS 2.0 Risk Assessment Guidelines
- The lifecycle for Changes to the PCI DSS and PA-DSS.
- Guidance for PCI DSS Scoping and Segmentation

Segmenting the network to include only systems that process credit card data can decrease the scope of a PCI assessment. PCI has a specific scope for Acquiring Banks, Data Processors, and Merchants only. Other industries are not in scope for PCI. There are 4 level of merchant types.[30]

Level 1 requirements are for Merchants with over 6 million transactions annually. Level 2 requirements are for Merchants with between 1 and 6 million transactions annually. Level 3 requirements are for Merchants with between 20,000 and 1 million transactions annually. Level 4 requirements are for Merchants with Less than 20,000 transactions annually.

PCI is state law in some cases. In Minnesota, the law prohibits the retention of some types of payment card data subsequent to 48 hours after authorization of the transaction.[31] Nevada incorporated the standard into state law, requiring compliance of merchants doing business in that state with the current PCI-DSS, and shields compliant entities from liability. In Washington state, PCI is incorporated into state law. Companies are not required to be compliant to PCI-DSS, but compliant entities are shielded from liability in the event of a data breach.[32]

Companies that handle less than six million transactions per year can self-assess; those whose transaction volumes exceeds six million require a third-party assessor. Qualified Security Assessor (QSA) companies are independent companies that have been qualified by the PCI Security Standards Council to validate a firm's adherence to PCI DSS. QSA are individuals who are employed by a QSA Company which satisfied QSA requirements. These independent groups must be certified by PCI Security Council for compliance confirmation in organization procedures.[33]

"An Internal Security Assessor is an individual who has earned a certificate from the PCI Security Standards Company for their sponsoring organization."[34] This certified individual can perform PCI self-assessments for their organization. The ISA program is designed for Level 2 merchants to meet the new Mastercard compliance validation requirements. ISA certification empowers a firm to do an inward appraisal of the company to propose security solutions for the PCI DSS compliance.

A Report on Compliance (RoC) is a required to be filed by all level 1 merchants.[35] The RoC form is used to verify for Visa merchants that the merchant being audited is compliant with the PCI DSS standard. The RoC confirms policies, strategies, approaches & workflows are implemented appropriately by the firm for the protection of cardholder data against fraud. A "RoC Reporting Template" is available on the PCI SSC site and contains detailed guidelines about how to fill out the RoC.

The PCI DSS Self-Assessment Questionnaires (SAQs) are tools designed to assist merchants and service providers validation the report details of their PCI DSS self-assessment. The Self-Assessment Questionnaire is required to be completed by merchants every year and submitted to their transactional bank. The SAQ is an Attestation of Compliance (AOC) where each SAQ question is replied to based upon an internal PCI DSS self-evaluation. Each SAQ question is replied to with either yes or no.

The PCI Security Council can withdraw credit card privileges for noncompliance. Fines for PCI noncompliance vary from US$5,000 to US$100,000 per month until the merchants achieve compliance. These fines are easily outflanked by credit monitoring fees, laws suits, and actions by state and federal governments that can result from noncompliance. In the case of Target, the total cost of data breach was over US$200 million. This included an US$18.5 million legal settlement with 47 state attorneys general.[36]

Notes

1. James P. Melendres, Aloke S. Chakravarty, Snell & Wilmer, "The EU general data protection regulation", May 22, 2018, https://www.swlaw.com/publications/legal-alerts/2544.
2. PCI security standards council, "Securing the future of payments together", 2020, https://www.pcisecuritystandards.org.
3. NIST, "Path forward to support adaption and adoption of cybersecurity framework", February 2018, https://www.nist.gov/system/files/documents/2018/02/06/session_iii_-_barrett_csf.pdf.
4. ISO. "ISO/IEC 27001 information security management", 2020, https://www.iso.org/isoiec-27001-information-security.html.
5. Meanie Watson, IT Governance, "Top 4 cybersecurity frameworks", January 17, 2019, https://www.itgovernanceusa.com/blog/top-4-cybersecurity-frameworks.
6. NIST, "Small and medium business perspectives", July 15, 2020, https://www.nist.gov/cyberframework/small-and-medium-business-perspectives.
7. NIST, "National institute of Standards and Technologies", 2020, https://www.nist.gov/.
8. NIST, "New to framework", September 23, 2020, https://www.nist.gov/cyberframework/new-framework.
9. NIST, "Frameworkdocuments", October 2, 2020, https://www.nist.gov/cyberframework/framework.
10. NIST, "Questions and answers", September 23, 2020, https://www.nist.gov/cyberframework/frequently-asked-questions/framework-basics#framework.
11. NIST, "An introduction to the components of the framework", June 15, 2020, https://www.nist.gov/cyberframework/online-learning/components-framework.
12. NIST, "An introduction to the components of the framework", June 15, 2020, https://www.nist.gov/cyberframework/online-learning/components-framework.
13. NIST, "An introduction to the components of the framework", June 15, 2020, https://www.nist.gov/cyberframework/online-learning/components-framework.

14. NIST, "An introduction to the components of the framework", June 15, 2020, https://www.nist.gov/cyberframework/online-learning/components-framework.
15. NIST, "An introduction to the components of the framework", June 15, 2020, https://www.nist.gov/cyberframework/online-learning/components-framework.
16. NIST, "An introduction to the components of the framework", June 15, 2020, https://www.nist.gov/cyberframework/online-learning/components-framework.
17. NIST, "An introduction to the components of the framework", June 15, 2020, https://www.nist.gov/cyberframework/online-learning/components-framework.
18. ISO, "Publicly available standards", 2020, https://standards.iso.org/ittf/PubliclyAvailableStandards/.
19. Wikipedia, "ISO/IEC 27000-series", October 6, 2020, https://en.wikipedia.org/wiki/ISO/IEC_27000-series.
20. 27001 Academy, "ISO 27001 vs. ISO 27002", 2020, https://advisera.com/27001academy/knowledgebase/iso-27001-vs-iso-27002/.
21. Compliance Forge, "Which framework is right for my business", 2020, https://www.complianceforge.com/faq/nist-800-53-vs-iso-27002-vs-nist-csf.html.
22. Technetsolutions, "Difference between ISO 27001 and 27002 standard", April 29,2019, https://technetsolutions.net/difference-between-iso-27001-and-27002-standard/.
23. CIS, "The 20 CIS controls & resources", 2020, https://www.cisecurity.org/controls/cis-controls-list/,
24. CIS, "CIS controls version 7-Whats old, whats new", 2020, https://www.cisecurity.org/blog/cis-controls-version-7-whats-old-whats-new/.
25. CIS, "Powerful best practices", 2020, https://learn.cisecurity.org/cis-controls-download.
26. PCI, "Security Standards Council", 2020, https://www.pcisecuritystandards.org/.
27. Isitzen, "PCI DSS," February 7, 2020, https://www.isitzen.com/tech/2020/2/pci-dss.
28. PCI, "Document library," 2020, https://www.pcisecuritystandards.org/document_library#agreement.
29. PCI, "Maintaining payment security", 2020, https://www.pcisecuritystandards.org/pci_security/maintaining_payment_security.
30. Otava, "Guide to PCI compliance levels and merchant types", January 19, 2012, https://www.otava.com/blog/guide-to-pci-compliance-levels-merchant-types/.
31. Jaikumar Vijayan, Computer World, "Minnesota becomes first state to make core PCI requirement a law", May 23, 2007, https://www.computerworld.com/article/2541431/minnesota-becomes-first-state-to-make-core-pci-requirement-a-law.html#:~:text=PCI%20specifically%20prohibits%20companies%20from,the%20PCI%20requirement%20into%20law.
32. Jones Day, "Nevada imposes new requirements for credit card transactions and data transfers",July 2009,https://www.jonesday.com/en/insights/2009/08/nevada-imposes-new-requirements-for-credit-card-transactions-and-data-transfers#:~:text=Nevada's%20recent%20amendment%2C%20S.B.&text=227%20requires%20all%20companies%20doing,with%20respect%20to%20those%20transactions.%22.
33. PCI, "Qualified security assessors," 2020, https://www.pcisecuritystandards.org/assessors_and_solutions/qualified_security_assessors.
34. PCI, "Internal security assessors (ISA) program," 2020, https://www.pcisecuritystandards.org/assessors_and_solutions/become_isa.
35. Margaret Rouse, Tech Target, "Report on compliance (ROC)", June 2010, https://searchsecurity.techtarget.com/definition/Report-on-Compliance-ROC#:~:text=A%20Report%20on%20Compliance%20(ROC,Visa%20transactions%20in%20a%20year.
36. Jeff Peters, Varonis, "What is PCI compliance: Requirements and penalties", 2020, https://www.varonis.com/blog/pci-compliance/.

11 ENTERPRISE CYBERSECURITY PROGRAMS

We must endeavor to raise security awareness, that secURity is everyone's responsibility.
Les Correia, Global Head of Application Security, Estée Lauder Companies Inc.

Digital enterprises—enterprise risks

Digital business is driving innovation at a high rate of speed in the financial sector. The financial industry is the most targeted sector by cybercriminals due to its almost complete reliance on digital assets and the rigorous regulatory requirements regarding cyber risk programs.

Cybersecurity risk is related to the impact and likelihood of the consequences affecting the confidentiality, availability, and/or integrity of the data.

Other industries that rely heavily on supply chain, distribution, and logistics also have a heavy operational reliance on digital assets. In 2018, Distributed-Denial-of-Service (DDoS) attacks across supply chains using a top cloud provider led to a business interruption of up to six days with losses of approximately US$19 billion according to Lloyds.[2] Most of these losses were incurred in the manufacturing and trade sectors.

Disruption of the financial sector qualifies as a critical infrastructure event. In order to disrupt the financial sector, cyber-attacks would threaten multiple financial institutions simultaneously. Coordinated cyber-attacks on the banking sector using DDoS are realities that have been revealed in many countries. Some other examples of business disruption are given in the box below.

In 2018, 819 cyber incidents were identified in the financial industry, a significant increase from only 69 incidents reported in 2017.[3] The financial sector has new regulation from the New York State Department of Financial Services (NYS DFS) and has already experienced a number of data breaches from 2019 to 2020. In May 2019, First American Corporation suffered a data breach that compromised nearly 885 million files related to mortgage deeds, KrebsOnSecurity revealed.[4] The New York State Department of Financial Services is in the process of investigating and fining First American. NYSDFS can impose a penalty of US$1000 a record, making the fine on First American up to US$885 billion which would make them unsustainable.

DOI: 10.4324/9781003052616-13

DDoS Attacks on Multiple Financial Institutions

USA: In September 2012, the website of Bank of America, PNC, JPMorgan, US Bancorp, Wells Fargo were targeted and one month later the websites of BBT, Capital One, HSBC, Region Financial, SunTrust were also disrupted.

Czech Republic: On March 6, 2013, the websites of the central bank, three large banks, and the stock exchange were disrupted, with limited damages estimated at USD .5 million

Norway: On July 8, 2014, seven major financial institutions were attacked, leading to disrupted services during the day.

Finland: End-2014, three banks (Op Pohjola, Danske Bank and Nordea) suffered DDoS attacks that rendered their online services unavailable and for one bank prevented customers from withdrawing cash and making card payments.

Figure 11.1 DDoS Attacks on Mulitple Financial Institutions[5]

According to the Deposit Account Fraud Survey Study of the American Bankers Association (ABA), financial sector fraud losses were US$2.2 billion in 2016.[6] Some steps to deter fraud have been proposed by the American Bankers Association (ABA).

Digital assets are interconnected between firms. It is estimated that a cyber-attack will have a 20% chance of impacting more than two banks. The IMF working paper on Cyber Risk in the Financial Sector shows expected shortfalls, value at risk and net income with the average loss due to cyber-attacks for the countries in the ORX sample amounts to US$97 billion or 9% of bank net income.[7] Cyber risk is the biggest emerging exposure for all types of financial institutions which includes both central bank and fintech firms.

	Baseline		Scenario 2 (severe)	
	Independence			
	% net income	USD bn	% net income	USD bn
Average	9	97	26	268
VaR (95%)	14	147	34	352
ES (95%)	18	187	40	409
VaR 99%	19	201	41	427
ES (99%)	27	281	52	539
	Assuming 20% dependence*			
Average	12	127	34	351
VaR (95%)	18	184	43	446
ES (95%)	22	229	49	509
VaR 99%	24	248	51	529
ES (99%)	32	329	62	642

Note: VaR is the Value-at-Risk, ES is the Expected Shortfall. Net income data based on a sample of 7,947 banks for 2016.
*It is assumed that each cyber attack has a 20% probability to affect two or more firms.
Sources: ORX News, SNL, and staff calculations.

Figure 11.2 Aggregate Loss Due to Cyber Attacks in Banking[8]

Cybersecurity programs are people, process, tools, and insurance. In this chapter we will focus on components of a cybersecurity program. We discussed people and roles earlier in Chapter 6. Processes use policies and procedures that are related to establishing cybersecurity goals and the methods used to baseline and achieve those goals. Cybersecurity tools are security solutions that identify, protect against, detect, respond, or recover from a cyber event. We will discuss tools in detail in part 3 of this book. Cyber insurance is a risk transfer mechanism that is covered in part 7 of this book.

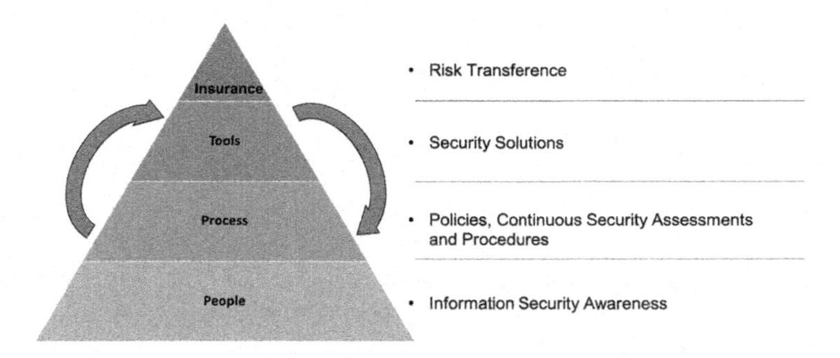

Figure 11.3 Cybersecurity Program Components

Cybersecurity program elements

There are several security program categories that align to most framework control tests. These include organizational oversight and leadership, logical and physical access, products and services lifecycle, systems, and security operations, monitoring and event management, quality and continuity of service, program auditing, testing and certification, and business process controls.

Organizational oversight and leadership

Oversight and leadership looks in detail at how there is tone at the top, enforcement, and support from senior management. For organizations, cybersecurity requires not only a strong culture of collaboration and communication but also support and commitment from executive leadership. Companies need to identify internal stakeholders and their backups for the various cybersecurity roles including the system owners, IT support people, compliance leaders, and secure commitment from internal leadership. Regardless of the maturity of the company, it is essential that organizations maintain centralized oversight of cybersecurity and compliance activities to ensure that the governance systems are consistent across the various business divisions and that the whole enterprise is compliant at all times and can increase resiliency homogenously.

It can be challenging for decentralized teams to implement centralized oversight. Using a RACI chart can help to segment out which roles own certain functions. Ownership and responsibility are sometimes used interchangeably. They are not the same. Ownership represents an individual who is accountable. You can look for documentation in legal contracts and formal business documents that include job descriptions and corporate policies to help define who is accountable. Responsibilities are for those who must work regarding specific assigned activities, tasks, or functions and ensuring that they are met. Responsibilities can be shared across individuals and teams.

Role	Responsibilities
Executive Sponsors, leader, Owner	• Authority to provide direction and budget • Accountable for the risk
Compliance Managers	• Manages ongoing compliance efforts with the IT and security teams • Security assessments framework experts • Works with the regulators and legal team on compliance requirements
Information Security Team	Responsible for the security controls applied across the business. This includes overall accountability for: • Information security • Policy • Acceptable use guideline • Awareness • Incident response
Business Unit Managers	• Ensures business unit payment card controls are enforced • Assists in removing payment card information from processes • Helps make processes compliant
Audit, Risk Management Team	Guides risk assessment and governance responsibilities.
Information Technology Team	The staff or outsourced third-party providing and operating the organization's computer network(s). IT Administrator/s are vital to identify due to their span of responsibility.
Third-Party Service Providers	Outsourced processes, technology, staffing, or purchased solutions
All Staff (organization)	Understanding of their responsibilities to protect cardholder data

Figure 11.4 Cyber Program Roles and Responsibilities

If there is more than one regulation, a best practice is to ascertain who has ownership of compliance activities for each law. Some options are to segment networks to de-scope some requirements (such as the PCI or HIPAA). In terms of privacy regulations, the best practice is to use the requirements that have the largest scope and apply them uniformly across the organization.

Logical and physical access

Logical and physical access looks at physical security and identify, authorization management controls. This category has to maintain effective access control practices across a diverse set of individuals, roles, and systems required for most organizations. Ensuring that only authorized individuals can access the resources requires well planned communication channels and teamwork within and between business units. In a large organization, using a centralized access control system is highly recommended due to the volume of individuals, systems, sites, and privileges that large or complex organizations have to manage. Substantial thought and planning must go into designing and maintaining the architecture, processes, and components of the access-control system from the security architects to the IAM specialists.

Products and services lifecycle

The products and services lifecycle looks at the controls in place for the development of systems and products to ensure security is baked in at development. Secure software development is a best practice that is related to cybersecurity. Software development teams play a critical role in the security of an organization where there is innovation and a large number of home-grown systems. Unfortunately, often these teams receive minimal cybersecurity training and are not aware of how important their role is and more so how it fits into the larger picture of the organization's compliance or security posture.

The SecureDevOps team focuses on ensuring that there is a well-developed lifecycle that includes security requirements when developing software. The cybersecurity program should include education that defines the best practices for secure software development. Some risky areas include: third party supply chain systems, legacy systems, and independent systems.

SecureDevOps teams should incorporate not only secure coding training and must ensure that the training is addressing the software languages, frameworks, and toolsets that are used. Training has to align with the development process. Issues should be identified using standard tools and techniques, such as code reviews, quality-assurance checks, penetration testing, and vulnerability scanning. Having a red team from an outside third-party identify areas of weakness can be important. Their feedback can be incorporated into the training materials.

Ensuring that changes are made to software based on incorporating changes needed to eliminate flaws found from data breach findings, business interruptions, and other findings from security assessments are also reflected in the updates to the training materials in a timely manner.

Some DevOps teams try and cut corners by promoting code to production without the permission of the database administrator (DBA). This is a bad practice and will fail on any compliance review for separation of duties.

Systems and security operations

Systems and security operations teams look at how incidents are detected, monitored and how events and incidents are managed. The quality and continuity of service needs to be baked into the related security procedures.

Program auditing, testing, and certification

Program auditing, testing, and certification looks at the level 3 audit team and their testing processes. Audits and assessments can impact the service provider functions of organizations. Having numerous audits and redundant cybersecurity control assessments is a waste of resources. Staggering or overlapping timeframes for each assessment along with potentially unique assessment processes for each assessment type is required for best practice. Conducting multiple different audit processes may require evidence to be provided from a common set of digital assets. Different cyber risks may not be consistent based on technologies, data types, and the results of the audit can potentially result in a considerable amount of duplicated effort if not managed properly.

Business process controls

Business process controls looks at separation of duties and related cybersecurity initiatives. This ties back into the DevOps issue discussed above and integrated cyber risk management programs.

Each CISO will have a series of initiatives to prioritize. Integrated cyber risk management is built for just that. Integrated cybersecurity risk allows for the prioritization of scarce resources based on impacts and the ability to manage the dynamic interplay of cybersecurity incidents, vulnerabilities, and threats. These initiatives prescribe policies, procedures, and tools and how they are used by different team members to address them and may include:

- Network and infrastructure security
- Endpoint and mobile device security
- Applications security
- Cloud security
- Threat and vulnerability management
- Security awareness and training program
- Security monitoring and operations management
- Security governance

Cyber risk management

Cyber risk management ensures that the cybersecurity program is being understood in context. It provides a mechanism to prioritize the needs of the cybersecurity program. Cyber risk management is not vulnerability management. It includes the quantification of cybersecurity exposures and the measurement of the digital asset cyber likelihood that are used to prioritize remediation work by the organization. Cyber risk management provides strategic use cases that include protecting the digital assets, managing vendor risk, quantifying cyber insurance needs, and cyber M&A activities.

Audit management

Audit management is the verification of the effectiveness of the cybersecurity program. Auditors examine the evidence supplied of the management and security controls within an information technology infrastructure and recommend ways to enhance the programs effectiveness.

Notes

1. David Bogoslaw, Corporate Secretary, "Cyber-security risk has increased in last 2 years, say directors and GCs", June 2, 2015, https://www.corporatesecretary.com/articles/boardroom/30185/cyber-security-risk-has-increased-last-2-years-say-directors-and-gcs.
2. Sean Michael Kerner, eWeek, "Lloyd's estimates the impact of a U.S. cloud outage at $19 billion", January 24, 2018, https://www.eweek.com/cloud/lloyd-s-estimates-the-impact-of-a-u.s.-cloud-outage-at-19-billion.

3. Warwick Ashford, Computerweekly.com, "High jump in cyber incidents reported by finance sector", July 1, 2019, https://www.computerweekly.com/news/252466038/Huge-jump-in-cyber-incidents-reported-by-finance-sector.
4. Brian Krebs, Krebs on Security, "NY charges first American financial for massive data leak ", July 20, 2020, https://krebsonsecurity.com/2020/07/ny-charges-first-american-financial-for-massive-data-leak/#:~:text=Jul%2020-,NY%20Charges%20First%20American%20Financial%20for%20Massive%20Data%20Leak,deals%20going%20back%20to%202003.
5. IMF Working Paper, "Cyber risk for the financial sector: A framework or quantitative assessment", June 2018, file:///C:/Users/eevan/Downloads/wp18143%20(3).pdf.
6. Security, "Banks stop $17 billion in fraud attempts in 2016", February 22, 2018, https://www.securitymagazine.com/articles/88711-banks-stop-17-billion-in-fraud-attempts-in-2016#:~:text=American%20Bankers%20Association%20Deposit%20Account,Center%20for%20Payments%20and%20Cybersecurity.&text=Despite%20that%2048%20percent%20increase,16%20percent%20to%20%242.2%20billion.
7. IMF Working paper, "Cyber risk for the financial sector: A framework for quantitative assessment", June 2018, https://www.imf.org/~/media/Files/Publications/WP/2018/wp18143.ashx.
8. IMF Working Paper, "Cyber risk for the financial sector: A framework or quantitative assessment", June 2018, file:///C:/Users/eevan/Downloads/wp18143%20(3).pdf.

12 ORGANIZATIONAL CYBER MATURITIES

Cyber Maturity is not for the faint of heart.

Ariel Evans, CEO Cyber Innovative Technologies, Inc.

Category	Level 1 **Unaware**	Level 2 **Tactical**	Level 3 **Focused**	Level 4 **Strategic**	Level 5 **Pervasive**
Security Team	No one	1 -2 people - IT centric	3 + - BU centric	Large - Supplemented	Large - internal
Security Tools	None	Firewalls, IDS, some VMS	Level 2 + some SIEM	Level 3 + outsourced SOC	All tools
Governance	None	IT Involvement	BU Involvement	Board Involvement	Board Involvement
Reporting	None	IT focused Spreadsheets	BU Focused Spreadsheets	Data Driven (integrated)	Highly Data Driven (integrated)
Security Lead	None	Security Manager	CISO or security manager	CISO	CISO
Privacy Lead	None	Lawyer	Lawyer, DPO	DPO	DPO
Risk Management	None	Vulnerability Focused	Audit, Incident Focused, some risk	Some integrated Cyber Risk Management	Cyber Integrated with ERM
Leadership	None	IT focused	BU Involvement	C and Board Level	C and Board Level
CISO Reporting	None	CIO	CIO, CISO	CIO, CRO, CFO, CISO	CRO and Board
Security Investments	Minimal	Compliance Focused	Incident Response Focused	Audit Focused	Integration Focused
Cyber Insurance Coverage	None	$1-2 million	$3-25 million	$25-100 million	$100's of millions
Asset Management	None	Excel	System based	Integrated system based	Integrated system based
Strategy	None	Basic Network Focus	Layered Tools	Threat Intelligence	AI, Busines Process Automation

Figure 12.1 Cybersecurity Maturities[2]

A maturity model approach has been adopted by the Department of Defense (DoD) to better evaluate and improve the cybersecurity posture of the Defense Industrial Base (DIB). It is my hunch that this will move into the commercial space to ensure that appropriate levels of cybersecurity practices and processes are in place to protect other types of data. This maturity model looks at organizational characteristics to compare maturities across five levels.

The characteristics we inventoried, and their mappings are:

1 Cyber Governance—How involved is the business in the governance of cybersecurity. Is there no involvement, involvement at the IT level, BU level or board?

DOI: 10.4324/9781003052616-14

— Unaware Level—No involvement
— Tactical Level—Information Technology involvement only
— Focused Level—Business Unit involvement
— Strategic Level—Board involvement
— Pervasive Level—Board involvement with a Cyber Audit Committee

2 Reporting Methods—How are cyber reports for the board created? Who creates the reports and is the data from spreadsheets or from integrated systems?

— Unaware Level—No board reporting
— Tactical Level—Information technology focused spreadsheets
— Focused Level—Business unit focused spreadsheets
— Strategic Level—Data driven from integrated systems (one or two systems)
— Pervasive Level—Data driven from highly integrated systems (over three systems)

3 Security Team—How many people are on the team, are they dedicated full time resources, are they from the IT, business unit or security department?

— Unaware Level—No one
— Tactical Level—1-2 people, IT centric
— Focused Level—3 + people, Business Unit centric
— Strategic Level—Large and supplemented from managed services and consulting teams
— Pervasive Level—Large, internal security department teams

4 Security Tools—Which cybersecurity tools are used, how are they used, what teams use them?

— Unaware Level—None
— Tactical Level—Basic off the shelf Firewalls, IDS, some VMS
— Focused Level—Tactical plus some have SIEM
— Strategic Level—Focused plus SIEM with security event correlation and/or User and Entity Behavior Analytics (UEBA), and outsourced SOC
— Pervasive Level—All types of cyber tools are used

5 Risk Management Program—Is it risk or simply vulnerability or incident focused?

— Unaware Level—None
— Tactical Level—Not true risk, vulnerability focus
— Focused Level—Incident and Audit focused
— Strategic Level—Integrated Cyber Risk Focus
— Pervasive Level—Integrated plus driven by Enterprise Risk Team

6 Vendor Management—Are third-parties being assessed and to what level?

— Unaware Level—None
— Tactical Level—Know they need to start one

— Focused Level—Initial Programs
— Strategic Level—More Mature Programs
— Pervasive Level—Integrated with Cyber Risk programs

7 Security Reporting—Who does the Head of Security/Security Manager or CISO report to?

— Unaware Level—None
— Tactical Level—CTO
— Focused Level—CIO, CISO
— Strategic Level—COO, CFO
— Pervasive Level—Board of Directors

8 Decision Maker—How many decision makers for cyber purchases are there?

— Unaware Level—None
— Tactical Level—One
— Focused Level—Two
— Strategic Level—Three
— Pervasive Level—More than Three

9 Security Lead—What role is accountable for cybersecurity?

— Unaware Level—None
— Tactical Level—CIO or Security Manager
— Focused Level—CISO
— Strategic Level—CFO
— Pervasive Level—CEO

10 Privacy Lead—Is there a privacy lead and who is it?

— Unaware Level—None
— Tactical Level—Lawyer
— Focused Level—CISO
— Strategic Level—Data Privacy Officer
— Pervasive Level—Data Privacy Officer with strong Cyber Background.

11 Leadership—Who is driving security purchases?

— Unaware Level—None
— Tactical Level—Information Technology focused
— Focused Level—Business Unit Involvement
— Strategic Level—C-Level
— Pervasive Level—C-Level and Board

12 Security Investment—What is the level of security investment?

— Unaware Level—Minimal
— Tactical Level—Compliance Focused

- Focused Level—Incident Response Focused
- Strategic Level—Audit or Risk Focused
- Pervasive Level—Integration Focused

13 Cybersecurity Exposures—How much baseline cyber exposures are there?

- Unaware Level—Small
- Tactical Level—Medium
- Focused Level—Medium to Large
- Strategic Level—Large
- Pervasive Level—Very Large

14 Weaknesses—What are the most glaring weaknesses in the cyber program?

- Unaware Level—There is no program in place at all
- Tactical Level—Not enough people, process and tools, no cloud security, not enough staff
- Focused Level—insufficient and/or ineffective security governance. This would include, but is not limited to, ongoing maintenance of security solutions, also revisiting/refreshing the security program roadmap
- Strategic Level—Limited cloud security, struggling with vendor management, not enough internal staff
- Pervasive Level—High CISO turnover, struggling with cloud security

15 Cyber Insurance—How much cyber insurance does the firm carry?

- Unaware Level—None
- Tactical Level—US$2 million or less
- Focused Level—US$3–25 million
- Strategic Level—US$25–100 million
- Pervasive Level—Over US$100 million

16 Digital Asset Management—Is it done with spreadsheets, systems, integrated systems?

- Unaware Level—None
- Tactical Level—Spreadsheets
- Focused Level—System-based but not updated
- Strategic Level—Integrated systems
- Pervasive Level—Highly integrated systems

17 Disaster Recovery Program—to what level is there confidence in the DR plan?

- Unaware Level—None
- Tactical Level—Written DR plan
- Focused Level—Written and tested DR plan
- Strategic Level—Regular Table-tops with IT
- Pervasive Level—Regular Table-tops with Business and IT

18 Cyber Tool Strategy—What is the focus of cybersecurity tool purchases?

- — Unaware Level—None
- — Tactical Level—Basic Network Focus
- — Focused Level—Layered Tools
- — Strategic Level—Threat Intelligence
- — Pervasive Level—AI, Business Process Automation

Typical characteristics of company maturities

Companies with unaware maturities

Unaware companies have very limited people process and tools. They do not have a cyber risk program. If they are even looking at security, it is solely from an IT perspective. There are no dedicated cyber teams. These are mostly very small companies with revenues less than US$50 million. Their motto is security by obscurity.

Companies with tactical maturities

Tactical companies have some sort of team for cybersecurity in place. They may have a security manager, however, there is usually no C-Level executive with cyber authority. They may have one or two people on a security team, however, not a resource dedicated solely to cyber. Some of these companies have revenue over a billion dollars a year. In most cases there is a heavy focus on compliance at this level of maturity, and there are basic security tools that are limited to off-the-shelf tools with limited customizations. This is not an organization that is looking at cyber from an enterprise risk perspective and is doing cybersecurity begrudgingly. They have an IT mindset.

As an example, let us look at a firm with several regional offices in the U.S. IT and security are all decentralized across each regional office. There is a security manager in one office and only three IT people working on cyber related projects in a 5000-person organization. They are woefully understaffed. They have some tactical tools with a basic network focus and limited customization. Good news is that after their maturity assessments, they understood the need to make a shift from a compliance/IT focus to an audit/risk focus and to align their cybersecurity program in terms of risk.

Companies with focused maturities

Here, the business is starting to be involved in cybersecurity and understand their role. The business has a seat at the cyber table. They understand that if they have a breach the impact will be devastating. Focused maturities have senior leadership and reporting structures that are starting to involve the business in decision making, planning, and cyber response. They have started to standardize incident management procedures and operationally integrate multiple threat intelligence sources. They tend to implement more layered defense tactics and leverage more types of security technology, at times with too heavy a reliance on technology solutions alone.

The security investments they make are typically in technology addressing audit findings. They are starting to migrate out of the compliance mindset. The security leadership is more centralized and influential, asking for more input from the business, but they still have limited security control over cloud services. They are starting to look at cyber insurance as a strategy. They are asking questions, such as: Do we need cyber insurance? How much to we need? Is it the right coverage limits? What is our ransomware strategy? Cyber insurance brokers cannot benchmark limits adequacy without using a digital asset approach. This is one of the use cases that we will be exploring in detail in the cyber insurance section of this book.

Companies with strategic maturities

This level has integrated people, process, and tools in their cybersecurity program. They are proactive about security and risk management. They customize and extend their incident management, endpoint, and threat intelligence capabilities into company operations, prioritizing according to critical company processes and systems. Their security teams are larger, with more resources available to manage advanced security operations. They realize they need specialist security partners to support their operations through better coverage of the threat landscape and a perspective on priority issues and actions. There is a security leader, who is a C-level executive, they are integrating security thinking into business strategy and operations planning.

Companies with pervasive maturities

These companies embrace cybersecurity as an enterprise risk. They limit the impact of security threats, first by sophisticated integration of detection and protection capabilities and second through well-planned remediation and recovery activities, even when their inherent risk is larger. They standardize and embed security activities within and across business operations and integrate, but do not solely rely upon, advanced techniques like automation and artificial intelligence into their security platforms and infrastructure, which enables scaling. The whole business is engaged in security planning and execution. They have large security teams spread across internal staff and partners and a C-level CISO who provides regular reports on security issues to the Board. They have cyber insurance and a vendor risk program in place.

Industry maturities

In terms of industry maturities, we have banking, financial, and insurance typically at pervasive levels. This is due to the early regulatory influence in these industries. Healthcare and telco are typically at the strategic levels with programs in place but not enough prioritization across key risk areas. Manufacturing, energy, utilities, and retail are usually tactical. Education, construction, and legal are unaware.

Other findings

Security operations tend to be outsourced at the lower-level maturity and then companies will bring security operational resources back in-house as their maturity grows.

The more mature the company, the more the business is involved in cybersecurity.

Cybersecurity tools are layered point solutions that perform specific functions. Companies start with firewalls and buy more tools as they mature.

Notes

1. Ariel Evans, "Managing cyber risk", 2019, Routledge 52 Vanderbilt Avenue, New York, NY 10017.
2. Maryellen Evans, Digital Asset Based Cyber Risk Algorithmic Engine, Integrated Cyber Risk Methodology and Automated Cyber Risk Management System. US 2020/0106801 Al, United States Patent and Trademark Office, April 2, 2020.

PART III
CYBERSECURITY TOOLS

13 CYBERSECURITY POLICIES

As a Global CISO, the best advice I can give is to block traffic from any countries that you can and don't try to do something different for every part of the world or region. Pick and choose what you're going to use from a defined policy and procedure first. Ideally, from a global perspective pick the policy from the most onerous country or region with the strictest requirements you have to comply with and implement them globally.

Michael Meyer, Chief Risk Officer and Chief Innovation Offer at MRS BPO

Cybersecurity policies and their components

Cybersecurity policies legally outline each person's responsibilities for protecting digital assets. These cybersecurity policies act as a means to benchmark goals and tie back the risk reduction from the cybersecurity program to confidentiality, integrity, and availability. This chapter will introduce the concept of cybersecurity policies and how they are used to set the standards of behavior for cyber related activities, such as the encryption of email attachments and restrictions on the use of social media, etc.

Cybersecurity programs use policies to measure their effectiveness. Most companies start with high-level policies for mechanisms, such as acceptable use, password, and incident response and as they mature, they add more sophisticated ones.

Policies are statements of requirements that explicitly define the security expectations of the mechanism(s). They provide justification that the mechanism meets policy through assurance evidence and approvals based on evidence. The security mechanisms must be designed and implemented to meet the requirements of the policy.

Cybersecurity procedures are a collection of related, structured activities or tasks by people or equipment in which a specific sequence produces a cybersecurity goal.

There are many online resources that address specific security policy requirements for companies. These include the Department of Health and Human Service's Healthcare Insurance Portability and Accountability Act (HIPAA), the PCI Security Council's Data Security Standard (PCI-DSS), and European Union's General Data Protection Regulation (GDPR).

Best practices can be used to create a set of cybersecurity policies for various categories of cybersecurity requirements, such as antivirus software, encryption, the use of cloud applications, etc. The SANS Institute provides free templates of cybersecurity policies.[3] There are dozens of templates that include everything from password protection to creating a digital signature policy.

DOI: 10.4324/9781003052616-16

Cybersecurity policies should prioritize the areas of primary importance to the organization. That typically is related to protecting the most sensitive and regulated data, and the security measures needed to address the causes of a prior data breach or business interruption. Tying the cybersecurity, privacy, and risk programs to the policies is a critical part of thought leadership.

The policy must be easy to read and understand. Technical information should be provided in referenced documents in guidelines and procedures. Responsible parties must understand how to meet the requirements in the policy. If the encryption policy states that it is required to encrypt all personal identifiable information (PII) it has to define exactly which specific encryption software is approved and the procedure to encrypt the data.

The components of a solid cybersecurity policy should include the following sections:

Overview: This is a brief summary of the intentions behind the cybersecurity policy.

Purpose: This is the reason for creating the cybersecurity policy.

Scope: The scope defines who and what the cybersecurity policy applies to. This includes what type of digital or physical assets and what type of people in terms of their employment category and roles.

Policy Statements: This is a set of specific statements that apply to the scope of the cybersecurity policy with respect to the purpose and the mechanisms to be put in place.

Roles/responsibilities: This defines which roles are responsible for the specific implementation of the policy statements. Stakeholders can include both internal and external resources. Having an RACI chart that defines cybersecurity roles and responsibilities, accountability and who are informed or consulted should be part of the policy.

Related Policies, Guidelines and Procedures: This is a set of references to other documents that relate directly to this cybersecurity policy.

Monitoring/reporting: This defines how exactly the cybersecurity policy will be monitored and by whom. This includes how often is it reviewed and updated.

Enforcement: This states what compliance measures will be taken to enforce the policy and which roles carry out the enforcement and how.

Exceptions: These relate to roles or assets that are excluded from the policy.

Definitions: These are statements defining the terminology used in the cybersecurity policy.

Revision History: This is a table of when, by whom and what was revised.

Types of cybersecurity policies

Common cybersecurity policies include but are not limited to:

- Acceptable Use—An acceptable use policy defines the set of rules that restrict the ways in which the digital assets (such as network, website, or systems) may be used and sets guidelines as to how they should be used.

- Access Control—The access control policy outlines the cybersecurity controls that are required to be in place to obtain both physical access to the computer hardware and those for logical access to the software in order to limit access to computer networks and data to those with a business need.
- Anti-Virus—This policy states the recommended processes to address malware-related problems.
- Clean Desk—A clean desk policy instructs that all employees keep a desk free of confidential and sensitive information. Clean desk policies are best practices to reduce the risk of document theft, fraud, or a security breach. Sensitive information like passwords should not be written and left unattended and visible in plain site on anyone's desk.
- Data Breach Response Policy and Procedures—The data breach policy outlines what needs to be done to limit a data breach and the procedure to follow to remediate a data breach. A data breach response plan is a documented step by step procedure that is used to reduce the risk associated with unauthorized access and to mitigate the damage caused when a breach occurs. All universities teach an assumption of breach model. This means that it is not an if, it is when. Every company should have a data breach response policy and breach response plan. Details on the steps in the plan, the team roles and responsibilities need to be documented and reviewed by each team member.
- Data Privacy—A data privacy policy is a legal document in privacy law that states the way an organization collects, uses, and protects the individual's sensitive data.
- Data Retention and Disposal Policy—This policy defines the time periods for retention and the methods used for disposal of data.
- Email Policy—The purpose of an email policy is to ensure the proper use of the email system and make users aware of what is deemed as acceptable and unacceptable use of the email system.
- Email Retention Policy—The email retention policy defines what information can be sent or received via email, if it should be retained and for how long. Email information should be categorized into four main classifications (with retention guidelines), such as administrative correspondence or fiscal correspondence (4 years), general correspondence (1 year), and ephemeral correspondence (retain until read, and then destroy).
- Encryption—An encryption policy designates what type and level of encryption is acceptable for different types of data.
- Network Policies—Network policies are sets of rules that describe who is authorized to do different actions on the network. It outlines the conditions, constraints, and settings that are approved. This includes who manages connections and under which circumstance users can or cannot connect.
- Password Protection Policy—A password policy is a set of rules that outline the best practice for the use and protection of passwords. It includes acceptable password lengths, characters, and rules governing password sharing as some examples. A password policy is essential part of an organization's official regulations and should be taught as part of security awareness program at a minimum.

- Remote Access—The purpose of this policy is to define rules and requirements for connecting to a company's network from any host. These rules and requirements are designed to minimize the potential exposure to a company from damage which may result from unauthorized use of their resources. Potential damage includes the loss of sensitive or confidential company data, intellectual property, damage to public image, damage to the businesses' critical internal systems, and fines or other financial liabilities incurred as a result of those losses.
- Risk Assessment—This policy is used to define the requirements for periodic digital asset cybersecurity risk assessments for the purpose of determining areas of vulnerability, and to initiate appropriate remediation.
- Server Security—The purpose of this policy is to establish standards for the base configuration of internal server equipment that is owned and/or operated by the company. The effective implementation of this policy will minimize unauthorized access to proprietary information and technology.
- Social Media—A social media policy outlines how an organization and its employees should conduct themselves using online social media platforms on the Web. It helps protect your company's online reputation and encourages employees to also get involved in sharing about the company to their online network.
- VPN Policy—The purpose of this policy is to provide guidelines for Remote Access IPSec or L2TP Virtual Private Network (VPN) connections to the corporate network.

Example of an acceptable use policy[4]

Overview

Management intentions for publishing an Acceptable Use Policy are not to impose restrictions that are contrary to Cyber Innovative Technology's (CIT) established culture of openness, trust, and integrity. Management is committed to protecting CIT's employees, partners and the company from illegal actions, or cyber incidents that damage the firm, either knowingly or unknowingly.

All digital assets, regardless of the point of access, including, but not limited to, computer equipment, software, operating systems, storage media, network accounts providing electronic mail, World Wide Web browsing, and File Transfer Protocols, are the property of Cyber Innovative Technology, Inc. These systems are to be used only for business purposes. Business purposes are those that serve the interests of the company, and of our customers.

Effective security is a team effort. Every employee, contractor, and affiliate who deals with information and/or information systems must support this policy. It is everyone's responsibility to read, acknowledge, and understand these guidelines, and to conduct their activities accordingly.

Purpose

The purpose of this policy is to outline the acceptable use of computer equipment at Cyber Innovative Technology, Inc. These rules are in place to protect the employee and Cyber Innovative Technology, Inc. Inappropriate use exposes Cyber Innovative Technology,

Inc. to cybersecurity risks, including malware, viruses, worms, ransomware, and other attacks that can compromise networked systems and services, and legal issues.

Scope

This policy applies to the use of information, electronic and computing devices, and network resources that are used to conduct Cyber Innovative Technology, Inc. business or interact with internal networks and business systems, whether, owned or leased by CIT, the employee, or a third party. All employees, contractors, consultants, temporary, and other workers at Cyber Innovative Technology, Inc. and its subsidiaries are responsible for exercising good judgment regarding appropriate use of IT resources in accordance with CIT policies, procedures and standards, local, state, and federal laws, and regulation. Exceptions to this policy are documented in Section 5.2.

This policy applies to employees, contractors, consultants, temporaries, and other workers at CIT, including all personnel affiliated with third parties. This policy applies to all equipment that is owned or leased by Cyber Innovative Technology, Inc.

Policy

General Use and Ownership

1 Cyber Innovative Technology, Inc. proprietary information stored on electronic and computing devices whether owned or leased by CIT, the employee or a third party, remains the sole property of Cyber Innovative Technology, Inc. You must ensure through any means necessary that any information that is classified as proprietary is protected in accordance with the *Data Protection Standard*.
2 You have a responsibility to promptly report the theft, loss or unauthorized disclosure of Cyber Innovative Technology, Inc. proprietary information.
3 You may access, use or share Cyber Innovative Technology, Inc. proprietary information only to the extent it is authorized and necessary to fulfill your assigned job duties.
4 Everyone is responsible for exercising good judgment regarding the reasonableness of personal use. Each department is responsible for creating guidelines concerning personal use of systems that they own. In cases of uncertainty, please should consult your supervisor or manager.
5 For security and network maintenance purposes, authorized individuals have the authority to monitor equipment, systems and network traffic at any time, in alignment with the Audit Policy. The firm reserves the right to audit networks and systems on a periodic basis to ensure compliance with this policy.

Security and Proprietary Information

1 All mobile and computing devices that connect to the internal network must comply with the *Access Policy*.

2 Both Admin level and user level passwords must comply with the *Password Policy*. Providing passwords to another individual, either deliberately or through failure to secure its access, is prohibited.
3 All computing devices must be secured with a password-protected screen-saver which has an automatic activation feature set to 5 min or less. You must lock log off or lock the screen when the computer device is unattended.
4 It is prohibited to post from a CIT email address to newsgroups without a disclaimer stating that the opinions expressed are strictly the person who made them and are not necessarily those of CIT, unless posting is in the course of business duties.
5 In order to avoid the insertion of malware, everyone who has access to CIT systems must use extreme caution when opening e-mail attachments. This includes being on guard for emails that are received from unknown senders. Everyone is required to attend security awareness training that includes training on Phishing attacks.

Unacceptable Use

The following activities are unacceptable and are prohibited. Some individuals may be exempted from these restrictions if they correspond to their legitimate job duties. (e.g., systems administrators may need to disable network access of a host if that host is disrupting production services).

Under no circumstances is an employee of Cyber Innovative Technology, Inc. authorized to engage in any activity that is illegal under local, state, federal, or international law while utilizing CIT owned resources.

The lists below are a framework for activities which fall into the category of unacceptable use. This list is by no means exhaustive.

System and Network Activities

The following activities are strictly prohibited, with no exceptions:

1 Violations of the rights of any person or company protected by copyright, trade secret, patent or other intellectual property, or other laws or regulations, including, but not limited to, the installation of unlicensed software products for use by Cyber Innovative Technology, Inc.
2 Unauthorized copying of copyrighted material for which Cyber Innovative Technology, Inc. or the end user does not have an active license is strictly prohibited. This includes, but is not limited to, digitized copies of all copyrighted works, such as text, photographs from magazines, books, websites, or other copyrighted sources, copyrighted music, and the installation of any copyrighted software.
3 Accessing data, a network, server, or an account for any purpose other than conducting CIT business, even if you have authorized access, is prohibited.
4 Exporting software, data, intellectual property, technical information, encryption software or other prohibited technology or information, in violation of international or regional export control laws, is illegal.

5 Introduction of malicious code, viruses or programs into the network, server, computer or tablet that is the property of CIT or is used for CIT business purposes (e.g., botnets, viruses, worms, Trojan horses, e-mail bombs, etc.).
6 Sharing or revealing your account password to others or allowing use of your account by others. This includes anyone both inside and outside CIT regardless of where work is being done.
7 Using a Cyber Innovative Technology, Inc. digital asset to actively engage in using, procuring, or sharing material that is in violation of our sexual harassment policy and hostile workplace laws.
8 Making fraudulent offers of products, or services from any CIT account.
9 Making statements about cyber events expressly or implied, unless it is a part of normal job duties.
10 Causing a security breach or business interruption. Security breaches include, but are not limited to, unauthorized access to data of which the individual is not an intended recipient or logging into a server or account that the employee is not expressly authorized to access, unless these duties are within the scope of regular duties. For purposes of this section, "business interruption" includes, but is not limited to, ransomware attacks, network sniffing, floods to servers, packet spoofing, denial-of-service attacks, and forged routing information for malicious purposes.
11 Port scanning or security scanning is expressly prohibited unless prior preapproved.
12 Monitoring of the network that may intercept data not intended for the individual's host, unless this activity is a part of their normal job/duty.

Email

1 Sending "junk mail" or other advertising material to individuals who did not specifically request such material by opting in resulting in spam email.
2 Any form of inappropriate behavior via email, mobile, or telephone, including foul language, frequency, and/or the size of email.

Blogging and Social Media

1 Blogging can only be done by authorized employees and is subject to the terms and restrictions set forth in this Policy. Blogging from Cyber Innovative Technology's systems is also subject to monitoring.
2 Employees are prohibited from revealing any CIT confidential or proprietary information covered by CIT's Confidential Information policy when engaged in blogging.
3 Cyber Innovative Technology's trademarks, and logos may not be used in connection with any blogging activity unless indicated in the individual's job description. Exceptions to blogging are for the marketing team only.

Policy compliance

Compliance Measurement: The InfoSec team will verify compliance to this policy.

Exceptions: Any exception to the policy must be approved in writing by the InfoSec team in advance.

Noncompliance: An employee found to have violated this policy may be subject to disciplinary action, up to and including termination of employment.

Related standards, policies, and processes

Data Classification Policy
Data Protection Standard
Social Media Policy
Access Policy
Password Policy

Revision history

Change History Record

Issue	Description of Change	Approval	Date of Issue
1	Initial issue	Ariel Evans	1/15/19
2	Annual update		1/15/20

Figure 13.1 Revision History

Example of a privacy policy[5]

Overview

1. In this policy, the use of "we," "us," and "our" refers to Cyber Intelligence 4U.
2. We are committed to safeguarding the privacy of Cyber Intelligence 4U website visitors and product customers. We are active members of the International Association of Privacy Professionals (IAPP) and provide GDPR and Privacy education for customers.
3. This policy applies for citizens in the U.S. and EU where CIT is acting in the capacity of collecting and processing personal data, or as a data controller with respect to the personal data of visitors to our website and users of VRisk®.
4. We use cookies on our website to track information about visitors. Cookies are not 100% necessary for the provision of our website. A consent question will be provided as to the use of cookies when a visitor first comes to our website.
5. We comply with the following privacy regulations; the General Data Protection Regulation (GDPR), and all U.S. state privacy laws.

How we use your personal data

1 In this section, Cyber Intelligence 4U defines:

(a) the categories of personal data that we may process;
(b) the uses for which we may process your personal data; and
(c) the legal bases of the processing your personal data.

2 We may collect and process data about your use of our website. This data may include your IP address, geographical location, browser type and version, operating system, referral source, length of visit, page views and website navigation paths, as well as information about the timing, frequency and pattern of your service use. The source of the usage data is SharpSpring. This usage data may be processed for the purposes of analyzing the use of the website and services.
3 We may process your website user account data which may include your name, mobile phone number, and email address. This account data may be processed for the purposes of operating our website, providing our services, ensuring the security of our website, maintaining back-ups of our databases, and communicating with you.
4 We may collect and process information contained in a from that you submit to us regarding services. The data may be processed for the purposes of offering, marketing, and selling relevant goods and/or services to you.
5 We may process information relating to transactions that you entered in to our website. This data may include your name, address, phone number, transaction information, and credit card details. We do not store credit card data and are PCI compliant.

Providing your personal data to others

1 Your personal data held in our website database will be stored on the servers of our hosting services providers Godaddy.com and CPanel.com
2 We may disclose your personal data where such disclosure is necessary for compliance with a legal request that we are required to comply with.

Data retention

1 Personal data that we process for any purpose or purposes shall not be kept for longer than is necessary for business purposes.
2 As stated above, we may retain your personal data when it is necessary for compliance with a legal directive.

Your rights

1 In this Section, we have listed the rights that you have under the U.S. and EU data protection laws. We honor these rights for our U.S. website visitors and customers elevating the standard of care.

2 Your principal rights are:

(a) the right to access copies of your personal data;
(b) the right to fix inaccurate personal data and to complete incomplete personal data;
(c) the right to deletion of your personal data;
(d) the right to restrict processing of your personal data;
(e) the right to object to processing of your personal data;
(f) the right to transfer your personal data to another organization or to you;
(g) the right to complain to an E.U. supervisory authority about our processing of your personal data;
(h) the right to withdraw consent of our processing of your personal data; and
(i) all requests should be made via our website or to our marketing department in writing. You must provide proof of identity.

On receipt of your request and verification of your identity Cyber Intelligence 4U will provide you an update on your request within one month.

About cookies

1 A cookie is a file containing an identifier that is to a Web browser and is stored by the browser. The identifier is then sent back to the originating server each time the browser requests a page from the server.
2 A persistent cookie is stored by a Web browser and remains valid until its set expiry date. A session cookie will expire at the end of the user session, when the Web browser is closed.

Cookie use

1 We use cookies for:

(a) We use cookies to identify when you visit our website and as you navigate our website, and to determine if you are logged into the website.
(b) We use cookies to store information about your preferences and to personalize the website for your interests.
(c) We use cookies to prevent fraudulent use of login credentials.
(d) We use cookies to help us to analyze performance of our website.

Cookies used by our service providers

1 Our service providers use cookies, and those cookies may be stored on your computer when you visit our website.
2 We use Google Analytics and SharpSpring. They gather information about the use of our website by means of cookies and single-pixels. The information gathered is used to create reports about the use of our website.

Managing cookies

1 Web browsers will allow anyone the ability to refuse to accept cookies and to delete cookies. The steps vary from browser to browser, and from version to version. Up-to-date information about blocking and deleting cookies for Google, Mozilla, Opera, IE, and Safari are available via these links:

(a) https://support.google.com/chrome/answer/95647 (Chrome);
(b) https://support.mozilla.org/en-US/kb/enable-and-disable-cookies-website-preferences (Firefox);
(c) https://help.opera.com/en/latest/security-and-privacy/ (Opera);
(d) https://support.microsoft.com/en-gb/help/17442/windows-internet-explorer-delete-manage-cookies (Internet Explorer);
(e) https://support.apple.com/en-gb/guide/safari/manage-cookies-and-website-data-sfri11471/mac (Safari);

2 Blocking all cookies can have a negative impact upon the usability of many websites.
3 If you block cookies, you will not be able to use all the features on our website.

Amendments

1 We may update this policy by publishing a new version on our website.

Our details

1 This website is owned and operated by Cyber Intelligence 4U
2 We are registered in The United States of America
3 Our principal place of business is at 555 Madison Avenue, New York, New York, 10021
4 You can contact us:

(a) by post, to the postal address given above
(b) using our website contact form
(c) by telephone, on the contact number published on our website

Credit

1 This document was modified using a template from SEQ Legal (https://seqlegal.com/free-legal-documents/privacy-policy).

Creating the policies

Depending upon your firm's cybersecurity maturity, the CIO or CISO is usually responsible for all information security policies. Other stakeholders should contribute to creating the policy based on their expertise and roles within the organization. The board and C-level executives must outline and prioritize the business needs for cybersecurity and are responsible to adequately budget the needed resources to support the cybersecurity program.

The General Council (GC) and legal team must ensure that the policies meet legal requirements and comply with all federal and state regulations.

The Human Resources (HR) department is responsible for training and enforcing employee related policies. There has to be a documented process that ensures that employees have read and understood the policy and what the consequences are for those who violate it.

The Vendor Cyber Risk Manager (VCRM) is responsible for vendor cybersecurity. This includes the vendor risk policy, vetting IT service, technology, and cloud service vendors, managing the contracts, and enforcing the contract provisions. The VCRM team has to verify that a third party's cybersecurity meets the organization's cybersecurity requirements. This starts with the cybersecurity policies for third parties.

Board members and audit committees of public companies and associations must review and approve cybersecurity policies. They may be involved in policy creation depending on their expertise and the needs of the organization.

When creating cybersecurity policies, it is critical to include the people who will be managing and enforcing the policies. For example, include the audit team on the technical policy requirements and the IT/security person who is the subject matter expert on encryption or access management.

Notes

1. FTI Journal, "Managing cyber risk: Job #1 for directors and general counsel", July 2014, https://www.ftijournal.com/article/managing-cyber-risk-job-1-for-directors-and-general-counsel.
2. Verizon, "2020 Data Breach Investigations Report", 2020, https://enterprise.verizon.com/resources/reports/dbir/.
3. Sans, "Security policy templates", 2020, https://www.sans.org/information-security-policy/.
4. Cyber Innovative Tech, 2020, https://cyberinnovativetech.com/.
5. Cyber Intelligence 4U, 2020, https://cyberintelu.com/.

14 CYBERSECURITY TOOLS

We always talk about there's a lack of funding, a lack of support, a lack of tools and gadgets or gizmos, but when I look back at the 19 years I've been doing this and see where the real weaknesses are, it's usually a lack of strategy. It's that we have all this stuff in place, but we don't have a head coach who's seeing the whole playing field, who understands where all the pieces fit together and who has devised a strategy to make it all work.

Shawn Tuma—Cybersecurity and data privacy attorney
at Spencer Fane LLP

Cyber tool purpose

Cyber tools are point solutions that either identify a cyber event, protect digital assets, detect vulnerabilities, threats, or incidents, respond to them, or recover from them. The five pillars of the NIST Cybersecurity Framework are: Identify, Detect, Protect, Respond, and Recover. The NIST Cybersecurity Framework provides a policy framework of computer security guidance for how private sector organizations in the United States can assess and improve their ability to prevent, detect, and respond to cyber-attacks.

A cybersecurity tool can be associated with policy statements to measure the effectiveness of a policy. Policies are a set of statements of security requirements that explicitly define the security expectations of the mechanisms related to a given policy. They provide justification that the mechanisms in place meet policy expectations through assurance evidence and approvals based on evidence. They outline specific entities and executable actions that are designed and implemented to meet the requirements of the policy.

As an example, an encryption policy states that it is in place to assure integrity of data and provides specific mechanisms to achieve that goal. In this example, the strength of the cipher suite has to be defined explicitly to be effective.

Detection cybersecurity tools

Detection is the action or process of identifying the presence of something concealed. This includes the detect of activity considered anomalous. This activity is typically associated with a cybersecurity incident. The potential impact of these activities must be established, and alert thresholds defined. Other detection functions

DOI: 10.4324/9781003052616-17

are end-to-end monitoring of digital assets in order to demonstrate security issues and understand the effectiveness of the safeguards put in place. The digital assets, including the network, physical environments, user, and service provider activity should all be monitored regularly. Vulnerability scanning is an important part of this. Detection processes need to work to maintain all processes and procedures related to the detection of anomalous activity and protections against cybersecurity events. The people aspect of detection has to be in job descriptions so roles and responsibilities will align with compliance needs. Let us explore different detection tools and what they do.

Firewalls

Firewalls are a detection tool. A firewall is an access control mechanism. It keeps the bad guys out and lets the good guys in. When you hear about "perimeter security"— firewalls are the first thing that comes to mind.

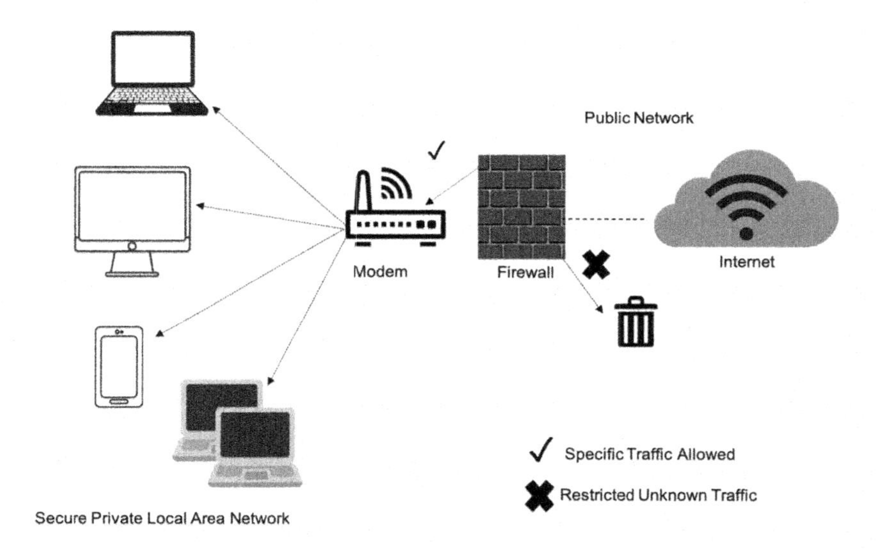

Figure 14.1 Firewalls

Many firewalls are embedded in devices and they come for free when you buy the device. These include routers, modems, etc. A firewall monitors all of the unencrypted traffic that comes into the network and it detects possible attacks. Most companies have a firewall. What it does not do is monitor malicious activities that originate INSIDE the network. A firewall looks at what is coming in through your network and protects from unwanted incoming network traffic. Most unaware companies will have a firewall.

Common firewall vendors include Fortinet FortiGate, Cisco ASA, Sophos UTM, pfSense, Meraki MX Firewalls, WatchGuard XTM, Palo Alto, Checkpoint, and Juniper SRX, among others.

Intrusion detection system (IDS)

In addition to firewalls, systems are needed to detect anything already lurking in the network. An Intrusion Detection System (IDS) monitors the traffic both outside and inside the network. There are two types—one that looks only at certain points and one that looks at the hosts (a host is a device that communicates with other hosts on a network and may offer information resources, services, and applications to users or other nodes on the network). The important point about IDS is that it monitors both the inbound and the outbound traffic. Palo Alto and Checkpoint are famous IDS vendors that manufacture this type of cybersecurity tool. There are many others.

Vulnerability management scanners

Vulnerably Management Scanners are in the Identify category. Vulnerability scanning is a cyclical automated process that can identify network, application, and security vulnerabilities. It can be done by either an internal or external team. If internal, the IT department usually does the scanning. This scan can also be performed by attackers trying to find points of entry into your network.

They are looking at discovering weaknesses in systems in a cyclical manner. They start out with discovery, then prioritization, do an assessment, reporting, remediating, and verifying.

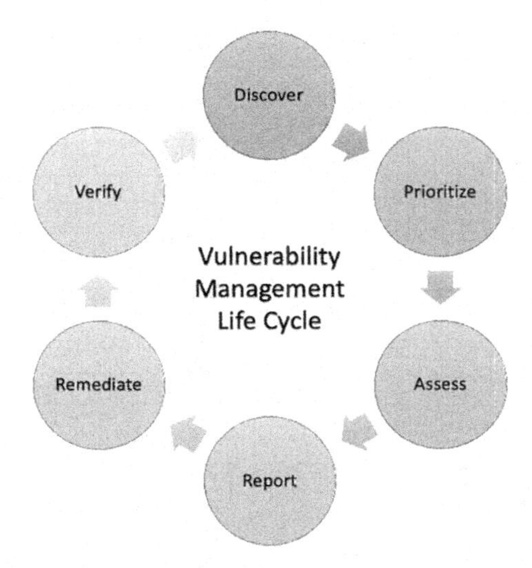

Image 14.1 Vulnerability Management Scanner Lifecycle

Vulnerability scanners compare details about the target attack surface using a database of common vulnerability exposures (CVEs). The database contains known flaws, coding bugs, packet construction anomalies, default configurations, and potential vectors to sensitive data that can be exploited by attackers.

A vulnerability scanning service uses software running from the standpoint of the person or organization inspecting the attack surface in question. The VMS process uses software that will identify and classify the system weaknesses and generates a report of its findings. The findings in the report are used to identify opportunities for an organization to improve their security posture.

Qualys, Tenable, and Rapid7 are some of the most popular vendors out there but there are about 20–30 vendors in this area. This technology has been around for a few decades. Most of your medium maturity companies have a VMS. A VMS provides an excellent approach to integrate and automate security processes.

VMS data can be fed into risk management software to show in near real time how vulnerabilities increase the residual risk likelihood of digital assets.

Security incident and event management

Security Incident and Event Management systems better known as SIEMs are technologies that have been in existence for more than a decade, initially evolving from the log management discipline. A SIEM collects security data from network devices, servers, domain controllers, and more. SIEM stores, normalizes, aggregates, and applies analytics to that data to discover trends, detect threats, and enable organizations to investigate any alerts.

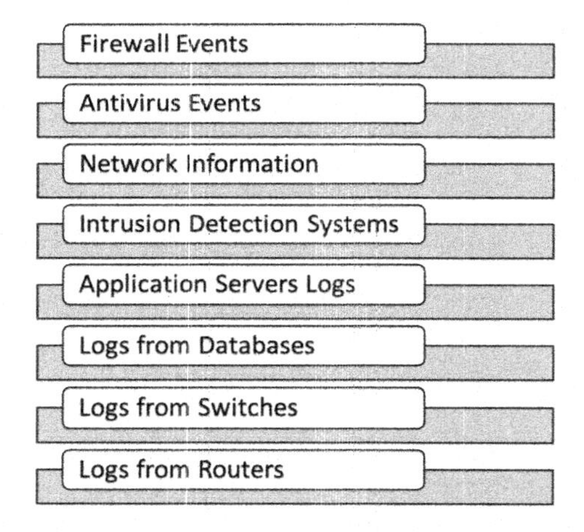

Image 14.2 Security Incident Event Management System Components

The SIEM is a triple winner. It identifies, protects, and detects. It is a tool that analyses security events to determine if they are an incident versus a false positive. It monitors the network traffic and looks for abnormalities. There are a set of rules that are configured in the SIEM. They are not easy to get up and running. You need to know details about your network infrastructures to design the rules and prescribe what you want to monitor. The rules have to be written, then implemented, tested, and rolled out. It is a large project to get one of these up and running. A lot of your midsize companies are going to outsource this to a Managed Security

Service Provider or MSSP. This is great for these size companies since they typically do not have the internal people to set it up, manage and monitor it.

Some SIEM vendors and systems include IBM QRadar, HP ArcSight, Logrthym, and Splunk. Once the SIEM is configured, it has security devices that it is monitoring, network services servers, and applications, it collects the data, it does the analysis in the engine using different rules and algorithms. Then it puts it in a data base, then it gets reported, then they analyze it. The issue with SIEMs is that you have a lot of false positives or noise. If you only have a few people on your security team, it is hard to keep up with this. You would need to do a lot of filtering and make rules and algorithms tighter until you got to the point where you actually would be effective. This means more budget is needed for resources. These are some of the pros and cons with this type of cyber tool.

Protection cybersecurity tools

Protection tools are like detection tools; however, they prevent someone or something from inflecting harm or injury. These include access controls to ensure confidentiality, awareness training that ensures that personnel can efficiently carry out the protection tasks outlined in the company's policies and with third parties. Also included are cybersecurity tools that protect stop malicious activities before they cause harm. We will explore different tools that are preventative.

Security awareness

Security awareness training programs are a set of instructional guidelines and quizzes that enforce learning. A good security awareness program should educate employees about corporate policies and procedures for working with information technology. Some awareness training customizes simulations in your environments, such as fake emails and work with your teams to see how many people are clicking on phishing emails. They provide statistics to see which departments need more training.

Security awareness programs have very high return on investment. As an example, one of my customers was clicking six malicious emails per month on average in each department and they had 100 departments. After cybersecurity awareness training, they reduced the click rate to one click per month per department. These tools are relatively inexpensive. They include training across many different types of awareness, such as acceptable use, phishing, passwords, encryption, etc. The method is to test, train, engage, track, retest, measure, and repeat. Security awareness training needs to be done consistently to build muscle memory.

Encryption

Encryption protects the privacy of the data. Encryption has been around a long time and there are many types. Encryption simply scrambles data in a way that only the authorized parties can actually use it. It uses a key methodology to encrypt and decrypt the data. There are different types of keys- asymmetric and symmetric.

Symmetric Key Algorithms are algorithms that produce similar or exactly the same encryption keys for both the encryption of plaintext and the decryption of ciphertext.

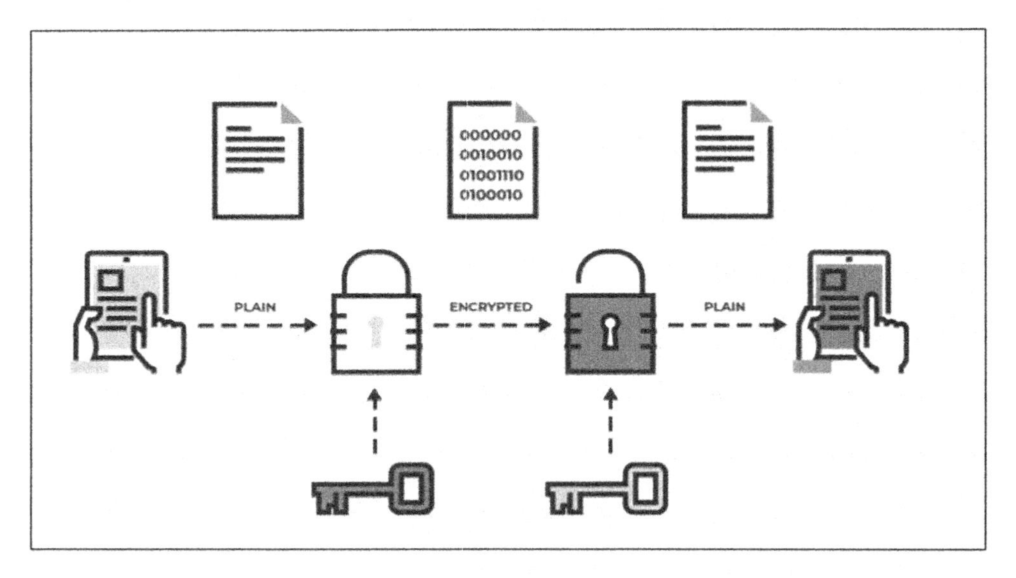

Image 14.3 Encryption

Asymmetric Key Algorithms use algorithms that use unique keys for the encryption of plaintext and the decryption of ciphertext.

Encryption can be done at different levels of the data lifecycle. This includes encryption at rest (inactive data that is physically stored in databases, spreadsheets, tapes, etc.) or in transit (data that is active and flows over untrusted or trusted networks) or in use (spreadsheet, word documents, etc.).

One of the issues you are going to see in the cloud that relates to encryption is the topic of key management. Key management requires resources for setting up rules, managing and maintaining them. Best practices and some compliance regulations require that keys be rotated and replaced every year. PCI requires companies to be compliant with key management. PCI also has deprecated TSL 1.0 and is no longer approved for encryption use with credit card data.

Some of the compliance frameworks will tell you exactly which protocols you can and cannot use. The government is very prescriptive about this.

SSL

How can you recognize if the Web application you are using is secure? Secure Socket Layer (SSL) provides a protocol that creates a secure connection between a Web server and your browser via encryption. That means that the data you're transmitting to the Web server is protected from unwanted snoops. In the Web application URL, you will see a security symbol and the URL starts with https. This verifies that SSL is being used to connect. When you see https in your Web browser, you know that application is using SSL certificates.

Image 14.4 Secure Socket Layer

What does this protect? What kind of attack can happen on Web browsers? If you don't use SSL, the firm is vulnerable to a man in the middle attack. A man-in-the-middle attack happens when the attacker secretly relays and may also alter the communications between two parties that have an expectation of privacy.

What does this protect? What kind of attack can happen on Web browsers? If you don't use SSL, you are vulnerable to a man-in-the-middle attack. A man-in-the-middle attack is an attack where the attacker secretly relays and possibly alters the communications between two parties who believe that they are directly communicating with each other.

SSL certificates can be self-signed or managed by a certificate authority. A certificate authority or certification authority is an entity that issues digital certificates. A digital certificate certifies the ownership of a public key by the named subject of the certificate.

A public key is a cryptographic key that can be obtained and used by anyone to encrypt messages intended for a specific recipient. The encrypted messages can be deciphered only by using a private key that is known only to the recipient.

The certificate authority acts as a trusted third party—trusted both by the subject (owner) of the certificate and by the party relying upon the certificate. The format of these certificates is specified by the X.509 standard. One particularly common use for certificate authorities is to sign certificates used in HTTPS, the secure browsing protocol for the World Wide Web.

Some common certificate authority vendors are Symantec, Comodo, and GoDaddy with over three-fourths of all issued TLS certificates. The certificate comes with the public key, the browser checks the certificate and makes sure it is authorized by the trusted provider and then it goes ahead and encrypts the data and sends it to the Web server.

SSL and TLS are both cryptographic protocols that provide authentication and data encryption between servers, machines, and applications operating over a network (e.g., a client connecting to a Web server). Transport Layer Security (TLS) is a new version of SSL and has more protocols to address vulnerabilities and support stronger more secure cipher suites and algorithms.

SSL was originally developed by Netscape in 1995 with SSL 2.0 (1.0 was never released to the public). A number of vulnerabilities were found in version 2.0 and it was quickly replaced by SSL 3.0 in 1996. Versions 2.0 and 3.0 are sometimes written as SSLv2 and SSLv3. TLS was introduced as a new version of SSL and was based on SSLv3.

A Brute Force attack is when an attacker wants to get your private keys so they can decrypt your data. This is done via trial and error with the attacking computer effectively making guesses one after another. When quantum computing becomes available, computing power and performance will increase, making it possible to obtain a private key more easily. Today's key infrastructures are not going to be useful in terms of a quantum world. There needs to be an innovative strategy in the works today for encryption and Quantum. In theory, all the Public Key Infrastructure (PKI) infrastructures that we have today probably won't work.

PKI is a board term that is used to establish to describe the management of public key encryption. It is one of the most common forms of internet encryption. PKI is baked into every Web browser in use today to secure traffic across the public internet. It is also used by organizations to secure their internal communications and access to connected devices. The public cryptographic keys are part of the encryption process and may be used to help authenticate the identity of the communicating parties or devices.

Penetration testing

Before you can roll out a product into production, you need to do penetration (pen) testing. Pen testing uses hacking techniques to try and find vulnerabilities in the code that will allow an attacker to get inside the organization and do malicious things. Pen testers use a variety of different methods, including code injections, password cracking, and phishing. This particular type of tool is in used to identify vulnerabilities and should be baked into the secure software development lifecycle.

Image 14.5 Penetration Testing

Pen testing is a planned event. Pen testing processes will identify target systems and define a particular goal. They review all the available information and use different procedures to check the goals that they are trying to check.

There are three types of pen tests: White Box, Black Box, and Grey Box. White box testing provides background and system information to set up the tests (e.g., SIEM system and other specific data). Black box testing provides only basic or no information except the company name. Gray box testing is a combination of both black and white testing where there is limited knowledge of the target that is shared with the auditor.

Pen tests will show if a system is vulnerable to attacks, how sufficient the defenses were, and details about which defenses were defeated. All issues discovered should be reported to the system owner.

The National Cyber Security Center[1] describes penetration testing as the following: "A method for gaining assurance in the security of an IT system by attempting to breach some or all of that system's security, using the same tools and techniques as an adversary might."

Goals of penetration tests can vary. The primary goal is usually to identify vulnerabilities that can be exploited by cyber-criminals. Security audits require penetration tests. Most regulations (NYS DFS Part 500, etc.) and guidelines (PCI-DSS) require penetration testing on an annual or quarterly basis, and after system changes.

There are many frameworks and methodologies that exist for conducting penetration tests. These include the Open Source Security Testing Methodology Manual (OSSTMM)[2], the Penetration Testing Execution Standard (PTES),[3] the NIST Special Publication 800-115,[4] the Information System Security Assessment Framework (ISSAF),[5] and the OWASP Testing Guide.[6]

Identification cybersecurity tools

Identification tools pinpoint all of the digital assets that must be protected that are in the company's infrastructure. Identification makes cyber manageable and helps combat shadow IT bad practices where IT assets fall under the radar of protective efforts. Identify also encompasses recognizing the potential risks that could impact the systems the business uses to support its daily operations and critical corporate activities. Identification tools allow the CISO to effectively prioritize the enterprise's cybersecurity efforts based on the cyber risk to the digital assets that they use and the specific threats that could potentially impact these assets. We will explore different tools that are used in the identification process of cybersecurity.

Cyber risk management

Cyber risk management is a new science. Cyber risk management platforms address the identify needs of the company; however, they do more than that. They prioritize risk reduction activities and add the resiliency data that is so needed in today's enterprise.

The Identify function includes five key categories: Asset Management, Business Environment, Governance, Risk Assessment, and Risk Management.

Asset Management functions can be baked into the cyber risk platforms and they provide a method for the CISO and cyber stakeholders to identify the systems, devices, users, data, and technologies that support crown jewel, business critical or business crucial processes paving a road to manage them according to their critical importance.

Asset management platforms should also map the business environment across the owners of the digital assets to involve key stakeholders in the cybersecurity program.

Governance functions are also needed in the cyber risk management platform for the CISO, and cyber stakeholders seek to work together across all the policies and procedures for managing and monitoring regulatory, operational, legal, and reputational risk related to cybersecurity.

The risk assessment is needed for the CISOs and their security stakeholders to ensure a full understanding of the cybersecurity risks that measure the impact exposures and likelihoods associated with the business.

Cyber risk has two metrics—exposures which are potential financial losses based on what an attacker damages and cyber risk scores that are empirically derived based on the impact and likelihood of damage to the digital asset. Exposures are data exfiltration, business interruption, and regulatory loss. Scores look at the likelihood an attack will cause damage. Inherent risk is the baseline of cyber resiliency, security assessments demonstrate the effectiveness of cyber controls, and residual risk causes inherent risk to rise and is based on data from the cybersecurity tools. This lies the foundation to incorporate AI into cybersecurity.

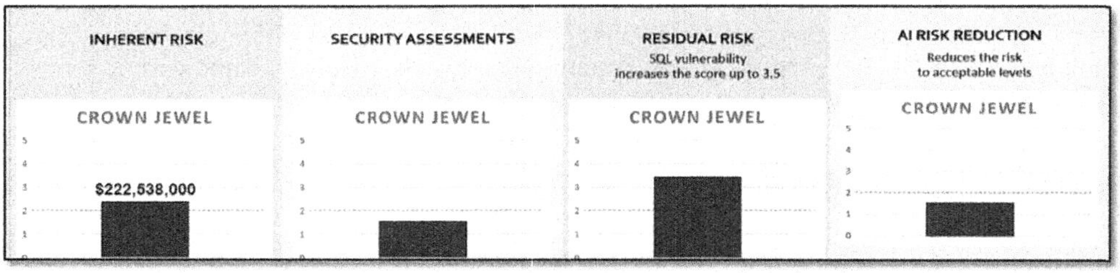

Image 14.6 Cyber Risk Management Lifecycle

The attacker attacks the digital assets. They steal your data, interrupt your business, and cause regulatory fines and penalties. The digital asset approach allows for use cases, including cyber insurance qualifications, prioritization of resources, M&A, and allows for an integration approach using security assessments and cyber tool data.

Lastly, cyber risk management provides a risk management strategy that prioritizes risk reduction based on impacts and likelihoods, risk tolerances, and demonstrates cyber resiliency.

We review cyber risk management in detail in part 8 of this book.

As per Gartner,[7] by 2025, 60% of global IT risk management (ITRM) buyers will depend on risk management solutions to aggregate digital risks in their business ecosystem, up from 15% in 2019.

Through 2025, 50% of ITRM solutions will evolve to support digital risk management capabilities, including cloud, operational technology (OT), Internet of Things (IoT), and the social media environments of digital businesses, up from less than 30% in 2019.

Vendors include Cyber Innovative Technologies, RiskLens, and Security Scorecard.

Vendor cyber risk management

Vendor cyber risk management is third party cyber risk management and is required by new privacy regulations, including NYS DFS Part 500, the GDPR, the insurance data security act, and the CCPA, among others. Sixty-three percent of reported breaches are attributed to vendors.[8] Cloud service providers, management consulting vendors and product vendors all touch an organization's digital assets. Most companies send the majority of their private and sensitive data to third parties to be processed and/or shared with business partners. Understanding the cyber exposures is critical to know how to reduce risk and manage the vendor relationship. The risk of the first party is inherited by the third party. For example, Facebook had a US$5 billion fine when their vendor Cambridge Analytica suffered had a breach of their data. Vendors without good cyber hygiene present a very high risk to companies.

A vendor risk management solution should measure exposures and score the vendor's risk in alignment to the digital assets in the context of what they provide. A product vendor should ensure that they provide patches and bake security into the technology. A company has to ensure that their service vendor's (data processor, management consultant, etc.) cybersecurity posture is aligned to the expectations of the company to protect the confidentiality, integrity, and availability of their data. A cloud service vendor has a shared responsibility model with the organization that has to be understood and measured.

We review vendor cyber risk management in detail in part 10 of this book.

Cyber Risk Management vendors include Cyber Innovative Technologies and Bitsight.

Protection cybersecurity tools

Data loss prevention

Data loss prevention (aka DLP) is a software product that helps a network administrator control what data end users can transfer outside the organization.

Data loss prevention software identifies data that needs extra protection or that may be exfiltrated and helps to prevent data breaches. DLP monitors, detects and blocks sensitive data that has been identified while in use at the endpoints, in transit via network traffic, and at rest when being stored in a database.

DLP first identifies confidential or sensitive information that will be in scope to protect. Firms use compliance regulations to determine which data is in scope. DLP is sometimes confused with data discovery. DLP uses data discovery as one of the processes to identify data in scope.

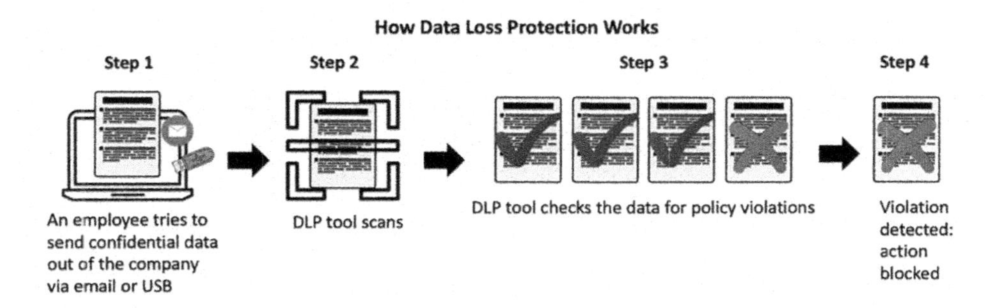

Image 14.7 Data Loss Prevention

Data can exist in different formats. Data that is in free-form is referred to as structured. Examples are data in a file such as a spreadsheet. Unstructured data is data that is in a text or media format in text documents like Microsoft Word, PDF files, and video. Approximately, 80% of all data is unstructured and 20% structured.[9]

Data loss events turn into data leakage in cases where media that contains sensitive information is lost or stolen if acquired by an unauthorized person. A data leak is possible without losing the data on the originating side.

DLP is very hard to implement. It has a high failure rate. DLP must also be configured with rules like the SIEM. The rules have to be approved by the business in many cases and these rules will limit their ability to send data outside the organization. Most employees do not like DLP because it may block their outgoing emails. This tool is great for privacy regulation. Because this prevents privacy data from being sent outside the organization that is blocked due to business reasons. DLP protects privacy data, which could include Social Security Numbers, emails, phone numbers, etc. RSA and Websense are popular DLP vendors.

Advanced threat protection

Advanced threat protection (ATP) refers to a category of security solutions that defend against sophisticated malware or hacking-based attacks targeting sensitive data. Advanced threat protection solutions can be available as software, a managed service, or a hybrid of the two.

Advanced threat protection is a tool that companies use to block malware. Why is this significant? It doesn't deliver the payload; therefore, nothing is exfiltrated and there are no remediation costs. What's great about preventative tools is that all the respond and recover activities and costs are unnecessary. The approaches that each vendor uses may differ as to in-memory versus out-of-memory attacks. As this technology matures, it will be interesting to see the return on investment and effectiveness.

Over 80% of attacks happen on the endpoint and advanced evasive threats pose the biggest risk. Antivirus can handle commodity malware, but file-less attacks are 10x more likely to breach the business. Advanced threat protection is designed to preemptively prevent the most dangerous endpoint attacks. This includes zero-day, evasive, unknown malware, ransomware, and browser-based attacks. A zero-day threat is a threat that exploits an unknown computer security vulnerability. The term is derived from the age of the exploit, which takes place before or on the first (or "zeroth") day of a developer's awareness of the exploit or bug. Attackers exploit zero-day vulnerabilities through different vectors. Vendors include Carbon Black, ZScaler, Morphisec, and others.

Cyber simulation range

Attack simulations show how your network and security controls would perform against real-world attack scenarios. They can provide recommendations that can help your company improve network segmentation, update IPS signatures, use compensating controls, and more.

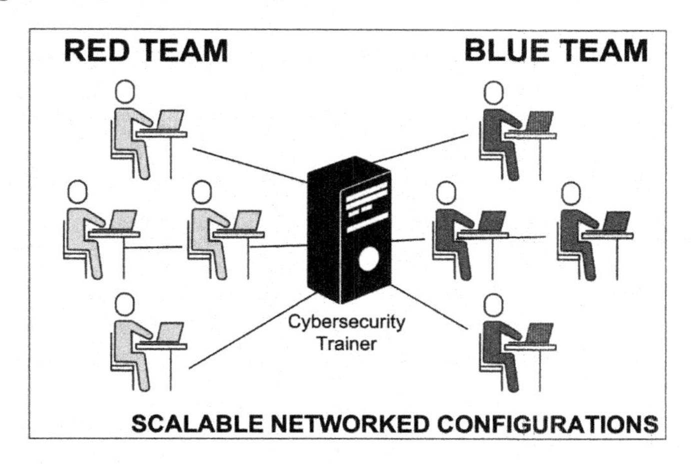

Image 14.8 Cyber Simulations

This typically is a combination of software and teams that are training to increase their cyber skills. Simulations can be used to benchmark skill levels and help to increase skills to respond to evolving threats. There are several levels of teams, red, blue, and purple that work on cyber simulations.

A cyber range is a virtual environment that is used for cyberwarfare training by individuals or teams. The cyber range can measure the skills and determine deficiencies in the analyst's capabilities in various domains like Web, LINUX, and Windows exploitation.

Cyber teams are divided into red, blue, and purple based on different factors. Red Teams are the attackers. Red Teams are usually outside contractors. The Red Team has basic knowledge of how to break in and what security is already in place at the firm. When attackers know what security is being used by a company, they can avoid attacks that would be identified. Most large organizations have internal Red Teams and supplement them with contractors to provide independent testing. Red Team members are proficient with all forms of digital attacks. This includes social engineering methods that are used to access the systems of the firm. The Red Team will try everything they can to hack into sensitive systems. The Red Team has an agreement in place that they are not legally liable for any attacks that succeed into privileged systems.

Blue Teams are usually members of the IT Security or Data Security divisions of the company who is being tested. Blue Teams are defensive in nature and will be continually hardening system and network security. They engage with the Red Team during a simulated attack. The first attack does not involve the Blue Team directly, however during the reattack phase the Red Team will test if the vulnerabilities have been patched. Blue team simulations use specific cyber tools to increase their skill sets (SIEM or VMS that the company has purchased).

During an audit both teams work together and document what tests were performed, which exploits succeeded, and the details of what went wrong. The Red Team provides system and network logs of all the operations performed, and the Blue Team documents the corrective actions that were taken on each vulnerability or exploit found in the testing process.

Purple Teams are a single group that do both Red and Blue testing. They can be a third party, or employees of the company. Purple teams do not focus exclusively on either attacking or defending. Purple teams have to have excellent offensive and defensive skills. Many times, a person with a specific specialty is needed like SCADA.

Having Red, Blue, and Purple teams keep up their skills is vital to making the company reduce cyber risk. Constantly testing against the latest vulnerabilities has to be a proactive program in all companies.

Cyber threat intelligence

Cyber Threat Intelligence (CTI) uses a collection of threat intelligence data from multiple sources, such as Open Source Intelligence (OSINT), Social Media Intelligence (SOCMINT), Human Intelligence (HUMINT), technical intelligence or intelligence from the deep, and dark web to spot threats. CTI's focuses on three areas: cybercrime, hacktivism, and cyberespionage via advanced persistent threat (APT) or cyber spying.

Cyber Threat Intelligence uses services and software in the deep and dark web to identify and track cyber-criminals and thwart their plans. They act as spies that identify different cyber-criminal relationships by scanning the deep and dark web, looking for malicious activity and clandestine conversations, and they provide data to organizations about reconnaissance activities and threats. They look for confidential data that cyber-criminals are selling. CTI vendors have a semi-automated platform, and they can show you dashboards and reports your threat profile on the deep and dark web. These tools and services are very expensive. They cost between US$120k and US$300k. Some vendors include Carbon Black, Kela, SixGill, and others. These vendors are usually employed by companies that are large targets of espionage or blackmail.

Cyber kill chain

The Cyber Kill Chain was invented by Lockheed Martin and it lays out the steps that attackers take to exploit your infrastructure. The first thing they do is reconnaissance. How do they do this? Port scanning, social engineering, job boards, etc. They try to figure out who they want to attack. Then, they weaponize. They couple exploits with backdoors, and they deliver payloads. They deliver payloads via email, Web, and USB—any weakness that they can exploit. They will install malware on your system and steal your data and disturb your business. Here are the steps in the Cyber Kill Chain.

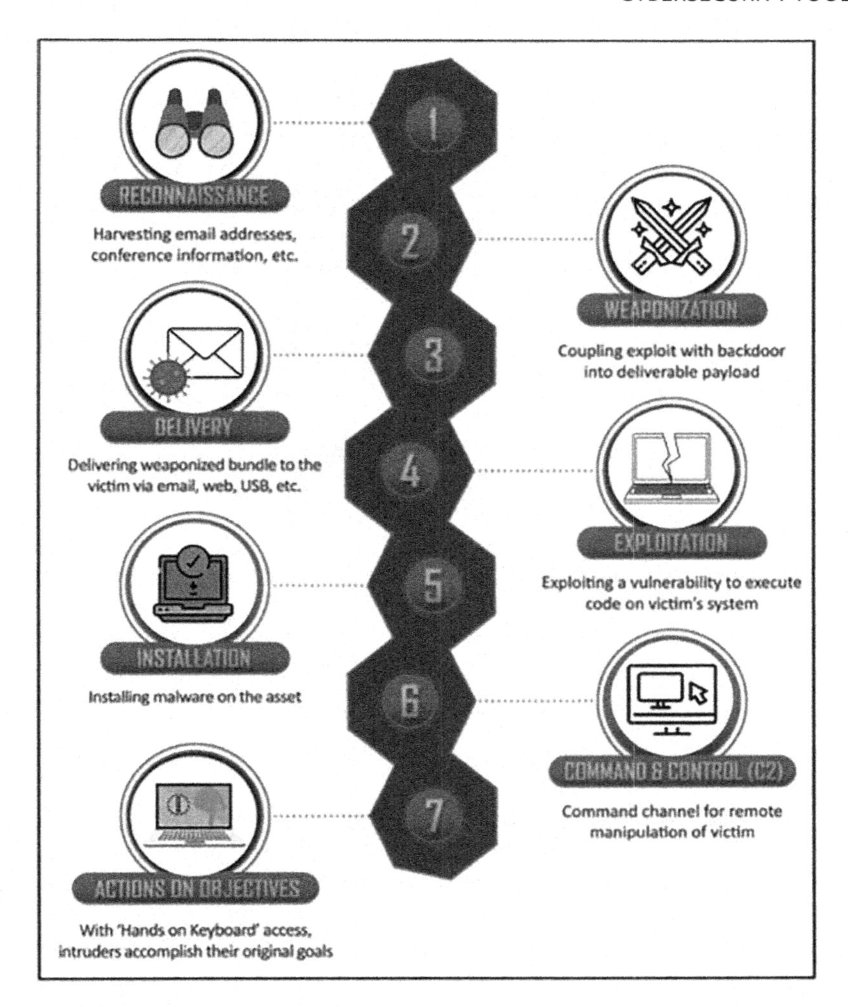

Image 14.9 The Kill Chain

Reconnaissance: The intruder selects their target, researches it, and attempts to identify vulnerabilities in the target network.

Weaponization: The intruder creates a remote access malware weapon, such as a virus or worm, tailored to one or more vulnerabilities.

Delivery: The intruder transmits the weapon to target (e.g., via email attachments, websites, or USB drives).

Exploitation: The malware is designed as a weapon with program code triggers, which take actions on a targeted network to exploit a vulnerability.

Installation: The malware weapon installs an access point (e.g., "backdoor") usable by intruder.

Command and Control: The malware enables the intruder to have "hands on the keyboard" persistent access to target network.

Actions on Objective: The intruder takes action to achieve their goals, such as data exfiltration, data destruction, or encryption for ransom.

Cyber tool maturity

As a company increases its cyber maturity it will buy tools to automate and fill the gaps in their programs. Companies start with firewalls and IDS's. Unaware companies have little to no security tools. Tactical companies typically have firewalls and IDS. Focused companies will include vulnerability management scanners and maybe data loss prevention tools. Strategic companies have advanced tools including advanced threat prevention. Pervasive companies are using AI and business process automation.

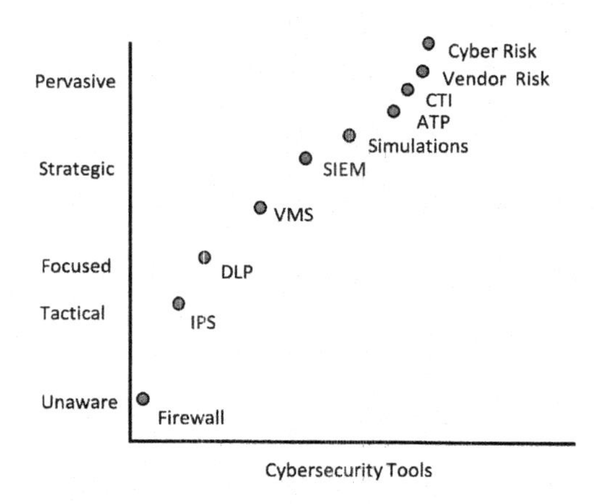

Image 14.10 Cyber Tool Maturities[10]

Unaware and tactical companies have no vendor risk management program. Focused companies have started initial vendor risk management programs. Initial programs will have a vendor inventory and some basic information about the vendor's security program. Strategic companies have more mature vendor risk management programs. More mature vendor management programs have extensive questionnaires; however, many are not in context. Pervasive companies have integrated vendor risk management programs. Integrated vendor risk management programs look at vendors in context and utilize digital asset risk metrics.

Companies with a tactical maturity typically implement basic network protection, relying heavily on using off-the-shelf tools and technology with limited customization. They have a compliance mindset.

Focused maturity companies typically have Firewalls, IDS, and some VMS as security tools. Companies with a focused maturity are likely to have started to standardize incident management procedures and operationally integrate multiple threat intelligence sources. They tend to implement more layered defense tactics and leverage more types of security technology, at times with too heavy a reliance on technology solutions alone. Their security investments they make are typically in technology addressing audit findings.

Strategic maturities have integrated people, process, and tools. They are proactive about security and risk management. They customize and extend their incident management, endpoint and threat intelligence capabilities into company operations, prioritized according to critical company processes, and systems. They realize they need specialist security partners to support their operations through better coverage of the threat landscape and a perspective on priority issues and actions. They do regular table-top exercises and focus on threat intelligence cyber strategy and investments.

Companies with pervasive maturities limit the impact of security threats, first by sophisticated integration of detection and protection capabilities and second through well-planned remediation and recovery activities, even when their inherent risk is larger. They standardize and embed security activities within and across business operations and integrate, but do not solely rely upon, advanced techniques like automation and artificial intelligence into their security platforms and infrastructure, which enables scaling. They do regular and frequent table-top exercises. Security investments are AI and BPM focused.

Notes

1. National Cyber Security Centre, "Penetration testing", August 8, 2017, https://www.ncsc.gov.uk/guidance/penetration-testing.
2. Kirkpatrick Price, "What you need to know about OSSTMM", October 3, 2019, https://kirkpatrickprice.com/blog/what-you-need-to-know-about-osstmm/.
3. PTES, "High level organization of the standard", August 16, 2014, http://www.pentest-standard.org/index.php/Main_Page.
4. NIST, "Technical guide to information security testing and assessment", September 2008, https://tsapps.nist.gov/publication/get_pdf.cfm?pub_id=152164.
5. OISSG, "Information systems security assessment framework (ISSAF) Draft 0.2.1B", May 1, 2006, http://cuchillac.net/archivos/pre_seguridad_pymes/2_hakeo_etico/lects/metodologia_oissg.pdf.
6. OWASP, "OWASP web security testing guide", 2020, https://owasp.org/www-project-web-security-testing-guide/.
7. Gartner, "Allgress named a challenger in Gartner 2019 Magic Quadrant for IT Risk Management", 2019, https://static1.squarespace.com/static/58d04b7fbf629abc5cba10ec/t/5d800a8e1dcea74b3ca28fb9/1568672398551/Gartner+2019+MQ+for+IT+Risk+Management.pdf.
8. Mahmood Sher-Jan, 20iapp, "Surprising stats on third-party vendor risk and breach likelihood", August 21, 2017, https://iapp.org/news/a/surprising-stats-on-third-party-vendor-risk-and-breach-likelihood/.
9. Timothy King, Data Management Solutions Review, "80 percent of your data will be unstructured in five years", March 28, 2019, https://solutionsreview.com/data-management/80-percent-of-your-data-will-be-unstructured-in-five-years/.
10. Maryellen Evans, Digital Asset Based Cyber Risk Algorithmic Engine, Integrated Cyber Risk Methodology and Automated Cyber Risk Management System. US 2020/0106801 Al United States Patent and Trademark Office, April 2, 2020.

PART IV

CYBERSECURITY REGULATION AND FRAMEWORKS

15 US FEDERAL REGULATION

Other countries unite behind cyber regulation, our country is outsourcing privacy and security to the states and only stepping in on egregious issues. We need federal cyber regulation to reduce redundancy and keep up with global standards.

Ajay Singh, Corporate Adviser and Fellow Institute of Directors

FAIR information act[1]

In all of my public speaking around data security and privacy, I emphasize key ideas about the relationship between regulation and security. Security is a component of FAIR information practices. This law came into being in 1973 in the Nixon administration. The department of Health and Human Services formed a taskforce to consider the security of healthcare and government data. They understood the need for policies that would allow computerization to move forward while recognizing that privacy would be entirely different than in a paper driven world. They composed this code of FAIR information practices that has five clauses—openness, disclosure, secondary use, correction; and security. In Europe, there is a new regulation that focuses on privacy. It is interesting to note that the US early on started to look at privacy due to the revolution in computer technology, however, in my opinion, dropped the ball. The GDPR is a set of similar ideas that is much more prescriptive with bonafide enforcement capabilities that are strong. Conversely, the US enforcement capabilities were not tested until very recently with the fines for the Facebook data breach.

The first requirement of FAIR is transparency. You need to know what the data you are collecting will be used for. This must be known at the point at or before the data is actually collected. Notice must be given and there must be limits on use and sharing.

The second requirement is choice. People need to be able to opt in or opt out and consent to changes. Third is the right to access your data and make corrections to it. Fourth, there has to be specific time frames and ways your data is protected and disposed of, and notification if your data is breached. Lastly, there must be accountability and auditing.[2]

These principles are the bedrock of privacy regulation in the US. Probably one of the weakest expressions of them in the US is in the Gramm–Leach–Bliley Act where they have very minimal respect paid to these core aspects, what is really at risk and needs to be protected. The Gramm–Leach–Bliley Act requires financial institutions and companies that offer financial products or services (loans, financial or

DOI: 10.4324/9781003052616-19

investment advice, or insurance) to explain their information-sharing practices to consumers and to safeguard sensitive data.[3]

These principles all tie into the cybersecurity triad of confidentiality, integrity, and availability. Let us now look at some perspective cyber related regulations.

HIPAA

The Health Insurance Portability and Accountability Act (HIPAA) was passed in 1996.[4] HIPAA is a federal law and a national standard that was designed to protect medical records and other personal health information. HIPAA protects protected health information (PHI) that identifies an individual and is maintained or exchanged electronically or in hard copy.

Any data elements that could be used to identify a person should be protected. The protection is over the lifecycle of the information as long as the information is in the hands of a covered entity or a business associate. The protections apply regardless of the form of the information; both electronic and nonelectronic forms are in scope.

Covered entities are defined in the HIPAA as:

1. Health plans
2. Health care clearinghouses
3. Health care providers who electronically transmit any health information in connection with transactions for which HHS has adopted standards

A "business associate" is a person or entity who is not a member of the workforce of a covered entity, that performs functions or activities on behalf of, or provides certain services to, a covered entity that allows for access by the business associate to PHI.

HIPAA, also known as Public Law 104-191, is enforced by the US Department of Health and Human Services. At HHS.org there are many free resources to see how you can comply with the HIPAA security rule and it will reference the NIST cybersecurity framework.

Healthcare organizations must understand the HIPAA Security Rule to comply with HIPAA requirements. The HIPAA Security Rule consists of the administrative, physical, and technical safeguards and their mechanisms and procedures that must be in place to ensure the integrity of Protected Health Information (PHI).

Administrative	Technical	Physical
Designate responsible individual	Threat detection and response	Disaster recovery plan
Perform a risk assessment	Access privileges	Visitor access control to premises
Employee training and discipline	Encryption	Employee access control to records containing PII

Figure 15.1 Cybersecurity Safeguards

The Administrative Safeguards are focused on the requirement to conduct ongoing risk (correct reference is a control) assessments in order to identify vulnerabilities that will impact the integrity of PHI.

One bone to pick with how this law is written is the use of the term *risk*. This term is incorrectly used. Risk is derived from impact and likelihood metrics. The assessments that are required in HIPAA are security control assessments across administrative, physical, and technical requirements. Administrative safeguards establish the security management process and control the management of information access to ensure the integrity of PHI. Proper information access includes the management of who, when, and how PHI can be accessed, and monitored. Risk assessments that measure the effectiveness of access controls are critical to prevent data breaches and the imposition of rigorous fines and sanctions.

The physical safeguards focus on the mechanisms that should be in place to prevent unauthorized access to PHI, and protect data from physical threats like fire, flood, and environmental hazards.

The physical requirements include both physical access to facilities in which computer equipment lives and the access of personnel entering the facilities, as well as to how PHI is digitally accessed by and stored on computer equipment.

Healthcare is innovative and mobile. Many providers communicate using devices to patients. The administrative safeguards are extremely important in these instances. A Bring Your Own Device (BYOD) policy must be in place to ensure that safeguards on mobile devices are in place properly. Medical professionals use personal mobile devices to support their workflows, preform clinical testing, and other key functions. There must be a suitable policy in place to guide medical professionals about appropriate use of these technologies and the best practices to reduce cyber risk.

Eighty-seven percent of doctors use a Smartphone at work to support their workflow according to a Manhattan Research/Physician Channel Adoption Study.[5] The physical cybersecurity requirements stipulate that any device used to access PHI must have an automatic log-off facility so PHI cannot be accessed by unauthorized personnel when a workstation or mobile device is left unattended.

The technical safeguards focus on the cybersecurity controls that must be in place to ensure data security when PHI is being communicated on an electronic network in use, flight and at rest.

USB flash drives, mobile devices, and other computer equipment should be considered when developing and implementing cybersecurity policies about data retention, transfer, and disposal of PHI. Mechanisms must be in place to ensure that PHI can be deleted remotely in the event that a personal mobile device or USB drive is lost or stolen.

There are three types of technical controls for HIPAA: access controls, audit controls, and integrity controls. Access and audit controls define how staff accessing PHI must authenticate their identity. Integrity controls provide the instructions of how PHI data at rest (stored in databases) should be stored to ensure its integrity.

Data must also be protected in flight. The technical safeguards when PHI is in transit include measures that ensure confidentiality and protect against the interception of messages or third-party retrieval of messages that are transmitted over an electronic network.

Healthcare organizations have the responsibility to ensure that all emails and text messages that contain PHI are secure. This is a difficult requirement to fulfill. Copies of messages may remain indefinitely on cloud service providers' environments. The options are to be either encrypt every email and SMS message or prohibit medical professionals to send PHI in an electronic communication.

The logistics of encrypting every email and every SMS is a massive undertaking and not practical in most situations. It is typically not cost-effective or practical to find an encryption approach that fits through diverse operating systems and multiple platforms and complies with the other HIPAA data protection specifications.

Most healthcare organizations have implemented secure messaging solutions to avoid this issue. Secure messaging solutions work via messaging applications that can be downloaded onto a computer or mobile device irrespective of the operating system. They provide compliance for this requirement by encrypting and encapsulating all communications containing PHI within a healthcare organization's private communications network.

Using this solution, security measures are in place to prevent the accidental or malicious disclosure of PHI. Preset message lifespans can be put in place to ensure that communications are automatically deleted from a user's app after a preset period of time. Identity and Access Management Systems (IAM), automatic archiving of messages and forcing log offs using automated techniques are part of solutions to meet HIPAA data security requirements. Sixty-seven percent of nurses use Smartphones at work according to an American Nurse Today study.[6]

The federal fines for HIPAA noncompliance are based on the level of perceived negligence found within your organization at the time of the HIPAA violation. These fines and consequences can range from US$100 to US$50,000 per record, with a maximum penalty of US$1.5 million per year for each violation. This is a significant fine.

The health sector is the fifth largest of the US economy. HIPAA applies to two defined categories: covered entities and business associates. Medical device manufacturers are not defined as covered entities. However, they can be engaged in regulated activities but as a general matter, they might be handling the same kind of information with identifying information types and known conditions or treatment history. Clinical Research Organizations (CROs) typically have terabytes of data and are not required to comply with HIPAA. Who will protect data under these circumstances? The Federal Trade Commission (FTC) has jurisdiction here. Health information is considered sensitive personal data just like financial data. This means that fair information principles apply to this type of data.

Many companies try and skirt around the business associate label. Regardless of whether the firm meets the exact definition, it is a best practice to document the expectations and obligations around the security of healthcare and PII. This requirement is leaking into the new vendor provisions that we see in NYS DFS, the insurance data security act and other legislation. Sensitive data sets need to be protected by contract without regard to whether it is covered entity or business associate.

Many firms purposely did not sign a business associate agreement to avoid having to comply with HIPAA. This loophole stayed in place until the mid-2000s. In 2009,

Health and Human Services Agency (HHS) fixed that rule and changed the language to ensure that a company is a business associate by virtue of their activities. If you do not sign a business associate agreement with a business associate, the covered entity is in violation of the requirement that all business associates have an agreement.

Health and Human Services Agency has an Office of Civil Rights (OCR) that handles all manner of privacy or security complaints from patients that come in a variety of ways. Patients can complain about how a doctor mishandled their data. Organizations must report a data breach within 60 days that affects over 500 users. Every report of a data breach of over 500 affected users will be investigated to some level. As part of the investigation a risk analysis and risk management plan are required. There will be a full audit. There must be a process in place for collecting and logging individual events. Fines are levied based on neglect, which is determined based on a culture of noncompliance. Tone at the top is critical to rebut this.

Violations of HIPAA are rigorous. HIPAA sets up per violation fines and penalties capping them at US$1.5 million. Any organization can have multiple violations. Examples of violations include not having a device control policy, poor or nonexistent risk assessments, no risk management plan, etc.

As an example, if you are creating an app for the iPhone and Apple has a security control that is hard coded into the phone and you disable that control, you must replace it with a compensating control. That is a rule of the FTC.

HHS enforcement moves very slowly. The FTC tries to wrap up enforcement activities in six to eight months depending on the complexity. This is due to differences in staffing and the auditing approaches. The FTC is very surgical, asking questions and getting back to companies within 10 to14 days. HHS is heavy on auditing and views a breach as requiring an audit. They usually work regionally and have limited staff with one person working on hundreds of breaches. Additionally, they need expert help when things get very technical since they do not have the staff to address it. HHS is very sensitive to gross negligence. As an example, when PHI is being accessed by a business associate on a laptop and it is stolen and not properly encrypted. There is also a great deal of improper discarding of paper record cases when companies are in bankruptcy or winding down.

Shadow IT plays heavily into the Office of Civil Rights (OCR) fines. As an example, a tri-state hospital had an excellent risk analysis with all of their clinical care systems. It is an academic medical institution. Doctors and faculty do a great deal of research projects. One doctor was doing unapproved research on the side and he set up a very simple application for his OR schedule for the people in his department and it was not deemed sensitive. He set up an opening in the firewall to allow people to remote in to schedule appointments. He had patient information in the system, and he linked in through central IT. He was an authorized person doing something authorized. However, there was no risk assessment of this application. The hospital only focused on the top ten systems. He decommissioned his servers and did not close the opening in the firewall. Google was able to crawl the server that held all the patient data. Someone had died that had been in the ICU and their loved one had been on the internet trying to write their obituary and they found their ICU records. This is really bad. In all, this issue affected about 6,000 people.

SEC regulation and enforcement

The Office of Compliance Inspections and Examinations (OCIE)[7] conducts the SEC's National Exam Program. OCIE's mission is to "protect investors, ensure market integrity and support responsible capital formation through risk-focused strategies that: (1) improve compliance; (2) prevent fraud; (3) monitor risk; and (4) inform policy. The results of the OCIE's examinations are used by the SEC to inform rule-making initiatives, identify and monitor risks, improve industry practices, and pursue misconduct."[8]

"On February 20, 2018, the Securities and Exchange Commission[9] voted unanimously to approve a statement and interpretive guidance to assist public companies in preparing disclosures about cybersecurity risks and incidents."

"I believe that providing the Commission's views on these matters will promote clearer and more robust disclosure by companies about cybersecurity risks and incidents, resulting in more complete information being available to investors," said SEC Chairman Jay Clayton. "In particular, I urge public companies to examine their controls and procedures, with not only their securities law disclosure obligations in mind but also reputational considerations around sales of securities by executives."

The guidance reflects new and timely views from the SEC about public companies' disclosure obligations under existing law with respect to cybersecurity risk and incidents. It also speaks to the importance of cybersecurity policies and procedures, incident disclosure controls, and procedures in the context of cybersecurity.

The SEC states that companies should disclose the risks associated with cybersecurity programs and incidents if these risks arise in connection with acquisitions. They want firms to consider the occurrence of prior cybersecurity incidents, including their severity and frequency. Firms should measure the probability of the occurrence and potential magnitude of cybersecurity incidents, the adequacy of preventative actions taken to reduce cybersecurity risks and the associated costs, including, if appropriate, discussing the limits of the company's ability to prevent or mitigate certain cybersecurity risks.

Guidance relates to the company's business and operations that give rise to material cybersecurity risks and the potential costs and consequences of such risks, including industry-specific risks and third-party supplier and service provider risks.

Costs associated with maintaining cybersecurity protections, in conjunction with cyber insurance coverage relating to cybersecurity incidents should be part of a firm's strategy.

Reputational, operational, and legal risk should be considered. A gap analysis of existing cyber regulations that may affect the requirements to which companies are subject relating to cybersecurity and the associated costs to companies should be considered.

It is required for companies regulated by the SEC to inform them if there is a data breach and if there is an investigation they need to be told early on. Most companies are frequently meeting with regulators. Relationships tend to be fairly open conversations. As part of their enforcement authority the SEC will examine the safeguards rule to determine if any enforcement action needs to happen.

Let us look at some enforcement action of the SEC. A good example is a 2013 breach that was traced back to China is RT Jones Capital Equities data breach. The attackers breached the Web server and over 100,000 prospective clients' records were exposed. R.T. Jones failed to notify the individuals. They were censured and fined with a relatively small amount. The fine is a statement that the SEC is making to wake up companies to pay attention to their compliance with Reg SP,[10] conduct periodic risk assessments, have minimal access controls in place like a firewall, and have an incident response plan and encrypt the PII that was stored on the server. This early fine should have been a shot across the bow to other investment firms.

In 2016, a nonfirm email system that was used to conduct firm business was breached in the case of Craig Scott Capital. Here, think of Hilary Clinton and most others in the federal government that used nonauthorized email servers. In cybersecurity this is a big no-no. The firm was forwarding faxes to personal email addresses of administrative assistants on a grand scale. The faxes included PII data. The firm had a prohibition in their written policies and procedures against this type of behavior. Their policies were incomplete without prescriptive ways to ensure this practice was not done. This is a gross departure from the standard of care and a typical root cause of data breaches that is embarrassing. The firm was fined US$100,000 and the individual management US$25,000 each.

Morgan Stanley was also made an example of in 2016. Morgan Stanley used internet portals where advisors could pull reports on customer income and holdings. There was a written policy in place prohibiting the use of information beyond the business need. In terms of the fair information practices, if you are given information you must disclose how you are going to use it for legitimate purposes. At Morgan Stanley, it is alleged the controls were not entirely effective because attackers got the reports without going through the controls. The controls were not tested or monitored for suspicious activity. Gailen March found and exploited the flaws in the controls, which was a criminal act. He amassed data on 730k customer accounts and uploaded it to a personal server that was hacked. The data then showed up on the dark web and then they had to disclose it to all of their customers. It was a complex pattern that showed the importance to test the controls and monitor your portals. These data sites must be very secure with granular controls and logging capabilities embedded in the tools so they will have a complete audit trail on who accessed, downloaded, or transferred data. In many instances, the off-boarding procedures when someone leaves the company were not adhered to and continued to have active credentials. This can provide competitors with easy access to privileged data.

Federal Trade Commission (FTC)

The ability to understand if a company where you are a shareholder has had a breach has changed over the past decade. In 2011, the basic rules were that if there was a material loss or the risk of a material loss that you did not have to disclose it. This was due to the financial function and the legal function not having the expertise and visibility into IT to make risk assessments that could signify a material loss. A big change at the FTC is to allow the business to have the right conversations and connections to understand cybersecurity.

Woodrow Wilson signed the Federal Trade Commission Act of 1914[11] to outlaw unfair methods of competition and unfair acts or practices that affect commerce. The inspiration and motivation for this act started in the late 19th century, when the Sherman Act was passed as part of an antitrust movement to prevent manufacturers from joining price-fixing cartels. After the case *Northern Securities Co. v. United States*, which dismantled a J. P. Morgan company, antitrust enforcement became institutionalized. Soon after, Roosevelt created the Bureau of Corporations, an agency that reported on the economy and businesses across U.S. industries. The Bureau of Corporations was the predecessor to the Federal Trade Commission. In 1913, President Wilson expanded the powers of this agency by signing the Federal Trade Commission's Act along with the Clayton Antitrust Act. The Federal Trade Commission Act focused on business reform to protect consumers against methods of deception in advertisement, forcing the business to be upfront and truthful about items being sold.

The Federal Trade Commission Act empowers the FTC to prevent unfair methods of competition, and unfair or deceptive acts or practices in or affecting commerce; seek monetary redress and other relief for conduct injurious to consumers; prescribe trade regulation rules defining with specificity acts or practices that are unfair or deceptive, and establishing requirements designed to prevent such acts or practices; conduct investigations relating to the organization, business, practices, and management of entities engaged in commerce; and make reports and legislative recommendations to Congress.

The US Federal Trade Commission acts in a dual capacity—as an anti-trust anti-authority. Consumer protection should be understood as a subset of anti-trust authority to prohibit tricksters gaining market share and revenue over competitors through illegal practices. In terms of cybersecurity, if a company is doing false advertising or tricking consumers by monetizing their data in unexpected ways this would come under the governance of the FTC. Facebook was fined US$5 billion for these types of business practices.

The FTC addresses deceptive practices and fraud. Deception is easy to understand. Deception is different than fraud. Fraud in the law has really specific elements. Fraud says I told you something, it was not true, you relied on it, it caused you harm, I can collect the damages and I did it on purpose. Deception is not a fraud. It has a much lower bar to prove. Deception is the tendency to mislead. It is an error of omission. In order to understand this transaction, I needed to be told particular things that I was not told at all.

The FTC focuses heavily on FAIR information practices and can use privacy policies as a lever. All companies must post privacy policies. It would be a deceptive or a nonfair practice if it were not posted. A privacy policy is really just a pledge of accountability. It is not a waiver. A waiver is when you want to go bungee jumping off a bridge and you say okay, I get it, I throw my body off of here and no matter what happens I cannot sue. A pledge says that as part of my fair information practice, you have the right to transparency and that the privacy policy is accurate, complete, and its fully implemented. The FTC is the authority that has become our data protection regulator, similar to what they have in Europe.

The FTC is really a political body, an independent agency of the federal government. It is not part of the Executive Branch itself. The president nominates and the Senate confirms the FTC commissioners. The FTC can be lobbied, just like big business lobbies senators for their votes on a bill.

The EU–US Privacy Shield Framework[12] provides a method for companies to transfer personal data to the United States from the European Union (EU) in a way that is consistent with EU law. To join the Privacy Shield Framework, a company must self-certify to the Department of Commerce that it complies with the Privacy Shield Principles. A company's failure to comply with the Principles is enforceable under Section 5 of the FTC Act prohibiting unfair and deceptive acts. The FTC has committed to make enforcement of the Framework a high priority and will work together with EU privacy authorities to protect consumer privacy on both sides of the Atlantic. The Framework replaces the US–EU Safe Harbor Program.

The Department of Commerce has created a Fact Sheet with an overview of the protections provided and how the program works. More detailed information is available at the Department of Commerce Privacy Shield Website.

Facebook and the FTC

The FTC's bold and unprecedented move to fine Facebook US$5 billion for its role in the Cambridge Analytica data breach has everyone's attention. Specifically, the FTC fined Facebook because it violated the law by failing to protect data from third parties. It also served up ads through the use of phone numbers that were provided for security authentication, and lied to users that its facial recognition software was turned off by default.

Facebook's FTC settlement is the largest fine ever levied for data privacy violations and contains an extraordinary remedial order which mandates the formation of a board-level privacy committee and rigorous privacy requirements, among other things. Let us look at how this monumental resolution, which had strong dissents from two FTC Commissioners, is shaping the data privacy enforcement climate, the specific obligations in the order and compliance takeaways.

The US$5-billion FTC Facebook settlement, is the largest and is preceded by the US$575-million FTC Equifax settlement and the announcement by the UK Information Commissioner's Office (ICO) of GBP 183 million fine on British Airways following data breaches. These fines have changed the enforcement landscape for data privacy and data security for years to come indicating a new era of aggressive data privacy and data security enforcement on both sides of the pond.

The Equifax and Facebook cases together are milestones that accompany a new era for the FTC in flexing its muscle in privacy and data security matters. There is an increasing awareness by the government and the general public of the ginormous power of big data and the associated potential for misuse and harm—making this just the tip of the iceberg. We are going to see more enforcement actions down the line, whether from the FTC or other agencies.

The FTC Order is centered around Facebook's violation of a previous 2012 Order. It charges violations of Section 5 of the FTC Act and among other things, requires Facebook to adopt policies and procedures going forward that will be costly and require a major change in culture. The top dog at Facebook answered "I don't know" countless times in his two days of congressional hearings. The disgust was obvious when Rep Debbie Dingel (D-MI) said, "As CEO, you didn't know some key facts," toward the end of the second day of Zuckerberg's Congressional hearings.

Facebook has to change their policy and procedures regarding representations of data use, sharing of nonpublic user information, the deletion of certain information, use of telephone numbers given for multi-factor authentication purposes, enhanced security around passwords, and new facial recognition templates. It also mandates Facebook implement a rigorous privacy program and be subject to independent privacy program assessments, establish a board-level committee for privacy and the provide honest reporting of certain incidents to the FTC.

SEC Commissioners Rohit Chopra and Rebecca Kelly Slaughter each wrote strong dissenting arguments that the Order did not go far enough in terms of the fine or the remedial measures and was just a slap on the wrist to a law scoffing company with outsized global influence and revenue. They also noted that there was no individual liability in the face of insurmountable evidence of cybersecurity neglect. "Facebook's officers and directors were legally bound to ensure compliance with the 2012 Order, yet the proposed settlement grants a gift of immunity for their failure to do so," Chopra wrote.[13]

The criticism of the settlement reveals that there is appetite for even more robust fines and stricter requirements. The next arena, however, may be Congress.

I often frequently hear privacy and cybersecurity professionals lament the lack of consolidated guidance in the US around acceptable data privacy practices.

This case demonstrates the heightened awareness around data privacy and presents a good opportunity to sell boards on the importance of strong privacy programs. It is good to see that both the FTC and SEC are making it clear that their patience with misleading data privacy and usage practices has run its course. Privacy is the new order of the day, and it is now on the agenda of executives and boards.

The FTC Order resolves all claims related to Facebook's alleged violation of the 2012 consent order. Another issue with the order is that the settlement agreements cover conduct not specifically related to the privacy allegations at hand. The idea that there can be a settlement that provides immunity for unidentified misconduct has never been seen. The remedial steps in the Order are now the most stringent privacy program in the world.

The Order establishes a new framework for FTC settlements and provides a model for what the FTC would consider to be a strong privacy program for businesses that engage in processing and storing large amounts of personal data.

Since Facebook is a repeat offender, the many elements of the Order are not new. Requirements for Facebook to be honest with its users in how it uses their data was always a requirement. The Order requires that Facebook not misrepresent, "expressly or by implication," its maintenance of the security and privacy of "Covered Information," as the Complaint charges that it did in the past. Covered Information includes geolocation information sufficient that is used to identify a street name and name of city or town, IP addresses, User IDs, or other persistent unique identifier data that can be combined to identify a user over time and across different devices.[14]

Facebook cannot mislead users about the extent to which a consumer can control the privacy of their data and the steps to implement those privacy controls, and to which third parties their data is accessible and to what degree.

The Order prohibits Facebook from sharing the nonpublic information of a user with a third party without clear and conspicuous disclosure and affirmative express consent.

The Order states that Facebook must ensure that the information that a user requested to be deleted is not available to a third party within 30 days of deletion and that data that Facebook controls is deleted or de-identified within 120 days.

Facebook must only use phone numbers provided for a security purpose as prescribed and not to sell advertisements or share the number with third parties for purposes other than what the person has agreed to.

Facebook's fate

The FTC has mandated a rigorous privacy program for Facebook. Facebook must implement the privacy program within 180 days of the Order. Requirements include:

- **Document the Program.** Produce written documentation of the program details, implementation, and maintenance that are overseen by the Chief Executive Officer (Mark Zuckerberg) and an Independent Privacy Committee that will function at the board-level at least once a year.
- **Create an Independent Committee.** Create an Independent Privacy Committee which is to receive a quarterly report about the privacy program and meet quarterly with Security Assessors.
- **Hire an independent Chief Privacy Officer.** Ensure employment of a designated employee(s), as a "Chief Privacy Officer for Product" (CPO), to run the privacy program. Oversight of the CPO will be from the Independent Privacy Committee.
- **Conduct Annual Risk Assessments.** Formalize a written risk assessment program that will assess privacy risks at least annually. This includes internal and external risk categories and third-party privacy risk.
- **Third Party Incident Response Plan.** Provide a written and tested incident response plan that provides within 30 days an assessment and mitigation in cases where Facebook has verified that the privacy data of 500 or more users was accessed, collected, used, or shared by a third party in violation of Facebook's terms. This includes annual third-party certifications, and monitoring and enforcement against third parties that violate contract terms
- **Product Risk.** Conduct privacy review of new products services or practices, that produce a detailed written report about any privacy risks and safeguards that are being used to mitigate these risks.

- **Privacy Reviews.** Produce a quarterly report from the CPO to the CEO of these reviews and all privacy decisions, in advance of meetings of the Independent Privacy Commission
- **Access Controls.** Ensure that controls that limit employee access to Covered Information and that protect information shared with affiliates are in place.
- **Consent.** Provide for disclosure and consent for face recognition software.
- **Implement Privacy Training Programs.** Establish regular employee and contractor privacy training programs.
- **Engage the Use of Outside Experts.** Seek program guidance from independent third parties on how to design, develop, and maintain the privacy program.
- **Monitor the Program.** Monitor and evaluate the program annually.

Many of the requirements are aligned to the principle of privacy by design. GDPR has requirements for privacy by design, however at this time there are not regulations in the US that address that principle. It stands to reason that this type of requirements will be enacted into US privacy law and any firm that is collecting, processing, or using PII should use the most stringent aspects of requirements to avoid redundancy and high costs.

This Order should act as a warning for any company that uses consumer data. Implementing these types of program provisions will be costly. The Order requires biennial assessments from independent third-party professionals (Security Assessors) with the initial assessment due in 180 days after the mandated privacy program is put into place and then once every two years for 20 years. The Security Assessors must ensure that they did not rely primary on assertions or attestations made by Facebook's management.

The CEO and other Facebook Officers must sign the privacy certifications annually. Facebook must submit a report to the Security Assessor and to the FTC within 30 days after a Privacy Incident and follow up every 30 days until the incident is fully remediated.

One of the most glaring aspects of the Facebook Data Breach was the lack of governance. In addition to the creation of an Independent Privacy Committee, the level of board involvement is the key part of the settlement and demonstrates the FTC's tone at the top structural requirements.

In 2018, the SEC provided guidance for public companies to prioritize cybersecurity and bake it into their business functions at the board level. Privacy, risk, compliance, and cybersecurity are interdependent functions. Privacy has to be understood in context of cybersecurity not as a separate domain.

The FTC Chairman Joe Simons said the settlement is "unprecedented in the history of the FTC" and is designed "to change Facebook's entire privacy culture to decrease the likelihood of continued violations."[15]

The FTC Order will require major structural changes at Facebook. On the positive side, privacy programs will increase the value of Facebook's offerings by protecting its key asset—data.

Wyndham Worldwide—security, the FTC's role

The first company to challenge the FTC was Wyndham Worldwide, a hospitality company that franchises and manages hotels and sells timeshares. It also licensed its brand name to 90 independently owned hotels. Its computer network is in Phoenix, Arizona which connects its data center with the property management systems of each of the Wyndham-branded hotels.

Wyndham filed a motion to dismiss an FTC complaint that cited weak data security practices which led to three data breaches. The motion was dismissed on August 25th, 2015. This decision is noteworthy since it makes clear that the FTC is the "top cop" regulatory agency looking over privacy and security practices of private business. This marked the understanding that the FTC is here to stay in the data privacy and security space.

The Commission has regulated privacy and cybersecurity practices for years through its authority, under Section 5 of the FTC Act, to regulate "unfair or deceptive" acts or trade practices. Using that authority, the Commission has brought more than 200 enforcement actions against companies involving data privacy or security practices. Wyndham was one of the first regulated companies to challenge the FTC's authority in the cybersecurity and data privacy areas, and had Wyndham prevailed, the FTC would likely have had to look to Congress to restore its power to regulate in the space.

Companies typically settle these cases in the early stages, so no federal appellate court has ever had a chance to weigh in on whether Section 5 of the FTC Act[16] actually gives the FTC the authority to "regulate" data privacy and security. The Third Circuit Court of Appeals (Court) has now said that it can. The decision is a significant victory for the FTC, which has now had its authority to regulate data privacy and cybersecurity affirmed by a federal court of appeals.

The FTC alleged that Wyndham Worldwide and its subsidiaries had serious cybersecurity deficiencies which without a doubt had unnecessarily exposed consumers' personal data to unauthorized access and theft. The FTC claims that the deficiencies included, for example, the storage of payment card information in clear readable text and the use of easily-guessed passwords. Among the other allegations are that Wyndham failed to: use firewalls between the property management systems and the corporate network; update information security policies; restrict the access of third-party vendors to its network; employ measures to detect and prevent unauthorized access to its network; and follow incident response procedures to prevent the same malware from being used in a subsequent attack.[17]

In 2008 and 2009, Wyndham suffered three data breaches. In the first breach, in April 2008, hackers broke into the local network of a hotel in Phoenix and used the "brute-force method—repeatedly guessing users' login IDs and passwords—to access an administrator account in Wyndham's network," the Court said. The hackers were able to obtain unencrypted information for over 500,000 accounts which they sent to a domain in Russia.

The second attack was in March 2009, when hackers accessed Wyndham's network through an administrative account. Wyndham found out about the attack two months later when consumers filed complaints about fraudulent credit card charges. Wyndham then discovered that memory scraping malware that was used in the previous attack was present on the computer systems in more than 30 hotels. The FTC claims this was the result of insufficient incident response plans. In this second attack, hackers obtained payment card information for approximately 50,000 consumers.

The third attack, in late 2009, was the result of Wyndham's failure to limit access between the hotel's property management systems, Wyndham's network and the internet, the FTC says. The hackers had access to the servers of multiple hotels and obtained payment card information for about 69,000 consumers. Again, Wyndham only learned of the intrusion when consumers complained of fraudulent charges to credit card companies in 2010.

The FTC says that the breach resulted in at least US$10.6 million in fraud loss, plus financial injury because of consumers' "unreimbursed fraudulent charges, increased costs, and lost access to funds or credit" and also that consumers "expended time and money resolving fraudulent charges and mitigating subsequent harm."

Wyndham moved to dismiss the complaint and the New Jersey court denied that motion. The Third Circuit granted an interlocutory appeal on two issues—(1) whether the FTC has the authority to regulate cybersecurity under the unfairness prong of 15 USC §45(a); and (2) if so, whether Wyndham had fair notice that its specific cybersecurity practices could fall short of that provision.

The Court noted that though the FTC's deception claim was not before them on the appeal, the FTC also alleged that Wyndham published a privacy policy on its website that "overstates the company's cybersecurity."

The Court rejected all of Wyndham's arguments that its behavior did not fall under the unfairness prong of the FTC Act—15 USC §45(a).

The Court held that unfair conduct does not need to be unscrupulous or unethical. As for Wyndham's argument that a practice is only unfair if it is not equitable, the Court said, "A company does not act equitably when it publishes a privacy policy to attract customers who are concerned about data privacy, fails to make good on that promise by investing inadequate resources in cybersecurity, exposes its unsuspecting customers to substantial financial injury, and retains the profits of their business."[18]

The fact that Wyndham was a victim of the breaches does not insulate it from the FTC complaint, the Court said. "[T]hat a company's conduct was not *the most* proximate cause of an injury generally does not immunize liability from foreseeable harms," the Court said (emphasis in original), noting that the second and third breaches were foreseeable.

It also held that an unfairness claim may also be brought on the basis of likely rather than actual injury. "This is a significant holding," Gottlieb said, "because it means that the FTC has authority to bring data privacy and security actions against companies even where no actual harm to consumers has been shown, which makes the FTC's reach more expansive than lawsuits that could be filed, for example, by class action plaintiffs."

The Court disposed of Wyndham's other arguments such as the idea that "fairness" under §45(a) does not encompass cybersecurity because of subsequent legislation that does, such as the Fair Credit Reporting Act and the Children's Online Privacy Act.

One of the most egregious portions of the opinion, which involved Wyndham's slippery slope argument that if the FTC could regulate Wyndham's data security practices, then the FTC could regulate locks on hotel doors, require armed guards at hotel doors and could sue supermarkets that are "sloppy about sweeping up banana peels."[19]

The Court said: "The argument is alarmist to say the least. And it invites the tart retort that, were Wyndham a supermarket, leaving so many banana peels all over the place that 619,000 customers fall hardly suggests it should be immune from liability under 45(a)."[20]

Wyndham also argued that notwithstanding whether its conduct was unfair, the FTC failed to give fair notice of the specific cybersecurity standards needed by the company. The Court said that "Wyndham was not entitled to know with ascertainable certainty the FTC's interpretation of what cybersecurity practices are required by §45(a)" but it was entitled to "fair notice that its conduct could fall within the meaning of the statue."

This level of notice required is low, the Court said, because the FTC Act is a civil statute that regulates economic activities—and businesses are expected to "consult relevant legislation in advance of action."

Gottlieb said that it is significant that "the Third Circuit was unpersuaded by Wyndham's argument that the FTC was required to define with clarity its standards for what constitutes reasonable data privacy and security practices."

He added, "In particular, the Court noted that the availability of previous consent decrees offered fair notice to Wyndham regarding the type of conduct that rises to the level of an unfair or deceptive data security practice. Companies seeking clarity on the types of practices that might lead to FTC investigation or enforcement actions would therefore be well advised to pay attention to FTC consent decrees as they are released."

"This entire action now moves back to the District Court to continue the trial on the merits," Larose said, "and that is where we will see the real takeaways. The litigation will now focus on whether Wyndham's actions directly contributed to not one or two hacks, but three, and we may see some further specificity and clarity on the ground rules for 'reasonable' or 'adequate' cybersecurity litigated in a court and not in consent decrees or settlement agreements."

A company spokesman for Wyndham, Michael Valentino, told *Reuters* that "safeguarding personal information remains a top priority" for Wyndham. "We believe the facts will show the FTC's allegations are unfounded."

In its statement,[21] the FTC lauded the victory. "Today's Third Circuit Court of Appeals decision reaffirms the FTC's authority to hold companies accountable for failing to safeguard consumer data," FTC Chairwoman Edith Ramirez said. "It is not only appropriate, but critical, that the FTC has the ability to take action on behalf of consumers when companies fail to take reasonable steps to secure sensitive consumer information."[22]

Lab MD—an FTC defeat

In July of 2015, the FTC suffered its first loss in a data breach security case. In the first such case to reach a full adjudication, an administrative law judge dismissed the agency's complaint against LabMD, Inc. regarding two alleged cybersecurity incidents at LabMD. The Administrative Law Judge (ALJ) held, in a lengthy Initial Decision, that the FTC did not meet its burden on the first prong of the three-part test in Section 5(n) of the FTC Act—that LabMD's conduct caused, or is likely to cause, substantial consumer injury.

Section 5(n) of the FTC Act provides that a practice can be deemed "unfair" if: 1) the act or practice causes or is likely to cause substantial injury to consumers; 2) the injury is not reasonably avoidable by consumers themselves; and 3) the injury is not outweighed by countervailing benefits to consumers or to competition.[23]

The FTC filed an unfairness claim against LabMD in connection with two security incidents regarding files containing personal information of LabMD customers.

In October 2012, the ALJ said that the Sacramento Police Department found paper copies of "day sheets"[24] containing personal information of LabMD customers, as well as copied checks and a money order payable to LabMD in the possession of individuals who later pleaded guilty to identity theft. The FTC claimed that the discovery of this information showed the insufficient data security practices of LabMD. The ALJ said that the FTC failed to show how LabMD's data practices led to the disclosure of the information.[25]

This cancer testing lab is now closed. The CEO who owned it wrote a book criticizing the FTC. One of the employees in 2008 used peer to peer downloading software that allowed a vulnerability to be exploited and leaked patient files. LabMD found out about it by a security vendor called Diversa. Diversa discovered it and asked to be hired to clean it up. The CEO of the lab says he was blackmailed into allowing Diversa to clean it up or else they would have told the regulators. Diversa sought revenge and went to the FTC anyway. The FTC went after LabMD. The FTC realized they could not call any witnesses because both sides were biased.

LifeLock-identity protection gone wrong

LifeLock Inc. is an American identity theft protection company that provides a system that monitors for identity theft, the use of personal information, and credit score changes.

LifeLock was ordered to a US$100 million settlement by the Federal Trade Commission for contempt charges where it violated the terms of a 2010 federal court order that required the company to secure consumers' personal information and prohibits the company from deceptive advertising. At the time, this was the largest monetary award obtained by the Commission in an order enforcement action.

"This settlement demonstrates the Commission's commitment to enforcing the orders it has in place against companies, including orders requiring reasonable security for consumer data," said FTC Chairwoman Edith Ramirez. "The fact that consumers paid LifeLock for help in protecting their sensitive personal information makes the charges in this case particularly troubling."

LifeLock violated several components of the 2010 order including that LifeLock failed to establish and maintain a comprehensive information security program to protect users' sensitive personal information, including their social security, credit card, and bank account numbers, falsely advertised that it protected consumers' sensitive data with the same high-level safeguards used by financial institutions, and falsely advertised that it would send alerts "as soon as" it received any indication that a consumer may be a victim of identity theft.

Under the terms of the 2015 settlement, LifeLock is required to deposit US$100 million into the registry of the US District Court for the District of Arizona.

Federal Communications Commission (FCC)

On November 5, 2015, the Federal Communications Commission's Enforcement Bureau has entered a US$595,000 settlement with Cox Communications. The settlement is to resolve an investigation into whether the company failed to properly protect its customers' personal information when the company's electronic data systems were breached in 2014. As a result, third parties had access to the personal information of Cox's subscribers. Cox has approximately six million subscribers nationwide.[26]

This action represents the FCC's first privacy and data security enforcement action with a cable operator. "Cable companies have a wealth of sensitive information about us, from our credit card numbers to our pay-per-view selections," said Enforcement Bureau Chief Travis LeBlanc. "This investigation shows the real harm that can be done by a digital identity thief with enough information to change your passwords, lock you out of your own accounts, post your personal data on the web, and harass you through social media. We appreciate that Cox will now take robust steps to keep their customers' information safe online and off."

The Enforcement Bureau's investigation found that Cox's electronic data systems were breached in August 2014 by a hacker that pretended to be from Cox's information technology department and convinced both a Cox customer service representative and Cox contractor to enter their account IDs and passwords into a fake, or "phishing," website. With those stolen credentials, the hacker gained unauthorized access to Cox customers' PII. The hacker then posted some customers' information on social media sites, changed some customers' account passwords, and shared the compromised account credentials with other cybercriminals.

The FCC found that, at the time of the breach, Cox's data security systems did not include basic controls that might have prevented the use of the compromised credentials. Cox never reported the breach to the FCC as required by law.

The settlement requires Cox to identify all affected customers, notify them of the data breach, and provide one year of free credit monitoring services to those affected. Additionally, Cox must adopt a comprehensive cybersecurity program that includes annual system audits, internal threat monitoring, and penetration testing. The FTC will monitor Cox's compliance for seven years.

Data breach notification laws

State governments

All states require notification where there is a reasonable likelihood of unauthorized acquisition of personal information of state residents. All states have specific notification requirements. Most are 72 hours; however, Colorado is the most aggressive with a 30-hour window for notification.

Federal government

Federal notification requirements are sector-specific (HIPAA, GLBA). Uniform federal notification requirements have been proposed but not adopted yet.

EU General Data Protection Regulation (2018 effective date)

Requires notification of relevant data protection authority within 72 hours for any breach of "personal data," except if breach is unlikely to result in risk to personal rights/freedoms. Notification to individuals must be made "without undue delay."

Key concepts that determine enforcement

The following are key areas that will determine if the FTC or other agency will act to enforce. Having these requirements will be helpful to prevent enforcement actions.

Digital Asset Inventory: A digital asset inventory is a security requirement that allows you to know what consumer information the company has and which employees or third-parties have access to it.

Minimization: Limiting the data a company collects and retains based on legitimate business needs to minimize extraordinary exposures.

Formal Program: The program should afford the ability to protect the information by assessing risks and implementing protections in certain key areas—physical security, electronic security, employee training, and oversight of service providers.

Deletion: The ability to properly dispose of information after it is no longer needed.

Manage Breaches: Having a plan in place to respond to security incidents, should they occur.

Discretion not to enforce

There are many instances where the regulatory body will not sue. These include:

- Where there were isolated errors with unexpected, inadvertent consequences to security.
- In cases of malicious attack involving great sophistication (actually fairly rare).
- The events were not foreseeable.
- The risks were insignificant relative to other risks requiring mitigation.
- Prompt attention to third party reports of vulnerabilities was paid.
- There was a lack of access/use of exploitable personal information (no harm).
- There was no over-promising to consumers.

Considerations impacting the decision to investigate/sue

Other considerations that the regulatory body will look at include:

- Was the risk foreseeable at the time of the compromise?
- What is the nature/magnitude of the event relative to other risks that required mitigation?
- What were costs/benefits to protecting against the event?
- Were overall data security practices reasonable?

- What was the duration/scope of the compromise?
- What is the level of consumer injury?
- What type of information was disclosed without authorization?
- What was the overall response to the incident (timely, accurate notice, credit monitoring, and restitution?)

Notes

1. Wikipedia, "FTC fair information practice", March 9, 2020. https://en.wikipedia.org/wiki/FTC_fair_information_practice.
2. Wikipedia, "FTC fair information practice", December 4, 2020, https://en.wikipedia.org/wiki/FTC_fair_information_practice.
3. Federal Trade Commission, "Gramm-Leach-Bliley Act", July 2, 2002, https://www.ftc.gov/tips-advice/business-center/privacy-and-security/gramm-leach-bliley-act.
4. CDC, "Health Insurance Portability and Accountability Act of 1996 (HIPPA)", September 14, 2018, https://www.cdc.gov/phlp/publications/topic/hipaa.html.
5. C. Lee Ventola, P&T, "Mobile devices and apps for health care professionals: Uses and benefits," May 2014, https://www.ncbi.nlm.nih.gov/pmc/articles/PMC4029126/#:~:text=The%20June%202012%20Manhattan%20Research,99%25%20who%20use%20a%20computer.
6. Sue Montgomery, Working Nurse, "Nurses using smartphones and tablets at work", 2020, https://www.workingnurse.com/articles/Nurses-Using-Smartphones-and-Tablets-at-Work#:~:text=THE%20BYOD%20TREND&text=Spyglass%20found%20that%20nurses%20at,their%20personal%20smartphones%20for%20work.
7. U.S. Securities and Exchange Commission, "Office of Compliance Inspections and Examinations", April 16, 2020, https://www.sec.gov/ocie.
8. U.S. Securities and Exchange Commission, "SEC adopts statement and interpretive guidance on public company cybersecurity disclosures", February 21, 2018, https://www.sec.gov/news/press-release/2018-22.
9. U.S. Security and Exchange Commission, "SEC adopts statement and interpretive guidance on public company cybersecurity disclosures", February 21, 2018, https://www.sec.gov/news/press-release/2018-22.
10. U.S. Securities and exchange commission, "Regulation S-P", June 22, 2000, https://www.sec.gov/spotlight/regulation-s-p.htm.
11. Britannica, "Federal Trade Commission Act 1914," 2020, https://www.britannica.com/event/Federal-Trade-Commission-Act.
12. Privacy Shield Framework, "Privacy shield overview", 2020, https://www.privacyshield.gov/Program-Overview.
13. Siva Vaidhyanathan, The Guardian, "Billion-dollar fines can't stop Google and Facebook. That's peanuts for them", July 26, 2019, https://www.theguardian.com/commentisfree/2019/jul/26/google-facebook-regulation-ftc-settlement.
14. Rebecca Hughes, Cybersecurity Law Report, "How Facebook's $%-billion FTC settlement is shaping compliance expectations", August 8, 2019, https://www.huntonak.com/images/content/5/8/v2/58734/How%20Facebooks%205-Billion%20FTC%20Settlement%20Is%20Shaping%20Compliance%20Exp.pdf.
15. Marcy Gordon and Barbara Ortutay, The Washington Times, "FTC fines Facebook $5B, adds oversight for privacy mishaps", July 24, 2019, https://www.washingtontimes.com/news/2019/jul/24/ftc-fines-facebook-5b-adds-oversight-for-privacy-m/.
16. FederalReserve.gov, "Federal Trade Commission Act Section 5: Unfair or deceptive acts or practices", 2020, https://www.federalreserve.gov/boarddocs/supmanual/cch/ftca.pdf.

17. Smith Debnam Narron Drake Saintsing & Meyers LLP, Lexology, "Lessons to be learned from Wyndham Hotels data breach", February 2, 2016, https://www.lexology.com/library/detail.aspx?g=4e7666a0-72b6-413b-b444-62d07426a71c.
18. Jason N. Smolanoff, Kroll, "Do not forget about privacy", February 21, 2019, https://www.kroll.com/en/insights/publications/cyber/tips-company-cyber-enforcement/do-not-forget-about-privacy.
19. Dykema, "Hard lessons from the Wyndham decision: What businesses must know about the FTC's authority to regulate data security", September 1, 2015, https://www.dykema.com/resources-alerts-hard-lessons-from-the-wyndham-decision_09-01-2015.html.
20. U.S. court affirms FTC authority to enforce data breach rules. https://www.eweek.com/security/u.s.-court-affirms-ftc-authority-to-enforce-data-breach-rules.
21. Federal Trade Commission, "Statement from FTC chairwoman Edith Ramirez on appellate ruling in the Wyndham Hotels and Resorts matter", August 24, 2015, https://www.ftc.gov/news-events/press-releases/2015/08/statement-ftc-chairwoman-edith-ramirez-appellate-ruling-wyndham.
22 Federal Trade Commission, "Statement from FTC Chairwoman Edith Ramirez on Appellate Ruling in the Wyndham Hotels and Resorts Matter", August 24, 2015, https://www.ftc.gov/news-events/press-releases/2015/08/statement-ftc-chairwoman-edith-ramirez-appellate-ruling-wyndham.
23. Joe Shapiro, White and Williams, LLP, "Administrative law judge rules against FTC in Data Security Enforcement Action" November 19, 2015, https://www.whiteandwilliams.com/resources-alerts-Administrative-Law-Judge-Rules-Against-FTC-in-Data-Security-Enforcement-Action.html.
24. Federal Trade Commission, "United States of America before the Federal Trade Commission", September 21, 2016, https://www.ftc.gov/system/files/documents/cases/160921labmdoppsurreply.pdf.
25. Federal Trade Commission, "FTC files complaint against LabMD for failing to protect Consumer's privacy", August 29, 2013, https://www.ftc.gov/news-events/press-releases/2013/08/ftc-files-complaint-against-labmd-failing-protect-consumers.
26. Federal Communications Commission, "Cox Communications to pay $595,000 to settle data breach investigation", November 5, 2015, https://www.fcc.gov/document/cox-communications-pay-595000-settle-data-breach-investigation#:~:text=Cox%20Communications%20to%20Pay%20%24595%2C000,Breach%20Investigation%20%7C%20Federal%20Communications%20Commission.

16 US STATE REGULATIONS

California and New York adopted sweeping cybersecurity regulations, and more states are following. Increasingly concerned about data privacy, hacking and fraud, organizations must now meet a duty of care for reasonable cybersecurity.

JT Jacoby, CISO, International Rescue Committee

US privacy laws

In the US at the state level, the impetus for comprehensive privacy bills is in full gear. As of this writing, over half the states have some level of privacy legislation in the works. This comes on the heels of the California Consumer Privacy Act that was passed in 2018.[1] The International Association of Privacy Professionals (IAPPs) Westin Research Center[2] has compiled research for each state's privacy laws and proposed comprehensive privacy bills from across the US and updates this to stay up to date of the changing state-privacy landscape as new legislation is passed or proposed.

Many of the bills being considered will not pass the legislative process to become law. Each state has the ability to craft legislation that differs in terms of data elements, breach notification timelines, and a host of other provisions regarding the use and collection of privacy data. Doing a state-by-state comparison of the key provisions in each bill needs to be understood to scope privacy security requirements properly. IAPP does not report on bills that are voted down or die in committee.

IAPP has identified 17 provisions that commonly appear in comprehensive privacy statutes. The 17 common privacy provisions are broken into two categories—9 relate to consumer rights and 8 relate to business obligations. Let's explain the legislative process that will be helpful in dissecting state privacy regulatory status.

Each state legislature has a unique legislative calendar and different legislative procedures; this set of columns generalizes those different legislative procedures into six categories:[3]

- Introduced—A bill has been introduced on a legislative chamber floor but has not yet moved into committee.
- In Committee—A bill is moving through the various committees in its chamber of origin.
- Crossed Chamber—A bill has passed a vote in its chamber of origin and moved to the opposite chamber of the legislature (e.g., a state house of representatives passed a bill and it moved to the state senate).

DOI: 10.4324/9781003052616-20

- Cross Committee—A bill is moving through the various committees in its nonoriginating chamber.
- Passed—Both chambers of the legislature have passed the bill.
- Signed—The governor signed the bill and it is now law.

State	Legislative Process	Statute/Bill (Hyperlinks)	Common Name	Consumer Rights									Business Obligations							
				To Access to Collected	To Access to Shared	To Rectification	To Deletion	To Restriction	To Portability	To Opt-Out	Against Solely Automated Decision Making	Private Right of Action	Strict Age-based Opt-In	Notice/Transparency Requirement	Data Breach Notification	Risk Assessment	Prohibition on Discrimination	Purpose Limitation	Processing Limitation	Fiduciary Duty
California		**Ca. Civ. Code §§ 1798.100 - .199**	**California Consumer Privacy Act**	**x**	**x**		**x**		**x**	**x**		**s**	**16**	**x**			**x**			
~~*Connecticut*~~		~~*HB 1108/SB 1108*~~																		
Hawaii		*SB 418*[i]		*x*	*x*		*x*		*x*	*x*			*16*	*x*	*x*		*x*			
~~*Hawaii*~~		~~*HCR 225*~~																		
Illinois		*HB 3358*	*Data Transparency and Privacy Act*		*x*					*x*				*x*						
~~*Louisiana*~~		~~*HR 249*~~																		
Maine		**LD 946**[ii]	**An Act To Protect the Privacy of Online Consumer Information**					**x**		**in**				**x**			**x**			
~~*Maryland*~~		~~*SB 613*~~	~~*Online Consumer Protection Act*~~	~~*x*~~	~~*x*~~		~~*x*~~		~~*x*~~	~~*x*~~				~~*x*~~			~~*x*~~			
Massachusetts		*SD 341/S 120*		*x*	*x*		*x*		*x*	*x*		*x*	*18*	*x*			*x*			
Minnesota		*HF 2917/SF 2912*		*x*	*x*	*x*	*x*	*x*	*x*	*x*	*x*			*x*		*x*			*x*	
Nevada		**SB 220/Chapter 603A**								**x**				**x**	**x**					

Image 16.1 Privacy Provisions[4]

State	Legislative Process	Statute/Bill (Hyperlinks)	Common Name	To Access to Collected	To Access to Shared	To Rectification	To Deletion	To Restriction	To Portability	To Opt-Out	Against Solely Automated Decision Making	Private Right of Action	Strict Age-based Opt-In	Notice/Transparency Requirement	Data Breach Notification	Risk Assessment	Prohibition on Discrimination	Purpose Limitation	Processing Limitation	Fiduciary Duty
New Jersey		*S2834*			*x*					*x*				*x*			*x*			
~~*New Mexico*~~		~~*SB 176*~~	~~*Consumer Information Privacy Act*~~	~~*x*~~	~~*x*~~		~~*x*~~		~~*x*~~	~~*x*~~		~~*s*~~	~~*18*~~	~~*x*~~			~~*x*~~			
New York		*SB S5642*[iii]	*New York Privacy Act*	*x*	*x*	*x*	*x*	*x*	*x*	*x*	*x*	*x*		*x*	*x*				*x*	*x*
~~*North Dakota*~~		~~*HB 1485*~~																		
Pennsylvania		*HB 1049*	*Consumer Data Privacy Act*	*x*	*x*		*x*			*x*		*s*	*16*	*x*			*x*			
Rhode Island		*HB 5930/S0234*	*Consumer Privacy Protection Act*	*x*	*x*		*x*		*x*	*x*		*x*	*16*	*x*			*x*			
~~*Texas*~~		~~*HB 4390*[iv]~~	~~*Texas Privacy Protection Act*~~																	
Washington		*SB 5376*	*Washington Privacy Act*	*x*	*x*	*x*	*x*	*x*	*x*	*x*	*x*			*x*	*x*	*x*				

In Session: MA, NJ, PA

Introduced / In Committee / Crossed Chamber / Cross Committee / Passed / Signed

Bold - passed law
Italics - proposed bill, not passed
s - private right of action for security violations only
in - opt-in consent requirement
~~Black strikethrough - bill postponed indefinitely~~
~~Purple strikethrough - task force substituted for comprehensive bill~~

[i] Hawaii SB 418 is pending while the task force has been adopted.
[ii] Maine LD 946 applies only to internet service providers.
[iii] New York SB S5642 includes a broad consumer right to opt-out of any processing, not just the sale of personal information.
[iv] Texas HB 4390 is a GDPR-style restriction-based bill that prohibits a business from collecting or processing information except under certain circumstances.

Legislative Process: Introduced > In Committee > Crossed Chamber > Cross Committee > Passed > Signed

iapp **Last updated: 10/15/2019**

Image 16.2 Legislative Process[5]

The consumer rights common privacy provisions align to new privacy legislation and the GDPR. These include the following:[6]

- **The right of access to personal information collected**—The right for a consumer to access from a business or data controller the information collected, or categories of information collected about the consumer. This right may only exist if a business sells information to a third party.
- **The right of access to personal information shared with a third party**—The right for a consumer to access personal information shared with third parties.
- **The right to rectification**—The right for a consumer to request that incorrect or outdated personal information be corrected or updated, but not deleted.
- **The right to deletion**—The right for a consumer to request deletion of personal information about the consumer under certain conditions.
- **The right to restriction of processing**—The right for a consumer to restrict a business's ability to process personal information about the consumer.
- **The right to data portability**—The right for a consumer to request personal information about the consumer be disclosed in a common file format.
- **The right to opt out of the sale of personal information**—The right for a consumer to opt out of the sale of personal information about the consumer to third parties.
- **The right against solely automated decision making**—A prohibition against a business making decisions about a consumer-based solely on an automated process without human input.
- **A consumer private right of action**—The right for a consumer to seek civil damages from a business for violations of a statute.

Business obligations

- **A strict opt-in for the sale of personal information of a consumer less than a certain age**—A restriction placed on a business to treat consumers under a certain age with an opt-in default for the sale of their personal information.
- **Notice/transparency requirements**—An obligation placed on a business to provide notice to consumers about certain data practices, privacy operations, and/or privacy programs.
- **Data breach notification**—An obligation placed on a business to notify consumers and/or enforcement authorities about a privacy or security breach.
- **Mandated risk assessment**—An obligation placed on a business to conduct formal risk assessments of privacy and/or security projects or procedures.

- **A prohibition on discrimination against a consumer for exercising a right**—A prohibition against a business treating a consumer who exercises a consumer right differently than a consumer who does not exercise a right.
- **A purpose limitation**—An EU General Data Protection Regulation-style restrictive structure that prohibits the collection of personal information except for a specific purpose.
- **A processing limitation**—A GDPR-style restrictive structure that prohibits the processing of personal information except for a specific purpose.
- **Fiduciary duty**—An obligation imposed on a business/controller to exercise the duties of care, loyalty, and confidentiality (or similar) and act in the best interest of the consumer.

CCPA

The California Consumer Privacy Act (CCPA)[7] is a state statute intended to enhance privacy rights and consumer protection for residents of California. The bill was signed into law by Jerry Brown, the Governor of California, on June 28, 2018. The office name of the bill is AB-375. The CCPA became effective on January 1, 2020.

The Act sets forth provisions for California residents who have the right to:

- know which data elements are being collected about them;
- know if their personal data is being sold and to whom;
- know if their personal data is being disclosed and to whom;
- opt out of the sale of personal data;
- have access to review their personal data for accuracy;
- request that their personal data is deleted; and
- ensure that they are not discriminated against for exercising their privacy rights.

The CCPA applies to any business that collects California consumers' personal information, does business in the state of California, and satisfies at least one of these three minimum thresholds:

- Annual gross revenues are in excess of US$25 million.
- Buys or sells the personal data of 50,000 or more either consumers, households or both.
- Makes more than half of its annual revenue by selling California consumers' personal data.

Under CCPA, organizations are required to "implement and maintain reasonable security procedures and practices" in protecting consumer data.

If a business is collecting California consumer data, the law does not apply if the entire transactional process took place outside of California, no sale of the consumer data occurred in California, and no PII was collected from the consumer in California.

This law applies to brick and mortar and online businesses. The law expressly says it is "not limited to information collected electronically or over the Internet, but [the law applies] to the collection and sale of all personal information collected by a business from consumers." This definition is overly expansive and applies to almost all businesses (offline or on). The IAPP has (conservatively) estimated that over a half-million businesses are regulated by the law, "the vast majority of which are small- to medium-sized enterprises."[8]

CCPA was meant to be for a colossus like Google and Facebook, however small businesses have to adhere to the same requirements as these giants. The issue here is that the law applies to any business that "receives...the personal information of" 50k+ consumers. This includes the "receipt" of credit cards. The 50k threshold is meet by any business that has an average of 137 unique credit card sales per day. This would put many restaurants, coffee shops, and other small retailers in scope.[9]

If a tiny ad-supported website received over 50k unique IP addresses a year, that would put them in scope. Treating small business the same as Google and Facebook imposes massive costs on small businesses that are not manageable for most of them. Solutions for the Small Medium Entity (SME) need to be in place to leverage across these new privacy laws. Imagine an SME that does business in CA and other states who enact their own privacy regulations. It would be impossible to afford and manage.

CCPA requirements address the following needs:

- Defining process requirements for consent of minors under the age of 13 years by parental or guardian consent forms.
- Requiring an Opt-Out provision with a "Do Not Sell My Personal Information" link on the home page of business website.
- Having multiple methods for submitting data access requests, including, at a minimum, a toll-free telephone number.
- Clear and timely privacy policies with an updated description of California residents' rights.
- Privacy notices must be accessible and have alternative methods to access them clear to the consumer.

The following finds can be imposed for violation of CCPA:

- The California Attorney General's Office may prosecute the company instead of allowing civil suits to be brought against it.
- In lieu of any California Attorney General Action, civil class action lawsuits can be filed that may pay statutory damages between US$100 and US$750 for each California resident and incident, or actual damages, whichever is greater, and any other relief a court deems proper.
- A fine up to US$7,500 for each intentional violation and US$2,500 for each unintentional violation- a violation is the loss of a record.

CCPA defines personal information as information that identifies, relates to, or describes, is reasonably capable of being associated with, or could reasonably be linked, directly or indirectly, with a particular consumer or household. The issue here is *reasonably capable of being associated with*. That is very broad. Data elements include the following:

- A real name or alias
- Consumer's postal address
- A unique personal identifier such as a social security number or identity number
- An online identifier
- An internet protocol (IP) address
- A consumer's email address
- An account name
- A social security number
- Driver's license number
- Passport number

In terms of the provision that allows the scope to include data that relates to, describes, or is capable of being associated with, a particular individual, this can make the scope unmanageable. In addition to the scope above it can also include but not be limited to, their signature, physical characteristics or description, address, telephone number, insurance policy number, education, employment, employment history, bank account number, credit card number, debit card number, or any other financial information, medical information, or health insurance information.

CCPA does not consider Publicly Available Information as personal information. Public information is data that is prepared, owned, used, or retained by any US public agency for official business. The law regulates the use, collection and protection of consumers' "personal information." CCPA broadly defines "consumer" as any natural person, of both the regulated business and its business customers and vendors.

"It's well-known in privacy circles that attempts to distinguish personal information from nonpersonal information are likely to be under-or overly-inclusive."[10] In this case, CCPA took the overinclusive route to a new level. Publicly available data that is provided by the government and fits the purpose that is not compatible with the purpose for which the data is maintained and made available from the agency is out of scope.

Combinations of data that can be associated with a unique individual is important to understand CCPA. When 3 PII data elements are combined the likelihood to identify a person uniquely is over 80%. "As an example, knowing someone is "male" does not uniquely identify them; but knowing a person's birthdate, zip code, and gender allows the accurate unique identification of 87% of the population."[11]

Because of these abilities to associate data to uniquely identify someone, gender information qualifies as PII because it is "capable of being associated with" a unique California consumer. All data about a consumer meets this "capable of being associated with" provision.

Consumer data that is deidentified is not in scope for CCPA. This can be related to data that cannot reasonably identify a person since there are technical safeguards implemented that prohibit reidentification of the consumer, or business processes that are in place that specifically prohibit reidentification of the information to name a few.

Additionally, data that is in the form of aggregate consumer information applies to "information that relates to a group or category of consumers, from which individual consumer identities have been removed, that is not linked or reasonably linkable to any consumer or household, including via a device is exempt from CCPA requirements.

GDPR is broader than CCPA. The major differences between CCPA and the European Union's GDPR are related to the scope, geography, and requirements to protect the privacy data. GDPR covers all personal data regardless of source of the data. CCPA scope is for data that was provided by a consumer and excludes personal data that was purchased by, or acquired through, third parties.

A summary of the law's primary obligations are:

> A consumer may request, and the business shall disclose categories and specific personal information that they have collected.

Disclosure of Generic Collection Practices Upon Collection: At or before collection of a consumer's personal information, a business shall "inform consumers as to the categories of personal information to be collected and the purposes for which the categories of personal information shall be used." The business shall not collect undisclosed categories, or make undisclosed uses, of personal information.

Erasure: Upon a consumer's request, a business shall delete any personal information about the consumer that the business collected from the consumer.

Businesses can refuse deletion requests when it "is necessary for the business or service provider to maintain the consumer's personal information" to: 1) complete the transaction or a reasonably anticipated transaction; 2) find, prevent, or prosecute security breaches or illegal activity; 3) "Debug to identify and repair errors that impair existing intended functionality"; 4) exercise free speech (of the business or a third party) or "exercise another right provided for by law"; 5) comply with the California ECPA; 6) engage in certain types of research in limited cases; 7) "enable solely internal uses that are reasonably aligned with the expectations of the consumer based on the consumer's relationship with the business"; 8) comply with a legal obligation; or 9) "Otherwise use the consumer's personal information, internally, in a lawful manner that is compatible with the context in which the consumer provided the information."

Disclosures About Collected Personal Information to the Consumer: Upon a consumer's request, a business shall disclose to the consumer the: 1) "categories of personal information it has collected about that consumer"; 2) "categories of sources from which the personal information is collected"; 3) "business or commercial purpose for collecting or selling personal information"; 4) "categories of third parties with whom the business shares personal information"; and 5) "specific pieces of personal information it has collected about that consumer." The last element should be provided in a format to facilitate data portability.

Disclosures About Sold/Disclosed Personal Information to the Consumer: If a business sells consumer information (where "sell" includes disclosing or disseminating the information "for monetary or other valuable consideration" or "discloses it for a business purpose" (a narrowly defined term) upon a consumer's request, a business shall disclose to the consumer the categories of personal information that the business: 1) "collected about the consumer"; 2) "sold about the consumer and the categories of third parties to whom the personal information was sold, by category or categories of personal information for each third party to whom the personal information was sold"; and 3) "disclosed about the consumer for a business purpose."

Request Mechanisms: The law specifies many operational details about how consumers may make their requests and how businesses must and cannot treat those requests. Among other things, for the disclosures about collected and sold/disclosed personal information, the business must allow the consumer to make requests by at least two methods, including a toll-free number and a website (if the business has a website).

Opt-Out of Data Sales: Consumers can opt-out of sales of their personal information, and the business can't ask them to change that for at least 12 months.

Opt-In for Data Sales Related to Minors: A business that knows (or "willfully disregards" the consumer's age) personal information relates to consumers under 16 may not sell the personal information unless the consumer (ages 13–16) or parent/guardian (under 13) opts-in.

Opt-Out of Third-Party Data Resales: "A third party shall not sell personal information about a consumer that has been sold to the third party by a business unless the consumer has received explicit notice and is provided an opportunity to exercise the right to opt out."

Specifications for Disclosing Opt-Out of Data Sales: If a business sells personal information, then it must "provide a clear and conspicuous link on the business' Internet homepage, titled 'Do Not Sell My Personal Information,' to an Internet Web page that enables a consumer, or a person authorized by the consumer, to opt out of the sale of the consumer's personal information."

Specifications for Privacy Policies: Among other requirements, a business' privacy policy must notify consumers about their erasure rights, collections and sales/disclosures of personal information, the opt-out/opt-in rights for data sales, and restrictions on privacy-based discrimination.

Anti-Discrimination: "A business shall not discriminate against a consumer because the consumer exercised any of the consumer's rights under this title," though a business may charge "a consumer a different price or rate, or [provide] a different level or quality of goods or services to the consumer, if that difference is reasonably related to the value provided to the consumer by the consumer's data." Businesses may offer "financial incentives" (an undefined term) to compensate for the collection, sale, or deletion of data, but not if the financial incentives are "unjust, unreasonable, coercive, or usurious in nature."

CCPA authorizes the California Attorney General's office to further adopt regulations that enhance the rights of California consumers. This includes designating additional categories of personal information "to address changes in technology, data collection practices, obstacles to implementation, and privacy concerns." This was done in terms of IoT technology with the nation's first IoT cybersecurity law, California SB-327, which went into effect January 1st, 2020.

CCPA gives businesses a 30-day period to cure any issues following a written notice. The only exception to the law that creates a private cause of legal action is when "nonencrypted or nonredacted PII is subject to an unauthorized access and data is exfiltration, stolen, or the disclosure is a result of the business' failure to implement and maintain reasonable security procedures and programs that are appropriate to the nature of the PII."

If a business does not cure the issues within 30-days, the consumer can move forward with civil litigation. They must notify the California Attorney General's office of the pending lawsuit. The AG can opt to either do nothing, in which case the lawsuit can continue, express an intention to prosecute the defendant, in which case the pending civil lawsuit will stop if the AG actually prosecutes within 6 months, or unilaterally veto the lawsuit.

Maine: an act to protect the privacy of online customer information[12]

Maine has a very limited Act that is short in scope, reach, sanctions, and remedies. The Maine act applies to customers of broadband internet access service that are physically located and billed for service received in Maine.

Customers personal information that is defined as personal identifying information is protected. This includes but is not limited to:

- Customer's name.
- Billing information.
- Social security number.
- Billing address.
- Demographic data information from a customer's use of broadband internet access service.
- Web browsing history.

The definition of "customers" under this act is not as broad as the definition of "consumers" under the CCPA. This Maine law is only to protect customers that subscribe to broadband services and are physically located in Maine and billed for services received in Maine to be protected under the law. CCPA protects California residents, online and offline, even when they are physically outside the state.

CCPA does not discriminate on the data relating to a California resident or household. It protects it all. Under the Maine law, its scope is to protect data relating to broadband services and not to other data elements.

The Maine law is limited to providers of broadband internet access service operating within the state of Maine. The term "Provider" means a person who provides broadband internet access service. CCPA applies to most businesses world-wide and in all industries.

To comply with Maine's law, the provider must provide notice, seek express opt-in consent before collecting personal information, and protect personal information. The broadband providers must give notices of its obligations and customers' rights under the law at the point of sale and on their public facing website. This is similar to CCPA, in as much as it has prescriptive details about disclosing the opt-out right. A best practice would be to have this as a security requirement regardless of the geography scope.

As expected, broadband providers must take reasonable measures to protect customer personal information from unauthorized use, disclosure, or access. However, the Maine law does not provide for fines or remedies for specific security violations.

The law states that if a provider violates Title 35-A on Public Utilities, causes or permits a violation of the title or omits to do anything that the title requires it to do it may be liable in damages to the person injured as a result.

For violations where the entity willfully did not put protections or follow the law, the Maine Public Utilities Commission can impose an administrative penalty for each violation (record) in an amount that does not exceed US$5,000 or .25% of the annual gross revenue that the provider received from sales in Maine, whichever amount is lower. This is not much incentive to be cyber resilient.

For each day that a violation continues it constitutes a separate offense with a maximum administrative penalty for any related series of violations that may not exceed US$500,000 or 5% of the provider's annual gross revenue that the provider received from sales in Maine, whichever amount is lower.

Nevada's Senate Bill 220[13]

The law provides protection to consumers who reside in the state of Nevada.

The law prescribes that it protects covered information. Covered information is defined as "any one or more of the following items of personally identifiable information about a consumer collected by an operator through an internet website or online service and maintained by the operator in an accessible form, such as a first and last name. Any other information concerning a person collected from the person through the internet website or online service of the operator and maintained by the operator in combination with an identifier in a form that makes the information personally identifiable."

Nevada's law is narrow in its scope. It defines a consumer as "a person who seeks or acquires, by purchase or lease, any good, service, money or credit for personal, and family or household purposes." The Nevada law only protects consumers when seeking or acquiring those things online. Nevada protects the consumer regardless of if the purchase was done physically in Nevada.

Nevada law's does not extend to household information and is limited to information collected by a business online. The law applies to operators and defines them as a person who owns or operates an internet website or online service for commercial purposes; collects and maintains covered information from Nevada resident consumers who use or visit the internet website or online service. It purposefully directs its activities toward Nevada, consummates some transaction with Nevada or a resident thereof, purposefully avails itself of the privilege of conducting activities in Nevada or otherwise engages in any activity that constitutes sufficient nexus with Nevada to satisfy the requirements of the United States Constitution.

Nevada's law applies to many businesses without a pure physical presence in the state of Nevada but who operate a commercial website that can be accessed by Nevada residents. Therefore, the operator can be in any state.

Financial institutions that are subject to the Gramm–Leach–Bliley Act and entities that are subject to HIPAA are out of scope. Third parties that operate, host, or manage an internet website or online service on behalf of its owner, and generally, manufacturers of motor vehicles or persons who repairs or services motor vehicles are also exempt.

In terms of cybersecurity process requirements, every operator of an online service purposefully addressed to Nevada consumers must establish a designated request address through which a consumer may submit a verified request directing the operator not to make any sale of any covered information the operator has collected or will collect about the consumer and respond to such requests.

Most businesses do not sell PII for monetary considerations. In contrast to CCPA, where the scope includes any exchange of personal information for any valuable consideration, monetary, or otherwise. CCPA means any contract is in scope.

As in most states, operators must provide a privacy notice with information about its data collection practices. Best practices align to a new requirement to establish a designated request address in addition to an email address, toll-free number, or internet website with a form to make consumer requests about their data.

In terms of fines, the Nevada Attorney General can bring a civil action for an injunction or impose penalties of up to US$5,000 for each violation (record).

Colorado protection for consumer data privacy[14]

In 2013 after Target was breached, the state of Colorado started to propose legislation to protect consumer's privacy. Colorado realized that their laws were comparatively weak.

The bill was introduced in Colorado House of Representatives on January 19, 2018. It was spearheaded by the Colorado Attorney General's office with bi-partisan support in House and Senate. It underwent significant revisions with six published versions. The bill passed both the House and Senate without a single "no" vote. It was signed into law by the Governor on May 29, 2018 and is effective September 1, 2018.

There are three key new information security requirements:

1 To implement and maintain reasonable security measures to protect documents containing personal identifying information.
2 To contractually require third-party service providers to implement and maintain reasonable security measures.
3 To implement a written policy to dispose of documents containing personal identifying information.

There are significant changes to state's breach notification statute. There is a new obligation to notify the Attorney General within 30 days. This is the shortest time frame in the United States. There are no carve outs for HIPAA and GLBA regulated entities and there is an expanded definition of "personal information" to include medical information and log-in credentials.

The law applies to covered entities, government entities and third-party service providers. A covered entity is defined as a person that maintains, owns, or licenses PII in the course of the person's business, vocation, or occupation." C.R.S 6-1-102(6) defines "person" as "an individual, corporation, business trust, estate, trust, partnership, unincorporated association, or two or more thereof having a joint or common interest, or any other legal or commercial entity."

A Governmental "entity" is defined as: "[T]he state and any state agency or institution, including the judicial department, county, city, and country, incorporated city or town, school district, special improvement district, authority, and every other kind of district, instrumentally, or political subdivision of the state organized pursuant to law."

Third-party service providers are excluded from definitions of "covered entity" and "governmental entity." They are defined as "any entity that has been contracted to maintain, store or process personal information on behalf of a covered entity or governmental entity."

There is a new requirement to implement and maintain "reasonable security procedures and practices." This applies to "a covered entity that maintains, owns, or licenses personal identifying information of an individual residing in the state shall implement and maintain reasonable security procedures and practices that are appropriate to the nature of the personal identifying information and the nature and size of the business and its operations." It was purposefully drafted to be broad instead of prescriptive and it is expected that standards will develop through lawsuits, Attorney General enforcement actions, and potentially written guidance from Attorney General's office.

Colorado's definition of privacy data is:

1 Social Security Number.
2 Personal identification number.

3 Password.
4 Pass code.
5 Official state or government issued driver's license or identification card number.
6 Passport number.
7 Biometric data -[U]nique biometric data generated from measurements or analysis of human body characteristics for the purpose of authenticating the individual when he or she accesses an online account.
8 Employer, student, or military identification number.
9 Financial transaction device—[A]ny instrument or device whether known as a credit card, banking card, debit card, electronic fund transfer card, or guaranteed check card, or account number representing a financial account or affecting the financial interest, standing, or obligation of or to the account holder that can be used to obtain cash, goods, property, or services or to make financial payments, but shall not include a "check," a "negotiable order of withdrawal," and a "share draft" as defined in section 18-5-205" *See* C.R.S 18-5-701.

Colorado has a new requirement to ensure protections are in place when PII is transferred to third-party service providers. The covered entity is exempt if it agrees to provide its own security protection for the information it discloses to a third-party service provider.

If not, the covered entity shall require that the third-party service provider implement and maintain reasonable security procedures and practices that are:

(a) Appropriate to the nature of the personal identifying information disclosed to the third-party service provider.

This is vague, however at a minimum it means is that encryption should be in place based on data classification. *Reasonable* has to be defined in context.

(b) Reasonably designed to help protect the personal identifying information from unauthorized access, use, modification, disclosure, or destruction.

This is also vague and should have more specifics as to what reasonable protection is exactly.

An exception was enacted when a covered entity retains security responsibility and implements controls to protect PII from unauthorized disclosure or to eliminate third-party's access, "disclosure of personal identifying information does not include disclosure of information to a third-party under circumstances where the covered entity retains primary responsibility for implementing and maintaining reasonable security procedures and practices appropriate to the nature of the personal identifying information and the covered entity implements and maintains technical controls that are reasonably designed to: (a) help protect the personal identifying information from unauthorized access, use, modification, disclosure, or destruction or (b) effectively eliminate the third-party's ability to access the personal identifying information, notwithstanding the third-party's physical possession of the personal identifying information."

The law added electronic documents to the scope in terms of adding it to the existing law that required the proper disposal of paper documents. Both are now in scope.

The law requires a written policy that must state that when paper or electronic documents are no longer needed, "the covered entity shall destroy or arrange for the destruction of such documents....by shredding, erasing, or otherwise modifying" the PII to make it unreadable or indecipherable. This requires that a data retention and disposal policy address these specific requirements and define types of data with retention time limits and other business rules that apply to cyber risk reduction.

When a covered entity is regulated by federal law, the federal law requirements can be used to comply with the Colorado law in reference to data disposal of personal identifying information. If the entity is in scope for HIPAA and/or GLBA they would qualify for this. Be aware that PII is a broad definition and that PHI is a subset of PII. Ensuring that companies do a digital asset inventory and data type will provide a clear line of sight into data type gaps and how to use this limited safe harbor.

Colorado law prescribes requirements for a Written Information Security Program (WISP). The firm is required to develop and implement a WISP that contains administrative, technical, and physical safeguards to protect PII such as:

The requirement for a written data retention and disposal policy is a new requirement. The third-party vendor management program requires you to identify third parties to which company transfers PII, identify protections, if any, used to transfer PII (e.g., encryption), and develop a mechanism to evaluate security procedures being used by third-parties (e.g., vendor questionnaire). Companies must use contract language that satisfies C.R.S 6-1-713.5.

There are scope changes related to data elements. The former CO law defined "personal information" as an individual's first name/initial and last name, in combination with: Individual's Social Security Number, or Driver's license number or nonoperating identification license number; or financial account or credit card number in combination with any required security code, access code, or password that would permit access to the account.

The new law is broader and defines "personal information" as an individual's first name/initial and last name, in combination with Social Security Number, or driver's license or ID card number, or student, military, or passport ID number, or medical information, or health insurance information; or biometric data.

These changes are consistent with recent movement to expand the types of information that trigger data breach notifications to consumers. Twenty percent of states have enacted legislation or amended statutes in 2017 and 2018. Today all 50 states have data breach notification laws.

The prior law stated for data breach notification that notification must be done in the most expedient manner possible and without any unreasonable delay. The new law states that it cannot be done later than 30 days after there is sufficient evidence to conclude that a security breach has taken place.

Colorado, as of this writing, has the shortest breach notification timeline in the US and in the world. Fines for a violation have skyrocketed recently to US$20,000 per record, ten times the original US$2,000 per record fine.

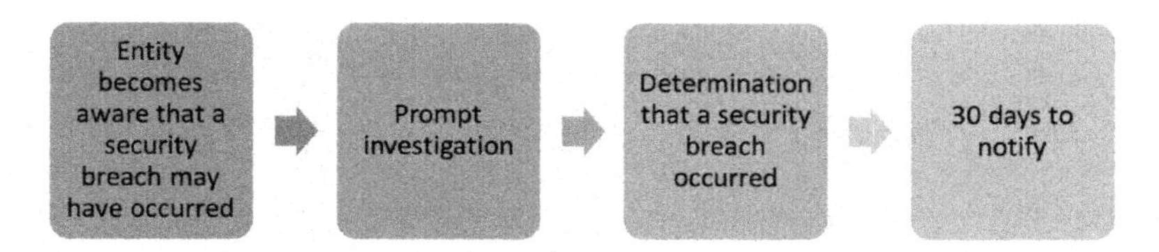

Figure 16.1 Data Breach Investigation Steps

Notification for online breaches require that in addition to standard notice, must also direct person to immediately change their password and security question(s) and answer(s) and take other steps appropriate to protect the online account and all other online accounts with same login info. If the email account is compromised, notice shall be provided to the individuals when they are connected to the online account from an internet protocol address or online location that they are known to customarily use.

The notice contents must include: the approximate date of the breach, a brief description of the personal information included in the breach, information that the resident can use to contact the covered entity, toll-free numbers and addresses for consumer reporting agencies, and a toll-free number, address and website address for the FTC.

The Attorney General must be contacted if the breach is over 500 residents and the credit reporting agencies if the breach is over 1,000 residents.

In terms of encryption, it is defined to mean that data is rendered unusable, unreadable, or indecipherable to an unauthorized person through a security technology generally accepted in the field of information security. If there is a breach of encrypted data that is not classified as personal information, the firm must disclose if the encryption key was also acquired or was reasonably believed to have been acquired in the security breach.

Third-party obligations apply to an entity that has been contracted to maintain, store or process personal information on behalf of a covered entity. They must notify the covered entity of any security breach in the most expedient time possible and without unreasonable delay and cooperate with the covered entity in the event of a security breach that compromises such computerized data. The notification obligations remain with the owner, the third-party is not required to provide notice to affected individuals unless an agreement between the parties provides otherwise.

There is a limited safe harbor in place for the Colorado law. Firms are compliant if they are regulated by state or federal law and maintain written procedures for a security breach pursuant to the laws, rules, regulations, guidance, or guidelines established by its regulator, but they must still provide notice to Attorney General;

and if there is a conflict on the notification timing, the law with the shortest time-frame controls.

In terms of the incident response plan, C.R.S. 6-1-716(3) creates a safe harbor if an entity maintains its own notifications procedures as part of an information security policy and the procedures are consistent with the timing requirements of the statute and the entity provides notice in accordance with its policies. We recommend that you have an incident response plan that you feel confident giving to the AG's office, vet and retain outside counsel that are cybersecurity experts and forensic firms. The statute requires a covered entity to conduct a "prompt investigation" as soon as it becomes aware that a security event may have occurred. You do not have time to waste in locating and securing outside consultants to conduct the investigation after the breach. In terms of third-party contracts, you must examine how the risk of loss is allocated in third-party contracts in event of a breach and consider indemnification and insurance provisions to mitigate risk and analyze use of encryption, redaction, etc.

Insurance data security act[15]

The National Association of Insurance Commissioners (NAICs) is the US standard-setting and regulatory support organization created and governed by the chief insurance regulators from the 50 states, the District of Columbia and five US territories. The NAIC using state insurance regulators establishes standards and best practices and coordinates regulatory oversight.

In 2019, the NAIC focused on eight issues central to our mission of protecting policyholders and advancing the state-based policy agenda. The NAIC's strategic priorities for 2019 included Data, Innovation, and Cyber.

The NAIC adopted a Data Security Model Law with the goal of having it adopted in all states within a few years.[16] So far, eight states have adopted a version of the Model Law and it looks like more are on the way.

The NAIC adopted a Data Security Model Law in November 2017. The Model Law will provide a benchmark for any cybersecurity program in the insurance industry. The requirements in the Model Law align to other data security frameworks, such as the HIPAA Security Rule and the New York State Department of Financial Services (NYDFS) regulations (specifically the 23 NYCRR 500). Licensees are subject to the Model Law where the state has adopted a version of the Model Law.

The insurance industry is a mass collector of significant amounts of sensitive, nonpublic information including personal information. Outside of the financial industry, insurance-related businesses are one of the most targeted industries for cyberattacks. Small and mid-sized insurance companies face the same risks as a colossus like AIG and Zurich and are in scope for the model law.

In the spring of 2018, South Carolina was the first state to adopt the Model Law followed by Ohio and Michigan in late 2018. In 2019, Mississippis Governor signed that state's version of the Model Law, followed by Alabama, Delaware, and Connecticut. In 2020, New Hampshire followed suit.

Those eight states have enacted a version of the NAIC's Model Law with some differences. The breach notification deadline in the NAIC's Model Law is 72 hours. In Ohio, Connecticut, and Delaware, it is three business days, and ten days in Michigan.

Smaller firms with less than ten employees and independent contractors are exempt from the information security program requirement. Some states that have adopted the Model Law have changed that exception. In Michigan it is less than 25 employees and independent contractors. However, all are required to provide notification in the case of certain cybersecurity events.

The Model Law generally applies to "Licensees." "Licensees are defined as any person licensed, authorized to operate, or registered, or required to be licensed, authorized, or registered pursuant to the insurance laws of this State but shall not include a purchasing group or a risk retention group chartered and licensed in a state other than this State or a Licensee that is acting as an assuming insurer that is domiciled in another state or jurisdiction."[17]

Some businesses are in scope that require a license, but are not a dedicated insurance business, such as car rental companies and travel agencies that offer insurance packages in connection with their primary business.

Requirements

Under the Model Law, licensees must maintain a comprehensive, written Information Security Program. The Program should be appropriate to the size and complexity of the licensee, the nature and scope of the licensee's activities, including its use of third-party service providers, and the sensitivity of the nonpublic information collected, processed, and maintained by the licensee. The Program must meet administrative, technical, and physical safeguards and preform a risk assessment. In short, the Program cannot be an "off-the-shelf" set of policies and procedures.

Companies must make risk-based decisions on which security controls should be implemented and ensure the Board and/or executive management is overseeing the program. The firm must have a third-party vendor program and require third-party service providers to maintain reasonable safeguards. An incident response plan must be in place and notification mechanism to the insurance commissioner of a cybersecurity event within 72 hours or less as prescribed by the state law.

The Model Law protects both personal information and "nonpublic information." Nonpublic information includes business related information that if tampered with, or if there is an unauthorized access, use or disclosure, would cause a material adverse impact to the licensee's business, operations, or security.

Scope for PII under the Model Law includes:

i Social Security number
ii Driver's license number or nondriver identification card number
iii Account number, credit, or debit card number

iv Any security code, access code, or password that would permit access to a consumer's financial account, or
v Biometric records
vi Certain health information concerning a consumer that relates to the consumer's physical, mental or behavioral health or condition
vii Data about the provision of health care
viii Data related to the payment for the provision of health care

Insurance firms that operate in multiple states need to track state adoption of the Model Law. In all compliance programs, the best practice is to the adopt the most stringent aspects of the applicable cyber regulations into one compliance program.

NYD DFS part 500

The New York State Department of Financial Services (DFS or NYSDFS) is the department of the New York state government responsible for regulating financial services and products, including those subject to the New York insurance, banking, and financial services laws.[18]

New York State Department of Financial Services (NYDFS) protect consumers by ensuring the safety and soundness of the financial institution. To this effect they have created a new cybersecurity regulation. This new law applies to any New York State registered entity providing financial services including insurance companies, banks, as well as financial services institutions. The new law is 23 NYCRR 500 and is part 500 of the NYDFS's overall body of regulation.

23 NYCRR 500 requires entities in scope to assess their cybersecurity risk profiles and implement a comprehensive cyber risk management plan that recognizes and mitigates that risk.

The NYDFS Cybersecurity Regulation covers any organization that is regulated by the Department of Financial Services. This includes licensed lenders, state-chartered banks, trust companies, service contract providers, private bankers, mortgage companies, insurance companies doing business in New York State, and non-U.S. banks licensed to operate in New York State.

The regulation does not apply to organizations with fewer than 10 employees, or less than US$5 million in gross annual revenue for three years, or less than US$10 million in year-end total assets.

NYS DFS is covered in detail later in this book. Here, is a high-level checklist of requirements:

- Establish an effective cybersecurity program.
- Create and maintain a written cybersecurity policy.
- Designate a chief information security officer (CISO).
- Hire qualified cybersecurity personnel or utilize third-party providers.
- Establish an incident response plan.

- Submit notification of incidents to the NYDFS (within 72 hours).
- CISO must file annual cybersecurity report.
- Regularly conduct penetration testing and vulnerability management.
- Conduct bi-annual risk assessments.
- Maintain an audit trail.
- Implement application security protocols.

Our next chapter focuses exclusively on New York State DFS Part 500.

Notes

1. Mitchell Noordyke, IAAP, "US State comprehensive privacy law comparison", April 18,2019, https://iapp.org/news/a/us-state-comprehensive-privacy-law-comparison/.
2. IAAP, "Westin Center updates US State comprehensive privacy law comparison table", July 18, 2019, https://iapp.org/news/a/westin-center-updates-u-s-state-comprehensive-privacy-law-comparison-table.
3. Sarah Rippy, IAAP, "US State comprehensive privacy law comparison," February 11, 2020, https://iapp.org/resources/article/state-comparison-table/.
4. Sarah Rippy, IAAP, "US State comprehensive privacy law comparison", February 11, 2020, https://iapp.org/resources/article/state-comparison-table/. Image as Courtesy of IAPP.
5. Sarah Rippy, IAAP, "US State comprehensive privacy law comparison", February 11, 2020, https://iapp.org/resources/article/state-comparison-table/. Image as Courtesy of IAPP.
6. Sarah Rippy, IAAP, "US State comprehensive privacy law comparison", February 11, 2020, https://iapp.org/resources/article/state-comparison-table/.
7. Wikipedia, "California Consumer Privacy Act", August 25, 2020, https://en.wikipedia.org/wiki/California_Consumer_Privacy_Act.
8. Rita Heimes, IAAP, "New California privacy law to affect more than half a million US companies", July 2, 2018, https://iapp.org/news/a/new-california-privacy-law-to-affect-more-than-half-a-million-us-companies/.
9. California Consumer Privacy Act Overview, "An introduction to the California Consumer Privacy Act (CCPA)", July 9, 2018, https://northerndistrictpracticeprogram.org/wp-content/uploads/2018/09/Intro-to-CCPA.pdf.
10. Eric Goldman, Technology & Marketing Law Blog, "A privacy bomb is about to be dropped on the California economy and the global internet", June 27, 2018, https://blog.ericgoldman.org/archives/2018/06/a-privacy-bomb-is-about-to-be-dropped-on-the-california-economy-and-the-global-internet.htm.
11. Hacker News, "87% of US population are uniquely identified by", August 10, 2011, https://news.ycombinator.com/item?id=2942967.
12. Office of Governor Janet T. Mills, State of Maine, "Governor Mills signs internet privacy legislation", June 6, 2019, https://www.maine.gov/governor/mills/news/governor-mills-signs-internet-privacy-legislation-2019-06-06.
13. Nevada State Legislature, "Selected session 80th (2019) session", December 9, 2020, https://www.leg.state.nv.us/App/NELIS/REL/80th2019/Bill/6365/Text.
14. Phil Weiser, Colorado Attorney General, "Colorado's consumer data protection laws: FAQ's for businesses and government agencies", 2019, https://coag.gov/resources/data-protection-laws/.
15. National Association of Insurance Commissioners, "Insurance data security model law", 4th quarter 2017, https://content.naic.org/sites/default/files/inline-files/MDL-668.pdf.

16. National Association of Insurance Commissioners & The center for insurance policy and research, "The NAIC insurance data security model law", June 2020, https://www.naic.org/documents/cmte_legislative_liaison_brief_data_security_model_law.pdf.
17. National Association of Insurance Commissioners & The center for insurance policy and research, "The NAIC insurance data security model law", June 2020, https://www.naic.org/documents/cmte_legislative_liaison_brief_data_security_model_law.pdf.
18. New York State Department of Financial Services, "New York State Department of Financial Services 23 NYCRR 500", 2020, https://www.dfs.ny.gov/docs/legal/regulations/adoptions/dfsrf500txt.pdf.

17 NEW YORK STATE DEPARTMENT OF FINANCIAL SERVICE PART 500

DFS has good intentions in what they are trying to do but lack the technical knowhow to implement meaningful changes to the industry. The regulations give the illusion of security, and that is not the same thing as implementing actual security measures to protect financial institutions. This chapter provides meaningful information to pivot your cybersecurity program to obtain both DFS compliance and real cybersecurity.

Theodore Tomita III, Executive Vice President & CTO/CISO at Catskill Hudson Bank

Definitions

NYS DFS defines the following:

(a) An "Affiliate" is any Person that controls, is controlled by, or is under common control with another Person. For purposes of this subsection, control means the possession, direct or indirect, of the power to direct or cause the direction of the management and policies of a Person, whether through the ownership of stock of such Person or otherwise.

(b) An "Authorized User" is any Person (employee or third party) that participates in the business operations of a Covered Entity and is authorized to access and use any Information Systems and data of the Covered Entity.

(c) A "Covered Entity" is any Person who is operating under or required to operate under a license, registration, charter, certificate, permit, accreditation, or similar authorization under the Banking Law, the Insurance Law, or the Financial Services Law.

(d) A "Cybersecurity Event" is any act or attempt, regardless of whether it is successful or unsuccessful, to gain unauthorized access to, disrupt, or misuse an Information System or information stored on such Information System.

(e) An "Information System" is a discrete set of electronic information resources organized for the collection, processing, maintenance, use, sharing, dissemination, or disposition of electronic information, as well as any specialized system, such as industrial/process controls systems, telephone switching and private branch exchange systems, and environmental control systems.

DOI: 10.4324/9781003052616-21

(f) "Multifactor Authentication" is an authentication mechanism that uses the verification of at least two of the following types of authentication factors:

— knowledge factors, such as a password; or
— possession factors, such as a token or text message on a mobile phone; or
— inherence factors, such as a biometric characteristic.

Furthermore, NYS DFS defines,

(g) "Nonpublic Information" is any electronic information that is not Publicly Available Information and is:

1. Business-related information of a Covered Entity the tampering with which, or unauthorized disclosure, access or use of which, would cause a material adverse impact to the business, operations, or security of the Covered Entity.
2. Any information concerning an individual which because of name, number, personal mark, or other identifier can be used to identify such individual, in combination with any one or more of the following data elements: (i) social security number; (ii) drivers' license number or nondriver identification card number; (iii) account number and credit or debit card number; (iv) any security code, access code, or password that would permit access to an individual's financial account; or (v) biometric records.
3. Any information or data, except age or gender, in any form or medium created by or derived from a health care provider or an individual and that relates to (i) the past, present, or future physical, mental, or behavioral health or condition of any individual or a member of the individual's family; (ii) the provision of health care to any individual; or (iii) payment for the provision of health care to any individual.

(h) "Penetration Testing" is a test methodology in which assessors attempt to circumvent or defeat the security features of an Information System by attempting penetration of databases or controls from outside or inside the Covered Entity's Information Systems.

(i) A "Person" is any individual or any nongovernmental entity, including but not limited to any nongovernmental partnership, corporation, branch, agency, or association.

(j) "Publicly Available Information" is any information that a Covered Entity has a reasonable basis to believe is lawfully made available to the general public from: federal, state, or local government records; widely distributed media; or disclosures to the general public that are required to be made by federal, state, or local law. (1) For the purposes of this subsection, a Covered Entity has a reasonable basis to believe that information is lawfully made available to the general public if the Covered Entity has taken steps to determine: (i) that the information is of the type that is available to the general public and (ii) whether an individual can direct that the information not be made available to the general public and, if so, that such individual has not done so.

(k) A "Risk Assessment" is an annual assessment of the security controls of a Covered Entity that it is required to conduct under section 500.09 of this Part.

(l) Risk-Based Authentication means any risk-based system of authentication that detects anomalies or changes in the normal use patterns of a person and requires additional verification of the person's identity when such deviations or changes are detected, such as through the use of challenge questions.

(m) A "Senior Officer" is any senior individual or individuals (acting collectively or as a committee) responsible for the management, operations, security, information systems, compliance, and/or risk of a Covered Entity, including a branch or agency of a foreign banking organization subject to this Part.

(n) A "Third-Party Service Provider" is any person that (i) is not an Affiliate of the Covered Entity; (ii) provides services to the Covered Entity; and (iii) maintains, processes, or otherwise is permitted access to Nonpublic Information through its provision of services to the Covered Entity.

Requirements

The requirements are listed from sections 2 through 17.

- Section 500.02: Cybersecurity Program
- Section 500.03: Cybersecurity Policy
- Section 500.04: Chief Information Security Officer
- Section 500.05: Penetration Testing and Vulnerability Assessments
- Section 500.06: Audit Trail
- Section 500.07: Access Privileges
- Section 500.08: Application Security
- Section 500.09: Risk Assessment
- Section 500.10: Cybersecurity Personnel and Intelligence
- Section 500.11: Third-Party Service Provider Security Policy
- Section 500.12: Multi-Factor Authentication
- Section 500.13: Limitations on Data Retention
- Section 500.14: Training and Monitoring
- Section 500.15: Encryption of non-public Information
- Section 500.16: Incident Response Plan
- Section 500.17: Notices to Superintendent

Exceptions for each requirement are defined below:

Exemption	Exempt From	Still Required
500.19 (a) (1) Fewer than 10 employees working in NYS 500.19 (a) (2) Less than $5 million in gross annual revenue 500.19 (a) (3) Less than $10 million in year-end total assets	500.04- Chief Information Security Officer 500.05- Penetration Testing and Vulnerability Assessments 500.06- Audit Trail 500.08- Application Security 500.10- Cybersecurity Personnel and Intelligence 500.12- Multi-Factor Authentication 500.14- Training and Monitoring 500.15- Encryption of Nonpublic Information 500.16- Incident Response Plan	500.02- Cybersecurity Program 500.03- Cybersecurity Policy 500.07- Access Privileges 500.09- Risk Assessment 500.11- Third Party Service Provider Security Policy 500.13- Limitations on Data Retention 500.17- Notices to Superintendent 500.18- Confidentiality 500.19- Exemptions 500.20- Enforcement 500.21- Effective Date 500.22- Transitional Periods 500.23- Severability

Image 17.1 NYS DFS Exceptions Sections 500.19 (a) (1), (2), and (3)[3]

Exemption	Exempt From	Still Required
500.19 (c) Does not control any information systems and nonpublic information 500.19 (d) Captive insurance companies that do not control nonpublic information other than information relating to its corporate parent company	500.02- Cybersecurity Program 500.03- Cybersecurity Policy 500.04- Chief Information Security Officer 500.05- Penetration Testing and Vulnerability Assessments 500.06- Audit Trail 500.07- Access Privileges 500.08- Application Security 500.10- Cybersecurity Personnel and Intelligence 500.12- Multi-Factor Authentication 500.14- Training and Monitoring 500.15- Encryption of Nonpublic Information 500.16- Incident Response Plan	500.09- Risk Assessment 500.11- Third Party Service Provider Security Policy 500.13- Limitations on Data Retention 500.17- Notices to Superintendent 500.18- Confidentiality 500.19- Exemptions 500.20- Enforcement 500.21- Effective Date 500.22- Transitional Periods 500.23- Severability

Image 17.2 NYS DFS Exceptions Sections 500.19 (c) and (d)[4]

Timelines

Let's examine some key dates associated with this law. Effective March 1, 2017, the Superintendent of Financial Services established 23 NYCRR Part 500, as a regulation that stipulated cybersecurity requirements for financial services companies. Companies had two years to get ready to be compliant with this law. Enforcement started March 1, 2019. At that point, many CISOs simply resigned. They were not going to assume legal liability for companies that refused to give them enough budget or resources to be able to meet all the NYS DFS Part 500 requirements. Every February, companies have to certify with NYS DFS that they were compliant the previous year.

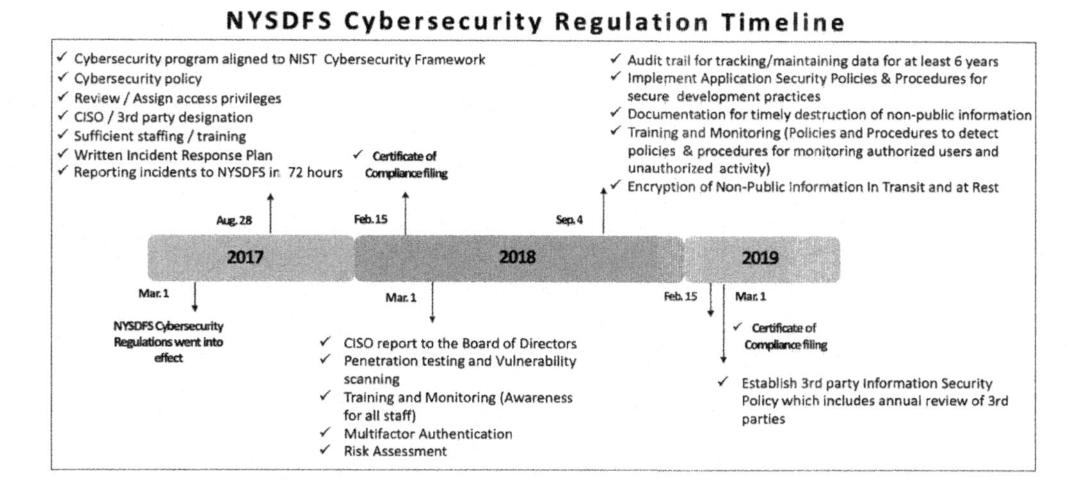

Figure 17.1 NYS DFS Cybersecurity Regulation Timeline

It will take most companies two years to be compliant. This timeline is a best practice to break up the requirements in a logical manner. Every February 15, each regulated entity under NYS DFS has to certify. The issue we see today is that most do not certify fully. Each certificate of compliance is only for the previous calendar year, everything up until December 31st.

The first step is to set up the security program. Many folks think that the security program is all their documentation. This is not correct; the cybersecurity program is a document in and of itself, however, it must include all the policies and procedures that describe how you manage cyber risk. These policies include the access control, encryption, and password standards, to name a few. Policies must be crafted and reviewed annually.

The CISO role needs to be assigned to a qualified individual.

This person will be directly accountable for the cybersecurity program. Sometimes you see an information security manager or some other title attempting to fill this role. DFS is clear that it is a senior role. Regulators want to see that there is a *local* function that carries that role. We have seen cases where a foreign bank has a global CISO only; there is no local CISO to fill the function. Many firms will indicate to the examiners that they have a global CISO, so there is no need to have a local CISO. The regulators will not accept that. Your firm is required to have a local CISO. If you have an incident that occurs in the foreign home office and one that occurs in New York, is he or she going to split time between both places? Of course not.

Additionally, there is a stipulation where the CISO has to report to the board annually on the status of the program. To be clear, what the examiners have said is that when there is a global CISO who reports to a board, and the board is overseas, it will not satisfy the NYS DFS requirement. You have to have a local function and the security operations team must report to a local committee or the local board. There is a great deal of misunderstanding about the CISO function pertaining to this law. There also needs to be specific training for staff and an incident response plan in place. Incidents must be reported to NYDFS within 72 hours.

Below is an explanation of each set of requirements.[5]

Section 500.02 cybersecurity program

A cybersecurity program must be put in place and maintained. The program must be able to assess risk, accept or mitigate it, and report clearly on it.

> (a) Each Covered Entity shall maintain a cybersecurity program designed to protect the confidentiality, integrity, and availability of the Covered Entity's Information Systems.

This includes all the policies and procedures that are required to be in place. Policies are covered in deeper detail in the next requirement.

> (b) The cybersecurity program shall be based on the Covered Entity's Risk Assessment and designed to perform the following core cybersecurity functions:
>
> 1 Identify and assess internal and external cybersecurity risks that may threaten the security or integrity of nonpublic Information stored on the Covered Entity's Information Systems.
> 2 Use defensive infrastructure and the implementation of policies and procedures to protect the Covered Entity's Information Systems, and the nonpublic Information stored on those Information Systems, from unauthorized access, use, or other malicious acts.
> 3 Detect Cybersecurity Events.
> 4 Respond to identified or detected Cybersecurity Events to mitigate any negative effects.
> 5 Recover from Cybersecurity Events and restore normal operations and services.
> 6 Fulfill applicable regulatory reporting obligations.

The language here is not well defined. NYS DFS uses the word *risk* incorrectly. That they are defining here is a cybersecurity control assessment. We will address cyber risk in the following chapters.

> (c) A Covered Entity may meet the requirement(s) of this Part by adopting the relevant and applicable provisions of a cybersecurity program maintained by an Affiliate, provided that such provisions satisfy the requirements of this Part, as applicable to the Covered Entity.

A frequently asked question about this provision is: Can the same entity be a Covered Entity, an Authorized User, and a Third-Party Service Provider? The answer is yes, depending on the facts and circumstances, the same entity can be a Covered Entity, an Authorized User, and a Third-Party Service Provider. An example of this is an independent insurance agent who works with multiple insurance companies. They are a Covered Entity with its own obligation to establish and maintain a cybersecurity program designed to protect the confidentiality, integrity, and availability of its Information Systems and Nonpublic Information. They are also defined as a third party.

Another frequently asked question about this provision is: Are subsidiaries and other affiliates of a firm in scope? Yes, they are. If a subsidiary or other affiliate presents risks to the Information Systems or the Nonpublic Information stored on those Information Systems, those risks must be evaluated and addressed in the Covered Entity's Risk Assessment, cybersecurity program, and cybersecurity policies. See 23 NYCRR Sections 500.09, 500.02, and 500.03.

(d) All documentation and information relevant to the Covered Entity's cybersecurity program shall be made available to the superintendent upon request.

This means that the firm has to have everything at the ready and not scramble at the last moment to get the documentation.

Control assessment

The NYS DFS Part 500[6] requires that the firm uses a control framework for the security assessment. While regulators do not mandate NIST, it is a popular framework. Many banks use the "FFIEC CAT/FSSCC ACAT" first and foremost and complement it with NIST and/or CIS and/or ISO2700.

The CISO is ultimately responsible to make this program work. The CISO needs a reporting structure that he or she can have confidence in when they need to get budget and resources to comply with this law.

Remember that cloud services are shared responsibility models. Regulators are clear that if the firm uses a cloud provider, it is still responsible to protect the data. This means due diligence reviews and ongoing monitoring of the cloud service vendors.

Most cloud service security assessments rely on SOC 2 reports. These are just check the box reports that are done by accountants. Accountants know zero about cybersecurity. Having a robust vendor program is critical to ensure that you understand how much cyber risk you are truly carrying.

500.03 cybersecurity policy

NYSDFS has made it very clear what should be in the cybersecurity policy. If you look at these elements below from a–n there is nothing new here. It is simply recycled the NYSDFS way.

(a) Information security. The information security program outlines your cyber strategy and approach. It includes policies, procedures, monitoring, reporting, governance, and all aspects of how the CISO manages cybersecurity.

(b) Data governance and data classification. Data governance classification is how the firm identifies and manages the laws related to cybersecurity. Data classification is critical to know if multiple regulations are pertaining to the digital assets.

(c) A digital asset inventory is essential. Your digital asset inventory needs to match what's actually in place. Digital assets are systems, technologies that are associated to the data classification.

If the digital asset inventory is incomplete, then you will not know what you have to protect. This applies to all laptops and workstations and assets in the cloud. Everything has to be tracked. If you have your inventory up to date, it takes less time to address the vulnerabilities. You will not be able to prioritize vulnerabilities unless you know which assets they are associated to. If it is up to date you can simply run a query or look at the report and see what assets need to be addressed by determining the impact. Data classification, digital asset inventories, and vulnerability management go together.

(d) Access control and management. Policies and procedures must be in place. Tools to automate access control are encouraged. A semiannual review of users should be done to ensure no one has unauthorized access.

(e) Business continuity and disaster recovery planning and resources. This part of the security program is essential. Having a business continuity program (BCP) with disaster recovery plans that are tested are required. Knowing the RTOs and RPO is part of that plan.

(f) Systems, operations, and availability concerns.

(g) Systems network security. This includes the network policies and procedures that show how you manage your network. No one should be an exception when it comes to the network security policy. This needs to be clear when cybersecurity training is set up. It doesn't matter if you are the cleaning person or the CEO.

(h) Systems and network monitoring. This includes the network policies and procedures that show how you monitor your network.

(i) Systems application and development and QA. There are too many times when a system goes live, and IT hears about it at the last minute. There are so many things that need to be done before and after a system goes live. Security is often thought of as a roadblock. Ensuring all security mechanisms are in place will slow everything down. However, if your colleagues still want to proceed without cybersecurity signing off you must make them put it in writing that they moved forward without your "Okay." Most likely they will not sign any document like that If you don't have it in writing and something happens, then they will blame the CISO.

(j) Physical security. Typically, firms will have a facilities manager or someone that does the security that is tied to computers, card systems, cameras, etc. You need a relationship with the physical security team. Here's an example why. There was an alert that someone had tried to use a thumb drive to download information. Forensics went in and found that it was a senior person from the auditing department. When they were confronted, they denied it was them. They said they weren't at work that day. The logs then had to be pulled off all the card access records of that day from the physical security people. Turns out, this person didn't use that card at work that day. Perhaps they gained entrance by tailgating and walking in after someone else. A review of the cameras from that day showed that the person was in their office that day. This emphasizes the need to have a good relationship with the physical security team. It is important to know how often they recycle their tapes. In this example, the tape was very helpful.

(k) Customer data privacy. Many requirements provide details that are required, including sections 500.12 and 500.13.
(l) Vendor risk management. Vendor risk management programs must be in place. We cover this in detail as it relates to section 500.11.
(m) Risk management. Periodic risk assessments are required. We cover this in detail as it relates to section 500.09.
(n) Incident response. Written incident response plans are mandatory. We cover this in detail as it relates to section 500.16.

The NYSDFS requirements that are laid are nothing new. The question is how effective your program is and how well did you implement it. What you do in practice and how you document it must be in sync. If someone questions the program, it is critical that you can show you are following what was written and approved. If you deviate from the policy and procedure, then you could get in trouble. If there is something being done in practice that should be documented, you need to get your procedures updated. Then, when you execute it no one can say you are not doing your job. This is why it is at the top of the priorities for the DFS.

500.04 CISO

Many companies get confused with this requirement. If your firm is regulated by NYSDFS, they must have a CISO function. We mentioned the importance of this position earlier. The regulation states that they must have someone in the US. If there is no such function, it's an automatic write up. If a firm doesn't want to hire a full-time person, there are options. Firms can use a third-party service provider. There are many virtual CISOs or outsourced CISO options. It comes down to resources and budget. Sometimes it's better to work with a third-party service provider instead of hiring a full-time person based on budget and resources. The third party must report to a Senior Management in the firm such as the Chief Operating Officer, or to Chief Compliance Officer, however, it cannot be IT. If a firm has a global CISO, and they get the cyber report from the US office and report it to the board, it will be considered not compliant with regulation.

(a) Each Covered Entity shall designate a qualified individual responsible for overseeing and implementing the Covered Entity's cybersecurity program and enforcing its cybersecurity policy (for purposes of this Part, "Chief Information Security Officer" or "CISO"). The CISO may be employed by the Covered Entity, one of its Affiliates or a Third-Party Service Provider. To the extent this requirement is met using a Third-Party Service Provider or an Affiliate, the Covered Entity shall:

1. retain responsibility for compliance with this Part;
2. designate a senior member of the Covered Entity's personnel responsible for direction and oversight of the Third-Party Service Provider; and
3. require the Third-Party Service Provider to maintain a cybersecurity program that protects the Covered Entity in accordance with the requirements of this Part.

(b) The CISO of each Covered Entity shall report in writing at least annually to the Covered Entity's board of directors or equivalent governing body. If no such board of directors or equivalent governing body exists, such report shall be timely presented to a Senior Officer of the Covered Entity responsible for the Covered Entity's cybersecurity program. The CISO shall report on the Covered Entity's cybersecurity program and material cybersecurity risks.

The CISO must ensure that the cyber program includes at a minimum the following program features:

1. Ensuring the confidentiality of nonpublic Information and the integrity and security of the Covered Entity's Information Systems
2. Cybersecurity policies and procedures
3. Measurement of material cybersecurity risks to the Covered Entity
4. Understanding the overall effectiveness of the Covered Entity's cybersecurity program
5. Incident response for any material Cybersecurity Events

A frequently asked question about the CISO is: Does the CISO have to report in writing at least annually to the board of directors? Can this requirement be met by reporting to an authorized subcommittee of the board? The answer is no. DFS emphasizes that a well-informed board is a critical part of an effective cybersecurity program. The CISO's reporting to the full board is crucial to enable the board to assess the governance, funding, structure, and effectiveness of the cybersecurity program as well as compliance with Part 500 and other applicable laws or regulations.

Another frequently asked question is: Can a Covered Entity use an employee of an Affiliate as its Chief Information Security Officer ("CISO") to satisfy the requirements of 500.04(a)(2)-(3)? As per DFS, to the extent it utilizes an employee of an Affiliate to serve as the CISO for purposes of 500.04(a), the Affiliate is not considered a Third-Party Service Provider.

500.05 pen testing and vulnerability assessments

Here, we are going to talk about penetration testing and vulnerability assessments. Again, as I mentioned earlier, there is nothing specifically different or new with the regulations from DFS. And the key is that the requirement is read and understood.

The requirement states:

The cybersecurity program for each Covered Entity shall include monitoring and testing, developed in accordance with the Covered Entity's Risk Assessment, designed to assess the effectiveness of the Covered Entity's cybersecurity program. The monitoring and testing shall include continuous monitoring or periodic Penetration Testing and vulnerability assessments. Absent effective continuous monitoring, or other systems to detect, on an ongoing basis, changes in Information Systems that may create or indicate vulnerabilities, Covered Entities shall conduct:

(a) Annual Penetration Testing of the Covered Entity's Information Systems determined each given year based on relevant identified risks in accordance with the Risk Assessment.
(b) Biannual vulnerability assessments, including any systematic scans or reviews of Information Systems reasonably designed to identify publicly known cybersecurity vulnerabilities in the Covered Entity's Information Systems based on the Risk Assessment.

When it comes to the pen testing and vulnerability assessments requirements it is very straightforward. One of the key differences is in (b), where it says biannual vulnerability assessments should be done. There are firms where they do it quarterly, which is fine, that can still be done. At a minimum, there should be at least two vulnerability assessments a year that are being done.

The pen testing is required annually. Typically, this is done by an outside firm. It is very important that the scope of the pen tests is clearly defined. It has to be understood that it includes internal testing as well as external. Sometimes firms will just do the external part. Internal pen testing is also required. That includes many different things, such as government social engineering and phishing exercises.

The key here is that the pen testing and the vulnerability assessments are done by a third party. They should be independent and unbiased.

IP addresses and vulnerabilities must be looked at in context. Who is your audience for the pen test report and a scan? There is a huge gap here that must be understood in context. What most CISOs do is that they run the scans and the report is provided to the CIO. That's not enough, because when the scan is run, it only shows the level of the vulnerability, not the asset it is associated to. The report will show a Level 5 vulnerability with a particular IP address. Is that IP address for your internal phone system or is that IP address for your money transfer system? That's what management must know. What needs to happen here is to take the testing report and turn it into something that makes business sense.

What most CISOs do is they take the report, and they present it to the IT department saying we have 500 vulnerabilities, 400 are Level 5, 200 are Level 4, and so on. That is not valuable information. When you do your pen testing and get the results, you must provide a clear line of sight to the management and leadership what the report actually means. As an example, if an IP address or a range of IP addresses have Level 5 critical vulnerabilities, the report must align those IP addresses to the digital assets they are associated to. Is this an IP address for some firewall device or for your money transfer system? This is about the prioritization of remediation work and is a must for the cybersecurity program.

Typically, IT wants to show a small number of vulnerabilities. This is not the point. I've been in situations where there are 900 issues coming. The head of IT asks, how can we reduce the number? He or she is not looking at the data in context. It's not how many vulnerabilities you have. It's what systems, especially critical systems, are being impacted. That's what the CISO has to understand and communicate; otherwise, it is rubbish.

If you have a third party do the testing they are at a serious disadvantage. The third party does not know your environment. When they run their scans and they do their internal scanning of the workstations, the CISO must analyze the report to see which of the critical systems are being impacted. This is why integrated digital asset risk management is so valuable to the CISO. Firms must classify the digital assets. It is a requirement. CISOs must work with third parties to ensure the most critical systems are prioritized. They must be prioritized and then patched.

In many instances where a third party does a pen test and they explain a report to the management, the leadership doesn't understand what they are saying. The report has to be delivered in a context in business language. That is the job of the CISO to ensure that the report is useful.

If the report is not understood in context, then the IT person will put it in the patch schedule to fix the vulnerably. The next cycle of patching could be every quarter. If a report with level 5 vulnerabilities was given to the business owner of that application, they would be greatly upset to see these issues were not fixed immediately. Remember, the CISO is not working for IT, they are working for the firm.

Another frequently asked question is: What would serve as continuous monitoring for purposes of 23 NYCRR 500.05? This can be done through many different technical and procedural tools, control assessments, and systems. To be considered effective, continuous monitoring must have the ability on an ongoing basis to detect changes or activities within Information Systems. Monitoring for the existence of system vulnerabilities or malicious activity is required. Noncontinuous monitoring of Information Systems includes the periodic manual review of system and network logs, firewall configurations, and other nonautomated practices and would not satisfy the requirement for effective continuous monitoring.

500.06 audit trail

Each Covered Entity shall securely maintain systems that to the extent applicable and based on its Risk Assessment:

1. Are designed to reconstruct material financial transactions sufficient to support normal operations and obligations of the Covered Entity; and include audit trails designed to detect and respond to Cybersecurity Events that have a reasonable likelihood of materially harming any material part of the normal operations of the Covered Entity.
2. Each Covered Entity shall maintain records required by section 500.06(a)(1) of this Part for not fewer than five years and shall maintain records required by section 500.06(a)(2) of this Part for not fewer than three years.

An audit trail has two parts: first, each covered entity has to maintain systems to the extent applicable and based on risk assessment. This means the firm must be able to reconstruct material financial transactions and it must be sufficient to support normal operations. What that is saying is that if when there is an incident where loses a financial transaction due to a cyber event like a DoS attack, it must be recovered or reconstructed. This is a business continuity requirement that states the firm must recover data and transactions that were done at a certain point in time. To fill this requirement, most firms are looking into real-time recovery with a very short window where they can recover the most recent transactions.

The second part requires firms to include audit trails designed to detect and respond to cyber events. This would be done in the SIEM. The SIEM collects security events so that if something happens to that system, you don't have to collect the logs and parse the information.

The issue with audit trails is that they are very simple, but sometimes difficult to implement. The audit trails have to be able to "respond to cyber events". So where do your cyber events occur? In your digital assets. The applications, operating systems, network, and databases. Everything is pretty straightforward with systems. System Admins can pull the Windows logs or the Linux logs from your network devices.

Some firms struggle with database audits. It is required to track security events that occur at the database level. As an example, for each application, there is an application ID. The interface, the user logs are in the application and each database has a separate I.D. and password. What happens in the background? That ID and password are pulling information from some database. Many times, firms and most developers take shortcuts. They form a connection pool. This is where when you log into the database you are mapped to an ID. This allows the firm to have multiple users connecting to the database, all mapping to the same database ID. There is no way to see if this is 1 or 10 users logging in, since there is not ten separate database I.D.s for each person. Many developers tie the application I.D. to the database.

Therefore, there is no way to distinguish the security events in this case. If a user deleted a table through the interface it will show up on the database logs, but you won't know which user actually executed that event. DFS states that this is a no-go. There must be bonafide audit trails. There are many tools out there that work like a sniffer. It can be used to see who did what with each I.D. because the request has to come back, so it ties the two together.

The proper way to meet this requirement is to turn on the log at the database level and see how it affects the performance and the response time. In terms of retention, DFS is saying to keep data no more than three years. There are a lot of regulations that require keeping it longer. A cross reference of all the regulations is required to establish what data types must be retained and for how long.

500.07 access privileges

As part of its cybersecurity program, based on the Covered Entity's Risk Assessment, each Covered Entity shall limit user access privileges to Information Systems that provide access to nonpublic Information and shall periodically review such access privileges.

The key points here are to have an:

- Effective Onboarding and Off-boarding Processes
- User Entitlement Process

This means ensuring that employees and consultants are provided the correct credentials in a timely manner and that those credentials are disabled on the day that they are no longer with the firm. The regulation requires that the user entitlement review be done twice a year. It can be done more often, and most firms do this more than twice a year. It is critical to know who has access to your data and to ensure that when they leave, they no longer have access to your data. Typically, the user IDs are not deleted, they are disabled. This allows management to still check email or files for any users.

500.08 application security

(a) Each Covered Entity's cybersecurity program shall include written procedures, guidelines, and standards designed to ensure the use of secure development practices for in-house developed applications utilized by the Covered Entity, and procedures for evaluating, assessing, or testing the security of externally developed applications utilized by the Covered Entity within the context of the Covered Entity's technology environment.

(b) All such procedures, guidelines, and standards shall be periodically reviewed, assessed, and updated as necessary by the CISO (or a qualified designee) of the Covered Entity.

The key point is that the firm has clear written procedures that address the secure software development lifecycle. As mentioned earlier, sometimes security is notified the date an application is going live. Proper procedures will prevent this type of behavior. The best practice is for teams to be notified well in advance. Code reviews are required. When applications are poorly designed the firm will be open to SQL Injections and Cross Site Scripting. Code reviews should catch these vulnerabilities. DFS requires checking the application security procedures to ensure that a code check is actually done. Backdoors are typically created by developers that provide a shortcut into the application. Having unrealistic deadlines adds to this practice. Backdoors must be documented so that they can be sealed off before going live. Roles and responsibilities of the developers, security administrators, and others must be documented.

The CISO is ultimately responsible for the application security. That also includes external applications. The CISO must ensure the controls are working as expected for third-party built code. Many times, the third party follows their own procedures that are not aligned to yours. Any new systems being brought into the firm require the CISO to have a way to review and approve its uses before it is productionized. This process must be part of your application security documentation. If it is documented and implemented it, DFS will see that the firm is complying. If it is in practice and not documented, DFS will indicate that the firm is not complying. The firm's documentation and approval processes cannot be stressed enough. Proper application security procedures are one of the most important principles used to reduce vulnerabilities.

500.09 risk assessment

(a) Each Covered Entity shall conduct a periodic Risk Assessment of the Covered Entity's Information Systems sufficient to inform the design of the cybersecurity program as required by this Part. Such Risk Assessment shall be updated as reasonably necessary to address changes to the Covered Entity's Information Systems, nonpublic Information, or business operations. The Covered Entity's Risk Assessment shall allow for revision of controls to respond to technological developments and evolving threats and shall consider the particular risks of the Covered Entity's business operations related to cybersecurity, Nonpublic Information collected or stored, Information Systems utilized, and the availability and effectiveness of controls to protect Nonpublic Information and Information Systems.

(b) The Risk Assessment shall be carried out in accordance with written policies and procedures and shall be documented. Such policies and procedures shall include:

1 criteria for the evaluation and categorization of identified cybersecurity risks or threats facing the Covered Entity;

2 criteria for the assessment of the confidentiality, integrity, security, and availability of the Covered Entity's Information Systems and Nonpublic

Information, including the adequacy of existing controls in the context of identified risks; and

3 requirements describing how identified risks will be mitigated or accepted based on the Risk Assessment and how the cybersecurity program will address the risks.

This requirement is a combination of a risk and a security assessment. It needs to be very detailed. If it is done right, it takes anywhere from 3–6 months. That's why it is typically done once a year and should be described in the security policy. DFS incorrectly calls a security control assessment a risk assessment. The "risk assessment" must be documented and include key points. They require pen testing, vulnerability scanning, and a vulnerability assessment. A risk assessment is based on the impact and likelihood and is a dynamic set of data. Cyber Risk Management Platforms measure the impact and likelihood associated with digital assets that allows for the prioritization of risk.

A configuration assessment is also required. Servers, databases, and networks must be configured a certain way based on policies that are in place and how the firm needs to assess them. Most times when the firm builds a system, they use a standard build. What happens if it gets changed? Was it authorized? This must be taken into account when the firm assesses the environment from a configuration point of view.

Physical security is required. How effective are the cameras, card system, etc.?

A vendor risk assessment must be done. If the third parties have weak security, then why are you using them? There are cases where the business overrules security and insists on using vendors with poor cybersecurity hygiene. In these cases, as a CISO, the risk must be identified, and risk mitigation procedures put in place. Vendor risk assessments must be presented to management to prioritize risk remediation. The CISO must put the assessment details in writing so that management understands what the risks are. Management should define what they expect the vendor to correct and within what time frame. This puts the ball in the vendor's court. The business needs to decide if they can accept vendor risk and for how long.

Data requirements must be documented and verified. A digital asset inventory with a data map must be done to identify where data lives. Encryption requirements and access rights must be documented.

The DFS report needs to capture all the elements of the security and risk analysis in business language. Your audience is not technical. They must understand if the program is effective and where the gaps are.

500.10 personnel

(a) Cybersecurity Personnel and Intelligence. In addition to the requirements set forth in section 500.04(a) of this Part, each Covered Entity shall:

1 utilize qualified cybersecurity personnel of the Covered Entity, an Affiliate, or a Third-Party Service Provider sufficient to manage the Covered Entity's cybersecurity risks and to perform or oversee the

performance of the core cybersecurity functions specified in section 500.02(b)(1)–(6) of this Part;

2 provide cybersecurity personnel with cybersecurity updates and training sufficient to address relevant cybersecurity risks; and

3 verify that key cybersecurity personnel take steps to maintain current knowledge of changing cybersecurity threats and countermeasures.

(b) A Covered Entity may choose to utilize an Affiliate or qualified Third-Party Service Provider to assist in complying with the requirements set forth in this Part, subject to the requirements set forth in section 500.11 of this Part.

What examiners are looking for is the evidence that the security function has competent people that know what they are doing. The former CISO at Equifax had a music degree. Why was she in that position? NYS DFS Examiners will be closely scrutinizing the bank CISO to ensure that she/he has the requisite qualifications and experience to be a competent CISO. They must be able to speak freely without any issue of being reprimanded about doing their job. This is why it distinctly says qualified people. The team must be able to speak in both the business and technical language. Most CISOs today only are only technical. They need to be able to speak both languages. This is where training comes in.

500.11 Third-party service providers

Each Covered Entity shall implement written policies and procedures designed to ensure the security of Information Systems and nonpublic Information that are accessible to, or held by, Third-Party Service Providers. Such policies and procedures shall be based on the Risk Assessment of the Covered Entity and shall address to the extent applicable:

- The identification and risk assessment of Third-Party Service Providers.
- Minimum cybersecurity practices required to be met by such Third-Party Service Providers in order for them to do business with the Covered Entity.
- Due diligence processes used to evaluate the adequacy of cybersecurity practices of such Third-Party Service Providers.
- Periodic assessment of such Third-Party Service Providers based on the risk they present and the continued adequacy of their cybersecurity practices.

Such policies and procedures shall include relevant guidelines for due diligence and/or contractual protections relating to Third-Party Service Providers including to the extent applicable guidelines addressing:

- The Third-Party Service Provider's policies and procedures for access controls, including its use of Multifactor Authentication as required by section 500.12 of this Part, to limit access to relevant Information Systems and nonpublic Information.

- The Third-Party Service Provider's policies and procedures for use of encryption as required by section 500.15 of this Part to protect nonpublic Information in transit and at rest.
- Notice to be provided to the Covered Entity in the event of a Cybersecurity Event directly impacting the Covered Entity's Information Systems or the Covered Entity's nonpublic Information being held by the Third-Party Service Provider.
- Representations and warranties addressing the Third-Party Service Provider's cybersecurity policies and procedures that relate to the security of the Covered Entity's Information Systems or nonpublic Information.

There are limited exceptions to the requirements. As an example, an agent, employee, representative, or designee of a Covered Entity who is itself a Covered Entity need not develop its own Third-Party Information Security Policy pursuant to this section if the agent, employee, representative, or designee follows the policy of the Covered Entity that is required to comply with this Part.

Sixty-three percent of reported data breaches are due to third parties. Third parties can be service providers that implement IT projects, systems or technology providers that provide technologies or consolidated sets of technologies, or cloud service providers that provide cloud infrastructure. Any vendor that is touching your data must be included.

It is recommended to include all vendors. It may not be apparent that the vendor has any relationship to your data. As an example, let's explore Fazio Mechanical. They are an HVAC vendor that had access to Target's systems. Vendors can have hidden risks. Target's data was breached due to the third-party HVAC vendor's poor access control hygiene. A phishing email was sent to employees at Fazio Mechanical. "Citadel"—a trojan malware was inserted. Fazio Mechanical's vendor credentials were stolen by attackers and used to access Target's network. Attackers then exploited a Web application vulnerability at Target using a SQL injection. Once the backdoor was created, the attackers took their time conducting reconnaissance to locate the servers they wanted to steal data from. After the servers were located the attackers probably used a "pass-the-hash" attack to steal an Admin access token that was create a new Admin account. As a result, 70 million customers' PII was stolen. The servers did not store the credit card number associated with the PII. The attackers then went after the point-of-sale (POS) machines. Attackers next installed malware onto POS machines to copy all the credit and debit card data used for purchases. After copying the data from the POS, the data was then forwarded to servers in America and Brazil to wait for the attackers to retrieve it at their convenience and sell it on the dark web.

Many companies have adopted a cloud first strategy with noncore applications moving into the cloud. Cloud service security is tricky. It is a shared responsibility model between the organization and the cloud service provider. The organization is responsible to protect its data and provide the customer service regardless if it is on-premise or in the cloud. Documentation is critical with vendors.

Vendor management starts with a vendor inventory. Not only who they are but what type of vendor they are. Vendors can have more than one function. As an example, Salesforce is both a cloud service and a system vendor. It is not enough to have a list of applications that are vendor supported. You have to know the vendor and what they provide you.

Second, it is required to know what data the vendor touches and what type of asset they work with. As an example, Salesforce handles privacy data and personally identifiable information (PII). Privacy data is defined as EU citizen data and PII is US personal data using the NIST definition. Why do you need to know this? The rules are different based on the types of data. Salesforce is a business-critical asset in most cases. The asset classification relates to the prioritization of resources in the event of a cyber issue and the level of risk tolerance. Vendors that are working with crown jewel assets will receive the greatest amount of scrutiny by an examiner.

Many likelihood factors must be known about vendors. How do they access your systems? Where do they access your systems? How many of your records do they have? We discuss vendor risk management in depth in the vendor risk management chapters.

Examiners may ask for a SOC 2 report. A SOC 2 is an audited report done by a CPA firm like KPMG or Deloitte which is supposedly designed to provide assurances about the effectiveness of controls in place at a service organization that are relevant to the security, availability, or processing integrity of the system used to process clients' information, or the confidentiality or privacy of that information. It is, in my opinion, not very valuable; however, it was what the industry knows.

A risk assessment of a vendor has to focus on what is important. How much data exfiltration, business interruption, and regulatory exposures do you have with the vendor?

A security control assessment is required. How effective are the vendor's cybersecurity controls? The NIST cybersecurity control assessment should be reviewed in depth. Security issues should be prioritized to fix based on the risk assessment.

Data breach response plans must be detailed with a communications framework in place and detailed incident response plans are required. Procedures should include guidelines for due diligence and contractual protections. All third parties should connect using multifactor authentication. Nonpublic Information (NPI) must be encrypted in transit and at rest for cloud service providers that have sensitive data on their network.

Security incidents must be communicated by the third party to your firm within a specific timeframe. It is recommended to put in the contract contractual protections that in the event of a breach, they have 72 hours to report it to you. If they do not notify you and the breach is made public, the examiners are going to come after your firm and ask why it was not reported it to them within 72 hours. All 50 states have data breach notification laws.

Contract language is critical. In particular, ensure that the vendor does not try to wiggle out of taking responsibility for a data breach. We have seen language in contracts that stipulate that if there's a breach, that is not the vendor's fault and they still expect to still get paid; regardless, they will accept no responsibility. Signing this type of contract is a mistake and will have to be revisited so that proper language is in place. The security team should be involved in the contract process to prevent this type of behavior. A big issue with vendor management today is the business selects the vendor and cybersecurity team is not involved. This must change and should be baked into a policy that prohibits this behavior.

500.12 Multifactor authentication

Based on its Risk Assessment, each Covered Entity shall use effective controls, which may include Multifactor Authentication or Risk-Based Authentication, to protect against unauthorized access to nonpublic Information or Information Systems.

Multifactor Authentication shall be utilized for any individual accessing the Covered Entity's internal networks from an external network, unless the Covered Entity's CISO has approved in writing the use of reasonably equivalent or more secure access controls.

Remote access connection to your firm requires multifactor authentication for nonpublic information. This includes if you access a third-party system that has critical information. Whether it be hard tokens or soft tokens only multifactor will do. The examiner will accept nothing less.

500.13 Limits on data retention

As part of its cybersecurity program, each Covered Entity shall include policies and procedures for the secure disposal on a periodic basis of any nonpublic Information identified in section 500.01(g)(2)-(3) of this Part that is no longer necessary for business operations or for other legitimate business purposes of the Covered Entity, except where such information is otherwise required to be retained by law or regulation, or where targeted disposal is not reasonably feasible due to the manner in which the information is maintained.

The examiners will look at the policies for data retention. They should include policies for secure disposal on a periodic basis of any nonpublic information. The retention policies must be kept up to date. This relates back to knowing where your data is on premise or with a third party. If you have data that's at a third party, they have to be included in the policy, especially when it comes to destruction or legal hold requirements.

This must be managed properly. The location of the data must be known and who is managing it and when and how it is being disposed of. One challenge here is that when you have a critical document that is sent via an email to ten people, you now have ten copies. When you delete the original you still those ten copies. A mechanism must be put in place to figure out how to manage your critical data and make sure when you destroy it is indeed gone from everywhere. One solution may be to use SharePoint. With SharePoint when you share a file by email you send a link instead of sharing a file. There are other solutions of this type. The key is to know where your data is so when it comes to destroying it that allows the effective implementation of those procedures.

500.14 Training and monitoring

As part of its cybersecurity program, each Covered Entity shall:

(a) implement risk-based policies, procedures, and controls designed to monitor the activity of Authorized Users and detect unauthorized access or use of, or tampering with, Nonpublic Information by such Authorized Users; and
(b) provide regular cybersecurity awareness training for all personnel that is updated to reflect risks identified by the Covered Entity in its Risk Assessment.

This requirement speaks to ensuring that your employees are properly trained. This includes management and the board. Examiners will ask how you know that your training is effective. One method is to have a quiz afterward that the person signs off on. This documents that they have understood the training.

As an example, in one case, an individual went to a Dropbox website and uploaded customer information. It was found on an audit. HR was asked to pull his awareness training program record. The person clearly signed off on the training and HR used that to discipline the employee.

500.15 Encryption of nonpublic information (NPI)

(a) As part of its cybersecurity program, based on its Risk Assessment, each Covered Entity shall implement controls, including encryption, to protect nonpublic Information held or transmitted by the Covered Entity both in transit over external networks and at rest.

1 To the extent a Covered Entity determines that encryption of nonpublic Information in transit over external networks is infeasible, the Covered Entity may instead secure such nonpublic Information using effective alternative compensating controls reviewed and approved by the Covered Entity's CISO.
2 To the extent a Covered Entity determines that encryption of nonpublic Information at rest is infeasible, the Covered Entity may instead secure such nonpublic Information using effective alternative compensating controls reviewed and approved by the Covered Entity's CISO.

(b) To the extent that a Covered Entity is utilizing compensating controls under (a) above, the feasibility of encryption and effectiveness of the compensating controls shall be reviewed by the CISO at least annually.

This requirement is to make sure that nonpublic information is encrypted at rest and in transit.

500.16 Incident response plan

As part of its cybersecurity program, each Covered Entity shall establish a written incident response plan designed to promptly respond to, and recover from, any Cybersecurity Event materially affecting the confidentiality, integrity, or availability of the Covered Entity's Information Systems or the continuing functionality of any aspect of the Covered Entity's business or operations.

Such incident response plan shall address the following areas:

- The internal processes for responding to a Cybersecurity Event.
- The goals of the incident response plan.
- The definition of clear roles, responsibilities, and levels of decision-making authority.
- External and internal communications and information sharing.
- Identification of requirements for the remediation of any identified weaknesses in Information Systems and associated controls.
- Documentation and reporting regarding Cybersecurity Events and related incident response activities.
- The evaluation and revision as necessary of the incident response plan following a Cybersecurity Event.

There is nothing new here. If you have an incident whether internally or with a third-party there should be a documented process in place that outlines step by step how to deal with it. DFS lays this out including what your plan should include in terms of the internal processes, goals of the plan, role and responsibilities, communication and information sharing, remediation of any weaknesses, how to report the event, and evaluate and revise the plan as necessary.

500.17 Notices to the superintendent

(a) Notice of Cybersecurity Event. Each Covered Entity shall notify the superintendent as promptly as possible but in no event later than 72 hours from a determination that a Cybersecurity Event has occurred that is either of the following:

1. Cybersecurity Events impacting the Covered Entity of which notice is required to be provided to any government body, self-regulatory agency, or any other supervisory body; or
2. Cybersecurity Events that have a reasonable likelihood of materially harming any material part of the normal operation(s) of the Covered Entity.

(b) Annually, each Covered Entity shall submit to the superintendent a written statement covering the prior calendar year. This statement shall be submitted by February 15 in such form set forth as Appendix A, certifying that the Covered Entity is in compliance with the requirements set forth in this Part. Each Covered Entity shall maintain for examination by the Department all records, schedules, and data supporting this certificate for a period of five years.

To the extent a Covered Entity has identified areas, systems, or processes that require material improvement, updating or redesign, the Covered Entity shall document the identification and the remedial efforts planned and underway to address such areas, systems, or processes. Such documentation must be available for inspection by the superintendent.

The key here is to notify within 72 hours. Sometimes there is confusion here. What exactly is needed to report? Is it minor issues or just breaches? The easiest way to address this is to categorize the event. There are different ways to do this. Not every incident needs to be reported to DFS or your customers. For example, an employee is accessing your network remotely. They forget their password and try 50 times. That is going to trigger a lot of events that do not necessarily need to be reported. It can be innocent where they just forgot their password. However, when it is not innocent, and it is someone trying to gain unauthorized access into an account, that is another issue. This is why categorizing the events and how they are impacting the business and customers is critical by breaking events down into severity levels. Similarly, when a vulnerability report is run, you break down the event by associating the IP address to the digital asset. Forgotten passwords do not need to be reported. It is just a mistake and is categorized as a level 1 event. Higher level issues where it is clearly an unauthorized attempt to get to your data must be reported.

The first step is to define what is reportable and use that. Care must be taken to be clear about how you justify the categories of what is reportable. If it impacts your business operations, you must report it, even if it is internal. As an example, if someone internally makes a mistake that impacted customers even if it wasn't intentional, it is a reportable event to DFS. If you do not meet the 72 hours deadline, you may have issues with DFS. If you have third parties that have your data and they have an issue, they may need to report to you, but you may not need to report to DFS. Each case must be clearly defined.

Notes

1. Wikipedia, "New York State Department of Financial Services", September 8, 2020, https://en.wikipedia.org/wiki/New_York_State_Department_of_Financial_Services.
2. New York State Department of Financial Services, "New York State Department of Financial Services 23 NYCRR 500", https://www.dfs.ny.gov/docs/legal/regulations/adoptions/dfsrf500txt.pdf.
3. New York State Department of Financial Services, "FAQ's: NYCRR Part 500-Cybersecurity", 2020, https://www.dfs.ny.gov/industry_guidance/cyber_faqs.
4. New York State Department of Financial Services, "FAQ's: NYCRR Part 500-Cybersecurity", 2020, https://www.dfs.ny.gov/industry_guidance/cyber_faqs.
5. New York State Department of Financial Services, "New York State Department of Financial Services 23 NYCRR 500", https://www.dfs.ny.gov/docs/legal/regulations/adoptions/dfsrf500txt.pdf.
6. Cyber resilience: An important new role for storage. https://www.ibm.com/downloads/cas/K3MQPOZX.

18 INDUSTRY CYBERSECURITY STANDARDS

PCI Standards emphasize the importance of people, process and technology when it comes to protecting payment information. This guidance can help businesses focus on the 'people' part of the equation and build a greater culture of security awareness and vigilance across their organizations.

Troy Leach, CTO PCI SSC

PCI-DSS in depth

Let's look at the PCI-DSS in detail. The Payment Card Industry Data Security Standard (PCI-DSS) is an information security standard for organizations that use or process data and is governed by the PCI Security council members—Mastercard, Visa, American Express, JBC, and Discover.

The PCI Standard is a mandated guideline from the card brands and is administered by the Payment Card Industry Security Standards Council. The standard was created to reduce credit card fraud. Compliance must be validated annually or quarterly, either by an external Qualified Security Assessor (QSA) or by a firm-specific Internal Security Assessor (ISA) who creates a Report on Compliance for organizations handling large volumes of transactions, or by Self-Assessment Questionnaire (SAQ) for companies handling smaller volumes. The latest version of the standard is V.3.2.1 that was released in May of 2018. Version 4 is due out in mid-2021.

PCI-DSS compliance is required for banks, merchants, and data processors. PCI-DSS has the following six control objectives[4]:

- Build and Maintain a Secure Network and Systems
- Protect Cardholder Data
- Maintain a Vulnerability Management Program
- Implement Strong Access Control Measures
- Regularly Monitor and Test Networks
- Maintain an Information Security Policy

There are 12 sets of requirements within the six control objectives. These include[5]:

- Installing and maintaining a firewall configuration to protect cardholder data. The purpose of a firewall is to scan all network traffic and block untrusted networks from accessing the system.

DOI: 10.4324/9781003052616-22

- Changing vendor-supplied defaults for system passwords and other security parameters. Default passwords are easily discovered through public information and can be used by malicious individuals to gain unauthorized access to systems.
- Protecting stored cardholder data. Encryption, hashing, masking, and truncation are methods used to protect cardholder data.
- Encrypting transmission of cardholder data over open, public networks. Strong encryption, including using only trusted keys and certifications, reduces the risk of being targeted by malicious individuals through hacking.
- Protecting all systems against malware and performing regular updates of anti-virus software. Malware can enter a network in numerous ways, including internet use, employee email, mobile devices, and/or storage devices. Up-to-date anti-virus software or supplemental anti-malware software will reduce the risk of exploitation via malware.
- Developing and maintaining secure systems and applications. Vulnerabilities in systems and applications allow unscrupulous individuals to gain privileged access. Security patches should be immediately installed to fix vulnerabilities and prevent exploitation and compromise of cardholder data.
- Restricting access to cardholder data to only authorized personnel. Systems and processes must be used to restrict access to cardholder data on a "need to know" basis.
- Identifying and authenticating access to system components. Each person with access to system components should be assigned a unique identification (ID) that allows accountability of access to critical data systems.
- Restricting physical access to cardholder data. Physical access to cardholder data or systems that hold this data must be secure to prevent unauthorized access or removal of data.
- Tracking and monitoring all access to cardholder data and network resources. Logging mechanisms should be in place to track user activities that are critical to prevent, detect, or minimize the impact of data compromises.
- Testing security systems and processes regularly. New vulnerabilities are continuously discovered. Systems, processes, and software need to be tested frequently to uncover vulnerabilities that could be used by malicious individuals.
- Maintaining an information security policy for all personnel. A strong security policy includes making personnel understand the sensitivity of data and their responsibility to protect it.

PCI has several supplemental guidelines regarding the use of technologies, approaches, and special testing requirements. These include but are not limited to Penetration Testing, Code Reviews and Application Firewalls Clarified, Applicability in an EMV Environment, Virtualization Guidelines, Tokenization Guidelines, Risk Assessment Guidelines, and Scoping and Segmentation.

PCI scope

PCI has a specific scope for merchants, banks, and data processors. Segmenting the network to include only systems that process credit card data can decrease the scope of a PCI assessment.

PCI requirements for merchants are based on transaction volume. Level 1 requirements are for merchants with over 6 million transactions annually. Level 2 requirements are for merchants with between 1 and 6 million transactions annually. Level 3 requirements are for merchants with between 20,000 and 1 million transactions annually and level 4 requirements are for merchants with less than 20,000 transactions annually.

PCI standards have been incorporated into state law in some cases. In Minnesota, there is a law prohibiting the retention of some types of payment card data beyond 48 hours after authorization of the transaction. Nevada requires merchants doing business in that state to comply with the current PCI DSS and shields compliant entities from liability. In Washington, PCI DSS was incorporated into state law. Unlike Nevada's law, entities are not required to comply with it, but compliant entities are shielded from liability in the event of a data breach.

Some companies can self-assess, but most require a third-party assessor. A Qualified Security Assessor (QSA) is an individual bearing a certificate that has been provided by the PCI Security Standards Council. This certified person can audit merchants for Payment Card Industry Data Security Standard (PCI DSS) compliance. QSAs are independent groups/entities which have been certified by PCI SSC for compliance confirmation in organization procedures.

An Internal Security Assessor (ISA) is an individual who has earned a certificate from the PCI Security Standards Council on behalf of their sponsoring organization. This certified person has the ability to perform PCI self-assessments for their organization. This ISA program was designed to help Level 2 merchants meet the new Mastercard compliance validation requirements. ISA certification empowers a worker to do an internal appraisal of his/her organization and propose security solutions/controls for PCI DSS compliance. As the ISAs are sponsored by the organization for the PCI SSC affirmation, they are in charge of cooperation and participation with QSAs.

A Report on Compliance (ROC) is a form that has to be filled by all level 1 merchants and Visa merchants undergoing a PCI DSS audit. The ROC form is used to verify that the merchant being audited is compliant with the PCI DSS standard. The ROC confirms that policies, strategies, approaches, and workflows are appropriately developed and implemented by the organization for the protection of cardholders against scams and fraud involving card-based business transactions. A template "ROC Reporting Template" is available on the PCI SSC site and contains detailed guidelines about the ROC.

The Self-Assessment Questionnaire is a set of questionnaire documents that merchants are required to complete every year and submit to their transaction bank. The questionnaires are validation tools intended to assist merchants and service providers reporting the results of their PCI DSS self-assessment. Another component of the SAQ is an Attestation of Compliance (AOC). This is where each SAQ question is answered based on the internal PCI DSS self-evaluation. Each SAQ question must be replied to with either "yes" or "no." In the event that a question has the appropriate response "no," the firm is required to explain its future implementation plans.

Case Study: Heartland Payment Systems

Heartland Payment Systems was another landmark PCI-related case. Heartland is a leading payment processing company. In 2008, they reported that their systems had been compromised by malware. Heartland at the time handled over 100 million transactions per month for more than 250,000 businesses. Heartland failed to detect the breach and was alerted by Visa and MasterCard of suspicious transactions.[6] The data consisted of PCI-regulated data, including credit card numbers, expiration dates, and a subset of the exposed data also included credit card names.

In 2007, Heartland assured financial institutions that the sensitive financial information entrusted to the processor was secure. In December of 2007, unauthorized persons hacked into Heartland's computer network and gained access to the confidential financial data associated with approximately 130 million credit cards and debit cards.[7]

In November 2008, the PCI determined that controls in place were insufficient. Heartland executives were "well aware ... that the bare minimum PCI-DSS standards were insufficient to protect it from an attack by sophisticated hackers," the complaint says.

In January 2009, suspicious files were found (indicating that the breach had occurred) on Heartland's proprietary "Passport" application. Passport was used to process credit card and debit card transactions and send payments to merchants. On January 20, 2009, Heartland publicly disclosed the breach. On the day after the data breach was announced, Heartland conducted a webinar about the data breach for its high-level employees, sales representatives, and/or relationship managers. The complaint says Heartland relationship managers were told that "PCI compliance was not a big deal."[8]

On March 14, 2009, Visa removed Heartland from its published list of PCI-DSS compliant service providers and on April of 2009, Heartland was recertified as PCI compliant.

Heartland would eventually provide over US$145 million in compensation for fraudulent payments. The total loss for companies, banks, and insurers would be estimated at over US$200 million. Albert Gonzalez, the mastermind behind the Heartland Payment Systems breach and the breaches that affected TJX, Office Max, and restaurant chain Dave & Busters, was sentenced in March 2010 to two consecutive 20-year terms after pleading guilty. All class action lawsuits were dropped.

Remediation and consumer credit costs to Heartland were a little over US$200 million. However, within days of announcing the breach, Heartland stock price fell by 50% and further declined within months by 77%. As a direct result of the hapless security program, Heartland was not able to process credit card data for several months and lost hundreds of customers.[9]

Notes

1. Wikipedia, "Albert Gonzalez", August 19, 2020, https://en.wikipedia.org/wiki/Albert_Gonzalez.
2. Claire Suddath, Time, "Master hacker Albert Gonzalez", August 19, 2009, http://content.time.com/time/business/article/0,8599,1917345,00.html.
3. Melanie Watson, IT Governance, "Top 4 cybersecurity frameworks", January 17, 2019, https://www.itgovernanceusa.com/blog/top-4-cybersecurity-frameworks.
4. Official PCI Security Standards Council Site - Verify PCI .... https://www.pcisecuritystandards.org/pci_security/maintaining_payment_security
5. Payment Card Industry (PCI) Data Security Standard. https://citadel-information.com/wp-content/uploads/PCI_DSS_v3-1.pdf
6. The Associated Press, Security on NBC News.com, "Heartland payment systems hacked", January 20, 2009, http://www.nbcnews.com/id/28758856/ns/technology_and_science-security/t/heartland-payment-systems-hacked/#.X2JFpWhKhPY.
7. Linda McGlasson, Bank info security, "Heartland breach: Inside look at the Plaintiff's case", October 8, 2009, https://www.bankinfosecurity.com/heartland-breach-inside-look-at-plaintiffs-case-a-1844.
8. Heartland Breach: Inside look at the Plaintiffs' Case. https://www.bankinfosecurity.com/heartland-breach-inside-look-at-plaintiffs-case-a-1844.
9. Michael Gordover, Observe IT, "Throwback Thursday: Lessons learned from the 2008 Heartland breach", March 19, 2015, https://www.observeit.com/blog/throwback-thursday-lessons-learned-from-the-2008-heartland-breach/.

PART V

INCIDENT RESPONSE, AUDIT, AND FORENSICS

19 CYBERSECURITY INCIDENT RESPONSE

It takes 20 years to build a reputation and a few minutes of cyber-incident to ruin it.

Stephane Nappo, CISO Group SEB

Incident response teams

An incident response team is a centralized team that is responsible for responding to a cybersecurity incident. The team will receive a notification of a security breach or business interruption, analyze, and implement the incident response plan. The team usually includes the following people:

- **Incident Response Manager:** The manager oversees and prioritizes the different steps in managing the incident. They also interface with the other stakeholders in the firm—including the CISO, legal team, corporate security team members, HR team, etc.—and coordinate communications.
- **CISO:** The buck stops with the CISO. The CISO coordinates with the Incident Response Manager and documents the issues to report to the board. The CISO has to be able to explain the incident, update the status to stakeholders, and outline the required steps to address the incident. The CISO also works with the legal team to coordinate communication both internally and externally about the incident.
- **General Counsel:** They work with the CISO and team on communications to regulators, State Attorneys General, the public, and law enforcement. They work with HR on internal communications. They also provide advice regarding liability issues in the event that an incident involves PII, PHI, etc.
- **Human Resources:** They will be involved if an employee is involved in the incident and will be responsible for their discipline.
- **Security Analysts:** Analysts are the key people who review cyber events and identify when an incident has actually occurred. They help determine what, when, and how.
- Forensics professionals are typically responsible for recovering key artifacts of data and maintaining the chain of custody of the evidence to ensure that it can be used in a court of law.

DOI: 10.4324/9781003052616-24

- **Cyber Threat Intelligence Specialists:** They complement the security analysts by providing threat intelligence and context to the incident.
- **Senior Management:** They are ultimately responsible for all cybersecurity incidents. They provide the budget for the incident response team.
- **Audit:** Audit works with the incident response team in providing the methodology for risk, vulnerability, and threat assessments.
- **Public Relations (PR):** This team ensures that the issue is communicated properly to external stakeholders, such as investors and the press.

Incident response steps

Incident response is a set of steps for teams to respond to incidents. In order for the incident response teams to be successful, a coordinated and organized approach is needed, for companies to effectively address the wide range of security incidents that a company may experience. There are several steps that every response program needs to have to be effective.

Step 1: preparation

Without proper preparation, the incident response will most likely fail as seen by Equifax and many others. Having a set of predetermined guidelines will increase the chances of success. Having a comprehensive plan must be in place to support all team members. The plan should address the following steps:

1. **Development and Documentation of the IR Policies:** The establishment of well-defined policies, and procedures, with roles and responsibilities outlined in detail.
2. **Creation of Communication Guidelines:** The creation of the communication standards and guidelines that outline roles, timing, and process to enable seamless communication during and after an incident.
3. **Utilization of External Threat Intelligence Feeds:** Collecting data from dark web sources that allow for the analysis of threat intelligence feeds.
4. **Performance of Cyber Hunting Exercises:** For more mature companies, conduct operational threat hunting exercises that identify incidents occurring within your infrastructure. This allows for a more proactive incident response.
5. **Understanding Your Threat Detection Capabilities:** Work to ensure that the current threat detection capabilities are sufficient and update the risk assessment programs.
6. Providing employee training, especially to spot phishing or BEC attacks and avoid dangerous websites.
7. Establishing resources for testing, training, and providing guidance. NIST and SANS both have many guides including:

NIST Guide to Test, Training, and Exercise Programs for IT Plans and Capabilities: https://csrc.nist.gov/publications/detail/sp/800-84/final

SANS Guide: SANS Institute Incident Handling Guide: https://www.sans.org/reading-room/whitepapers/incident/incident-handlers-handbook-33901

Step 2: incident detection and reporting

The focus of this step is to monitor security events in order to identify events, detect incident, alert management, and report on potential security incidents.

Firms use firewalls, IDS, and DLP systems to monitor security events. Preventing data loss is a critical aspect of this step. SIEM systems will detect potential security incidents by correlating alerts. Having a ticketing process for incidents that documents initial findings, alerts stakeholders, and assigns an initial incident classification is needed. The reporting process should include specified triggers for the escalation of regulatory-related incidents. Quarterly or semi-annual reviews of successful and denied attacks are a good way to adjust detection and reporting.

Step 3: triage and analysis

Properly scoping and understanding the security incident is the focus of this step. Resources collecting data from tools for analysis will identify indicators of compromise. Individuals need to have in-depth skills and an understanding of system responses, digital forensics, memory analysis, and malware analysis, among others.

It is important to focus on the legal repercussions of compromises as well as the technical. This can include filing an insurance claim, reporting requirements, and customer/client notifications, among others. This would also be a good spot to begin prepping the PR response.

Analysis on endpoints, artifacts, and the malware is a part of this step.

Endpoint Analysis: It determines what traces have been left behind by the threat actor.

Artifact Timeline Analysis: It gathers the artifacts that are needed to build a timeline of nefarious activities. Forensics will analyze bit-for-bit copies of data and capture RAM that is used to analyze and identify the key artifacts to determine what occurred on a computer device or devices at issue.

Malware Analysis: The team will investigate the malicious malware that was used by the attacker and document the functionalities of the malware. They use behavioral analytics to investigate how the malicious program executes in a Virtual Machine (VM) and they monitor its behavior. The team will also use reverse engineering techniques to scope out the malware functionality and come up with its signature.

Enterprise threat hunting is used to analyze systems and the event logs to determine the scope of compromise. All compromised accounts, machines, etc. must be documented to ensure the effective containment and neutralization of the threat is effectively performed.

Step 4: containment and neutralization

The strategy for containment and neutralization uses the threat intelligence and indicators of compromise that have been gathered during step 3. Once the system is restored and security is verified, normal operations can resume.

Shutdowns must be coordinated. After all of the identified affected systems that have been compromised are known, a coordinated shutdown of these devices is performed. Proper timing is essential, and a notification must be sent to all IR team members involved.

Wiping clean the infected devices and rebuilding the operating system from the ground up is required. All passwords must be changed to any compromised accounts.

Identified domains and IP addresses that were leveraged by threat actors for command and control need to have threat mitigation controls in place to block the communication from all points of egress connected to these domains.

Step 5: post incident activities

After the incident is resolved, the team must ensure that information regarding the incident is properly documented into a "lessons learned" that will be used to prevent similar occurrences from happening again in the future.

An incident report that documents the details of the incident is used for lessons learned to improve the incident response plan. New or updated security measures will be recommended to keep this type of security incident from reoccurring.

Closely monitoring activities related to the incident will aim to prevent cybercriminals from repeating the incident. This requires careful scrutiny of the SIEM logs for any indications that could be associated with the prior incident.

Updating the organization's threat intelligence feeds is recommended, as well as identifying new preventative measures to prevent future incidents.

It is also critical to perform an incident review to gain cross-functional support and ensure the proper implementation of new security initiatives such as the focus on the legal, financial, and reputational fallout of the event. Here is where legal really earns their stripes.

Best practices steps

There are best practices to follow when creating and using an incident response plan. These include:

1. Having a Digital Asset Inventory. This identifies which data is the most important to protect and can be used in prioritization. Companies process and store terabytes of data, but they have limited resources to protect it. Having a line of sight on prioritization is priceless.
2. Keep it Simple. The incident response plan needs to be easy to understand and implement. It must outline specific procedures and avoid being vague.

According to the Cybersecurity Unit at the US Department of Justice,[1] the procedures should, at the minimum, address the following items:

— "Who is largely responsible for each step (e.g., initial containment, threat elimination, recovery) in the incident response plan and how to contact them, day or night.
— How to proceed if those individuals are unreachable, including who will serve as their backup and how to reach them.
— Which data needs the greatest protection (i.e., mission-critical data and data containing personal information).
— How to preserve data related to the breach in a forensically sound manner.
— What criteria to use to determine who should be notified about the data breach (e.g., affected customers, the general public).
— When and how to notify law enforcement and cyber-incident reporting organizations."

3 Use Templates from Industry Bodies. Templates save time and money. Many organizations specialize in these documents. The Incident Response Policies and Plans resources page on the Incident Response Consortium website provides free guides. The American Institute of Certified Public Accountants (AICPA)[2] has a free incident response plan template, which is downloadable and adaptable.
4 Coordinate the incident response plan with policies and procedures. There will be materials in other plans and procedures that reference the incident response plan. The Disaster Recovery (DR) plan has to align with the IR plan.
5 Keep the IR plan up to date and test it regularly. It is important to run table-top exercises of the incident response to ensure everyone is ready, discover any issues and correct them before the breach. Table-top exercises allow the staff to practice the process, which will eliminate confusion in the event of an actual breach. Minimally, this should be done once a year. Best practices require an annual review and update of the IR plan. Updates have to be shared and understood by the teams.
6 Don't panic and follow the plan. Have confidence in your plan and follow it.
7 Look to continuously improve the plan. Ensure that you have continuous monitoring in place and look that they have not inserted a RAT that allows them to come back into your systems. Review the incident and identify any problems and update the plan.

Notes

1. United States Department of Justice, "Best practices for victim response and reporting of cyberincidents", September 2018, https://www.justice.gov/criminal-ccips/file/1096971/download.
2. American Institute of Public Accountants, "Incident response plan", September 16, 2020, www.aicpa.org.

20 DIGITAL FORENSICS METHODS

In Cybersecurity, when you have eliminated the likely, whatever remains, however improbable, must be the truth.

Ariel Evans, CEO Cyber Innovative Technologies

What a forensics analyst does

Computer forensics investigators provide many companies with different services that are based on gathering digital information. These may include investigating computer systems and data in order to present information in a court of law to demonstrate how an unauthorized user accessed a system, altered or stole data. A digital forensics analyst does many activities in the course of their job that focus on protecting the computer system, recovering files, analyzing data, providing reports, suggestions, and feedback, and testifying in court when required. Computer forensics training will help develop the skills necessary for a successful career in this field.

Forensic analysts have an avid interest in technology and the desire to constantly learn to stay abreast of the latest technological advances. They need the ability to effectively communicate both verbally and in writing regarding all elements of a successful digital forensic investigation. Having good analytical and problem-solving skills are also key requirements. It is helpful to have experience in a computer-related role. Backgrounds in law enforcement are also beneficial.

The salary range for computer forensics analysts and investigators is usually over six figures and varies widely depending on geography, whether the job is in the commercial sector or in the public sector. The Bureau of Labor Statistics (BLS) states that the occupation of information security analysts with digital experience is expected to grow by 28% between 2016 and 2026.[1]

Technology forensic challenges

I will start by discussing the major technology trends that have made the forensic space more complex over the past 20–30 years in the context of how we conduct forensic investigations. Everyone today has a cell phone and some folks have more than one cell phone, one for personal use and the other for work. Corporations used to have landline phones. Landlines made conducting investigations easy because

DOI: 10.4324/9781003052616-25

you could simply pull the call records from the phone company. One issue faced by companies today is the trend to bring your own device (BYOD). This changes the ownership, privacy, and control over the phone. The employer may not have issued the equipment and therefore, they have little to no control over the mobile phone.

Couple this with the huge increases in miniaturization and computer processing power, particularly for mass storage. It is very easy to exfiltrate large amounts of data without raising any red flags. Remember the microdot? During the cold war, it was common to send out enemy secrets in the form of a microdot sometimes under a postage stamp. Today, a similarly sized device can hold 260 gigs of data. It is easier than ever to data out.

Ten years ago, many of us were still using low speed internet and ten years before that, dial up. Today, high-speed internet is taken for granted. It is another new vector for exfiltrating large amounts of information. This attack surface has almost five billion users today and has grown 600% in the past ten years.

Biometric acquisition systems are everywhere. Biometrics are a means to measure the physical characteristics of a person to verify their unique identity. These can include physiological traits, such as fingerprints and retinae images, or behavioral characteristics, such as the unique way you would complete a security authentication puzzle. Consumers can now get high grade biometrics systems for their own security, which creates huge problems for people who are trying to conduct investigations. Biometric identification data is kept in databases and they can be hacked.

There has been a huge worldwide spread of the cellular data network. Cellular networks all have international standards. Those standards were built with an assumption of trust that all major users and telecoms were playing fairly and respecting peoples' privacy. That of course we know is not the case. The standards are publicly available and easily exploitable making them simple to gain rogue access to a switching system and find the location of any cell phone or eavesdrop on any conversation that is not sent over an encrypted calling device. This issue impacts national security and critical infrastructure security.

Social and file sharing systems are used as a first step in many hackers' arsenals to profile the targets on social media and spoof their way into that person's devices or organization.

Let us also include video and video game systems as another mechanism to consider. Multiplayer games like Halo have their own protocols for communicating with one another and until recently there was concern in the government that those protocols were beyond the reach of surveillance systems. They are certainly beyond the reach of private sector surveillance. Video games can serve as a vector for the illicit sharing and transmission of information.

As you build and evaluate your network, these are the things you need to be thinking about. Policies like BYOD, social media, and gaming need to be considered in terms of their risks and the ability to investigate them. There has been an explosion of vendors and new protocols. Complexity in cybersecurity is not typically a good thing. Good security design is usually a simple security design.

There has been a huge increase in the attack surface and opportunities for exploitation. An internal attack surface is a part of a network or organization that is open and exposed to vulnerability and exploitation. The two examples that most people can relate to are Cisco VOIP phones and HP printers that run on the network. Until recently, both had serious vulnerabilities. The Cisco vulnerability allowed the phones to be reprogrammed to allow illicit eavesdropping. The HP printers had a vulnerability that allowed attackers to send a rogue pdf to the printer where the printer would print something but then turn itself into a promiscuous listening device that lived on the network and allowed for external mapping. From a forensics perspective, this is challenging. The more things connected to your network, the more points and potential points of entry into the network. That means figuring out where a rogue attacker or bad actor is coming from is more difficult.

A big part of investigations is attributing and assigning blame for a cyber-attack that exfiltrated data. Investigators must figure out exactly how sensitive company information was removed. Increasingly, that is just not possible. Similarly, the layperson's knowledge has increasingly little resemblance to reality. Expectation management in digital forensics becomes very important. With Covid-19, most people are working from home and that is unfortunate for investigative purposes. Using a Virtual Desktop Interface (VDI) or Virtual Private Network (VPN) is more critical today than ever.

There has been a huge convergence between trivial and nontrivial security. High speed government grade cryptography that ten years ago would have been illegal to take outside the USA is now on the cell phone of every single person. It has gotten much easier for bad people to cover up their tracks. Finally, even at the IT leadership level, there is a very poor shared understanding of what kind of information is being captured and logged.

Cyber enabled investigations—definitions

Why would a company conduct an internal investigation? Perhaps, they received an anonymous letter saying the company is doing something unethical. Maybe they have user behaviors that trigger alarms or a data breach. The exfiltrated data may be intellectual property (IP), company secrets, long-term company strategy, etc. It could be PHI or PII data that is regulated by national and international laws.

Reporting obligations change from state to state but generally if a company's data has been compromised or business interrupted due to a cyber event, it needs to be reported. There are many aspects to reporting. What if you have four records that all belong to the same person? This would cause over-reporting. This will cost four times more. Another consequence is the firm may under-report. This can become a major regulatory issue and may get the firm sued, which could be worse. The digital asset approach prevents over- or under-reporting. All companies have an obligation to know what data and the regulations that you must comply with for reporting. NYS DFS Part 500 requires reporting for business interruption and data loss.

Sometimes a firm is running an investigation and running compliance audits because they want to make sure your organization is in good health. We like to think of investigations as a way to lawfully find the truth and understand risk. One of the goals of an investigation should be to not increase risk in the conduct of the investigation. What are some risks about running an internal investigation in response to a government demand or anonymous letter to the CEO? You could be burdened by the knowledge of what you find. The firm could have reporting obligations or things that they need to tell their regulator or tell the government. They could lose control.

Here are some terms that apply to digital forensics.

Evidence—In the traditional sense is when an investigator goes to a crime scene and is trying to figure out who stole a bunch of petty cash. In the old days, there was a petty cash container, it has been pried open, and there are camera feeds, fingerprints, and timecards that need to be reviewed. That is hard evidence. What is the evidence in the cyber setting? Access logs, digital forensics, Security Incident and Event Management (SIEM) information. Information that is trustworthy that we can rely on since it is retrieved using documented and repeatable methods. This is how cyber investigations are hugely different than traditional physical investigations.

Investigation goal—It is the reason an investigator is in the room. The goal may be to report to a regulator or inspector general that is requiring you to investigate a data breach, or shareholders have sued you for breach of fiduciary duty, or the CEO is curious. Goals must be clear and defined from day one in order not to overreach and burden you with the knowledge.

The investigative plan—It is the steps the investigator is going to take to achieve the goal or advance toward the goal.

Privileged communication—Client attorney privilege is immune from disclosure. When the investigator is thinking about how to structure an investigation they need to be thinking about if what they are doing is privileged or whether they are creating discoverable information that could really sink a company. The concept of privilege is very different in different countries. It is imperative to speak with the council about this before it is too late.

A covert investigative method—It is anything you can do when the subject of the investigation is not aware of it. Examples include imaging a computer, pulling call logs, etc. These are different from known overt methods where the subject knows you are investing them.

Chain of custody—It is the document that explains how the information an investigator retrieved made its way from where it was to where it is. This needs to be documented or else it cannot be used in court. In digital forensics, this is defined in legal contexts as the chronological documentation of digital evidence and/or paper trails that record the sequence of custody, control, transfer, analysis, and disposition of physical or electronic evidence.

Cyber-enabled investigation—goals

Some goals can be:

- To understand anomalous behavior
- To identify the source of a problem
- To respond to a regulator

- To prepare for a lawsuit
- To gather evidence in the hopes that someone who has wronged your organization will be prosecuted

It is important that the goal does not create any unforeseen risks. Something happened and the firm received a demand from the regulator. The investigator needs to help figure out what is going on inside the organization. The first thing the investigator needs to do is set the goal. Who does the investigator need in the room, what access is needed, and what risks are being creating in the process? The risk of finding something that is needed to report on is important to understand. Maybe the investigator finds out two employees are romantically involved. How does the investigator make sure leadership is aware of the future challenges that may arise without unwanted surprises?

Digital forensics processes include identification, perseveration, collection, examination, interpretation, documentation, and evidence preservation. A digital forensic investigation consists of four major components: acquisition of imaging, evidence gathering, analysis, and reporting.

To acquire digital evidence, the computer must be imaged. This process is the imaging of the computer's memory (RAM) to create an exact sector level duplicate of the storage medium.[2] The priority of any digital forensics investigations is to recover hard evidence of a criminal activity. Imaged evidence must be validated as accurate by comparing the acquired image (or logical copy) and original media/data.

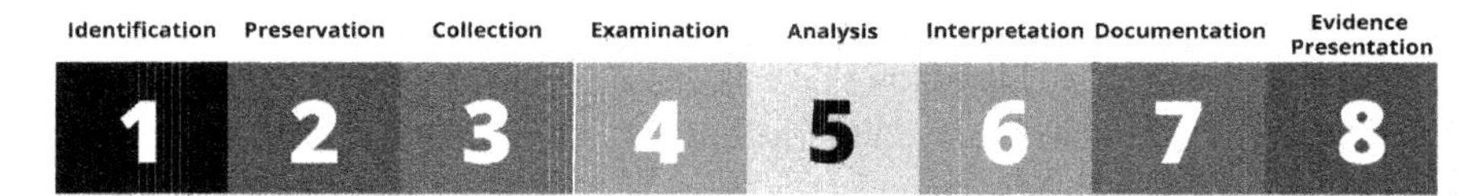

Figure 20.1 Digital Forensics Processes

In the evidence gathering phase, the forensics investigator will use keyword searches across digital media, investigate users' activities, and recover deleted files, and get the operating system registry information.

The evidence recovered is reviewed and the investigator will use that data to reconstruct events or actions and to verify deductions. When an investigation is complete, the data is formally documented in business terms.

Digital evidence must be adjudicated and recognized according to case law. Digital evidence must be collected as per guidelines that are cited in the Evidence Act and Criminal Procedure Code applicable to the geographic location of the cybercrime. The digital evidence must have integrity and authenticity. Integrity is looking for unaltered evidence (either the original or the copy). Authenticity is the ability to confirm the integrity of information by comparing original images versus copies. Documenting the chain of custody from the crime scene will help to establish the authenticity of evidence.

Cyber-enabled investigation—evidence

Physical collection of evidence is a bit different than evidence collection for an IT-enabled investigation. The admissibility of digital evidence is based on the tools used to extract it. In the US, the Daubert standard is applied, and a judge is responsible for ensuring that the digital imaging processes and software used to obtain it are acceptable.

Sometimes, the investigator starts an investigation not even knowing what they are looking for. The evidence they need may be in use by the wrong people when they need it. Spoilation is a huge risk. It is easy to destroy data these days or change a file. A cyber investigator cannot take photos of a company's computer system. If there was a crime or problem on organizational property, the investigator can just go in. But if you have a BYOD policy, the investigator cannot just go and search someone's cell phone depending on what is allowed in the organization's BYOD policies. Searching someone's personal cell phone and then firing them is a high risk.

The process to search data is multistep. First, consult with organizational leaders and legal counsel. The investigation must be done quietly. Second, start with doing covert imaging of as much data as possible. It is important that the company does not outright act like it does not trust the employees. One of the major shortcomings of modern server-based email platforms is that when you delete a message it gets deleted off the server. In most cases after 30 days, the messages are gone for good. In G Suite, you can turn on Vault for users if you are worried about deletion. It appears to be deleted but still resides in the system.

Companies should have logging turned on and then do the overt forensics work. You need to generate some pretext for this, such as we have a virus, and we need to update your computer. If you must image the hard drive, you make a perfect forensic image and return the device to the user. Next, the investigator does searches. Along the way every step the process and findings need to be documented. It is advisable not to let the IT department do this. The risk of them trying to do this themselves and it is failing is too large.

What kind of information can you expect to get from a laptop or a phone? Registry information, emails, network shares recently accessed which shows what people were on which drives, recent Wi-Fi access points, and a lot of raw random data from the browser's cache. All that data can be combined to produce interesting results. The investigator can see regular phone call logs and text messages, photos, and GPS locations. They can get a ton of information from electronic devices. It also allows us to get a lot of information about physical items. Every time someone prints something, there is a series of tiny yellow dots on the paper that show the investigator where it was printed and the time. This is true of government printers and many corporate printers as well.

Another common way for someone to steal information from your company is with a USB. If the USB port is not disabled, we strongly encourage you to disable it. The most effective way for people to steal data these days is to bring a personal cell phone into the workspace and just take photographs of the screen. The personal cell phone is generally off limits to company investigators. It is certainly not off-limits to our friends in the federal and state government. Many folks think that post-Edward Snowden, your data was not being gathered and you have more privacy rights. Wrong.

Investigations and privacy

Let us look at San Bernardino, the single most deadly act of terror on United States territory since the Boston bombers and was more deadly than in the Boston area. The shooter had a locked iPhone. The shooter is dead. The government used the normal court process to get access to the phone. This involves going to court and using the All-Writs Act,[3] which allows federal courts to have the power to do whatever is needed to force compliance with a lawful order.

The FBI wanted that phone data, and they used the All-Writs Act to get it. They sought and received a court order from a magistrate judge compelling Apple to defeat its own security system. Apple and several other organizations challenged the magistrate's order. The process to appeal from a magistrate is to appeal to a district court judge who is a presidentially nominated and Senate-confirmed district court judge that needs to see that this is outside the power of the All-Writs Act.

This order also creates massive security problems. You are asking Apple to create a government version of their own iOS. Whenever we create a government version of anything it is going to get leaked. This creates a huge debate inside the computer science, security, and engineering community about whether this is legitimate. Apple's argument was probably bolstered by the fact that the NSA shortly thereafter lost several extraordinarily top-secret computer exploitation tools. If the government's secret keeper cannot keep secrets, how can they expect us to?

In the end, the government withdrew its request when they were able to procure from a third-party vendor a service that allowed them to unlock the iPhone. This issue is still completely untested, unresolved by higher courts, whether it is inside the government's power to compel that kind of that kind of access. I think it is very much an open question. There are several constitutional provisions that are implicated, and there is a major public policy dispute about it.

Are we safer if everybody's communications are more secure or are we less safe? Anyone who is interested in this policy issue may wish to familiarize themselves with the Clipper Chip debate in the late 1990s. The Clipper Chip[4] was a chipset that was developed and promoted by the United States National Security Agency (NSA) as an encryption device that secured "voice and data messages" with a built-in backdoor. It was intended to be adopted by telecommunications companies for voice transmission. Clipper was a proposal from President Clinton's administration to compel the use of public key escrow encryption in all communications devices. The algorithm that they were going to use was called Skipjack, and Skipjack had a feature where in addition to working as a point-to-point crypto device, there could be a central repository of master keys that the National Security Agency would hold.

The idea was to mandate this as a lawful method of encryption and to make illegal all other kinds of encryption. This sparked a huge public debate over privacy issues. This was a time before 9/11 and a period of general safety and security. Ultimately, the Clinton administration backed down off it. Before they backed down, by the way, a computer scientist named Matt Belaid, who now teaches at the University of Pennsylvania, found a fatal error in the skipjack encryption algorithm that would have let anybody defeat it.

Now there are available, relatively unbreakable forms of ways to conduct encrypted communications and encrypted discussions such as WhatsApp. There is an application that allows you to have a point-to-point encrypted discussion with another individual. This is an open issue in the government today. Lots of journalists use it. It is streamlined and secure.

The most secure systems do not have backdoors. If you put a backdoor in, somebody will find it and they will access it. Your system will be compromised. There is a big open question about complying with an order from the government. You will be compelled to comply because if you do not, you may be this year's poster child the day after terrorists use your systems to perpetrate their act.

There is a Mike Tyson quote, "everyone has a plan until they get punched in the mouth." When you do an investigation, you must make sure you know exactly what you are doing and have a written plan. It must state your goals, the steps you will take and how restricted you need the investigative team. You will want it to be as small as possible.

Some things to consider are if it will go into litigation or if you think the firm may terminate someone. There could be a lawsuit. Imaging computers by people who know what they are doing is costly. It could cost US$10,000 a laptop to do imaging and analysis. If you are looking at a pool of 50 people, it gets prohibitively expensive awfully quick. Start by pulling the Office 365 and exchange server data. This is cheap to do. It is important to layout the plan, the resources, and the costs with different options of the level of analysis.

Cyber-enabled investigations—process

As I said, the first step is to figure out the exact goal. The desired outcome of the investigation is very important. Senior leaders will often say, "we've got to figure out what's going on. We've got to investigate this." I already talked about why that might not always be a good idea. You need to know what the specific desired outcome is, and how can you manage their expectations so that they understand what you are and are not likely to find. The process consists of:

- Consulting with organizational leadership to determine the desired outcome.
- Assess trust and needs.
- Assemble the case leadership team.
- Make a list of the information you need.
- Assess the best way to gather it.
- Assess deadlines—subpoena response date, upcoming reporting requirement, state, or federal reporting requirements, other organizational needs.
- Conduct covert steps first (i.e., imaging, log activation, etc.)

- Conduct overt activities (i.e., interviewing) in a deliberate and disciplined matter.
- Keep track of everything.
- Follow the process and be disciplined.

Banks do a lot of mole hunts for supervisory data. John's bank has an insufficient capital cushion. It could sink John's bank. Mole hunts finds where there is supervisory information that has been leaked. When you have that, you have a universe of people who might have access to it. You cannot just image all their computers. You cannot just check every Facebook page to see which one leaked it. Expectation management is very important.

The team assembly is extremely important. You need to figure out who you can trust. If the investigator cannot trust the IT lead, that is a big problem, and this happens all the time. Most security teams are not well supported and do not have the tools they need.

Figure out the information that is needed in the investigation and what it is going to prove. It is very rare that you find an actual smoking gun. As an example, a leak happened on January 2nd. Who was in the office on January 2nd? Who was on travel on January 2nd? Who got a bad HR rating?

It is particularly important for publicly traded organizations who might have reporting obligations to know the deadlines. Understanding what regulations are in place is very important. If you are investigating a potential PII breach, you must know the notification window for the Attorney General Office. In some cases, it is 14 days. Regulations and the timing of notifications are very critical to get right. A conversation about deadlines and whether you can meet them needs to happen in the beginning. Always do the covert work first. Always do the covert work first. Always do the covert work first. This is very, very, very important.

The next are overt activities like interviewing and documenting. It is critical to keep track of everything. Ensure that the lawyers are aware of what you are tracking. Be careful about what you do put and do not put in writing. Remember that the investigation and the notes and the information you create during the investigation can be discoverable if there's litigation. There is an old saying attributable to Attorney General Ed Meese. Ed Meese once said "say you are sorry with flowers and chocolate. Just never say you're sorry in writing." Every piece of information you generate, you should assume it is going to be in court or in a newspaper. Most importantly, follow the process. Be disciplined and invest in your investigation.

Traditional interview methods

The traditional method of being interrogated by the police or an intelligence community asset is useful in cyber forensics. When it comes time to do this overt work, you might be doing it yourself. You do not want the IT people, especially the IT leads doing it for several reasons.

The room needs to be put together so that the individual feels pressured to talk. Typically, a hot room with no windows and a chair and a table blocking the exit. Having a big imposing guy sitting right there in front of the door and another off in the corner that is blocking the exit while somebody is taking notes is very intimidating. This is the kind of pressure that a trained interrogator is going to know how to apply. When this person leaves the room, they will know that they are the focus of the investigation.

The basic tactical tasks of an interrogation are revealing the components of a crime or incident; establishing the circumstances, including the place and time of actions significant for the investigation; identifying the ways and motives of their fulfilment and occurrence; understanding the features of the persons participating in it; identifying subjects for the interrogation; determining the extent of caused damage; and identifying other witnesses and persons involved in issue.

If this is a cybercrime, it is reasonable to collect data about places of residence, study, work, leisure, etc. Tax inspectors, law enforcement officers, co-workers, neighbors, and those that are familiar with the subject can provide such data. For incidents, it can be important to review data from the personnel file.

In the interrogation phase of a forensics investigation, the investigator may want to find out whether an individual showed inappropriate interest in the firm's digital assets, if outsiders had unauthorized access to the server rooms, if there were any failures in the operation of the software, if there was a theft of data, or any failures in operation of hardware, networks, or other computer protection mechanisms.[5]

The investigator should obtain various cybersecurity program information. This includes how well controls are in place, how often the software is checked for viruses and the results of recent checks, and how often the software is patched and the rules of patch management. The investigator should have an inventory of the digital assets (software, hardware, processes, and data) and if they are purchased or homegrown with a list of vendors. Investigators should get all the access policies and procedures, and cybersecurity program information including the methods of information protection, tools used, etc.

During the investigation, it needs to be determined whether there was unauthorized access to data, when it happened, and how it happened. If there is illegal access, it is necessary to interrogate people that have means, motive, and opportunity in the firm. This includes users, programmers, risk managers, IT managers, business unit owners, etc.

At the beginning of the interrogation, it is important to find out the computer skills and experience of those suspected, and who had access on the day of the incident to narrow the scope of the suspects.

Highly skilled cybercriminals are repeat offenders. They are serial criminals who expertly conceal their actions. These individuals are usually involved with organized criminal groups, and are highly skilled and operationalized. If the crime is committed by this type of group, the investigator needs to establish if there was collusion and who initiated the crime. Other details such as the time, place, and roles between accomplices and the actions related to the crime must be determined.

When questioning a suspect, it is important to establish the following:

- Where the activity occurred
- Which methods were used to gain physical access into the facility if the accused claims if the event happened inside the firm

- How they gained access
- The sources of data that were compromised
- The digital assets they exfiltrated
- How they carried out the crime
- Technical tricks and ruses they used to gain unauthorized access
- The use of a USB or other ways they concealed their activities
- Bribes or other means that they used an individual with an official position for illegal access

Cyber-enabled investigations—special issues

Remember, your goal is to reduce risk, not increase it. What are the kinds of major risks that you might encounter if you run a broad cyber investigation?

- Unclear IT policies—These will have to be updated and may put egg on the policy owners' faces if they are not up to the grade.
- Unlawful searches—You might find you may create risk by conducting unlawful searches if you are not disciplined about the communications.
- Generation of incorrect documentation along the way—You may create incorrect information that could mislead people down the line that could come up in court.
- Alienation of organization members.
- Uncovering evidence of a crime, or information that creates new legal obligations.
- You risk spoilation, which is the destruction of evidence.

What happens if you find child pornography on a company computer? Unfortunately, this dreadful thing happens a lot. If the company computer is hosting child pornography and you become aware of it, that's a big problem and you have to do something. It is breaking the law at both the federal and state levels.

The child pornography law

Images of child pornography are not protected under the US Constitution. The possession and distribution of child pornography is illegal under both state and federal laws. Many people download files from the internet that contains pornographic images. Over 20% of all internet pornography involves children.[6]

In some cases, individuals are misdirected to internet sites that they did not intend to visit that contain child pornography. Charges may be made against innocent individuals who were fooled into visiting these sites.

Section 2256 of Title 18, United States Code, defines child pornography as any visual depiction of sexually explicit conduct involving a minor (someone under 18 years of age). This includes pictures, videos, and graphics that are digital or computer-generated. Altering a photograph or video to appear as if it is a minor can be considered child pornography. Artistic drawings that are used in scientific, academic, or have other nonillegal value are not in the scope of child pornography.[7]

Individuals must knowingly possess, distribute, or receive child pornography to be charged with this sex crime. The court has to prove there was intent on the part of the defendant. Many internet investigators track which computers access child pornography websites or download pornographic materials. Individuals that download hundreds of images or are repeatedly accessing a website with child pornography will be hard pressed to prove that they had no intent to possess these illegal images.

Defenses to child pornography charges

Most accused persons say that they did not know that what they were downloading or accessing was child pornography. Possession of adult pornography is legal. Some individuals may unwittingly access child pornography material that they thought was okay because they were on an adult site.

When a computer has multiple users, an accused can argue that they were not the only party using that machine. Police must have probable cause to search a person's computer for child pornography. If a search was conducted without probable cause and without a warrant, the items obtained during the search may be fruit of the poisoned tree and stand as inadmissible.

Punishment for child pornography possession or distribution

Child pornography charges can be prosecuted in both federal and state court and carry hefty criminal punishments. First-time offenses can result in 15–30 years in prison plus extended time in supervised sex offender release programs. In addition, if convicted, the person is required to be registered in the National Sex Offender Public Website.[8]

Cyber-enabled investigations—government demand

When the government wants something from you, they are going to send you a warrant. You might get a search warrant. You might be ordered to help the government comply with a wiretap warrant. You might get a special warrant from a secret court in Washington called the Foreign Intelligence Surveillance Act Court[9] (FISC), the FISC will use a classified demand for information, and you will be compelled to provide it. You may not tell anyone about it, because sharing classified information is unlawful. You might get a national security letter, which is a special investigative tool that the FBI uses to compel you to provide what they are requesting. It is illegal for you to tell anyone that you are giving to the FBI in this case.

Child pornography case study[10]

John Eric Shaffer could not fix some technical issues with his computer. He took it to a computer repair shop named CompuGig. Shaffer described the problems he had with the technician. This included that he could not access the internet. CompuGig's computer technicians performed a series of tests as requested by John. They determined that the laptop's hard drive had failed. To fix it, it required removing the old hard drive and installing a new hard drive. The computer company followed procedure and called John Shaffer, explained the findings and solution. They requested and received an "approval" to replace the equipment, transfer the files, and upload the old hard drive.

While transferring the files from John's old hard drive to the new hard drive, the computer repair person experienced difficulties in transferring the images. This required manual access to open individual files. In opening the files, the technician came across suspicious images that he believed to be sexually explicit photographs of minors.

The computer technician that was repairing the computer did not intentionally search to see if the laptop contained pornographic images. The computer technician upon discovering the images of young girls which appeared to sexually explicit in nature, promptly informed his boss of the discovery. A senior company executive then contacted the police.

Once reported to the police, the police reviewed the alleged images by having the computer technician demonstrate how he came upon the explicit images. Law enforcement authorities interviewed John Shaffer about the images. He admitted that his computer contained images with girls as young as eight years old. He also identified the folders containing the images. Shaffer also self-incriminated himself in writing to admitting to the possession of 72 digital images of children engaged in actual or simulated sexual acts.

The police charged Shaffer with criminal possession of child pornography. He was also charged with using the internet to commit, cause, or facilitate the commission of the felony of sexual abuse of children.

Shaffer then sought legal counsel who accused the police of conducting a warrantless search to obtain evidence against him. In the accusation, he claimed the police violated his constitutional rights to privacy. He told the court that he only provided his incriminating statement after the police unlawfully conducted their illegal search and seizure. The court suppressed his motion.

They ruled that it was unreasonable for Shaffer to expect a right to privacy when providing his computer to an outside repair service. Previous prior case law supported that the act of a technician who unintentionally finds child pornography on a computer and reports it to law enforcement authorities is admissible in a court of law.

In the prior case law, the courts determined that the defendant should have known there is a strong chance that any illegal images will be discovered when leaving the hard drive at the repair shop, which exposed the potential to detect illegal images. The Supreme Court concluded that the police came to CompuGig at the request of the store owners and that they did not illegally engage in a warrantless search.

Notes

1. U.S, Bureau of Labor Statistics, "Information security analysts", September 1, 2020, https://www.bls.gov/ooh/computer-and-information-technology/information-security-analysts.htm.

2. Abdul Khader Sarmathy, Secure Reading, "Digital forensics overview in a nutshell!", October 16, 2010, https://securereading.com/digital-forensics/.
3. Legal Information Institute, "28 U.S. code 1651. Writs", 2020, https://www.law.cornell.edu/uscode/text/28/1651.
4. Electronic Privacy Information Center, "The clipper chip", 2020, https://www.epic.org/crypto/clipper/.
5. Vasili Polivanyuk, Computer Crime Research Center, "Interrogation of suspects in investigating computer crime", 2002, http://www.crime-research.org/library/Polivan1003eng.html.
6. Child Pornography: Patterns From NIBRS. https://www.ojp.gov/pdffiles1/ojjdp/204911.pdf
7. Citizen's Guide To U.S. Federal Law On Child Pornography. https://www.justice.gov/criminal-ceos/citizens-guide-us-federal-law-child-pornography
8. Citizen's Guide To U.S. Federal Law On Child Pornography. https://www.justice.gov/criminal-ceos/citizens-guide-us-federal-law-child-pornography
9. United States Foreign Intelligence Surveillance Court, "Recent public filings", December 2, 2020, https://www.fisc.uscourts.gov/.
10. Joseph D. Seletyn, Esq. Prothonotary, FindLaw, No. 435 WDA 2017, "Commonwealth of Pennsylvania v. Eric John Shaffer", December 21, 2017, https://caselaw.findlaw.com/pa-superior-court/1883707.html.

21 CYBERSECURITY AUDITING

Over seventy percent of the of the Earth's surface is covered with water. The remaining thirty percent is covered with auditors from headquarters.

Barnet Margolis, Global Head of Internal Audit at Cantor Fitzgerald

The basics

A cybersecurity or an IT audit is the examination and evaluation of an organization's information technology infrastructure, policies, and operations. IT auditors examine physical and digital security controls, business and financial controls that involve information technology systems.

Auditing myths

A myth is a belief that is inaccurate and widely held. Myths can tell us about assumptions that we and others make about each other. Sometime a myth has some element of truth in it which makes it harder to dispel.

The modern internal cybersecurity/IT audit profession has been around for less than a century. We will examine some myths that have a grain of truth and explore them what makes them a myth. Eliminating these untruths can lead an organization towards a more cyber resilient path.

Myth #1: internal auditors are accountants by training[1]

IT auditing evolved out of financial auditing. One of the most common misperceptions about IT auditing is that the auditors solely focus on a companies' financial records. A solid audit or accounting background is only useful for audits that address financial risks.

IT auditors may address fraud risks, compliance issues, and operational issues. These are unrelated to accounting. IT auditors' backgrounds may be specific to the technologies they audit or specific to the reasons for the audit. The best IT auditors have analytical and critical thinking abilities, data mining skills, consulting, advisory, business acumen, and IT skills.

Typically, in vendor cyber risk management the company will require the vendor to provide a SOC II report. A SOC report is a verifiable auditing report which

DOI: 10.4324/9781003052616-26

is performed by a Certified Public Accountant (CPA) designated by the American Institute of Certified Public Accountants (AICPA). It is a collection of offered services of a CPA concerning the systematic controls in a service organization.

A SOC 1 Audit is focused on internal controls related to financial reporting (ICFR). A SOC 2 Audit is focused on information and IT security identified by any of 5 Trust Services Categories: security, confidentiality, information privacy, processing integrity, and availability.

I do not think that this is very useful. This type of an audit report is done by accounting firms like KPMG and PWC. Most of these types of auditors are not skilled in cybersecurity and are only trained in looking at financials.

Myth #2: auditors are the enemy; they are nitpickers and fault-finders

Another myth is that IT internal auditors pick apart everything and ruin the reputations of the people who do the "real work." Many people see IT auditors as a distraction.

From my experience, internal IT auditors may not always be very skilled in cybersecurity policy, practices, and techniques. This misperception often times stems from IT auditors, including the Head of IT Audit, not knowing how to socialize and manage complex and/or challenging findings, and the associated risks.

In reality, of course, IT audit's focus is on the major risks. IT Audit resources are limited, and auditors have no time to focus too much attention on minor issues. They must limit their focus and time to address the major risks and controls. Auditors prefer to report on a US$2 million cost savings rather than on a US$2 error!

If an audit is done correctly with the right team and there's good communication between the auditee or the client and management, that is not going to be the case. First of all, there is a limit as far as the number of hours and resources that can be spent on an audit. The audit team has to have a specific scope for the audit, and they have to stick to that scope. We need to all be careful with scope creep. Clients have the right to verbalize if they think the audit team is going in a wrong direction.

Myth #3: do not ask—do not tell

If auditors believe people are not being honest, they will increase the scope of the audit to determine whether other important information is being withheld.

It is important to ask to get together and discuss things if you believe that the audit is not focused in the right area. When an audit is announced, some people will feel it is best not to talk about things that are not working properly or things that are not fixed due to lack or budget or resources. This can create a lot of unnecessary work in an audit.

However, on the other hand, it is important to think about what you say so that something is not said out of context. The last thing you want is to start raising red flags that do not exist. Be mindful of the scope and work within its parameters to keep focus and prevent finding things that are not relevant. Stick to the topics.

There are times when you do have to raise a red flag. As an example, the auditor may want to review physical security at a specific data center. Maybe in this case 10%

of your systems, your card readers are actually not working at this moment because you are upgrading your systems. You need to voice that. There is no point for an auditor to come in and write up something that you already have identified. One of the important things is that you identify and understand what your risks are and what your controls are so you can actually self-identify your own issues.

If you are addressing them and you have evidence that you are working on something, those are things to bring onto account because those are things that auditor may have to keep into mind. There are those things that audit will have to test no matter what.

Myth #4: internal auditors are robots that select their audit targets and use standard checklists to audit the same things exactly the same way each and every time

This applies more to a SOC I report, since a SOC II Type 2 report includes technology and security controls; these likely will change over time due to changes in technologies, tools, processes, etc.

That should not be the case. There are situations where there are exceptions concerning key financial controls. Financial controls are tested every year when there is a SOC audit. They do test the same things the same way each time.

Auditing professional standards require risk-based plans to determine priorities. Based on the risk, a repeat audit may be in order. In terms of compliance reviews, audits are routinely required by regulators. In this case a specific checklist is used that is updated based on the regulator. Internal auditing is evolving with new technologies like IoT and cloud.

Doing an annual IT audit involves circling back to find out if anything is changed. Has the management changed? Has there been any changes in the industry? Are there any issues that have impact to the company systems? What is being done to the systems in terms of innovation, upgrades, and projects? All of this should be factored in.

One positive aspect could be that you used to have these controls that were done manually and now they are automated. That is a new item that an auditor would want to check. How were they designed, tested, and implemented? How do you know that they are working properly, and everything is accurate? Are they being monitored? Where is the evidence to support this? Is the system locked down and following a documented change control process? Automated controls will save time and money and will be relied upon. The auditor will choose several tests and verify that things work properly.

Myth #5: internal audit is a police function

It may seem that way depending on the culture of the organization. It can be very challenging to be an auditor in a company that is growing rapidly through mergers and acquisition. Large companies will have little understanding of what is going on at a regional level if they are consolidating and centralizing systems. Having limited staff and resources without regional oversight is not a best practice.

From an auditing perspective it makes things harder if there is no expert that knows country regulations. Once regulations come into play, culturally it can get difficult. Audit needs to form partnerships with all of the business units to get the cooperation that they need and have the business be in front of the auditing processes. Auditors are not just supposed to find faults. They are supposed to be trusted advisors with the business to have an atmosphere of cooperation where a manager can call up audit and voice a concern and get suggestions and help from audit. Audit should help and advise.

In my experience, the best auditors create a relationship with their customers. Accusing or aggressive behavior will cause resistance. Cooperation will allow everyone to accomplish their objectives and improve the cybersecurity posture of the firm.

Auditors have to be careful to not cross the line and provide all the help since they will be auditing them at some point in the future. They have to keep their independence. The partnership with the business allows the auditors to be better at their jobs.

Audit is really a monitoring function. Everybody, no matter what, whether it is enterprise risk management, whether it is corporate security, or information security will be reviewed. In public companies, auditors have an obligation to report to the audit committee. And the audit committee then also reports to the board of directors. It is ultimately a way to look after the stakeholders, the interests of the stakeholders, investors, and people who have a lot committed in the organization.

Objectives of an IT audit

IT audit objectives must demonstrate the effectiveness of the cybersecurity controls. These audit objectives align to compliance with legal and regulatory requirements. Requirements demonstrate the level of confidentiality, integrity, and availability of the digital assets.

Businesses want to protect the information assets. The first step to do this is the digital asset inventory that we have spoken about in prior chapters. These include systems, software, hardware, devices, communication infrastructure, asset owners, and vendors.

Other objectives can be:

- Ensure the privacy of internal and external stakeholders
- Protect the reputation of the firm
- Comply with federal and state laws, industry guidelines, and contracts
- Ensure confidentiality, integrity, and availability of the digital assets

To achieve the above, the business' cybersecurity controls must be designed properly, and operate effectively.

IT audit strategies

There are two audit strategies—compliance testing and substantive testing. Compliance testing is collecting evidence to ascertain if an organization has effective control procedures that map to specific compliance objectives. Conversely, substantive testing is collecting evidence to test the confidentiality, integrity, and availability of the digital assets.

Compliance testing of controls is when an organization has a set of control objectives and the auditor looks for evidence that the controls are in place. As an example, if the change control policy states that all application changes must go through the change control process, the auditor will look at the current configuration of the routers and compare it to the previous configuration file to see if they are different. If they are different the supporting change control documentation and approvals must be in place. Do not be surprised to find that network administrators, when they are simply re-sequencing rules, forget to put the change through change control.[2]

Substantive testing involves physical testing. For example, the organization has a backup policy and procedure in place that requires 3 generations (grandfather, father, and son) be in place at an offsite facility. The auditor would do a physical inventory of the tapes and compare that inventory to the organizations inventory to ensure that all 3 generations were present.[3]

The audit report must have evidence that supports the findings. Auditors have to understand the organizational structure, have access to the IT policies, procedures, documentation and standards, digital asset inventory and exposures, cyber risk scores, and the team members that will participate in the audit. Personnel must be interviewed to verify information and to observe the processes and employee performance where required. Testing of controls and the results of the tests must be documented.

Process deviations should be documented in terms of what an individual actually does versus what the process and procedures say should be done. Reviewing proper control implementation is a key part of the audit. Having on-sight inspections provide insight as to how a particular control is being managed.

Application controls

Application controls are used by the systems that are processing transactions and data. Application controls are used to ensure the integrity of the data and are controls related to the business processes. Evidence is needed to demonstrate that the procedures are in place that are effective to protect the data, and that the data has integrity.

General controls apply across the entire organization and extend to the digital asset infrastructure and support services. General controls include accounting, operational, administrative, security policies and procedures, secure design, adequate documentation, technical, administrative, and physical safeguards.

The initial tasks to audit an application are related to the digital asset inventory process which includes mapping the applications and data flows. Mapping starts with reviewing the documentation and investigating what data types are processed and stored and how the data moves when processed from application to application. This data map can be held in a cyber risk management platform or can be obtained by using interviews with the system owners, data guardians, and system administrators.

The digital asset inventory allows us to have a strategy that prioritizes which controls to look at first based on which assets are the most important to the firm. Testing the controls, documenting, and translating the test results and any other audit evidence to the business provides important information to bridge the gaps in a logical manner.

IT audit control reviews

Once all the evidence is gathered, the auditor will review and determine if the operations audited are well controlled and effective. Compensating controls must be considered. A weakness in one area which is compensated for with a strong control in another adjacent area may cancel out the risk. The auditor must include these findings in the audit report.

Key recipients of audit reports

The recipients of audit reports are typically the Chief Information Risk Officer, Chief Information Officer, the CISO and in some cases, depending on how the structure is set up, a CSO. The CSO is the Chief Security Officer who typically takes care of your physical security. In an organization with a mature information security program, other possible key recipients of audit reports include the COO, department heads, and business division heads, among others. Chief security officers and chief information security officers may work together on a day-to-day basis.

Auditors are not fraud investigators. It is important that you do not have any personal relationships with the teams that you are auditing to ensure that you are not biased on the audit.

Types of audits

There are many different types of audits:

Information and application audits are referred to as integrated audits because you may have both the IT and financial teams involved. Accounting reviews require that they also review IT controls which are used in financial systems. The IT auditor works as a team to audit the systems with the financial team. Most likely, the financial team's work may be done much sooner than the IT team. This is mainly due to the fact that many transactions go through multiple systems. The audit should be scoped to include the operational perspective. Ensuring that there is systems documentation in place saves time and limits scope creep.

Data Center audits—Cloud service providers including Microsoft, Amazon, and Google provide infrastructure, platforms, or software to process and/or store data. There must be an agreement that outlines the security controls and delineates who is responsible for specific controls and the hand offs between the organization and the CSP. This is a must.

Many data centers have everything doubled for their Disaster Recovery (DR) program. Do not assume that just because a data center is large that they have more controls and security. Key areas to inquire include: Are the computer rooms locked down? Who has a key? Is that a fake or a real camera? Is it recording? Double check all the physical security devices. Auditors are in the trust and verify business. Test everything to verify that they actually work. Look at the company, the cybersecurity policies, and make sure nothing has changed since they signed the agreement. Understand the controls that are required and understand what needs to be reviewed and the success requirements.

System Development Audits—Secure software development is the bridge to reduce vulnerabilities. It is very critical for the organization to have this in place. You must have a secure software development process in place regardless of if you are using Agile or Waterfall project methods. Separation of duties and other security requirements are a must. Having a DevOps team in place does not mean you can promote code from development to production without the database administrators doing a code review. I saw this when I was CISO and wrote it up as a separation of duties violation in spite of the head of DevOps being best friends with the CEO. DevOps has to follow procedures to promote code according to the rules with no exceptions. Baking security into the products will pay off in the long run.

IT governance, business continuity, and disaster recovery are all very critical functions. You need to have these program elements in place to keep your business running when a cyber disaster hits. This requires strong program and project management. Audit has to know about projects that are in flight, milestones, and due dates.

The 4 phases of an audit

There are four phases to an audit. Let us go into details about the four phases of an audit: Planning, Fieldwork, Reporting, and Follow up.

Stage 1: planning an IT audit

There are two phases in planning the IT audit: Prioritizing the audit and preparing for the audit kickoff.

Prioritization

The first phase is to plan to succeed by prioritizing what is most important to audit. This requires gathering information about the digital assets and to create a project plan. Digital asset risk-based auditing uses impacts and likelihoods to assess risk and prioritize decisions for the IT auditor that relates to decisions regarding compliance testing or substantive testing. In a digital asset risk-based approach, IT auditors are prioritizing testing internal and operational controls based on which digital assets are most important to protect. Digital asset risk assessments drive a cost-benefit methodology that aligns to risk reduction. In this phase, the IT auditor needs to have:

- Specific business information and industry knowledge
- Any prior year's audit results
- Regulatory laws and guidelines
- Inherent digital asset scoring and control assessments

"Inherent risks" are the risks without controls in place that exist due to behavioral and user attributes and the evaluation of the cybersecurity control assessments that demonstrate the effectiveness of the controls. As an example of control effectiveness, we want to look across the infrastructure for security gaps and prioritize audit findings based on inherent cyber risk scores.

In this phase, to gain an understanding of the existing infrastructure and internal control structure, the IT auditor needs to identify seven other areas/items:

- Digital asset inventory
- Digital asset exposures
- Control environment
- Control procedures
- Detection risk assessment
- Control risk assessment
- Equate total risk

Once the IT auditor has gathered the information for planning and understands the cybersecurity controls to prioritize based on the risk assessment, they are ready to begin the audit. An up-to-date digital asset inventory and exposure quantification is needed here to assist you in selecting the applications to audit which support the most critical or sensitive business functions.

Preparing for the audit kickoff

The planning stage kicks off with a letter that is issued by the auditors that informs the teams involved in the audit that an audit is going to be taking place. There should be sufficient notice for teams to prepare. The more time the better. Teams are busy and will need to be resourced for the audit. Their time needs to be planned, initial documentation has to be collected and resources made available.

Depending on the auditors, they may already know the IT environment. They may have a set agenda of what they want to review and talk about. If the auditors do not understand your IT environment, or if this is a new audit, they will have some preliminary questions they need to ask.

You should have a complete inventory of your digital assets, including systems, your hardware, your software, technologies, data types processed, where they are located, ownership, vendors, and their relationships. In other words, all the information about them. Where they are physically located? Where are all of your network closets? Where are your wiring closets? Where are your data centers? What is your infrastructure vs. what you are outsourcing? Do you have contracts and agreements with those people? Teams must have those at the ready for the auditors.

Have copies of the approved policies and procedures ready for the auditor's review. Drafts are not acceptable. These documents must be signed, dated, include all the revision information, and information about the next revision date. All policies and procedures must be updated regularly. If it is not documented, it does not officially exist. There will be a lot of IT project work happening and it all has to be documented to eliminate unnecessary confusion. The auditor has to compare to see if the work is being done to specifications.

Auditors have different technical skills, some of them may be good at testing active directories, UNIX systems, mainframes... Some of them may know how to test different types of security systems. No one auditor knows everything. They audit team has to also determine what skills they will need to perform the audit.

Provide the auditor all your documentation ahead of time including processes, procedures, flow charts, data mappings, and other useful documentation. They will need to review as much as possible to be ready to ask pertinent questions and to confirm assumptions and ask about things that were not clear. If it is an application or system they are reviewing, they will want to see it. An auditor has to justify why they are looking at certain areas. If they do not have documentation from you, you are going to need to start creating it.

Providing evidence from prior audits to the auditor tells the history of the digital asset, its strengths, and weaknesses. If you have fixed something in the past, be upfront about it and show what was done, and what was fixed. If it was not tested, the auditors will test it. They will see if they get the same issue or if it has been resolved. Be prepared to show evidence and have the status tracked in case something is not complete, planned or simply not done. The key is to know why it was not fixed, or how it was fixed to ensure that it can be retested. Maybe you had something that took a higher priority, and you could not get to test this in time. There needs to be proof that this project is inflight, the status and an actual end date. Auditors must be shown that you are taking cybersecurity seriously.

For issues that are still open, be prepared to present status and evidence that progress is being tracked and reported to senior IT Management and Information Risk. Depending on the control, you may have to wait a full year to do a test. If it is an annual control, you may need to wait to see if it is fixed or not. Are there any issues that have come up since then? Provide all the updates to the auditors.

The audit team also must have any updates on the business and on the team members. This is the opportunity where you start talking about lessons learned from previous audits. This will also be done when the audit report is being issued. Communication is critical with the auditors and the business and it needs to be a 2-way conversation and should happen during field work as well.

After you receive an announcement letter, there will be a kickoff meeting. You need to have your team assembled and ask the auditors who they need. Let them tell you who they need. Do not just bring one or two people. Bring your whole team and then let them decide who is really needed or not. The boots on the ground people will be needed to help answer any questions. They will be asking questions about the business, systems, controls, and risks to scope the audit properly.

Discuss how long the period testing will cover. Will they cover half a year? Full year? These questions are all fair game because you do not have resources to be dedicating full time to this over vast amounts of time. Do not be afraid to ask the auditors questions. You want to test for 1 year...why are you testing the first 6 months when we are implementing controls in the second half of the year?

Step 2: fieldwork: environment walkthrough and interviews

Once you are done planning, you have your scope and the areas you will cover, and the teams are defined and ready to go. The plan is in place. It is now time to schedule a walkthrough of the environment and the interviews. Make sure your team is ready. Let audit schedule their meetings but make sure they manage everything. Auditors have the right to speak to some people individually. Some people feel threatened and do not tell the whole truth when they have someone looking over their shoulder. However, sometimes there is a rational reason you do not want that person alone in the room. Make expectations clear before each meeting. When the meeting is getting scheduled, ensure that you have provided the auditor with a competent, knowledgeable person who knows what is going on, is confident in the process, and good at explaining themselves…and knows when to hold their tongue. If you have a new team member and you want to sit in, just explain that to the auditor.

As soon as the audit team identifies an anomaly, there needs to be a check to make sure that the analysis and testing were done correctly. This should be brought to the control owner. Does this make sense to you based on what we discussed? Remember the auditor is still learning about your digital assets or company if they are external auditors. Based on what the auditor was initially told they will test and confirm findings with the owners.

If the owner indicates that the test was not done right, then they will need to rescope it and it should be done over. However, it could also be that they found something and may need to write it up better. Those discussions allow the auditors and the owners to learn from each other.

Ensure that the information is written up properly. A comma can make a world of difference. The way it is written is very important. Putting everything you have done into writing needs to be clearly understood by anyone reading it. The right context is very important and hardest part to get right.

If you are being audited there is nothing that prevents you from asking, "how is it going? Is there anything I need to know now?" Do not wait until the report goes out because then it is too late.

Controls that are in place will most likely be in scope for testing. If something does not exist, there is no need to test it. Perhaps something should be in place, but it cannot be tested because you do not have it. Be transparent, show the controls you have in place, and indicate that they will find a few flaws and let them test. Do not wait for the auditor to find it and say that you knew about that, you are wasting everyone's time.

As auditors find anomalies, they will bring it up to your team and verify them. Work with the auditors before they give the draft report. Provide information about who may fix certain issues and speak to them soonest to understand how long they may need and the dependencies. Ultimately you will sign off that you are taking care of it, but it may be someone other than you that is fixing that. That needs to be done before that audit report goes out.

Steps 3: reporting

A draft report must be provided to all the stakeholders. There should be nothing new coming up on that report at this point. The audit team needs to obtain management corrective actions and target dates. This is the point in the process where a lot of issues start occurring. Teams need to calculate how long it will take to fix something, keeping in mind your resources, priorities, etc. This must be thought through thoroughly. Fixing things may take months. If you are fixing something and every month you are getting a report from a system of the status, you may need a few months of reports to know if you are making real change.

There are two things to keep in mind when fixing, the design of the control and the operating effectiveness. Is the control designed properly? Is that the issue? Or is it operationally ineffective? As an example, take a signature process. A claim check being sent out for anything over US$99,000 requires three approvals. One person is out on vacation. This person keeps getting an email to approve the payment. They are out of the office and the process is stalled. It is important to know if there a regulation tied to that payment. In this case the person out did not do anything wrong, however the process was not set up to delegate the approvals to someone else. There should have been an alternate approver. This is a design flaw in the control process.

Once management owners have signed off on the draft report, the final report can be issued. When that happens, all the dates on the report are final, and there should be no changes. Do not wait for the draft from the auditors. Start talking with them regularly during the audit. To clear the audit report may actually take twice the amount of time of the actual audit itself. System owners must be consulted about how issues need to be resolved, they must have a plan, timeline, and resourcing to execute it.

Steps 4: follow up

Use project management best practices when auditing and in the follow up. This includes what, how, when, who and the dependencies. Ensure that you have realistic target dates. The action plan must align with the issues identified. Make sure what you are saying you are going to resolve actually makes sense for that issue. If the issue talks about removing access for terminated employees, do not distract the team, and talk about something else. Everything you are going to fix needs to be measurable to ensure that it is verified as complete. That is why it is important to have the right person who is going to fix it, in an understandable project format, with the correct information for the auditor.

If management is using other projects to fix the current issue, ensure mitigating controls are considered as a short-term solution until the other project has been completed and the control re-tested.

Introduction to cloud auditing

Cloud computing,[4] as defined by the National Institute of Standards and Technology (NIST), is "a model for enabling ubiquitous, convenient, on-demand network access to a shared pool of configurable computing resources (e.g., networks, servers, storage, applications, and services) that can be rapidly provisioned, and released with minimal management effort or service provider interaction." Cloud computing is also described as the use of computing resources provided over a network, that typically require less interaction between the organization and infrastructure provider.

Three service models are commonly implemented in the cloud. These include software as a service (SaaS), platform as a service (PaaS), and infrastructure as a service (IaaS). In each of these service types, some security requirements will be different. Cloud security audits focus on the cloud security requirements across the cloud service.

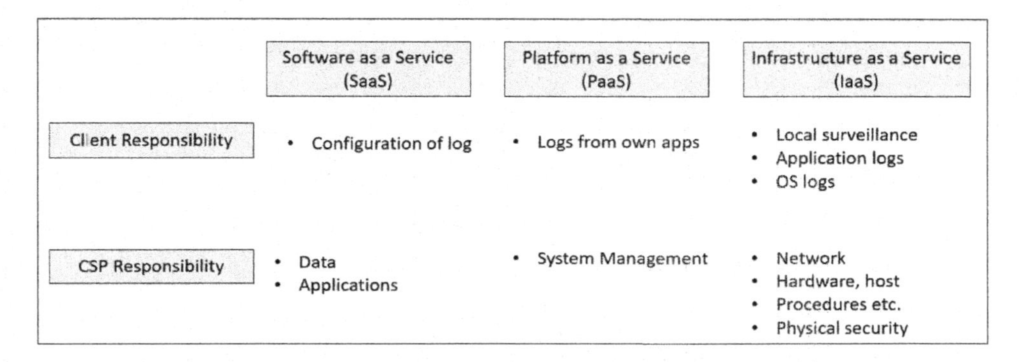

Figure 21.1 Cloud Audit Responsibilities

Cloud services are shared responsibility models between the organization and the cloud service provider (CSP). The cloud service provider is responsible for the physical server, hardware, network units, the physical buildings, and the procedures concerning the operation of hardware. IaaS providers have the most administration burden. SaaS have the least amount of functional responsibility and therefore the least burden.

Organizations are responsible to protect the data that they provide to cloud service providers. This requires that you know exactly what data is provided, where the data is being stored and how it is being protected.

Cloud vs. IT auditing

IT audits are either internal or external. Internal audits are done by an organization's own employees, concerning specific organizational processes, and focus primarily on optimization of the cyber resiliency. External audits are done by a third-party. Audits all focus on the perspective on an organization's ability to meet security requirements or regulations and tie back issues to confidentiality, integrity, and availability.

But what happens when an organization migrates to the cloud? The cloud computing shared responsibility model exposes novel security issues to protect the data. This shared security model poses new challenges for the security auditor. The Cloud

Security Alliance (CSA) is in the process of standardizing cloud requirements for confidentiality, integrity, and availability auditing.

The Cloud Security Alliance is a nonprofit group that is using best practices to educate practitioners and help secure the many forms of cloud computing. CSA and its member groups will cover all aspects of cloud computing in the forms of SaaS, PaaS, IaaS, etc.[5]

Here we will focus on the differences between cloud security auditing vs. traditional IT auditing practices. These will help to illustrate special important provisions for cloud security audits. A cloud infrastructure is the result of a relationship between the organization, cloud service providers, and end users. The CSP must protect data from cybersecurity threats and ensure that the users' availability is not compromised. The organization owns the data and must verify that the cloud service provider has adequate controls in place to ensure confidentiality and integrity of the user data. This shared relationship is difficult to manage.

Traditional IT auditing and cloud security auditing share similar control concerns, however a cloud security auditor must address unique issues that are not handled in traditional IT security audits. The most critical aspect of a cloud audit is to ensure that the auditor has sufficient knowledge of cloud security controls. This includes not only the unique cloud terminology and a working knowledge of a cloud system's digital framework, the agreements in place between the CSP and the organizations relating to the cybersecurity controls. There are several skills that a cloud auditor has to be an expert in. These include encryption, colocation, technology, regulation, and scope.

Cloud skills: encryption

It is typically going to violate a compliance requirement to store sensitive data in plaintext. Regardless of whether the data is in an on-premise system or in the cloud, the information can be exploited by hackers. Encrypting the sensitive data on-premise first before transmitting it to the CSP is one method that can be used. The risk is that a system administrator may abuse their privileges. If encryption is done in the cloud, the cloud service provider's encryption and decryption tools must be secure.[6]

Encryption always has performance issues. When data is encrypted at rest there will be a decrease in the query response times. Encryption uses heavy computational resources. A best practice is to use encryption only where sensitive data is not accessed frequently (for instance, archived customer information).

Amazon's Simple Storage Service (S3) provides encryption by default. Care must be taken not to have double encryption in these cases. Some solutions do not provide encryption by default, leaving it up to customers to decide. Amazon's Elastic Compute Cloud service is an example.

Third-party services can allow clients to encrypt the data before sending it to a CSP. Data in transit is usually encrypted using technologies, such as Secure Socket Layer (SSL). If the organization depends solely on the CSP for encryption, it must allow the CSP to control its encryption and decryption keys, therefore the CSP would have access to all the data it stores. In a public cloud with multitenant residency, this is not a safe practice. In this case, if one part of the cloud is compromised, all parts of the cloud could be compromised as well.

A better practice is for encryption and decryption to take place outside the reach of a CSP. As newer innovations approach encrypting and decrypting issues like this, cloud storage data may not take as much extra computational resources. Fully homomorphic encryption allows encrypted queries to search encrypted texts without search engine decryption. Homomorphic encryption has the potential to solve the security issue of encrypted data at rest in both traditional IT and cloud infrastructures.

Cloud auditing also introduces additional privacy issues. A balance has to be struck between auditors that need to keep their queries cloaked, and what the audited organization wants to ensure the privacy of all its encrypted data. Auditors have to have just enough access to the organization's data to complete their work, but not be allowed to copy or remove any data.

In some cases, the CSP might not be willing or able to disclose certain cryptographic information, even under auditing circumstances. To help mitigate this problem, the Payment Card Industry Cloud Special Interest Group recommends that cryptographic keys and the encryption algorithm information be stored and managed independently from the cloud service.

Cloud skills: colocation

The primary benefit of using the cloud is multitenancy. Multiple organizations can share one cloud service's physical systems driving down the costs. This leads to unique security concerns. Each organization's systems must be isolated. Care must be in place to prevent gaining administrative access to the shared physical hardware. Unauthorized access will result in violations of integrity and confidentiality. Cloud auditors need to understand colocation and how and why it is used in the cloud environment.

Cloud skills: technologies

Cloud computing uses virtual machines (VMs). This is where one physical machine will host many tenants. Each tenant uses an instance of the VM. This results in many hosts that need to be audited. Standardizing using a master VM image that is verified for security will make the auditing manageable.

Technologies like hypervisors are required to be audited. Hypervisors are used to insulate VMs from the physical hardware and have vulnerabilities. The very nature of hypervisors makes them vulnerable to being exploited. Thus, they require specific security measures and controls to minimize associated risks.

Knowing the business relationships of the VMs that are in the same service is critical to understand. Hypervisors can be configured in many ways and provide a challenge to the cloud auditors.

Technologies like firewalls, virtual switches, and storage are in scope for a cloud audit. Auditors must be aware of these technologies and how they are used in the cloud. Cloud audits typically are much longer than an IT audit due to the technology complexity.

Cloud skills: regulation

Cross border regulations must be considered in a cloud audit. Country law varies and each organization's compliance requirements can be based on what type of data is stored in the CSP's physical location. As an example, Israel banking data cannot be stored on AWS. The AWS EMEA cloud service sits in Amsterdam. Banking data can only be in stored in the state of Israel. Before an investment in cloud, it is critical to know where the CSP stores your data.

Regulations to consider when using frameworks

Cybersecurity regulations can be based on data types, geography of data stored or processed, location of the storage or processing, industry, and other special requirements. A one-size fits-all cloud audit will not satisfy all the requirements and each audit should be tailored to these needs. Different audit requirements are needed for healthcare for the HIPAA regulation, credit card for PCI audits, privacy for CCPA and GDPR audits and Federal Risk and Authorization Management Program (FedRAMP) for U.S. regulations as just a few examples.

Emerging frameworks

Today, cloud computing security audits do not have any recognized standard frameworks. Traditional IT security audits can choose from a vast array of frameworks like NIST cybersecurity, ISO 27001, COBIT, ITIL, etc. Cloud security auditors are being forced to fall back on the use of one of these traditional IT security audit frameworks.

ISO 27001 and ISO 27002 provide only limited help for cloud auditors. The ISO 27000 series does not mention the different encryption scenarios cloud auditors must understand. ISO has been working on developing a new cloud-specific security standard—ISO/International Electrotechnical Commission (IEC) 27017. This standard will focus on the information security aspects of cloud computing and provide recommendations on implementing cloud-specific information security controls. This standard will supplement the guidance in ISO/IEC 27002 and other ISO27k standards.

No official standards exist as of today to standardize the digital asset infrastructure and security of cloud environments. The PCI DSS Cloud Special Interest Group has some recommendations for cloud security. PCI has several examples that can be used for cloud environments:

- Traditional separation of servers for each client's cardholder data.
- Virtualized servers that are dedicated to each client and its cardholder data environment.

- Applications that run in separate logical partitions and have separate database management images with no sharing of resources, such as disk storage.

To underline the importance of proper colocation security, the PCI DSS Cloud Special Interest Group issued this statement regarding multitenancy: "Without adequate segmentation, all clients of the shared infrastructure, as well as the CSP, would need to be verified as being PCI-DSS-compliant in order for any one client to be assured of the compliance of the environment."[7] The Payment Card Council uses a Qualified Security Assessor cloud supplement to address how auditors handle PCI-DSS certifications in the cloud.

NIST 800-144 offers specific guidelines on security and privacy in public cloud computing.[8]

Notes

1. Richard Chambers, IA Internal Auditor, "Five classic myths about internal auditing", June 20, 2012, https://iaonline.theiia.org/five-classic-myths-about-internal-auditing#:~:text=Myth%20%231%3A,auditors%20are%20accountants%20by%20training.&text=But%20internal%20auditors%20commonly%20address,as%20the%20operations%20they%20audit.
2. Kenneth Magee, Infosec, "IT auditing and controls—planning the IT audit", 2020, https://resources.infosecinstitute.com/itac-planning/#gref.
3. Kenneth Magee, Infosec, "IT auditing and controls—planning the IT audit", 2020, https://resources.infosecinstitute.com/itac-planning/#gref.
4. NIST, "Final version of NIST cloud computing definition published", October 25, 2011, https://www.nist.gov/news-events/news/2011/10/final-version-nist-cloud-computing-definition-published#:~:text=According%20to%20the%20official%20NIST,and%20released%20with%20minimal%20management.
5. Cloud Security Alliance, https://cloudsecurityalliance.org/.
6. William Aiken, InfoQ, "Cloud security auditing: Challenges and emerging approaches", March 8, 2015, https://www.infoq.com/articles/cloud-security-auditing-challenges-and-emerging-approaches/.
7. PCI Cloud Special Interest Group, https://www.pcisecuritystandards.org/pdfs/PCI_SSC_Cloud_Guidelines_v3.pdf?agreement=true&time=1565135042827.
8. NIST, "NIST released special publication 800-144 guidelines on security and privacy in public cloud computing", January 22, 2012, https://csrc.nist.gov/News/2012/NIST-Released-Special-Publication-800-144.

PART VI

CYBERSECURITY RISK MANAGEMENT

22 CYBERSECURITY FINANCIAL EXPOSURES

Cybercrime is the greatest threat to every company and people resource, in the world. "I like to keep the focus on corporate and individual accountabilities."

Andre Bromes, CISO, Company Confidential

Digital assets

Digital assets are systems, technologies, business processes, and the data that they process and store.

Data is the information that is processed and stored. Cybercriminals steal data. Data breaches are reportable in all 50 states and to state Attorneys General and to various regulators. Depending upon what type of data your company processes and stores, your industry and geography, it will be regulated by one or more entities. Data can be classified into different types including privacy, personally identifiable information (PII), credit card, intellectual property, customer data, supply chain data, controlled unclassified information (CUI), etc. Many regulators use the number of records stolen to apply fines. Understanding what data type(s) you have can help to answer questions related to financial exposures. These questions include, "How much financial exposure do I have?" and "Which regulations is my firm in scope for?"

A system is a consolidated set of technologies that provides the basis for collecting, creating, storing, processing, and distributing data. Most systems have to have an annual cybersecurity assessment to determine the effectiveness of their cybersecurity controls.

Technologies are computer-related components that typically consist of hardware, software, databases, messaging, endpoint, devices, etc. Systems are associated to technologies in a many-to-many relationship model. A many-to-many relationship is a type of cardinality that refers to the relationship between two entities A and B in which A may contain a parent instance for which there are many children in B and vice versa.

As an example, databases are where records are stored. When a vulnerability, such as a SQL injection is exploited in a database, it can have a ripple effect in terms of increasing the financial exposure since several systems use that database version. It is essential to know how much financial exposure you have for each system. The system exposure is directly related to the technology exposure. It is critical to understand which technologies are utilized in your systems. More regulation is being put in place that is specific to the technology level.

DOI: 10.4324/9781003052616-28

California became the first state to regulate the security of IoT devices beginning on January 1, 2020. California's existing data privacy laws protect only personal information with no express requirement to the technologies used. The new law is designed to provide requirements that protect the security of both IoT devices, and any information contained on IoT devices.

The law requires an IoT manufacturer who sells a connected device in California to equip the device with a reasonable security feature or features that are all of the following: "(1) Appropriate to the nature and function of the device. (2) Appropriate to the information it may collect, contain, or transmit. (3) Designed to protect the device and any information contained therein from unauthorized access, destruction, use, modification, or disclosure." Please refer to 2018 Cal. egis. Serv. Ch. 886 (S.B. 327) (to be codified at Cal. Civ. Code § 1798.91.04(a)).[2]

Business processes are a set of digital rules that are utilized by one or more systems to take inputs, transform them, and produce outputs which are reported or used by other systems. Financial loss from the interruption of business processes can be felt throughout the entire organization in the form of a ransomware attack or on a system-by-system basis in the form of a denial-of-service attack.

Financial exposure types

Hackers, nation states, and other nefarious types attack the digital assets. Financial exposures are the potential impacts a firm would have in the event of a successful cyberattack. There are three types of financial exposures related to cybersecurity attacks: Data Exfiltration, Business Interruption, and Regulatory Loss. Within each there are subcategories. Let's break them down.

Data exfiltration

Cybercriminals want to steal your data. Typically, this happens through a phishing email that inserts malware that exfiltrates the data. When personal data is stolen, there is a series of activities that must be undertaken. Notifications have to be sent out to each person, forensic examinations must be conducted to investigate the cause, call centers have to be set up to help those affected, and a host of other related costs are incurred. These costs are called the cost of a record. Some of these costs are insurable.

The cybercriminal may commit financial or healthcare fraud by selling this data on the dark Web to exploit it for financial gain. Data exfiltration compromises data confidentiality. The company has not protected sensitive information from being accessed by unauthorized parties. A cybercriminal can also alter data that would result in an integrity violation as well as a confidentiality issue.

Business interruption

The second type of financial exposure is a business interruption. Business interruptions are when the firm loses revenue due to the system being unavailable. Business interruption can be from a ransomware or denial-of-service attack.

In a denial-of-service attack, the attackers will flood a Web application server with traffic and shut it down. Denial-of-service is a cyber-attack in which the cybercriminal makes a computer or network resource unavailable to its intended users by disrupting services of a host connected to the internet. This attack is done system by system.

Ransomware is a type of malware that inserts a virus which encrypts the firm's digital assets and perpetually blocks access to them unless a ransom is paid, or the systems are restored. Ransomware attacks are malware that is delivered via phishing emails similar to a data exfiltration attack. However, in this instance the malware encrypts the entire infrastructure. This attack is an organization level attack that is specific to the on-premise systems of the firm, not the systems that are in a cloud.

Regulatory fines

The third category of financial exposures are regulatory exposures. In the case of a data breach or business interruption, regulatory bodies may levy penalties and fines based on the type of data you process and store in systems technologies. These fines may also be based on geography, industry, and/or technology. There are regulatory fines related to privacy, healthcare, insurance, financial, credit card, and other data types. In addition to fines, regulators can pull business privileges, such as in the case of credit card or the DoD.

Each regulation was enacted to protect specific types of sensitive data. The Payment Card Industry guideline applies only to credit card data. The U.S. Department of Health and Human Services regulates U.S. healthcare data. Both healthcare and credit card data are categories of privacy data. EU citizen privacy data is regulated by the European Supervisory Authority using the GDPR and in the United States by the Attorneys General on a state-by-state basis.

Data exfiltration, business interruption, and regulatory losses make up the firm's digital asset financial exposure. The board of directors has the fiduciary duty to protect the digital assets. Digital asset financial exposure quantification is the only method that has defensible values according to the analyst and academic communities.

Digital asset financial quantifications

This section provides a step-by-step process to quantify financial exposures.

Step 1: digital asset inventory

You cannot protect what you cannot see. It is impossible to protect a digital asset if you don't know anything about it or that it even exists. Any business that does not do an inventory goes out of business. There simply are no excuses for not doing this. A digital asset inventory is a map of your infrastructure that identifies the systems, technologies, business processes, and data that are being processed and stored.

It is required to know if these are on-premise or cloud assets and where they are physically located. This information is used in determining the scope of cybersecurity assessments in the following chapters.

There are two approaches to identify digital assets: automated and manual.

Automated: The automated approach uses tools to identify digital assets. These are tools that typically put collection agents on all your servers to identify what exists. This however will provide a partial picture and the firm needs to use interviews to verify the information and fill in the blanks.

There are tools that can be used to identify the systems and networks. Free tools, such as Nmap, can be used to automatically identify where servers exist. Nmap is an open-source network scanner that will discover hosts and services on the computer network. Nmap accomplishes this by sending packets and analyzing the packet responses. Additionally, tools can scan and provide a list or a range of IP addresses to be searched. There are other tools that firms can buy that are more robust to help here.

Using these types of tools allows most firms to identify roughly 80% of their infrastructure. The other 20% will be missed, even when using a tool. Verification must be done to have an accurate inventory.

Manual: the manual approach uses interviews to inventory the digital assets. The best way to do this is using a business unit by business unit approach. Start by getting an organization chart and speaking with all of the business unit owners. They will provide access to the system owners in their unit to help inventory the digital assets.

Find out as much as you can about the system from the business side, and then move to the technology team. It is important to see how the system is configured and where the various components reside. The system and network administrators that support applications running on the systems can help you to drill down from the high-level information to the more technical aspects of each system.

For small to midsized firms, Excel can be used. However, in order to be used in context of cyber risk management, Excel is not effective. It is a starting point if there are no other alternatives. For larger firms, managing thousands of systems requires an asset management system. Examples of platforms with asset management include Cyber Innovative Technologies VRisk, ServiceNow and others.

Each asset must be classified in terms of importance: crown jewel, business critical, or crucial. Asset classification is used to set risk tolerances and in remediation prioritization.

Digital asset inventories should include the following information:

- System Legal Name: The name of the system that was purchased or what was developed in house
- Systems Number: A unique identifying number of each system
- System Type: Homegrown (in house developed) or purchased
- Vendor Name: If purchased
- Business Unit (BU) Name: BU that owns the system
- System Owner: The accountable person in the BU for the system
- Data Types: The types of data that is processed and stored by the system
- Asset Classifications: The importance of the asset (critical, standard, etc. or crown jewel, business critical, and business crucial)
- RTO: The recovery time objective of the system

- Cost to restore: The cost to restore the system
- Number of Records: Unique count of PII records that the system processes
- Environment Type: Cloud vs. on Premise
- If cloud: Deployment model (SaaS, IaaS, and PaaS) and type (Private, Public, and Hybrid)
- Specific technologies used: Operating Systems, Databases, IoT device, Web application server, etc. and their version (needed for patch analysis)

To answer these questions, you need to conduct interviews with the system owners, IT, and security teams. Below is an example of a digital asset inventory.

Digital Asset Classification	System Number	System Name	System Description	System Owner	Classification	Cloud Deployment Models Used	Cloud Service Models Used	Vendor Name and Product or Service Provided
Business Crucial	1	Agent Commissions	Commission processing system	Joe Smith	Financial, PII	SaaS	Public	
Crown Jewel	2	Guidewire PolicyCenter	Policy System	Tom Jones	Underwriting , PII			Guidewire
Business Crucial	3	VRisk	Cyber Risk Management System	Sally Kargbo		SaaS	Public	Cyber Innovative Technologies
Business Crucial	4	Homeland Tracker	OFAC reporting	Janet Rims	PII	SaaS	Public	
Business Crucial	5	Legacy Billing System	Legacy Billing System	Jeff Wells	PII			

Figure 22.1 Digital Asset Inventory Example[3]

In the next section we move to Step 2: Exposure Modeling.

Step 2: exposure modeling

Data exfiltration modeling

Data exfiltration happens when attackers (individual cyber criminals, organized criminals, and nation-states) steal the organization's information. In 2020, we saw a huge data breach at the adult live-streaming website CAM4.[4] This popular live-streaming adult website had over 7 terabytes of data and the breach exposed over 10 billion PII records.[5]

Other notable mentions in terms of record loss in 2020 are:

- Advanced Info Service (AIS)—8.3 billion records
- Keepnet Labs—5 billion records
- BlueKai—billions of records
- Whisper—900 million records
- Sina Weibo—538 million records
- Estée Lauder—440 million records
- Broadvoice—350 million records
- Wattpad—268 million records
- Microsoft—250 million records

- Facebook—267 million records
- Instagram, TikTok, and YouTube—235 million records
- Cit0Day—226 million records
- Unprotected Google Cloud Server—201 million records

The costs associated with data exfiltration are legal, notification expenses, forensics, remediation, monitoring, and public relations (PR) costs. Cyber insurance will pay for all these costs except remediation. The 2017 Cost of Data Breach Study from the Ponemon Institute, sponsored by IBM, puts the cost at US$242 per data record.[6]

The data exfiltration cost of the breach is based on the number of records taken. Again, you must know which systems process or store which type of data as we discussed in asset classification in the previous chapter. The calculation below provides a digital asset algorithm to calculate data exfiltration loss.

$$\text{Data Exfiltration Loss} = \text{number of records} * \text{cost per record}$$

In the case of Equifax 149 million records were breached, therefore the cost is 149M records* US$141 per record = US$21B. Note that at the time of the breach their market cap was US$17.2B. Their stock went down 31% erasing US$5B off their value on September 7, 2018.

Use cases for data exfiltration calculations include reducing uninsurable exposures, prioritizing risk reduction initiatives, and aligning exposures to cyber insurance limits and sublimits.

Uninsurable Exposures: many companies store hundreds of millions of records in a database without a business reason. This results in billions of dollars of exposures. These exposures are not insurable. The highest written cyber policy to data is US$750 million. That is the equivalent of approx. 4 million records. The recommendation here is to archive records to reduce that exposure. The table below shows a real-word example for an e-commerce company that had old employees in their database and over US$100 million of uninsurable financial exposure.

System Name	# of Records	Data Exfiltration Exposure	Data Exfiltration Exposure over Aggregate Insurance Limit Amount	Excess Records	CI Records
Peoplesoft HR	4,000,000	$800,000,000	$400,000,000	2,000,000	2,000,000
CRM System	20,000,000	$4,000,000,000	$3,600,000,000	18,000,000	2,000,000
Payroll System	2,500,000	$500,000,000	$100,000,000	500,000	2,000,000

Figure 22.2 Uninsurable Exposures

In this example, the cost of a record is US$200, and your cyber insurance aggregate limit is US$400 million. This equates to a maximum in each system of 2 million records in the database. Any records above that number will not be covered and the firm will incur the costs.

Business interruption: denial-of-service

Business interruption happens when the authorized users cannot access an application. Let's look at a denial-of-service attack. In February 2020, Amazon Web Services (AWS) reported they were hit by a 2.3 terabit-per-second (Tbps) distributed denial-of-service (DDoS) attack![7] This attack replaced GitHub as the largest DDoS attack to date. GitHub had a 1.35 Tbps attack against its site in 2018.[8]

How do we calculate business interruption costs from a DoS attack? DoS and DDoS are system level attacks. Therefore, we are calculating the revenue loss related to each system. It is critical to know which business processes are related to the system.

As an example, let's look at one process interruption for a bank where the wire transfer process was made unavailable. Most companies have done business continuity management (BCM) exercises as part of their disaster recovery programs. The BCM program looks at each process and determines the cost to restore it, and the recovery time objective (RTO). The recovery time objective is the duration of time within which a business process must be restored after a disaster in order to avoid unacceptable consequences associated with a break in continuity. The cost to restore is the amount of resources and time needed to restore the system. For a DoS attack business interruption costs are as follows:

$$\text{Business Interruption Loss} = (\text{Average Hourly System Revenue} * \text{RTO}) + \text{Cost to Restore}$$

In our example, if the average amount of wire transfer fees an hour is US$100,000 and the RTO is 4 hours and the cost to restore is US$20,000 the business interruption loss from a DOS attack is US$420,000. This simple calculation is used in business continuity management programs today and is updated routinely as part of best practices. This is frankly, nothing new. If your organization has done business continuity management work, you most likely have these figures handy already.

Business interruption: ransomware

Business interruption from ransomware happens when the authorized users cannot access the corporate infrastructure. This happens typically when the cybercriminal sends a phishing email which inserts malware that encrypts all the file servers of the on-premise systems. In December 2019, Israel experienced a series of cyber-attacks. Bleeping Computer reported that the Habana Labs, a developer of AI processors, allegedly suffered a cyber-attack involving the Pay2Key ransomware on December 13, 2020. Sensitive data was stolen that included everything from source code to various business documents.[9]

This attack is just one of many attacks against Israeli-based companies being targeted by ransomware operations in 2020, after the assassination of Iran's top Nuclear Scientist.[10]

In November 2020, Shirbit Insurance, an Israeli insurance provider that serves many government employees was ransomed. On December 1, 2020, the Israel

National Cyber Directorate (INCD) and Capital Market Authority announced an investigation.

This is an ongoing ransomware campaign that's going south fast. The hackers initially demanded 50 Bitcoin in exchange for not publishing the company's sensitive client information. Shirbit missed the first payment deadline and the attacker increased the demand to 100 BTC and, later to 200 BTC. In today's dollars, 200 BTC would equal more than US$3.8 million approximately. Shirbit representatives are refusing to pay the hackers. As a result, the hackers have released three batches of Shirbit information via their Telegram channel. The Times of Israel reports that the attackers most likely have sold some of the stolen data to an unknown third party.[11]

How do we calculate business interruption costs from a ransomware attack? Ransomware is an organizational attack where the entire on-premise infrastructure is unavailable. Therefore, we are calculating the revenue loss related to entire organization on-premise systems. There are other costs associated with ransomware that are financial amplifiers. These include lawsuits, operational costs, etc.

Ransomware will shop the entire supply chain. The revenue of the firm should be used in the calculation based on revenue from the on-premise systems. Cloud systems are not involved in a ransomware attack. It is important to determine the Ransomware Recovery Time Objective. Similar to the RTO, it is the duration of time within which the business must be restored after a ransomware attack in order to avoid unacceptable consequences associated with a break in continuity.

Business Interruption Ransomware Loss = (Average Hourly Organizational Revenue * RRTO * Percent of On-Premise Systems) + Cost to Restore on Premise Systems

Regulatory losses

Regulatory fines are penalties levied against organizations for noncompliance with data security directives. The most well-known are the GDPR which relates to European Union citizen privacy data, healthcare that is regulated using HIPAA policies and standards and are enforced by the U.S. Department of Health and Human Services, along with its Office of Civil Rights (OCR), and the Payment Card Industry Data Security Standard (PCI-DSS)[12] which relates to credit card data.

This loss is based on the type of data the breach has impacted. Fines can also be industry specific, geography specific or technology specific. Regulators can be an industry body like the Payment Card Industry or governmental focused like the Federal Information Security Management Act (FISMA) or the European Union Supervisory Authority.

FISMA is aimed at those that doing business with the United States Federal Government. The new Cybersecurity Maturity Model Capability (CMMC) regulation from the U.S. Department of Defense (DoD) for third-party assessments of DoD defense contractors is coming into effect soon.

Cyber insurance companies will pay against claims related to GDPR, PCI, and other regulatory types of losses notwithstanding the company has taken steps to ensure that the digital assets are protected.

For GDPR privacy breaches of EU citizen data, the fines can be 20M EUR or 4% of annual revenue, whichever is higher. This is a turning point in cyber. As of January 2021, regulations have been minimally effective in changing an organization's cyber posture. The fines have been too low, and the enforcement has been too weak. GDPR is expected to save more than 2 billion EUR per year as there will just be a single set of rules to comply with rather than different ones in different countries. This is very different than in the United States where each state has its own data breach laws and enforcement is at the state level.

California's new privacy law that went into effect in January 2020, makes it easier for consumers to sue companies after a data breach. It gives the state's attorney general more authority to fine companies that don't adhere to the new regulation. Fines are set at US$7,500 a record.[13]

Each nation state in the European Union will have enforcement teams and will share information with other nation states. GDPR considers a personal data breach as a breach that has led to the accidental or unlawful destruction, loss, alteration, unauthorized disclosure of, or access to, personal data transmitted, stored, or otherwise processed. Notification timelines start from the moment the organization becomes aware of the breach. A notice must be provided without undue delay and, where feasible, not later than 72 hours after the firm having become aware of it.

The Payment Card Industry Data Security Standard is a guideline for banks, merchants, and data processors who process credit card data. It has fines of US$500K per incident and can suspend card privileges. It not a well enforced guideline. Only four states have adopted PCI as state law. These include MN, NV, MA, and WA. Each has minimal provisions and compliant entities are shielded from liability in the event of a data breach.[14]

For U.S. businesses, privacy law compliance involves a changing patchwork of Federal and State laws. These include the following:

Federal Trade Commission (FTC)

The FTC has tried 130 spam and spyware cases and more than 50 general privacy lawsuits. Since 2002, the FTC has brought more than dozens of cases against companies for using unfair or deceptive practices that put consumers' personal data at unreasonable risk. Some better-known cases are:

- Facebook—US$5 billion fine for privacy violations
- Equifax—US$575 million fine as part of settlement with FTC, CFPB, and States related to 2017 data breach

GDPR (EU Supervisory Authority)

Since 2018, the European Supervisory Authority has made headlines for GDPR violations with numerous companies. These include British Airways, Marriot International Hotels, and others. U.S. companies that process EU citizen data are in scope.

Key GDPR actions include the following metrics:[15]

- Google—largest fine to date in 2020—50 million EUR (US$56.6 million).
- Over 220 fines have been handed out for GDPR violations in the first ten months of 2020.
- The total amount of fines issued by the EU in 2020 exceeds 175 million EUR.
- Between 2018 and 2019, the average number of fines issued per month increased by 260%.
- In July 2020, a total of 45 fines (the highest number of fines issued in a single month since the GDPR was introduced) were levied against violators.
- Only 20% of US, UK, and EU companies are fully GDPR compliant.
- The primary cause of data loss reported to the Information Commissioner's Office (ICO) to date is misdirected emails.

2020 fines include:

- Google—50 million EUR (US$56.6 million)
- H&M—35 million EUR (US$41 million)
- TIM—27.8 million EUR (US$31.5 million)
- British Airways—22 million EUR (US$26 million)
- Marriott—20.4 million EUR (US$23.8 million)
- Wind—17 million EUR (US$20 million)
- Google—7 million EUR (US$7.9 million)

Securities & Exchange Commission (SEC)

The SEC has recently issued important new guidance on cyber with risk assessments as a requirement. See www.sec.gov/rules/interp/2018/33-10459.pdf to read the guidance.

Other SEC highlights include the following cases:

- MORGAN STANLEY SMITH BARNEY, SEC FILE NO. 3-17280 (June 8, 2016)—fined US$1M and censured
- R.T. JONES CAPITAL EQUITIES, SEC FILE NO. 3-16827 (September 22, 2015)—fined US$75K and censured
- CRAIGSCOTTCAPITAL,SECFILENO. 3-17206 (April 12, 2016)—finedUS$100K and censured

U.S. Department of Health and Human Services (HHS)

Health and Human Services recently is leading the way with several data breach and privacy cases. The maximum penalty for each violation of a specific HIPAA requirement increased to US$59,522 (up from US$58,490), with a calendar-year cap of US$1,785,651 (up from US$1,754,698)[16] for all violations of an identical provision.

Minimum HIPAA penalties have increased to US$119 per record (up from US$117) for a covered entity or business associate that did not know and could not have known by exercising reasonable diligence about the violation. Violations due to reasonable causes that do not fall into the category of willful neglect, also have an increased minimum penalty to US$1,191 (up from US$1,170). The minimum penalty increased to US$11,904 (up from US$11,698) for violations that are due to willful neglect and corrected within 30 days of when the covered entity or business associate knew, or should have known by exercising reasonable diligence about the violation.[17]

Recently HHS implemented H.R. 789. This will require HHS and the OCR to recognize the cyber practices of covered entities and business associates prior to making certain determinations including the levying of fines. This law is expected to have a significant impact on the frequency and size of fines imposed by HHS.

Based on the data you process and the number of records, an algorithm can be created to demonstrate your losses. As an example, if you are a merchant that processes orders in the EU you are in scope for GDPR. Your maximum fine is 4% of revenue. If you are a pharmaceutical company with business in the EU and the United States, you have two aspects to consider: GDPR and HIPAA.

In addition to financial impacts, there are operational, legal and reputational losses. These amplify financial impacts and have their own inter-relationships. We will discuss these in more detail shortly.

Cyber exposure amplification

Financial losses can be amplified by other key criteria. These amplifiers include Reputational loss, Operational loss, and Legal (ROLF) amplifiers of Financial losses. This is a more subjective measurement that can influence the objective financial measures we have just discussed.

Reputational Risk Amplification—Reputationally, if there is national or international press release regarding a data breach, the sales will drop as a direct result of this information. For example, Target's sales fell by 46% year-one post breach in the fourth quarter of 2013 to US$520 million. Reputational risk is the risk associated with the trust in the company. Reputational risk amplifies financial risk from two perspectives—both in terms of lost sales and stock price. If the reputation impact is rumor and worry it may not be as concerning as if it is international press with a major loss of clients. However, rumors can have devastating consequences. Companies have very few mechanisms to control the occurrences of rumors, however it is critical to catch them early and address them as soon as possible (e.g., corporate communications). Listening to chatter beyond in the deep and dark web to detect sentiments, rumors, etc. is useful.

In term of stock impacts, in the case of Equifax, organizations that utilize Equifax to provide credit checks on potential employees have lost trust in them. Stock plummeted 25% and many customers are discontinuing the use of their service. This amplifies the financial losses Equifax will have, their credit liquidity, bond ratings, and a host of macroeconomic and microeconomic factors. The relationship between reputational risk and financial risk can be translated from a qualitative perspective into a quantitative metric using risk amplification algorithms.

Operational Risk Amplification—Operational risk is the prospect of loss resulting from inadequate or failed procedures, systems, or policies.[18] Operational risk also amplifies financial risk. Minor impacts in which there is no client impact is different from a complete stop of activities where revenue will be lost, and possible fines can be imposed. Most organizations have Service Level Agreements (SLAs) in place with their customers. These SLAs have financial consequences if uptime is impacted or other levels of service are degraded. SLAs with operational risk can amplify financial risk.

Cyber events that result in a complete stop of activities can have a huge direct financial impact based on this operational impact amplification. As an example, Merck had to borrow 1.8 million doses from the Pediatric National Stockpile in response to the NotPetya attack. This was the entire U.S. emergency supply. It took Merck 18 months to replenish this store, which was valued at US$240 million.[19] Additionally, typically, 31% of employees and executives are let go after a data breach leading to further operational losses.

Regulatory Risk Amplification—Regulatory risk is defined as risk of having privileges withdrawn by a regulator, or having conditions applied by a regulator that adversely impact the economic value of an enterprise.[20] Regulatory risk also amplifies financial risk. In the case of the payment card industry credit card privileges may be withdrawn resulting in a loss of revenue. In Luxembourg, regulators may reprimand or in the case of a serious breach they may fine, request dismissal of management, threaten to withdraw authorization, and take criminal action. These scenarios also lead to increased legal costs and financial loss.

Vendor Risk Amplification—Another often-misunderstood cyber risk is third party risk. As noted earlier, the third-party outsourcing trend will only accelerate as more and more talent is outsourced. Third party risk is a major concern in cybersecurity. Depending on which statistic you read, 39–63% of breaches are caused by third parties.[21] Many organizations use many third-party suppliers and vendors from organizations or countries with poor cybersecurity practices. Their cybersecurity issues are inherited by the first party. The cyber insurance industry is keen on reducing this type of risk since it is the one settling these claims. One of the most well-known third-party breaches is the case of Target. Target had a third-party data breach where a HVAC vendor's credentials were stolen. The breach resulted in 40 million credit and debit card numbers and 70 million records of personal information stolen. Third-party risk can directly impact and amplify the financial risk if the organization has not taken measures to manage vendor risk. Recently I spoke to Paul Ferrillo, Partner at McDermott, Will & Emory, and author of "Navigating the Cybersecurity Storm." His primary concerns in cybersecurity are vendors and IoT. These risks if not addressed today will haunt us for decades to come. We will discuss vendors and IoT in detail in the following chapters.

Financial exposure quantification use cases

Cyber exposures are the financial exposures related to what cyber insurance companies will pay claims against. They are directly aligned to the damage a cybercriminal can do.

These three types of calculations are used to:

- Baseline and measure cyber resilience
- Optimize resource prioritization for maximum cyber risk reduction
- Obtain cyber insurance limits adequacy
- Identify uninsurable cyber exposures
- Calculate third-party exposures
- Provide a cybersecurity tool ROI and roadmap
- Provide cyber budgeting aligned to standard budgeting methodologies

How to apply these use cases will be discussed more in the following chapters.

Notes

1. Thich Nhat Hanh, Nature's Web of Life, "Interbeing-no man is an island", June 27, 2019, https://www.freshvista.com/2019/interbeing-no-man-is-an-island/.
2. Jones Day, "California to regulate security of IoT devices", October 2018, https://www.jonesday.com/en/insights/2018/10/california-to-regulate-security-of-iot-devices#:~:text=On%20September%2028%2C%202018%2C%20California,effect%20on%20January%201%2C%202020.
3. Maryellen Evans, Digital Asset Based Cyber Risk Algorithmic Engine, Integrated Cyber Risk Methodology And Automated Cyber Risk Management System. US 2020/0106801 Al, United States Patent and Trademark Office, April 2, 2020.
4. Alina Bizga, Security Boulevard, "CAM4 data leak exposes personal data of millions of users", May 5, 2020, https://securityboulevard.com/2020/05/cam4-data-leak-exposes-personal-data-of-millions-of-users/.
5. Maria Henriquez, Security, "The top 10 data breaches of 2020", December 3, 2020, https://www.securitymagazine.com/articles/94076-the-top-10-data-breaches-of-2020#:~:text=Facebook's%20data%20breach%20%E2%80%93%20267,YouTube%20breach%20%E2%80%93%20235%20million%20records&text=Unprotected%20Google%20Cloud%20Server%20breach,MGM%20%E2%80%93%20142%20million%20records.
6. IBM, "How much would a data breach cost your business?", 2020, https://www.ibm.com/security/data-breach.
7. Jon Porter, The Verge, "Amazon says it mitigated the largest DDoS attack ever recorded", June 18, 2020, https://www.theverge.com/2020/6/18/21295337/amazon-aws-biggest-ddos-attack-ever-2-3-tbps-shield-github-netscout-arbor.
8. Casey Crane, Hashed Out, "DDoS attacks. The largest DDoS attacks in history", June 25, 2020, https://www.thesslstore.com/blog/largest-ddos-attack-in-history/#:~:text=Amazon%20Web%20Services%20(AWS)%20reports,of%20service%20(DDoS)%20attack!&text=At%20the%20time%2C%20this%20made,biggest%20DDoS%20attack%20in%20history.
9. Casey Crane, Hashed Out, "Recent ransomware attacks: Latest ransomware attack news in 2020", December 15, 2020, https://www.thesslstore.com/blog/recent-ransomware-attacks-latest-ransomware-attack-news/.

10. First, "Pay2Key—The plot thickens", December 7, 2020, https://www.first.org/blog/20201207-Pay2Key.
11. Toi Staff, The Times of Israel, "Hackers appear to begin selling data they stole from Shirbit insurance firm", December 7, 2020, https://www.timesofisrael.com/hackers-appear-to-begin-selling-data-they-stole-from-insurance-firm/.
12. PCI Security Standards Council, "Securing the future of payments together", 2020, https://www.pcisecuritystandards.org/.
13. Maria Korolov, CSO, "California Consumer Privacy Act (CCPA): What you need to know to be compliant", July 7, 2020, https://www.csoonline.com/article/3292578/california-consumer-privacy-act-what-you-need-to-know-to-be-compliant.html.
14. Tom Kemp, Forbes, "Buckle up with cybersecurity...It's the law", February 1, 2012, https://www.forbes.com/sites/tomkemp/2012/02/01/buckle-up-with-cybersecurity-its-the-law/?sh=4faac1851d72.
15. Tessian, "11 biggest GDPR fines of 2020 (So far)", November 15, 2020, https://www.tessian.com/blog/biggest-gdpr-fines-2020/.
16. Mercer, "HHS adjusts 2020 HIPAA, other civil monetary penalties", January 23, 2020, https://www.mercer.com/our-thinking/law-and-policy-group/hhs-adjusts-2020-hipaa-other-civil-monetary-penalties.html#:~:text=HIPAA%20privacy%20and%20security,violations%20of%20an%20identical%20provision.
17. Mercer, "HHS adjusts 2020 HIPAA, other civil monetary penalties", January 23, 2020, https://www.mercer.com/our-thinking/law-and-policy-group/hhs-adjusts-2020-hipaa-other-civil-monetary-penalties.html#:~:text=HIPAA%20privacy%20and%20security,violations%20of%20an%20identical%20provision.
18. The Risk Management Association, "Operational risk management training & resources", 2019, https://www.rmahq.org/operational-risk/#:~:text=The%20definition%20of%20operational%20risk,of%20an%20institution's%20business%20functions.
19. Riley Griffin, Bloomberg, The Philadelphia Inquirer, "Merck cyberattack's $1.3 billion question: Was it an act of war?", December 3, 2019, https://www.inquirer.com/wires/bloomberg/merck-cyberattack-20191203.html#:~:text=Merck%20had%20to%20borrow%201.8,medicine%20wasn't%20affected.).
20. SOHA, "Third party access is a major source of data breaches, yet not an IT priority", 2016, https://static1.squarespace.com/static/56b3cadb59827ecd82b02b43/t/5906176a893fc052557a0646/1493571436523/Soha_Systems_Third_Party_Advisory_Group_2016_IT_Survey_Report.pdf.
21. Thor Olavsrud, CIO, "11 steps attackers took to crack Target", September 2, 2014, https://www.cio.com/article/2600345/11-steps-attackers-took-to-crack-target.html.

23 DIGITAL ASSET CYBER RISK MODELING AND SCORING

If you don't invest in risk management, it doesn't matter what business you're in, it's a risky business.

Fred Eslami, Alternative Risk Transfer and Cyber Security Leader at A.M. Best

Cyber risk scores

There are three levels of cyber risk scores that are aligned to the cybersecurity lifecycle: inherent cyber risk, mitigating cyber risk, and residual cyber risk. Each score is a collection of attributes and relationships that are related to each other. Using this approach allows firms to understand risk, privacy, compliance, and security using metrics that are defensible. It can allow companies to apply AI to reduce cyber risk using non-human intervention. This chapter will focus on inherent cyber risk.

Inherent cyber risk

Inherent means existing in something as a permanent, essential, or a characteristic attribute. Digital assets have characteristic attributes that influence cyber risk. They influence the degree of an impact and/or likelihood of a cyber event. These attributes are characteristics that the asset is 'born with.' This is a static attribute unless the characteristics are altered. These attribute categories include:

- **Technology attributes**: The specific technologies that are components of the systems. As one example, assets that are in a SaaS cloud are inherently risker than those in an IaaS cloud. IaaS cloud services are more prescriptive than SaaS cloud services which is typically spun up with the same virtual machine images. This makes it easier for a hacker to know the infrastructure to plan an attack.
- **User attributes**: The characteristic ways that the asset is used by people. As one example, the more users of a system, the higher the likelihood of a data breach. Employees are the weakest link in cybersecurity. They click on malware links that lead to data breaches and business interruptions. Therefore, the more people using a system, the higher the likelihood of a cyber event.

DOI: 10.4324/9781003052616-29

- **Protection attributes**: The protection characteristics that are baked into the asset. As one example, IoT technology typically has no administrative access controls for system administrators to limit access. That makes systems with IoT technologies inherently more risker than those without IoT technologies. In system admin parlance, IoT technology is 'wide open' to exploitation since there are typically no access control mechanisms built into the technology. This is why an IoT device made in China will sell for 50 cents and one made in the US will sell for $5. Security costs money.

Identifying these attributes is the first essential step to creating an inherent cyber risk score. An inherent cyber risk score is an empirical value that can be used to compare cyber risk sans security control (which mitigate risk) information. Comparing these attributes provides a way to understand cyber risk in context and identify areas that can be adjusted to reduce inherent risk. It provides for ranking and prioritizing of digital assets that may be used by CISOs and cyber risk managers to have a defensible approach to risk reduction.

After the assets have been identified and the categories of behaviors analyzed, the categories are collated across the firm in a gap analysis. The firm can identify the gaps in the assets in terms of usage, technologies, protection mechanisms, etc.

System Name	2FA is in place for this system	System enforces separation of duties through assigned access authorizations	System enforces assigned authorizations for controlling access to the system in accordance with applicable policy	User privileges on the information system are consistent with the documented user authorizations
PeopleSoft HR	Yes	Yes	Yes	Yes
Legacy Policy	No	Yes	Yes	Yes
SAP Financials	Yes	Yes	Yes	Yes
Imageright	No	Yes	Yes	Yes

Figure 23.1 Cyber Control Gaps

As an example, in terms of Two Factor Authentication (2FA): it is observed that 70% of the digital assets have two factor authentication in place and 30% do not. Your next questions should be: "Which assets don't have 2FA in place? What asset types are they? Are they crown jewel assets, such as a trading system or an asset that is connected directly to it? How much are their exposures?" These questions will help to prioritize your next steps. Should you put two factor authentication in place for a digital asset whose exposures are high and is a crown jewel? Most likely yes.

Digital asset cyber risk scoring provides a defensible line of sight into cyber risk remediation prioritization and reduction. Inherent cyber risk is the risk without cybersecurity controls in place and provides a baseline to begin measuring cyber risk. Baselines are used as minimums or starting points for comparisons of gaps in asset characteristics and/or controls.

Inherent cyber risk is also what I refer to a "cybergeddon" risk. This is analogous to 'if there is zero percent effectiveness of cybersecurity controls' and represents the worst-case scenario analysis.

Inherent risk is important since it provides an understanding of each digital asset in the context of how it behaves and where improvements can be made to reduce it. The digital asset behavioral characteristics influence how easy it is for a cybercriminal to exploit it.

Inherent cyber risk is based on two factors: impact and likelihood. Impact is the potential financial loss. Likelihood is the probability that a cyber event will cause a loss. In this chapter we will dive into defining how to calculate inherent cyber scores using impacts and likelihoods and the key concepts related to the cybersecurity lifecycle and how it relates to cyber risk metrics.

The cybersecurity lifecycle

Any company that uses digital assets has cyber risk. Since most of the assets of a firm are digital, it is clear that cyber risk is now the most important aspect of your business to manage. Cyber risk is inherent in any business enterprise, and sound cyber risk management is an essential aspect of running a successful business. The goal is to be cyber resilient to the highest degree possible.

Cybersecurity has a lifecycle, similar to how software development has a life cycle. The cybersecurity lifecycle is a term that outlines the process for identifying risks or vulnerabilities, measuring protection, detect and manage risk, responding to threats and vulnerabilities, remediating incidents, and monitoring cybersecurity. *Unlike the software development lifecycle, the cybersecurity lifecycle is a dynamic lifecycle that requires constant attention and continuous monitoring and remediation.*

Too many CISOs ignore this reality for too long. The days of any CISO not recognizing and executing their security program from a lifecycle approach should be long gone. CISOs that do not recognize this are doomed to fail and are those whose organizations are most vulnerable.

The cybersecurity lifecycle processes include identifying digital assets, quantifying cyber exposures, baselining cyber resiliency by measuring the inherent cyber risk, accessing security control effectiveness by using a control assessment like ISO 27001, and monitoring the security of the digital assets by ingesting cybersecurity tool data to prioritize cyber risk remediation of the digital assets. Using this lifecycle model provides a guide to ensure that cybersecurity resiliency is measured and continually being improved.

Companies must remove themselves from the compliance mindset that the cybersecurity program is over once you complete the security control assessment and check the box that it is done. The cybersecurity lifecycle of identify, detect, and access, protect, monitor, and remediate (respond/recover) is a continuous process of cyber risk management which will lead to resilience.

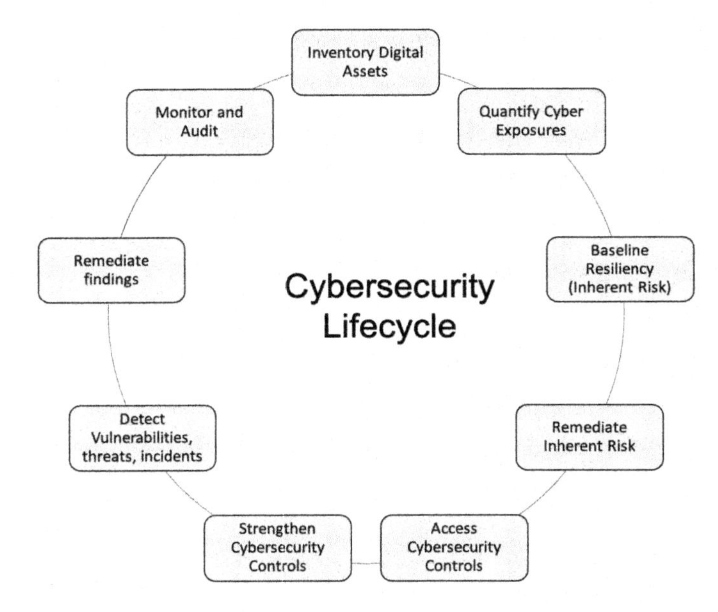

Figure 23.2 Cybersecurity Lifecycle

The next section will provide insights into the effectiveness of cyber controls related to the inherent cyber risk scores. We will continue with a discussion of cyber risk thresholds, what they are, why they are useful, and delve into the attributes needed to create an inherent cyber risk score for each digital asset.

Cyber risk thresholds

Digital asset classifications are used to set cyber risk thresholds. Crown jewels will have the lowest thresholds, followed by business critical, and then business crucial. Once the firm has inventoried the digital assets and classified the data, they should quantify the financial exposures and calculate the cyber risk scores based on their asset characteristics.

Asset classifications are important in cyber risk strategy and the prioritization of remediation work. We use three types of classifications—crown jewel, business critical, and business crucial. Other scales, such as high, medium, and low are just as useful. The point is which one is more important and use it set up remediation work.

A crown jewel strategy is how most firms start a cyber risk management program. Some firms will have tens of thousands of digital assets. Typically, 15% of them will be classified as crown jewels. The firm should start to quantify and score these assets first.

A crown jewel asset refers to a company's most prized or valuable assets in terms of its profitability and future prospects. A failure of this type of system may result in the company going out of business. Examples of types of crown jewel systems include:

Safety Critical Systems: these are systems whose failure may result in injury, loss of life or serious environmental damage. An example of a safety-critical system is a control system for a chemical manufacturing plant.

Mission Critical Systems: these are systems whose failure may result in the failure of some goal-directed activity. An example of a mission-critical system is a navigational system for a spacecraft.

Transactional Systems: these are systems whose failure may result in the failure of some goal-directed activity. An example of a transactional system is one that processes privacy data when the company sells trust (i.e., Equifax).

A business-critical system is a system whose failure may result in very high costs for the business using that system but does not create unsustainability. An example of a business-critical system is the customer accounting system in a bank.

A business crucial system is a system whose failure is not critical but has significant impact.

Digital assets can also be classified as target assets in the case of a merger and acquisition.

The cyber risk score is empirical. An empirical score relies on a comprehensive and diverse set of cyber risk data, based on how exposures are calculated, to determine the risk profile of any organization. It can be on any scale, such as 0 to 5, 0 to 10 or 0 to 100, 0 to 1000, etc. The only condition is that the scale is the same across inherent cyber risk scoring, mitigation scoring and residual risk scoring.

As an example, if I am using a scale of 0–5, I would make the crown jewel threshold 2, the business critical a 2.75 and the business crucial a 3.5 perhaps. The idea is to test out the numbers that you get from your scoring and adjust to show a striation of metrics that uses common sense and logic. Let's move on to how we actually calculate an inherent cyber risk score.

Inherent cyber risk modeling

A cyber risk score is an empirical score based on impact and likelihood metrics, to determine the risk profile of the digital assets of any organization. It is done for each digital asset.

Our approach focuses on the attributes that the cybercriminal attacks: the digital assets. Scoring of digital assets allow companies to create Advanced User and Asset Behavioral (AUAB) analytics with capabilities that allow for enabling the identification of high-risk user and entity behaviors that represent problematic security postures. These can be analyzed across the infrastructure and prioritized in terms of adjusting those asset characteristics.

Cyber Risk Scores are a combination of algorithms of impact and likelihood that use weighted criteria to score empirically. Impact is the degree to which a cyber-issue may have an adverse outcome on the organization. Likelihood is a probability a cyber-attack will cause damage.

As an example, the Prime Minister's office of Israel recognizes 3 * impact + likelihood as the algorithm for their cyber risk score.[1]

There are many impacts attribute types that can be used to calculate cyber risk scores. These include Security Innovation, Asset Criticality, Regulatory Attributes, Reputational Attributes, Exposures, Recovery Time Objectives, Stock Amplifiers, Legal Amplifiers, etc.

There are many likelihood attributes that can be used to calculate cyber risk scores, these include the number of users, the types of users, system locations, system access mechanisms, the skills needed to breach the system, the localization of a data breach, proximity to breach, interconnectivity, etc. We will be reviewing and explaining a host of attributes used in calculations.

Asset attributes can be aligned to privacy attributes. Asset attributes that make the asset more likely to be breached increase risk and therefore decrease confidentiality and integrity. Integrity and confidentiality are privacy metrics. These calculations are used in the Privacy Impact Assessment and represent a Data Privacy Impact Assessment (DPIA) score.

Inherent cyber risk scoring uses a set of questions related to digital asset attributes to create a baseline of understanding which digital assets are inherently the riskiest. Crown jewel asset strategies stipulate that crown jewel assets should be monitored continuously to ensure that any findings, vulnerabilities, or incidents are prioritized appropriately. Based on the risk scores, we can provide a matrix of prioritization that will focus on the reducing the risk in a logic and mindful manner.

Inherent cyber risk attributes

Cyber risk scoring questions must be understood in context. The examples below outline key attributes that are measured by the business owner and may have input from other organizational members, like the IT, BCM, or Compliance teams to name a few. Each metric must be modeled based on the criteria described below.

Likelihood attributes

1 User Number Risk. Users are individuals who access systems. They use credentials (user id and password) to gain access. According to the 2016 State of Cybersecurity in Small and Medium-Sized Businesses,[2] negligent employees or contractors are the number-one cause of data breaches in small and midsize businesses, accounting for 48% of all incidents. The more users, the higher the likelihood of a data breach.

Determine the maximum number of users and use that as the highest weight in your model. Create the weighting to reflect the appropriate level of likelihood. See the example below.

Answer	Weight
0-100	2
101-250	4
251-500	6
501-1000	8
Over 1000	10
Not answered	10

Figure 23.3 Likelihood Metric: Number of Users Example[3]

2 User Type Risk. Users can be internal employees, customers, vendors, or a combination of these. External users increase likelihood more than internal users. Vendors are third parties that are associated with over 63% of data breaches. The more different type of users, the higher the likelihood. When looking at likelihood, using combinations of users is important in your scoring. The following figure is one example of this metric.

Answer	Weight
Employees	2
Customers	4
Vendors	6
Employees & Customers	8
Employees & Vendors	8
Customers & Vendors	8
Employees, Customers and Vendors	10
Not answered	10

Figure 23.4 Likelihood Metric: Types of Users Example[4]

3 Access Risk. Is the system located on a secure isolated segment, on a cloud service, on the corporate network, on a customer network or a vendor network? Internal isolated systems have less likelihood than cloud hosted systems. Vendor networks are more likely to have breaches than a customer network, etc. The example below outlines one approach to this.

Answer	Weight
Secured isolated segment	2
Corporate network	4
Cloud service	6
Customer network	8
Vendor network	10
Not answered	10

Figure 23.5 Likelihood Metric: Access Risk Example[5]

4 Cloud Deployment Model Risk. Is a cloud technology as a service being used? What type of deployment model is used? Infrastructure as a Service (Iaas), Platform as a service (Paas), or Software as a Service (Saas)? IaaS has less likelihood to be breached due to the lack of similarity of the infrastructure, than a Paas offering and SaaS offering. The more the organization controls the cloud, the less likely there will be a breach.

A study conducted by the Ponemon Institute entitled "Man in Cloud Attack" reports[6] found that over 50% of the professionals surveyed had a strong belief that their organization's security measures to protect data on cloud services are suboptimal. The study used several scenarios to test the belief. The report concluded that overall data breaching was three times more likely to occur for businesses that utilize the cloud than those that utilize on-premise environments.

Answer	Weight
Infrastructure as a Service (Iaas)	4
Platform as a Service (Paas)	6
Software as a Service (Saas)	10
Not answered	10

Figure 23.6 Likelihood Metric: Cloud Deployment Model Example[7]

5 Type of Cloud Service Model Risk. What category of cloud service do you use? Private, hybrid, public? A public cloud infrastructure is when the cloud service provider makes resources available to the public via the internet and deployment is shared across multiple tenants (multi-tenant) via the internet. This increases the likelihood of a data breach.

Hybrid clouds are a solution that combines a private cloud with one or more public cloud services, using proprietary software that enable communication between each distinct service. Private clouds are a computing model that offers a proprietary environment where there is no sharing of resources, and the cloud is dedicated to a single business entity (single tenant). Private cloud service providers use extended, virtualized computing resources via physical components stored on-premises or at a vendor's datacenter. These are the least likely to have a cyber incident.

Answer	Weight
Private	6
Hybrid	8
Public	10
Not answered	10

Figure 23.7 Likelihood Metric: Cloud Service Model Example[8]

6 Geo-Political Risk. Where the data centers are physically sitting will influence likelihood. There are a number of categories that are analyzed from malware rates to cybersecurity-related legislation to defining cyber geo-political risk. Many sources exist that provide relevant data to rank cyber risk.

Denmark has been identified as the most cyber-secure country in the world, taking over from Japan in 2019. Denmark is followed by Sweden, Germany, Ireland, and Japan as the best performing countries. France, Canada, and the United States were all pushed out of the top five most cyber-secure countries in 2019.[9] Algeria is the least cyber-secure country in the world with no cyber legislation except one vague privacy law in place. Some categories to score geo-political cyber likelihood are:

— Percentage of mobile malware infections
— Number of financial malware attacks
— Percent of computer malware
— Percentage of telnet attacks (by originating country)
— Percentage of attacks by crypto miners
— Least prepared for cyber-attacks
— Worst up-to-date legislation for cybersecurity

The figure below outlines a model for geo-political cyber risk.

Answer	Weight
Sweden	2
Germany	4
UK	6
USA	6
Peru	8
Russia	10
Not answered	10

Figure 23.8 Likelihood Metric: Geo-Political Risk Model Example[10]

7 Resource Risk. Does breaching or interrupting this system take sophisticated actors, such as nation state teams that were used in the Stuxnet attack or does attacking this system need only one guy in a dark room with a hoodie and red bull? This risk looks at the quality and quantity of resources needed to cause a cyber event.

Answer	Weight
None	0
Minimal	6
Moderate	8
Nation State Resources	10
Not Answered	10

Figure 23.9 Likelihood Metric: Resource Level Example[11]

8 Technology Risk. Does this system use technology that has no administrative access capabilities? Typically, IoT is a culprit here. Scada technology requires detailed knowledge of how it works. This attribute is related to the ease to breach or interrupt the digital asset.

Answer	Weight
Non-Cloud/IoT	2
Cloud	6
IoT	8
IoT & Cloud	10
Not Answered	10

Figure 23.10 Likelihood Metric: Technology Risk Example[12]

9 Vendor Access Risk. Does a third party support this system? Third parties are responsible for the majority of data breaches. What is the level of access? How is it controlled? Vendor access risk is critical to understand.

Answer	Weight
None	2
Individual Access	6
Admin Access	10
Not answered	10

Figure 23.11 Likelihood Metric: Third-Party Risk Example[13]

10 Vendor Rating Risk. Has a third-party risk assessment been done on the vendor? What are the results? Have they been deemed high, medium, or low risk? What level of assessment risk does the vendor have related to the digital assets that they are working with.

Answer	Weight
Low Risk	2
Medium Risk	6
High Risk	10
Not done or not answered	10

Figure 23.12 Likelihood Metric: Third-Party Risk Assessment Example[14]

11 Prior Breach Risk. How often are cyber-criminals attempting to get access to this system and have they been successful? Was there an attempt, in what time frame, are hackers constantly trying to breach the system, was there already a breach? Understanding it an asset is a target relates to the likelihood it will be breached.

Answer	Weight
No attempts	2
Single attempt	4
Repeated attempts in past 3 months	4
Breached in the past 3 months	6
Breached in the past 6 months	8
Breached in the past year	10
Not answered	10

Figure 23.13 Likelihood Metric: Prior Breach Attempts Example[15]

12 Development Risk. Is there a deep knowledge of the system and infrastructure like with a home-grown system needs, some knowledge, general knowledge like with an off the shelf product? Homegrown systems have specs that are internal, whereas off the shelf products have specs that are all over the internet.

Answer	Weight
Deep knowledge of the system and infrastructure: Home-grown system	2
Some knowledge: Hybrid system	6
General knowledge: Off the shelf product	10
Not answered	10

Figure 23.14 Likelihood Metric: Prior Breach Attempts Example[16]

13 Attack Proximity Risk. What is the proximity needed to breach the system? Is it direct physical access like with a switch, admin rights, user rights, protocols through a DMZ and firewall like with a Web application, or anonymous public access?

Answer	Weight
Direct physical access like with a switch	2
Admin rights	4
User rights, protocols through a DMZ and firewall like with a web application	6
Anonymous public access	10
Not answered	10

Figure 23.15 Likelihood Metric: Attack Proximity Example[17]

14 Breach Localization Risk. How localized are the effects of the breach? Would it be isolated to the system, system and network, external network, all systems in the area, outside the system (supply chain), crown jewel? This is a very important metric. The reason Equifax was such a disaster is because it was not understood that the breach effects were not isolated when that system was left unpatched, rather the breach impacted the crown jewel assets.

Answer	Weight
Isolated to the system	2
System and network	4
External network	6
All systems in the area	8
Outside the system (supply chain)	10
Crown jewel	10
Not answered	10

Figure 23.16 Likelihood Metric: Localization Risk Example[18]

15 Interface Number Risk. How many interfaces exist in the system? The more interfaces the higher the likelihood of a data breach.

Answer	Weight
0	0
1-1	4
5-6	6
7-10	8
More than 10	10
Not answered	10

Figure 23.17 Likelihood Metric: Interface Number Risk Example[19]

16 Interface Type Risk. What is the nature of the system interfaces? Intra-organizational, external interfaces with suppliers, interfaces with the general public? External with suppliers would be more likely than internal.

Answer	Weight
None	0
Intra-organizational interfaces	6
External interfaces with suppliers	8
Interfaces to the general public	10
Not Answered	10

Figure 23.18 Likelihood Metric: Interface Type Example[20]

17 Remote Access Risk. How are remote workers connecting? Via 2FA, via an encrypted channel, via a commercial takeover software??

Answer	Weight
None	0
Via two factor authentication (2FA)	4
Via an encrypted channel	6
Via a commercial takeover software	8
Not Answered	10

Figure 23.19 Likelihood Metric: Remote Access Example[21]

18 Permission Risk. What is the current level of compartmentalization of permissions in the systems? Full compartmental permissions by groups and roles, individual compartmental permissions per employee, basic compartmental permissions (manager and user), no compartmental permissions. Roles and groups afford the least likelihood. Other areas to explore here are the onboarding and offboarding processes and entitlement procedures.

Answer	Weight
Full compartmentalization (permissions by groups and roles)	0
Individual compartmentalization (individual permissions per employee)	4
Basic compartmentalization (Manager and User)	6
None	8
Not Answered	10

Figure 23.20 Likelihood Metric: Permission Example[22]

19 Patch Policy Risk. What is the current update level of the system? Are you using the most recent version, up to three versions back, more than three versions back, versions that are no longer supported? The more recent the patching the less likely you will have a cyber event.

Answer	Weight
Installing full updates at least once a quarter	4
Installing security updates at least once a quarter	6
Critical security updates at least once a quarter	8
No orderly updating process in place	10
Not Answered	10

Figure 23.21 Likelihood Metric: Patching Policy Example[23]

20 Patch Frequency Risk. What is the policy for updating the software and the security patches? Are you installing full updates at least once a quarter, installing security updates only once a quarter, critical security updates only

at least once a quarter, no orderly updating process? The more rigor, the less likely you will have a cyber event.

Answer	Weight
The most recent version	2
Up to 3 versions back	6
More than 3 versions back	8
Versions that are no longer supported by the manufacturer (End of Life)	10
Not Answered	10

Figure 23.22 Likelihood Metric: Patch Frequency Example[24]

21 Physical Security. What is the physical security level of the system? Is there a visitor policy? Is the company physically accessible to authorized individuals only? Are cameras in place? Having proper physical security lessens the likelihood of cyber events.

Answer	Weight
Accessible to authorized individuals only badging, visitor policy and cameras are in place.	4
Accessible to authorized individuals only badging, and visitor policy are in place.	6
Accessible to authorized individuals only and visitor policy is in place.	8
No badging, visitor policy or cameras in place.	10
Not Answered	10

Figure 23.23 Likelihood Metric: Physical Security Example[25]

22 Inherent Access Control. What is the level of access control embedded in the technology? Is it bolted on? Is it unsupported, end of life (EOL)?

Systems that are end of life have no patches available to prevent vulnerabilities from impacting them and as a result carry significant risks of something going wrong from a vulnerability. An example is a system that runs on Windows XP. There are still over 250M users running applications on XP.

Answer	Weight
Access control baked in	2
Access control not baked in	6
End of Life	10
Not answered	10

Figure 23.24 Likelihood Metric: Inherent Access Control Example[26]

Each attribute question is weighted to differentiate which attributes are most important to the organization.

Impact attributes

Impact is the degree to which a cyber issue may have an adverse outcome on the organization. Impact attributes will increase the level of damage. These can include the following attributes: types of technology, complexity of attacks, dependencies, sensitivity of data, reputation damage, stock damage, legal damage, recovery times, and cost of restoring systems. Here are some examples.

1 Asset Type. What is the dependency of the asset type? How important is the digital asset? Crown jewel assets will have higher impacts than business critical and business crucial.

Answer	Weight
Business Crucial	4
Business Critical	6
Crown Jewel	8
Not answered	10

Figure 23.25 Impact Metric: Asset Type Example[27]

2 Maximum Regulatory Impact. What is the degree of regulatory impact? How many regulations does this system fall under and which ones? Some are more costly than others, like GDPR. The more regulations the more potential impact on the organization. Different ones have higher impacts and must be considered in context.

Answer	Weight
PCI	4
CCPA	6
HIPAA	8
GDPR	10
Not Answered	10

Figure 23.26 Impact Metric: Maximum Regulatory Impact Example[28]

3 What is the degree of potential reputational damage?

Reputational impact can be measured in many ways:

— rumor(s)
— worry of isolated client(s)
— coverage in national press and many information requests from clients

— coverage in specialized press and loss of some clients or a strategic client
— coverage in all national media with mass departure of clients
— coverage in international press and departure of all clients

OR

— customer facing system
— crown jewel
— many privacy records

Finding the one that fits your organization is important.

Answer	Weight
Worry of isolated client(s)	2
Coverage in national press and many information requests from clients	4
Coverage in specialized press and loss of some clients or a strategic client	6
Coverage in all national media with mass departure of clients	8
Coverage in international press and departure of all clients	10
Not answered	10

Figure 23.27 Impact Metric: Reputational Damage Example 1[29]

Answer	Weight
No customer data and not a crown jewel	2
Customer data and not a crown jewel	4
No customer data but a crown jewel	6
Customer data, crown jewel and few privacy records	8
Customer data, crown jewel and many privacy records	10
Not answered	10

Figure 23.28 Impact Metric: Reputational Damage Example 2[30]

4 Regulatory Penalties. Regulatory penalties and fines are on the rise and can be unsustainable. What is your maximum regulatory fine?

— US$500M
— US$100–500M
— US$50–100M

— US$25–50M
— under 25M

The higher the fines, the higher the impact.

Answer	Weight
$500M	2
$100-500M	4
$50-100M	6
$25-50M	8
Under $25M	10
Not answered	10

Figure 23.29 Impact Metric: Regulatory Penalties Example[31]

5 Risk Interdependencies. How many risk interdependencies are there for this system? The more interferences, the more impact.

— Reputational, Operational, Legal and Financial
— Reputational, Operational, and Legal
— Reputational and Operational
— Operational and Legal
— Legal and Financial
— Reputational, Legal and Financial
— Operational, Legal and Financial
— Only one—operational, legal, financial, or reputational

Answer	Weight
Reputational or Operational or Legal or Financial	4
Reputational and Operational	6
Operational and Legal	6
Legal and Financial	6
Reputational, Legal and Financial	8
Operational, Legal and Financial	8
Reputational, Operational, and Legal	8
Reputational, Operation, Legal and Financial	10
Not answered	10

Figure 23.30 Impact Metric: Risk Interdependency Security Example[32]

6 RTO. What is the System recovery time objective (RTO) impact? Do you have a service level agreement? This is the time the system needs to be back on-line in the case of business interruption.

— 0–4 hours
— 5–12 hours
— 12–24 hours
— 24–48 hours
— over 48 hours

If the RTO is shorter, the higher the impact.

Answer	Weight
0-4 hours	2
5-12 hours	4
12-24 hours	6
24-48 hours	8
Over 48 hours	10
Not answered	10

Figure 23.31 Impact Metric: Recovery Time Objective Example[33]

7 Cost of Restoring the System. What is the cost of restoring the system?

— Less than US$10k
— US$10–25k
— US$25–50k
— US$50–100k
— Over US$100k

The higher the cost of restoring, the higher the impact.

Answer	Weight
Less than $10K	2
$10-25K	4
$25-50K	6
$50-100K	8
Over $100K	10
Not answered	10

Figure 23.32 Impact Metric: Cost of Restoring the System Example[34]

8 Privacy Records. How many privacy records do you have in this system?

— 0
— 1–100k
— 100k–2500k
— 250k–500k
— 500k–1 million
— over 1 million

The more records the system processes, the higher the impact.

Answer	Weight
0	0
1 to 100K	2
100 to 2500K	4
250K to 500K	6
500K to 1M	8
Over 1M	10
Not answered	10

Figure 23.33 Impact Metric: Privacy Record Damage Example[35]

9 Stock Damage. Are you a public company? What will a data breach do to your market cap? Looking at stock prices in your industry can act as a guide.

— 50% loss of stock price
— 25% loss of stock price
— 10% loss of stock price
— 5% loss of stock price.

In the case of Equifax, the stock price decreased by 31%. This is a good barometer to use if it is a customer facing privacy data system.

Answer	Weight
5% loss of stock price	4
10% loss of stock price	6
25% loss of stock price	8
50% loss of stock price	10
Not answered	10

Figure 23.34 Impact Metric: Stock Damage Example[36]

Each attribute question is weighted to differentiate which attributes are most important to the organization.

Creating the inherent cyber risk score for each system

After each impact and likelihood question and answers are created, an algorithm is crafted to generate the inherent risk score. Each impact and likelihood question is weighted independently. Each digital asset is scored separately.

In this example, we will use a scoring range of 0 to 5. Here is a simple algorithm that is the average score.

Inherent Cyber Risk Score for a Digital Asset = Average of Impact Score * Average of Likelihood Score

Step 1: Select a Maximum Question Score for Impact Questions.

i.e., we will select 5 in this example.

Step 2: Calculate the summary of the Maximum Question Scores for all the Impact questions.

i.e., 10 impact questions are all weighted at a maximum of 5. This would produce a maximum question summary score equal to 50. (5*10).

Step 3: Select a Maximum Answer Score for Impact Answers.

i.e., we will select 5 in this example.

Step 4: Calculate the summary of the Maximum Answer Scores for all the answers.

i.e., 10 answers have a maximum score of 5 would be equal to 50. (5*10)

Step 5: Calculate the Impact Risk Score for each question. Multiply the question score by the answer score.

i.e., Question 1 has a weight of 5 and an answer value of 3, therefore (3*5) = 15. Continue for all 10 questions and sum the scores. If all had an answer of 3 then the likelihood score (3*5*10) = 150.

Step 6: Select a Maximum Question Score for Likelihood Questions.

i.e., we will select 5 in this example.

Step 7: Calculate the summary of the Maximum Question Scores for all the Likelihood questions.

i.e., 10 Likelihood questions are all weighted at a maximum of 5. This would produce a maximum question summary score equal to 50. (5*10).

Step 8: Select a Maximum Answer Score for Likelihood Answers.

i.e., we will select 5 in this example.

Step 9: Calculate the summary of the Maximum Answer Scores for all the Likelihood answers.

i.e., 10 answers have a maximum Likelihood score of 5 would be equal to 50. (5*10)

Step 10: Calculate the Likelihood Risk Score for each question. Multiply the question score by the answer score.

i.e., Question 1 has a weight of 5 and an answer value of 3, therefore (3*5) = 15 .... Continue for all 10 questions and sum the scores. If all had an answer of 3 then the likelihood score (3*5*10) = 150.

Step 11: Create an Inherent Cyber Risk Calculation – Israeli Prime Minister uses (3*Impact) + Likelihood. (3*150) + 150 = 600 for that system.

Step 12: Preform the calculation on each digital asset.

Inherent cyber risk score use cases

Inherent cybersecurity risk can be used as a benchmark for measuring cyber resiliency. If an asset is a crown jewel with a high inherent cyber risk score, controls and monitoring should be put in place to reduce the inherent risk to a more acceptable level.

System	Inherent Risk Score
Trading System	.71
Torrent Flood	.59
Hancock Bank	.42
FaveRates	.42
Guidewire ClaimCenter	.40
Core Commissions	.40

Figure 23.35 Measuring Cyber Resiliency[37]

The inherent cyber risk scores can be used to identify the digital assets that have the highest scores related to privacy, technology, or other risk types. Assets that have the higher inherent cyber risk scores should be investigated to spot trends across the infrastructure to implement risk reduction techniques. As an example, if there are thousands of users on a system, one recommendation would be to review the off-boarding procedures to ensure all those users are authorized and to tighten up the process by offboarding more frequently. Another would be to check the entitlement process in the Identify Access Management (IAM) system.

System Name	Confidentiality Score	Integrity Score	Financial Exposure
Trading System	.53	.53	$ 203,209,900
Peoplesoft HR	.52	.52	$ 129,289,900
HireRight	.49	.49	$ 400,715,400
AlwaysCare	.48	.48	$ 160,320,100
Guidewire Claims Center	.48	.48	$ 116,320,200
Payroll System	.36	.36	$ 176,220,200

Figure 23.36 Measuring Privacy Risk[38]

Once the inherent risk is determined the risk tolerance will be shown in terms of the asset classification. Cyber risk data related to assets that are crown jewels would be reviewed to minimize risk. An asset classification heat map can be used to spot trends easily.

Crown Jewel System Name	Cyber Risk Score	Financial Exposure
Torrent Flood	.77	$ 63,048,600
SAP Financials	.66	$ 11,113,200
Peoplesoft HR	.64	$ 80,283,400
FaveRates	.64	$ 103,559,300
Guidewire ClaimCenter	.63	$ 187,800,500
Commercial Property System	.63	$ 1,087,800

Figure 23.37 Measuring Crown Jewel Risk[39]

A security assessment will measure the effectiveness of the controls in place. Each control has a weight and a score that are used to show how inherent risk is lowered. We will move on to the next chapter and focus on residual risk reduction from cybersecurity controls.

Notes

1. NIST, "Cybersecurity framework success story", 2020, https://www.nist.gov/system/files/documents/2020/07/23/Israeli%20National%20Cyber%20Directorate%20Success%20Story%20062920%20508.pdf.
2. Pomemon Institute, "2016 state of cybersecurity in small & medium-sized businesses (SMB)", June 2016, https://www.keepersecurity.com/assets/pdf/The_2016_State_of_SMB_Cybersecurity_Research_by_Keeper_and_Ponemon.pdf.
3. Evans, Maryellen. Digital Asset Based Cyber Risk Algorithmic Engine, Integrated Cyber Risk Methodology and Automated Cyber Risk Management System. US 2020/0106801 Al, United States Patent and Trademark Office, April 2, 2020.
4. Evans, Maryellen. Digital Asset Based Cyber Risk Algorithmic Engine, Integrated Cyber Risk Methodology and Automated Cyber Risk Management System. US 2020/0106801 Al, United States Patent and Trademark Office, April 2, 2020/.
5. Evans, Maryellen. Digital Asset Based Cyber Risk Algorithmic Engine, Integrated Cyber Risk Methodology and Automated Cyber Risk Management System. US 2020/0106801 Al, United States Patent and Trademark Office, April 2, 2020.
6. American Journal of Information Science and Computer Engineering, "Security issues, threats and possible solutions in cloud computing", May 5, 2019, http://www.aiscience.org/journal/paperInfo/ajisce?paperId=4446.
7. Maryellen Evans, Digital Asset Based Cyber Risk Algorithmic Engine, Integrated Cyber Risk Methodology and Automated Cyber Risk Management System. US 2020/0106801 Al, United States Patent and Trademark Office, April 2, 2020.
8. Maryellen Evans, Digital Asset Based Cyber Risk Algorithmic Engine, Integrated Cyber Risk Methodology and Automated Cyber Risk Management System. US 2020/0106801 Al, United States Patent and Trademark Office, April 2, 2020.

9. Comparitech, "Which countries have the worst (and best) cybersecurity?", March 3, 2020, https://www.comparitech.com/blog/vpn-privacy/cybersecurity-by-country/.
10. Maryellen Evans, Digital Asset Based Cyber Risk Algorithmic Engine, Integrated Cyber Risk Methodology and Automated Cyber Risk Management System. US 2020/0106801 Al, United States Patent and Trademark Office, April 2, 2020.
11. Maryellen Evans, Digital Asset Based Cyber Risk Algorithmic Engine, Integrated Cyber Risk Methodology and Automated Cyber Risk Management System. US 2020/0106801 Al, United States Patent and Trademark Office, April 2, 2020.
12. Maryellen Evans, Digital Asset Based Cyber Risk Algorithmic Engine, Integrated Cyber Risk Methodology and Automated Cyber Risk Management System. US 2020/0106801 Al, United States Patent and Trademark Office, April 2, 2020.
13. Maryellen Evans, Digital Asset Based Cyber Risk Algorithmic Engine, Integrated Cyber Risk Methodology and Automated Cyber Risk Management System. US 2020/0106801 Al, United States Patent and Trademark Office, April 2, 2020.
14. Maryellen Evans, Digital Asset Based Cyber Risk Algorithmic Engine, Integrated Cyber Risk Methodology and Automated Cyber Risk Management System. US 2020/0106801 Al, United States Patent and Trademark Office, April 2, 2020.
15. Maryellen Evans, Digital Asset Based Cyber Risk Algorithmic Engine, Integrated Cyber Risk Methodology and Automated Cyber Risk Management System. US 2020/0106801 Al, United States Patent and Trademark Office, April 2, 2020.
16. Maryellen Evans, Digital Asset Based Cyber Risk Algorithmic Engine, Integrated Cyber Risk Methodology and Automated Cyber Risk Management System. US 2020/0106801 Al, United States Patent and Trademark Office, April 2, 2020.
17. Maryellen Evans, Digital Asset Based Cyber Risk Algorithmic Engine, Integrated Cyber Risk Methodology and Automated Cyber Risk Management System. US 2020/0106801 Al, United States Patent and Trademark Office, April 2, 2020.
18. Maryellen Evans, Digital Asset Based Cyber Risk Algorithmic Engine, Integrated Cyber Risk Methodology and Automated Cyber Risk Management System. US 2020/0106801 Al, United States Patent and Trademark Office, April 2, 2020.
19. Maryellen Evans, Digital Asset Based Cyber Risk Algorithmic Engine, Integrated Cyber Risk Methodology and Automated Cyber Risk Management System. US 2020/0106801 Al, United States Patent and Trademark Office, April 2, 2020.
20. Maryellen Evans, Digital Asset Based Cyber Risk Algorithmic Engine, Integrated Cyber Risk Methodology and Automated Cyber Risk Management System. US 2020/0106801 Al, United States Patent and Trademark Office, April 2, 2020.
21. Maryellen Evans, Digital Asset Based Cyber Risk Algorithmic Engine, Integrated Cyber Risk Methodology and Automated Cyber Risk Management System. US 2020/0106801 Al, United States Patent and Trademark Office, April 2, 2020.
22. Maryellen Evans, Digital Asset Based Cyber Risk Algorithmic Engine, Integrated Cyber Risk Methodology and Automated Cyber Risk Management System. US 2020/0106801 Al, United States Patent and Trademark Office, April 2, 2020.
23. Maryellen Evans, Digital Asset Based Cyber Risk Algorithmic Engine, Integrated Cyber Risk Methodology and Automated Cyber Risk Management System. US 2020/0106801 Al, United States Patent and Trademark Office, April 2, 2020.
24. Maryellen Evans, Digital Asset Based Cyber Risk Algorithmic Engine, Integrated Cyber Risk Methodology and Automated Cyber Risk Management System. US 2020/0106801 Al, United States Patent and Trademark Office, April 2, 2020.
25. Maryellen Evans, Digital Asset Based Cyber Risk Algorithmic Engine, Integrated Cyber Risk Methodology and Automated Cyber Risk Management System. US 2020/0106801 Al, United States Patent and Trademark Office, April 2, 2020.
26. Maryellen Evans, Digital Asset Based Cyber Risk Algorithmic Engine, Integrated Cyber Risk Methodology and Automated Cyber Risk Management System. US 2020/0106801 Al, United States Patent and Trademark Office, April 2, 2020.

27. Maryellen Evans, Digital Asset Based Cyber Risk Algorithmic Engine, Integrated Cyber Risk Methodology and Automated Cyber Risk Management System. US 2020/0106801 Al, United States Patent and Trademark Office, April 2, 2020.
28. Maryellen Evans, Digital Asset Based Cyber Risk Algorithmic Engine, Integrated Cyber Risk Methodology and Automated Cyber Risk Management System. US 2020/0106801 Al, United States Patent and Trademark Office, April 2, 2020.
29. Maryellen Evans, Digital Asset Based Cyber Risk Algorithmic Engine, Integrated Cyber Risk Methodology and Automated Cyber Risk Management System. US 2020/0106801 Al, United States Patent and Trademark Office, April 2, 2020.
30. Maryellen Evans, Digital Asset Based Cyber Risk Algorithmic Engine, Integrated Cyber Risk Methodology and Automated Cyber Risk Management System. US 2020/0106801 Al, United States Patent and Trademark Office, April 2, 2020.
31. Maryellen Evans, Digital Asset Based Cyber Risk Algorithmic Engine, Integrated Cyber Risk Methodology and Automated Cyber Risk Management System. US 2020/0106801 Al, United States Patent and Trademark Office, April 2, 2020.
32. Maryellen Evans, Digital Asset Based Cyber Risk Algorithmic Engine, Integrated Cyber Risk Methodology and Automated Cyber Risk Management System. US 2020/0106801 Al, United States Patent and Trademark Office, April 2, 2020.
33. Maryellen Evans, Digital Asset Based Cyber Risk Algorithmic Engine, Integrated Cyber Risk Methodology and Automated Cyber Risk Management System. US 2020/0106801 Al, United States Patent and Trademark Office, April 2, 2020.
34. Maryellen Evans, Digital Asset Based Cyber Risk Algorithmic Engine, Integrated Cyber Risk Methodology and Automated Cyber Risk Management System. US 2020/0106801 Al, United States Patent and Trademark Office, April 2, 2020.
35. Maryellen Evans, Digital Asset Based Cyber Risk Algorithmic Engine, Integrated Cyber Risk Methodology and Automated Cyber Risk Management System. US 2020/0106801 Al, United States Patent and Trademark Office, April 2, 2020.
36. Maryellen Evans, Digital Asset Based Cyber Risk Algorithmic Engine, Integrated Cyber Risk Methodology and Automated Cyber Risk Management System. US 2020/0106801 Al, United States Patent and Trademark Office, April 2, 2020.
37. Maryellen Evans, Digital Asset Based Cyber Risk Algorithmic Engine, Integrated Cyber Risk Methodology and Automated Cyber Risk Management System. US 2020/0106801 Al, United States Patent and Trademark Office, April 2, 2020.
38. Maryellen Evans, Digital Asset Based Cyber Risk Algorithmic Engine, Integrated Cyber Risk Methodology and Automated Cyber Risk Management System. US 2020/0106801 Al, United States Patent and Trademark Office, April 2, 2020.
39. Maryellen Evans, Digital Asset Based Cyber Risk Algorithmic Engine, Integrated Cyber Risk Methodology and Automated Cyber Risk Management System. US 2020/0106801 Al, United States Patent and Trademark Office, April 2, 2020.

24 CYBERSECURITY CONTROL ASSESSMENTS AND CYBER RISK

Security program design must start with a risk assessment: enterprise risk, business risk, regulatory risk, technology risk, industry risk. And you must keep looking at what's happening in the world right now that could heighten these.

Tim Callahan, SVP & Global CISO, Aflac

Nothing new here

A cybersecurity control assessment is a required as part of any organization's cyber risk management and compliance strategy. Cybersecurity control assessments are nothing new. They have been in place for decades in many different forms.

Various industries stipulate a legal obligation to perform a cybersecurity control assessment. For example, under HIPAA (Health Insurance Portability and Accountability Act) all "covered entities" must perform a cybersecurity control assessment. Additionally, the PCI Security Council, NYS DFS, and other federal government agencies require annual cybersecurity control assessments.

Note: Many of these regulations call a control assessment a risk assessment. As you can see from reading this book, they are not the same. We have to use the right language in cybersecurity, risk, and compliance or we will never be able to communicate effectively. That NIST 800-53, NIST CSF, ISO 27001, PIC-DSS, and the other required assessments do is test controls, not measure risk.

Typically, your organization will have in-house IT personnel that can assist or do a cybersecurity control assessment. IT staff must understand the digital assets. System owners that own and understand various information flows and the data will be involved in the assessment. Knowing how to test the control is the key to a good assessment.

Getting started

Each control assessment has a scope. The scope will be dictated by the regulations and data processed by the systems and stored in the associated databases. The assessment team will need to know which business owners and IT teams support the application.

A framework will either be prescribed by the regulator as with the PCI (PCI-DSS) or can be chosen based on preferences of the CISO or team doing the assessment.

DOI: 10.4324/9781003052616-30

Knowing the controls to assess is critical. Planning is essential, will saving time and money.

Step 1: Scope and prioritization of the assessment. Which systems process the data that are in scope for the assessment? If it is GDPR, then it is systems that process EU citizen privacy data. Each system should be prioritized based on the amount of financial exposures and inherent likelihood scores. Those systems have the most risk.

Step 2: Identify potential assessment redundancy.

Many teams work in silos. As an example, the PCI team and the HIPAA team don't know what each other are working on. This creates the potential that two teams will be testing the same controls on the same system. In this example, this leads to double the cost for the firm. Ideally, there should be management oversight to prevent this. The different teams should know about each other and identify which systems are in scope and work together on the control assessments.

Step 3: Identify precursor controls.

Know the precursor controls.[1] According to NIST, these are controls that should be assessed prior to assessing a specific control. That is, controls, whose assessment would most likely produce information either required in order to make the determinations of this controls effectiveness or be helpful in doing so.

Example of a control

There are hundreds of controls in different frameworks. This is an example of how to start to break down the control into the needed tasks and evidence required for the NIST 800-53 framework, control AC-1 related to access control policies and procedures. This control is a basic control that is required in every framework regardless of industry, controls or organization, system, technology of data level. In this example, we choose the organizational level. This means that only one access control policy and procedure is used at the firm. This would be typical in a small to medium enterprise, however, not at a large firm.

The example below blows out each control test and the evidence to support the control is effectively in place.

Unique ID.#: AC-1
Control Name: Access Control Policy and Procedures
Framework: NIST 800-53
Level of Control: Organizational

Detailed breakdown of control requirements:

The organization:

(a) Develops, documents, and disseminates to defined personnel or roles who must implement or adhere to the control as follows:

Translation for management and the testing team: Requirement 1. The policy is written and approved. It is not in a draft form. Draft forms are unacceptable. Requirement 2. The policy was crafted with the people who have to use it such as the system administrators, etc.

1 An access control policy that addresses the purpose, scope, roles, responsibilities, enforcement, mechanisms required, related policies and procedures, monitoring/reporting, exceptions, definitions, and revision history; and

Translation for management and the testing team: Requirement 3. The policy has the required components to be effective, including enforcement and monitoring. It has documented multiple mechanisms that are required to demonstrate that it is effective.

2 Procedures that facilitate the implementation of the access control policy and the associated access controls; and

Translation for the testing team: Requirement 4. The procedure mechanisms tie back to the policy statement. There will be several of these that are needed to ensure that the policy mechanisms are effective.

(b) Ensure that there are reviews and updates to the current:

1 Access control policy reviewed and/or updated annually; and

Translation for the testing team: Requirement 5. The access control policy is reviewed and updated annually and there is a revision history to prove it.

2 Access control procedures reviewed and/or updated annually.

Translation for the testing team: Requirement 6. The access control policy is reviewed and updated annually and there is a revision history to prove it.

Assessment project planning

> By failing to prepare, you are preparing to fail.
>
> Benjamin Franklin

Each section of the framework will require the assessor to examine, interview, and/or test the control. A project plan that defines the type of action required, the person required to perform that action and the evidence needed to demonstrate effectiveness provides a logic method to test the control.

The project plan should be broken down into Milestones that tie to the test itself; Tasks, Start Dates, End Dates, Resources, Evidence Required and Prerequisites needed, and comments. Each task is uniquely identified and the required evidence, which is the deliverable for the task, is clearly stated.

Task Id	Milestone	Task	Owner	Desc.	Start Date	End Date	Dependency	Comments
1	Access Control Assessment	Obtain Access Control Policy	Joe		1/1/21	1/3/21		
2		Review Access Control Policy	Joe		1/2/21	1/4/21	1	
3		Obtain Access Control Procedure	Joe		1/1/21	1/3/21		
4		Review Access Control Procedure	Joe		1/2/21	1/4/21	3	
5		Determine list of roles/responsibilities	Joe		1/4/21	1/5/21	2.4	
6		Align to policy and procedures	Joe		1/5/21	1/6/21	2.4	
7		Obtain DocuSign Policy and Procedure Acknowledgements	Joe		1/1/21	1/3/21		
8		Compare Acknowledgements	Joe		1/2/21	1/4/21	7	
9		Obtain Review Process	Joe		1/1/21	1/3/21		
10		Review Review Process	Joe		1/2/21	1/4/21	9	

Figure 24.1 Project Plan Example for a Task

Example project plan task and evidence breakdown for AC-1

Obtain the access control policy and procedures or other relevant documents. Investigate and place into evidence whether:

Task 1: evidence that the organizing develops, documents, and disseminates to defined personnel or roles who must implement or adhere to the control as follows: an access control policy that addresses the purpose, scope, roles, responsibilities, enforcement, mechanisms required, related policies and procedures, monitoring/reporting, exceptions, definitions, and revision history; and

Task 1: Obtain the written access control policy

Evidence 1: Written and approved Access Control Policy

Task 2: Review the access control policy for best practice components

Evidence 2: The policy was crafted with all the best practice components.

Task 3: The policy and procedure were crafted by the people who have to use it, such as the system administrators, etc.

Evidence 3: List of policy and procedure creators.

Task 4: Review the access control policy for required mechanisms

Evidence 4: The policy has documented multiple mechanisms that are required to demonstrate that it is effective.

Task 5: Obtain the written access control procedure

Evidence 5. The procedure mechanisms tie back to the policy statement. There will be several of these that are needed to ensure that the policy mechanisms are effective.

Task 6: Obtain the review schedule and revision history for the policy.

Evidence 6: The access control policy reviewed and/or updated annually; and there is a revision history.

Task 7: Obtain the review schedule and revision history for the procedure.

Evidence 7. The access control procedure is reviewed and updated annually and there is a revision history to prove it.

Each task will utilize the identified assessment method with the appropriate required level of rigor and detail evidence requirements that will be judged to be sufficient or ruled insufficient. The task should also be specific to the scope and any interdependencies. The tasks should provide the evidence details that would satisfy an auditor's level of confidence and assurance for the specific control.

Security assessment mitigating risk scoring

Similar to our Inherent Cyber Risk Scoring modeling, each control can be given a weight and each control answer can be weighted in terms of the control effectiveness. It is important to use the same scale the was used for the Inherent Cyber Risk Score.

Cybersecurity control answer weight

Each control will have a series of answers that are weighted based on the evidence obtained.

Answer weight score: 1

This is the lowest answer weight score and will create a lower score associated with the greatest confidence that the control is in place.

All seven criteria are met. The organization develops and documents the access control policy in alignment to the cybersecurity requirements. The organization develops and documents access control procedures, and the organization disseminates the access control policy and procedures to appropriate roles within the organization. The responsible parties within the organization acknowledge they have read and understood the access control policy and procedures, and the organization updates access control policy and procedures when organizational review indicates updates are required. The policy best practices and mechanisms are tiled back to the policy requirements.

Evidence:

Evidence 1: Written and approved Access Control Policy.

Evidence 2: The policy was crafted with all the best practice components.

Evidence 3: List of policy and procedure creators.

Evidence 4: The policy has documented multiple mechanisms that are required to demonstrate that it is effective.

Evidence 5: The procedure mechanisms tie back to the policy statement. There will be several of these that are needed to ensure that the policy mechanisms are effective.

Evidence 6: The access control policy reviewed and/or updated annually; and there is a revision history.

Evidence 7: The access control procedure is reviewed and updated annually and there is a revision history to prove it.

Answer weight score 2

The organization has 5 out of 7 pieces of evidence. Typically, the annual review will be missing.

Answer weight score 3

The organization has 4 out of 7 pieces of evidence. Typically, the annual review and the signed policy and procedure acknowledgement forms will be missing.

Answer weight score 4

The organization has 3 out of 7 pieces of evidence. Typically, the annual review, the signed policy and procedure acknowledgement forms, and list of responsible parties for the policy and procedures will be missing.

Answer weight score 5

The organization has 0 to 2 out of 7 pieces of evidence.

Score	Description	Evidence in Place
1	All 7 Criteria are in place.	1. There is a written and approved Access Control Policy and Procedure in place. 2. The policy was crafted with all the best practice components.
2	6 our of 7 Criteria are in place.	3. There is a list of policy and procedure creators. 4. The policy has documented multiple mechanisms that are required to demonstrate that it is effective.
3	5 our of 7 Criteria are in place.	5. The procedure mechanisms tie back to the policy statements. There will be several of these that are needed to ensure that the policy mechanisms are effective.
4	4 our of 7 Criteria are in place.	6. The access control policy is reviewed and/or updated annually; and there is a revision history.
5	3 or less of 7 Criteria are in place.	7. The access control procedure is reviewed and/or updated annually; and there is a revision history.

Figure 24.2 Assessment Answer Weighting Example

Cybersecurity control question weight

Next, we address the question weights. Some questions will be weighted higher than others. The lowest and best risk score associated to the certainty the control is in place.

This has to be done for all the controls. There are 169 controls that are part of the NIST 800-53 v4 and would need to be planned as above and weighted. They include the following categories and subcategories of tests:

Access control: includes tests for account management, access enforcement, information flow enforcement, separation of duties, least privilege, unsuccessful logon attempts, system use notification, concurrent session lock, session lock, session termination, permitted actions without identification or authentication, remote access, wireless access, access control for mobile devices, use of external information systems, information sharing, and publicly accessible content.

Security awareness and training: tests include security awareness and training policy and procedures, security awareness training, role-based security training, and security training records.

Audit and accountability: tests include audit and accountability policy and procedures, audit events, content of audit records, audit storage capacity, response to audit processing failures, audit review, analysis, and reporting, audit reduction and report generation, time stamps, protection of audit information, audit record retention. Audit generation security assessment and authorization tests include security assessment and authorization policy and procedures, security assessments, system interconnection, plan of action and milestones, security authorization, continuous monitoring, penetration testing, and internal system connections.

Configuration management: tests include configuration management policy and procedures, baseline configuration, configuration change control, security impact analysis, access restrictions for change, configuration settings, least functionality, information system component inventory, configuration management plan, software usage restrictions, and user-installed software.

Contingency planning: tests include contingency planning policy and procedures contingency plan, contingency training, contingency plan testing, alternate storage site, alternate processing site, telecommunications services, information system backup, and information system recovery and reconstitution.

Identification and authorization: tests include identification and authentication policy and procedures, identification, and authentication (organizational users), device identification and authentication, identifier management, authenticator management, authenticator feedback, cryptographic module authentication, and identification and authentication (non-organizational users).

Incident response: tests include incident response policy and procedures, incident response training, and incident response testing.

Incident handling: tests include incident handling, incident monitoring, incident reporting, incident response assistance, incident response plan, and information spillage response, system.

Maintenance: tests include maintenance policy and procedures, controlled maintenance, maintenance tools, nonlocal maintenance, maintenance personnel, and timely maintenance.

Media protection: tests include media protection policy and procedures, media access, media marking, media storage, media transport, media sanitization, and media use.

Physical and environmental protection: tests include physical and environmental protection policy and procedures, physical access authorizations, physical access control, access control for transmission medium, access control for output devices, monitoring physical access, visitor access records, power equipment and cabling, emergency shutoff, emergency power, emergency lighting, fire protection, temperature and humidity controls, water damage protection, delivery and removal, and alternate work site.

Planning: tests include security planning policy and procedures, system security plan, rules of behavior, and an information security architecture.

Personnel security: tests include personnel security policy and procedures, position risk designation, personnel screening, personnel termination, personnel transfer, access agreements, third-party personnel security, and personnel sanctions.

Risk assessment: tests include risk assessment policy and procedures, security categorization, risk assessment, and vulnerability scanning.

System services: tests include system and services acquisition policy and procedures, allocation of resources, system development life cycle, acquisition process, information system documentation, security engineering principles, external information system services, developer configuration management, and developer security testing and evaluation.

Systems and communications: tests include system and communications protection policy and procedures, application partitioning, information in shared resources, denial-of-service protection, boundary protection, transmission confidentiality and integrity, network disconnect, cryptographic key establishment and management, cryptographic protection, collaborative computing devices, public key infrastructure certificates, mobile code, voice over internet protocol, secure name/address resolution service (authoritative source), secure name/address resolution service (recursive or caching resolver), architecture and provisioning for name/address resolution service, session authenticity, protection of information at rest, and process isolation.

System and information: tests include system and information integrity policy and procedures, flaw remediation, malicious code protection, information system monitoring, security alerts, advisories, and directives, security function verification, software, firmware, and information integrity, spam protection, information input validation, error handling, information output handling and retention, and memory protection.

Transparency: tests include inventory of personally identifiable information, privacy incident response, privacy notice, system of records notices and privacy act statements, dissemination of privacy program information, internal use, and information sharing with third parties.

Cybersecurity assessment mitigating risk score modeling

Remember that cyber risk scores are empirical scores that rely on comprehensive and diverse data. In this case the data is the effectiveness of the controls. It is done for each digital asset.

The cyber assessment scores are summarized, and the average score is used to calculate the effectiveness of the controls. Here are the steps to follow.

Step 1: Number of Controls: Determine the number of controls you will include. In this example we will include all 169.

Step 2: Control Weighting: Determine the weight of each control test. In this example, I assume a scale of 0 to 5.

Step 3: Test Weighting: Determine the possible answers for each test and map them to a control test weight.

Step 4: Answer Weight: Determine the weight for each answer.

Step 5: Control Test Results: Preform the control tests.

Step 6: Score for each Test: Multiply the answer weights by the question weights for each control test.

Step 7: 100% Effectiveness Score: Determine 100% effectiveness by summing the maximum value of the answer weights by the sum of the question weights. In this case 169* 5 = 845.

Step 8: Control Test Score: Calculate the raw scores for each control test by multiplying the answer weights by the question weights.

Step 9: Summary Control Test Score: Summarize all the control test scores.

Step 10: Average Mitigating Risk Score: Calculate the *control effectiveness average* by taking the sum of the control test scores and dividing them by the number of control tests.

Step 11: Post Assessment Score: Calculate the *post assessment score* by multiplying the inherent cyber risk score by (1- the Average Mitigating Risk Score).

If the inherent risk score of the digital asset was 2.5 and (1—the Average Mitigating Risk Score is 80% (.8)) then the Post assessment score is .5.

The purpose of this is to provide for gap analysis of the mitigating controls and trends analysis across the trends across the digital asset infrastructure.

Trends analysis

Using the digital asset approach allows for each control to be accessed across the infrastructure. Let's go take a look at some control scores and understand what the trends are telling us.

System	Policy and Procedures	Separation of Duties	Unsuccessful Login Attempts	Least Privilege
SAP Financials	3	5	3	3
Peoplesoft HR	3	5	1	1
Guidewire ClaimsCenter	2	5	1	1
Payroll System	1	5	1	1

Figure 24.3 Control Trends Analysis

It is obvious that there is an issue with Separation of Duties (SoD). In cybersecurity, SoD is used to avoid conflicts of interest that could lead to fraud, and to prevent control failures that could result in data theft or security breaches.

As an example, if one person is performing both the development and testing of a system, they are more likely to be pushing the testing thorough prematurely. Perhaps a bonus is tied to this. Many developers open and leave backdoors that can be exploited by cybercriminals. A Quality Assurance (QA) person would find these and insist that they be closed.

The finding would be that the company is ignoring separation of duties and needs to implement a process to ensure that they are in place.

A second observation could be that SAP Financials has an average mitigating score that shows the controls are 40% less in place than other crown jewels systems. The firm will want to strengthen the controls for SAP Financials to prevent a claim of willful neglect if the system is breached.

Many trends can be correlated and spotted to help the firm see how economies of scale can be utilized to shore up control effectiveness when one process is impacting the entire infrastructure as in the SoD example.

Note

1. NIST, "FISMA implementation project", December 3, 2020, https://csrc.nist.gov/projects/risk-management/security-assessment/assessment-cases-overview.

PART VII

THE GENERAL DATA PROTECTION REGULATION (GDPR) AND PRIVACY

25 GDPR OVERVIEW

The cybersecurity and privacy regulatory landscape has evolved on a global scale and is now in a state of constant and consistent change. In the US alone, many states have plans to enact new privacy regulations over the next two years. Compound that with consumer awareness and expectations around transparency, the time is now to build a global privacy program that can keep pace, maintain trust and stay ahead of these changes.

Jo Ann Lengua Davaris, Vice President, Global Privacy,
Booking Holdings Inc.

Privacy—2020 and beyond

What is Privacy? Privacy is described as "the condition or state of being free from public attention to, intrusion into, or interference with one's acts or decisions."[4]

Privacy is a person's right to choose and to determine whether, how, and to what extent information about oneself is communicated to others.

The expectation of privacy is described as "a belief in the existence of the right to be free of governmental intrusion in regard to a particular place or thing."[5]

The time to learn about GDPR is over. Fourteen months after the EU's General Data Protection Regulation (GDPR) took effect, the world of data privacy has shifted its focus from guidance to stepped-up enforcement, according to PWC. The large fines on three multinationals levied by two data protection authorities (DPAs) in 2019 are just the beginning of active and rigorous enforcement.[6]

Will 2020 also mark the shift to consumers exercising their rights over their data? Companies are adding significant resources to meet customer requests for their data, according to a recent PWC survey of preparedness for the California Consumer Privacy Act (CCPA).[7]

There are many similarities between GDPR and other global regulations relating to data protection and privacy. GDPR has a greater financial impact, and its scope is more extensive than any others.

Privacy penalties

The US$5 billion penalty against Facebook is the largest fine ever imposed on any company for violating the right to data privacy. It is almost 20 times greater than the largest privacy or data security penalty ever imposed worldwide as of January 2020.

DOI: 10.4324/9781003052616-32

Privacy penalties are making history. British Airways also made history with a record US$230 million penalty. Marriott was fined $124 million and Equifax agreed to pay a minimum of US$575 million for its 2017 breach. In July 2019, the credit ratings agency agreed to pay US$575 million in a settlement with the Federal Trade Commission. This rose shortly afterward to US$700 million. The fine is related to the company's "failure to take reasonable steps to secure its network."[8]

US$300 million of Equifax's fine will go to a fund that gives affected consumers free credit monitoring services. US$125 million will be added to this fund if the initial payment is not enough to compensate consumers. US$175 million will go to 48 states, the District of Columbia and Puerto Rico for compensation. US$100 million will go to the Consumer Financial Protection Bureau (CFPB). The settlement requires Equifax to obtain third-party assessments of its information security program every two years.

"Companies that profit from personal information have an extra responsibility to protect and secure that data," said FTC Chairman Joe Simons. "Equifax failed to take basic steps that may have prevented the breach that affected approximately 147 million consumers."[9]

Equifax was fined US$625,000 in the UK for its 2017 data breach. This was the maximum fine allowed under the pre-GDPR Data Protection Act 1998. Uber's poor handling of its 2016 breach cost it almost US$150 million.[10]

GDPR influences include the Gramm-Leach-Bliley Act (GLBA) which is being investigated as a national privacy regulation. The Gramm-Leach-Bliley Act was enacted to protect consumer financial privacy. Its provisions limit when a financial institution can disclose a consumer's nonpublic personal information to nonaffiliated third parties.

Introducing the GDPR

The General Data Protection Regulation[11] passed by the European Union (EU) Parliament & Council is a regulation in EU law on data protection and privacy, replacing the Data Protection Directive (Directive 95/46/EC). Formally adopted 25 May 2016, it became effective 25 May 2018.

The EU has had a directive on data protection and privacy since 1995. The directive was not implemented homogenously across the EU. The EU saw the need for rigorous enforcement and has changed the directive to a regulation making it is legally binding and the regulation has created data privacy consistency across the EU. GDPR is saving more than 2 billion EUR per year by eliminating redundancy across the EU nation states.[12]

GDPR governs all conduct with respect to processing personally identifiable information (PII) for all individual residents of the EU.

GDPR has global impact on all businesses, irrespective of their location. The scope includes those which process PII of EU residents in the context of products and services they provide; those which monitor the activity of EU residents; or which are deemed to be "established" in the EU, which includes any real and effective activity in the EU.

GDPR personal data terminology[13]

The GDPR scope defines EU citizen personal data as any information relating to an individual. The information can be related to either their private, professional, or public life. It includes names, images, email address, bank details, social media posts, medical information, and even a computer's IP address.

A Data Subject is a person whose data is collected, stored, or processed. Data Owner may be used in lieu of the term Data Subject.

A Data Controller is an organization that collects data from EU residents.

A Data Processor is an organization that processes data on behalf of a Data Subject or Data Controller (e.g., cloud service provider). Note that Data Controllers can be both Controller and Processor.

GDPR data elements include: passport number, driver's license number, logins/passwords, email or IP address, financial data, mental/physical health or other medical information, race/ethnicity/religious affiliations, sexual orientation, political opinions, and biometric data.

GDPR fines[14]

The maximum penalties are 20M EUR or 4% of global turnover, whichever is higher. These fines are related to the articles associated with the data subject rights and could result in a company going out of business. GDPR enforcement is targeted to make organizations proactive about their cybersecurity from the top down and to prevent data breaches of EU nationals from occurring.

The following fines and sanctions can be imposed for violations of GDPR:

Article 83 paragraph 4 dictates the general conditions for imposing administrative fines. When deciding whether to impose an administrative fine and the amount of that fine the Supervisory Authority will consider among other things, the nature, gravity, and duration of the violation. It will take into account the number of data subjects affected and the level of damage suffered by them, whether the act was intentional or negligent, any actions taken by the controller or data processor to mitigate the damage suffered by data subjects, any previous infringements, the degree of cooperation with the supervisory authority, how the violation was reported, and any other mitigating or aggravating factors related to the issue.

GDPR has two tiers of financial penalties. Less severe violations may result in a fine of up to 10 million EUR, or 2% of the firm's worldwide annual revenue from the preceding financial year, whichever amount is higher.[15] This would stem from any violations of the following:

- For Controllers and Data Processors: Articles 8, 11, 25–39, 42, and 43 are rules that address the governing of data protection, the lawful basis for processing, and more.
- For Certification bodies: Articles 42 and 43 are rules that govern that their evaluations and assessments without bias and via a transparent process.

- For Monitoring bodies: Article 41 is a rule to ensure that they demonstrate independence and follow established procedure in handling complaints or reported infringements in an impartial and transparent manner.

A warning will be provided in writing in cases of a first and non-intentional non-compliance violation. In addition, periodic audits and a fine of up to 10 million EUR or 2% of the annual worldwide turnover of the preceding financial year, whichever is greater, is possible, if there has been an infringement of the following provisions of this article.

Article 83 paragraphs 5 and 6 provide for a fine of up to 20 million EUR or 4% of the annual worldwide turnover of the preceding financial year, whichever is greater. It is typically related to infringement of the basic principles for processing, including conditions for consent for Articles 5, 6, 7, and 9, the data subjects' rights for Articles 12 to 22, the transfers of personal data to a recipient in a third country or an international organization for Articles 44 to 49, any obligations pursuant to member state law adopted under Chapter IX, and noncompliance with an order or a temporary or definitive limitation on processing or the suspension of data flows by the supervisory authority for Article 58(2) or failure to provide access in violation of Article 58(1).

It is important to note that violation of the rights of the data subjects (Articles 12–22) have the highest penalties. These requirements are heavy on policies, process and procedures being in place. The effectiveness of the policies, processes and procedures is dependent upon the identification of where all the privacy data lives. This relates back to Article 1. Without a digital asset inventory, you cannot be compliant with any of the GDPR articles.

More severe violations relate to the principles of the right to privacy and the right of the data subject to have their data updated, or to be forgotten. These more severe types of infringements of the rights of the data subject could carry a fine of up to 20 million EUR, or 4% of the firm's worldwide annual revenue from the preceding financial year, whichever amount is higher. This would stem from any violations of the following:

- Articles 5, 6, and 9 which relate to the basic principles for processing. These articles stipulate that data processing must be done in a lawful, fair, and transparent manner. Data must be collected and processed for a specific purpose, kept accurate and up to date, and processed in a manner that ensures its security.
- Article 6 provides six lawful reasons to process data. Organizations must meet one of the six requirements. Specific types of personal data, such as race, political opinions, religion, trade union membership, sexual orientation, health, and biometric data are prohibited except under specific circumstances.
- Article 7 provides the conditions for consent and outlines the documentation requirements to prove consent.
- Articles 12–22 are the most important data subjects' rights. Data Subjects have a right to know what data an organization is collecting and what they

are doing with it. They may obtain a copy of the data collected, have erroneous data corrected, and in some circumstance have the right to have the data deleted (forgotten). Data Subjects have a right to transfer their data to another organization upon request.

- Articles 44–49 relate to the transfer of data to an international organization or a recipient in a third country. The European Commission must decide that a country or organization ensures an adequate level of protection before data can be transferred out of the EU.
- Nation State Specific Laws: Chapter IX grants EU member states the ability to pass additional data protection laws as long as they are in accordance with the GDPR. Violations of these additional nation-state laws faces GDPR administrative fines.
- Supervisory Orders: Non-compliance with an order by a supervisory authority will incur a huge fine, regardless of what the original violation was.

Article 82: These fines above are only those that are done at the level of the Supervisory Authority. Data Subjects have the right to seek compensation from organizations that cause them material or non-material damage as a result of a GDPR violations.

GDPR compliance

Complying with GDPR requirements will reduce the chances of triggering a Data Protection Authority (DPA) to investigate your company's privacy practices. DPAs can and will impose a fine on companies of up to 4% of annual global turnover for violations of data subject rights. Member states have added more requirements and fines. As an example, the Netherlands has more than doubled its fining capacity to 10% of annual revenues for violation of Data Subject rights. Many European privacy advocates are pressuring DPAs to enforce the fines and up the ante.

I advise multinationals that must be compliant with GDPR to adopt these stringent requirements across the firm and to communicate this privacy posture to the DPAs that have jurisdiction over their major European operations.

Supervisory Authorities cooperate together and provide information sharing, mutual assistance, and organizing joint operations. If there is an GDPR incident and a firm has multiple locations in the EU, it will have a single SA lead the investigation. This lead authority will be based on the location of a company's main establishment and where the main processing activities take place. This one-stop shop approach is based on Articles 46–55 and reduces redundancies to supervise all the processing activities of that business throughout the EU. The European Data Protection Board (EDPB) coordinates all the Supervisory Authorities activities.

GDPR has a 72-hour breach notification requirement. However, if you are a multinational, I recommend that you look at the states you process data in and use the most stringent data breach notification requirement. In Colorado, the requirement is 30 hours. This is the shortest time-frame to data by any regulatory body.

There are exceptions to GDPR when data is processed in an employment capacity or for national security purposes. Check the requirements thoroughly to understand the context of the requirement for your firm. Ensuring that there is visibility into each requirement will boost a corporations' compliance visibility with EU data-protection authorities. Compliance with each requirement will reduce the chances of triggering a EU Data Protection Authority (DPA) to investigate a company's privacy practices.

Breaking down the rights of the data subjects

What are the major components of GDPR? There are two major categories of requirements for GDPR: the enforcement of the Rights of the Data Subjects in relationship to their data and a Privacy Impact Assessment (PIA) to guarantee systems that process GDPR data have acceptable levels of confidentiality and integrity and manage risk in this context. The PIA is covered in depth in Chapter 28.

Key areas to understand for the right of the data subjects are:

- Article 15: The Right to Access Personal Data. Under GDPR, data subjects have the right to access the data collected on them by a data controller. The data controller has 30 days to respond an access request.
- Article 16: The Right to Rectification. Data subjects have the right to request their data be updated.
- Article 17: The Right to Erasure. The right to have data deleted, aka the right to be forgotten, allows a data subject to stop all processing of their data and request their personal data be erased.
- Article 18: The Right to Restrict Data Processing. Data subjects can request that all processing of their personal data be stopped.
- Article 19: The Right to be Notified. Data subjects must be notified about the use of their personal data in an obvious manner and be informed about the actions that can be taken if they feel their rights are being violated. This notification requirements extends to data subjects if they have had any rectification or erasure of their personal data under Articles 16, 17, and 18.
- Article 20: The Right to Data Portability. A data subject can request that their personal data file be sent to a third party electronically. Data must be provided in a machine-readable format which is commonly used such as a csv file if doing so is technically feasible.
- Article 21: The Right to Object: Any request to stop data processing that is denied by a data controller can be objected to by the data subject.
- Article 22: The Right to Reject Automated Decision-Making. Data subjects may refuse have their data automatically processed in certain circumstances.

The privacy impact assessment (PIA)

Privacy metrics and key performance indicators (KPIs)

Privacy metrics include confidentiality and integrity. Availability is not a privacy metric. Confidentiality is the ability to ensure that only authorized and approved users have access to the data. Integrity is ability to ensure that the data is unaltered and is consistent, accurate, and trustworthy over its entire life cycle.

Measuring privacy metrics is the only known defensible method to ensure that the level of integrity and confidentiality are at acceptable levels. This meets the requirements for Article 5f. There are many digital asset attributes that influence the likelihood of a data breach which violates the rights of the data subjects to have confidentiality and integrity. These must be measured in context to benchmark these scores in the privacy impact assessment, areas identified for improvement to reduce the risk and monitored on a routine basis.

Privacy metrics must be benchmarked, and thresholds of acceptable risk defined based on the amount of impact. In terms of GDPR or CCPA, this related back to regulatory fines. We will provide a detailed methodology to benchmark privacy metrics in the following chapters.

GDPR case study

British Airways (BA) is part of the International Consolidated Airlines Group S.A. (IAG) and is the largest international carrier in the UK. BA is headquartered in London, England, near its main hub at Heathrow Airport. The corporate head office for IAG is in London, UK. Formed in January 2011, IAG is the parent company of British Airways and other airlines. It is a Spanish registered company with shares traded on the London Stock Exchange, Spanish Stock Exchange and FTSE 100 Index. BA has over 45,000 employees and made 13,290 million GBP in revenue is 2019.[16]

2018	2018	2018	2018	2019	2020
March British Airlines frequent flyer accounts hacked BA claimed that no personal information had been swiped	**April** 185,000 transactions compromised	**July** 244,000 transactions compromised	**September** BA states affected transactions are 380,000+ RiskIQ published analysis of the data breach and cites Magecart as the actors behind the attack	**July** BA fined 183.4 million ($230M) by ICO	**April** BA has had their GDPR regulation fines deferred until later in 2020

Figure 25.1 British Airlines Timeline[17]

BA has had multiple cyber related incidents. The Information Commissioner's Office (ICO) has issued a notice to fine British Airways 183.39M GBP (approx. US$230M) for violations of the General Data Protection Regulation (GDPR). The fine is 1.5% of BA's global turnover for the year.

In March of 2015, British Airways frequent-flyer accounts were hacked. A third-party used information obtained elsewhere on the internet, via an automated process, to try to gain access to accounts.

In September of 2018, they suffered a data breach on their booking website and app. The hackers had carried out a "sophisticated, malicious criminal attack" on BA's website. Users of British Airways' website were diverted to a fraudulent site. Through this false site, details of customer information were harvested by the attackers.

According to cybersecurity firm RisklQ, the hack was just 22 lines of JavaScript (code), embedded into the company's website.[18] The malicious code stole data when customers entered their details into a payment form. The form was sent to an attacker-controlled server when a user clicked or tapped a submission button. The attackers were so bold that they set up a Secure Socket Layer certificate for this server to fake it as a legitimate site by showing a credential that confirms the server has Web encryption enabled to protect data in transit. A security firm reported that credit card skimming malware was installed by hackers on British Airways' website and was to blame for a data breach of over 380,000 credit cards.

Most recently in August of 2019, their e-ticketing system was breached. A security bug was discovered with the potential to expose sensitive data. BA included passenger details in the URL parameters that directed the passenger from the email to the British Airways website. This was used to streamline the user experience so that when they were logged in automatically, they could view their itinerary and check in for their flight. The passenger details included in the URL parameters included the booking reference number, and user surname. Both data elements were exposed because the link was unencrypted. This means anyone snooping on the same public Wi-Fi network can easily intercept the link request and use the information to gain access to the passenger's online itinerary to steal more information or even manipulate the booking information. The airline check-in links were unencrypted and easily intercepted, enabling unauthorized third parties to view and change passengers' flight booking details and personal information.

Earlier in July 2019, Wandera's threat research team observed that passenger details were being sent unencrypted when a user on their network logged into the British Airways e-ticketing system. BA was unaware of the issue. Wandera notified British Airways of the vulnerable link. BA did not seem to take any action after learning about the vulnerability.

The 2015 breach could have been prevented by using unique and stronger passwords to protect accounts, different passwords for different accounts, enabling Multi-Factor Authorization (MFA) and remaining vigilant on account activity.

The 2018 breach could have been prevented by improving Configuration Management practices and using a correctly configured Web Application Firewalling (WAF), which inspects and filters traffic on websites.

The 2019 breach could have been prevented by using encryption through the check-in process, requiring User Authentication where PII is accessible and editable and having patching of systems on a regular basis. As per Willie Walsh, CEO of BA's parent company IAG SA, "The technology failed only because the people behind it failed in some capacity."[19]

How to start a privacy program

A digital asset inventory is the first step to understanding your data. It is critical to identify which systems are in scope for privacy risk assessments and to quantify your financial exposures. Digital asset inventories are needed to allow companies to comply with all the data subject rights. Not knowing which systems process the privacy data is a recipe for failure. For example, let's take the right to rectification. How can you put a process together that provides for this without knowing where that data subject's data is being stored to delete it? You can't! If your firm does not have an asset inventory application then you can do it in excel by asking questions of the system owners such as the ones below will provide context.

- Which systems process GDPR data? Some obvious examples include Customer Relationship Management (CRM), HR systems, payroll systems and the systems that feed data to them or are fed by them. Don't forget unstructured data that are on laptops and in non-inventoried shadow IT systems like a Microsoft Access database. Excel resources and asset management systems are available as a mechanism to document this.
- Which devices are involved? (Cloud, USB, File Shares...) These are all in scope. Furthermore, the laws are starting to pivot to single out and address innovative technologies. Innovative technologies typically have no security built into them. Technologies are the components of systems. They will make a system more inherently risky by their very nature. Systems that process privacy must have a level of assurance that they are protecting the privacy data.

Mapping systems, and technologies like devices is the best place to start. Documenting where the data lives, and where it is processed defines the scope of the compliance intuitive. New policies and processes will need to be created or enhanced to protect the rights of the data subjects.

The GDPR program is rigorous. Some of the starting requirements that are important are that businesses must:

- Appoint a Data Protection Officer (DPO) to be accountable for all data privacy protections and activities. The role of the DPO is to think like a regulator, who is enforcing this regulation. Responsibility is to ensure that the company or organization is correctly protecting individuals' personal data according to current legislation. Other responsibilities include managing the GDPR and Privacy Program, communicating to Board on privacy issues and with the EU DPA, offering advice on privacy matters, monitoring GDPR and privacy compliance, liaising with the authorities and addressing privacy risks.
- Maintain a data privacy notice and provide notice at all points of data collection.
- Maintain policies & procedures to respond to requests from data subjects (i.e., access, update, portability, erasure, opt out).
- Maintain a data breach or incident response plan, including a log to track incidents as well as protocols to notify regulators as well as impacted individuals.
- Use standard contractual clauses and binding corporate rules to ensure compliant cross border data transfers.

- Create data processing inventories and integrate data privacy principles for encryption, de-identification of PII, automated processing, restricted access, and record retention into information security programs.
- Influence marketing practices and technology projects with Privacy by Design principles.

GDPR evidence requirements

If your firm has a data breach, the EU supervisory authority is going to ask for evidence of the GDPR program. A GDPR program requires forms, policies, and procedures in order to comply with each of the data subject related rights in terms of use and collection of personal data. As an example, to comply with Article 15—Right to Erasure, the firm has to have a form for the data subject to fill out and request to be forgotten. A set of processes and procedures have to be written that address each step of what has to be done to delete the data subject rights data, including approving, deleting, auditing, and notifying. The systems that are processing the data subjects' personal information have to have a privacy impact and security control assessment done.

The following chapters explore in depth the GDPR articles in layman's terms, how to collect GDPR evidence and the Privacy Impact Assessment (PIA).

Notes

1. Anne Gherini, Inc., "Why US based startups are panicking about this new regulation. Many have heard the warnings and neglected to act. GDPR's compliance deadline is approaching and the fines are heavy," February 28, 2018, https://www.inc.com/anne-gherini/fifty-two-percent-of-us-businesses-are-affected-by-this-new-regulation.html.
2. Clint Boulton, CIO, "U.S. companies spending millions to satisfy Europe's GDPR", January 26, 2017, https://www.cio.com/article/3161920/article.html.
3. Jonathan Crowl, Skyword, "The impact of GDRP for American companies might be bigger than you think", February 14, 2018, https://www.skyword.com/contentstandard/the-impact-of-gdpr-for-american-companies-might-be-bigger-than-you-think/.
4. Justice SA Bobde, Scroll.in, "What does privacy actually mean? Excerpts from the Supreme court judgement", August 24, 2017, https://scroll.in/article/848349/what-does-privacy-actually-mean-excerpts-from-the-supreme-court-judgment#:~:text=%E2%80%9C'Privacy'%20is%20'%5B,right%20to%20be%20let%20alone.
5. LegalLingo, "Nom Clause", 2020, https://legal-lingo.com/nom-clause.
6. PWC, "Top policy trends 2019", 2019, https://www.pwc.com/us/en/library/risk-regulatory/strategic-policy/top-policy-trends-2019.html.
7. PWC, "What you don't know about the California Consumer Privacy Act", 2020, https://www.pwc.com/us/en/services/consulting/cybersecurity/california-consumer-privacy-act/what-to-know-about-ccpa.html.
8. Federal Trade Commission, "Equifax to pay $575 million as part of settlement with FTC, CFPB, and States related to 2017 data breach", July 22, 2019, https://www.ftc.gov/news-events/press-releases/2019/07/equifax-pay-575-million-part-settlement-ftc-cfpb-states-related.
9. Federal Trade Commission, "Equifax to pay $575 million as part of settlement with FTC, CFPB, and States related to 2017 data breach", July 22, 2019, https://www.ftc.gov/news-events/press-releases/2019/07/equifax-pay-575-million-part-settlement-ftc-cfpb-states-related.

10. Dan Swinhoe, CSO, "The biggest data breach fines, penalties and settlements so far", December 4, 2020, https://www.csoonline.com/article/3410278/the-biggest-data-breach-fines-penalties-and-settlements-so-far.html#:~:text=Uber's%20poor%20handling%20of%20its,Services%20collecting%20increasingly%20large%20fines.
11. Intersoft consulting, "General data protection regulation GDPR", May 25, 2018, https://gdpr-info.eu/.
12. Danny Palmer, ZDNet, "What is GDPR? Everything you need to know about the new general data protection regulations", May 17, 2019, https://www.zdnet.com/article/gdpr-an-executive-guide-to-what-you-need-to-know/.
13. GDPR.EU, "What is GDPR, the EU's new data protection law?," 2020, https://gdpr.eu/what-is-gdpr/.
14. GDPR.EU, "What are the GDPR's fines?," 2020, https://gdpr.eu/fines/.
15. GDPR.EU, "What are the GDPR's fines?," 2020, https://gdpr.eu/fines/.
16. IAG, "Newsroom," 2020, https://www.iairgroup.com/en/newsroom.
17. Holly Graceful, Graceful Security, "British Airways breach timeline", July 22, 2019, https://gracefulsecurity.com/british-airways-breach-timeline/.
18. Ivan Mehta, TNW, "It took hackers just 22 lines of code to steal British Airway's customer data", September 12, 2018, https://thenextweb.com/security/2018/09/12/hackers-used-22-line-code-stole-british-airways-data/#:~:text=Programs-,It%20took%20hackers%20just%2022%20lines%20of,steal%20British%20Airways'%20customer%20data&text=Last%20week%2C%20British%20Airways%20acknowledged,380%2C000%20customers'%20data%20being%20compromised.&text=RiskIQ%20found%20that%20the%20script,before%20the%20data%20breach%20began.
19. Andy Patrizio, Network World, "British Airway's outage, like most data center outages, was caused by humans", June 8, 2017, https://www.networkworld.com/article/3200105/british-airways-outage-like-most-data-center-outages-was-caused-by-humans.html.

26 GDPR ARTICLES

There are only two types of companies: those that know that they have been hacked and those that don't know that they have been hacked. Which are you?

Jordan Jeffer, Cybersecurity Risk Leader, Investigations and Threat Intelligence at Mastercard

CHAPTER 1: GENERAL PROVISIONS

Article 1—subject matter and objectives[1]

1 This Regulation lays down rules relating to the protection of natural persons with regard to the processing of personal data and rules relating to the free movement of personal data.
2 This Regulation protects fundamental rights and freedoms of natural persons and in particular their right to the protection of personal data.
3 The free movement of personal data within the Union shall be neither restricted nor prohibited for reasons connected with the protection of natural persons with regard to the processing of personal data.

The first question every company must ask is "are we in scope for GDPR?" In order to be able to know that, there must be a mechanism that identifies GDPR data in each system. This determines the scope of the GDPR and privacy program.

Systems that process or store EU citizen data can be identified with an automated tool that identifies which servers have privacy data, or manually. If done manually, an excel spreadsheet can be used to map systems, technologies, and data types. Data can also be mapped in an asset management system like the VRisk Cyber Risk Management Platform or others.[2] Knowing where the data lives is required to be able to have effective procedures for erasure, rectification, and portability as well as the ability to conduct a privacy impact assessment to name a few.

Refer to the appendix for a typical excel spreadsheet example.

Article 1 has 8 requirements which include:

- Privacy Notice—"A privacy notice is a statement made to a data subject that describes how the organization collects, uses, retains, and discloses

DOI: 10.4324/9781003052616-33

personal information. A privacy notice is sometimes referred to as a privacy statement, a fair processing statement, or sometimes a privacy policy." [3]

- Privacy Notice Register—This is a list of all the privacy policies that have been created with issue numbers, date, target data subjects, locations used, legal basis for processing, and withdrawal reason and dates.
- GDPR System Register—This is a list of all systems in scope for the PIA and security control assessment.
- "Privacy Policy—This is an internal statement that governs an organization or entity's handling practices of personal information. It is directed at the users of the personal information. A privacy policy instructs employees on the collection and the use of the data, as well as any specific rights the data subjects may have.
- Information Security Policy—This is an information security policy (ISP) that is a set of rules, policies and procedures designed to ensure all users and networks within an organization meet minimum IT security and data protection security requirements."
- Data Protection Policy—A data protection policy is a type of security policy that aims to design, implement, guide, monitor, and manage security over an organization's data. It primarily aims at securing and protecting logical data stored, consumed, and managed by an organization.
- Data Subject Consent Form—This is a form used to obtain consent to process a data subject's personal data from the company.
- Privacy Impact Assessment—This is a risk assessment of the confidentiality and integrity of the privacy data that is being processed by the systems.

Article 2—material scope[4]

This article applies to the processing of personal data wholly or partly by automated means. It also applies to the processing other than by automated means of personal data which form part of a filing system or are intended to form part of a filing system.

The firm needs to know what mechanism(s) is in place for identifying which systems are processing personal data wholly or partly by automated means. Automated processing will have higher levels of data confidence and therefore less risk.

Article 2 has five requirements. All are also required for article 1. They are:

- GDPR System Register—This is a list of all systems in scope for the PIA and security control assessment.
- "Privacy Policy—This is an internal statement that governs an organization or entity's handling practices of personal information. It is directed at the users of the personal information. A privacy policy instructs employees on the collection and the use of the data, as well as any specific rights the data subjects may have.

- Information Security Policy—This is an information security policy (ISP) that is a set of rules, policies and procedures designed to ensure all users and networks within an organization meet minimum IT security, and data protection security requirements."
- Data Protection Policy—A data protection policy is a type of security policy that aims to design, implement, guide, monitor, and manage security over an organization's data. It primarily aims at securing and protecting logical data stored, consumed, and managed by an organization.
- Data Subject Consent Form—This is a form used to obtain consent to process a data subject's personal data from the company.
- Privacy Impact Assessment—This is a risk assessment of the confidentiality and integrity of the privacy data that is being processed by the systems.

Article 3—territorial scope[5]

1 This article applies to the processing of personal data in the context of the activities of an establishment of a controller or a processor in the Union, regardless of whether the processing takes place in the Union or not.
2 This article applies to the processing of personal data of data subjects who are in the Union by a controller or processor not established in the Union, where the processing activities are related to:

   (a) The offering of goods or services, irrespective of whether a payment of the data subject is required, to such data subjects in the Union; or
   (b) The monitoring of their behavior as far as their behavior takes place within the Union.

3 This article applies to the processing of personal data by a controller not established in the Union, but in a place where Member State law applies by virtue of public international law.

Questions to ask in include: Is there a mechanism in place for identifying the systems that process personal data for people in the European Union whether is it processed in the EU or elsewhere? This mechanism should differentiate which country and state the data subject is mapped to for inclusion of U.S. privacy laws. I recommend here that if you are a U.S. entity that is processing EU data that you use one program for privacy compliance. Each state is crafting new legislation for privacy and the idea of mapping hundreds of privacy requirements is daunting. As indicated in the previous chapter, best practice is to adopt the most stringent aspects of the applicable laws into one compliance program.

This article will scope the requirement for the Privacy Impact Assessment (PIA) and other requirements. Article 3 has the same requirements as article 2.

Article 4—definitions[6]

There are no specific requirements for article 4. The definitions are used in all the forms, policies, procedures, and assessments required for GDPR.

The purposes of this article:

"personal data" means any information relating to an identified or identifiable natural person ("data subject"); an identifiable natural person is one who can be identified, directly or indirectly, in particular by reference to an identifier, such as a name, an identification number, location data, an online identifier or to one or more factors specific to the physical, physiological, genetic, mental, economic, cultural, or social identity of that natural person;

"processing" means any operation or set of operations which is performed on personal data or on sets of personal data, whether or not by automated means, such as collection, recording, organization, structuring, storage, adaptation or alteration, retrieval, consultation, use, disclosure by transmission, dissemination or otherwise making available, alignment or combination, restriction, erasure, or destruction;

"restriction of processing" means the marking of stored personal data with the aim of limiting their processing in the future;

"profiling" means any form of automated processing of personal data consisting of the use of personal data to evaluate certain personal aspects relating to a natural person, in particular to analyze or predict aspects concerning that natural person's performance at work, economic situation, health, personal preferences, interests, reliability, behavior, location, or movements;

"pseudonymization" means the processing of personal data in such a manner that the personal data can no longer be attributed to a specific data subject without the use of additional information, provided that such additional information is kept separately and is subject to technical and organizational measures to ensure that the personal data are not attributed to an identified or identifiable natural person;

"filing system" means any structured set of personal data which are accessible according to specific criteria, whether centralized, decentralized or dispersed on a functional or geographical basis;

"controller" means the natural or legal person, public authority, agency, or other body which, alone or jointly with others, determines the purposes, and means of the processing of personal data; where the purposes and means of such processing are determined by Union or Member State law, the controller or the specific criteria for its nomination may be provided for by Union or Member State law;

More definitions include:

"processor" means a natural or legal person, public authority, agency, or other body which processes personal data on behalf of the controller;

"recipient" means a natural or legal person, public authority, agency, or another body, to which the personal data are disclosed, whether a third party or not. However, public authorities which may receive personal data in the framework of a particular inquiry in accordance with Union or Member State law shall not be regarded as recipients; the processing of those data by those public authorities shall follow the applicable data protection rules according to the purposes of the processing;

"third party" means a natural or legal person, public authority, agency, or body other than the data subject, controller, processor, and persons who under the direct authority of the controller or processor are authorized to process personal data;

"consent" of the data subject means any freely given, specific, informed, and unambiguous indication of the data subject's wishes by which he or she, by a statement or by a clear affirmative action, signifies agreement to the processing of personal data relating to him or her;

"personal data breach" means a breach of security leading to the accidental or unlawful destruction, loss, alteration, unauthorized disclosure of, or access to, personal data transmitted, stored, or otherwise processed;

"genetic data" means personal data relating to the inherited or acquired genetic characteristics of a natural person which give unique information about the physiology or the health of that natural person and which result, in particular, from an analysis of a biological sample from the natural person in question;

"biometric data" means personal data resulting from specific technical processing relating to the physical, physiological, or behavioral characteristics of a natural person, which allow or confirm the unique identification of that natural person, such as facial images or dactyloscopic data;

"data concerning health" means personal data related to the physical or mental health of a natural person, including the provision of health care services, which reveal information about his or her health status;

Furthermore, we define

"main establishment" as:

as regards a controller with establishments in more than one Member State, the place of its central administration in the Union, unless the decisions on the purposes and means of the processing of personal data are taken in another establishment of the controller in the Union and the latter establishment has the power to have such decisions implemented, in which case the establishment having taken such decisions is to be considered to be the main establishment;

as regards a processor with establishments in more than one Member State, the place of its central administration in the Union, or, if the processor has no central administration in the Union, the establishment of the processor in the Union where the main processing activities in the context of the activities of an establishment of the processor take place to the extent that the processor is subject to specific obligations under this Regulation;

"representative" means a natural or legal person established in the Union who, designated by the controller or processor in writing pursuant to Article 27, represents the controller or processor with regard to their respective obligations under this Regulation;

"enterprise" means a natural or legal person engaged in an economic activity, irrespective of its legal form, including partnerships or associations regularly engaged in an economic activity;

"group of undertakings" means a controlling undertaking and its controlled undertakings;

"binding corporate rules" means personal data protection policies which are adhered to by a controller or processor established on the territory of a Member State for transfers or a set of transfers of personal data to a controller or processor in one or more third countries within a group of undertakings, or group of enterprises engaged in a joint economic activity;

When looking at the supervisory authority, GDPR defines the following:

"supervisory authority" means an independent public authority which is established by a Member State pursuant to Article 51;

"supervisory authority concerned" means a supervisory authority which is concerned by the processing of personal data because:

the controller or processor is established on the territory of the Member State of that supervisory authority;

data subjects residing in the Member State of that supervisory authority are substantially affected or likely to be substantially affected by the processing; or a complaint has been lodged with that supervisory authority;

"cross-border processing" means either:

processing of personal data which takes place in the context of the activities of establishments in more than one Member State of a controller or processor in the Union where the controller or processor is established in more than one Member State; or

processing of personal data which takes place in the context of the activities of a single establishment of a controller or processor in the Union, but which substantially affects or is likely to substantially affect data subjects in more than one Member State.

"relevant and reasoned objection" means an objection to a draft decision as to whether there is an infringement of this Regulation, or whether envisaged action in relation to the controller or processor complies with this Regulation, which clearly demonstrates the significance of the risks posed by the draft decision as regards the fundamental rights and freedoms of data subjects and, where applicable, the free flow of personal data within the Union;

"information society service" means a service as defined in point (b) of Article 1(1) of Directive (EU) 2015/1535 of the European Parliament and of the Council;

"international organization" means an organization and its subordinate bodies governed by public international law, or any other body which is set up by, or on the basis of, an agreement between two or more countries.

CHAPTER 5: PRINCIPLES

Article 5—principles relating to the processing of personal data[7]

Article 5 requires that personal data shall be:

(a) processed lawfully, fairly, and in a transparent manner in relation to the data subject ("lawfulness, fairness, and transparency");

(b) collected for specified, explicit, and legitimate purposes and not further processed in a manner that is incompatible with those purposes; further processing for archiving purposes in the public interest, scientific or historical research purposes or statistical purposes shall, in accordance with Article 89(1), not be considered to be incompatible with the initial purposes ("purpose limitation");

(c) adequate, relevant, and limited to what is necessary in relation to the purposes for which they are processed ("data minimization");
(d) accurate and, where necessary, kept up to date; every reasonable step must be taken to ensure that personal data that are inaccurate, having regard to the purposes for which they are processed, are erased, or rectified without delay ("accuracy");
(e) kept in a form which permits identification of data subjects for no longer than is necessary for the purposes for which the personal data are processed; personal data may be stored for longer periods insofar as the personal data will be processed solely for archiving purposes in the public interest, scientific or historical research purposes or statistical purposes in accordance with Article 89(1) subject to implementation of the appropriate technical and organizational measures required by this Regulation in order to safeguard the rights and freedoms of the data subject ("storage limitation");
(f) processed in a manner that ensures appropriate security of the personal data, including protection against unauthorized or unlawful processing and against accidental loss, destruction, or damage, using appropriate technical or organizational measures ("integrity and confidentiality").

The controller shall be responsible for, and be able to demonstrate compliance with, paragraph 1 ("accountability").

The firm must have a mechanism in place that ensures personal data is processed lawfully, fairly, and transparently. This relates to the privacy policy. The data must be collected for specified, explicit, and legitimate purposes only. The data must be adequate, relevant, and limited. The data must be accurate. The data must not be kept no longer than needed.

Here we define metrics that are system specific. The system metrics must be measured to ensure it is processed securely in terms of integrity and confidentiality. This requires program reviews and the privacy impact assessment to comply with article 5f. This requires a Privacy Impact Assessment. Article 5 also requires the Data Protection Policy is in place that addresses all the requirements above.

Article 6—lawfulness of processing[8]

1 Processing shall be lawful only if, and to the extent that, at least one of the following applies:

(a) the data subject has given consent to the processing of his or her personal data for one or more specific purposes;
(b) processing is necessary for the performance of a contract to which the data subject is party or in order to take steps at the request of the data subject prior to entering into a contract;
(c) processing is necessary for compliance with a legal obligation to which the controller is subject;
(d) processing is necessary in order to protect the vital interests of the data subject or of another natural person;

(e) processing is necessary for the performance of a task carried out in the public interest or in the exercise of official authority vested in the controller;
(f) processing is necessary for the purposes of the legitimate interests pursued by the controller or by a third party, except where such interests are overridden by the interests or fundamental rights and freedoms of the data subject which require protection of personal data, in particular where the data subject is a child.

The point of 6(f) of the first subparagraph shall not apply to processing carried out by public authorities in the performance of their tasks.

2 Member States may maintain or introduce more specific provisions to adapt the application of the rules of this Regulation with regard to processing for compliance with points (c) and (e) of paragraph 1 by determining more precisely specific requirements for the processing and other measures to ensure lawful and fair processing including for other specific processing situations as provided for in Chapter IX.
3 The basis for the processing referred to in point (c) and (e) of paragraph 1 shall be laid down by:

(a) Union law; or
(b) Member State law to which the controller is subject.

The purpose of the processing shall be determined in that legal basis or, as regards the processing referred to in point (e) of paragraph 1, shall be necessary for the performance of a task carried out in the public interest or in the exercise of official authority vested in the controller. That legal basis may contain specific provisions to adapt the application of rules of this Regulation, inter alia: the general conditions governing the lawfulness of processing by the controller; the types of data which are subject to the processing; the data subjects concerned; the entities to, and the purposes for which, the personal data may be disclosed; the purpose limitation; storage periods; and processing operations and processing procedures, including measures to ensure lawful and fair processing, such as those for other specific processing situations as provided for in Chapter IX. The Union or the Member State law shall meet an objective of public interest and be proportionate to the legitimate aim pursued.

4 Where the processing for a purpose other than that for which the personal data have been collected is not based on the data subject's consent or on a Union or Member State law which constitutes a necessary and proportionate measure in a democratic society to safeguard the objectives referred to in Article 23(1), the controller shall, in order to ascertain whether processing for another purpose is compatible with the purpose for which the personal data are initially collected, take into account, inter alia:

(a) any link between the purposes for which the personal data have been collected and the purposes of the intended further processing;

(b) the context in which the personal data have been collected, in particular regarding the relationship between data subjects and the controller;
(c) the nature of the personal data, in particular whether special categories of personal data are processed, pursuant to Article 9, or whether personal data related to criminal convictions and offences are processed, pursuant to Article 10;
(d) the possible consequences of the intended further processing for data subjects;
(e) the existence of appropriate safeguards, which may include encryption or pseudonymization.

Questions to ask regarding the policies and procedures are: Is there a mechanism in place to ensure that:

(a) The stated purpose is clear? And there is consent to process?
(b) It is required by a contract?
(c) It is necessary for other compliance reasons?
(d) It is necessary to protect someone's vital interests?
(e) It is required for public interest or an official authority?
(f) It is limited due to the subject is a child?

Required forms to meet this article's needs are the Data Subject Consent and Withdrawal Forms, and the Parental Consent and Withdrawal Forms. Procedures needs are Access Control Rules and Rights Procedure, and the Subject Access Request Record Procedure.

The data subject consent form should state that the data subject is granting the organization and third-party processors authority to process their personal data for an explicit purpose and the legitimate reason for processing their personal data.

Article 7—conditions for consent[9]

Article 7 states:

1 Where processing is based on consent, the controller shall be able to demonstrate that the data subject has consented to processing of his or her personal data.

If the data subject's consent is given in the context of a written declaration which also concerns other matters, the request for consent shall be presented in a manner which is clearly distinguishable from the other matters, in an intelligible and easily accessible form, using clear and plain language.

2 Any part of such a declaration which constitutes an infringement of this Regulation shall not be binding.
3 The data subject shall have the right to withdraw his or her consent at any time.
4 The withdrawal of consent shall not affect the lawfulness of processing based on consent before its withdrawal. Prior to giving consent, the data subject shall be informed thereof. It shall be as easy to withdraw as to give consent.

5 When assessing whether consent is freely given, utmost account shall be taken of whether, inter alia, the performance of a contract, including the provision of a service, is conditional on consent to the processing of personal data that is not necessary for the performance of that contract.

Things to conder in article 7 are if there is a mechanism to verify the data subject's consent was freely given and they can withdraw it easily at any time?

The Data Subject Consent Form and the Data Subject Consent Withdrawal Forms are required. The Consent Procedure, Withdrawal of Consent Procedure, Retention of Records Procedure, and Withdrawal of Consent Procedure are the required procedures. A Data and Retention and Disposal Schedule is also required.

Article 8—conditions applicable to child's consent in relation to information society services[10]

Article 8 states:

1 Where point (a) of Article 6(1) applies, in relation to the offer of information society services directly to a child, the processing of the personal data of a child shall be lawful where the child is at least 16 years old. Where the child is below the age of 16 years, such processing shall be lawful only if and to the extent that consent is given or authorized by the holder of parental responsibility over the child. States may provide by law for a lower age for those purposes provided that such lower age is not below 13 years.

2 The controller shall make reasonable efforts to verify in such cases that consent is given or authorized by the holder of parental responsibility over the child, taking into consideration available technology.

3 Paragraph 1 shall not affect the general contract law of Member States, such as the rules on the validity, formation, or effect of a contract in relation to a child. Is there a mechanism that allows for special restrictions that apply to consent by/for children?

The Parental Consent and Withdrawal Forms are required. The Data Protection Policy and the Consent Procedure are needed.

Article 9—processing of special categories of personal data[11]

Article 9 states:

1 Processing of personal data revealing racial or ethnic origin, political opinions, religious or philosophical beliefs, or trade union membership, and the processing of genetic data, biometric data for the purpose of uniquely identifying a natural person, data concerning health or data concerning a natural person's sex life or sexual orientation shall be prohibited.

2 Paragraph 1 shall not apply if one of the following applies:

(a) the data subject has given explicit consent to the processing of those personal data for one or more specified purposes, except where Union or Member State law provide that the prohibition referred to in paragraph 1 may not be lifted by the data subject;
(b) processing is necessary for the purposes of carrying out the obligations and exercising specific rights of the controller or of the data subject in the field of employment and social security and social protection law in so far as it is authorized by Union or Member State law or a collective agreement pursuant to Member State law providing for appropriate safeguards for the fundamental rights and the interests of the data subject;
(c) processing is necessary to protect the vital interests of the data subject or of another natural person where the data subject is physically or legally incapable of giving consent;
(d) processing is carried out in the course of its legitimate activities with appropriate safeguards by a foundation, association or any other not-for-profit body with a political, philosophical, religious or trade union aim and on condition that the processing relates solely to the members or to former members of the body or to persons who have regular contact with it in connection with its purposes and that the personal data are not disclosed outside that body without the consent of the data subjects;

Additionally, in relationship to special categories, GDPR states the following:

(e) processing relates to personal data which are manifestly made public by the data subject;
(f) processing is necessary for the establishment, exercise, or defense of legal claims or whenever courts are acting in their judicial capacity;
(g) processing is necessary for reasons of substantial public interest, on the basis of Union or Member State law which shall be proportionate to the aim pursued, respect the essence of the right to data protection and provide for suitable and specific measures to safeguard the fundamental rights and the interests of the data subject;
(h) processing is necessary for the purposes of preventive or occupational medicine, for the assessment of the working capacity of the employee, medical diagnosis, the provision of health or social care or treatment or the management of health or social care systems and services on the basis of Union or Member State law or pursuant to contract with a health professional and subject to the conditions and safeguards referred to in paragraph 3;
(i) processing is necessary for reasons of public interest in the area of public health, such as protecting against serious cross-border threats to health or ensuring high standards of quality and safety of health care and of medicinal products or medical devices, on the basis of Union

or Member State law which provides for suitable and specific measures to safeguard the rights and freedoms of the data subject, in particular professional secrecy;

(j) processing is necessary for archiving purposes in the public interest, scientific or historical research purposes or statistical purposes in accordance with Article 89(1) based on Union or Member State law which shall be proportionate to the aim pursued, respect the essence of the right to data protection and provide for suitable and specific measures to safeguard the fundamental rights and the interests of the data subject.

Additionally, GDPR states the following:

3 Personal data referred to in paragraph 1 may be processed for the purposes referred to in point (h) of paragraph 2 when those data are processed by or under the responsibility of a professional subject to the obligation of professional secrecy under Union or Member State law or rules established by national competent bodies or by another person also subject to an obligation of secrecy under Union or Member State law or rules established by national competent bodies.

4 Member States may maintain or introduce further conditions, including limitations, with regard to the processing of genetic data, biometric data or data concerning health.

Forms required are the Data Subject Consent Form and the Parental Consent Form.

If consent is obtained—Systems and databases should be inventoried to identify where these sensitive data processing is done. Additional controls are required on these data elements. Encryption is most widely used. The Consent Procedure is required.

Article 10—processing of personal data relating to criminal convictions and offences[12]

Article 10 states that processing of personal data relating to criminal convictions and offences, or related security measures based on Article 6(1) shall be carried out only under the control of official authority. It can also be carried out when the processing is authorized by Union or Member State law providing for appropriate safeguards for the rights and freedoms of data subjects. Any comprehensive register of criminal convictions shall be kept only under the control of official authority.

Questions to answer are is there a mechanism for specific circumstances relating to criminal convictions and offenses?

The Form required is the Data Subject Consent Form. Procedures are Access Control Rules and Rights Procedure and the Subject Access Request Record Procedure.

If this relates to your type of business, a specific identifier must be used to flag this type of sensitive criminal information. Systems and databases must be inventoried to identify where this sensitive data processing is done. Additional controls are required on these data elements. Encryption is most widely used.

Article 11—processing which does not require identification[13]

Article 11 states:

1 If the purposes for which a controller processes personal data do not or do no longer require the identification of a data subject by the controller, the controller shall not be obliged to maintain, acquire, or process additional information in order to identify the data subject for the sole purpose of complying with this Regulation.
2 Where, in cases referred to in paragraph 1 of this Article, the controller is able to demonstrate that it is not in a position to identify the data subject, the controller shall inform the data subject accordingly, if possible. In such cases, Articles 15 to 20 shall not apply except where the data subject, for the purpose of exercising his or her rights under those articles, provides additional information enabling his or her identification.

In terms of data online, GDPR suggests in the case when identification should include the digital identification of a data subject, (i.e., through an authentication mechanism, such as the same credentials, used by the data subject to log in to the online service offered by the data controller) to use industry recognized standards, such as that of NIST's digital identity guidelines. They provide a mechanism to apply state-of-the-art methods of identification, authentication, and authorization, which belong to the foundational support, the key concepts and tenets of information security.

CHAPTER 3: RIGHTS OF THE DATA SUBJECT

Article 12—transparent information, communication, and modalities for the exercise of the rights of the data subject[14]

Article 12 states:

1 The controller shall take appropriate measures to provide any information referred to in Articles 13 and 14 and any communication under Articles 15 to 22 and 34 relating to processing to the data subject in a concise, transparent, intelligible and easily accessible form, using clear and plain language, in particular for any information addressed specifically to a child. The information shall be provided in writing, or by other means, including, where appropriate, by electronic means. When requested by the data subject, the information may be provided orally, provided that the identity of the data subject is proven by other means.
2 The controller shall facilitate the exercise of data subject rights under Articles 15 to 22. In the cases referred to in Article 11(2), the controller shall not refuse to act on the request of the data subject for exercising his or her rights under Articles 15 to 22, unless the controller demonstrates that it is not in a position to identify the data subject.

3 The controller shall provide information on action taken on a request under Articles 15 to 22 to the data subject without undue delay and in any event within one month of receipt of the request. That period may be extended by two further months where necessary, considering the complexity and number of the requests. The controller shall inform the data subject of any such extension within one month of receipt of the request, together with the reasons for the delay. Where the data subject makes the request by electronic form means, the information shall be provided by electronic means where possible, unless otherwise requested by the data subject.
4 If the controller does not act on the request of the data subject, the controller shall inform the data subject without delay and at the latest within one month of receipt of the request of the reasons for not acting and on the possibility of lodging a complaint with a supervisory authority and seeking a judicial remedy.

Additionally, GDPR states the following:

5 Information provided under Articles 13 and 14 and any communication and any actions taken under Articles 15 to 22 and 34 shall be provided free of charge. Where requests from a data subject are manifestly unfounded or excessive, in particular because of their repetitive character, the controller may either:

(a) charge a reasonable fee considering the administrative costs of providing the information or communication or taking the action requested; or
(b) refuse to act on the request.

The controller shall bear the burden of demonstrating the manifestly unfounded or excessive character of the request.

6 Without prejudice to Article 11, where the controller has reasonable doubts concerning the identity of the natural person making the request referred to in Articles 15 to 21, the controller may request the provision of additional information necessary to confirm the identity of the data subject.
7 The information to be provided to data subjects pursuant to Articles 13 and 14 may be provided in combination with standardized icons in order to give in an easily visible, intelligible and clearly legible manner a meaningful overview of the intended processing. Where the icons are presented electronically, they shall be machine-readable.
8 The Commission shall be empowered to adopt delegated acts in accordance with Article 92 for the purpose of determining the information to be presented by the icons and the procedures for providing standardized icons.

Article 12 seeks to understand if there is a mechanism in place for communications with data subjects that ensures they are transparent, clear, and easily understood.

The Forms required are the Parental Consent and Consent Withdrawal Forms. The Data Protection Policy is also required.

Article 13—information to be provided where personal data are collected from the data subject[15]

Article 13 states:

1 Where personal data relating to a data subject are collected from the data subject, the controller shall, at the time when personal data are obtained, provide the data subject with all of the following information:

(a) the identity and the contact details of the controller and, where applicable, of the controller's representative;
(b) the contact details of the data protection officer, where applicable;
(c) the purposes of the processing for which the personal data are intended as well as the legal basis for the processing;
(d) where the processing is based on point (f) of Article 6(1), the legitimate interests pursued by the controller or by a third party;
(e) the recipients or categories of recipients of the personal data, if any;
(f) where applicable, the fact that the controller intends to transfer personal data to a third country or international organization and the existence or absence of an adequacy decision by the Commission, or in the case of transfers referred to in Article 46 or 47, or the second subparagraph of Article 49(1), reference to the appropriate or suitable safeguards and the means by which to obtain a copy of them or where they have been made available.

Additionally, GDPR states the following:

2 In addition to the information referred to in paragraph 1, the controller shall, at the time when personal data are obtained, provide the data subject with the following further information necessary to ensure fair and transparent processing:

(a) the period for which the personal data will be stored, or if that is not possible, the criteria used to determine that period;
(b) the existence of the right to request from the controller access to and rectification or erasure of personal data or restriction of processing concerning the data subject or to object to processing as well as the right to data portability;
(c) where the processing is based on point (a) of Article 6(1) or point (a) of Article 9(2), the existence of the right to withdraw consent at any time, without affecting the lawfulness of processing based on consent before its withdrawal;
(d) the right to lodge a complaint with a supervisory authority;
(e) whether the provision of personal data is a statutory or contractual requirement, or a requirement necessary to enter into a contract, as well as whether the data subject is obliged to provide the personal data and of the possible consequences of failure to provide such data;

(f) the existence of automated decision-making, including profiling, referred to in Article 22(1) and (4) and, at least in those cases, meaningful information about the logic involved, as well as the significance and the envisaged consequences of such processing for the data subject.

3 Where the controller intends to further process the personal data for a purpose other than that for which the personal data were collected, the controller shall provide the data subject prior to that further processing with information on that other purpose and with any relevant further information as referred to in paragraph 2.
4 Paragraphs 1, 2, and 3 shall not apply where and insofar as the data subject already has the information.

Article 13 seeks to understand if there is a mechanism for the provision of fair processing information in terms of if their info will be exported (especially outside the EU), how long the info will be held, their rights and how to enquire/complain etc.

Privacy notices inform individuals about how organizations use their personal data and their rights under the Data Protection Act. They also allow organizations to meet their obligations under the act to provide fair processing information to such individuals.

The Privacy Notice is required, along with the Retention of Records Procedure.

Article 14—information to be provided where personal data have not been obtained from the data subject[16]

Article 14 states:

1 Where personal data have not been obtained from the data subject, the controller shall provide the data subject with the following information:

(a) the identity and the contact details of the controller and, where applicable, of the controller's representative;
(b) the contact details of the data protection officer, where applicable;
(c) the purposes of the processing for which the personal data are intended as well as the legal basis for the processing;
(d) the categories of personal data concerned;
(e) the recipients or categories of recipients of the personal data, if any;
(f) where applicable, that the controller intends to transfer personal data to a recipient in a third country or international organization and the existence or absence of an adequacy decision by the Commission, or in the case of transfers referred to in Article 46 or 47, or the second subparagraph of Article 49(1), reference to the appropriate or suitable safeguards and the means to obtain a copy of them or where they have been made available.

2 In addition to the information referred to in paragraph 1, the controller shall provide the data subject with the following information necessary to ensure fair and transparent processing in respect of the data subject:

(a) the period for which the personal data will be stored, or if that is not possible, the criteria used to determine that period;
(b) where the processing is based on point (f) of Article 6(1), the legitimate interests pursued by the controller or by a third party;
(c) the existence of the right to request from the controller access to and rectification or erasure of personal data or restriction of processing concerning the data subject and to object to processing as well as the right to data portability;
(d) where processing is based on point (a) of Article 6(1) or point (a) of Article 9(2), the existence of the right to withdraw consent at any time, without affecting the lawfulness of processing based on consent before its withdrawal;
(e) the right to lodge a complaint with a supervisory authority;
(f) from which source the personal data originate, and if applicable, whether it came from publicly accessible sources;

Additionally, GDPR states the following:

3 The controller shall provide the information referred to in paragraphs 1 and 2:

(a) within a reasonable period after obtaining the personal data, but at the latest within one month, having regard to the specific circumstances in which the personal data are processed;
(b) if the personal data are to be used for communication with the data subject, at the latest at the time of the first communication to that data subject; or
(c) if a disclosure to another recipient is envisaged, at the latest when the personal data are first disclosed.

4 Where the controller intends to further process the personal data for a purpose other than that for which the personal data were obtained, the controller shall provide the data subject prior to that further processing with information on that other purpose and with any relevant further information as referred to in paragraph 2.
5 Paragraphs 1 to 4 shall not apply where and insofar as:

(a) the data subject already has the information;
(b) the provision of such information proves impossible or would involve a disproportionate effort, in particular for processing for archiving purposes in the public interest, scientific or historical research purposes or statistical purposes, subject to the conditions and safeguards referred to in Article 89(1) or in so far as the obligation referred to in paragraph 1 of this Article is likely to render impossible or seriously impair the

achievement of the objectives of that processing. In such cases the controller shall take appropriate measures to protect the data subject's rights and freedoms and legitimate interests, including making the information publicly available;

(c) obtaining or disclosure is expressly laid down by Union or Member State law to which the controller is subject and which provides appropriate measures to protect the data subject's legitimate interests; or

(d) Where the personal data must remain confidential subject to an obligation of professional secrecy regulated by Union or Member State law, including a statutory obligation of secrecy.

Article 14 sets forth information data subjects should receive "at the time when personal data are obtained," and includes a list too long for most opt-in notices and more easily covered in a privacy statement.

The Privacy Notice is required.

Article 15—right of access by the data subject[17]

Article 15 states:

1 The data subject shall have the right to obtain from the controller confirmation as to whether or not personal data concerning him or her are being processed, and, where that is the case, access to the personal data and the following information:

(a) the purposes of the processing;
(b) the categories of personal data concerned;
(c) the recipients or categories of recipient to whom the personal data have been or will be disclosed, in particular recipients in third countries or international organizations;
(d) where possible, the envisaged period for which the personal data will be stored, or, if not possible, the criteria used to determine that period;
(e) the existence of the right to request from the controller rectification or erasure of personal data or restriction of processing of personal data concerning the data subject or to object to such processing;
(f) the right to lodge a complaint with a supervisory authority;
(g) where the personal data are not collected from the data subject, any available information as to their source;
(h) the existence of automated decision-making, including profiling, referred to in Article 22(1) and (4) and, at least in those cases, meaningful information about the logic involved, as well as the significance and the envisaged consequences of such processing for the data subject.

2 Where personal data are transferred to a third country or to an international organization, the data subject shall have the right to be informed of the appropriate safeguards pursuant to Article 46 relating to the transfer.

3 The controller shall provide a copy of the personal data undergoing processing. For any further copies requested by the data subject, the controller may charge a reasonable fee based on administrative costs. Where the data subject makes the request by electronic means, and unless otherwise requested by the data subject, the information shall be provided in a commonly used electronic form.
4 The right to obtain a copy referred to in paragraph 3 shall not adversely affect the rights and freedoms of others.

Article 15 is asking if there a mechanism in place for people to find out whether the organization holds their personal info, what it is being used for, to whom it may be disclosed etc., and be informed of the right to complain, get it corrected, insist on it being erased etc.

The subject access request forms allow the data subject to request this information and must include a phone number, email and addresses to communicate with the organization to complain and/or request erasure. For the company to be able to know how to answer all these questions there needs to be several processes in place to identify where the data lives, how it is used, and have the ability to erase it.

The Subject Access Request Form is required. The Subject Access Request Record Procedure, the Rectification Procedure and the Erasure Procedure are required.

Article 16—right to rectification[18]

Article 16 speaks to the data subject's right to obtain from the controller, without undue delay. The rectification of inaccurate personal data concerning him or her. Considering the purposes of the processing, the data subject shall have the right to have incomplete personal data completed, including by means of providing a supplementary statement.

Is there a mechanism in place for people to get their personal info corrected, completed, clarified etc.?

The subject access request forms allow the data subject to request to update their information and must include a phone number, email and addresses to communicate to the organization to complain and/or request erasure. For the company to be able to correct the data and verify completion there must be a procedure in place to find the data, update the data and provide an audit trail.

The Subject Access Request Form, The Subject Access Request Record Procedure, the Rectification Procedure, the Audit Schedule, and the Audit Lead Report are required.

Article 17—right to erasure ("right to be forgotten")[19]

Article 17 states:

1 The data subject shall have the right to obtain from the controller the erasure of personal data concerning him or her without undue delay and the

controller shall have the obligation to erase personal data without undue delay where one of the following grounds applies:

(a) the personal data are no longer necessary in relation to the purposes for which they were collected or otherwise processed;
(b) the data subject withdraws consent on which the processing is based according to point (a) of Article 6(1), or point (a) of Article 9(2), and where there is no other legal ground for the processing;
(c) the data subject objects to the processing pursuant to Article 21(1) and there are no overriding legitimate grounds for the processing, or the data subject objects to the processing pursuant to Article 21(2);
(d) the personal data have been unlawfully processed;
(e) the personal data have to be erased for compliance with a legal obligation in Union or Member State law to which the controller is subject;
(f) the personal data have been collected in relation to the offer of information society services referred to in Article 8(1).

2 Where the controller has made the personal data public and is obliged pursuant to paragraph 1 to erase the personal data, the controller, taking account of available technology and the cost of implementation, shall take reasonable steps, including technical measures, to inform controllers which are processing the personal data that the data subject has requested the erasure by such controllers of any links to, or copy or replication of, those personal data.

Additionally, GDPR states the following:

3 Paragraphs 1 and 2 shall not apply to the extent that processing is necessary:

(a) for exercising the right of freedom of expression and information;
(b) for compliance with a legal obligation which requires processing by Union or Member State law to which the controller is subject or for the performance of a task carried out in the public interest or in the exercise of official authority vested in the controller;
(c) for reasons of public interest in the area of public health in accordance with points (h) and (i) of Article 9(2) as well as Article 9(3);
(d) for archiving purposes in the public interest, scientific or historical research purposes or statistical purposes in accordance with Article 89(1) in so far as the right referred to in paragraph 1 is likely to render impossible or seriously impair the achievement of the objectives of that processing; or
(e) for the establishment, exercise, or defense of legal claims.

This article requires that there be a mechanism in place for people that have the right to be forgotten, i.e., to have their personal info erased and no longer used.

The subject access request forms allow the data subject to request erasure. For the company to be able to erase the data and verify completion there must be a procedure in place to find the data, erase the data, and provide an audit trail. See the Operations Procedure in VRisk.

The Subject Access Request Form, the Subject Access Request Record Procedure, the Erasure Procedure, the Audit Schedule, and the Audit Lead Report are required.

Article 18—right to restriction of processing[20]

Article 18 states:

1 The data subject shall have the right to obtain from the controller restriction of processing where one of the following applies:

 (a) the accuracy of the personal data is contested by the data subject, for a period enabling the controller to verify the accuracy of the personal data;
 (b) the processing is unlawful and the data subject opposes the erasure of the personal data and requests the restriction of their use instead; the controller no longer needs the personal data for the purposes of the processing, but they are required by the data subject for the establishment, exercise or defense of legal claims; the data subject has objected to processing pursuant to Article 21(1) pending the verification whether the legitimate grounds of the controller override those of the data subject.

2 Where processing has been restricted under paragraph 1, such personal data shall, with the exception of storage, only be processed with the data subject's consent or for the establishment, exercise, or defense of legal claims or for the protection of the rights of another natural or legal person or for reasons of important public interest of the Union or of a Member State.

 (a) A data subject who has obtained restriction of processing pursuant to paragraph 1 shall be informed by the controller before the restriction of processing is lifted.

Article 18 requires that there be a mechanism in place for people to have a right to restrict processing of their personal info.

The subject access request forms allow the data subject to request the right to restrict the processing of their personal info. For the company to be able to restrict processing of the personal info, there must be a procedure in place to find the data, restrict the processing of the data, and provide an audit trail.

The Withdrawal of Consent Procedure is required. The Subject Access Request Form, the Subject Access Request Record Procedure, the Audit Schedule, and the Audit Lead Report are required.

Article 19—notification obligation regarding rectification or erasure of personal data or restriction of processing[21]

Article 19 states that the controller shall communicate any rectification or erasure of personal data or restriction of processing carried out in accordance with Article 16, Article 17(1), and Article 18 to each recipient to whom the personal data have been disclosed, unless this proves impossible or involves disproportionate effort. The controller shall inform the data subject about those recipients if the data subject requests it.

There needs to be a mechanism in place for people to know the outcome of requests to have their personal info corrected, completed, erased, restricted, etc.

The procedures for erasure, correction, and restriction should have an explicit process to inform the data subject of the completion of their requests. The Operations Procedure, the Rectification Procedure, the Erasure Procedure, and the Communications Procedure are required.

Article 20—right to data portability[22]

Article 20 needs to know if there a mechanism in place for people to obtain a usable 'portable' electronic copy of their personal data to pass to a different controller.

1 The data subject shall have the right to receive the personal data concerning him or her, which he or she has provided to a controller, in a structured, commonly used, and machine-readable format and have the right to transmit those data to another controller without hindrance from the controller to which the personal data have been provided, where:

 (a) the processing is based on consent pursuant to point (a) of Article 6(1) or point (a) of Article 9(2) or on a contract pursuant to point (b) of Article 6(1); and
 (b) the processing is carried out by automated means.

2 In exercising his or her right to data portability pursuant to paragraph 1, the data subject shall have the right to have the personal data transmitted directly from one controller to another, where technically feasible.
3 The exercise of the right referred to in paragraph 1 of this Article shall be without prejudice to Article 17. That right shall not apply to processing necessary for the performance of a task carried out in the public interest or in the exercise of official authority vested in the controller.
4 The right referred to in paragraph 1 shall not adversely affect the rights and freedoms of others.

The Data Portability Procedure is required.

Article 21—right to object[23]

Article 21 states:

1 The data subject shall have the right to object, on grounds relating to his or her particular situation, at any time to processing of personal data concerning him or her which is based on point (e) or (f) of Article 6(1), including profiling based on those provisions. The controller shall no longer process the personal data unless the controller demonstrates compelling legitimate grounds for the processing which override the interests, rights, and freedoms of the data subject or for the establishment, exercise, or defense of legal claims.

2 Where personal data are processed for direct marketing purposes, the data subject shall have the right to object at any time to processing of personal data concerning him or her for such marketing, which includes profiling to the extent that it is related to such direct marketing.
3 Where the data subject objects to processing for direct marketing purposes, the personal data shall no longer be processed for such purposes.
4 At the latest at the time of the first communication with the data subject, the right referred to in paragraphs 1 and 2 shall be explicitly brought to the attention of the data subject and shall be presented clearly and separately from any other information.
5 In the context of the use of information society services, and notwithstanding Directive 2002/58/EC, the data subject may exercise his or her right to object by automated means using technical specifications.
6 Where personal data are processed for scientific or historical research purposes or statistical purposes pursuant to Article 89(1), the data subject, on grounds relating to his or her particular situation, shall have the right to object to processing of personal data concerning him or her, unless the processing is necessary for the performance of a task carried out for reasons of public interest.

There must be a mechanism in place for people to object to their information being used for profiling and marketing purposes.

There must be a process in place to allow the data subject to object via phone, email, and mail. The Communications Procedure and the Operations Procedure are required.

Article 22—automated individual decision-making, including profiling[24]

Article 22 states:

1 The data subject shall have the right not to be subject to a decision based solely on automated processing, including profiling, which produces legal effects concerning him or her or similarly significantly affects him or her.
2 Paragraph 1 shall not apply if the decision:

    (a) is necessary for entering into, or performance of, a contract between the data subject, and a data controller;
    (b) is authorized by Union or Member State law to which the controller is subject, and which also lays down suitable measures to safeguard the data subject's rights and freedoms and legitimate interests; or
    (c) is based on the data subject's explicit consent.

3 In the cases referred to in points (a) and (c) of paragraph 2, the data controller shall implement suitable measures to safeguard the data subject's rights and freedoms and legitimate interests, at least the right to obtain human intervention on the part of the controller, to express his or her point of view and to contest the decision.

4 Decisions referred to in paragraph 2 shall not be based on special categories of personal data referred to in Article 9(1), unless point (a) or (g) of Article 9(2) applies and suitable measures to safeguard the data subject's rights and freedoms and legitimate interests are in place.

There must be a documented process in place with business rules that review the effectiveness of the automatic processing of personal data. The Operations Procedure is required.

Article 23—restrictions[25]

Article 23 states:

1 Union or Member State law to which the data controller or processor is subject may restrict by way of a legislative measure the scope of the obligations and rights provided for in Articles 12 to 22 and Article 34, as well as Article 5 in so far as its provisions correspond to the rights and obligations provided for in Articles 12 to 22, when such a restriction respects the essence of the fundamental rights and freedoms and is a necessary and proportionate measure in a democratic society to safeguard:

(a) national security;
(b) defense;
(c) public security;
(d) the prevention, investigation, detection or prosecution of criminal offences or the execution of criminal penalties, including the safeguarding against and the prevention of threats to public security;
(e) other important objectives of general public interest of the Union or of a Member State, in particular an important economic or financial interest of the Union or of a Member State, including monetary, budgetary and taxation a matters, public health, and social security;
(f) the protection of judicial independence and judicial proceedings;
(g) the prevention, investigation, detection, and prosecution of breaches of ethics for regulated professions;
(h) a monitoring, inspection or regulatory function connected, even occasionally, to the exercise of official authority in the cases referred to in points (a) to (e) and (g);
(i) the protection of the data subject or the rights and freedoms of others;
(j) the enforcement of civil law claims.

2 In particular, any legislative measure referred to in paragraph 1 shall contain specific provisions at least, where relevant, as to:

(a) the purposes of the processing or categories of processing;
(b) the categories of personal data;
(c) the scope of the restrictions introduced;
(d) the safeguards to prevent abuse or unlawful access or transfer;

(e) the specification of the controller or categories of controllers;
(f) the storage periods and the applicable safeguards considering the nature, scope and purposes of the processing or categories of processing;
(g) the risks to the rights and freedoms of data subjects; and
(h) the right of data subjects to be informed about the restriction unless that may be prejudicial to the purpose of the restriction.

The Data Protection Officer must be abreast of all national laws and how the laws override rights and restrictions for national security or other purposes. The DPO Job Responsibilities Document is required.

CHAPTER 4—CONTROLLER AND PROCESSOR RESPONSIBILITIES

Article 24—responsibility of the controller[26]

Article 24 states:

1 Considering the nature, scope, context, and purposes of processing as well as the risks of varying likelihood and severity for the rights and freedoms of natural persons, the controller shall implement appropriate technical and organizational measures to ensure and to be able to demonstrate that processing is performed in accordance with this Regulation. Those measures shall be reviewed and updated where necessary.
2 Where proportionate in relation to processing activities, the measures referred to in paragraph 1 shall include the implementation of appropriate data protection policies by the controller.
3 Adherence to approved codes of conduct as referred to in Article 40 or approved certification mechanisms as referred to in Article 42 may be used as an element by which to demonstrate compliance with the obligations of the controller.

Is there a Data Protection Officer (DPO) in place that acts as the "controller" and is responsible for implementing appropriate privacy controls (including policies and codes of conduct) considering the risks, rights, and other requirements within and perhaps beyond GDPR?

A DPO is responsible to implement policies and privacy controls that include a privacy impact assessment to measure risk and effectiveness of privacy controls and other requirements.

The Rationale for a DPO document, the Data Protection Officer (DPO) Job Responsibilities, and the Data Protection Officer (DPO) Job Description are required.

Article 25—data protection by design and by default[27]

Article 25 states:

1 Taking into account the state of the art, the cost of implementation and the nature, scope, context and purposes of processing as well as the risks of varying likelihood and severity for rights and freedoms of natural persons

posed by the processing, the controller shall, both at the time of the determination of the means for processing and at the time of the processing itself, implement appropriate technical, and organizational measures, such as pseudonymization, which are designed to implement data-protection principles, such as data minimization, in an effective manner and to integrate the necessary safeguards into the processing in order to meet the requirements of this regulation and protect the rights of data subjects.

2 The controller shall implement appropriate technical and organizational measures for ensuring that, by default, only personal data which are necessary for each specific purpose of the processing are processed. That obligation applies to the amount of personal data collected, the extent of their processing, the period of their storage and their accessibility. In particular, such measures shall ensure that by default personal data are not made accessible without the individual's intervention to an indefinite number of natural persons.
3 An approved certification mechanism pursuant to Article 42 may be used as an element to demonstrate compliance with the requirements set out in paragraphs 1 and 2 of this Article.

Is there a mechanism in place for privacy by design? The software development lifecycle policy and procedures should include privacy requirements that are embedded in the design and not bolted on afterwards. The DPO should be a part of this process. The SDLC Policy, the Data Protection Officer (DPO) Job Responsibilities, and the Governance Procedure are required.

Article 26—joint controllers[28]

Article 26 states:

1 Where two or more controllers jointly determine the purposes and means of processing, they shall be joint controllers. They shall in a transparent manner determine their respective responsibilities for compliance with the obligations under this Regulation, in particular as regards the exercising of the rights of the data subject and their respective duties to provide the information referred to in Articles 13 and 14, by means of an arrangement between them unless, and in so far as, the respective responsibilities of the controllers are determined by Union or Member State law to which the controllers are subject. The arrangement may designate a contact point for data subjects.
2 The arrangement referred to in paragraph 1 shall duly reflect the respective roles and relationships of the joint controllers vis-à-vis the data subjects. The essence of the arrangement shall be made available to the data subject.
3 Irrespective of the terms of the arrangement referred to in paragraph 1, the data subject may exercise his or her rights under this Regulation in respect of and against each of the controllers.

The DPO should have processes and procedures set up to collaborate with teams across the organization including compliance, security, business owners, data stewards, governance teams, and development teams. The Data Protection Officer (DPO) Job Responsibilities and the Governance Procedure are required.

Article 27—representatives of controllers or processors not established in the Union[29]

Article 27 states:

1. Where Article 3(2) applies, the controller or the processor shall designate in writing a representative in the Union.
2. The obligation laid down in paragraph 1 of this Article shall not apply to:
   (a) processing which is occasional, does not include, on a large scale, processing of special categories of data as referred to in Article 9(1) or processing of personal data relating to criminal convictions and offences referred to in Article 10, and is unlikely to result in a risk to the rights and freedoms of natural persons, taking into account the nature, context, scope, and purposes of the processing; or
   (b) a public authority or body.
3. The representative shall be established in one of the Member States where the data subjects, whose personal data are processed in relation to the offering of goods or services to them, or whose behavior is monitored, are.
4. The representative shall be mandated by the controller or processor to be addressed in addition to or instead of the controller or the processor by, in particular, supervisory authorities and data subjects, on all issues related to processing, for the purposes of ensuring compliance with this Regulation.
5. The designation of a representative by the controller or processor shall be without prejudice to legal actions which could be initiated against the controller or the processor themselves.

GDPR requires for organizations outside Europe, to have a formal privacy representative. And inside Europe if they meet certain conditions (e.g., they routinely supply goods and services to, or monitor Europeans).

Privacy is now one of the top 3 business concerns. A formal privacy representative should be appointed for organizations outside of the EU. The Data Protection Officer (DPO) Job Responsibilities and the Rationale for a Data Protection Officer (DPO) are required.

Article 28—processor[30]

Article 28 states:

1 Where processing is to be carried out on behalf of a controller, the controller shall use only processors providing sufficient guarantees to implement appropriate technical and organizational measures in such a manner that processing will meet the requirements of this Regulation and ensure the protection of the rights of the data subject.
2 The processor shall not engage another processor without prior specific or general written authorization of the controller. In the case of general written authorization, the processor shall inform the controller of any intended changes concerning the addition or replacement of other processors, thereby giving the controller the opportunity to object to such changes.
3 Processing by a processor shall be governed by a contract or other legal act under Union or Member State law, that is binding on the processor with regard to the controller and that sets out the subject-matter and duration of the processing, the nature and purpose of the processing, the type of personal data and categories of data subjects and the obligations and rights of the controller. That contract or other legal act shall stipulate, in particular, that the processor:

   (a) processes the personal data only on documented instructions from the controller, including with regard to transfers of personal data to a third country or an international organization, unless required to do so by Union or Member State law to which the processor is subject; in such a case, the processor shall inform the controller of that legal requirement before processing, unless that law prohibits such information on important grounds of public interest;
   (b) ensures that persons authorized to process the personal data have committed themselves to confidentiality or are under an appropriate statutory obligation of confidentiality;
   (c) takes all measures required pursuant to Article 32;
   (d) respects the conditions referred to in paragraphs 2 and 4 for engaging another processor;
   (e) considering the nature of the processing, assists the controller by appropriate technical and organizational measures, insofar as this is possible, for the fulfillment of the controller's obligation to respond to requests for exercising the data subject's rights laid down in Chapter III;
   (f) assists the controller in ensuring compliance with the obligations pursuant to Articles 32–36 considering the nature of processing and the information available to the processor;

Additionally, GDPR states the following:

4 Where a processor engages another processor for carrying out specific processing activities on behalf of the controller, the same data protection obligations as set out in the contract or other legal act between the controller and the processor as referred to in paragraph 3 shall be imposed on that other processor by way of a contract or other legal act under Union or Member State law, in particular providing sufficient guarantees to implement appropriate

technical and organizational measures in such a manner that the processing will meet the requirements of this Regulation. Where that other processor fails to fulfill its data protection obligations, the initial processor shall remain fully liable to the controller for the performance of that other processor's obligations.

5 Adherence of a processor to an approved code of conduct as referred to in Article 40 or an approved certification mechanism as referred to in Article 42 may be used as an element by which to demonstrate sufficient guarantees as referred to in paragraphs 1 and 4 of this Article.
6 Without prejudice to an individual contract between the controller and the processor, the contract or the other legal act referred to in paragraphs 3 and 4 of this Article may be based, in whole or in part, on standard contractual clauses referred to in paragraphs 7 and 8 of this Article, including when they are part of a certification granted to the controller or processor pursuant to Articles 42 and 43.
7 The Commission may lay down standard contractual clauses for the matters referred to in paragraph 3 and 4 of this Article and in accordance with the examination procedure referred to in Article 93(2).
8 A supervisory authority may adopt standard contractual clauses for the matters referred to in paragraph 3 and 4 of this Article and in accordance with the consistency mechanism referred to in Article 63.
9 The contract or the other legal act referred to in paragraphs 3 and 4 shall be in writing, including in electronic form.
10 Without prejudice to Articles 82, 83, and 84, if a processor infringes this Regulation by determining the purposes and means of processing, the processor shall be considered to be a controller in respect of that processing.

Is there a mechanism in place to ensure processors only process personal info in accordance with instructions from the controller and applicable laws? This applies to the vendor agreements the firm has with Cloud Service Providers and other third-parties.

If an organization uses one or more third parties to process personal info ("processors"), can it ensure they too are compliant with GDPR?

Vendor relationship management processes and procedures must ensure that third parties that process personal information are compliant with the GDPR. This can also be a role of the DPO if there is no vendor management team.

The Data Protection Officer (DPO) Job Responsibilities and the Rationale for a Data Protection Officer (DPO) are required.

Article 29—processing under the authority of the controller or processor[31]

Article 29 states:

1 The processor and any person acting under the authority of the controller or of the processor, who has access to personal data, shall not process those data except on instructions from the controller, unless required to do so by Union or Member State law.

2 The DPO must have a process to review the data processors mechanisms to ensure processing is lawful and correct. The Data Protection Officer (DPO) Job Responsibilities and the Data Processor Mechanism Review Procedure are required.

Article 30—records of processing activities[32]

Article 30 states:

1 Each controller and, where applicable, the controller's representative, shall maintain a record of processing activities under its responsibility.

   (a) That record shall contain all of the following information:
   (b) the name and contact details of the controller and, where applicable, the joint controller, the controller's representative, and the data protection officer;
   (c) the purposes of the processing;
   (d) a description of the categories of data subjects and of the categories of personal data;
   (e) the categories of recipients to whom the personal data have been or will be disclosed including recipients in third countries or international organizations;
   (f) where applicable, transfers of personal data to a third country or an international organization, including the identification of that third country or international organization and, in the case of transfers referred to in the second subparagraph of Article 49(1), the documentation of suitable safeguards;
   (g) where possible, the envisaged time limits for erasure of the different categories of data;
   (h) Where possible, a general description of the technical and organizational security measures referred to in Article 32(1).

2 Each processor and, where applicable, the processor's representative shall maintain a record of all categories of processing activities carried out on behalf of a controller, containing:

   (a) the name and contact details of the processor or processors and of each controller on behalf of which the processor is acting, and, where applicable, of the controller's or the processor's representative, and the data protection officer;
   (b) the categories of processing carried out on behalf of each controller;
   (c) where applicable, transfers of personal data to a third country or an international organization, including the identification of that third country or international organization and, in the case of transfers referred to in the second subparagraph of Article 49(1), the documentation of suitable safeguards;
   (d) where possible, a general description of the technical and organizational security measures referred to in Article 32(1).

Additionally, GDPR states the following:

3 The records referred to in paragraphs 1 and 2 shall be in writing, including in electronic form.
4 The controller or the processor and, where applicable, the controller's or the processor's representative, shall make the record available to the supervisory authority on request.
5 The obligations referred to in paragraphs 1 and 2 shall not apply to an enterprise or an organization employing fewer than 250 persons unless the processing it carries out is likely to result in a risk to the rights and freedoms of data subjects, the processing is not occasional, or the processing includes special categories of data as referred to in Article 9(1) or personal data relating to criminal convictions and offences referred to in Article 10.

Is there a mechanism in place for controllers to maintain documentation concerning privacy, e.g., the purposes for which personal info is gathered and processed, "categories" of data subjects and personal data etc.?

Data classification processes and procedures should be in place to identify which systems and technologies process categories of data. The DPO should have processes documented related to purposes for which personal info is gathered and processed. VRisk allows for categorization of data processed in system and stored in databases. The Data Classification Procedure is required.

Article 31—cooperation with the supervisory authority[33]

Article 31 states:

1 The controller and the processor and, where applicable, their representatives, shall cooperate, on request, with the supervisory authority in the performance of its tasks.
2 Is there a policy in place to ensure that organizations cooperate with the authorities, e.g., privacy or data protection ombudsmen?
3 The DPO must have a process and procedure in place that has identified authorities and the means to contact them and cooperate with them. The Contact with Authorities Work Instruction is required.

Article 32—security of processing[34]

Article 32 states:

1 Considering the state of the art, the costs of implementation and the nature, scope, context, and purposes of processing as well as the risk of varying likelihood and severity for the rights and freedoms of natural persons, the controller and the processor shall implement appropriate technical and organizational measures to ensure a level of security appropriate to the risk, including inter alia as appropriate:

(a) the pseudonymization and encryption of personal data;
(b) the ability to ensure the ongoing confidentiality, integrity, availability, and resilience of processing systems and services;
(c) the ability to restore the availability and access to personal data in a timely manner in the event of a physical or technical incident;
(d) a process for regularly testing, assessing, and evaluating the effectiveness of technical and organizational measures for ensuring the security of the processing.

2 In assessing the appropriate level of security account shall be taken in particular of the risks that are presented by processing, in particular from accidental or unlawful destruction, loss, alteration, unauthorized disclosure of, or access to personal data transmitted, stored, or otherwise processed.
3 Adherence to an approved code of conduct as referred to in Article 40 or an approved certification mechanism as referred to in Article 42 may be used as an element by which to demonstrate compliance with the requirements set out in paragraph 1 of this Article.
4 The controller and processor shall take steps to ensure that any natural person acting under the authority of the controller or the processor who has access to personal data does not process them except on instructions from the controller unless he or she is required to do so by Union or Member State law.

Are there mechanisms in place to ensure that organizations implement, operate, and maintain appropriate technical and organizational security measures for personal info, addressing the information risks? A Privacy Impact Assessment and a Security Control Assessment are required.

Article 33—notification of a personal data breach to the supervisory authority[35]

Article 33 states:

1 In the case of a personal data breach, the controller shall without undue delay and, where feasible, not later than 72 hours after having become aware of it, notify the personal data breach to the supervisory authority competent in accordance with Article 55, unless the personal data breach is unlikely to result in a risk to the rights and freedoms of natural persons.

Where the notification to the supervisory authority is not made within 72 hours, it shall be accompanied by reasons for the delay.
2 The processor shall notify the controller without undue delay after becoming aware of a personal data breach.
3 The notification referred to in paragraph 1 shall at least:

(a) describe the nature of the personal data breach including where possible, the categories and approximate number of data subjects concerned, and the categories and approximate number of personal data records concerned;

(b) communicate the name and contact details of the data protection officer or other contact point where more information can be obtained;
(c) describe the likely consequences of the personal data breach;
(d) describe the measures taken or proposed to be taken by the controller to address the personal data breach, including, where appropriate, measures to mitigate its possible adverse effects.

4 Where, and in so far as, it is not possible to provide the information at the same time, the information may be provided in phases without undue further delay.
5 The controller shall document any personal data breaches, comprising the facts relating to the personal data breach, its effects, and the remedial action taken. That documentation shall enable the supervisory authority to verify compliance with this Article.

Is there a mechanism in place to notify the authorities promptly (within 3 days of becoming aware of them unless delays are justified) for privacy breaches that have exposed or harmed personal information? The Personal Data Breach Notification Procedure is required.

Article 34—communication of a personal data breach to the data subject[36]

Article 34 states:

1 When the personal data breach is likely to result in a high risk to the rights and freedoms of natural persons, the controller shall communicate the personal data breach to the data subject without undue delay.
2 The communication to the data subject referred to in paragraph 1 of this Article shall describe in clear and plain language the nature of the personal data breach and contain at least the information and measures referred to in points (b), (c), and (d) of Article 33(3).
3 The communication to the data subject referred to in paragraph 1 shall not be required if any of the following conditions are met:

(a) the controller has implemented appropriate technical and organizational protection measures, and those measures were applied to the personal data affected by the personal data breach, in particular those that render the personal data unintelligible to any person who is not authorized to access it, such as encryption;
(b) the controller has taken subsequent measures which ensure that the high risk to the rights and freedoms of data subjects referred to in paragraph 1 is no longer likely to materialize;

(c) it would involve disproportionate effort. In such a case, there shall instead be a public communication or similar measure whereby the data subjects are informed in an equally effective manner.

4 If the controller has not already communicated the personal data breach to the data subject, the supervisory authority, having considered the likelihood of the personal data breach resulting in a high risk, may require it to do so or may decide that any of the conditions referred to in paragraph 3 are met.

Is there a mechanism in place to notify the authorities promptly for privacy breaches that have exposed or harmed personal info and hence are likely to harm their interests "without undue delay?" The Personal Data Breach Notification Procedure is required.

Article 35—data protection impact assessment (DPIA)[37]

Article 35 states:

1 Where a type of processing in particular using new technologies, and considering the nature, scope, context, and purposes of the processing, is likely to result in a high risk to the rights and freedoms of natural persons, the controller shall, prior to the processing, carry out an assessment of the impact of the envisaged processing operations on the protection of personal data.
2 A single assessment may address a set of similar processing operations that present similar high risks.
3 The controller shall seek the advice of the data protection officer, where designated, when carrying out a data protection impact assessment.

(a) A data protection impact assessment referred to in paragraph 1 shall in particular be required in the case of:
(b) a systematic and extensive evaluation of personal aspects relating to natural persons which is based on automated processing, including profiling, and on which decisions are based that produce legal effects concerning the natural person or similarly significantly affect the natural person;
(c) processing on a large scale of special categories of data referred to in Article 9(1), or of personal data relating to criminal convictions and offences referred to in Article 10; or
(d) a systematic monitoring of a publicly accessible area on a large scale.

4 The supervisory authority shall establish and make public a list of the kind of processing operations which are subject to the requirement for a data protection impact assessment pursuant to paragraph 1. The supervisory authority shall communicate those lists to the Board referred to in Article 68.

Additionally, GDPR states the following:

5 The supervisory authority may also establish and make public a list of the kind of processing operations for which no data protection impact assessment is required. The supervisory authority shall communicate those lists to the Board.

6 Prior to the adoption of the lists referred to in paragraphs 4 and 5, the competent supervisory authority shall apply the consistency mechanism referred to in Article 63 where such lists involve processing activities which are related to the offering of goods or services to data subjects or to the monitoring of their behavior in several Member States, or may substantially affect the free movement of personal data within the Union.

7 The assessment shall contain at least:

   (a) a systematic description of the envisaged processing operations and the purposes of the processing, including, where applicable, the legitimate interest pursued by the controller;
   (b) an assessment of the necessity and proportionality of the processing operations in relation to the purposes;
   (c) an assessment of the risks to the rights and freedoms of data subjects referred to in paragraph 1; and
   (d) the measures envisaged to address the risks, including safeguards, security measures and mechanisms to ensure the protection of personal data and to demonstrate compliance with this Regulation considering the rights and legitimate interests of data subjects, and other persons concerned.

8 Compliance with approved codes of conduct referred to in Article 40 by the relevant controllers or processors shall be taken into due account in assessing the impact of the processing operations performed by such controllers or processors, in particular for the purposes of a data protection impact assessment.

9 Where appropriate, the controller shall seek the views of data subjects or their representatives on the intended processing, without prejudice to the protection of commercial or public interests or the security of processing operations.

10 Where processing pursuant to point (c) or (e) of Article 6(1) has a legal basis in Union law or in the law of the Member State to which the controller is subject, that law regulates the specific processing operation or set of operations in question, and a data protection impact assessment has already been carried out as part of a general impact assessment in the context of the adoption of that legal basis, paragraphs 1–7 shall not apply unless Member States deem it to be necessary to carry out such an assessment prior to processing activities.

11 Where necessary, the controller shall carry out a review to assess if processing is performed in accordance with the data protection impact assessment at least when there is a change of the risk represented by processing operations.

Is there a mechanism in place to access privacy risks, including potential impacts, particularly where new technologies/systems/arrangements are being considered, or otherwise where risks may be? Is there a mechanism to rank Significantly risky situations? A Privacy Impact Assessment is required that measures confidentiality and integrity of the systems that are processing data. Anything less does not meet the requirement.

Article 36—prior consultation[38]

Article 36 states:

1 The controller shall consult the supervisory authority prior to processing where a data protection impact assessment under Article 35 indicates that the processing would result in a high risk in the absence of measures taken by the controller to mitigate the risk.
2 Where the supervisory authority is of the opinion that the intended processing referred to in paragraph 1 would infringe this Regulation, in particular where the controller has insufficiently identified or mitigated the risk, the supervisory authority shall, within period of up to eight weeks of receipt of the request for consultation, provide written advice to the controller and, where applicable to the processor, and may use any of its powers referred to in Article 58. That period may be extended by six weeks, considering the complexity of the intended processing. The supervisory authority shall inform the controller and, where applicable, the processor, of any such extension within one month of receipt of the request for consultation together with the reasons for the delay. Those periods may be suspended until the supervisory authority has obtained information it has requested for the purposes of the consultation.
3 When consulting the supervisory authority pursuant to paragraph 1, the controller shall provide the supervisory authority with:

   (a) where applicable, the respective responsibilities of the controller, joint controllers and processors involved in the processing, in particular for processing within a group of undertakings;
   (b) the purposes and means of the intended processing;
   (c) the measures and safeguards provided to protect the rights and freedoms of data subjects pursuant to this Regulation;
   (d) where applicable, the contact details of the data protection officer;
   (e) the data protection impact assessment provided for in Article 35; and
   (f) any other information requested by the supervisory authority.

4 Member States shall consult the supervisory authority during the preparation of a proposal for a legislative measure to be adopted by a national parliament, or of a regulatory measure based on such a legislative measure, which relates to processing.

5 Notwithstanding paragraph 1, Member State law may require controllers to consult with, and obtain prior authorization from, the supervisory authority in relation to processing by a controller for the performance of a task carried out by the controller in the public interest, including processing in relation to social protection and public health.

Is there a mechanism to notify authorities for privacy risks assessed as "high?" The DPIA, Contact with Authorities Work Instruction, and Procedures are needed.

Article 37—designation of the data protection officer[39]

Article 37 states:

1 The controller and the processor shall designate a data protection officer in any case where:

(a) the processing is carried out by a public authority or body, except for courts acting in their judicial capacity;
(b) the core activities of the controller or the processor consist of processing operations which, by virtue of their nature, their scope and/or their purposes, require regular and systematic monitoring of data subjects on a large scale; or
(c) the core activities of the controller or the processor consist of processing on a large scale of special categories of data pursuant to Article 9 or personal data relating to criminal convictions and offences referred to in Article 10.

A group of undertakings may appoint a single data protection officer provided that a data protection officer is easily accessible from each establishment.

2 Where the controller or the processor is a public authority or body, a single data protection officer may be designated for several such authorities or bodies, taking account of their organizational structure and size.
3 In cases other than those referred to in paragraph 1, the controller or processor or associations and other bodies representing categories of controllers or processors may or, where required by Union or Member State law shall, designate a data protection officer.
4 The data protection officer may act for such associations and other bodies representing controllers or processors.
5 The data protection officer shall be designated on the basis of professional qualities and, in particular, expert knowledge of data protection law and practices and the ability to fulfill the tasks referred to in Article 39.
6 The data protection officer may be a staff member of the controller or processor or fulfill the tasks on the basis of a service contract.
7 The controller or the processor shall publish the contact details of the data protection officer and communicate them to the supervisory authority.

Is there a data protection officer position? The Rationale for a DPO is required. I highly do not recommend that attorneys are hired for this position. It is the equivalent of Equifax hiring a music major as their CISO. They are not qualified. They have no cybersecurity or IT training which is pivotal to be effective in this position.

Article 38—position of the data protection officer[40]

Article 38 states:

1 The controller and the processor shall ensure that the data protection officer is involved, properly and in a timely manner, in all issues which relate to the protection of personal data.
2 The controller and processor shall support the data protection officer in performing the tasks referred to in Article 39 by providing resources necessary to carry out those tasks and access to personal data and processing operations, and to maintain his or her expert knowledge.
3 The controller and processor shall ensure that the data protection officer does not receive any instructions regarding the exercise of those tasks. He or she shall not be dismissed or penalized by the controller or the processor for performing his tasks. The data protection officer shall directly report to the highest management level of the controller or the processor.
4 Data subjects may contact the data protection officer with regard to all issues related to processing of their personal data and to the exercise of their rights under this Regulation.
5 The data protection officer shall be bound by secrecy or confidentiality concerning the performance of his or her tasks, in accordance with Union or Member State law.
6 The data protection officer may fulfill other tasks and duties. The controller or processor shall ensure that any such tasks and duties do not result in a conflict of interests.

Is the DPO supported by the organization and engaged in privacy matters? The Information Security Policy and the Data Protection Officer (DPO) Job Responsibilities are required.

Article 39—tasks of the data protection officer[41]

Article 39 states:

1 The data protection officer shall have at least the following tasks:

(a) to inform and advise the controller or the processor and the employees who carry out processing of their obligations pursuant to this Regulation and to other Union or Member State data protection provisions;

(b) to monitor compliance with this Regulation, with other Union or Member State data protection provisions and with the policies of the controller or processor in relation to the protection of personal data, including the assignment of responsibilities, awareness-raising and training of staff involved in processing operations, and the related audits;
(c) to provide advice were requested as regards the data protection impact assessment and monitor its performance pursuant to Article 35;
(d) to cooperate with the supervisory authority;
(e) to act as the contact point for the supervisory authority on issues relating to processing, including the prior consultation referred to in Article 36, and to consult, where appropriate, with regard to any other matter.

2 The data protection officer shall in the performance of his or her tasks have due regard to the risk associated with processing operations, considering the nature, scope, context, and purposes of processing.

Does the DPO offer advice on privacy matters, monitor compliance, liaise with the authorities, act as a contact point, address privacy risks etc.? Data Protection Officer (DPO) Job Responsibilities is required.

Article 40—codes of conduct[42]

Article 40 states:

1 The Member States, the supervisory authorities, the Board, and the Commission shall encourage the drawing up of codes of conduct intended to contribute to the proper application of this Regulation, taking account of the specific features of the various processing sectors and the specific needs of micro, small, and medium-sized enterprises.
2 Associations and other bodies representing categories of controllers or processors may prepare codes of conduct, or amend or extend such codes, for the purpose of specifying the application of this Regulation, such as with regard to:

(a) fair and transparent processing;
(b) the legitimate interests pursued by controllers in specific contexts;
(c) the collection of personal data;
(d) the pseudonymization of personal data;
(e) the information provided to the public and to data subjects;
(f) the exercise of the rights of data subjects;
(g) the information provided to, and the protection of, children, and the manner in which the consent of the holders of parental responsibility over children is to be obtained;
(h) the measures and procedures referred to in Articles 24 and 25 and the measures to ensure security of processing referred to in Article 32;

(i) the notification of personal data breaches to supervisory authorities and the communication of such personal data breaches to data subjects;
(j) the transfer of personal data to third countries or international organizations; or
(k) out-of-court proceedings and other dispute resolution procedures for resolving disputes between controllers and data subjects with regard to processing, without prejudice to the rights of data subjects pursuant to Articles 77 and 79.

Additionally, GDPR states the following:

3 In addition to adherence by controllers or processors subject to this Regulation, codes of conduct approved pursuant to paragraph 5 of this Article and having general validity pursuant to paragraph 9 of this Article may also be adhered to by controllers or processors that are not subject to this Regulation pursuant to Article 3 in order to provide appropriate safeguards within the framework of personal data transfers to third countries or international organizations under the terms referred to in point (e) of Article 46(2). Such controllers or processors shall make binding and enforceable commitments, via contractual or other legally binding instruments, to apply those appropriate safeguards including with regard to the rights of data subjects.
4 A code of conduct referred to in paragraph 2 of this Article shall contain mechanisms which enable the body referred to in Article 41(1) to carry out the mandatory monitoring of compliance with its provisions by the controllers or processors which undertake to apply it, without prejudice to the tasks and powers of supervisory authorities competent pursuant to Article 55 or 56.
5 Associations and other bodies referred to in paragraph 2 of this Article which intend to prepare a code of conduct or to amend or extend an existing code shall submit the draft code, amendment or extension to the supervisory authority which is competent pursuant to Article 55. The supervisory authority shall provide an opinion on whether the draft code, amendment or extension complies with this Regulation and shall approve that draft code, amendment, or extension if it finds that it provides sufficient appropriate safeguards.
6 Where the draft code, or amendment or extension is approved in accordance with paragraph 5, and where the code of conduct concerned does not relate to processing activities in several Member States, the supervisory authority shall register and publish the code.
7 Where a draft code of conduct relates to processing activities in several Member States, the supervisory authority which is competent pursuant to Article 55 shall, before approving the draft code, amendment or extension, submit it in the procedure referred to in Article 63 to the Board which shall provide an opinion on whether the draft code, amendment or extension

complies with this Regulation or, in the situation referred to in paragraph 3 of this Article, provides appropriate safeguards.

8 Where the opinion referred to in paragraph 7 confirms that the draft code, amendment, or extension complies with this Regulation, or, in the situation referred to in paragraph 3, provides appropriate safeguards, the Board shall submit its opinion to the Commission.

9 The Commission may, by way of implementing acts, decide that the approved code of conduct, amendment or extension submitted to it pursuant to paragraph 8 of this Article have general validity within the Union. Those implementing acts shall be adopted in accordance with the examination procedure set out in Article 93(2).

10 The Commission shall ensure appropriate publicity for the approved codes which have been decided as having general validity in accordance with paragraph 9.

11 The Board shall collate all approved codes of conduct, amendments and extensions in a register and shall make them publicly available by way of appropriate means.

Is there a mechanism to align the GDPR assessment process with other codes of conduct, regulations, and guidelines? Having a Cybersecurity Control Mapping Framework is required.

Article 41—monitoring of approved codes of conduct[43]

Article 41 states:

1 Without prejudice to the tasks and powers of the competent supervisory authority under Articles 57 and 58, the monitoring of compliance with a code of conduct pursuant to Article 40 may be carried out by a body which has an appropriate level of expertise in relation to the subject-matter of the code and is accredited for that purpose by the competent supervisory authority.

2 A body as referred to in paragraph 1 may be accredited to monitor compliance with a code of conduct where that body has:

(a) demonstrated its independence and expertise in relation to the subject-matter of the code to the satisfaction of the competent supervisory authority;

(b) established procedures which allow it to assess the eligibility of controllers and processors concerned to apply the code, to monitor their compliance with its provisions and to periodically review its operation;

(c) established procedures and structures to handle complaints about infringements of the code or the manner in which the code has been, or is being, implemented by a controller or processor, and to make those procedures and structures transparent to data subjects and the public; and

(d) demonstrated to the satisfaction of the competent supervisory authority that its tasks and duties do not result in a conflict of interests.

3 The competent supervisory authority shall submit the draft requirements for accreditation of a body as referred to in paragraph 1 of this Article to the Board pursuant to the consistency mechanism referred to in Article 63.
4 Without prejudice to the tasks and powers of the competent supervisory authority and the provisions of Chapter VIII, a body as referred to in paragraph 1 of this Article shall, subject to appropriate safeguards, take appropriate action in cases of infringement of the code by a controller or processor, including suspension or exclusion of the controller or processor concerned from the code. It shall inform the competent supervisory authority of such actions and the reasons for taking them.
5 The competent supervisory authority shall revoke the accreditation of a body as referred to in paragraph 1 if the requirements for accreditation are not, or are no longer, met or where actions taken by the body infringe this Regulation.
6 This Article shall not apply to processing carried out by public authorities and bodies.

Is there a mechanism to demonstrate the GDPR assessment process with other codes of conduct, regulations, and guidelines? A Cybersecurity Control Mapping Framework is required.

Article 42—certification[44]

Article 42 states:

1 The Member States, the supervisory authorities, the Board, and the Commission shall encourage, in particular at Union level, the establishment of data protection certification mechanisms and of data protection seals and marks, for the purpose of demonstrating compliance with this Regulation of processing operations by controllers and processors. The specific needs of micro, small, and medium-sized enterprises shall be considered.
2 In addition to adherence by controllers or processors subject to this Regulation, data protection certification mechanisms, seals or marks approved pursuant to paragraph 5 of this Article may be established for the purpose of demonstrating the existence of appropriate safeguards provided by controllers or processors that are not subject to this Regulation pursuant to Article 3 within the framework of personal data transfers to third countries or international organizations under the terms referred to in point (f) of Article 46(2). Such controllers or processors shall make binding and enforceable commitments, via contractual or other legally binding instruments, to apply those appropriate safeguards, including with regard to the rights of data subjects.
3 The certification shall be voluntary and available via a process that is transparent
4 A certification pursuant to this Article does not reduce the responsibility of the controller or the processor for compliance with this Regulation and

is without prejudice to the tasks and powers of the supervisory authorities which are competent pursuant to Article 55 or 56.

Additionally, GDPR states the following:

5 A certification pursuant to this Article shall be issued by the certification bodies referred to in Article 43 or by the competent supervisory authority, on the basis of criteria approved by that competent supervisory authority pursuant to Article 58(3) or by the Board pursuant to Article 63. Where the criteria are approved by the Board, this may result in a common certification, the European Data Protection Seal.
6 The controller or processor which submits its processing to the certification mechanism shall provide the certification body referred to in Article 43, or where applicable, the competent supervisory authority, with all information and access to its processing activities which are necessary to conduct the certification procedure.
7 Certification shall be issued to a controller or processor for a maximum period of three years and may be renewed, under the same conditions, provided that the relevant criteria continue to be met. Certification shall be withdrawn, as applicable, by the certification bodies referred to in Article 43 or by the competent supervisory authority where the criteria for the certification are not or are no longer met.
8 The Board shall collate all certification mechanisms and data protection seals and marks in a register and shall make them publicly available by any appropriate means.

Article 43—certification bodies[45]

Article 43 states:

1 Without prejudice to the tasks and powers of the competent supervisory authority under Articles 57 and 58, certification bodies which have an appropriate level of expertise in relation to data protection shall, after informing the supervisory authority in order to allow it to exercise its powers pursuant to point (h) of Article 58(2) where necessary, issue, and renew certification. Member States shall ensure that those certification bodies are accredited by one or both of the following:

   (a) the supervisory authority which is competent pursuant to Article 55 or 56;
   (b) the national accreditation body named in accordance with Regulation (EC) No 765/2008 of the European Parliament and of the Council[1] in accordance with EN-ISO/IEC 17065/2012 and with the additional requirements established by the supervisory authority which is competent pursuant to Article 55 or 56.

2 Certification bodies referred to in paragraph 1 shall be accredited in accordance with that paragraph only where they have:

 (a) demonstrated their independence and expertise in relation to the subject-matter of the certification to the satisfaction of the competent supervisory authority;
 (b) undertaken to respect the criteria referred to in Article 42(5) and approved by the supervisory authority which is competent pursuant to Article 55 or 56 or by the Board pursuant to Article 63;
 (c) established procedures for the issuing, periodic review and withdrawal of data protection certification, seals, and marks;
 (d) established procedures and structures to handle complaints about infringements of the certification or the manner in which the certification has been, or is being, implemented by the controller or processor, and to make those procedures and structures transparent to data subjects and the public; and
 (e) demonstrated, to the satisfaction of the competent supervisory authority, that their tasks and duties do not result in a conflict of interests.

Additionally, GDPR states the following:

3 The accreditation of certification bodies as referred to in paragraphs 1 and 2 of this Article shall take place on the basis of requirements approved by the supervisory authority which is competent pursuant to Article 55 or 56 or by the Board pursuant to Article 63. In the case of accreditation pursuant to point (b) of paragraph 1 of this Article, those requirements shall complement those envisaged in Regulation (EC) No 765/2008 and the technical rules that describe the methods and procedures of the certification bodies.
4 The certification bodies referred to in paragraph 1 shall be responsible for the proper assessment leading to the certification or the withdrawal of such certification without prejudice to the responsibility of the controller or processor for compliance with this Regulation. The accreditation shall be issued for a maximum period of five years and may be renewed on the same conditions provided that the certification body meets the requirements set out in this Article.
5 The certification bodies referred to in paragraph 1 shall provide the competent supervisory authorities with the reasons for granting or withdrawing the requested certification.
6 The requirements referred to in paragraph 3 of this Article and the criteria referred to in Article 42(5) shall be made public by the supervisory authority in an easily accessible form. The supervisory authorities shall also transmit those requirements and criteria to the Board.
7 Without prejudice to Chapter VIII, the competent supervisory authority or the national accreditation body shall revoke an accreditation of a certification body pursuant to paragraph 1 of this Article where the conditions for

the accreditation are not, or are no longer, met or where actions taken by a certification body infringe this Regulation.

8 The Commission shall be empowered to adopt delegated acts in accordance with Article 92 for the purpose of specifying the requirements to be taken into account for the data protection certification mechanisms referred to in Article 42(1).
9 The Commission may adopt implementing acts laying down technical standards for certification mechanisms and data protection seals and marks, and mechanisms to promote and recognize those certification mechanisms, seals, and marks. Those implementing acts shall be adopted in accordance with the examination procedure referred to in Article 93(2).

CHAPTER 5—TRANSFERS OF PERSONAL DATA TO THIRD COUNTRIES OR INTERNATIONAL ORGANIZATIONS

Article 44—general principle for transfers[46]

Article 44 speaks to the transfer of personal data which is intended for processing after transfer to a third country or to an international organization. It states that this is appropriate only if the other provisions of the GDPR articles have been complied with by the controller and processor.

Article 44—Is there a mechanism for international transfers and processing of personal info to be complaint with GDPR?

Transfers of personal data to 3rd countries or international organizations Procedure is required. Is there a mechanism in place to identify which systems transfer GDPR data and to which locations that are identified as adequate? Compliance involves ensuring that suitable contracts/agreements and GDPR privacy controls are in. Some integrated cyber risk and privacy platforms show where data is transferred and can tag entitles with adequate or inadequate privacy arrangements and systems that use them.

Article 45—transfers on the basis of an adequacy decision[47]

Article 45 states:

1 A transfer of personal data to a third country or an international organization may take place where the Commission has decided that the third country, a territory or one or more specified sectors within that third country, or the international organization in question ensures an adequate level of protection. Such a transfer shall not require any specific authorization.
2 When assessing the adequacy of the level of protection, the Commission shall, in particular, take account of the following elements:

(a) the rule of law, respect for human rights and fundamental freedoms, relevant legislation, both general and sectoral, including concerning public security, defense, national security and criminal law and the access of public authorities to personal data, as well as the implementation of such legislation, data protection rules, professional rules, and security measures, including rules for the onward transfer of personal data to another third country or international organization which are complied with in that country or international organization, case-law, as well as effective and enforceable data subject rights and effective administrative and judicial redress for the data subjects whose personal data are being transferred;

(b) the existence and effective functioning of one or more independent supervisory authorities in the third country or to which an international organization is subject, with responsibility for ensuring and enforcing compliance with the data protection rules, including adequate enforcement powers, for assisting and advising the data subjects in exercising their rights and for cooperation with the supervisory authorities of the Member States; and

(c) the international commitments the third country or international organization concerned has entered into, or other obligations arising from legally binding conventions or instruments as well as from its participation in multilateral or regional systems, in particular in relation to the protection of personal data.

Additionally, GDPR states the following:

3 The Commission, after assessing the adequacy of the level of protection, may decide, by means of implementing act, that a third country, a territory or one or more specified sectors within a third country, or an international organization ensures an adequate level of protection within the meaning of paragraph 2 of this Article. The implementing act shall provide for a mechanism for a periodic review, at least every four years, which shall consider all relevant developments in the third country or international organization. The implementing act shall specify its territorial and sectoral application and, where applicable, identify the supervisory authority or authorities referred to in point (b) of paragraph 2 of this Article. The implementing act shall be adopted in accordance with the examination procedure referred to in Article 93(2).

4 The Commission shall, on an ongoing basis, monitor developments in third countries and international organizations that could affect the functioning of decisions adopted pursuant to paragraph 3 of this Article and decisions adopted on the basis of Article 25(6) of Directive 95/46/EC.

5 The Commission shall, where available information reveals, in particular following the review referred to in paragraph 3 of this Article, that a third country, a territory or one or more specified sectors within a third country, or an international organization no longer ensures an adequate level of protection within the meaning of paragraph 2 of this Article, to the extent

necessary, repeal, amend or suspend the decision referred to in paragraph 3 of this Article by means of implementing acts without retro-active effect. Those implementing acts shall be adopted in accordance with the examination procedure referred to in Article 93(2). On duly justified imperative grounds of urgency, the Commission shall adopt immediately applicable implementing acts in accordance with the procedure referred to in Article 93(3).

6 The Commission shall enter into consultations with the third country or international organization with a view to remedying the situation giving rise to the decision made pursuant to paragraph 5.

7 A decision pursuant to paragraph 5 of this Article is without prejudice to transfers of personal data to the third country, a territory or one or more specified sectors within that third country, or the international organization in question pursuant to Articles 46–49.

8 The Commission shall publish in the Official Journal of the European Union and on its website a list of the third countries, territories, and specified sectors within a third country and international organizations for which it has decided that an adequate level of protection is or is no longer ensured.

9 Decisions adopted by the Commission on the basis of Article 25(6) of Directive 95/46/EC shall remain in force until amended, replaced or repealed by a Commission Decision adopted in accordance with paragraph 3 or 5 of this Article.

Article 46—transfers subject to appropriate safeguards[48]

Article 46 states:

1 In the absence of a decision pursuant to Article 45(3), a controller or processor may transfer personal data to a third country or an international organization only if the controller or processor has provided appropriate safeguards, and on condition that enforceable data subject rights and effective legal remedies for data subjects are available.

2 The appropriate safeguards referred to in paragraph 1 may be provided for, without requiring any specific authorization from a supervisory authority, by:

(a) a legally binding and enforceable instrument between public authorities or bodies;

(b) binding corporate rules in accordance with Article 47;

(c) standard data protection clauses adopted by the Commission in accordance with the examination procedure referred to in Article 93(2);

(d) standard data protection clauses adopted by a supervisory authority and approved by the Commission pursuant to the examination procedure referred to in Article 93(2);

(e) an approved code of conduct pursuant to Article 40 together with binding and enforceable commitments of the controller or processor in the third country to apply the appropriate safeguards, including as regards data subjects' rights; or

(f) an approved certification mechanism pursuant to Article 42 together with binding and enforceable commitments of the controller or processor in the third country to apply the appropriate safeguards, including as regards data subjects' rights.

3 Subject to the authorization from the competent supervisory authority, the appropriate safeguards referred to in paragraph 1 may also be provided for, in particular, by:

(a) contractual clauses between the controller or processor and the controller, processor, or the recipient of the personal data in the third country or international organization; or

(b) provisions to be inserted into administrative arrangements between public authorities or bodies which include enforceable and effective data subject rights.

4 The supervisory authority shall apply the consistency mechanism referred to in Article 63 in the cases referred to in paragraph 3 of this Article.

5 Authorizations by a Member State or supervisory authority on the basis of Article 26(2) of Directive 95/46/EC shall remain valid until amended, replaced or repealed, if necessary, by that supervisory authority. 2Decisions adopted by the Commission on the basis of Article 26(4) of Directive 95/46/EC shall remain in force until amended, replaced or repealed, if necessary, by a Commission Decision adopted in accordance with paragraph 2 of this Article.

There must be a mechanism in place to identify which systems transfer GDPR data and to which locations that are identified as not adequate. Additionally, there must be a mechanism in place for the organization to verify the implementation and adequacy of privacy controls before transferring personal data to such countries, and subsequently, e.g., suitable contractual clauses and compliance activities? Integrated Cyber Risk Management Platforms can show where data is transferred and can tag entitles with adequate or inadequate privacy arrangements and systems that use them.

Article 47—binding corporate rules[49]

Article 47 states:

1 competent supervisory authority shall approve binding corporate rules in accordance with the consistency mechanism set out in Article 63, provided that they:

(a) are legally binding and apply to and are enforced by every member concerned of the group of undertakings, or group of enterprises engaged in a joint economic activity, including their employees;

(b) expressly confer enforceable rights on data subjects with regard to the processing of their personal data; and
(c) fulfill the requirements laid down in paragraph 2.

Additionally, GDPR states the following:

2 The binding corporate rules referred to in paragraph 1 shall specify at least:

(a) the structure and contact details of the group of undertakings, or group of enterprises engaged in a joint economic activity and of each of its members;
(b) the data transfers or set of transfers, including the categories of personal data, the type of processing and its purposes, the type of data subjects affected and the identification of the third country or countries in question;
(c) their legally binding nature, both internally and externally;
(d) the application of the general data protection principles, in particular purpose limitation, data minimization, limited storage periods, data quality, data protection by design and by default, legal basis for processing, processing of special categories of personal data, measures to ensure data security, and the requirements in respect of onward transfers to bodies not bound by the binding corporate rules;
(e) the rights of data subjects in regard to processing and the means to exercise those rights, including the right not to be subject to decisions based solely on automated processing, including profiling in accordance with Article 22, the right to lodge a complaint with the competent supervisory authority and before the competent courts of the Member States in accordance with Article 79, and to obtain redress and, where appropriate, compensation for a breach of the binding corporate rules;
(f) the acceptance by the controller or processor established on the territory of a Member State of liability for any breaches of the binding corporate rules by any member concerned not established in the Union; the controller or the processor shall be exempt from that liability, in whole or in part, only if it proves that that member is not responsible for the event giving rise to the damage;
(g) how the information on the binding corporate rules, in particular on the provisions referred to in points (d), (e), and (f) of this paragraph is provided to the data subjects in addition to Articles 13 and 14;
(h) the tasks of any data protection officer designated in accordance with Article 37 or any other person or entity in charge of the monitoring compliance with the binding corporate rules within the group of undertakings, or group of enterprises engaged in a joint economic activity, as well as monitoring training, and complaint-handling;

Additionally, GDPR states the following:

(i) the complaint procedures must include;

(j) the mechanisms within the group of undertakings, or group of enterprises engaged in a joint economic activity for ensuring the verification of compliance with the binding corporate rules. Such mechanisms shall include data protection audits and methods for ensuring corrective actions to protect the rights of the data subject. Results of such verification should be communicated to the person or entity referred to in point (h) and to the board of the controlling undertaking of a group of undertakings, or of the group of enterprises engaged in a joint economic activity, and should be available upon request to the competent supervisory authority;
(k) the mechanisms for reporting and recording changes to the rules and reporting those changes to the supervisory authority;
(l) the cooperation mechanism with the supervisory authority to ensure compliance by any member of the group of undertakings, or group of enterprises engaged in a joint economic activity, in particular by making available to the supervisory authority the results of verifications of the measures referred to in point (j);
(m) the mechanisms for reporting to the competent supervisory authority any legal requirements to which a member of the group of undertakings, or group of enterprises engaged in a joint economic activity is subject in a third country which are likely to have a substantial adverse effect on the guarantees provided by the binding corporate rules; and
(n) the appropriate data protection training to personnel having permanent or regular access to personal data.

3 The Commission may specify the format and procedures for the exchange of information between controllers, processors, and supervisory authorities for binding corporate rules within the meaning of this Article. Those implementing acts shall be adopted in accordance with the examination procedure set out in Article 93(2).

There must be a mechanism in place for national authorities to approve legally-binding privacy rules permitting transfers to nonapproved countries. The List of Authorities and Key Suppliers and the Contact with Authorities Work Instruction are required.

Article 48—transfers or disclosures not authorized by union law[50]

Article 48 addresses any judgment of a court or tribunal and any decision of an administrative authority of a third country requiring a controller or processor to transfer or disclose personal data. It may only be recognized or enforceable in any manner if based on an international agreement, such as a mutual legal assistance treaty, in force between the requesting third country and the Union or a Member State, without prejudice to other grounds for transfer pursuant to this Chapter.

Article 49—derogations for specific situations[51]

Article 49 states:

1 In the absence of an adequacy decision pursuant to Article 45(3), or of appropriate safeguards pursuant to Article 46, including binding corporate rules, a transfer or a set of transfers of personal data to a third country or an international organization shall take place only on one of the following conditions:

(a) the data subject has explicitly consented to the proposed transfer, after having been informed of the possible risks of such transfers for the data subject due to the absence of an adequacy decision and appropriate safeguards;
(b) the transfer is necessary for the performance of a contract between the data subject and the controller, or the implementation of pre-contractual measures taken at the data subject's request;
(c) the transfer is necessary for the conclusion or performance of a contract concluded in the interest of the data subject between the controller and another natural or legal person;
(d) the transfer is necessary for important reasons of public interest;
(e) the transfer is necessary for the establishment, exercise, or defense of legal claims;
(f) the transfer is necessary in order to protect the vital interests of the data subject or of other persons, where the data subject is physically or legally incapable of giving consent;
(g) the transfer is made from a register which according to Union or Member State law is intended to provide information to the public and which is open to consultation either by the public in general or by any person who can demonstrate a legitimate interest, but only to the extent that the conditions laid down by Union or Member State law for consultation are fulfilled in the particular case.

Where a transfer could not be based on a provision in Article 45 or 46, including the provisions on binding corporate rules, and none of the derogations for a specific situation referred to in the first subparagraph of this paragraph is applicable, a transfer to a third country or an international organization may take place only if the transfer is not repetitive, concerns only a limited number of data subjects, is necessary for the purposes of compelling legitimate interests pursued by the controller which are not overridden by the interests or rights and freedoms of the data subject, and the controller has assessed all the circumstances surrounding the data transfer and has on the basis of that assessment provided suitable safeguards with regard to the protection of personal data. The controller shall inform the supervisory authority of the transfer. The controller shall, in addition to providing the information referred to in Articles 13 and 14, inform the data subject of the transfer and on the compelling legitimate interests pursued.

Additionally, GDPR states the following:

2 A transfer pursuant to point (g) of the first subparagraph of paragraph 1 shall not involve the entirety of the personal data or entire categories of the personal data contained in the register. Where the register is intended for consultation by persons having a legitimate interest, the transfer shall be made only at the request of those persons or if they are to be the recipients.
3 Points (a), (b), and (c) of the first subparagraph of paragraph 1 and the second subparagraph thereof shall not apply to activities carried out by public authorities in the exercise of their public powers.
4 The public interest referred to in point (d) of the first subparagraph of paragraph 1 shall be recognized in Union law or in the law of the Member State to which the controller is subject.
5 In the absence of an adequacy decision, Union or Member State law may, for important reasons of public interest, expressly set limits to the transfer of specific categories of personal data to a third country or an international organization. Member States shall notify such provisions to the Commission.
6 The controller or processor shall document the assessment as well as the suitable safeguards referred to in the second subparagraph of paragraph 1 of this Article in the records referred to in Article 30.

Is there a mechanism in place to measure the risk of data transfers that are to nonapproved countries? The Transfers of Personal Data to Third Countries or International and Organizations Procedure and the Privacy Impact Assessment are required.

Article 50—international cooperation for the protection of personal data[52]

Article 50 states:

1 In relation to third countries and international organizations, the Commission, and supervisory authorities shall take appropriate steps to:

(a) develop international cooperation mechanisms to facilitate the effective enforcement of legislation for the protection of personal data;
(b) provide international mutual assistance in the enforcement of legislation for the protection of personal data, including through notification, complaint referral, investigative assistance, and information exchange, subject to appropriate safeguards for the protection of personal data and other fundamental rights and freedoms;
(c) engage relevant stakeholders in discussion and activities aimed at furthering international cooperation in the enforcement of legislation for the protection of personal data;
(d) promote the exchange and documentation of personal data protection legislation and practice, including on jurisdictional conflicts with third countries.

Is there a mechanism to communicate with international authorities on privacy issues? The List of Authorities and Key Suppliers and the Contact with Authorities Work Instruction are required.

CHAPTERS 6, 7, 8, 9, 10, AND 11

This book addresses Enterprise cybersecurity requirements and not the requirements of the Supervisory Authorities. Therefore, the following are not addressed.

- articles 51–59 which are addressing Chapter 6 Independent Supervisory Authorities;
- articles 60–76 which are addressing Chapter 7 Cooperation and Consistency;
- articles 77–84 which are addressing Chapter 8 Remedies, liability, and penalties;
- articles 85–91 which are addressing Chapter 9 Provisions relating to specific processing situations;
- articles 92–93 which are addressing Chapter 10 Delegated acts and implementing acts;
- articles 94–99 which are addressing Chapter 11 Final provisions;

Articles 51–99 are not in scope for this book. However, relevant to penalties, member states can lay down criminal penalties for infringements of this regulation.

Summary

GDPR is a complex set of requirements that require a firm understanding of information technology, cybersecurity, privacy, and regulatory acumen. In this chapter we have laid out the types of queries that are needed to understand each article. Our next chapter will focus on the requirements and the evidence that is needed to comply from a cybersecurity perspective.

Notes

1. Intersoft consulting, "General data protection regulation (GDPR)", 2020, https://gdpr-info.eu/art-1-gdpr/.
2. Cyber Innovative Technologies, "Cyber innovative technologies", 2020, https://cyberinnovativetech.com/.
3. Bob Seigel, CSO United States, "Privacy policy or privacy notice: what's the difference", May 4, 2016, https://www.csoonline.com/article/3063601/privacy-policies-and-privacy-notices-whats-the-difference.html#:~:text=Privacy%20Notice%3A%20A%20statement%20made,or%20sometimes%20a%20privacy%20policy.
4. Intersoft consulting, "General data protection regulation (GDPR)", 2020, https://gdpr-info.eu/art-2-gdpr/.
5. Intersoft consulting, "General data protection regulation (GDPR)", 2020, https://gdpr-info.eu/art-3-gdpr/.
6. Intersoft consulting, "General data protection regulation (GDPR)", 2020, https://gdpr-info.eu/art-4-gdpr/.

7. Intersoft consulting, "General data protection regulation (GDPR)", 2020, https://gdpr-info.eu/art-5-gdpr/.
8. Intersoft consulting, "General data protection regulation (GDPR)", 2020, https://gdpr-info.eu/art-6-gdpr/.
9. Intersoft consulting, "General data protection regulation (GDPR)", 2020, https://gdpr-info.eu/art-7-gdpr/.
10. Intersoft consulting, "General data protection regulation (GDPR)", 2020, https://gdpr-info.eu/art-8-gdpr/.
11. Intersoft consulting, "General data protection regulation (GDPR)", 2020, https://gdpr-info.eu/art-9-gdpr/.
12. Intersoft consulting, "General data protection regulation (GDPR)", 2020, https://gdpr-info.eu/art-10-gdpr/.
13. Intersoft consulting, "General data protection regulation (GDPR)", 2020, https://gdpr-info.eu/art-11-gdpr/.
14. Intersoft consulting, "General data protection regulation (GDPR)", 2020, https://gdpr-info.eu/art-12-gdpr/.
15. Intersoft consulting, "General data protection regulation (GDPR)", 2020, https://gdpr-info.eu/art-13-gdpr/.
16. Intersoft consulting, "General data protection regulation (GDPR)", 2020, https://gdpr-info.eu/art-14-gdpr/.
17. Intersoft consulting, "General data protection regulation (GDPR)", 2020, https://gdpr-info.eu/art-15-gdpr/.
18. Intersoft consulting, "General data protection regulation (GDPR)", 2020, https://gdpr-info.eu/art-16-gdpr/.
19. Intersoft consulting, "General data protection regulation (GDPR)", 2020, https://gdpr-info.eu/art-17-gdpr/.
20. Intersoft consulting, "General data protection regulation (GDPR)", 2020, https://gdpr-info.eu/art-18-gdpr/.
21. Intersoft consulting, "General data protection regulation (GDPR)", 2020, https://gdpr-info.eu/art-19-gdpr/.
22. Intersoft consulting, "General data protection regulation (GDPR)", 2020, https://gdpr-info.eu/art-20-gdpr/.
23. Intersoft consulting, "General data protection regulation (GDPR)", 2020, https://gdpr-info.eu/art-21-gdpr/.
24. Intersoft consulting, "General data protection regulation (GDPR)", 2020, https://gdpr-info.eu/art-22-gdpr/.
25. Intersoft consulting, "General data protection regulation (GDPR)", 2020, https://gdpr-info.eu/art-23-gdpr/.
26. Intersoft consulting, "General data protection regulation (GDPR)", 2020, https://gdpr-info.eu/art-24-gdpr/.
27. Intersoft consulting, "General data protection regulation (GDPR)", 2020, https://gdpr-info.eu/art-25-gdpr/.
28. Intersoft consulting, "General data protection regulation (GDPR)", 2020, https://gdpr-info.eu/art-26-gdpr/.
29. Intersoft consulting, "General data protection regulation (GDPR)", 2020, https://gdpr-info.eu/art-27-gdpr/.
30. Intersoft consulting, "General data protection regulation (GDPR)", 2020, https://gdpr-info.eu/art-28-gdpr/.
31. Intersoft consulting, "General data protection regulation (GDPR)", 2020, https://gdpr-info.eu/art-29-gdpr/.
32. Intersoft consulting, "General data protection regulation (GDPR)", 2020, https://gdpr-info.eu/art-30-gdpr/.

33. Intersoft consulting, "General data protection regulation (GDPR)", 2020, https://gdpr-info.eu/art-31-gdpr/.
34. Intersoft consulting, "General data protection regulation (GDPR)", 2020, https://gdpr-info.eu/art-32-gdpr/.
35. Intersoft consulting, "General data protection regulation (GDPR)", 2020, https://gdpr-info.eu/art-33-gdpr/.
36. Intersoft consulting, "General data protection regulation (GDPR)", 2020, https://gdpr-info.eu/art-34-gdpr/.
37. Intersoft consulting, "General data protection regulation (GDPR)", 2020, https://gdpr-info.eu/art-35-gdpr/.
38. Intersoft consulting, "General data protection regulation (GDPR)", 2020, https://gdpr-info.eu/art-36-gdpr/.
39. Intersoft consulting, "General data protection regulation (GDPR)", 2020, https://gdpr-info.eu/art-37-gdpr/.
40. Intersoft consulting, "General data protection regulation (GDPR)", 2020, https://gdpr-info.eu/art-38-gdpr/.
41. Intersoft consulting, "General data protection regulation (GDPR)", 2020, https://gdpr-info.eu/art-39-gdpr/.
42. Intersoft consulting, "General data protection regulation (GDPR)", 2020, https://gdpr-info.eu/art-40-gdpr/.
43. Intersoft consulting, "General data protection regulation (GDPR)", 2020, https://gdpr-info.eu/art-41-gdpr/.
44. Intersoft consulting, "General data protection regulation (GDPR)", 2020, https://gdpr-info.eu/art-42-gdpr/.
45. Intersoft consulting, "General data protection regulation (GDPR)", 2020, https://gdpr-info.eu/art-43-gdpr/.
46. Intersoft consulting, "General data protection regulation (GDPR)", 2020, https://gdpr-info.eu/art-44-gdpr/.
47. Intersoft consulting, "General data protection regulation (GDPR)", 2020, https://gdpr-info.eu/art-45-gdpr/.
48. Intersoft consulting, "General data protection regulation (GDPR)", 2020, https://gdpr-info.eu/art-46-gdpr/.
49. Intersoft consulting, "General data protection regulation (GDPR)", 2020, https://gdpr-info.eu/art-47-gdpr/.
50. Intersoft consulting, "General data protection regulation (GDPR)", 2020, https://gdpr-info.eu/art-48-gdpr/.
51. Intersoft consulting, "General data protection regulation (GDPR)", 2020, https://gdpr-info.eu/art-49-gdpr/.
52. Intersoft consulting, "General data protection regulation (GDPR)", 2020, https://gdpr-info.eu/art-49-gdpr/.

27 GDPR EVIDENCE

If you are not able to fully comply with regulatory cybersecurity requirements, examiners do expect to see a realistic and approved strategic plan to get there.

Richard Hudson, Senior Manager Cybersecurity and Privacy at Treliant

Policies

There are five cybersecurity policies required for General Data Protection Regulation (GDPR). These include the Data Protection Policy, Privacy Policy, Information Security Policy, GDPR Training Policy, and the Access Control Policy.

Data protection policy

A data protection policy is an internal document that acts as the foundation of the organization's GDPR compliance program. It outlines GDPR's requirements for the employees and states how the organization will achieve compliance. This policy is required to meet compliance for articles 1–5, 8, 12–14, 24, and 32.

Privacy policy

A privacy policy is a statement or a legal document which is externally facing that records the means by which a party collects, uses, discloses, and manages a customer or client's personal data. It is a statement that governs an entity's handling practices of personal information. A privacy policy instructs employees on the collection and the use of the data, as well as any specific rights the data subjects may have. This policy is required to meet compliance for articles 1–5. Privacy policies must be posted on the company website.

Information security policy

An information security policy is an overarching internal document that references a set of policies issued by an organization to ensure that all employees and consultants that use its digital assets comply with rules and guidelines related to the security of the data that is owned by the organization whether it is processed or stored by the firm or by a third-party.

DOI: 10.4324/9781003052616-34

The Board of Directors and management must be committed to preserving the confidentiality, integrity and availability of all the digital assets to preserve their competitive edge, cash-flow, profitability, legal, regulatory and contractual compliance, and reputation. This policy outlines the goals for reducing information-related risks to acceptable levels. This policy is required to meet compliance for articles 1–5.

Access control policy

An access control policy is an internal document which outlines the controls placed on both physical access to the computer system (having locked access to where the system is physically located) and to the software in order to limit access to organizations digital asset. This policy is required to meet compliance for articles 30, 32, and 35.

GDPR training policy

This policy is an internal document which outlines the company GDPR training program and how to be compliant with GDPR requirements, and matters relating to data protection and privacy.

Employees are required to understand the risks to the organization. Risk may be financial and reputation or to themselves. These include potential disciplinary actions, including dismissal.

By relating to protecting their own data, employees can understand the significance of data protection laws like GDPR and their value. The requirements for the use, collection and security of personal data, why there are certain policies and procedures in place and, most importantly, why they must comply with those policies can be easily understood from a personal point of view.

GDPR begins with awareness. Controllers must ensure that this is a top-down program and ensure that the key people in the organization are aware of the law. Senior management must appreciate the impact on the firm and get behind the GDPR program. One of the risk areas is having staff that are not aware and in need of training.

This is a good time to check the firm's procedures and to work out how staff would react in certain situations. An example is in the case of a subject access request or other data subject rights request. If someone asks to have their personal data deleted, would your systems help you to locate and delete the data? Who will make the decisions about deletion? Would all staff know how to recognize a subject access request?

The GDPR introduces a duty on all organizations to report certain types of data breach to the Supervisory Authority and, in some cases, to notify individuals. Would all staff know how to recognize a data breach or security incident and how to react?

This policy is required to meet compliance for article 39.

Procedures

Procedures are a set of instructions that provide direction to achieve the goals of the policies they support. GDPR has organizational and system requirements that are related to procedures. Organizational procedures are procedures that are applicable across the entire organization and system procedures are specific to a system or set of systems. We will review the articles individually and map them to each one. These procedures relate to the use, collection, and system protections required for GDPR.

Consent procedure

The consent procedure outlines the steps needed for articles 6–9. The consent of the data subject is needed for processing of his or her personal data and is within the scope of this procedure. This procedure is needed to obtain consent from the data subject to collect and use their data.

Consent is defined as any statement that is freely given, specific, informed, and shows an unambiguous indication that the data subject wishes to allow for the processing of their personal data. This is typically done with an organizational form and procedure that relates back to the consent policy.

Explicit consent is required for the processing of sensitive personal data. Specific conditions apply to the validity of consent given by children in relation to information society services, with requirements to obtain and verify parental consent below certain age limits.

This procedure outlines the steps to obtain consent for adults and children. It ties back to the privacy notice register, subject consent form, and right to withdraw consent procedure.

Retention of records procedure

This procedure outlines rules for record types, periods to retain them, justification, and disposal methods. This procedure relates to the retention of records policy, information classification procedure, log of information assets for disposal, access control rule, retention, and disposal log. This procedure is for meeting compliance with article 7. The procedure can vary from system to system depending upon all the types of data that it processes.

Data portability procedure

The data portability procedure is used when transmitting data directly from one data controller to another. It addresses how the data will be provided and is related to achieving compliance with article 20.

Data protection policy review procedure

This procedure outlines the steps for doing a data protection impact assessment and is required for compliance with article 24. It outlines the appropriate controls that are required to be implemented to mitigate any risks identified as part of the DPIA process and subsequent decision to proceed with the processing. This is done at the organizational level for each system that processes EU citizen data.

Internal audit procedure

This procedure outlines the steps for an doing an internal audit of the GDPR program. It establishes the requirements for their planning, preparation, performance, reporting, following up, and closing down. It applies to achieving compliance with articles 28 and 47. The audit is at the organizational and system levels.

Communication procedure

This procedure addresses all internal and external communications related to personal data, data breaches, GDPR compliance and other topics related to data protection are within the scope of this procedure. Details will be documented related to the work instructions for internal or external communications. This procedure relates to compliance with articles 33 and 36. This an organizational level procedure.

Competence procedure

This procedure allows the data protection officer (DPO) to ensure that all necessary competences are documented and job descriptions are in order for the GDPR program. This procedure is needed for compliance with article 32. This an organizational level procedure.

Contact with authorities work instruction

This procedure is used for the requirement for contacting authorities under all relevant laws including the EU GDPR. It is required for compliance with articles 33 and 36. This an organizational level procedure.

Control of records procedure

This procedure relates to the control of records, whether analog or digital, and the retention requirements for each type. Emails containing personal data should be retained, archived and destroyed in line with this policy. It is required for compliance with article 32. This is a system level procedure.

Complaints procedure

This procedure addresses complaints from data subject(s) related to the processing of their personal data, the firms handling of requests from data subjects and the appeals process. It is required for compliance with article 47. This an organizational level procedure.

Managing third party service contracts

This procedure is in place to ensure that adequate technical and other resources that might be required are made available to manage and monitor the relationship with third parties. It is required for compliance with articles 44–50. This an organizational level procedure.

Managing sub-contract processing procedure

This procedure outlies the security requirements of its information processing facilities and information assets in relation to external parties. It is required for compliance with articles 28 and 29. This an organizational level procedure.

Secure disposal of storage media

This procedure addresses all manner of disposal media and the steps to secure it. It is required for compliance with article 32. This a system level procedure.

Subject access request procedure

This procedure relates to the steps for the firm to take related to the data subject's request for access to their information. It identifies the operating systems and applications that are required to be queried. It is required for compliance with articles 12–19, 21, and 22. This an organizational level procedure.

Subject access request record procedure

This procedure relates to the steps for the data subject to request access to organizational information as is their predetermined right to such information. It is required for compliance with articles 6, 7, 10, 12, and 30. This has components at the organizational and system level.

Transfers of personal data to third countries or international organizations procedure

This procedure applies where the firm wishes to transfer personal data to third countries or international Organizations outside of the EU for processing. This includes the onward transfer of personal data from a third country, or an international Organization to another third country, as well as to another international Organization within the scope of this procedure. It is required for compliance with articles 44–49. This an organizational level procedure.

Withdrawal of consent procedure

This procedure outlines the steps to withdraw consent. It is required for compliance with article 7. This an organizational level procedure.

Operations procedure

This procedure applies to all operational areas, including data protection and processing operation procedures and technology components and is used as a guide to minimize the negative impact of operations upon the personal information management system. This procedure is required for compliance with article 32. This a system level procedure.

Continuous improvement procedure

This procedure address how to continually improve the GDPR Compliance Management System's (VRisk) adequacy, suitability and effectiveness. This procedure is required for compliance with article 32. This an organizational level procedure.

Data breach procedure

This procedure is used in the event of a personal data breach under article 33 of the GDPR. Notification of a personal data breach must be made to the supervisory authority, and is required for compliance with article 34. Communication of a personal data breach must be made to the data subject promptly and clearly. This is at the organizational level procedure that is critical to get right.

Forms

GDPR requires forms and documentation for the use and collection requirements. We will review the requirements individually and map them to each form or document.

Competence matrix

The competence matrix is a log of the required competencies, who is filling the roles, their required qualifications and training. This is required for compliance with article 39.

Contact with authorities work instruction

This is a set of instructions on what to provide to the Supervisory Authority and their contract details. This is required for compliance with articles 31–33.

Data protection officer (DPO) job description

This document is the requirements for the HR team to utilize when filling the DPO position. It contains the roles, responsibilities needed to drive compliance with the EU GDPR and ensure ongoing compliance of all the core activities. This is required for compliance with article 38.

Data protection officer (DPO) job responsibilities

This document outlines in detail the responsibilities of the DPO. These include maintaining expert knowledge of data protection law and practices, as well as other professional qualities, to ensure that company complies with the requirements of the EU GDPR and relevant member state data protection law(s) and regulations. It outlines the reporting structure and requirements for demonstrating compliance with the GDPR. This includes that policies and procedures are kept up to date. The

DPO must plan and schedule data processing audits regularly, monitor core activities to ensure they comply with the EU GDPR. They are also the main contact point for employees and will liaise with all members of staff on matters of data protection. This is required for compliance with article 39.

Data subject consent form

This form is required to be filled out by the data subject to provide consent and must stipulate what the consent is for. This is required for compliance with articles 1, 6, 7, and 10.

Data subject consent withdrawal form

This form is required to be filled out by the data subject to withdraw their consent to have their data processed and stored. This is required for compliance with article 7.

Individual user rights agreement

This agreement from the data subject grants the firm access rights to their data. The data subject agrees that they understand and accept the rights and the business reasons for these access rights. They also agree to not breach the company's digital assets and to comply with the Acceptable Use Policy, its e-mail policy and its information security policy. This is required for compliance with article 6.

Log of information assets for disposal

This is a log of the schedule for disposal of digital assets. This is required for compliance with article 32.

Log of request to remove info assets from site

This is a register of all the digital assets that have been disposed, the method, retention periods by type, date of disposal, etc. This is required for compliance with article 32.

Parental consent form

This is a form used by the parent to provide consent for a company to process the data on behalf of a minor and the purpose of that collection. This is required for compliance with articles 6, 8, 12, 40, and 57.

Parental consent withdrawal form

This is the form needed for a parent to withdraw their consent for a minor to have their data processed. This is required for compliance with articles 6, 8, 12, 40, and 57.

Physical entry controls and security areas

This is a list of all the physical controls that are needed to prevent unauthorized access into buildings where GDPR data is being processed and stored. This is required for compliance with articles 25 and 35.

PIMS and GDPR objectives record

This is a log of the information management objectives, documents, responsibility, and dates that are required to be compliant with the GDPR. This is required for compliance with articles 1–4.

Privacy notice

This documents the terms and conditions for the data subjects regarding how the company will ensure their data privacy. The notice must be in a concise, transparent, intelligible, and easily accessible form. It must be written in clear and plain language, particularly for any information addressed specifically to a child, and posted in a timely manner. This is required for compliance with article 1.

Privacy notice register

This log documents the privacy notices, when they were issued and the targeted data subjects. This is required for compliance with article 1.

Rationale for a data protection officer

The GDPR requires the appointment of a DPO if your firm is a public authority or body, or if your firm carries out certain types of processing activities. This document addresses your firm's rationale for the appointment of a DPO. This is required for compliance with article 37.

Retention and disposal schedule

This log documents the record types, periods to retain them, justification, date of disposal, and disposal method. This is required for compliance with article 7.

Note

1. Intersoft consulting, "General Data Protection Regulation (GDPR)", 2020, https://gdpr-info.eu/art-2-gdpr/.

28 GDPR REQUIREMENTS

The data privacy impact assessment (DPIA)

The only truly secure system is one that is powered off, cast in a block of concrete and sealed in a lead-lined room with armed guards—and even then I have my doubts.

Professor Eugene Spafford

Privacy metrics and KPIs

Confidentiality, integrity, and availability are the foundation of any organization's security program. They function as goals and objectives for every cybersecurity program. Cybersecurity requirements require the measurement of these tenets of cybersecurity for each digital asset. *In the case of the privacy program, it is the same identical requirement, however, the scope is different. It is only for systems that process privacy data.*

Privacy metrics are confidentiality and integrity. Availability is not a privacy metric. Confidentiality is the ability to ensure that only authorized and approved users have access to the data. If this was not in place, it would violate a data subject's privacy. Integrity is the ability to ensure that the data is unaltered and is consistent, accurate, and trustworthy over its entire life cycle. As with confidentiality, if this is not in place it would violate a data subject's privacy. Availability is ensuring access is available to authorized users. If availability is not in place, it does not violate the data subject's rights.

Measuring privacy metrics is the only known defensible method to ensure that the level of integrity and confidentiality are at acceptable levels. This meets the requirements for article 5f. Article 5f states that the personal data shall be processed in a manner that ensures appropriate security of the personal data. This includes protections against unauthorized or unlawful processing, against accidental loss, (confidentiality) destruction or damage (integrity), by ensuring that appropriate technical or organizational measures are in place. The integrity and confidentiality of the data must be baselined to ensure this. Without measurements of confidentiality and integrity, this statement is useless. The DPIA provides these requirements metrics.

There are many digital asset attributes that influence the integrity and confidentiality of data. These must be measured and weighted in context to benchmark the inherent cyber risk scores that can be used in the Data Privacy Impact Assessment. The DPIA will identify areas for improvement to reduce the risk associated with integrity and confidentiality. It can also be used in conjunction with a security control

DOI: 10.4324/9781003052616-35

assessment like the NIST Cybersecurity Framework or ISO 27001 to show the effectiveness of the cybersecurity controls that are being used to protect the confidentiality and integrity of each digital asset that processes privacy data.

Data privacy impact assessment

What is a Data Privacy Impact Assessment? Some folks think a DPIA is being able to meet all the process requirements for all the GDPR articles. That is not accurate. If privacy were not related to digital assets, I would not even be writing this. Without metrics that measure the privacy of each digital asset that processes privacy data we have no foundation to stand on.

Understanding if the requirements for each article are in place provides a maturity assessment of the organization's privacy program and identifies gaps across specific requirements.

As an example, if there is no procedure in place to rectify the data subject's information, then that has to be put in place to satisfy the requirements for article 16. It does not impact the confidentiality or integrity. It looks at a specific data subject's rights to change incorrect data which requires a procedure. If there is not a rectification procedure in place, then there would be a finding of immature in relationship to that requirement to "of immature in" to "an immature finding in relationship to that requirement".

Now, let's look at a confidentiality example. It is required to have an access control policy and procedure in place. Access control policies define who and how access can be given to a digital asset. If there is no access control policy and procedure in place, then it violates confidentiality because anyone can access whatever they want. That is a privacy violation related to how well the cybersecurity program is in place. This is related to compliance with article 32.

Therefore, a DPIA is NOT how well each article is in place. It is how well the controls are in place to ensure integrity and confidentiality. This is just one reason why a lawyer is not even remotely qualified to be a DPO.

A DPIA has two sets of data to measure for each digital asset that process privacy data: confidentiality and integrity. First, the DPIA measures the asset behavioral characteristics that are being used to process privacy data. This is the inherent risk score that you learned about earlier. There is one difference; availability is not a concern with privacy.

As an example, let us look at a common system that processes privacy data: The Customer Relationship Management (CRM) system. All systems are made up of attributes that may be inherently riskier than others. If the CRM system has many interfaces, there are more points of ingress and egress (more points the cybercriminal can infiltrate) and that makes the risk of a confidentiality or integrity issue higher.

Likewise, if the CRM system has IoT technology in it, the risk of an integrity or confidentiality issue is higher because there are no access control mechanisms built into most IoT technologies. Without access control to stop unauthorized users from gaining access you have high integrity and confidentiality risk.

With user attributes: if the system is being used by vendors, and not employees, the privacy risk is higher. Vendors are not trusted, and employees are more trusted. There are many characteristics that define privacy metrics for integrity and confidentiality.

The second set of information to measure privacy impacts is related to the cybersecurity control assessment of the digital asset. The organization may pick any framework, unless regulations specify a specific one, to test the cybersecurity controls. The cybersecurity assessment is a set of cybersecurity control tests that mitigate confidentiality and integrity risk of each system by adding controls that decrease privacy risk. A cybersecurity assessment must be done for each system that processes privacy data to ensure that the controls are effective and protect the data sufficiently. We reviewed cybersecurity control assessments in Chapter 10.

The DPIA provides scores that need to be reviewed against privacy risk thresholds that are prescribed by the organization. These thresholds are used to determine if remediation actions need to be taken to align the level of confidentiality and integrity to GDPR standards for each system.

To start a DPIA, a digital asset inventory is needed of systems that process privacy data. This determines the scope of systems for the inherent risk assessment and control assessment.

Step 1: digital asset inventory

A digital asset inventory is the first step to understanding your data. It is critical to identify which systems are in scope for the DPIA. Digital asset inventories are needed not just for a DPIA, but for companies to be able to comply with all the data subject rights. Not knowing which systems process the privacy data is a recipe for failure. There are two methods to do a digital asset inventory. The first one is to ask questions of the system owners in each business unit to identify systems in scope. These include both on premise and cloud supported systems. This data can be captured in excel or an asset management system. Some questions are:

- Which systems process EU citizen data? Some obvious examples may include Customer Relationship Management (CRM), HR systems, payroll systems, clinical research systems, patient management systems, and the systems that feed data to them or are fed by them.
- Which technologies/devices are involved? (Cloud, USB, File Shares ...) The laws are starting to pivot to address innovative technologies. Innovative technologies typically have no security built into them. Technologies are the components of systems. They will make a system more inherently risky by their very nature. Systems that process privacy must have a level of assurance that they are protecting the privacy data.

Mapping systems and technologies/devices is the best place to start. Documenting the data and where it is processed defines the scope of any compliance intuitive. New policies and processes will need to be created or enhanced to protect the rights of the individual. The steps to perform a digital asset inventory are outlined in Chapter 22.

Step 2: people

The GDPR program is rigorous. Some of the starting requirements that are important are that businesses must plan to appoint or hire a Data Protection Officer (DPO) who will be accountable for all data privacy protections and activities. The role of the DPO is to think like a regulator preventing fines and penalties. Responsibilities include to ensure that the company or organization is correctly protecting the data subject's data according to current legislation. The DPO will manage the GDPR and Privacy Program, communicating to the Board on privacy issues and with the EU DPA, offering advice on privacy matters, monitoring GDPR and privacy compliance, liaising with the authorities, and addressing privacy risks. A GDPR training program is also required for all employees.

Step 3: policies and procedures

- Create and maintain a data privacy notice and provide notice at all points of data collection.
- Create and maintain policies and procedures to respond to requests from data subjects (i.e., access, update, portability, erasure, and opt out). See the previous chapter for a list of all policies and procedures required.
- Create and maintain a data breach or incident response plan, including a log to track incidents as well as protocols to notify regulators as well as impacted individuals.
- Ensure the use of standard contractual clauses and binding corporate rules to ensure compliant cross border data transfers.
- After creating a digital asset inventory, integrate data privacy principles for encryption, de-identification of PII, automated processing, restricted access, and record retention into information security programs.
- Influence marketing practices and technology projects with Privacy by Design principles.

Step 4: privacy risk modeling and scoring

As discussed earlier, a privacy impact assessment (PIA) is required to comply with the safeguards needed to meet Article 5's principles relating to processing of personal data. Article 5(f) states that the personal data shall be processed in a manner that ensures appropriate security of the personal data, including protection against unauthorized or unlawful processing and against accidental loss, destruction, or damage, using appropriate technical or organizational measures. This requires a baseline measurement of the integrity and confidentiality of each system that processes privacy data.

To meet this article there has to be a baseline measurement of confidentiality and integrity. Privacy risk scoring measures the confidentiality and integrity for each digital asset that processes or stores privacy data.

This means that GDPR requires benchmarking integrity and confidentiality and monitoring to ensure the confidentially and integrity of the digital assets are at and remain at acceptable tolerances.

Remember what confidentiality is—the ability to ensure that only authorized and approved users have access to the data. Remember that integrity is the ability to ensure that the data is unaltered and is consistent, accurate, and trustworthy over its entire life cycle. The digital asset has attributes that influence these two metrics.

Asset attributes that make the asset more likely to be breached increase risk and, therefore, decrease confidentiality and integrity. We will explore the attributes for confidentiality and integrity in detail and outline how to create an inherent cyber risk score for systems that process privacy data, aka privacy risk score. First, you define the information that you want to capture about the systems. This can be:

1 User Number Risk. Users are individuals who access systems. They use credentials (user id and password) to gain access. According to the 2016 State of Cybersecurity in Small and Medium-Sized Businesses, negligence by system users is the number-one cause of data breaches in small and mid-size businesses, accounting for 48% of all incidents. The more users, the higher the likelihood of a data breach.[1]
2 User Type Risk. Vendors are third parties that are associated with over 63% of data breaches. The more different type of users, the higher the likelihood. Users can be internal employees, customers, vendors, or a combination of these. External users increase likelihood more than internal users. When looking at likelihood, using combinations of users is important in your scoring.
3 Access Risk. Is the system located on a secure isolated segment, on a cloud service, on the corporate network, on a customer network or a vendor network? Internal isolated systems have less likelihood than cloud hosted systems. Vendor networks are more likely to have breach than a customer network, etc.
4 Cloud Deployment Model Risk. Is cloud technology Infrastructure as a service (Iaas), Platform as a service (Paas) or Software as a Service (Saas)? IaaS is less likely than a Paas offering and SaaS is less likely than a PaaS offering to be breached. The more the organization controls the less likely there will be a breach.

A study conducted by the Ponemon Institute entitled "Man In Cloud Attack," produced a report that concluded that, overall, data breaching was three times more likely to occur for businesses that utilize the cloud than those that don't.[2]

5 Cloud Service Model Risk. What category of cloud service? Private, hybrid, public? A public cloud is a type of cloud service in which the cloud service provider makes sharing resources available to the public via the internet and deployment is shared across multiple tenants (multitenant) via the internet. This increases the likelihood. Hybrid clouds are a solution that combines a private cloud with one or more public cloud services, using proprietary

software that enable communication between each distinct service. Private clouds are a computing model that offers a proprietary environment where there is no sharing of resources and the cloud is dedicated to a single business entity (single tenant).

6 Geo-Political Risk. Where your data centers are will influence likelihood. There are a number of categories that are analyzed from malware rates to cybersecurity-related legislation to define cyber geo-political risk. Many sources exist that provide relevant data to rank cyber risk. Denmark has been identified as the most cyber-secure country in the world, taking over from Japan in 2019. Algeria is the least cyber-secure country in the world with no cyber legislation except one vague privacy law in place. Some categories to score geo-political cyber likelihood are:[3]

— percentage of mobile malware infections,
— number of financial malware attacks,
— percent of computer malware,
— percentage of telnet attacks (by originating country),
— percentage of attacks by crypto miners,
— least prepared for cyber-attacks, and
— worst up-to-date legislation for cybersecurity.

7 Resource Risk. Does breaching or interrupting this system take sophisticated actors, such as nation state teams that were used in the Stuxnet attack or does attacking this system need only one guy in a dark room with a hoodie and Red Bull?

8 Technology Risk. Does this system use technology that has no administrative access capabilities? Typically, IoT is a culprit here. Scada technology requires detailed knowledge of how it works.

9 Vendor Support Risk. Does a third party support this system? Third parties are responsible for the majority of data breaches.

10 Vendor Rating Risk. Has a risk assessment been done on the third party? What are the results? Have they been deemed high, medium, or low risk?

11 Prior Breach Risk. How often are cybercriminals attempting to get access to this system and have they been successful? Was there an attempt, in what time frame, are hackers constantly trying to breach the system, was there already a breach?

12 Development Risk. Is there a deep knowledge of the system and infrastructure like with a home-grown system needs, some knowledge, general knowledge like with an off the shelf product? The skill levels influence confidentially, integrity, and accessibility.

13 Attack Proximity Risk. What is the proximity needed to breach the system? Direct physical access like with a switch, admin rights, user rights, protocols through a DMZ and firewall like with a Web application, or anonymous public access. The proximity to a breach influences confidentiality, integrity, and accessibility.

14 Breach Localization Risk. How localized are the effects of the breach? Isolated to the system, system and network, external network, all systems in the area, outside the system (supply chain), crown jewel. This is a very important metric. The reason Equifax was such a disaster is because it was not understood that the breach effects were not isolated when that system was left unpatched, rather the breach impacted the crown jewel assets. The localization influences confidentially, integrity, and accessibility.
15 Interface Risk. How many interfaces exist in the system? The more interfaces the higher the likelihood of a breach of confidentiality or integrity.
16 Interface Type Risk. What is the nature of the system interfaces? Intraorganizational, external interfaces with suppliers, interfaces with the general public.
17 Remote Access Risk. How are remote workers connecting? Via 2FA, via an encrypted channel, via a commercial takeover software.
18 Permission Risk. What is the current level of compartmental permissions in the systems? Full compartmental permissions by groups and roles, individual compartmental permissions per employee, basic compartmental permissions (manager and user), no compartmental permissions.
19 Patch Risk. What is the current update level of the system? Most recent version, up to three versions back, more than three versions back, versions that are no longer supported.
20 Patch Frequency Risk. What is the policy for update and security patches? Installing full updates at least once a quarter, installing security updates only once a quarter, critical security updates only at least once a quarter, no orderly updating process.
21 What is the physical security level of the system? Accessible to authorized individual only, Accessible to all employees of the organization, Accessible to external contractors, Accessible to all visitors of the organization.

Each attribute question is weighted to differentiate which attributes are most important to the organization. Each system provides the data and the DPIA baseline is created.

Data privacy impact assessment use cases

Identification of digital assets with the highest confidentiality and integrity risk

Nothing will ruin the GDPR program like a data breach. It is critical that the DPO and security team understand which digital assets have the highest amounts of privacy exposures. Each digital asset needs the risk exposure quantified and the privacy scored in terms of confidentiality and integrity. This will prioritize remediation work. We cover financial exposure calculations in Chapter 29.

Assets that have the higher risk scores for confidentiality and integrity should be investigated to spot trends across the digital assets and implement risk reduction techniques. As an example, if there are thousands of users on a system, the recommendation will be to review the off-boarding procedures to ensure all those users are authorized and to tighten up the process by doing it more frequently.

System Name	Business Unit	Privacy Risk Score	Financial Exposure
Guidewire Billing Center	Claims	.48	$4,205,112,000
Payment Center	Finance	.55	$1,061,302,000
Peoplesoft HR	HR	.26	$950,000,000
Salesforce	Sales	.60	$496,000,000
Trading System	Investment	.85	$596,000,000

Figure 28.1 Privacy Impact Assessment Example[4]

Risk registry

Each privacy risk needs to be identified and documented in the risk registry. The DPO should determine if the risk should be either accepted or prioritized to be fixed. The registry should align to project planning tasks for privacy risk reduction.

Risk Name	Risk Type	Control Maturity	Assessments/ Security Requirements
GDPR Article 20- Right to data portability- Data Portability Procedure not in place	GDPR Requirement	Non-existent	Access Control, Policies and Procedures
GDPR Article 32- Security of processing- Audit Schedule not in place	Requirement	Non-existent	Audit and Accountability
GDPR Article 7- Conditions for consent- Consent Procedure	GDPR Requirement – Rights of the Data Subject	Non-existent	Consent Procedure and Consent Form

Figure 28.2 Risk Registry Example[5]

Identification of gaps in the security controls

After the security control assessment is complete, the team needs to spot the trends in control gaps and prioritize the addition of more controls based on exposures and scores. Each control is weighted to differentiate controls that are most important to the organization.

GDPR Article	System(s)	Control Level	Control Score	Comments
17	All	Org	Non-existent	There is no right to erasure (right to be forgotten) procedure.
33	All	Org	Non-existent	There is no communication procedure in place for notification of a personal data breach to the supervisory authority.
35	All	Org	Non-existent	There is no Data Protection Impact Procedure in place.
38	All	Org	Non-existent	There is no DPO in place. There is no DPO job description in place.
39	All	Org	Non-existent	There is no DPO task description in place.

Figure 28.3 GDPR Gap Analysis Example[6]

Once gaps are identified, then the teams can prioritize any work that needs to be done to lower the risk and enhance the confidentiality and integrity.

GDPR is a complex set of requirements. Having an integrated approach that holistically works with the security team will provide a level of assurance for your firm and the regulators.

Notes

1. Ponemon Institute, "2016 State of cybersecurity in small & medium-sized businesses (SMB)", June 2016, https://www.keepersecurity.com/assets/pdf/The_2016_State_of_SMB_Cybersecurity_Research_by_Keeper_and_Ponemon.pdf.
2. American Journal of Information Science and Computer Engineering, "Security issues, threats and possible solutions in cloud computing", November 2, 2019, http://www.aiscience.org/journal/paperInfo/ajisce?paperId=4446.
3. Paul Bischoff, Comparitech, "Which countries have the worst (and best) cybersecurity?", March 3, 2020, https://www.comparitech.com/blog/vpn-privacy/cybersecurity-by-country/.
4. Maryellen Evans, Digital Asset Based Cyber Risk Algorithmic Engine, Integrated Cyber Risk Methodology and Automated Cyber Risk Management System. US 2020/0106801 Al, United States Patent and Trademark Office, April 2, 2020.
5. Maryellen Evans, Digital Asset Based Cyber Risk Algorithmic Engine, Integrated Cyber Risk Methodology and Automated Cyber Risk Management System. US 2020/0106801 Al, United States Patent and Trademark Office, April 2, 2020.
6. Maryellen Evans, Digital Asset Based Cyber Risk Algorithmic Engine, Integrated Cyber Risk Methodology and Automated Cyber Risk Management System. US 2020/0106801 Al, United States Patent and Trademark Office, April 2, 2020.

PART VIII

CYBERSECURITY RISK STRATEGY

29 CISO STRATEGIES

Cybersecurity is really problem solving. You know, there's a lot that you have to take in really quickly, there's a lot that you have to triage, and potentially, a lot of different ways to make sure that your customers are protected. So, it's really enabling people to see that they might have that skill set.

So, for example, it could be a healthcare person or somebody else who was a project manager or even a business systems analyst, right? Somebody who does those things over and over again. You can do that same job, you're just applying it to a different vertical, you're applying it to cybersecurity.

Aleta Jeffress, Chief Information & Digital Officer
for the City of Aurora, Colorado

CISO firings

CISOs are under fire. Literally and figuratively. Many CISOs are scapegoats and fall on their swords after a data breach. Securing a firm against cyber threats is not a one man or woman job. There are many circumstances leading up to a data breach which are not necessarily the fault of the CISO. However, most likely they are the first to go. Here are some of the most recent firings.

Capital One

In November 2019, the Wall Street Journal reported that Capital One had replaced the firm's CISO with the company's CIO while it looks for a full-time replacement.[1] Capital One announced an attacker took advantage of a misconfigured firewall and gained access to the personal information of over 100 million customers. The firm expects the incident to cost it between US$100 million and US$150 million on the short tail for customer notifications, credit monitoring, and legal support in 2019 alone.

Equifax

In 2017, Equifax lost the trust of a nation. An unpatched consumer complaint Web portal was compromised, and 143 million customer records were stolen. The U.S. House of Representatives Committee on Oversight and Government Reform said the incident was "entirely preventable," while U.S. Senate Permanent Subcommittee on Investigations accused the company of "neglect of cybersecurity."[2] The cost of

DOI: 10.4324/9781003052616-37

the incident is estimated to be US$1.35 billion in the short term and was already over US$5 billion in settled litigation in 2019 based on loss data from Advisen. The company paid US$700 million in fines to the Federal Trade Commission and others.

CSO Susan Mauldin and CIO David Webb "resigned" within one month after the breach. Equifax CEO Richard Smith "retired" in the wake of the breach. Susan Maudlin's lack of educational qualifications was a strong factor in the poor cybersecurity of Equifax. She had a degree in music.[3]

Poor patch management processes led to the attack being undetected for months. The company did not inform the public until compelled to by pressure from insiders. The company's poor handling of the incident was another large blemish on its reputation. Coupled with the fact that the firm admitted that the fund set up from the settlement would run out of money since too many people opted for cash rather than to trust the firm's free credit monitoring. As the icing on the cake, former Equifax CIO Jun Ying sold stock prior to the data breach and was convicted of insider trading and jailed for four months and fined US$55,000.[4]

Uber

In late 2017, Uber revealed that cybercriminals accessed Uber's private GitHub code repository. The firm's lack of basic cybersecurity (including a lack of multifactor authentication) allowed the hackers to use login credentials that were improperly stored to access the company's AWS Simple Storage Service (S3) instances that provides object storage through a Web service interface.[5]

Like Equifax, Uber failed to disclose the breach for over 12 months. CSO Joe Sullivan was fired due to his poor handling of the data breach that included being involved in a cover-up which took the form of ransom payment of over US$100,000 to the attackers.[6] This conspiracy was disguised as a bug bounty pay-out in exchange for deleting the data without releasing it. Uber's former security chief was charged with attempting to conceal from federal investigators a breach that over 57 million driver's and passenger's personal information was compromised. If convicted on both charges, Mr. Sullivan could face up to eight years in prison.[7]

Target

Target was the first to thrust the CISO and the Executives into the spotlight. Their eye-opening 3rd party attack resulted in a compromise to Target's payment systems and the theft of 40 million records in 2013.

CIO Beth Jacob "resigned" shortly after the attack at the company. The firm hired its first CISO, former GE CISO Brad Maiorino. CEO Gregg Steinhafel also "resigned" in the months following the breach.

JP Morgan

In 2015, CSO Jim Cummings and CISO Greg Rattray "resigned" in the wake of JPMorgan's 2014 data breach. Over 83 million accounts in the U.S. were stolen.

SONY

Amy Pascal was fired from SONY after the 2014 attack.

Facebook

Lack of corporate support led to Alex Stamos, Facebook's CSO, leaving the firm after three years due to a disagreement about the company's handling of the Cambridge Analytica scandal. Stamos favored a more open and direct response in disclosing what the company knew. He later told MSNBC that it was a "big mistake" that the company wasn't more forthcoming about the severity of the incident.[8]

The moral of the story is that the CISO is taking the brunt of blame for poor cybersecurity, regardless of if the Board, and Executives are providing enough budget. It is time to change the beat.

Digital cyber risk management

Making the business case for the cybersecurity program

According to Gartner, "By 2020, 60 percent of digital businesses will suffer major service failures due to the inability of the IT security team to manage digital risk in new technology and use cases."[9] Translation: the CISO must navigate these waters to show how they are protecting the digital assets and where they need financial support from the Executives. CISOs are at a disadvantage when it comes to budgeting. Most companies use a percentage of IT spends to carve out a cybersecurity budget. This is not logical or effective. Cybersecurity budgets should be based on risk reduction and return on investments as we will learn in this chapter.

Financial exposure assessment

CISOs have to explain the value of initiatives to Executives. Having an understanding of which digital assets need to be secured rigorously and prioritized in terms of monitoring or mitigation will go a long way to demonstrate the business value of cybersecurity programs and initiatives. The CISO has to put on a business hat. Chapters 22 and 23 provided the foundation to calculate financial exposures and cyber risk.

CISOs will be asked by Executives and the board about current cybersecurity news events and what the risk is? Let's take the recent SolarWinds breach. Austin, Texas-based SolarWinds disclosed in December that a compromise of its Orion software update servers earlier this year has resulted in malicious code being pushed to almost 18,000 customers that use its Orion platform. Most U.S. federal agencies and Fortune 500 firms use Orion to monitor the health of their IT networks and firewalls.[10] Is SolarWinds Orion in your digital asset inventory and what is the financial exposures? Orion by its nature is a very high-risk digital asset. It is an infrastructure monitoring and management platform; *therefore, the entire digital asset infrastructure is in scope for the financial exposures since it touches every digital asset.*

Understanding the types of financial losses related to digital assets is key not only in a time of crisis to plan mitigation and defensive initiatives against any possible advanced persistent threat (APT) that will impact their network but to understand what is most important about the digital asset. In the case of Orion, it was the security of SolarWinds development environment, was their vulnerability scans, pen tests, and security software development lifecycle in place? It seems not since the cybercriminal was able to insert malware into their software update to their customers. This is the worst cyber event since the NSA hacking tools were stolen in 2019. It is imperative that the CISO know what he or she is protecting and how.

When using a digital asset approach, the important information the board needs to support the CISO will be understood in context and budgets will be adjusted. If the Board has this data and they ignore it then they are open to shareholder actions, and a host of other legal mechanisms.

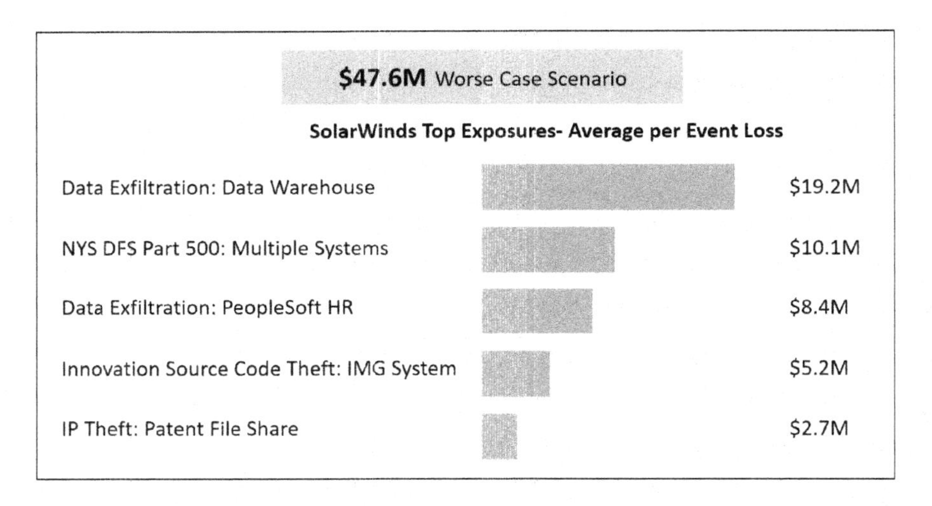

Figure 29.1 SolarWinds Financial Exposure Example

Inherent cyber risk assessment

A digital asset will be inherently more likely to be breached or interrupted based on the user and behavioral characteristics. The inherent cyber risk assessment identifies areas where the risk can be lowered. This is where IT and cybersecurity come together to understand the infrastructure and the issues the firm faces based on the asset and user behavior.

The CISO can use the inherent cyber risk scores to tighten up areas that are increasing the likelihood of a cyber event. These include identifying areas and pinpointing issues related to access control. As an example, seeing that there are thousands of users on a system would lead to investigating the off-boarding procedures to ensure that they are followed.

Cybersecurity assessment

Cybersecurity assessments allow a look at the control effectiveness. Doing a CIS Top 20 assessment will provide a good baseline of control value. This can put your feet on solid ground to determine control maturity. If you have a cyber maturity that is in the top 1/3 the firm would be mature enough for a deeper dive using a larger framework like ISO 27001 or the NIST Cybersecurity Framework. If the cyber maturity is low, then most likely there are some foundational issues that need attention right away and using a lighter framework would be a better approach.

The cybersecurity control assessment will identify control gaps in the program. Looking across the infrastructure can show trends and be correlated to the systems with the highest financial cyber risk exposure as a means to prioritize control strengthening.

Looking across the entire infrastructure and comparing the control effectiveness allows the CISO to identify trends in control weaknesses. As an example, if multifactor authentication (MFA) is in place for 80% of the systems, the CISO will need to look at the 20% that do not have MFA in place. Are their financial exposures high, are they connected to a crown jewel asset, what is it telling you from a risk perspective? The context has to be understood in order to allow a decision to either accept the risk of a weak control or take steps to strengthen it.

Integration of residual risk data from cyber tools

The board needs to understand the business impacts of cyber events. Many cybersecurity tools map to the technical components of the digital assets, such as IP addresses, but do not show which digital asset the issue is associated with. The digital asset methodology allows CISOs to integrate data from cyber tools, which allow the CISO to be able to prioritize remediation work and provide meaningful metrics to the board, ask for proper budget or let the chips fall on the head of the Board.

This is very meaningful when the regulators are looking at the cybersecurity program. IP addresses and vulnerabilities must be understood in context. Let's consider pen testing data. Many CISOs run the scans and the report is provided to the CIO. The report will show a Level 5 vulnerability with a particular IP address. Is that IP address for your internal phone system or is that IP address for your money transfer system? That's what management must know. What needs to happen here is to take the testing report and turn it into something that makes business sense.

An effective CISO will not just "run the scan" and turn over a report to the CISO. A good CISO should be able to lead the effort to address and deliver on this. The CISO should be capable of not only presenting to the CIO but also, if authorized, and to the Board.

Most CISOs I interact with, even those light on experience and training, would take a more involved, proactive approach if they had this type of data.

Unfortunately, what most CISOs do is they take the report, and they present it to the CIO with the number of vulnerabilities at Levels 5, 4, 3, 2, and 1. That is not in the right context. There is no business translation as to what it means. The better approach is for the CISO to link the vulnerabilities to the digital assets they are associated to. Treating the crown jewel systems less importantly than the business crucial systems is not the goal in cybersecurity. The goal is risk reduction. This translates back to budget and prioritization of remediation work.

Worst yet, the I.T. team has no context for cyber risk. They want to show a small number of vulnerabilities. It's not about how many vulnerabilities you have. It's what systems, especially critical systems, are being impacted. That's what the CISO has to explain to the board and Executives when providing useful information.

A third-party open testing team is at a serious disadvantage. The third-party does not know your digital assets. Correlating back this data to the digital assets is very valuable to the CISO. Firms are required to classify the digital assets. It is a requirement in every framework that is out there. CISOs must work with third parties to ensure the most critical systems are prioritized. They must be prioritized and then patched.

If the report is not understood in context, then the I.T. person will put the vulnerabilities into the patch schedule to be fixed. The next cycle of patching could be every quarter. Imagine your top business unit owner getting a report with level 5 vulnerabilities that were not patched to his or her critical systems. They would be more than upset to see these issues were not fixed immediately. Bottom line: the CISO, is not working for I.T., he or she is working for the firm.

Small medium enterprise disadvantage

Depending on the maturity of the firm, the CISO will have different cyber tools available for identification, protection, and detection of cyber events. As we discussed in Chapters 12 and 14, companies with lower maturities have limited cyber budget and tools. Considering over 98% of businesses are small medium enterprises (less than 100 workers) this puts most companies at a serious disadvantage.[11]

If we explore the CISO firings mentioned earlier, we will notice a laissez faire cybersecurity culture. This attitude comes from the top down. There has been a line drawn between the business and the cybersecurity that continues to plague CISOs. The lack of understanding of the meaningful metrics from cyber risk management handicaps CISOs who see cyber only as a technical challenge.

Digital asset methods integrate privacy, compliance, audit, and other teams with business process automation. The major benefit of implementing automated processes is that they eliminate many of the most time-consuming, repetitive tasks to free up resource time for more important undertakings.

Prioritization of resources

CISOs are faced with a shortage of talent and budget. This makes prioritization of resources a top concern. The Board and Executives want to understand when a cyber event happens which assets are impacted, what the financial losses will be, what caused the problem and how do we fix it, so it won't happen again.

For CISOs, prioritizing remediation work and initiatives can be based on digital asset scores correlated to gaps in the programs. Fixing one misconfiguration will increase cyber resiliency. However, knowing that specific vulnerabilities are hitting several digital assets and knowing which assets the vulnerabilities are connected with is critical in prioritizing cyber risk reduction. As an example, if you have a vulnerability that is associated with Oracle MySQL and you have 200 Oracle MySQL databases being used, then you need to know which assets that vulnerability impacts, and their exposures and to understand the business context needed to prioritize the work.

Perhaps privacy is your biggest concern. A view of the systems that process privacy data, their exposures and the gaps in the controls can be used to reduce cyber risk and increase confidentiality and integrity.

ROI and tool road mapping

Every CISO is asked what the Return on Investment (ROI) will be for the cybersecurity tool that they want to buy. Vendors struggle to articulate the value. That is not because it is not engineered well, it is because they don't understand the financial exposures that the firm has and how their tool reduces risk. Cyber tools identify, detect, protect, respond, or recover to cyber events.

ROI is based on cost and benefit analysis. The benefit must be understood in context. As an example, the benefit of an IoT credentialing tool is it will reduce data exfiltration risk for systems that use IoT. That means the CISO has to know which systems use IoT technology and relate the exposures to it. It does not reduce risk to a system that is not using IoT.

Likewise, a DDoS attack on critical Web application servers can be detected and damage prevented in many cases. As an example, AWS Shield is a managed Distributed Denial of Service (DDoS) protection service that safeguards applications running on AWS. Therefore, if you are running a high percentage in the cloud on AWS, this tool will reduce cyber risk related to DDoS attacks. It would have no benefit for on premise cyber exposure.

I go back time and time again to context. Context, context, context. Don't look for a silver bullet, look to understand what you are actually doing. You can't measure anything in cybersecurity unless you can map it to the digital asset and the type of financial exposure the tool mitigates. CISOs can make the business case using digital asset ROI analysis.

System Name	Business Unit	Security Tool	Quant Metric	Quant Value ($)	Risk Reduction (%)	Risk Reduction ($)	Tool Cost	ROI (%)
Always Care	Human Resources	Verizon IoT Security Credentialing	IoT Exposure	$30,951,500	5.00%	$1,547,500	$165,000	838%

Figure 29.2 Return on Investment Analysis

In addition, cyber tool road mapping can be done in the context of maximum risk reduction. Comparative analysis can make decision making easier and more transparent to those that hold the purse strings.

System Name	Business Unit	Security Tool	Quant Metric	Quant Value ($)	Risk Reduction (%)	Risk Reduction ($)	Tool Cost	ROI (%)
Always Care	Human Resources	IoT Security Credentialing	IoT Exposure	$30,951,500	5.00%	$1,547,500	$165,000	838%
Fiserv	Main Office	PCI Assessment	PCI Loss	$500,000	30%	$150,000	$27,500	445%
Salesforce	Main Office	Data Loss Prevention (DLP)	Data Exfiltration	$206,000,000	60%	123,600,000	$80,000	154,400%
Salesforce	Main Office	DDoS Shield	Business Interruption DoS	$136,900	15%	20,400	$7,000	194%

Figure 29.3 Cyber Tool Road Mapping

Cyber budgeting

Until now, there has been no way to correlate back risk reduction to the cyber spend. The digital asset approach allows companies to completely rethink how they can tie their cyber goals to their budgeting. Using 5–7% of IT spend cannot be correlated back to any business benefit.

All business units do cost based budgeting. They look at fixed and variable costs across capital and operational expenditures. Why not in cybersecurity? This type of approach can allow the organization to charge back the business units to protect their assets.

The business units own the assets. They are the ones who developed or purchased them. Why shouldn't they pay to protect them? If you buy a car or a house, you pay to maintain it and protect it. Using the digital asset approach, you can understand which tools protect either one, several or all the digital assets, and set up budgeting that makes fiscal sense.

Fixed costs are at both the operational level and the capital level. Operational fixed costs are people. This should include your cybersecurity team, such as the CISO, SOC analysts, security architects, etc. Operational fixed costs should be a shared resource across the enterprise. Security team costs can be shared across each business unit based on either the number of digital assets, the type of digital asset or other approaches that tie the business to the use of the cybersecurity team resources.

Capital costs would include the cybersecurity tools. Cybersecurity tools are licensed either by user, Central Processing Unit (CPU), annual subscriptions or open source under General Public Use (GPU). These are easy to understand. Each tool has a contract from the vendor with an end user licensing agreement (EULA). The key here is to understand what the tool protects the organization or specific asset types from. It is data exfiltration, business interruption, regulatory fines or a combination. Some tools will protect the entire organization, others only specific systems.

Variable costs have to do with the amount of unexpected remediation work that needs to be done to respond to an incident, threat, or vulnerability. There may be a tool that has to be purchased to help with this and resources that need to be deployed to fix the issue. Estimating variable costs can be done by taking an annual average over a one or two-year period and then updating it each quarter to get more data confidence based on these activities and re-estimate them for the next quarter.

Resource management

Resources are scarce. We have 2 million cybersecurity job openings in the U.S. alone. Using a digital asset strategy that prioritizes crown jewels to identify where the largest gaps are in the exposures, scores and controls is an effective approach to drive the budgeting, and resource prioritization. Cyber risk management platforms use this approach by integrating risk, compliance, privacy, resourcing, and budgeting functions. This integration allows for the pivoting of tasks and people when unexpected issues occur that need immediate attention. Cyber is dynamic and requires digital asset data to understand the impact of threats, vulnerabilities, and incidents that will happen unexpectedly all the time.

Notes

1. AnnaMaria Andriotis, The Wall Street Journal, "Capital One senior security officer being moved to new role", November 7, 2019, https://www.wsj.com/articles/capital-one-senior-security-officer-being-moved-to-new-role-11573144068.
2. Harper Neidig, The Hill, "Senate panel accuses Equifax of neglecting cybersecurity ahead of 2017 breach", March 7, 2019, https://thehill.com/policy/technology/433040-senate-panel-accuses-equifax-of-neglecting-cybersecurity-ahead-of-2017.
3. Brett Arends, Market Watch, "Opinion: Equifax hired a music major as Chief Security Officer and she has just retired", September 15, 2017, https://www.marketwatch.com/story/equifax-ceo-hired-a-music-major-as-the-companys-chief-security-officer-2017-09-15.
4. Dark Reading, "Former Equifax CIO sentenced to prison for insider trading", June 27, 2019, https://www.darkreading.com/attacks-breaches/former-equifax-cio-sentenced-to-prison-for-insider-trading/d/d-id/1335078#:~:text=Jun%20Ying%20is%20the%20second,supervised%20release%20for%20insider%20trading.
5. AWS, "Amazon Route 53 FAQs", 2021, https://aws.amazon.com/route53/faqs/#:~:text=Route%2053%20effectively%20connects%20user,to%20infrastructure%20outside%20of%20AWS.
6. Nicole Pelroth, Mike Issac, The New York Times, "Inside Uber's $100,000 payment to a hacker, and the fallout", January 12, 2018, https://www.nytimes.com/2018/01/12/technology/uber-hacker-payment-100000.html.
7. Kate Conger, The New York Times, "Former Uber Security Chief charged with concealing a hack", August 20, 2020, https://www.nytimes.com/2020/08/20/technology/joe-sullivan-uber-charged-hack.html.
8. Sissi Cao, Observer, "Ex-Facebook Security Chief Alex Stamos speaks up after bombshell NYT investigation", November 19, 2018, https://observer.com/2018/11/alex-stamos-facebook-security-chief-nyt-investigation/.

9. Gartner, "Gartner says by 2020, 60 percent of digital business will suffer major service failures due to the inability of IT security teams to manage digital risk", June 6, 2016, https://www.gartner.com/en/newsroom/press-releases/2016-06-06-gartner-says-by-2020-60-percent-of-digital-businesses-will-suffer-major-service-failures-due-to-the-inability-of-it-security-teams-to-manage-digital-risk.
10. Brian Krebs, Krebs on Security, "Malicious domain in SolarWinds hack turned into 'Killswitch'", December 20, 2020, https://krebsonsecurity.com/2020/12/malicious-domain-in-solarwinds-hack-turned-into-killswitch/.
11. Small Business & Entrepreneur Council, "Facts & data on small business and Entrepreneurship", 2018, https://sbecouncil.org/about-us/facts-and-data/#:~:text=Firms%20with%20fewer%20than%20100%20workers%20accounted%20for%2098.2%20percent.&text=Firms%20with%20fewer%20than%2020,workers%20increases%20to%2098.0%20percent.

30 CYBER IN THE BOARDROOM

Board oversight of cybersecurity is no longer a nice to have; it is a requirement. Investors, governments and regulators are demanding that boards demonstrate diligence and oversight.

Yoav Intrator, Former CEO JP Morgan Chase Israel

Target—the breach that brought it into the boardroom

In 2013, Target's data breach thrust the board front and center in the cyber battle. The CEO was fired and 7 out of 10 board members were ousted due to the data breach. This got the attention of companies and Boards around the world. Boards concluded that they had to understand cyber from a business perspective. They either needed to put an expert on the board to explain cybersecurity to them or they needed to understand it better themselves. Putting an expert on the board is not a scalable option.

Organizations need cyber accountability to be successful. The CEO, Board and Senior Executives must be able to defend the decisions that were made prior to the cyber event. Did money get spent on the right things? How much cyber risk was reduced? Which exposures? Does the Board understand the key components of the cyber program, and can they defend them to the key stakeholders? Without cyber risk management there is no accountability. Passing the buck and saying, "I did what the CISO told me to do," will not fly with stakeholders.

Let us take an example of a nondefensible incident and what should have been done. On March 8, 2017, the US CERT issued a notice to patch a critical vulnerability (CVE-2017-5638) in the Apache Struts application. Apache Struts is an open-source Web application framework for developing Java Enterprise Edition (EE) Web applications. In layman's terms, it is software that is used to create Web applications. The unpatched vulnerability failed to validate a user's credentials (user id and password) before letting it access sensitive internal functions.

Equifax's patch management policy required that patching occur within a 48-hour period. On March 15, the security team ran a vulnerability scan and found no vulnerabilities in the versions of Apache Struts. On May 13, cybercriminals gained access to sensitive data on the Equifax credit disputes portal due to the vulnerable unpatched version of Apache Struts. From mid-May to the end of July, Equifax's security team did not detect any illegal access.

DOI: 10.4324/9781003052616-38

On July 30, the attack was detected, and the disputes portal was taken offline and the next day the CEO was informed of the cyber incident. On August 2nd, Equifax implemented its incident response procedures, which included retaining a law firm and security forensic consultants. On September 4, it was determined that the personal information of 143 million people had been breached.

On September 7 Equifax's bungles reached the public. The company directed potential victims to a separate domain—equifaxsecurity2017.com—instead of simply building pages to handle the breach off of its main, trusted website, equifax.com. Equifax asked people to trust the security of the site, and to submit the last six digits of their Social Security number as a way of checking whether their information had been potentially compromised in the breach.[1]

I typed in Donald Trump 55-5555 and I was told my data was compromised. This showed that a sloppy breach response was in place.

Equifax says it learned about the mega-breach at the end of July, however they took roughly six weeks to disclose it. During that time, the company could have conceivably planned and executed a much more robust and reassuring way to help consumers.

On September 25, the CEO "stepped down," citing the breach as the primary reason. The CEO presented congressional testimony on October 4 and in December of 2018. The House Oversight Committee delivered its final report which concluded that a "lack of accountability and no clear lines of authority in Equifax's IT management structure existed, leading to an execution gap between IT policy development and operation."[2]

There are several indefensible positions here. These include:

- A crown jewel strategy was not in place.
- Vulnerability scans were not effective.
- The patch management policy was ignored.
- The extent of the risk was not understood.
- The breach notification was not only mismanaged, but it was also egregious.

The ability to have a defensible cyber story must be front and foremost in the mind of the CEO. This means that there must be a sound strategy based on meaningful metrics. The firm should have had effective vulnerability scanning in place for crown jewel assets, enforced their patch management policy, and had an effective strategy for communicating the breach to consumers.

Stuck in cyber jargon

A key issue, we face is the inability of the CISO to communicate properly with the board. When a CISO walks into the boardroom with a list of 300 vulnerabilities and announces, "This is my cyber program." the board is mystified. This is not a cyber program. It is a list of 300 vulnerabilities. And the board does not understand any of the cyber jargon of these vulnerabilities, such as man-in-the-middle attacks, SQL injections, or denial-of-service (DoS) attacks.

Cyber risk is an enterprise risk. It impacts business activities at all levels and can amplify other significant risks, including reputational, operational, legal, and regulatory risk. The organization's ability to successfully mitigate cyber risk requires mindful oversight by the Board of Directors. Organizational oversight is required by compliance regulations for decades now. Senior-level executives have to understand how dynamic cybersecurity actually is and demand the right information to make effective discussions about the cybersecurity program.

In a National Association of Corporate Directors (NACD) survey, less than 15% of directors said they were "very satisfied" with the quality of cybersecurity information they receive from management.[3] This chapter provides guidelines for effective board-level communication about cybersecurity matters.

What KPIs and the metrics can be digested and used by the board? The board understands business language which includes financial calculations, KPIs, ROIs, and other business-related information.

What does that mean? It means that they must have meaningful data that they can leverage for budgeting and cyber risk mitigation programs. The CISO has to speak to the Board in the language of cyber risk. One thing we see over and over again is vendors that label threats, vulnerabilities, and incidents as risk. They are not risk. Cyber risk consists of financial exposures related to data loss, business interruption, and regulatory fines. It also relates to the impact and likelihood of a digital asset throughout the entire cybersecurity lifecycle. Cyber Risk management is now front and center for board and CISOs. It is imperative that the cyber risk function speak to the board in a digestible way.

The role of a board of directors is to provide strategic oversight for the organization and hold management accountable for performance. Management is responsible for execution, including identifying, prioritizing, and managing cyber risks. While the specific information your board needs will vary depending upon the organization's industry, regulatory requirements, operating activities, geographic footprint, and risk profile, all boards are looking to management to translate technical, tactical details about cybersecurity into business terms: exposures, likelihood metrics, opportunities for risk reduction, and strategic implications that impact turnover, litigation, and budgeting.[4] We will explore four imperative areas that board members need to understand about cybersecurity.

The four-board cyber imperatives

There are four major initiatives/areas that the board needs to consider in their oversight strategy. These include:

- Protect the Digital Assets
- Third Party Cyber Risk Management
- Cyber Insurance
- M&A Cyber Strategy

First and foremost, the Board must protect the Digital Assets. There are many details that are required to do this, and we will examine them. We will focus on key takeaways with supporting data for Boards that provide insight on the condition of the organization's cybersecurity program and the business implications of cyber risks. Boards do not want large amounts of technical detail or operational, compliance-oriented metrics. Data is needed to show how effective the firm is at preventing data loss, business interruption, and regulatory fines.

The Board should be ensuring that the firm has an adequate Cyber Insurance Limit and set of Sub-limits. Most firms are woefully underinsured. Cyber insurance is part of the corporate strategy for cybersecurity that includes people, process tools, and insurance. Many companies are requiring that their vendors have cyber insurance.

New regulations are forcing Boards to guarantee that the company is managing third-party Cyber Risk effectively. Since 2018, four new laws that require vendor cyber risk management programs have gone into effect creating a further level of board oversight to be in place.

Boards also have to have a sound M&A strategy in regard to cybersecurity.

How can the CISO be successful with the board? Cyber roles have been evolving over the past decade. We first saw the CISO position come to life in 2011. This role focused solely on operational and tactical cybersecurity requirements. It traditionally has been someone with strong network background and technical skills. However, the ways that the board needs cyber related data is not technical. How is the role of the CISO changing? In some cases, we are seeing a new role called the Chief Digital Asset Officer (CDAOs) who acts to bridge the gap between the Board and a technical operationally focused CISO.

CDAOs focus on reporting, policies, and the cyber risk management functions. The operational CISO is focused on the day-to-day cyber operations and all of the cybersecurity initiatives that are being planned or in flight.

How the organization is structured is equally important in its cyber success. When there is a CISO reporting to a CIO we usually see trouble on the horizon. The CIO and CISO typically have diametrically opposing agendas. The CISO wants to slow things down by adding more security controls, assessments, and auditing. The CIO wants to speed things up and do the innovative work. They need to have things up 24/7. Having a CISO report to a CIO is not usually the most optimal approach to balance cybersecurity risk and innovation. One of the reasons for their often-contentious relationship in modern times is due to the fact that most difficult and visible initiatives and decisions are either security-driven or have security as a primary factor. Today, innovation almost always wins this battle over cybersecurity.

Digital asset exposures, risk, and cyber maturity review

We have been learning about the digital assets, their financial exposures, cyber risk, how they are holistically related to privacy, compliance, and security. In another five years over 95% of a business will be digital. We are already at over 85% today.

Financial exposures

There are four types of digital assets. A digital asset can be a system. It is the technologies that are the components of a system. It is also the business processes that run on those systems taking inputs and transforming them into outputs for analysis or reporting and it is also the type of data that is processed or stored in those systems and technologies. When a cybercriminal attacks an organization, they attack the digital assets. They steal the data and cause data exfiltration and regulatory fines. They may also interrupt the business processes through ransomware, or a DoS attack, causing revenue loss and possible regulatory fines as well.

Digital asset protection is the key to cyber resilience. Boards need to be able to measure the financial exposures and understand which digital assets have the most financial exposures. This provides the Board a defensible method to prioritize cyber risk reduction programs and to monitor digital assets that are the riskiest.

Inherent cyber risk

Each digital asset has a set of financial exposures and inherent cyber risk which is aligned to how likely it is to be breached. Inherent cyber risk is based on the characteristics of the digital asset (number of interfaces, number of users, etc.). High likelihood in key areas can be reduced using different risk reduction mechanisms.

Cybersecurity control (mitigating risk) assessments

Cybersecurity controls are used to mitigate the risk to digital assets. To properly protect digital assets, Boards need to provide proper budget which will be used to access, monitor, and strengthen the cybersecurity controls to reduce cyber risk to acceptable levels. Controls are codified in categories, such as access, encryption, etc. There are hundreds of controls that should be in place to achieve compliance in most firms for each digital asset. Ensuring proper mitigating controls are in place also lowers regulatory exposure.

Cybersecurity maturity

Cybersecurity has to be understood in context of maturity and resilience. Large companies may have every cyber tool under the sun, and smaller companies may have only basic off the shelf ones with little or no customization. Understanding the firm's cybersecurity maturity as described in Chapter 12 is an excellent starting point to benchmark the current maturity and to set cyber maturity and resiliency goals. The maturity analysis looks across the cybersecurity program to benchmark people, process, and tools and acts as a means to increase maturity in these key areas.

We suggest doing an evaluation of your company's organization maturity benchmark your firm's cyber maturity. It will provide valuable information about where you align to your peers and act as a starting point to set goals for people, process, and tool roadmaps.

Cybersecurity tools and residual cyber risk

Companies use cybersecurity tools to identify, protect, detect, respond, and recover from cyber events. Companies that are more mature can bake in cyber risk data from their tools to see how effective the tools are, calculate their ROI and measure their cyber risk reduction.

Now, let us explore key use cases, metrics and KPIs related to financial exposures, inherent cyber risk scores, security assessments, cyber tools, and the protection of the digital assets.

Protect the digital assets

In order to protect the digital assets, the board will be interested in the following:

- Big News Cyber Events: What do they mean to us?
- What are our most valuable digital assets? Which ones are crown jewels? How much financial exposure do they have?
- How much financial exposure do we have related to each exposure type: data breaches, ransomware attacks, business interruption from a DoS attack and regulatory penalties and fines? Which business units have the most exposures?
- How much hidden exposure do we have that is not covered by our cyber insurance policy?
- How does each digital asset compare in terms of the likelihood related to their cyber risk?
- How effective are our cybersecurity controls?
- Which digital assets are above their risk thresholds? By how much and why?
- What is our cyber tool roadmap? What are the ROIs related to our tools?
- What cybersecurity initiatives should we prioritize to lower risk?
- What is our current cyber resiliency and how do we increase it?
- Do we have enough cyber budget? If not, how much should we spend to achieve optimal resiliency? Do we have enough qualified resources?

Big news cyber events and what do they mean to us: SolarWinds example

This is a good example. When a board member reads this, they are going to panic. The CISO must be able to explain what the news is saying in layman's terms and outline the step-by-step plan.

In December of 2020, SolarWinds acknowledged its systems "experienced a highly sophisticated, manual supply chain attack on its SolarWinds Orion[5] Platform software builds for versions 2019.4 HF 5 through 2020.2.1, released between March 2020 and June 2020."[6]

Reuters broke the news about SolarWinds stating that it is believed that Russian hackers had been monitoring internal email traffic at the US Treasury and Commerce departments. Reuters reports the attackers were able to secretly alter the software updates released by SolarWinds for its Orion platform.[7]

The Cybersecurity and Infrastructure Security Agency (CISA) Computer Emergency Readiness Team (CERT), part of the Department of Homeland Security (DHS), issued Emergency Directive 21-01[8] on December 13, 2020 regarding this issue. "Treat all hosts monitored by the SolarWinds Orion monitoring software as compromised by threat actors and assume that further persistence mechanisms have been deployed," CISA advised.[9]

Microsoft, in their official blog post "Microsoft on the Issues," wrote that attackers added malicious code to software updates provided by SolarWinds for Orion users. "This results in the attacker gaining a foothold in the network, which the attacker can use to gain elevated credentials," Microsoft wrote.[10] This allows the hackers to use highly privileged accounts where they can add their own credentials to existing applications and services.

SolarWinds says it has over 300,000 customers, including 85% of the US Fortune 500, all ten of the top ten US telecommunications companies, all five branches of the US military, all of the top US accounting firms, the Pentagon, the State Department, the National Security Agency, the Department of Justice, and The White House.[11]

Now that you have had the bejesus scared out of you what steps do you take?

Step 1: Examine the Digital Asset Inventory to see if you have SolarWinds Orion. Using digital asset cyber risk analysis can visualize the exposures and the scope of the pending investigation.

Step 2: If no, assure the Board that you are not in scope for this issue.

Step 3: If yes, determine which systems are using SolarWinds.

Step 4: Disable all access to SolarWinds Platforms.

Step 5: Advise the board on which systems use SolarWinds and that they have been immediately disabled. Advise the board on the potential financial exposures.

Step 6: Start a forensics examination to see if there is a cyber event and what damage has been done. SolarWinds advised to exempt its products from antivirus scans and group policy object restrictions due to an issue that it may not work properly unless their file directories are exempted from antivirus scans and group policy object restrictions. A review of firewall policies and procedures and file directories needs to be accessed.

Step 7: CISO report of the cyber event to legal and the board.

Step 8: Legal Consultation with outside cyber attorneys on communication, potential lawsuits, and other associated needs.

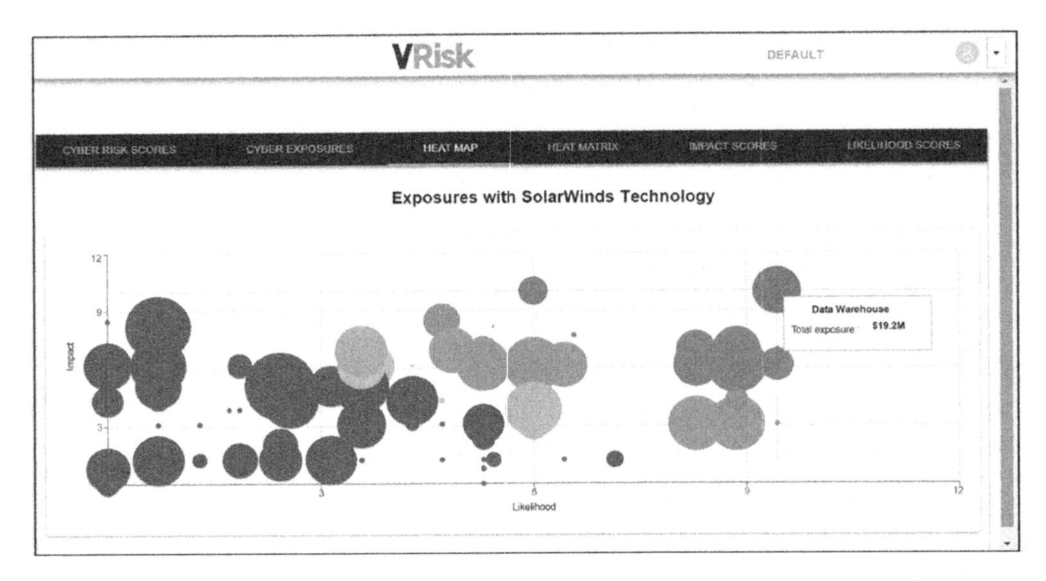

Image 30.1 Scope of SolarWinds Exposures and Investigation[12]

Set up a crown jewel strategy

Protecting the digital assets cannot be done in one fell swoop. Where do we start? Boards need to know which assets are the most valuable. Use a crown jewel strategy to start. The crown jewels are your most valuable assets. If there was a cyber-attack and a crown jewel were to be involved, it could make the company unsustainable. Most boards disagree on which digital assets are their crown jewels. When you get five board members into the room and ask them which are the top five digital assets, you typically are going to get 25 different. Digital asset financial exposure calculations easily solve this dilemma. The most important assets are the ones with the most financial exposures. Once you know this you can use it to prioritize the amount of protection, and monitoring needed accordingly.

Crown Jewel System Name	Cyber Risk Score	Financial Exposure
Guidewire Billing Center	.48	$ 4,205,112,100
Payment Center	.55	Lorem Ipsum $ 1,061,302,900
Salesforce	.60	$ 596,000,000
SAP Financials	.00	$ 401,960,200
Trading System	.51	$ 400,000,000
Exceed	.61	$ 255,133,300

Figure 30.1 Crown Jewel Strategy[13]

Understand which digital assets have the most exposure

Understanding which assets have the most exposures is critical. Data Exfiltration Exposures relate back to insertion of malware. This can be from many issues, including mis-configuration of systems or clicking on phishing emails. A cyber-criminal sends a phishing email, and their firm has malware inserted and the data is stolen. This usually needs to be reported to regulatory agencies.

There are a number of different things that a firm can do to try and avoid data exfiltration. These include cybersecurity awareness training, and Advanced Threat Prevention (ATP) technologies, among others.

DoS happens when Web application servers are flooded with traffic. Developing a distributed denial-of-service (DDoS) prevention plan based on regular security assessments is step one. When a DDoS attack hits, companies must be prepared to act. There is no time to think about the best steps to take. Key elements include a system checklist, forming a response team, and defining notification and escalation procedures. Make sure that the contact list includes internal and external contacts that should be informed about the attack.

Advanced intrusion prevention and threat management systems combine firewalls, VPN, anti-spam, content filtering, load balancing, and other layers of DDoS defense techniques to enable constant and consistent network protection to prevent a DDoS attack.

Understand what an outage means in financial terms. How much revenue will be lost? Are there SLAs in place that will have impacts? What about reputational impacts? DoS and DDoS are system by system metrics. In these attacks the cybercriminal is not going to shut down the entire infrastructure, they are going to select certain targets.

Ransomware is a type of malware that is typically delivered via phishing emails. Ransomware uses encryption to lock out the on-premise systems. The attack vector is usually coming in through a phishing email, however the payload is different than in data exfiltration. They are not going to steal your data; they are going to encrypt your infrastructure. This requires a ransomware strategy which we will discuss in detail in Chapter 33 when we look at a cost benefit analysis related to cyber insurance. Some important things to consider here is the level of confidence in your DR plans and the ransomware sublimit in your cyber insurance policy.

Regulatory fines are based on the type of data processed and/or geography, and/or industry and/or technology. In terms of privacy and regulatory requirements, fines will be related to data breaches and business interruptions based on type of data processed and geography. Many companies are now basing their privacy program requirements on the GDPR obligations.

Californians approved the California Privacy Rights Act (CPRA) to create a new consumer data privacy agency. In 2018, California adopted the California Consumer Privacy Act (CCPA) that went into effect in January 2020. Enforcement of CCPA began this past July.[14] The CPRA toughens privacy requirements and aligns California more with the GDPR.

This information provides valuable context for the board and helps them to work with the CISO to protect what is most important in a logical manner.

Discover lethal hidden exposures that are above your cyber insurance limit

Hidden exposures are exposures you do not expect to find. I see hidden exposures in the billions of dollars. Hidden exposures are due to the fact that some business units have decided they need an enormous number of records in their database. Every company should have a data retention and disposal policy that defines the lifecycle of data, when and how it is disposed or archived. Some business units ignore this key cybersecurity policy.

Let's look at a real life, real time example. First American Title Insurance Company has been charged by the NY State Department of Financial Services for exposing customer PII. This data includes bank account numbers, mortgage and tax records, Social Security Numbers, wire transaction receipts, and drivers' license images. First American Title Insurance Company is one of the largest providers of title insurance and in 2019, First American wrote more than 50,000 policies in New York State.

DFS has charged First American with multiple failures related to the handling of the data exposure of sensitive consumer information.[15] DFS alleges that First American:

- Failed to follow its cybersecurity policies.
- Neglected to conduct a security assessment and risk review of the misconfigured systems that lead to the data breach.
- Failed to understand the severity of the vulnerability associated with the system.
- Failed to investigate the vulnerability within the timeframe prescribed by their internal cybersecurity policies.

The data breach was discovered by an internal penetration test in December of 2018. First American grossly underestimated the seriousness of the vulnerability; and failed to follow the recommendations of its internal cybersecurity team to conduct further investigation into the vulnerability.

According to the charges, First American violated six provisions of the 23 NYCRR. Any violation of this law carries penalties of up to US$1,000 per violation. Each record of Nonpublic Information is counted as a separate violation and carries up to US$1,000 in penalties per record.[16]

If you consider the 50,000 records in New York State alone in 2019 you are looking at US$50 million in fines. However, the news is that First American Financial Corporation accidentally exposed 885 million records, most of them relating to mortgage deals going back 16 years.[17] This means that the total exposure is US$885 billion.

Fixing this is relatively simple. Archiving the excess records offline will remove them from the line of sight of the cybercriminal. The key is understanding the exposure is knowing how many records you need for business and ensuring that that exposure is not higher than your aggregate cyber limit. Boards want to avoid being the next First American.

System Name	Data Exfiltration	Record Count	Cyber Insurance Record Count	Excess Records
Smart Communications	$ 20M	100K	2M	0
Payment Center	$ 400M	2M	2M	0
Talent Nest	$ 10M	50K	2M	0
FastPASS	$ 40M	2.5M	2M	500K
Justifacts	$ 80M	4M	2M	2M

Figure 30.2 Hidden Exposures[18]

Level of digital asset likelihood and impact: inherent cyber risk

How does the impact and likelihood that a digital asset will be compromised compare to each other? Which ones are more inherently risky? To understand this, we look at the internet risk score that was based on the user and behavioral characteristics of each asset. We covered how to create this score in Chapter 23.

As an example, a system that uses IoT technology has more risk than one that does not. A system that has more users has a higher likelihood of a data breach. Inherent cyber risk scores can point out to the firm which assets need attention and can have their inherent risk reduced.

As an example, if there are over 5000 users on a system, management should access the effectiveness of the offboarding procedures and the authorizations for the system. Unnecessary users should be disabled. This will reduce the inherent cyber risk. Boards want to know which assets need more protection and why.

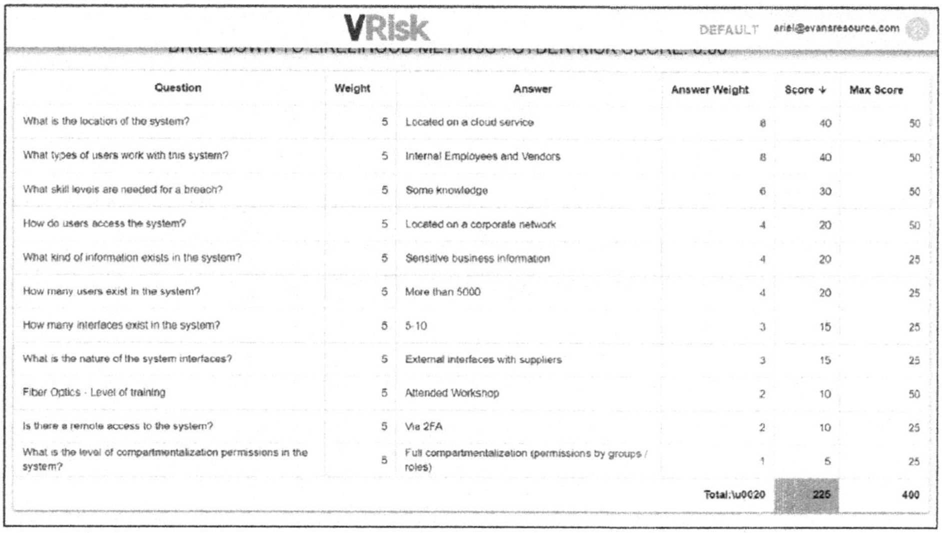

VRisk DEFAULT ariel@evansresource.com

Question	Weight	Answer	Answer Weight	Score ↓	Max Score
What is the location of the system?	5	Located on a cloud service	8	40	50
What types of users work with this system?	5	Internal Employees and Vendors	8	40	50
What skill levels are needed for a breach?	5	Some knowledge	6	30	50
How do users access the system?	5	Located on a corporate network	4	20	50
What kind of information exists in the system?	5	Sensitive business information	4	20	25
How many users exist in the system?	5	More than 5000	4	20	25
How many interfaces exist in the system?	5	5-10	3	15	25
What is the nature of the system interfaces?	5	External interfaces with suppliers	3	15	25
Fiber Optics - Level of training	5	Attended Workshop	2	10	50
Is there a remote access to the system?	5	Via 2FA	2	10	25
What is the level of compartmentalization permissions in the system?	5	Full compartmentalization (permissions by groups / roles)	1	5	25
			Total:\u0020	225	400

Image 30.2 Inherent Cyber Risk[19]

Cybersecurity control effectiveness: gaps in the cybersecurity program

When we compare the digital asset control assessments (mistakenly many times called risk assessments), it allows us to find gaps in the cybersecurity program controls. Control assessments look at the effectiveness of controls and we can analyze across the infrastructure patterns of gaps that can be strengthened to reduce cyber risk.

As an example, Multifactor Authentication (MFA) is required and the firm sees that 80% of the applications have MFA in place and 20% do not. The next question is which digital assets are in that 20%? Are they crown jewels, systems with high financial exposures or inherent cyber risk scores? Action can be taken to tighten controls that reduce the cyber risk in a logical prioritized fashion.

The gaps that can be identified across the controls include access risk, encryption risk, regulatory risk, reputation risk, and a host of others. Boards will want to know how effective the cyber controls are.

Cyber risk thresholds

Thresholds can be set based on the classification of the assets. Crown jewels would have the lowest thresholds. We can set a baseline cyber resilience and increase it by adding more controls or making them more effective.

Crown jewel assets will have the lowest thresholds. Management should identify any assets that are above the cyber risk threshold and look for trends across the thresholds.

Boards will want to know which assets are above tolerance and why.

Name	Description	Threshold
Business Critical	A business-critical system is a system whose failure may result in very high costs for the business using that system. An example of a business-critical system is the customer accounting system in a bank.	2.75
Business Crucial	A business crucial system is a system whose failure is not critical but has significant impact.	3
CIU	Classified Information	2.75
Crown Jewel	Crown jewel assets refer to a company's most prized or valuable assets in terms of its profitability and future prospects. A failure of this type of system results in the company going out of business. Examples include: Safety-Critical Systems - A system whose failure may result in injury, loss of life or serious environmental damage. An example of a safety-critical system is a control system for a chemical manufacturing plant. Mission-Critical Systems - A system whose failure may result in the failure of some goal-directed activity. An example of a mission-critical system is a navigational system for a spacecraft. Transactional Systems - A system whose failure may result in the failure of some goal-directed activity. An example is a transactional system is one that processes privacy data when the company sells trust. (i.e. Equifax)	2
Target Asset	M&A Target Asset	3

Figure 30.3 Cyber Risk Thresholds[20]

Cyber resiliency: the dynamic interplay of cyber

Cyber Resiliency is a measure of an entity's ability to continuously deliver the intended outcome despite adverse cyber events. It can be used to benchmark and define organizations goals in terms of cybersecurity. Exposures, inherent and residual risk scores are used to define resiliency.

We look at inherent risk, effectiveness of controls and residual risk. Each metric uses a weighting to and a formula. We covered this in detail in the cyber risk management module.

Resiliency goals need to be set for each asset classification. The first goal would be to reduce the exposures so that they are covered by the cyber insurance policy. The second goal is to work with the security controls and program for the crown jewel assets to lower the inherent risk first. After that, put more controls on second that align to maximum risk reduction and to manage more effectively any vulnerabilities, incidents, and threats that are directed at the crown jewel assets. Boards want to know which cyber events are impacting the company.

System	Threshold	Inherent Risk Score	Security Assessment Score	Residual Risk Score	Residual Risk Desc	Recommended Action
Trading System	2	2.3	1.5	4	SQL Injection Threat	Sanitize the SQL query
Peoplesoft HR	3	2	1	1	No threats, vulnerabilities or incidents detected	None
Guidewire ClaimsCenter	3	3	2.5	2.5	No threats, vulnerabilities or incidents detected	None
Payroll System	3	2.2	1.75	4	Zero Day Attack	Patch the application
Customer Portal	2	1.6	1	3.5	MITM Attack - Deprecated Chipher	Replace with an approved Chiper

Figure 30.4 Cyber Resiliency[21]

Cybersecurity tools roadmap and ROI

Cybersecurity tools reduce risk and have a return on investment related to the exposures that they reduce. Some tools will reduce risk at an organizational level, others at a systems level. It is critical to understand the context of the type of risk reduction the tool provides. Using a cost benefit analysis will not only provide a ROI but can be used as a cyber tool roadmap for budgeting the risk reduction programs.

Cyber budgeting

Cyber budgeting today is a percent of IT spend. IT spend has nothing to do with cybersecurity risk. Everyone knows that most cyber budgets are much too low. But the question is how low?

Until now, there has been no way to correlate back risk reduction to the cyber spend. The digital asset approach allows companies to completely rethink how they can tie their cyber goals to their budgeting.

We covered this approach in Chapter 29. Tying the budgeting to the board level from the CISO is a proactive approach that will allow the most use of scarce resources. We have two million job openings in the United States alone for skilled cybersecurity professionals. Using the crown jewel strategy to identify where the largest gaps are in the exposures, scores, and controls will drive the budgeting and resource prioritization. This approach allows for the pivoting of tasks and people when unexpected issues occur that need immediate attention. Cyber is dynamic and requires new data to understand the impact of threats, vulnerabilities, and incidents that will happen unexpectedly all the time.

Item	Charge Type	Amount	Comments
Licenses	Fixed Capital	$329,000	Cybersecurity Tool Licenses for DLP, SIEM and VMS
Cyber Team	Fixed Operational	$700,000	CISO, Sec Ops, Blue Team
Cybersecurity Findings	Variable Operational	$300,000	Average consulting costs for forensics and red team
Cyber Tools	Variable Capital	$50,000	Additional non-budgeted cyber tools
Total	All	$1,379,000	Annual budget needs

Figure 30.5 Cyber Budgeting[22]

Cyber insurance for boards

Most companies are drastically underinsured. In interactions and networking with other CISOs, cyber insurance is rarely a top agenda item. I think there are many reasons for that. Not just companies recognizing the need and role of cyber insurance, but also the insurers maturing their cyber insurance coverage model. This needs to change.

Cyber insurance is part of an effective cyber strategy. It is used to transfer risk. However, we have seen that most companies are woefully underinsured by 200 to 4000%. Digital asset exposures can be directly related back to how a cyber insurance company will pay a claim. Boards will be asking:

- Do we have enough cyber insurance? How much aggregate limit do we need?
- Are our sublimits on ransomware, business interruption and regulatory loss enough?
- What is our ransomware strategy?

Aggregate limit

The cyber insurance aggregate limit is the maximum amount of cyber insurance that can be claimed in a single year regardless of the attack vector. A data breach will most likely be the largest amount of exposure.

We compare the maximum exposure from data exfiltration with the sublimits to determine the highest amount. This will be the amount of aggregate limit your firm needs.

Dependent versus nondependent sublimits

Dependent and Nondependent types relate to where the cyber incident is taking place. Companies have on premise and cloud services that provide them infrastructure. Dependent is the risk in the cloud and nondependent is on-premise risk. These are two distinct and separate infrastructures that are mutually exclusive in terms of a cyber event.

Nondependent business interruption sublimit

Business interruption sublimit is related to a Denial of Service (DoS) attack on premise. This is when a system is not available due to a cybercriminal flooding the Web application server and shutting it down. Your revenue processing is stopped. You cannot process any transactions. That is what causes the financial damage. We consider the Recovery Time Objectives (RTOs) which indicates the maximum time the system can be down. We measure how much revenue should have been produced in that time and have the financial exposure of that system.

Dependent business interruption sublimit

Business interruption sublimit is related to a DoS attack for your systems on a cloud service. This is when a system is not available due to a cybercriminal flooding the Web application server and shutting it down. Your revenue processing is stopped. You cannot process any transactions. That is what causes the financial damage. We consider the RTOs which indicates the maximum time the system can be down. We measure how much revenue should have been produced in that time and have the financial exposure of that system.

Nondependent ransomware sublimit

Nondependent cyber extortion or ransomware impacts the entire on-premise corporate infrastructure. The key here is to ascertain the Ransomware Recovery Time Objective (RRTO). This is the amount of time from encryption to decryption and relates to the amount of time you must either pay the ransom or restore your entire infrastructure. There are many factors that influence it, such as reputational damage where people start to find out you have been ransomed. This can result in a loss of customers and cause more financial harm. It is not reportable unless you are a company that is regulated by the NYS FDS or other similar regulation, which requires you report operational cyber incidents. We take into consideration only the applications that are on-premise and not in the cloud. When you are being ransomed it isn't in the cloud systems that are impacted, it only impacts those that are on-premise.

Nondependent ransomware sublimit

Nondependent cyber extortion or ransomware impacts the cloud infrastructure. The key here is to ascertain the ransomware RTO. This is the amount of time from encryption to decryption and relates to the amount of time you must either pay the ransom or restore your entire infrastructure. There are many factors that influence it, such as reputational damage where people start to find out you've been ransomed. This can result in a loss of customers and cause you more financial harm. It is not reportable unless you are a company that is regulated by the NYS FDS, which requires you report operational cyber incidents. We also must know the percentage of applications that are on premise and not in the cloud. When you are being ransomed it isn't in the cloud systems that are impacted, it only impacts those that are on premise.

Regulatory sublimits

Regulatory fines may be paid for in some policies. This includes privacy, credit card, and other types of data that have been breached. Sublimits relate to the amount of money you may be fined. It is different for different regulations. HIPAA is based on the number of records, GDPR is based on annual revenue and/or 20 million EUR, whichever is higher, PCI is specific fine per incident and depending on what level merchant you are there are additional fines. Sublimit types may include:

- Privacy.
- GDPR.
- PCI.
- HIPAA.

Once the limits and sublimits are calculated the board can make the decision on how much to buy.

Limit	Amount	Comments
Aggregate	$400,000,000	Maximum Record Loss Costs
Dependent Ransomware Sublimit	$10,000,000	Ransomware Loss
Non- Dependent Ransomware Sublimit	$2,000,000	3rd Party Ransomware Loss
Dependent Business Interruption Sublimit	$1,500,000	DDoS Loss
Non-Dependent Business Interruption Sublimit	$1,000,000	3rd Party DDoS Loss
PCI Sublimit	$1,500,000	PCI Fines
CCPA Sublimit	$4,000,000	CCPA Fines
HIPAA Sublimit	$100,000,000	HIPAA Fines
GDPR Sublimit	$300,000,000	GDPR Fines

Figure 30.6 Cyber Insurance[23]

Ransomware strategy

Companies must have a ransomware strategy before they are hit with a ransomware attack. There is no time to find a cyber attorney, cyber forensics team and do the calculations needed to understand what the next best step is.

This strategy consists of a cost benefit analysis. The question is should you pay the ransom or should you restore? Here's a recipe to follow.

Step 1—What is your restoration readiness. Can you restore? First, you need to know if you have DR plans in place for the key systems. Second, you need to have tested them. Third, you need to have tested them recently and have a high level of confidence in the ability to restore. You must calculate the cost to restore all your systems.

As an example of what not to do: the city of Baltimore opted not to pay a ransom of US$87,000 in bitcoin. They spent US$18 million restoring their systems over a several month period. Obviously, they were not ready to restore.

Step 2—Do you have a relationship with an outside cyber attorney and forensics team on speed dial? If you are going to negotiate the ransom, then you have to have an experienced attorney spearhead this. It cannot be your General Counsel. You also will need to have an experienced ransomware forensics team that can decrypt the infrastructure and check that the criminals did not leave gifts behind for you. Many times they leave Random Access Trojans (RATs) so they can reransom you or steal your data. Many times, your insurance company will prescribe a panel of which firms you can use on their approved list.

Step 3—Calculating your trigger point. What is your Ransomware RTO? When do you have to be back up and running? Here you need to consider the revenue and reputational impacts. We think most companies need to be up within 48–72 hours maximum.

The Ransomware Trigger amount is equal to the RRTO * Revenue per hour * % of applications on premise.

If the cost of restoration is greater than the Ransomware Trigger Amount by 25% then I would opt to pay the ransom.

If the cost of restoration is less than the Ransomware Trigger Amount by 25% and you have high confidence in your ability to restore, then I would opt to restore.

Disclaimer- this is not legal advice, and we are not responsible for any damages you may incur. This topic is covered in length in Chapter 33.

Vendor cyber risk for boards

Vendors are responsible for 63% of reported breaches. A vendor cyber risk program is now required by many regulations. These include, but are not limited to, the PCI, GDPR, NYS DFS Part 500, and the insurance data security act.

Not all vendors are the same. However, most companies treat all vendors the same. Different vendors have different cyber risks depending on what they do with your digital assets.

- What relationships do we have with vendors associated to our digital assets?
- How much financial exposure and cyber risk do we have with these third-parties? How can we reduce it?
- How effective are the vendors' cyber controls?
- How can we continuously monitor a risky vendor?

Vendor relationships

First the firm needs to know what kind of vendor they have a contract with. Are they a service provider, system vendor, technology vendor, or cloud service provider? They can be a combination of different types. Each vendor type will need a different set of cybersecurity controls and information for your firm to evaluate their cyber risk properly. Contract reviews are important to understand what was agreed to from a cyber perspective. Ensure that there is language that addresses how a data breach will be handled, communicated, and remediated.

Vendor exposures

Vendor exposures are a very important metric to understand. If your firm is working with a cloud service provider, most likely your firm is sending them your data. How much financial exposure do you have with these vendors? How are they protecting your data? This relates back to how much dependent cyber insurance each vendor should carry.

What is the vendor's data retention and disposal policy? Does it meet your standards? How and what is triggering the disposal of your data? Vendors that are processing many records should be paid more attention. Vendor exposures will help a firm to prioritize the monitoring of vendors.

Vendor cybersecurity control assessments

Vendors must provide the initial information that is required, and the firm needs to check and verify that the vendor's cybersecurity controls are in place and how effective they are. However, this data must be collected in context. A Cloud Service Provider (CSP) is very different than a management consulting firm. You have to know which information is appropriate to which type of vendor and which vendor type(s) each one is.

This topic is so important that it will have its own textbook in 2021. Vendor risk management will be covered in *Vendor Cyber Risk Management—The Next Frontier in Cyber Resilience* in 2021.

Continuous monitoring

The US Department of Defense (DoD) has moved to a trust and verify model. They are requiring the use of 3rd party independent auditors to verify vendor data. This is a trend I see coming for all companies. Monitoring vendors will become an urgent requirement in the next few years. Having audit functionality in place will save time, money, and decrease vendor cyber risk.

We need to distinguish monitoring by means of periodic direct audits versus monitoring by using the services of third-party risk rating services which utilize various tools to monitor for vulnerabilities and associated risks. Audits and risk rating services are limited but both need to be considered whenever feasible.

The vendor risk management program should compare exposures and cyber risk scores and look for gaps. Vendors with high exposures and scores should be investigated into areas where exposures and risk can be lowered on a regular basis.

M&A cyber risk for boards

Many companies grow through M&A. Most are using simple due diligence checklists to look at the cybersecurity aspects of multimillion-dollar transactions. This does not provide any data on exposures. Cyber M&A exposures can be incorporated into M&A discussions in a short period of time to aid the acquirer in understanding that cyber risk they are signing up for. Using digital asset exposures and risk scoring boards can ask:

- We are planning to sell the company—how does our cyber resiliency impact our acquisition price?
- We are planning to buy a company—what financial exposure will we inherit? How effective is their cyber program?

Notes

1. Lily Hay Newman, Wired, "All the ways Equifax epically bungled its breach response", September 24, 2017, https://www.wired.com/story/equifax-breach-response/.
2. Kacy Zurkus, Info Security, "House report says Equifax breach was preventable", December 11, 2018, https://www.infosecurity-magazine.com/news/house-report-says-equifax-breach/.
3. National Cybersecurity Alliance, "Communicating with the board about cybersecurity: Making the business case", 2020, https://staysafeonline.org/wp-content/uploads/2017/09/Communicating-with-the-Board-about-Cybersecurity-Making-the-Business-Case.pdf.
4. National Cybersecurity Alliance, "Communicating with the board about cybersecurity: Making the business case", 2020, https://staysafeonline.org/wp-content/uploads/2017/09/Communicating-with-the-Board-about-Cybersecurity-Making-the-Business-Case.pdf.
5. SolarWinds, "How Orion platform products work", 2020, https://documentation.solarwinds.com/en/Success_Center/orionplatform/Content/Core-How-Orion-Works-sw1625.htm.
6. SolarWinds, "SolarWinds security advisory", December 31, 2020, https://www.solarwinds.com/securityadvisory.
7. Christopher Bing, Reuters, "Suspected Russian hackers spied on U.S. Treasury emails – sources", December 13, 2020, https://www.reuters.com/article/BigStory12/idUSKBN28N0PG.
8. United States Department of Homeland Security, "Mitigate SolarWinds Orion code compromise", December 13, 2020, https://cyber.dhs.gov/ed/21-01/.
9. United States Department of Homeland Security, "Mitigate SolarWinds Orion code compromise", December 13, 2020, https://cyber.dhs.gov/ed/21-01/.
10. Advice for incident responders on recovery from systemic .... https://www.microsoft.com/security/blog/2020/12/21/advice-for-incident-responders-on-recovery-from-systemic-identity-compromises/.
11. Brian Krebs, Krebs on Security, "U.S. Treasury, Commerce Depts. hacked through SolarWinds compromise", December 20, 2020, https://krebsonsecurity.com/2020/12/u-s-treasury-commerce-depts-hacked-through-solarwinds-compromise/.

12. Maryellen Evans, Digital Asset Based Cyber Risk Algorithmic Engine, Integrated Cyber Risk Methodology and Automated Cyber Risk Management System. US 2020/0106801 Al, United States Patent and Trademark Office, April 2, 2020.
13. Maryellen Evans, Digital Asset Based Cyber Risk Algorithmic Engine, Integrated Cyber Risk Methodology and Automated Cyber Risk Management System. US 2020/0106801 Al, United States Patent and Trademark Office, April 2, 2020.
14. Marla Korolav, CSO, "CPRA explained: New California privacy law ramps up restrictions on data use", December 21, 2020, https://www.csoonline.com/article/3601123/cpra-explained-new-california-privacy-law-ramps-up-restrictions-on-data-use.html?utm_source=Adestra&utm_medium=email&utm_content=Title%3A%20CPRA%20explained%3A%20New%20California%20privacy%20law%20ramps%20up%20restrictions%20on%20data%20use&utm_campaign=IDG%27s%20Top%20Enterprise%20Stories&utm_term=Editorial%20-%20IDG%27s%20Top%20Enterprise%20Stories&utm_date=20201224165328&huid=f0efb8c5-f767-4e35-b85f-3c6787847553.
15. SecurityMagazine,"NewYorkDFSchargestitleinsurerwithcybersecurityviolation",July28, 2020, https://www.securitymagazine.com/articles/92916-new-york-dfs-charges-title-insurer-with-cybersecurity-violation.
16. Security Magazine, "New York DFS charges title insurer with cybersecurity violation", July 28, 2020, https://www.securitymagazine.com/articles/92916-new-york-dfs-charges-title-insurer-with-cybersecurity-violation.
17. Chris Brook, Digital Guardian, "SEC looking into first American breach", September 25, 2020, https://digitalguardian.com/blog/sec-looking-first-american-breach#:~:text=When%20news%20broke%20earlier%20this,big%20corporation%20playing%20fast%20and.
18. Maryellen Evans, Digital Asset Based Cyber Risk Algorithmic Engine, Integrated Cyber Risk Methodology and Automated Cyber Risk Management System. US 2020/0106801 Al, United States Patent and Trademark Office, April 2, 2020.
19. Maryellen Evans, Digital Asset Based Cyber Risk Algorithmic Engine, Integrated Cyber Risk Methodology and Automated Cyber Risk Management System. US 2020/0106801 Al, United States Patent and Trademark Office, April 2, 2020.
20. Maryellen Evans, Digital Asset Based Cyber Risk Algorithmic Engine, Integrated Cyber Risk Methodology and Automated Cyber Risk Management System. US 2020/0106801 Al, United States Patent and Trademark Office, April 2, 2020.
21. Maryellen Evans, Digital Asset Based Cyber Risk Algorithmic Engine, Integrated Cyber Risk Methodology and Automated Cyber Risk Management System. US 2020/0106801 Al, United States Patent and Trademark Office, April 2, 2020.
22. Maryellen Evans, Digital Asset Based Cyber Risk Algorithmic Engine, Integrated Cyber Risk Methodology and Automated Cyber Risk Management System. US 2020/0106801 Al, United States Patent and Trademark Office, April 2, 2020.
23. Maryellen Evans, Digital Asset Based Cyber Risk Algorithmic Engine, Integrated Cyber Risk Methodology and Automated Cyber Risk Management System. US 2020/0106801 Al, United States Patent and Trademark Office, April 2, 2020.

PART IX
CYBERSECURITY INSURANCE

31 CYBER INSURANCE OVERVIEW

Digital connectedness has made the business world more of a true ecosystem with shared vulnerabilities and risks across entities. Business leaders have an obligation to consider cyber risk in this context and manage it from the top down.

Josh Stabiner, CISO at General Atlantic

What is cyber insurance?

Cyber insurance is a specialty line of insurance product intended to protect against risks that are related to internet connectivity and attacks against the digital assets. Cyber risks are typically excluded from traditional commercial general liability policies. Coverage provided by cyber insurance policies may include first-party and third-party coverages. First-party coverages are those that impact the company who is the data owner and may include insurance against losses from data exfiltration, cyber extortion, destruction, hacking, and business interruption from denial-of-service attacks. Third-party coverages focus on liability coverage which will indemnify companies for losses to others. Examples include data exfiltration or business interruption due to poor cyber safeguards, errors and omissions, and defamation. Benefits include regular cybersecurity auditing, post-incident public relations, forensic expenses, and criminal reward funds.

Cyber insurance is designed to protect a company from five cyber-related risks. These are usually defined as events associated with network security, privacy, interruption to your business, media liability, and errors and omissions. However, these terms confuse most companies and cyber professionals. These terms are used in ways that do not relate directly to how cyber professionals use them. We need a rethink to align the language to address the cyber market accordingly. The current context is not useful.

In university, this is taught as the following:

Network security: inadequate network security compromises confidentiality, availability, and integrity of data and is not the event to be insured. The actual loss event can be data exfiltration which is based on a data breach that may be due to a network security event. Other events that can be tied to network security are business interruption events. Both data exfiltration and business interruption can cause regulatory fines for privacy, credit card, or healthcare data violations. The loss for

DOI: 10.4324/9781003052616-40

data exfiltration is related to records stolen and/or fines levied. For business interruption, it is related to revenue interruption.

Privacy: privacy data is violated by confidentiality or integrity issues from either a network event, misconfigured system, or other types of vectors. It results in data exfiltration and regulatory fines.

Interruption to business is due to a ransomware or DoS event. The loss is related to revenue that cannot be processed.

Media liability is related to when media is corrupted or stolen.

Errors and omissions are for mistakes. A misconfigured system is a mistake so this is confusing.

This chapter will demystify the misaligned cyber insurance industry terms and get everyone to understand it from the proper context.

Brokers, carriers, and reinsurance companies

There are three types of firms in cyber insurance: brokers, carriers, and reinsurance firms. An insurance broker and an insurance agent differ based on who each represents. While a broker represents the insurance buyer, an agent represents one or more insurance companies. The insurance carrier is the company that holds your insurance policy and will pay the claim. An insurance carrier is not the same as an insurance agent. It is the company to which your insurance payments are sent and the company that pays if your firm files a covered claim.

Here are the top ten cyber insurance carriers to date.

Reinsurance companies are middle-men in the insurance triangle. They are an

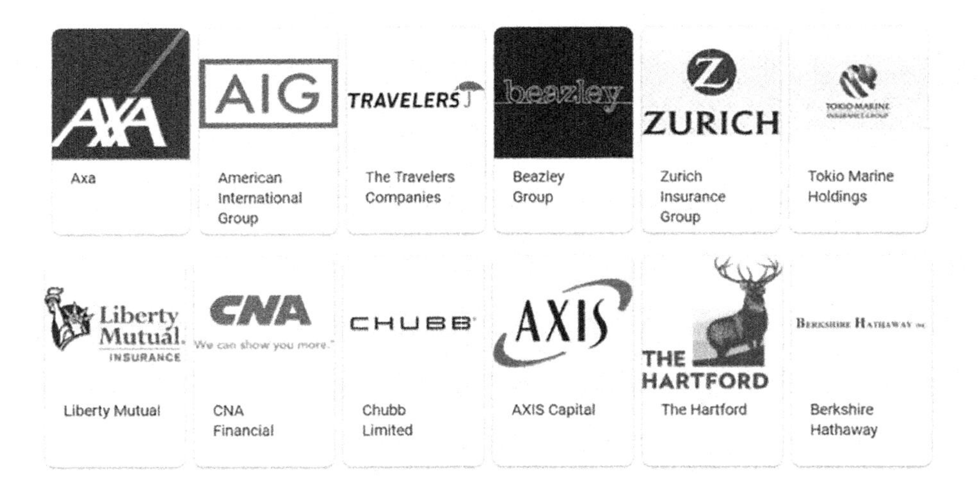

Figure 31.1 Top Cyber Insurance Carriers

insurance company which purchases policies from other insurance companies to diversify the risk in the event of a major claim.

A brief history of cyber insurance

In early 2000, the first cyber liability policies were developed for the Lloyd's of London market. The policy was spearheaded by a set of attorneys working closely with Lloyd's underwriter and several brokers. The policy created provided the third-party coverage and business interruption coverage for a limited set of cyber-related events.[3]

This initial policy focused only on business interruption. It was followed by coverage for regulatory exposures and the costs associated with a data breach, including credit monitoring costs, public relations costs, and the cost of restoring data. Afterward, third-party coverages for technology errors and omissions started to be sold to system integrators and developers. American International Group (AIG) and Chubb were the first carriers to enter the market. Today, there are more than 90 carriers in the cyber insurance market.

The highest written policy to date is US$750 million and is only affordable to the colossus. Most larger companies with US$50 billion in revenue are carrying around US$150 million in cyber coverage on the average. According to my research, we have seen companies underinsured by 200–4000%.[4] The issue is the total lack of understanding by the cyber insurance brokers and the firms of the actual financial exposures related to cyber events.

Allied Market Research published a report about the size of the global cyber insurance market. It estimated it to be US$4.85 billion in 2018 and predicted that it would increase to US$28.60 billion by 2026, registering a CAGR of 24.9% from 2019 to 2026.[5]

Components of a cyber insurance policy

An annual aggregate limit is the maximum amount an insurer carrier will pay for covered losses in a given single year.

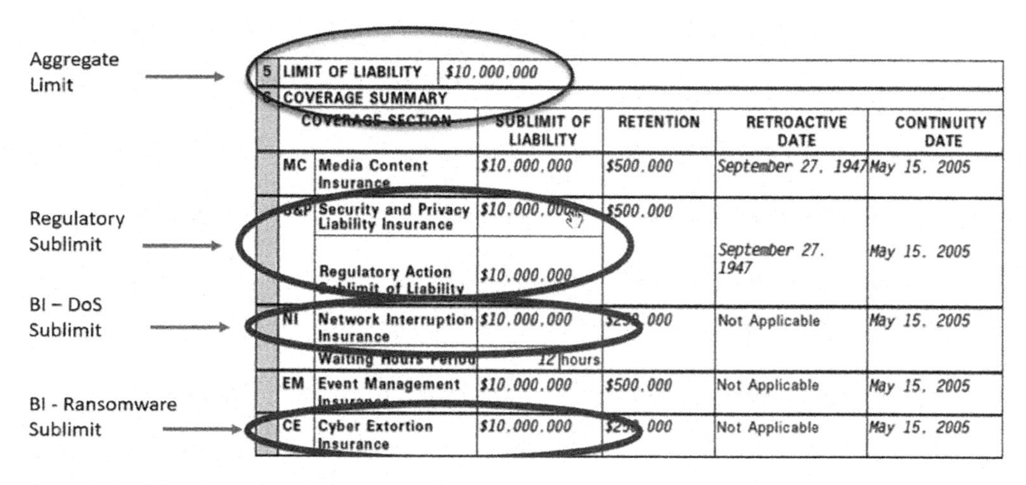

5	LIMIT OF LIABILITY	$10.000.000			
6	COVERAGE SUMMARY				
	COVERAGE SECTION	SUBLIMIT OF LIABILITY	RETENTION	RETROACTIVE DATE	CONTINUITY DATE
MC	Media Content Insurance	$10.000.000	$500.000	September 27. 1947	May 15. 2005
S&P	Security and Privacy Liability Insurance	$10.000.000	$500.000	September 27. 1947	May 15. 2005
	Regulatory Action Sublimit of Liability	$10.000.000			
NI	Network Interruption Insurance	$10.000.000	$2[illegible].000	Not Applicable	May 15. 2005
	Waiting Hours Period	12 hours			
EM	Event Management Insurance	$10.000.000	$500.000	Not Applicable	May 15. 2005
CE	Cyber Extortion Insurance	$10.000.000	$2[illegible].000	Not Applicable	May 15. 2005

Figure 31.2 Cyber Insurance Policy Example

A sublimit is part of the aggregate limit that applies to the specific type of loss. It is not in addition to the limit. These types of losses related to cyber events described above, include data exfiltration, business interruption due to a denial of service (DoS), distributed denial-of-service (DDoS) attacks, or ransomware attacks, and regulatory fines.

Levels of coverage

To understand the metrics on which claims are based, it is critical to understand a little cyber jargon and associate it back to the five levels of coverage.

Let's first look at network security. Network security coverage covers your business in the event of a network security failure, which can include a data breach due to a malware infection or business email compromise. These are typically losses due to data exfiltration that usually happens when an attacker inserts malware, usually from a phishing email, and steals the firm's data. Network security coverage includes first-party costs, which are expenses that you incur directly as a result of the cyber incident.

The costs related back to network security will be the cost of a record and the number of records stolen. Typically, this is the largest amount, however not always.

Types of cyber insurance limits

Business interruption: DoS sublimit

This is typically referred to in the policy as a business interruption sublimit, however, that is misleading. There are different types of business interruptions. System-level business interruptions are due to denial-of-service (DoS) attacks or DDoS attacks. When the entire infrastructure is involved it is at the organization level due to a ransomware attack. There is a separate cyber extortion sublimit. Therefore, a business interruption sublimit is due to a DoS attack. It is critical to read how the carrier has defined this type of limit. They may use different or misleading words. They are not cyber experts.

Remember that a sublimit is part of, rather than in addition to, the limit that would otherwise apply to the specific type of loss. It is the maximum amount available to pay for a type of loss, which in this case is from a DoS attack, or when multiple systems are attacked which is defined as a DDoS Attack.

DoS and DDoS are attacks that happen when the cybercriminal floods your Web application servers with traffic and shuts them down, therefore denying service to your users. This exposure is directly related to a loss of revenue, and recovery time objectives (the maximum tolerable length of time that an IT environment can be down after a failure or disaster occurs). DoS attacks on most critical systems will have a shorter recovery (1–6 hours) time objective (RTO).

Business interruption: ransomware sublimit

Let's look at another business interruption type—ransomware. Ransomware attacks typically happen when a cybercriminal sends a phishing email, someone clicks on it, and malware is inserted. This type of malware blocks accesses to a firm's digital assets unless a ransom is paid or the firm opts to restore all its systems. After the ransom is paid, a decryption key is provided to unlock the digital assets. Ransomware is on the rise and many companies opt to pay the ransom because they have low confidence in their ability to restore or the sheer expense related to restoring. But should the firm pay? We will discuss a ransomware strategy and what you need to know in the next chapter.

Business interruption coverage from ransomware is now being paid in the double-digit millions. Cyber extortion sublimits provide a solution for companies that face cyber hostage taking. When your digital assets, or the digital assets of a provider that you rely on to operate, go down due to a ransomware attack, ransomware sublimits allow firms to recover lost profits, fixed expenses, and extra costs incurred during the time your business was impacted.

Dependent versus nondependent sublimits

There will be two types of business interruption categories. Today, a large percentage of data and systems are off premise in a cloud. Dependent and Nondependent are categories that are related to where the cyber incident is taking place. Dependent is the risk in the cloud and nondependent is an on-premise risk.

Network event sublimit: data exfiltration

A network event typically means that a cybercriminal has stolen data from the firm. This is data exfiltration. This typically also happens from a phishing email when the malware delivered steals the firm's data.

Regulatory sublimits

Regulatory sublimits are based on the regulatory fines and penalties that happen when a regulator fines a company for misuse of data, business interruption, or a data breach. These fines vary depending on the regulation. This exposure can be directly related to the number of records, annual revenue, willful neglect, and other parameters.

Privacy liability coverage protects a company from liabilities which arise from a cyber incident that violates privacy regulations. These include third-party costs from liabilities required in a contractual obligation, costs related to regulatory investigations by monitoring bodies and law enforcement. They also defend an organization from consumer class action litigation and funding a potential settlement in the event of a cyber incident or data breach. They will pay for legal expenses, fines, and/or penalties incurred due to a regulatory investigation by a monitoring body or law enforcement; whether from the federal, state, local, and foreign government.

It is critical for companies to have insurance that protects them if a foreign governmental body investigates and levies a penalty for a privacy violation, such as the

EU Supervisory Authority for GDPR or the California Attorney General for CCPA. Let's not forget the US top privacy cop. The FTC most recently fined Facebook US$5 billion.

Regulatory loss is income lost due to fines or penalties associated with regulation. It can be related to privacy, healthcare, financial, and credit card data types. Some examples of regulatory bodies and the data they protect are:

- PCI Security Council—Credit Card Data
- EU Supervisor Authority—GDPR—EU Privacy Data
- Health and Human Services—HIPAA—Healthcare Data
- Federal Trade Commission—US Privacy Data
- California Attorney General—CCPA—California Residents

Aggregate limit

The cyber insurance aggregate limit must align to the maximum possible loss. This typically is directly related to data exfiltration exposure. When determining the aggregate limit each sublimit should be compared and the largest one used. Typically, the largest amount will be related to data exfiltration. Many companies have too many records in their databases which are not needed for business purposes. They do not archive them regularly and these increase data exfiltration exposure accordingly.

Media liability (media sublimit)

This coverage is related to intellectual property (IP) infringement or patent infringement. It often applies to online advertising risk, including social media posts, as well as printed advertising that can infringe another IP or patent.

This is more suited to media and entertainment companies to protect nonpatented IP. An inventory would need to be done of the IP value.

Errors and omissions (E&O sublimit)

When a cyber event keeps you from fulfilling your contractual obligations and delivering services to your customers E&O sublimits can be used. E&O sublimits are to cover claims that arise from mistakes related to performance or the failure to perform your services properly. This can include IT-related services, software, consulting, and extends to more traditional professional services like lawyers, doctors, architects, and engineers. E&O coverage addresses allegations of negligence or breach of contract. It covers legal defense costs or indemnification resulting from a lawsuit or dispute with your customers.

A review of all contractual obligations should be done and values need to be determined.

Notes

1. Bruce Schneier, Schneier on Security, "Cybersecurity insurance", April 12, 2018, https://www.schneier.com/blog/archives/2018/04/cybersecurity_i_1.html.

2. Josephine Wolff, Wired, "Cyberinsurance tackles the wildly unpredictable world of hacks", April 6, 2018, https://www.wired.com/story/cyberinsurance-tackles-the-wildly-unpredictable-world-of-hacks/.
3. Wikipedia, "Cyberinsurance", November 12, 2020, https://en.wikipedia.org/wiki/Cyber_insurance.
4. Cyber Innovative Technologies, "Cyber innovative technologies", 2020, https://cyberinnovativetech.com/.
5. Allied Market Research, "Cyber insurance market is expected to grow $28.60 billion by 2026: Says AMR", March 31, 2020, https://www.globenewswire.com/news-release/2020/03/31/2009314/0/en/Cyber-Insurance-Market-Is-Expected-to-Grow-28-60-Billion-by-2026-Says-AMR.html.

32 CALCULATING LIMITS ADEQUACY

For organizations downplaying ransomware defenses today, every day is a gamble that they can't afford later.

Andy Lin, CISO at Brighton Health Plan Solutions

Cyber insurance versus property and casualty insurance

Property and casualty insurance have been in existence for over 100 years, contrasted with cyber insurance that is in its infancy. Initially, carriers were baking cyber insurance coverage into property and casualty policies. Most recently, this has been shown not to be very effective and we are seeing brokers offering standalone cyber insurance policies. It is important to know the differences and the gaps between these two policy types.

Cyber insurance may pay for both first- and third-party expenses. A first party is your company, and all the coverage can be for on-premise digital assets and cloud-related exposures. As you learned earlier, cyber risk has financial exposures and there is a likelihood associated with the firm's digital assets that the asset can have a data breach or cyber event.

A third party is an institution or person that you outsource an activity to. In cyber insurance, outsourced vendors' third-party coverage is covering actions brought by the insured's customers/clients. When it comes to data, they are considered the third parties in most cases.

There are different types of third parties. Cloud service providers are vendors that store and process first-party data and provide either a system, infrastructure, or a platform as a service. Service vendors (typically called consultants) provide services in the form of management, IT, legal, accounting, or other services. Technology vendors are companies that your firm purchases IT technologies like databases and Web technologies. System vendors are third parties that provide your firm with entire sets of technologies bundled into a system.

Cyber insurance covers the financial damages associated with three types of cybersecurity losses: data breach, business interruption, and regulatory loss. This includes the first-party data breach response costs that are provided by servicer providers to mitigate a data breach.

DOI: 10.4324/9781003052616-41

First-party data breach response costs:

- Legal expenses: First-party legal expenses to triage the event, hiring third-party vendors, reviewing, and determining responsibilities under privacy breach law.
- Forensic expenses: First-party expenses related to investigating a system intrusion into an insured computer system.
- Credit/ID monitoring expenses: First-party expenses related to providing credit monitoring/ID monitoring services.
- Notification expenses: First-party expenses related to complying with privacy law notification requirements.
- Public relations expenses: First-party expenses related to hiring a public relations firm.

First Party (Breach Response Costs) Service Provider expenses to mitigate a breach event	
Legal Expenses	1st Party legal expenses to review and determine responsibilities under Privacy Breach Law
Forensic Investigations	1st Party expenses to investigate a system intrusion into an Insured Computer System
Credit / ID Monitoring Expense	1st Party expenses to provide credit monitoring / ID monitoring services
Notification Expense	1st Party expenses to comply with Privacy Law notification requirements
Public Relations	1st Party expenses to hire a Public Relations firm

Figure 32.1 First-Party Breach Response Costs

These costs relate directly to response expenses that the company will have. The next set of costs relate to operational losses.

First-party operational costs

First-party operational costs are those that are due to impacts on an organization's computer system. These include:

- Cyber extortion: Payments are to avert damage from a cybercriminal as a result of a threat to interrupt access to the insured's computer systems; payments also cover approved services such as computer forensics investigations.
- Data recovery: Expenses to recover data damaged on an insured computer system as a result of a failure of security.
- Business interruption: First-party reimbursement for lost income arising from an interruption to an insured's computer system as a result of a failure of security. These costs are related to the revenue processed by on-premise systems that the firm will lose in the event of a denial-of-service attack.

- Dependent business interruption (contingent): First-party reimbursement for lost income arising from an interruption to a dependent business computer system as a result of a failure of security. These costs are related to the revenue processed by systems in the cloud that the firm will lose in the event of a denial-of-service attack of their cloud service provider.
- System failure/dependent system failure: First-party reimbursement for lost income arising from an interruption to an insured or a dependent business computer system as a result of a system failure (any unplanned or unintentional outage).

First-party cyber crime

Social engineered crime is a funds transfer through fraudulent impersonation. Costs reimbursed will include for loss of funds due to a funds transfer initiated by an insured as a result of a fraudulent instruction by a third-party impersonating an employee, client, or vendor. This is typically done via a phishing exploit.

First Party (Operational Costs) Operational impact on an Organization computer system	
Cyber Extortion	Payments made to a party as a result of a threat to breach or an actual breach of an Insured's Computer System in order to avert a cyber attack or regain access to a computer system as a result of a cyber attack; includes payments for approved services such as computer forensics investigations
Data Recovery	1st Party expenses to recover data damaged on an Insured Computer System as a result of a Failure of Security
Business Interruption	1st Party loss for lost income from an interruption to an Insured Computer System as a result of a Failure of Security or System Failure
First Party Cyber Crime Theft of funds through social engineering or theft of telephone services - (Subject to lower limits)	
Social Engineering Crime (Funds transfer through fraudulent impersonation)	Loss of funds due to a funds transfer initiated by an Insured as a result of a fraudulent instruction by a third party impersonating an employee, client or vendor
Telephone Crime	1st Party loss resulting from unauthorized access to an Insured Telephone System by a third party

Figure 32.2 First-Party Operational Costs

Third-party liability

Third-party liability refers to an organization's liability as a result of a lawsuit or demand for money or injunctive relief due to a data breach or business interruption. These coverages include:

- Network Security Liability provides coverage if an Insured's computer system fails to prevent a data or privacy breach.

- Privacy Liability provides coverage if an Insured fails to protect the confidentiality of electronic or nonelectronic data that they own.
- Regulatory Liability provides coverage for litigation or investigations by Federal, State, Local, or Foreign regulators and related to fines and penalties where insurable by law. It usually covers GDPR, CCPA, NYDFS, HIPAA, Part 500, and other regulations with fines.
- PCI DSS Assessments Coverage provides coverage for contractual obligations, fines, and penalties levied under the terms of a Merchant Services Agreement due to noncompliance with the Payment Card Industry Data Security Standard (PCI-DSS) and as the result of a data breach. Note—it does not provide coverage if card privileges are revoked by the card brands.
- Media Liability covers the insured for intellectual property and personal injury perils that result from illegal dissemination of content.

Third Party Liability An organization's liability as a result of a lawsuit or demand for money or injunctive relief	
Network Security Liability	Provides liability coverage if an Insured's Computer System fails to prevent a Security Breach or a Privacy Breach
Privacy Liability	Provides liability coverage if an Insured fails to protect confidential electronic or non-electronic information in their care custody and control
Regulatory Liability	Coverage for lawsuits or investigations by Federal, State, or Foreign regulators relating to Privacy Laws (includes fines and penalties where insurable by law)
PCI DSS Assessments	Coverage for contractual assessments, fines and penalties owed under the terms of a Merchant Services Agreement due to non-compliance with the Payment Card Industry Data Security Standard (PCI-DSS) and as the result of a data breach
Media Liability	Covers the Insured for Intellectual Property and Personal Injury perils the result from dissemination of content (coverage for Patent and Trade Secrets are generally not provided)

Figure 32.3 Third Party Liability

Most coverages can be met with a cyber insurance stand-alone policy with the exceptions of imposter fraud and technology errors and omissions.

First-party privacy/network risks

- Physical damage to data only will be covered by General Liability (GL), Kidnap and Ransom (K&R), and cyber insurance policies.
- Virus/hacker damage to data only will be covered by GL, crime, K&R, and cyber insurance policies.
- A denial-of-service (DoS) attack will be covered by GL, crime, K&R, and cyber insurance policies.

- A business interruption loss from a security event will be covered by GL, crime, K&R, Errors and Omissions (E&O), and cyber insurance policies.
- An extortion or threat will be covered by all policy types: Property, GL, crime, K&R, E&O, and cyber insurance policies.
- Employee sabotage of data only will be covered by property, GL, K&R, and cyber insurance policies.
- Impostor fraud will be covered by property, GL, K&R, and E&O insurance policies.

Third-party privacy/network risks

- Theft/disclosure of private information will be covered by property, crime, K&R, and cyber insurance policies.
- Confidential corporate information breach will be covered by property, crime, K&R, and cyber insurance policies.
- Technology E&O Media liability (electronic content) will be covered by property, GL, crime, K&R, and E&O insurance policies.
- Media liability (electronic content) will be covered by property, crime, K&R, and cyber insurance policies.
- Privacy breach response and notification will be covered by property, GL, crime, K&R, and cyber insurance policies.
- Damage to third-party's data only will be covered by property, K&R, and cyber insurance policies.
- Regulatory privacy defense/fines will be covered by property, GL, crime, K&R, and cyber insurance policies.
- Virus/malicious code transmission will be covered by property, crime, K&R, and cyber insurance policies.

	Property	General Liability	Crime	K&R	E&O	Cyber
1st Party Privacy / Network Risks						
Physical damage to data only		x		x		✓
Virus/hacker damage to data only		x	x	x		✓
Denial of service (DOS) attack		x	x	x		✓
Business interruption loss from security event		x	x	x	x	✓
Extortion or threat	x	x	x	✓	x	✓
Employee sabotage of data only	x	x		x		✓
Impostor fraud	x	x		x	x	
3rd Party Privacy / Network Risks						
Theft/disclosure of private information	x		x	x		✓
Confidential corporate information breach	x		x	x		✓
Technology E&O	x	x	x	x	✓	
Media liability (electronic content)	x		x	x		✓
Privacy breach expense and notification	x	x	x	x		✓
Damage to 3rd party's data only	x			x		✓
Regulatory privacy defense / fines	x	x	x	x		✓
Virus/malicious code transmission	x		x	x		✓

Figure 32.4 Gap Analysis

Damage to physical property from a cyber attack is usually not covered in a cyber policy. In that case, a property policy is required for any company to protect their critical infrastructure. Some cyber policies will cover certain bodily or physical damage from a cyber attack. It is not always the case, but that is available on certain policies.

There is a cyber overlap for physical and nonphysical loss or damage to your electronic data, programs, or software. Careful consideration should be made to understand where one stops and the other begins.

Careful consideration needs to be made for business interruption from the loss or damage to electronic data or software for both dependent and contingent (third-party cloud service or supplier) business interruption to your organization from the loss or damage to your electronic data, programs, or software. There is no gap in coverage if cyber insurance is purchased for system failure associated with programming errors and property insurance does not cover programming errors.

Description of Cyber Event (Subject to exclusions and definitions)	A Property Policy (If cyber events coverage is provided)	A Cyber Policy (If cyber events coverage is provided)	Gap / Overlap
A) Damage to Physical Property from cyber attack	• Covered	• Not Covered	Not Applicable
B) Physical & Non-Physical loss or damage to your electronic data, programs or software	• Covered	• Covered for Non-Physical Only	Cyber Overlap (Coordination of waiting period and limit)
C) Business Interruption from the loss or damage to your electronic data, programs or software	• Covered for Unauthorized Access	• Covered for Unauthorized Access	Cyber Overlap (Coordination of waiting period and limit)
	• Covered for System Failure except for programming errors	• Covered for System Failure including programming errors	No Gap if cyber is purchased for system failure associated with programming errors
D) Contingent Business Interruption to your organization from the loss or damage to your electronic data, programs or software	• Covered for Unauthorized Access	• Covered for unauthorized access	Cyber Overlap (Coordination of waiting period and limit)
	• Covered for System Failure except for programming errors	• Covered for System Failure including programming errors	No Gap if cyber is purchased for system failure associated with programming errors

Figure 32.5 Property and Casualty Gap Analysis 1

Cyberterrorism coverage must carefully be considered. Most recently, Zurich and 30 other carriers denied coverage for the NotPetya Ransomware event to many insureds, including Mondelez and Merck.[1] The claim was denied for computer replacements under property coverages; the cyber coverages were actually paid out. Some carriers are claiming it was an act of war and therefore not covered by the cyber insurance policy.

Cyberterrorism coverage is for loss that results from damage to data or business interruption. The Terrorism Risk Insurance Act (TRIA) is a United States federal law enacted on November 26, 2002 that was created as a federal "backstop" for insurance claims related to acts of terrorism.[2] Property policies will be sufficient only if TRIA is triggered. Cyber insurance policies do not require it. There is no gap if cyber is purchased for a non-TRIA event.

There are unauthorized access exclusions in General Liability (GL) policies for the following events:

- *CGL 21 06*: Access or Disclosure of Confidential or Personal Information and Data-Related Liability—With Limited Bodily Injury Exception
- *CGL 21 07*: Access or Disclosure of Confidential or Personal Information and Data-Related Liability—Limited Bodily Injury Exception Not Included
- *CGL 21 08*: Access or Disclosure of Confidential or Personal Information (Coverage B Only)

Description of Cyber Event (Subject to exclusions and definitions)	A Property Policy (If cyber events coverage is provided)	A Cyber Policy (if cyber events coverage is provided)	Gap / Overlap
E) Cyberterrorism that results in damage to data or Business Interruption	• Covered if TRIA is triggered	• Covered for Cyberterrorism (No TRIA required)	No Gap if cyber is purchased for a non-TRIA event
F) Third Party Bodily Injury & Property Damage as a result of a cyber event	• Not Covered • No Third Party Property coverage afforded	• Not Covered	Not Applicable Please note: the General Liability may exclude unauthorized access
General Liability Policy: Unauthorized Access Exclusion			
• CGL 21 06: Exclusion — Access or Disclosure of Confidential or Personal Information and Data-Related Liability — With Limited Bodily Injury Exception • CGL 21 07: Exclusion — Access or Disclosure of Confidential or Personal Information and Data-Related Liability — Limited Bodily Injury Exception Not Included • CGL 21 08: Exclusion — Access or Disclosure of Confidential or Personal Information (Coverage B only)			

Figure 32.6 Property and Casualty Gap Analysis 2

Determining cyber insurance limits

Network sublimit

Data exfiltration exposure is calculated based on the number of records that could be stolen multiplied by the cost per record. A record is a set of data elements (name, phone number, etc.) stored in a database table. It is synonymous with a row. We discussed records in Chapter 2. For this calculation, we need to determine the number of unique records. We do not want to count the same record twice. The cost of the data breach is related to the notification. You will not be notifying someone twice if their records are stolen.

To obtain this information from a database, a Structured Query Language (SQL) query should be run by a Database Administrator (DBA) to determine the unique record count. Any junior DBA can do this. It requires them to know the primary key of the database and what data element will be used to query. In this case, it is a privacy data element that will uniquely identify the person. One example is to use the social security number. This will uniquely identify each person. The DBA will run the query and obtain the unique number of records.

The cost per record can be obtained from the IBM Ponemon Cost of a Data Breach Report. When considering the cost of a record it is important to have confidence in the data. The more data the higher the level of confidence. IBM Ponemon Cost of a Data Breach has been measuring the cost of a record for over 11 years and has the most data interviews to support their numbers.

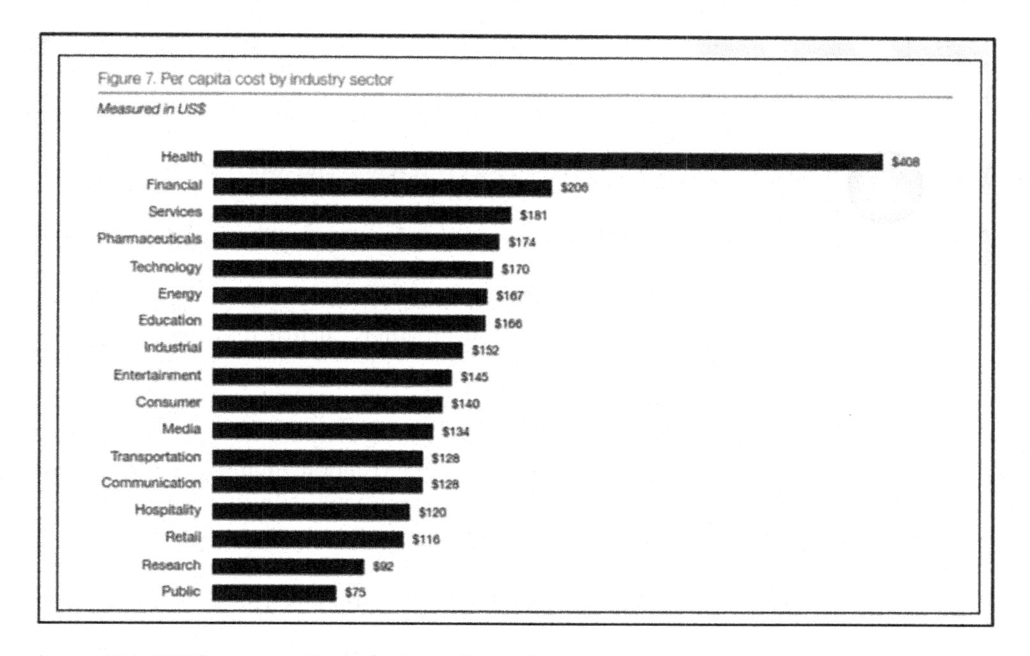

Image 32.1 IBM Pomemon Cost of a Record[3]

Fifty-two percent of the cost of a record is insurable and 48% is related to the remediation costs, which are uninsurable.[4] Insurable components include all costs in the previous chapter except the cost to remediate the incident.

Steps to calculate data exfiltration exposure

Step 1: Identify all the digital assets (systems and databases) that process privacy data. For cyber insurance, we only care about the privacy records. This includes PCI and PHI since they are a subset of privacy.
Step 2: Obtain the record counts for each system.
Step 3: Determine the cost per record.
Step 4: Calculate the data exfiltration amounts.
Step 5: Compare this amount against the other sublimits.

The aggregate limit will typically be the highest amount of data exfiltration if the other sublimits are not greater.

Data Exfiltration = Cost per Record * Number of Records

DoS sublimit

Business interruption can be due to a denial of service (DoS), Distributed denial-of-service (DDoS) attacks, or ransomware attack. There are two types of sublimits: dependent and nondependent. Dependent is related to interruptions in cloud services and nondependent is related to interruptions in on-premise systems.

Business interruption due to DoS is at a process level and is based on the RTO of the system, and revenue processed.

To calculate DoS business interruptions, follow these steps.

Step 1: Determine which systems process revenue and whether they are on a cloud or on-premise.
Step 2: Obtain the amount of annual revenue processed and RTO from the business owner for each system in scope.
Step 3: Calculate the hourly revenue processed.
Step 4: The system business interruption amount is calculated by multiplying the hourly revenue by the RTO.
Step 5: Compare all the calculations and determine the highest amounts for systems on-premise and for systems that are in a cloud. The on-premise calculation is the nondependent business interruption sublimit and the cloud calculation is the dependent business interruption sublimit.

Dependent business interruption sublimit
= Max (RTO * Revenue per Hour) – Cloud systems only.

Nondependent business interruption sublimit
= Max (RTO * Revenue per Hour) – On premise systems only.

Ransomware sublimit

The ransomware exposure is directly related to a loss of revenue that comes from the systems on-premise and the RRTO.

The RRTO is the time from the encryption to the time of decryption. Most companies will suffer reputational amplification of their financial loss if the ransom is not handled quickly and quietly or the systems are restored in less than 48 hours. Ransomware is on the rise. Business interruption coverage from ransomware is now being paid in the double-digit millions. Cyber extortion sublimits provide a solution for companies that face cyber hostage taking. When your digital assets, or the digital assets of a provider that you rely on to operate, goes down due to a ransomware attack, you can recover lost profits, and costs incurred during the time your business was impacted.

Step 1: Determine the annual revenue for on-premise systems and divide by the number of operational hours to get the revenue per hour.
Step 2: Determine the annual revenue for cloud systems and divide by the number of operational hours to get the revenue per hour.

Step 3: Determine the RRTO for the on-premise systems and for the cloud systems.
Step 4: Multiply the RRTO by the revenue per hour for cloud systems.
Step 5: Multiply the RRTO by the revenue per hour for the on-premise systems.
Step 6: Calculate the Dependent ransomware sublimit = (RRTO * Revenue per Hour) – Cloud systems only.
Step 7: Calculate the Nondependent ransomware sublimit = Max (RRTO * Revenue per Hour) – On premise systems only.

The maximum loss should be used for the ransomware sublimit. It is highly unlikely that a firm will have two ransomware events that are mutually exclusive (in the cloud and on premise).

Regulatory sublimits

Regulatory sublimits relate to defending the firm from fines that are levied for a privacy violation related to new regulations, such as GDPR and CCPA.

Let's look at a sublimit based on the GDPR. GDPR is the general data protection regulation that can have fines up to 4% of annual revenue or 20 million EUR, whichever is higher in the case of a data breach. Each regulation has to be considered in context. CCPA can levy a privacy fine of up to US$7500 a record. Each type of regulation has to be looked at in context.

Media liability (media sublimit)

Inventory the firm's Intellectual Property (IP) and determine its value.

Errors and omissions (E&O sublimit)

Inventory all contractual obligations. Identify where cyber-related issues will possibly prohibit payment.

Other considerations: uninsurable exposures

Many companies do not enforce their data retention and disposal policies and have not archived records appropriately. This creates a serious issue where systems have extraordinarily high amounts of records. They will not be covered by the cyber insurance policy since they are greater than the aggregate limit. The largest cyber insurance policy ever written as of January 2020 is US$750 million. Most companies cannot afford over US$100 million in limits.

If the firm has a US$400 million cyber insurance limit and they have a US$200 per record cost that equates to a total of 2 million records that can be exfiltrated. Any records greater than 2 million will not be covered by the insurance policy.

This leaves the company in dire straits if they have a data breach. In most cases, the company cannot be sustainable from an attack to systems where the records count exceeds the maximum number of records their cyber policy will cover.

It is recommended that the company archive records down to the maximum number associated to the cyber insurance limit to avoid this issue. Other solutions can be applied to segment the data or increase encryption effectiveness.

Notes

1. Riley Griffin, Katherine Chiglinsky, David Voreacos, Bloomberg, Insurance Journal, "Was it an act of war? That's Merck cyber attack's $1.3 billion insurance question", December 3, 2019, https://www.insurancejournal.com/news/national/2019/12/03/550039.htm.
2. U.S. Department of the Treasury, "Terrorism risk Insurance Program", 2020, https://home.treasury.gov/policy-issues/financial-markets-financial-institutions-and-fiscal-service/federal-insurance-office/terrorism-risk-insurance-program.
3. IBM Security, "Cost of a data breach report 2020", 2020, https://www.ibm.com/security/digital-assets/cost-data-breach-report/?cm_mmca1=000039JJ&cm_mmca2=10013747#/.
4. William C. Wagner, Taft, "Cyber Insurance: How do I determine my coverage needs?", April 16, 2015, https://www.privacyanddatasecurityinsight.com/2015/04/cyber-insurance-how-do-i-determine-my-coverage-needs/.

33 RANSOMWARE STRATEGIES

Ransomware is unique among cybercrime because in order for the attack to be successful, it requires the victim to become a willing accomplice after the fact.

James Scott, Sr. Fellow, Institute for Critical Infrastructure Technology

What is ransomware?

Ransomware is a type of malware that is typically delivered via phishing emails. The ransomware malware uses encryption to make your digital assets unavailable and causes significant business interruption losses. Some ransomware events are reportable to regulatory agencies and many companies are unprepared for a ransomware event.

Ransomware is a type of malware from cryptovirology. Cryptovirology[3] is a field that studies how to use cryptography to design powerful malicious software. There are only two ways to respond to a ransomware attack: (1) pay the ransom or (2) restore your systems. If you pay the ransom, the criminal will provide you the decryption key to unlock your file servers. Ransoms are typically demanded in digital currencies such as Bitcoin. These currencies are untraceable making prosecuting the perpetrators near impossible.

Ransomware attacks in phishing emails are typically carried out using a Trojan or a vulnerability in a network service. In computing, a Trojan horse, or Trojan, is malware which uses subterfuge to fool users of its true intent. The term is derived from the Ancient Greek story where soldiers hid within the Trojan Horse and entered the city of Troy leading to its downfall.[4] Ransomware trojans are disguised to appear as a legitimate link or file from an email that when the user clicks on it, they are tricked into downloading malware.

One well known example or a large-scale ransomware attack is the "WannaCry worm." The WannaCry ransomware attack began in May of 2017 and spread worldwide. This cyberattack used a ransomware cryptoworm, which traveled from computer to computer. It targeted computers running Microsoft's Windows operating systems. Once deployed, it encrypted data and then demanded ransom payments in Bitcoin. The cryptoworm propagated through a vulnerability in EternalBlue being used in older Windows systems. EternalBlue is a cyberattack exploit developed by the US National Security Agency (NSA). It was leaked by a hacker group named Shadow

DOI: 10.4324/9781003052616-42

Brokers on April 14, 2017, one month after Microsoft released patches for the vulnerability.[5] Microsoft released patches to close the exploit, however many companies had not applied the patch and by the time it was released it was too late. WannaCry had spread from organization to organization who had not applied the patch. Many infected companies were using out of date Windows systems or systems that were End of Life (EOL). EOL systems are not supported by the vendor any longer. These systems have no patch management abilities and include examples such as the Windows XP operating system. Over 250 million companies worldwide are still running XP. This is mainly due to the high cost of rip and replace.[6]

One reason for the high growth rate of ransomware is the level of organization in the dark web. As we discussed in our cybercrime chapter, the dark web is the new mafia. Many "as a service" offerings for ransomware require no technical knowledge to deploy and sell for as little as US$100. Cybercriminals have an entire ecosystem in the shadow market where pay masters are organizing relationships between malware developers, money launderers, and others. The level of sophistication is effective and highly profitable.

"There were 181.5 million ransomware attacks in the first six months of 2018. This marks a 229% increase over this same time frame in 2017."[7] McAfee showed in mid-2014, that it had collected more than double the number of samples of ransomware that quarter than it had in the same quarter of the previous year.[8] CryptoLocker was particularly successful in obtaining US$3 million before it was taken down by the FBI,[9] and since inception CryptoWall was estimated to have accrued over US$18 million by June 2015.[10]

Small and medium businesses with 250 to 5,000 employees account for almost half of cyber-attacks. They do not have the resources to invest in security as a large firm does and are easy pickings for cybercriminals.

There are different types of ransomware payloads. One method consists of delivering an application designed to lock the system until a payment is made, typically by setting the Windows Shell to itself. Another method is to modify the master boot record and/or partition table to prevent the operating system from booting until it is repaired.[11] The most sophisticated payloads encrypt files with strong ciphers that encrypt the victim's files in such a way that only the malware author has the needed decryption key.[12]

Ransomware variants

There are many types of ransomware variants and more are developed as I type. Here, are some of the most infamous and damaging ones to date.

Petya

Petya is related to the 2017 cyberattacks on Ukraine. In June of 2017, a modified version of Petya was used in a global cyberattack that was initially directed at the Ukraine.[13] Many security analysts believe that the attack was not meant to generate profit, but to cause disruption to the Ukrainian economy.[14]

Bad rabbit

Users in Russia and Ukraine reported a new ransomware attack in 2017, named "Bad Rabbit." This exploit follows a pattern similar to WannaCry and Petya by encrypting the user's file tables and then demanding a Bitcoin payment. ESET believed the ransomware was distributed via a bogus update to Adobe Flash software.[15] Victims included Interfax, Odessa International Airport, Kyiv Metro, and the Ministry of Infrastructure of Ukraine.[16] Other countries impacted were Turkey, Germany, Poland, Japan, South Korea, and the United States.[17] Interestingly, Bad Rabbit's code shares 57% of the code from Petya/NotPetya and forensics teams have linked it to the Petya attack in Ukraine.

WannaCry

We mentioned WannaCry earlier. This ransomware attack is noteworthy due to its unprecedented scale.[18] It spread throughout 150 countries and infected more than 230,000 computers worldwide.[19] WannaCry used 20 different languages to ransom users and demanded US$300 per computer and payment in Bitcoin.[20] WannaCry victims included Telefónica, FedEx, Deutsche Bank, Honda, Renault, Russia's Interior Ministry, and telecom MegaFon.[21] In Britain, the country's National Health Service (NHS) had to turn away patients or cancel scheduled operations from over 15 hospitals.[22] The companies were given a 7-day deadline from the day their computers were encrypted to pay the ransom or have their files deleted.[23]

CryptoLocker

CryptoLocker is an encrypting ransomware that appeared in 2013. Payments in Bitcoin or a prepaid cash voucher were required to be made within three days. The US Department of Justice issued an indictment against the Russian hacker Evgeniy Bogachev for his alleged involvement in the botnet.[24] It was estimated that US$3 million was extorted with the malware before it was shut down.[25]

TorrentLocker

In September 2014, a wave of ransomware targeted users in Australia, under the names CryptoWall and CryptoLocker. The ransomware trojans were spread using fraudulent emails claiming to be failed parcel delivery notices from Australia Post. Victims included the Australian Broadcasting Corporation, and its ABC News 24 was disrupted for half an hour and was shifted to Melbourne studios due to a CryptoWall infection on computers at its Sydney studio.[26] The TorrentLocker Trojan infected over 9,000 users in Australia and 11,700 infections in Turkey.[27]

CryptoWall

CryptoWall is similar to WannaCry in terms that both target Windows. CryptoWall was distributed as part of a malvertising campaign in late-September 2014. The campaign targeted several major websites where the ads were redirected to rogue websites that used browser plugin exploits to download the payload. Cleverly, the payload was signed with a digital signature in an effort to appear trustworthy to security software.[28] CryptoWall 3.0 used a payload written in JavaScript as part of an email attachment. The payload downloads executables disguised as JPG images. The malware creates new instances of explorer.exe and svchost.exe to communicate with its servers to avoid detection. When encrypting files, the malware also deletes volume shadow copies and installs spyware which steals passwords for Bitcoin wallets.[29] In June of 2015, the FBI reported that nearly 1,000 victims contacted their Internet Crime Complaint Center to report CryptoWall infections, and the FBI estimated losses of at least US$18 million.[30]

Reveton

Ransomware became troublesome in 2012. A Reveton payload is a malware that fraudulently claims that the user must pay a fine to the Metropolitan Police Service. Based on the Citadel Trojan, Reveton's payload displays a warning allegedly from a law enforcement agency claiming that the computer has been used for illegal activities and is commonly referred to as the "Police Trojan."[31] The tricky warning tells the victim that to unlock their computer, they have to pay a fine using a voucher from an anonymous prepaid cash service. To make the trick appear real, the screen displays the computer's IP address, while some versions display footage from a victim's webcam to give the illusion that the user is being spied upon.[32]

Reveton started in Russia, and began spreading in various European countries in early 2012.[33] Cleverly, the cybercriminals used templates with the logos of different law enforcement organizations to frighten the victim into payment. Another version displayed the logo of the royalty collection society PRS for Music, which specifically accused the user of illegally downloading music.[34]

In May 2012, threat researchers discovered templates for variations for the United States and Canada.[35] By August 2012, a new variant of Reveton was spreading in the United States. In February 2013, a Russian citizen was arrested by Spanish authorities in Dubai, for his relationship with a crime ring that was using Reveton.[36]

SamSam

SamSam started in 2016 and began to target JBoss servers. SamSam exploits vulnerabilities on weak servers.[37] The malware uses a Remote Desktop Protocol (RDP) to brute-force attack the computer. Victims of SamSam include the town of Farmington, New Mexico, the Colorado Department of Transportation, Davidson County, North Carolina, and the city of Atlanta.[38]

BOLO: Iranian nationals Mohammad Mehdi Shah Mansouri and Faramarz Shahi Savandi are wanted by the FBI for allegedly launching SamSam ransomware.[39] Allegedly these two cybercriminals made over US$6 million from ransomware and caused over US$30 million in damages using the malware.[40]

Syskey

Syskey is a utility that used to be included with Windows NT-based operating systems. Its purpose was to encrypt the user account database. The tool has been effectively used in ransomware attacks as a ruse. The cybercriminal would impersonate a technical support person and remote into the computer and use SysKey to lock the user out of their computer with a password known only to cybercriminal. Syskey was deprecated from Windows 10 and Windows Server in 2017.[41]

Proactive protection

Proactive measures will decrease costs. Prevention methods against ransomware will eliminate the respond and recover costs associated with data recovery specialists who restore systems. There are several preventative measures companies can consider.

Antivirus

Keeping antivirus software up to date is critical. Antivirus software will detect malware; however, it most likely will not detect a ransomware payload. If an attack is suspected or detected in its early stages, it takes time for the encryption to be put in place. Immediate removal of the malware before it has delivered its full payload will stop further damage to data.

Advanced threat prevention

Advanced Threat Prevention cybersecurity tools will quarantine suspicious emails and files that antiviruses may not defect. These precautionary measures for dealing with ransomware are somewhat effective.

Business continuity planning

Having a robust Business Continuity Management (BCM) program and proper backups are critical. Ransomware payloads will also attempt to delete any hot backups stored locally or that are accessible over the network, therefore it is a requirement to maintain "offline" backups of data. A proper back up strategy will remove the backup from the line of sight of the attacker. The scope of the attack is then limited. Any data that is stored in locations not accessible from an infected computer, (e.g., external storage drives or devices that do not have any connection to the network, including the internet), prevents them from being impacted by the ransomware. If your firm is using a cloud backup, please ensure that they are using append-only permissioning to the destination storage to ensure that the malware cannot delete or overwrite previous backups.

Best practices are to back up data regularly and verify the integrity of the backups. Testing the restoration process to ensure it is working properly is essential. Best practices include conducting an annual penetration test and vulnerability assessment. Make sure that you secure your backups. Ensure that the backups are not connected permanently to the computers and networks that they are backing up. This includes securing backups in the cloud and for on-premise environments, physically storing them offline. Some ransomware has the capability to lock cloud-based backups when systems continuously back up in real time. High confidence in backups is critical in ransomware recovery and response.[42]

Patch management and security awareness

Patch management will mitigate known vulnerabilities that can be leveraged by certain ransomware. Security training for the enterprise that focuses on good cyber hygiene, phishing, and network segmentation should be in place.

Decryption tools

There are security tools that can be used to decrypt files locked by ransomware. Successful recovery is not guaranteed.[43]

Free ransomware decryption tools can help decrypt files encrypted by the following forms of ransomware.[44]

Other helpful ideas to reduce ransomware risk are:

- Security Awareness Programs: One of the primary vectors of ransomware is phishing. There is a high ROI with automated training programs. Most companies see an 80% decrease in click rates within one month.[45]
- Spam Filters: Prevent phishing emails from reaching users. They authenticate inbound emails using technologies that prevent email spoofing.
- Email Scanning: Detects threats and will prevent the execution of malicious files.
- Firewalls: Block access to known malicious IP addresses.
- Employ the concept of least privilege: Ensures that admin rights are not abused.
- Access Controls: Limits the ability of users to interact with files.
- Disable Macro Scripts: Consider using secure viewing software to open Microsoft Office files transmitted via email instead of full office suite applications.
- Remote Desktop Protocol (RDP): Disable this if it is not being used.
- Application Whitelisting: Allows only approved programs to execute code.
- Virtual Desktops: Execute programs in a virtualized environment.
- Data Classification: Know what data is where to avoid regulatory fines and penalties.
- Network Segmentation: Use physical and logical separation of networks and data.

I'm ransomed! Now what???

There are two levels of response. The first one is to mitigate any further damage and the second one is to figure out if you will restore or pay the ransom. The later should be done *before you are ransomed!*

Mitigating further damage

If a ransomware is detected, disconnect the infected machines from the network. File systems typically keep snapshots of the data, and they are used to recover the contents of files from a point in time before the ransomware attack. Infected computers must be isolated immediately. Remove them from the network as soon as possible to prevent ransomware from spreading. Ensure that backups are free of malware and that you have secured your secure backup data or systems by taking them offline.

Immediately change all domain, online account passwords, and network passwords after removing the system from the network. Change all system passwords after the malware is removed from the system.

It is critical to collect and secure portions of the ransomed data that may exist. Make sure to delete registry values and files to stop the program from loading.

Implement your ransomware strategy

You may either be executing your business continuity plan or paying the ransom. The next section provides a strategy to figure out what is in the best interest of the firm.

Ransomware strategy

What is a ransomware strategy? A ransomware strategy is an approach to mitigate the damage from a ransomware attack. It addresses the factors that determine if you would opt to pay a ransom versus restoring your systems. It also addresses how to interact with the cybercriminal and the teams that are needed to work together in this scenario.

Cybercriminals will demand that you pay the ransom in a set short period of time. Usually up to 96 hours. There is no time to think about the steps that you need to take. Being prepared for this "when," not if, situation is critical. If the ransom is not paid, the files will remain encrypted permanently and there will be no choice but to restore your files. If the data is released then a data breach must be reported that could result in massive fines, reputation impacts, including stock price drops and customer loss.

Ransomware team

Ransomware attacks require companies to retain outside counsel and forensic teams that are experts in cybersecurity. In the case of a ransomware attack, they will negotiate the ransom and protect the company against Random Access Trojans (RATs) that may be hidden in the ransomware malware allowing attackers to have a back door to the company's environment.

Cost benefit analysis

Ransomware strategies include a cost benefit analysis. Should you pay or restore? First, you must ask, "can you restore?" Do you have a disaster recovery plan, and have you tested it recently? If the answer is "no," you do not have a choice and must pay the ransom or incur their wrath. The next thing to ask is, "what level of confidence do you have in the recovery plan?" If it is high, then it is time to look at the cost benefit analysis. The cost to restore must be known.

Another key factor to know is the Ransomware Recovery Time Objective (RRTO). The RRTO is the time from encryption to decryption. It is related to the risk amplifiers that you have. The RRTO is one of the main reasons that insurance companies have paid ransoms regularly. To their bean counters, it costs less to pay the ransom than to pay for an insured to recover all their data and/or systems. I actually think this has helped increase the rapidity of ransomware attacks in the United States.

How long can you be down without significantly losing money due to reputational or regulatory impacts? What if your customers cannot get access? How long before you think that they will go to a competitor? Do you have a Service Level Agreement (SLA) in place with partners that you provide data to that requires feeds every 6 hours? These are the aspects you have to take into consideration. What are you contractually bound to do? For financial services companies doing business in the State of NY, you are required to notify the NYS DFS. This will now be public information that you have had a cyber event.

If you experience a ransomware attack, are you required to notify the FBI? When your firm processes healthcare data and falls under HIPAA, you must report it as prescribed in the HIPAA reporting regulations. In many cases, your business is not legally required to make a report to the FBI. However, NYS DFS requires it be reported. Before you make a decision about whether or not to file a report with the FBI, it is suggested to carefully weigh the potential consequences to both your reputation and bottom line. Please take into account that (1) you have no control over whether the FBI shares information about your ransomware attack and (2) news of a ransomware attack could harm your company's interests.

However as per the FBI, "The FBI does not support paying a ransom in response to a ransomware attack. Paying a ransom doesn't guarantee you or your organization will get any data back. It also encourages perpetrators to target more victims and offers an incentive for others to get involved in this type of illegal activity."[46]

Know your RRTO. The RRTO is the period of time in which an enterprise's operations must be restored following a ransomware attack. It is calculated based on a number of factors typically determined by the CRO or Cyber Risk Manager. We find 72 hours to be the average across industries.

Some factors that might influence your RRTOs include:

1 Industry—Companies that are working with healthcare records or financial transactions will need to update their files more frequently than those dealing with data that is more static.
2 Partnering—Companies that are ingesting and sending data frequently will be updating their files more frequently than those that are partnering less.
3 Location of Data—Where your data is stored (on-premise or in the cloud) impacts RRTO. Cloud infrastructures are not in scope for a ransomware attack.

4 Regulatory—Numerous regulations contain clauses dealing with business availability. For example, the SOC 2 certification process requires a certain level of data availability and processing integrity. This can impact the acceptable amount of data loss following a service disruption.

To measure the amount of ransomware exposure, use the organizational revenue per hour from on-premise systems multiplied by the RRTO and compare that cost to your cost to restore.

Ransomware calculation

*Organizational revenue (from on premise systems) per hour * RRTO*

If the cost to restore is lower by 25% or more, restore, if not, pay the ransom. Please note that this is **not legal advice**, and I am **not responsible** for any losses your firm may incur if you utilize any information in this book. The other use case associated to this metric is the ransomware sublimit for your cyber insurance policy that is covered in the article above in section 6.

If the ransomware payment is made, the ransomware can be removed by supplying a program that will decrypt the files, or by sending an unlock code that undoes the payload's changes. There are several factors to consider in paying the ransom. There are serious risks to consider before paying the ransom. This is a critical decision that must consider the business implications and impacts to shareholders, employees, partners, and customers. The "restoration readiness" must be determined and understood. This is the cost, time, and technical feasibility of restoring the systems from backups.

Other factors to consider before opting to pay a ransom are:

- The cybercriminal may not provide the decryption keys.
- RATs can be left in your infrastructure that allow the cybercriminal to control your computer technology remotely. This allows them to look at local files, steal PII, acquire login credentials, and use the connection to download viruses which can be unwittingly spread across the company and to others.
- Many victims who paid the demand are targeted more than once by the same or other cybercriminals.
- Even after paying the ransom, some victims were asked to pay more.
- Paying may feel morally wrong since it encourages the cybercriminals.

In May 2020, the vendor Sophos reported that the global average cost to remediate a ransomware attack was US$761,106. This included downtime, resource time, device costs, network costs, lost revenues, and ransom paid. Over 90% of organizations that paid the ransom had their data restored according to this report.[47]

Cyber extortion sublimits

Cyber insurance is a part of an effective ransomware strategy and is covered in-depth in the previous two chapters.

Notes

1. Purplesec, "2020 Ransomware statistics, data & trends", 2020, https://purplesec.us/resources/cyber-security-statistics/ransomware/.
2. Deepen Desai, ZScaler, "30,000 percent increase in Covid-19-themed attacks", April 23, 2020, https://www.zscaler.com/blogs/security-research/30000-percent-increase-covid-19-themed-attacks.
3. Wikipedia, "Cryptovirology", December 5, 2020, https://en.wikipedia.org/wiki/Cryptovirology.
4. Wikipedia, "Trojan Horse (computing)", December 16, 2020, https://en.wikipedia.org/wiki/Trojan_horse_(computing).
5. David Goodin, Ars technica, "NSA-leaking shadow brokers just dumped its most damaging release yet", April 14, 2017, https://arstechnica.com/information-technology/2017/04/nsa-leaking-shadow-brokers-just-dumped-its-most-damaging-release-yet/#:~:text=The%20Shadow%20Brokers%E2%80%94the%20mysterious,target%20most%20versions%20of%20Microsoft.
6. Ellen Nakashima, Craig Timburg, The Washington Post, "NSA officials worried about the day its potent hacking tool would get loose. Then it did", May 16, 2017, https://www.washingtonpost.com/business/technology/nsa-officials-worried-about-the-day-its-potent-hacking-tool-would-get-loose-then-it-did/2017/05/16/50670b16-3978-11e7-a058-ddbb23c75d82_story.html.
7. Help Net Security, "Ransomware back in big way, 181.5 million attacks since January", July 11, 2018, https://www.helpnetsecurity.com/2018/07/11/2018-sonicwall-cyber-threat-report/.
8. Help Net Security, "Ransomware back in big way, 181.5 million attacks since January", July 11, 2018, https://www.helpnetsecurity.com/2018/07/11/2018-sonicwall-cyber-threat-report/.
9. Mark Ward, BBC News, "Cryptolocker victims to get files back for free", August 6, 2014, https://www.bbc.com/news/technology-28661463.
10. Sean Gallagher, Ars technica, "FBI says crypto ransomware has raked in >$18 million for cybercriminals", June 25, 2015, https://arstechnica.com/information-technology/2015/06/fbi-says-crypto-ransomware-has-raked-in-18-million-for-cybercriminals/.
11. Denis Maslennikov, Secure List, "And now, an MBR Ransomware", 2020, https://securelist.com/and-now-an-mbr-ransomware/30626/.
12. Cryptovirology.com, "our work on cryptovirology", 2020, https://www.cryptovirology.com/cryptovfiles/research.html.
13. Eric C., Safety Detectives, "Ransomware facts, trends & statistics for 2020", April 22, 2020, https://www.safetydetectives.com/blog/ransomware-statistics/.
14. Dan Goodin, Ars technica, "Tuesday's massive ransomware outbreak was, in fact, something much worse", June 28, 2017, https://arstechnica.com/information-technology/2017/06/petya-outbreak-was-a-chaos-sowing-wiper-not-profit-seeking-ransomware/.
15. BBC News, "Bad Rabbit' ransomware strikes Ukraine and Russia", October 24, 2017, https://www.bbc.com/news/technology-41740768.
16. Kyiv Post, The Guardian, "The Guardian: Bad rabbit – Game of Thrones-referencing ransomware hits Europe", October 25, 2017, https://www.kyivpost.com/technology/guardian-bad-rabbit-game-thrones-referencing-ransomware-hits-europe.html.
17. Selena Larson, CNN Business, "New ransomware attack hits Russia and spreads around globe", October 25, 2017, https://money.cnn.com/2017/10/24/technology/bad-rabbit-ransomware-attack/index.html.
18. BBC News, "Cyber-Attack: Europol says it was unprecedented in scale", May 13, 2017, https://www.bbc.com/news/world-europe-39907965#:~:text=A%20cyber%2Dattack%20that%20hit,%22to%20identify%20the%20culprits%22.

19. Pinterest, "The real victim of ransomware: Your local store owner", May 22, 2017, https://in.pinterest.com/pin/616078423996458775/.
20. Alfred Ng, CNET, "The real victim of ransomware: Your local store owner", May 22, 2017, https://www.cnet.com/news/wannacry-ransomware-real-victim-small-business-local-corner-store/#ftag=CAD590a51e
21. Reuters, "Honda halts Japan car plant after WannaCry virus hits computer network", June 21, 2017, https://www.reuters.com/article/us-honda-cyberattack/honda-halts-japan-car-plant-after-wannacry-virus-hits-computer-network-idUSKBN19C0EI.
22. The Guardian, "The NHS trusts hit by malware – full list", May 12, 2017, https://www.theguardian.com/society/2017/may/12/global-cyber-attack-nhs-trusts-malware.
23. Paul Mozur, Mark Scott, Vindu Goel, The New York Times, "Victims call hackers' bluff as ransomware deadline nears", May 19, 2017, https://www.nytimes.com/2017/05/19/business/hacking-malware-wanncry-ransomware-deadline.html.
24. The United States Department of Justice, "U.S. leads multi-national action against "Gameover Zeus" botnet and "Cryptolocker" ransomware, charges botnet administrator", June 2, 2014, https://www.justice.gov/opa/pr/us-leads-multi-national-action-against-gameover-zeus-botnet-and-cryptolocker-ransomware.
25. Mark Ward, BBC News, "Cryptolocker victims to get files back for free", August 6, 2014, https://www.bbc.com/news/technology-28661463#:~:text=All%20500%2C000%20victims%20of%20Cryptolocker,key%20to%20the%20scrambled%20files.
26. Patrick Budmar, ARN from IDG, "Australia specifically targeted by Cryptolocker: Symantec", October 3, 2014, https://www.arnnet.com.au/article/556598/australia-specifically-targeted-by-cryptolocker-symantec/.
27. Liam Tung, CSO, "Over 9000 PC's in Australia infected by TorrentLocker ransomware", December 17, 2014, https://www.csoonline.com/article/3501203/over-9-000-pcs-in-australia-infected-by-torrentlocker-ransomware.html.
28. Lucian Constantin, CSO, "Malvertising campaign delivers digitally signed CryptoWall ransomware", September 29, 2014, https://www.csoonline.com/article/2688343/malvertising-campaign-delivers-digitally-signed-cryptowall-ransomware.html.
29. Anthony Joe Melgarejo, Trend Micro, "CryptoWall 3.0 ransomware partners with FAREIT spyware", March 19, 2015, https://blog.trendmicro.com/trendlabs-security-intelligence/cryptowall-3-0-ransomware-partners-with-fareit-spyware/.
30. Sean Gallagher, Ars technica, "FBI says crypto ransomware has raked in > $18 million for cybercriminals", June 25, 2015, https://arstechnica.com/information-technology/2015/06/fbi-says-crypto-ransomware-has-raked-in-18-million-for-cybercriminals/.
31. John Leyden, The Register, "Fake cop trojan 'detects offensive materials' on PCs, demands money", April 5, 2012, https://www.theregister.com/2012/04/05/police_themed_ransomware/.
32. DarkReading, "Reveton malware freezes PCs, demands payment", August 16, 2012, https://www.darkreading.com/messages.asp?piddl_msgthreadid=2809&piddl_msgorder=.
33. Mehr Zum Thema, Computer Woche, "Ransom trojans spreading beyond Russian heartland", March 10, 2012, https://www.computerwoche.de/a/ransom-trojans-spreading-beyond-russian-heartland,2506789,2.
34. DarkReading, "Reveton malware freezes PC's, demands payment", August 16, 2012, https://www.darkreading.com/messages.asp?piddl_msgthreadid=2809&piddl_msgid=178139.
35. Lucian Constantin, Network World, "Police-themed ransomware starts targeting US and Canadian users", May 9, 2012, https://www.networkworld.com/article/2188411/police-themed-ransomware-starts-targeting-us-and-canadian-users.html.
36. Security Shelf, "Reveton 'police ransom' malware gang head arrested in Dubai", February 14, 2013, https://securityshelf.com/2013/02/14/reveton-police-ransom-malware-gang-head-arrested-in-dubai/.

37. Fahmida Y. Rashid, Info World, "Patch JBoss now to prevent SamSam ransomware attacks", April 19, 2016, https://www.infoworld.com/article/3058254/patch-jboss-now-to-prevent-samsam-ransomware-attacks.html.
38. Malware.News, "City of Atlanta hit with SamSam ransomware: 5 key things to know", March 1, 2018, https://malware.news/t/city-of-atlanta-hit-with-samsam-ransomware-5-key-things-to-know/18927.
39. Federal Bureau of Investigation, "Wanted by the FBI: Iranians indicted for SamSam ransomware hacking and extortion scheme", November 28, 2018, https://www.fbi.gov/audio-repository/wanted-podcast-samsam-ransomware-indictments-112818.mp3/view.
40. The United States Department of Justice, "Two Iranian men indicted for deploying ransomware to extort hospitals, municipalities, and public institutions, causing over $30 million in losses", November 28, 2018, https://www.justice.gov/opa/pr/two-iranian-men-indicted-deploying-ransomware-extort-hospitals-municipalities-and-public.
41. Windows Forum, "Syskey.exe utility is no longer supported in Windows 10, Windows server 2016 and Windows server 2019", July 26, 2019, https://windowsforum.com/threads/syskey-exe-utility-is-no-longer-supported-in-windows-10-windows-server-2016-and-windows-server-2019.245534/.
42. Federal Bureau of Investigation, "Scams and safety", 2020, https://www.fbi.gov/scams-and-safety/common-scams-and-crimes/ransomware#:~:text=Tips%20for%20Avoiding%20Ransomware&text=Keep%20operating%20systems%2C%20software%2C%20and,Secure%20your%20backups.
43. Jack Schofield, The Guardian, "How can I remove a ransomware infection?", July 28, 2016, https://www.theguardian.com/technology/askjack/2016/jul/28/how-can-i-remove-ransomware-infection.
44. Lucas Danes, 2Spywar, "The best ransomware removal tools of 2020", September 21, 2020, https://www.2-spyware.com/the-best-ransomware-removal-tools.
45. KnowBe4, "Phishing by industry 2020", 2020, https://www.knowbe4.com/hubfs/2020PhishingByIndustryBenchmarkingReport.pdf.
46. Federal Bureau of Investigation, "Scams and safety", 2020, https://www.fbi.gov/scams-and-safety/common-scams-and-crimes/ransomware#:~:text=The%20FBI%20does%20not%20support,will%20get%20any%20data%20back.&text=If%20you%20are%20a%20victim,or%20submit%20a%20tip%20online.
47. Sophos, "The state of ransomware 2020", 2020, https://secure2.sophos.com/en-us/content/state-of-ransomware.aspx.

PART X

CYBER VENDOR RISK MANAGEMENT

34 VENDOR CYBER RISK OVERVIEW

Vendors are responsible for more than half of data breaches and their breaches are typically an order of magnitude more costly than a first party data breach.

Alex Golbin, Global Head of Risk Assessments Business, IHS Markit

First, second, third, and fourth parties

A first party is your company and all the on-premise digital assets. As you learned earlier, this risk is the exposures and the likelihood that your company will have a data breach or cyber event.

Second-party cyber risk comes from your customers or members. Customers or members can log into your systems and touch your digital assets. Customers may not have antivirus or other security measures on devices, making it easier for hackers to gain access to your data.

A third party is an institution or person that you outsource an activity to. There are different types of third parties. Cloud service providers who store and process your data and provide you a software, infrastructure, or a platform as a service. Service vendors who provide you management, IT, legal, accounting, or other services. Technology vendors who you buy technologies from and system vendors who you buy systems from. Each has to be understood in context. More to follow on this shortly.

Unless a contract specifically forbids it, a vendor can transfer its rights and responsibilities to a fourth party.

Your institution outsources to third parties and those vendors outsource to other vendors. These are called fourth parties. This relates to your vendors' third-party cyber-risk management program.

Your firm owns the data it collects and is accountable to protect it. Your institution is also responsible for the life of that data when it is stored or processed by a third party. Consequently, your firm is also responsible for the activities of your vendors' third-party vendors (aka your fourth-party vendors). The more your third parties outsource to other vendors, the greater the costs and risks of vendor management.

The Statement on Standards for Attestation Engagements 18 (SSAE 18)[1] has a vendor management requirement that states you must define the scope and responsibilities of each third-party vendor you use and address security assessment findings, audits, and monitoring.

DOI: 10.4324/9781003052616-44

Vendors that have access to sensitive data put your firm at risk of a data breach. Other key concerns of the vendor portfolio include those that perform critical business services, interact with customers, or perform a sensitive highly publicized function that exposes your firm to reputational risk.

Top third-party breaches of 2018

Third-party breaches are the most expensive incidents for both enterprises and SMBs. In 2018, the average cost of a data breach has reached US$120k for SMBs, 36% higher than 2017 (US$88k).

Saks Fifth Avenue and Lord & Taylor

In April 2018, Saks Fifth Avenue and Lord & Taylor—a Hudson's Bay Company—had over 5 million records exposed.[2] Cybercriminals stole more than 5 million credit and debit card numbers from customers of Saks Fifth Avenue and Lord & Taylor by implanting software into an unsecure point of sale (POS) system, siphoning card numbers and information since May 2017. In this example, it shows how the parent company bears the reputational impact of breaches at its subsidiaries. Companies need to understand the digital asset relationships between their divisions and treat them as an extension of the organization. This third-party data breach illustrates the interconnectivity between parent and subsidiary organizations that hackers will exploit.

BestBuy, Sears, Kmart, and Delta

BestBuy, Sears, Kmart, and Delta data breaches were reported in April 2018 and May 2018. These companies had a large weak link in common. Chat and customer services vendor [24]7.ai was hacked, which lead to the compromise of hundreds of thousands of customer records being stolen at Best Buy, Sears, Kmart, and Delta. Understanding the interconnectivity of your digital assets and who owns and maintains their security is the key to understanding that the cyber risk strategies must address these relationships.

Corporation Service Company

In May 2018, Corporation Service Company reported that they had almost 6,000 records stolen.[3] CSC acts as a company that provides domain registration services and acts as an agent for service. Hackers stole personal information of CSC customers' Fortune 500 clients. According to SC Media, unauthorized access to CSC's network via a third party was detected during routine security monitoring. Cybercriminals stole a database table from the network that contained confidential CSC's client data.

This third-party breach illustrates the need to have a cyber risk program in place with vendors who you provide sensitive data to. Some of the biggest companies in the world were impacted by this breach. Most companies outsource over 60% of their services to third parties. Large enterprises will have thousands of these third parties in their digital ecosystem.

MyFitnessPal

In February 2018, MyFitnessPal—a subsidiary of Under Armour, reported the loss of over 150 million records plummeting Under Armour shares down 3%.[4] According to Reuters, approximately 150 million user accounts were hacked, with usernames, email addresses, and scrambled passwords all stolen. Growth through acquisition is a typical strategy and with each new acquisition comes more cyber risk. This illustrates that the parent company owns the risk.

Universal Music Group

In June 2018, Universal Music Group (UMG) was hacked when a contractor left data exposed by failing to protect an Apache Airflow server. Everything in their vendor supported cloud data storage was exposed to the open internet. This included proprietary security data, such as the internal file transfer protocol (FTP) credentials, AWS Secret Keys and passwords, and the internal and SQL root password. As demonstrated with Target and Facebook, the amount of damage a contractor with poor security hygiene can do is devastating. Understanding which digital assets contractors utilize is the key to locking down the areas where the crown jewels can be exposed. Data breaches will continue with third parties until a trust-and-verify model is put in place.

Applebee's

In January 2018, it was reported that Applebee's was hacked. According to Threatpost, malware on POS systems at more than 160 Applebee's restaurants was discovered, exposing credit card information collected from unknowing diners.[5] Most retailers use POS service providers to process credit card data. This has been an overall weak point across the world. Many retailers have immature cybersecurity programs and third-party programs are not even on their radar.

Chili's

In May 2018, Chili's reported that they suffered a point-of-sale attack with payment card data, including names and credit or debit numbers, stolen.[6] Supply chain cybersecurity needs to be prioritized since most companies are outsourcing the majority of these services.

My Heritage.com

In June 2018, My Heritage.com had almost 100 million accounts breached. A security researcher found an archive on a third-party server containing personal details of the MyHeritage users. This included hashed passwords and DNA test results.

MyHeritage stored the DNA test results on separate servers from the one that managed user accounts. According to BleepingComputer, the MyHeritage incident marks the biggest data breach of the year, and the biggest leak since last year's Equifax hack.[7]

Top third-party breaches of 2019

In 2019, a third-party breach costs, on average, was twice what a normal breach costs. These impacts are amplified by the loss of brand reputation, business, and decreases in stock price. The overall cost of failing to effectively evaluate third parties is about US$13 million.[8]

Quest Diagnostics

In June 2019, Quest Diagnostics reported the loss of almost 12 million patient records. An unauthorized user gained access to Quest Diagnostic's data from a third-party billing collections vendor—the American Medical Collection Agency (AMCA). The hacker dwelt in the system from August 2018 to March 2019. The data stolen included credit card numbers, bank account information, and social security numbers.

US Customs & Border Protection

US Customs & Border Protection reported that in June 2019, they had up to 100,000 records exposed, when hackers breached a database containing photos of license plates and travelers' faces.[9] The data was stolen via a subcontractor's network that had been compromised. This data included investigation records, department files, personal data, system credentials, and internal communication records. The data was exposed to the public via an open storage server that belonged to the Oklahoma Department of Securities. The database was publicly accessible to any IP address, and any files stored on the server were downloadable.

Facebook

Facebook was breached twice in April 2019 and had over 540 million records stolen. Third-party apps and programs that are provided by app developers accessed Facebook information. Cultura Colectiva—a digital media company based in Mexico, left over 540 million records of user IDs, account names, comments, and more exposed on a publicly accessible server. Secondly, Plaintext (unprotected) passwords and email addresses for 22,000 users were exposed via At the Pool, another third-party Facebook app.

Focus Brands Inc.

The restaurant franchising group, Focus Brands Inc., recently revealed in 2019 data breaches at Moe's Southwest Grill, McAllister's Deli, and Schlotzsky's. Once again, the breach was from hacked payment processing systems at a number of locations.

The Point-of-Sale (PoS) vendor was hacked, leaving payment information of countless customers vulnerable from April 2019 to July 2019.

Government breaches

Approximately 750,000 birth certificates of US citizens were stolen through an unnamed third-party service provider. The applications were publicly accessible on an AWS cloud platform, with no protection whatsoever applied. The applications include highly sensitive and personal data with names and details. The theft affected residents of states of California, New York, and Texas.[10]

According to Fidus Information Security, a UK-based penetration testing company, the third-party responsible for the leak, obtained copies of birth certificates and death certificates from state governments and provided this data as a service on the internet to citizens. The exposed database goes back as early as 2017.

This type of data can be harvested by attackers via phishing campaigns to be sold on the dark web. Vulnerable AWS buckets that re-left open are a typical configuration mistake leading to data exposures. Many are managed by third parties.

Regus

Records of more than 900 employees of Regus were published online on a Trello board. A third party, named Applause, conducted detailed reviews on the company's sales staff through camera-embedded "pens" that were filming in and around the office. Job performance details of more than 900 employees were recorded in a Trello spreadsheet that was accidentally published online.

The stolen data included names, addresses, other contact details, and job performance details. This breach falls under the purview of the UK's Information Commissioner's Office. The companies may be fined by ICO for the data breach under the GDPR.

Mercy Health-Lorain Hospital

In January 2020, Ohio based healthcare group, Mercy Health-Lorain Hospital notified patients about a data breach.[11] The third-party vendor RCM Enterprise Services was providing revenue cycle management services. It was discovered that the medical invoices that were mailed to patients included sensitive social security data.

Mitsubishi Electric

Mitsubishi Electric announced in June 2020 that it had suffered a data breach at the beginning of the year. Security engineers identified suspicious activity on the company network. Upon investigation, it was confirmed that "the network may have been subject to unauthorized access by third parties and that personal information and corporate confidential information may have been leaked to the outside." announced Mitsubishi.[12]

Purportedly, a Chinese hacker group gained access to a Mitsubishi subsidiary company's network in China and then laterally moved into systems located in key Mitsubishi Electric offices in Japan. It is unclear if any sensitive defense-related data connected to Mitsubishi's business partners or government clients' defense contracts was stolen.

According to Asahi Shimbun, the Japanese newspaper, the hackers accessed Mitsubishi's systems and exfiltrated data on joint projects, negotiations, orders from partners, and research documents. Data of more than 10 government organizations was stolen, including the information about the Defense Ministry, the Nuclear Regulation Authority, and the Agency for Natural Resources and Energy and sensitive data on private-sector companies in the critical infrastructure (power, telecommunications, railway, and auto industries).

BlueBear

Announced in early 2020, BlueBear was breached according to a recent report filed to the Office of California's Attorney General between October 1, 2019 and November 13, 2019. BlueBear is a network platform that provides accounting and management software for schools and districts across the United States.[13]

Personal information of the parents using Bluebear to pay school fees or purchase school supplies could have had their information stolen. The personal information at risk includes names, payment card number and expiration date, security codes, and account usernames and passwords.

P&N Bank

Australian P&N Bank notified customers about a data breach which put the personal and sensitive account information of customers at risk.[14] P&N Bank is a division of Police & Nurses Limited. The bank reported that the breach involved a system that is maintained and operated by a third-party hosting firm. The information exposed contained PII and included sensitive account number and account balance information.

Although details of the attack are unknown, access to P&N Bank's third-party CRM system took place on December 12 as it was undergoing an upgrade. Immediately, when the breach was discovered, the system in question was disconnected and shut down.

Top third-party breaches of 2020

Instagram

Instagram leads the pack with two data breaches so far in 2020. The first breach was blamed on a social media boosting service called Social Captain. Thousands of usernames and passwords were revealed to be in plaintext. Instagram influencers use the platform, boost the likes, and increase a user's Instagram followers. Users couple their Instagram accounts to the service. Instagram usernames and passwords are required to use the service.

TechCrunch reports, "Any user who viewed the web page source code on their Social Captain profile page could see their Instagram username and password in plain sight, so long as they had connected their account to the platform."[15]

A website vulnerability allowed unauthorized users to access any Social Captain user's profile without having to log in and access their Instagram login credentials. The exposed PII included usernames and passwords of 4700 users.

TechCrunch was alerted by an anonymous security researcher to the vulnerability. He provided a spreadsheet of about 10,000 scraped user accounts details. Scraping websites does not fall afoul of US computer hacking laws according to a recent court ruling.

Instagram said that storing login credentials in plaintext is a serious breach of its terms of service agreement.[16] Instagram is investigating and taking appropriate action. It is strongly recommended to never give passwords to anyone ever.

AmediCanna Dispensary, Bloom Medicinals, and Colorado Grow Company

AmediCanna Dispensary, Bloom Medicinals, and Colorado Grow Company were impacted by similar cyber issues. A vulnerable Amazon S3 bucket exposed approximately 30,000 marijuana users' records. The breach occurred through a point-of-sale software vendor, named THSuite.

Ohio-based medical marijuana dispensary, Bloom Medicinals, notified its patients as required by HIPAA. The same Amazon issue is associated with AmediCanna Dispensary and the Colorado Grow Company.

The exposed PII includes medical ID numbers, and the cannabis variety and quantity purchased.

Government and employee IDs were also breached. Revocation of state-awarded operating licenses is being explored by the Ohio Attorney General. These companies may also be fined due to HIPAA violations.

Cloud service providers

Third parties must be considered in their true context. A Cloud Service Provider is much different from a management consultant or an attorney.

Cloud Service Providers—A cloud service provider is a third-party company offering a cloud-based platform, infrastructure, application, or storage services.

- SaaS provides software as a service, where software is licensed on a subscription basis and is centrally hosted.
- PaaS provides a platform as a service that allows clients to develop, run, and manage applications without the complexity of building and maintaining the infrastructure typically associated with developing and launching an application.

- IaaS provides the infrastructure as a service, which is an instant computing infrastructure, provisioned and managed over the internet. Each resource is offered as a separate service component. Customers rent a particular service component for only as long as it is needed. As an example, with Microsoft Azure. Microsoft manages the infrastructure, the customer purchases, installs, configures, and manages their own software, operating systems, middleware, and applications.

Most of these models also provide data storage.

Service Providers—A third-party organization that provides services to the company. Examples include lawyers, accountants, doctors, IT companies, management consultants, etc.

System Vendors—Third-party organizations that provide a set of technologies that are sold as systems.

Technology Vendors—Third parties that sell technologies, such as databases, frameworks, languages, security tools, etc.

Vendor teams

Cyber Vendor Risk Management is becoming its own discipline. It is ideal if there is a centralized vendor or procurement team that is responsible for cyber risk. Team members will include the security team, internal security assessor (ISAs), legal team, and business owners. The procurement team ideally is the project management team that understands the requirements and evidence that will be acceptable to the firm. The security team helps to define the cybersecurity requirements and ensure that the vendor team understands what is required. The legal team will review the contract. Once the vendor has provided a risk assessment, the ISAs will review the evidence and discuss the results with the vendor team. Business owners provide input to key functions and vendor requirements across the firm.

Vendor contracts

A vendor's cybersecurity due diligence should begin prior to working with a firm. All vendors should establish and maintain a cyber risk strategy. This is a documented program strategy for identifying and managing their cybersecurity risks. An organization's cybersecurity strategy will be driven by laws and regulations that the organization is subject to, applicable industry standards, and the organization's assessment of its own tolerance for risk. Certain laws will mandate specific terms for vendor agreements. HIPAA requires a Business Associate Agreement. The US government has contract provisions in vendor agreements for companies doing business with the EU. This includes the Privacy Shield Principles.

Vendors that use subcontractors and suppliers (fourth parties) who may have access to your systems and data must have adequate third-party programs. Your vendor contracts must require an assignment clause, which provides your firm notice and consent before the vendor outsources any part of the contract. This gives a firm the ability to control fourth-party risk.

A digital asset inventory should be done of the data, systems, and business processes that the vendor will work with at the organization. Likewise, the organization should have an inventory of the systems and technologies the vendor is providing as well as the type of data to be processed or stored by the vendor.

Analyzing the digital asset interconnectivity and dependencies with the third parties is an element of starting a cybersecurity risk assessment.

Organizations should evaluate the inherent cybersecurity risk of people, processes, technology, and data that support an identified function. Companies must assess the effectiveness of cybersecurity controls to protect against the identified risk. Cyber risk assessments provide the basis for the application of appropriate controls and the development of remediation plans to mitigate risks and vulnerabilities down to reasonable and appropriate level.[17]

Vendor risk assessment program

Vendor risk assessment programs must be fit for purpose. Typical steps to set up a vendor risk assessment program include:

1. Vendor digital asset inventory and identification of vendor type(s).
   - The identification of digital asset goods or services provided in relationship to data that will be processed or stored by the vendor.
   - The type of access to systems given to a vendor and why.
   - The digital asset supported by the vendor.
   - Criticality of business service supported by the vendor.
   - The nature of service provided by the vendor and determination if the vendor directly interacts with your customers or handles other client-facing activities.
2. Identification of regulation(s) or industry standard(s) for the vendor to abide by.
   - Mapping of requirements across different regulations to reduce redundancy.
   - Ensure that the compliance program is aligned to applicable federal, state, and local laws.
3. Creation of a Vendor Questionnaire related to vendor type.
   - Ensure specific requirements are included in vendor questionnaires (i.e., ciphers required for encryption, etc.).
   - Include fourth-party requirements.
   - Select a Framework and ensure at a minimum:
     - Review of security policies and procedures and the enforcement of the vendor's security policies.
     - Effective incident response and business continuity/disaster recovery.

- Table-top exercises of DR plans are tested regularly and updated.
- Secure Software Development Life Cycle (SSDLC).
- Latest vulnerability scan.
- Latest pen test.
- Threat intelligence tools and processes.
- Disclosure of incidents/breaches and vulnerabilities the vendor identified in the vendor's systems.

4 Vendor Questionnaire and Evidence Review.

— Independent control attestations.
— Review evidence with Internal Security Assessor (ISA) Team.

5 Vendor Cyber Risk Profile Review.

— Determine data exfiltration and inherent vendor cyber risk.

6 Monitoring of vendor based on the risk profile.

Notes

1. Wikipedia, "SSAE No. 18", December 1, 2020, https://en.wikipedia.org/wiki/SSAE_No._18.
2. Jim Finkle, David Henry, Reuters, "Saks, Lord & Taylor hit by payment card data breach", June 19, 2017, https://cn.reuters.com/article/instant-article/idUSKCN1H91W7.
3. Zaid Shoorbajee, Cyber Scoop, "Hackers steal PII and payment info of thousands of California residents in company breach", May 21, 2018, https://www.cyberscoop.com/csc-california-data-breach/.
4. Tony Bradley, Forbes, "Security experts weigh in on massive data breach of 150 million MyFitnessPal accounts", May 30, 2018, https://www.forbes.com/sites/tonybradley/2018/03/30/security-experts-weigh-in-on-massive-data-breach-of-150-million-myfitnesspal-accounts/?sh=2390dc483bba.
5. Matthew J. Schwartz, Bank Info Security, "166 Applebee's restaurants hit with payment card malware", March 6, 2018, https://www.bankinfosecurity.com/172-applebees-restaurants-hit-payment-card-malware-a-10699#:~:text=On%20Friday%2C%20RMH%20Franchise%20Holdings,who%20dined%20at%20the%20restaurants.
6. Mary Hanbury, Business Insider, "Chili's restaurants were hit by a data breach that exposed customers' credit-card information", May 14, 2018, https://www.businessinsider.com/chilis-data-breach-2018-5?r=DE&IR=T#:~:text=On%20Saturday%2C%20its%20parent%20company,doesn't%20collect%20this%20information.
7. Catalin Cimpanu, Bleeping Computer, "MyHeritage genealogy site announces mega breach affecting 92 million accounts", June 5, 2018, https://www.bleepingcomputer.com/news/security/myheritage-genealogy-site-announces-mega-breach-affecting-92-million-accounts/.
8. Cyber GRX, "The worst third-party data breaches in 2019", June 2019, https://www.cybergrx.com/resources/research-and-insights/blog/the-worst-third-party-data-breaches-in-2019#:~:text=A%20third%2Dparty%20breach%20costs,parties%20is%20about%20%2413%20million.
9. Drew Harwell, Geoffrey A. Fowler, The Washington Post, "U.S. customs and border protection says photos of travelers were taken in a data breach", June 10, 2019, https://www.washingtonpost.com/technology/2019/06/10/us-customs-border-protection-says-photos-travelers-into-out-country-were-recently-taken-data-breach/.

10. Amer Owaida, We live security, "Data leak exposes 750,000 birth certificate applications", December 10, 2019, https://www.welivesecurity.com/2019/12/10/data-leak-exposes-750000-birth-certificate-applications/#:~:text=Over%20752%2C000%20birth%20certificate%20applications,the%20United%20States%2C%20TechCrunch%20reports.
11. DataBreaches.net, "Mercy Health Lorain Hospital laboratory patients notified of HIPAA breach due to contractor invoice printing error", January 7, 2020, https://www.databreaches.net/mercy-health-lorain-hospital-laboratory-patients-notified-of-hipaa-breach-due-to-contractor-invoice-printing-error/.
12. Sarah Coble, Info Security Group, "Mitsubishi Electric discloses information leak", January 20, 2020, https://www.infosecurity-magazine.com/news/mitsubishi-electric-discloses/.
13. CISO Mag, "Attackers compromised school management platform Blue Bear", January 6, 2020, https://cisomag.eccouncil.org/attackers-compromised-school-management-platform-blue-bear/.
14. Doug Olenick, SC Media, "Aussie P&N Bank suffers data breach", January 16, 2020, https://www.scmagazine.com/home/security-news/data-breach/aussie-pn-bank-suffers-data-breach/#:~:text=The%20Australian%20P%26N%20Bank%20reported,firm%2C%20was%20undergoing%20an%20upgrade.
15. Zack Whittaker, TechCrunch, "Social media boosting service exposed thousands of Instagram passwords", January 30, 2020, https://techcrunch.com/2020/01/30/social-captain-instagram-passwords/.
16. Zack Whittaker, TechCrunch, "Social media boosting service exposed thousands of Instagram passwords", January 30, 2020, https://techcrunch.com/2020/01/30/social-captain-instagram-passwords/.
17. American Bar Association (ABA) Cybersecurity Legal Task Force, Americanbar.org, "Vendor contracting project: Cybersecurity checklist", April 13,2017, https://www.americanbar.org/content/dam/aba/administrative/law_national_security/cyber-task-force-vendor-contracting.pdf.

35 VENDOR CYBERSECURITY REGULATIONS

I believe we will all be responsible for our own security—no vendor, service provider, or even government entity will save us.

Sean Martin, Founder ITPS Magazine Podcast

Regulations requiring vendor cyber risk programs

The PCI security council

The PCI Security Council (PCI SC) was formed in 2004 by the major card brands, including American Express, JBC, Visa, Mastercard, and Discover to protect cardholder data. It applies to merchants, acquiring banks, and data processors. Data processors are typically third parties; however, each of these three has first- and third-party relationships.

The PCI SC is one of the earliest governing bodies to have vendor cybersecurity requirements. They require all payment card service providers who process, transmit, and/or store payment card information to be compliant with the Payment Card Industry Data Security Standard (PCI-DSS).

Vendors must submit an Attestation of Compliance (AoC) every 12 months. An attestation is completed by a Qualified Security Assessor (QSA) and states that the organization is PCI DSS compliant. It is used as evidence that an organization has upheld security best practices to protect cardholder data. Each vendor submits an AOC as a service provider.

Each vendor must submit a quarterly Approved Scanning Vendor (ASV) report and the current years' penetration test of the external network. No vulnerabilities should exist that are scored 4.0 or higher by the CVSS in the Quarterly ASV scan report. The PCI Compliance team will only accept a maximum of three versions of an AOC from the same vendor for review in a 12-month period. The PCI Compliance team may request that the vendor provides a demo on their payment processing workflow through its services.[1]

Third-party service providers can store, process, or transmit cardholder data on behalf of the first party. They may also manage systems or technologies that store or process cardholder data. These may include payment systems, routers, firewalls, databases, physical security, and/or servers.

The use of a third party does not exclude the first party's responsibility to ensure that its cardholder data environment is secure. Clear policies and procedures must

DOI: 10.4324/9781003052616-45

be part of the vendor risk management program. These must outline all applicable security requirements, and ownership and auditing of those measures must be reported on regularly.

Proper due diligence and cyber risk analysis are critical components in the selection of any third-party vendor. Requirements from the PCI SC include four major components[2] when selecting vendors—proper due diligence, service correlation, a written cyber program, and monitoring of the third parties.

PCI requires Third-Party Service Provider (TPSP) Due Diligence for vendors that process or store cardholder data.[3] Vendors must be put through a rigorous vetting process using careful due diligence prior to establishment of the relationship.

PCI requires Service Correlation to the PCI DSS Requirements for TPSPs. This includes understanding how the services provided by TPSPs correspond to the applicable PCI DSS requirements.

PCI requires Written Agreements and Policies and Procedures for TPSPs. Detailed written agreements will ensure mutual understanding between the organization and its TPSP(s) concerning their respective responsibilities and obligations with respect to PCI DSS compliance requirements. PCI requires the firm to monitor Third-Party Service Provider Compliance Status.

National association of insurance commissioners (NAIC)[4]

The NAIC—Insurance Data Security Act (also known as the Model Law) requires the oversight of Third-Party Service Provider Arrangements. A Licensee (person, broker, carrier, and reinsurance firms that are required to be licensed, authorized, or registered pursuant to the insurance laws of this State) shall exercise due diligence in selecting its Third-Party Service Provider; and require the Third-Party Service Provider to implement the necessary administrative, technical, and physical safeguards to protect and secure the Information Systems and Nonpublic Information they have access to.

The third-party risk management program must have a formal process in place whereby:[5]

1 Risk is assessed based on the company's understanding of the third-party service providers information security program as well as by the company's ability to verify elements of the third-party service provider's security program;
2 Based on the company's risk, the company ranks vendors and uses a vendor's ranking to determine depth and frequency of review procedures performed related to ongoing vendor relationships;
3 The company determines appropriate access rights, based on the risk assessment and company business needs;
4 The company designs specific mitigation strategies, including network monitoring specific to third-party service providers and access controls, where appropriate.

If the Licensee suspects that a cybersecurity incident has occurred in a system maintained by a Third-Party Service Provider, the Licensee will perform a forensics investigation. During the investigation, it must be determined whether a Cybersecurity Incident has occurred. The nature and scope of the Cybersecurity Incident must be documented and any Nonpublic Information (NPI) that may have been involved in the Cybersecurity Incident identified. The firm must ensure that they restore the security of the Information Systems compromised in the Cybersecurity Event.

In the case of a cybersecurity incident, notification has to be provided in electronic form as directed by the Commissioner. Required information includes:

- Date of the occurrence of the Cybersecurity Incident;
- A description of how the information was compromised, including the specific roles and responsibilities of Third-Party Service Providers, if any;
- How the Cybersecurity Incident was identified;
- If any lost, stolen, or breached information has been recovered and if so, how this was done;
- Who discovered the Cybersecurity Incident;
- Whether a police report or other regulatory, government, or law enforcement agencies and, if so, when such notification was provided.

Third-party service providers must notify their affected Insurers and the Commissioner of Insurance in the state in which they are domiciled within 72 hours of a Cybersecurity Incident involving NPI that they are processing or storing on behalf of a Licensee.

Notification is also required to producers of record of all affected Consumers as soon as practicable as directed by the Commissioner if there is a Cybersecurity Incident involving NPI that is being processed or stored by its Third-Party Service Provider.

European Union—GDPR

Article 28 of the GDPR states that—If an organization uses one or more third parties to process personal info ("processors") it must ensure they are also compliant with GDPR.[6]

This requires a leader to oversee the vendor cyber risk management program and to put in place the program requirements that are needed.

Vendor relationship management processes and procedures must ensure that third parties that process personal information are complaint with the GDPR. This can also be a role of the DPO if there is no vendor management team. The Data Protection Officer (DPO) Job Responsibilities and the Rationale for a Data Protection Officer (DPO) are required.

State of CA—California Consumer Protection Act (CCPA)[7]

With respect to third-party risk, the CCPA recognizes, and places obligations on, service providers. These are defined as entities that process consumers' personal information (PI) on the business's behalf and third parties; these are defined as entities to whom the business shares or sells PI but do not directly collect PI from consumers. In particular, the CCPA emphasizes contractual requirements and the consumer's right to opt-out of the sale of personal information.

For service providers, businesses must maintain records of each service provider and the categories of PI disclosed to them. The organization must conduct due diligence on potential service providers prior to entering into a contract. The contracts must be reevaluated on at least an annual basis. The company must have a written contract with the service providers that prohibit them from retaining, using, or disclosing the PI for any purpose other than for the exact purposes of performing the services agreed to in the contract, or as otherwise, permitted by the CCPA. There must be language in the contract to help cure a violation of the CCPA. The service provider must notify the company without unreasonable delay upon experiencing a data breach. The contract must require the service provider to protect the PI disclosed to it by developing and maintaining reasonable security safeguards that are appropriate to the nature of the information.

In terms of Consumer Rights, the contract must require the service provider to delete a consumer's PI when you direct it to do so and obligate the service provider to assist you in complying with a consumer's request to know/to disclose the PI collected, shared, or sold. There must be processes in place that enable the company to notify a service provider when consumers exercise a right.

All categories of data that a third party touches must be documented and the business purpose of the data exchange with each third party clearly stated. Records must be maintained of third-party data exchanges in the preceding 12 months, including the categories of PI.

The third party must have accurate records of the data exchanges so that you can disclose to consumers the categories of PI sold and the categories of third parties to whom you have sold that PI. They must provide confirmation that your firm gave a consumer proper notice and the right to opt-out, and a signed attestation describing the notice, along with an example of the notice. They must have processes in place that guarantee the accuracy of the attestation. They must be able to cease selling a consumer's PI no later than 15 days after receipt of the consumer's request to opt-out of the sale of their PI.

Upon the receipt of a consumer's request to opt-out of the sale of PI, they must have processes in place to notify a third party of the consumer's request and to instruct the third party not to further sell that consumer's PI. They must maintain records of parties to whom they have sold a consumer's PI within the 90 days prior to the consumer's opt-out request.

New York State Department of Financial Services—NYCRR part 500[8]

Each Covered Entity (person operating under or required to operate under a license, registration, charter, certificate, permit, accreditation, or similar authorization under the Banking Law, the Insurance Law, or the Financial Services Law) must implement a set of written policies and procedures that are designed to safeguard the security of Information Systems and NPI that are processed or stored by a Third-Party Service Provider.

Requirements include that:

- these policies and procedures must be based on a Risk Assessment of the Covered Entity and identify all Third-Party Service Providers and access their cybersecurity practices to ensure that they met by such Third-Party Service Providers in order for them to do business with the Covered Entity;
- a rigorous due diligence is done to evaluate the adequacy of cybersecurity practices of such Third-Party Service Providers;
- periodic assessment of such Third-Party Service Providers based on the risk they present and the continued adequacy of their cybersecurity practices;
- the policies and procedures shall include relevant guidelines for due diligence and/or contractual protections relating to Third-Party Service Providers including, to the extent applicable, guidelines addressing:
  - the Third-Party Service Provider's policies and procedures for access controls;
  - the use of Multifactor Authentication as required by section 500.12;
  - the Third-Party Service Provider's policies and procedures for use of encryption as required by section 500.15 to protect NPI in transit and at rest;
  - notification process must be in place to the Covered Entity in the event of a Cybersecurity Incident directly impacting the Covered Entity's Information Systems or the Covered Entity's NPI that is processed or stored by the Third-Party Service Provider.

All the third-party risk management programs start with a vendor inventory, not only who they are but what type of vendor they are. Vendors can have more than one function. As an example, Salesforce is both a cloud service and a system vendor. It is not enough to have a list of applications that are vendor supported. You have to know the vendor and what they provide you.

A risk assessment of a vendor has to look at what is important. How much data exfiltration, business interruption, and regulatory risk do you have with the vendor?

Security Assessment. How effective is the vendor's cybersecurity controls? A NIST or ISO assessment should be reviewed in depth. Security issues should be prioritized to fix.

Vendor background checks and due diligence require more than a useless SOC 2 report.

The language about how data breaches will be handled in detail with a communication and incident response plan is required.

Procedures should include guidelines for due diligence, and contractual protections.

All third parties should connect using multifactor authentication.

Nonpublic information should be encrypted in transit and at rest for cloud service providers that have sensitive data on their network.

Security incidents must be communicated by the third party to your firm within a specific timeframe. It is recommended to put in the contractual protections that in the event of a breach, they have 72 hours to report it to you. If they do not notify you and the breach is made public, the examiners are going to come after you and ask why it was not reported it to them within 72 hours. All 50 states have data breach notification laws.

There are many issues with contracts. One instance, in particular, I recall is where the vendor told a company—"if there's a breach, that is not our fault, we expect to still get paid regardless and they accept no responsibility." The company signed it. When I saw the contract, I said, you know, you made a mistake, right? They had to revisit the contract and put the right language in because it wasn't reviewed properly. This had to go back to the business that engaged the vendor. The big issues with vendor management today are the business selects the vendor and cyber is not involved. This must change. This should be baked into a policy that allows for this issue to no longer exist.

Department of Defense (DoD)—CMMC[9]

The Department of Defense created a new program called the Cybersecurity Maturity Model Certification (CMMC). The DoD is requiring all contractors who handle sensitive DoD data to have a third-party maturity assessment in order to obtain DoD business. This requirement is effective on July 1, 2020.

The Office of the Under Secretary of Defense for Acquisition and Sustainment (OUSD (A&S)) recognizes that security is foundational to acquisition and should not be traded along with cost, schedule, and performance moving forward. The Department is committed to working with the Defense Industrial Base (DIB) sector to enhance the protection of controlled unclassified information (CUI) within the supply chain.

OUSD (A&S) is working with DoD stakeholders, University Affiliated Research Centers (UARCs), Federally Funded Research and Development Centers (FFRDC), and industry to develop the Cybersecurity Maturity Model Certification (CMMC).

The CMMC is a cybersecurity audit that measures the cybersecurity maturity levels of a company. The results from the Audit can range from "Basic Cybersecurity Hygiene" to "Advanced/Progressive." The intent of the DoD is to incorporate CMMC into Defense Federal Acquisition Regulation Supplement (DFARS) and use it as a requirement for contract awards.

CMMC Levels 1–3 have 110 security requirements, which are specified in NIST SP 800-171 rev1. CMMC incorporates additional practices and processes from other standards, references, and source materials. These include the NIST SP 800-53, the Aerospace Industries Association (AIA) National Aerospace Standard (NAS) 9933 "Critical Security Controls for Effective Capability in Cyber Defense," and the Computer Emergency Response Team (CERT) Resilience Management Model (RMM) v1.2.

The CMMC will review and combine various cybersecurity standards and best practices and map these controls and processes across several maturity levels that range from basic cyber hygiene to advanced. For a given CMMC level, the associated controls and processes, when implemented, will reduce risk against a specific set of cyber threats.

The CMMC effort builds upon existing regulation (DFARS 252.204-7012) that is based on trust by adding a verification component with respect to cybersecurity requirements.

The goal is for CMMC to be cost-effective and affordable for small businesses to implement at the lower CMMC levels. The intent is for certified independent third-party organizations to conduct audits and inform the DoD about vendor cyber risk.

Health and Human Services (HHS) HIPAA and HiTech acts[10]

Business Associates are third parties that are regulated by HIPAA. They are defined by HHS as any individual or organization that creates, receives, maintains, or transmits PHI on behalf of a Covered Entity (CE). It defines subcontractors as those that create, receive, maintain, or transmit PHI on behalf of a Business Associate.

For healthcare providers that are considered Covered Entities, your responsibilities include that you ensure that all your vendors who handle Protected Health Information (PHI) and are designated as Business Associates under HIPAA, and their subcontractors are compliant.

Twenty percent of all PHI breaches are caused by a Business Associate. If Business Associates or their Subcontractors get audited, so will the Covered Entity. Business associates include: administration, data processors, accountants, management consultants, IT system, and service providers, document disposal companies, EHR/EMR providers, leasing companies, call centers, document management services, lawyers, claim processors, technology vendors, financial services, data centers, telco vendors, cloud service providers, medical billers, and collection agencies, among others.

Vendors must follow the HIPAA Security Rule (2005) for electronic Protected Health Information. (ePHI). This includes:

1 Administrative Safeguards—Includes security management processes, workforce security, information access management, security training and awareness, contingency plan evaluation, and Business Associate contract
2 Physical Safeguards—Includes facility access controls, workstation use, workstation security, and device and media control
3 Technical Safeguards—Includes access control, audit control, integrity, personal or entity authentication, and transmission security

The HITECH Act of 2009 (Health Information Technology for Economic and Clinical Health Act) applies to business associates. It extends the privacy and security rules of HIPAA to Businesses Associates and their subcontractors.

The HITECH Act was enacted to promote the adoption of health information technology, named EHR (electronic health records). HITECH gives health providers technical requirements to hospitals and doctors who are using EHR. After 2009, this Act requires Business Associates to implement the same compliance documents and training as a Covered Entity.

The Omnibus Rule (2013)

Under the Omnibus Rule, Business Associates are independently responsible to comply with HIPAA privacy, security, and breach rule and are subject to fines.

First-party responsibilities with Business Associates include:

Having an up-to-date Business Associate Agreement (BAA) with each business associate is reviewed and updated every year. The agreement must confirm what data the Business Associate uses that is PHI, why the Business Associate (BA) was engaged and that how they will safeguard the PHI from misuse. The agreement governs the BA's creation, use, maintenance, and disclosure of PHI. The BA must comply with HIPAA Security, and help a Covered Entity (CE) satisfy privacy rules and treat subcontractors as Business Associates. Business Associates are directly liable for the following:

- use that is not permissible,
- disclosures,
- failures to provide breach notification to the CE,
- failure to provide a copy of the ePHI to either the CE, the individual, or the individual's designee, and
- failure to follow minimum necessary standards when using or disclosing and failure to provide an accounting of disclosures.

Business associates that do not comply with HIPAA are liable for Civil Penalties. These penalties are mandatory for willful neglect. The Health and Human Services Office for Civil Rights ("OCR") is responsible for enforcing the Privacy and Security Rule for HPAA Covered Entities.[11] OCR is required to impose HIPAA penalties if the Business Associate acted with willful neglect. This means that the Business Associate consciously, and intentionally failed to comply or showed reckless indifference to the obligation to comply with the HIPAA requirements.

A single action most often results in multiple violations. The loss of a record is a violation. As an example, the loss of a laptop containing records of 500 individuals is a loss of 500 records. This means in HIPAA language that it is 500 violations.

If there was a failure to implement the required policies and safeguards, each day the Covered Entity failed to have the required policy or safeguard in place constitutes a separate violation. HIPAA penalties add up quickly. The OCR has imposed millions of dollars in penalties and settlements over the past several years. Additionally, State Attorneys General have the authority to sue for HIPAA violations and recover penalties of US$25,000 per violation plus attorneys' fees. The following chart summarizes the tiered penalty structure:

Conduct of covered entity or business associate	Penalty
Did not know and, by exercising reasonable diligence, would not have known of the violation	$100 to $50,000 per violation; Up to $1,500,000 per identical violation per year
Violation due to reasonable cause and not willful neglect	$1,000 to $50,000 per violation; Up to $1,500,000 per identical violation per year
Violation due to willful neglect but the violation is corrected within 30 days after the covered entity knew or should have known of the violation	Mandatory fine of $10,000 to $50,000 per violation; Up to $1,500,000 per identical violation per year
Violation due to willful neglect, and the violation was not corrected within 30 days after the covered entity knew or should have known of the violation	Mandatory fine of not less than $50,000 per violation; Up to $1,500,000 per identical violation per year

Figure 35.1 HIPAA Fines[12]

HIPAA has the longest and one of the costliest penalties and settlements history in the United States. A single cyber event mostly likely results in multiple violations.[13] HIPAA considers willful neglect when imposing penalties. If the Business Associate did not act with willful neglect, the OCR may waive or reduce the penalties, depending on the circumstances. Willful negligence is indicated when the conduct is deliberate. Willful negligence involves behavior that is intended, and reckless.[14]

When the Business Associate was not willfully negligent and corrects the violation within 30 days, the OCR may choose not to impose any penalty. Having a plan and showing that changes were made to remediate the issue are key here. This is why having a cybersecurity program with policies and procedures that provide the requirements for the technical, physical, and administrative safeguards may protect the business associated from a very high penalty.

Furthermore, HIPAA violations may be a crime. Clinicians, healthcare staff members, data processors, insurance companies, among others have been prosecuted for improperly accessing, using, or disclosing PHI. The maximum criminal penalties under HIPAA include jail time of one year to ten years, and fines from US$25,000 to US$1,500,000 per violation.[15]

In a Memorandum of Opinion released in 2005, the Department of Justice (DOJ) makes a point of differentiating intent and knowledge. They define "knowingly" as referring to knowledge of the facts that comprise the offense and not the knowledge of the law being violated.[16]

Federal law prohibits any person from improperly obtaining or revealing PHI from a Covered Entity without authorization. Violations may result in the following criminal penalties.

Prohibited Conduct	Penalty
Knowingly obtaining or disclosing PHI without authorization.	Up to $50,000 fine and one year in prison
If done under false pretenses.	Up to $100,000 fine and five years in prison
If done with intent to sell, transfer, or use the PHI for commercial advantage, personal gain or malicious harm.	Up to $250,000 fine and ten years in prison
Prohibited Conduct	Penalty

Figure 35.2 HIPAA Criminal Penalties[17]

Business associates must report HIPAA breaches of unsecured PHI to Covered Entities that are affected. The Covered Entities must then notify affected individual(s) of the breach and HHS. The Covered Entity will have to incur the data exfiltration costs associated with the data breach, the costs of responding to the HHS investigation, and the potential penalties. Not reporting opens up both the business associates and the Covered Entity to civil penalties and open the firm up to civil lawsuits.

The privacy rules of HIPAA are very similar to GDPR. The Covered Entities and their business associates may not collect, use, or disclose PHI without the person's valid, HIPAA authorization.

The Business Associate needs to have a cybersecurity risk analysis preformed and the Covered Entity has to ensure that they have adequate security safeguards in place.

State of CO—Colorado Consumer Protection Act[18]

Colorado defines a third-party service provider as an entity which has been contracted to process or store personal information on behalf of a Covered Entity.

New requirements to ensure protections are in place when PII is transferred to third-party service providers:

Colorado requires that the third-party service provider implement and maintain reasonable security procedures and practices that are appropriate to the nature of the personal identifying information processes or stored by the third-party service provider; and that they use safeguards that are reasonably designed to protect the personal identifying information from unauthorized access, use, modification, disclosure, or destruction.

The Bill also was amended to include an exception where a Covered Entity retains security responsibility and implements controls to protect PII from unauthorized disclosure or to eliminate third-party's access:

> ... disclosure of personal identifying information does not include disclosure of information to a third party under circumstances where the covered entity retains primary responsibility for implementing and maintaining reasonable security procedures and practices appropriate to the nature of the personal

identifying information and the covered entity implements and maintains technical controls that are reasonably designed to:

(a) help protect the personal identifying information from unauthorized access, use, modification, disclosure, or destruction; or
(b) effectively eliminate the third-party's ability to access the personal identifying information, notwithstanding the third-party's physical possession of the personal identifying information

At the state level, Colorado now has the highest cost per record fine in the country as of this writing—a whopping US$20,000 a record.

Federal Trade Commission (FTC)—Graham Leach Bliley Act (GLBA)[19]

Companies in scope for GLBA are financial institutions, and those firms that offer financial products and services to individuals. These include loans, financial advice, investment advice, or insurance.

GLBA defines Nonpublic Personal Information (NPI) as all data that is Personally Identifiable Information (PII) and financial information that is provided by a customer to the financial institution, which results in a transaction with the customer.

Data that is generally public but has been made private (e.g. private emails, unlisted phone numbers, etc.), must be treated as nonpublic. GLBA definitions of NPI include an individual's income, social security number, marital status, amount of savings or investments, payment history, loan or deposit balance, credit or debit card purchases, account numbers, or consumer reports.

The Safeguards Rule requires financial institutions to create, implement, and maintain an all-inclusive cybersecurity plan which outlines the administrative, technical, and physical safeguards that are appropriate to an organization based on its size, complexity, and its financial activities. Safeguards should:

- ensure the confidentiality, integrity, and availability of all NPI,
- protect against the most common cyber threats, and
- protect against data breaches, and unauthorized access to NPI.

The cybersecurity plan must include:

- At least one employee who is responsible for the information security program and its safeguards.
- Have a risk management program that includes internal risks, third-party risks, and fourth-party risks to the confidentiality, integrity, and availability of NPI.
- Perform a rigorous cybersecurity risk assessment which assesses the effectiveness of the cybersecurity safeguards in place to mitigate all risk types.
- Regular testing of cybersecurity controls, systems, and procedures.

The Safeguards Rule forces financial institutions to take cyber risk management seriously by measuring their cybersecurity risk and the effectiveness of their controls, systems, and procedures to reduce that risk to acceptable levels.

Summary

Each vendor related regulation requires an understanding of the regulatory scope, cybersecurity programs, and the use of cybersecurity control framework in the vendor management and assessment processes. In Chapter 24, we provided an understanding of the controls across different frameworks. All frameworks aspire to provide a level of control effectiveness relative to administrative, technical, and physical safeguards that support confidentiality, integrity, and availability.

The next textbook in my cyber series is "Vendor Cyber Risk Management—The Next Frontier in Cybersecurity" and is a must for businesses. New roles and responsibilities are needed to manage these key program requirements for third-party cyber risk management. An understanding of how vendors impact cybersecurity is critical for this to be effective. Cyber touches every aspect of the business and is ubiquitous. Third parties are our supply chains. They are integrated with our business processes and cyber events impact the firm as the owner of the cyber risk.

Vendor cyber risk is complex since we now have smart interconnected devices and systems where risk is inherited from one system to another. This was the case of Target, Facebook, and SolarWinds, just to name a few. Vendors are not understood in their context and programs cannot be checklists only. They must understand how the vendor can damage the firm and act to prevent it. This next book is about how the business can have an effective approach to understand it and manage cyber vendor risk in context.

Notes

1. 42, "PCI compliance: Where does AOC, ROC, and SAQ stand for?", June 12, 2018, https://fortytwo.nl/pci-compliance-aoc-roc-saq/.
2. OneTrust Vendorpedia, "PCI DSS compliance: 3 key third-party risk management requirements", December 20, 2019, https://www. https://www.vendorpedia.com/blog/third-party-risk-requirements-for-pci-dss-compliance/.
3. PCI Security Standards Council, "Information supplement: Third-party security assurance", March 2016, https://www.pcisecuritystandards.org/documents/ThirdPartySecurityAssurance_March2016_FINAL.pdf.
4. NAIC, "National Association of Insurance Commissioners", 2021, https://content.naic.org/.
5. NAIC, "Insurance data security model law", 4th quarter 2017, https://content.naic.org/sites/default/files/inline-files/MDL-668.pdf?39.
6. Official Journal of the European Union, Regulation (EU) 2016/679 Of the European Parliament and the Council of 27 April 2016, "General Data Protection Regulation", April 27, 2016, https://gdprinfo.eu/.
7. Xavier Becerra, Attorney General, State of California Department of Justice, "California Consumer Privacy Act (CCPA)", 2021, https://www.oag.ca.gov/privacy/ccpa.

8. New York State Department of Financial Services, "FAQs: 23 NYCRR Part 500-Cybersecurity", December 10, 2020, https://www.dfs.ny.gov/industry_guidance/cyber_faqs.
9. Office of the Under Secretary of Defense for Acquisition & Sustainment, "CMMC FAQ's", December 10, 2020, https://www.acq.osd.mil/cmmc/faq.html.
10. U.S. Department of Health and Human Services, "Health Information Privacy", 2020, https://www.hhs.gov/hipaa/index.html.
11. U.S. Department of Health and Human Services, "HIPAA Enforcement", 2020, https://www.hhs.gov/hipaa/for-professionals/compliance-enforcement/index.html.
12. U.S. Government Publishing Office, "Content details 45 CFR 160.404-Amout of a civil money penalty", October 1, 2009, https://www.govinfo.gov/app/details/CFR-2009-title45-vol1/CFR-2009-title45-vol1-sec160-404.
13. U.S. Government Publishing Office, "Federal Register Department of Health and Human Services", January 25, 2013, https://www.govinfo.gov/content/pkg/FR-2013-01-25/pdf/2013-01073.pdf.
14. Pribanic & Pribanic, "Willful Negligence legal definition", 2019, https://pribanic.com/legal-glossary/willful-negligence-legal-definition/.
15. Legal Information Institute, Cornell Law School, "42 U.S. code 1320d-6—Wrongful disclosure of individually identifiable health information", 2020, https://www.law.cornell.edu/uscode/text/42/1320d-6.
16. U.S. Department of Justice, "Scope of criminal enforcement under 42 U.S.C. 130d-6, MEMORANDUM OPINION FOR THE GENERAL COUNSEL DEPARTMENT OF HEALTH AND HUMAN SERVICES AND THE SENIOR COUNSEL TO THE DEPUTY ATTORNEY GENERAL", June 1, 2005, https://www.justice.gov/sites/default/files/olc/opinions/attachments/2014/11/17/hipaa_final.htm.
17. Kim Stanger, Holland & Hart, "Complying with HIPAA: A checklist for business associates", October 26, 2015, https://www.hollandhart.com/showpublication.aspx?Show=26343.
18. Phil Weiser, Colorado Attorney General, "Consumer protection", 2019, https://coag.gov/office-sections/consumer-protection/.
19. Federal Trade Commission, "Gramm-Leach-Bliley Act", July 2, 2002, https://www.ftc.gov/tips-advice/business-center/privacy-and-security/gramm-leach-bliley-act.

THE WAY FORWARD

Most organizations are still tactically approaching cybersecurity issues from a technology perspective only. This is not just limiting, it is dangerous.

Professor Ariel Evans, CEO Cyber Innovative Technologies

Conclusion

Most organizations are now starting to understand how much cyber plays into their business risk. However, most organizations are still tactically approaching the issues from an IT point of view. This is not just limiting, it is dangerous. Thinking that you have outsourced your risk to a vendor, or cloud service is a fallacy. My next two books will take these topics head on from the business perspective.

Moreover, leaning solely on the IT team will only delay the inevitable. Unfortunately, many firms are still waiting for that big cyber breach to force them to understand cybersecurity from a business perspective and become proactive about their digital risk programs. This approach is like forcing a kid to drink their vitamin D fortified milk after they get rickets, instead of eating a balanced diet of meat, fish, and eggs that would have prevented the disease in the first place. Similarly, firms will be forced to start dealing with cyber and will take years to catch up to those with an effective cyber strategy. This is a competitive disadvantage.

Companies compete to be the first to the market with new technologies that will provide them first mover advantage, lower costs, and higher profits. However, in the race to be first, security is usually an afterthought. This is slowly starting to change. In Israel, most Fortune 2000 companies have an Innovation lab. This is forward thinking since Israel is both the cyber and startup nation, allowing companies to couple innovation and cyber together. The promise of innovation is vast, and the cyber risks are equally as vast.

In this Textbook, we have outlined the importance of using the digital asset approach in cyber risk management as a strategic imperative to prepare for the new innovations that will automate our lives and save us money and time. The digital asset methodology supports cyber risk management that uses AI to implement virtual patching and other novel cyber automated functions. Other innovations like Blockchain and IoT are increasing the attack surface. In these cases, the digital asset approach can be used to quantify the risk from the technology perspective. Having a digital asset approach will allow for defensible metrics that evolve with technology risks. Let's see what's coming in the next few years.

Innovation: autonomous economies and supply chain risk

In Dr. Yoav's Intrator's research "The Autonomous Economy: It's Sooner Than You Think,"[1], he asks you to "imagine a US-based health food chain that signs a contract with a Chinese tofu manufacturer, but this time the orchestration of the Design-Bid-Manufacture-Deliver process is fully automated and executed by using an autonomous contract. The intelligent orchestration and monitoring components start fairly early-on in the bidding process and continue into the manufacturing process, the packaging of the tofu, and eventually its delivery to a health food warehouse. The business processes used in this scenario are likely to include financing, insurance, payments, order management, bill of lading, product identification, product verification, quality assurance, and exceptions handling."

All these business processes use the latest technologies including IoT, Blockchain, and AI and are owned by multiple partners including the manufacturer, delivery company, insurance company, shipping company, air conditioning device manufacturer, etc.

As we have seen over and over, cybersecurity and regulation lag behind technology. Now I ask you to imagine a world where the security elements related to these technology innovations are baked in and not bolted on. Today's cybersecurity for the most part is bolted on as an afterthought.

Autonomous economies are interdependent. There is a direct relationship between the cybersecurity of the firm and supply chain partners. Over the past few years, we saw regulation catching up to technology in this respect. The SEC guidance of February 2018, California IoT Data Security Act, GDPR, and NYS Financial Services Part 500 all dictate that a cyber risk assessment must be done for the organization and the third-party supply chain. The issue here is there needs to be a firm understanding of the vendor technology, which digital assets they impact to understand the context of cybersecurity from the business perceptive.

IoT and digital asset cyber risk

The Internet of Things is an interconnected array of physical devices, including vehicles, home appliances, and corporate and government infrastructure. It is a combination of mechanical and electrical technology that includes electronics, software, sensors, actuators, and software which enables these Internet of Things to connect, collect, and exchange data.

IoT is a technology and therefore, a digital asset. We will see another vast explosion in IoT leading to autonomous solutions that drive efficiency. Most of the components of this technology do not have security built in. It is predicted that over 200 billion IoT devices will be in place by 2020.

If IoT products even have security, it is often using old and unpatched operating systems and software that are embedded in the device. Most times there is not even a way to change the default passwords on smart devices. A best practice with IoT security would be to have it on a network with restricted access. As with any network traffic, it should then be monitored.

Just now, we are starting to see cybersecurity point solutions designed for IoT. There will be a need for protecting and securing the network which connects the IoT devices to the back-end.

California recently enacted the California IoT Security Law. It is the first IoT law in the nation that requires all "connected devices" sold or offered for sale in California to have "reasonable security measures." Specifically, if a connected device is equipped with a means for authentication outside a local area network, to be deemed a "reasonable security" measure, the feature must meet one of the following requirements:

- the preprogrammed password is unique to each device manufactured; or
- the device contains a security feature that requires a user to generate a new means of authentication before access is granted to the device for the first time.

The digital asset approach inventories all technologies and can identify the assets in scope and provide for a security assessment related to these requirements.

Blockchain: trust by design

A blockchain is a digital distributed ledger that is available for all parties to see, providing transparency across the chain. The primary applications are in Initial Coin Offerings (ICOs), insurance, and supply chain management. Talk today is not so much about what security Blockchain needs as the fact that the ledger is immutable. Today, Blockchain is more of a mechanism to establish business trust than it is a security solution. As an example, Blockchain is being used across voting platforms, diamond sales, and in pharma to combat fraud. In general, Blockchains store data using sophisticated algorithms and innovative software rules that are extremely difficult for attackers to manipulate. However, no technology is 100% safe. Even the best-designed Blockchain systems can have security issues.

Why is Blockchain inherently more secure in principle? Let us look at how Bitcoin works as an example. Bitcoin's shared data is built into how each Bitcoin transaction is recorded in the ledger. The way it works is that a series of nodes owned by miners stores the ledger entry. This uses a consensus model that performs multiple calculations by different users to verify the validity of the transaction. When someone submits a transaction to the ledger, the nodes check to make sure the transaction is valid. A subset of them compete to package valid transactions into "blocks" and add them to a chain of previous ones. There is a cryptographic fingerprint unique to each block that makes it tamper proof.

The security element in Blockchain is the cryptographic fingerprint which is a hash. It provides proof that the miner who added the block to the Blockchain did the computational work. This is known as a "proof-of-work" protocol. Like with all hashes, altering the block would require generating a new hash. It is easy to verify if the block matches the hash. Additionally, all the nodes will update their respective copies of the Blockchain with the new block. This is one example of the consensus part of the Blockchain.

The hashes also serve as the links in the Blockchain where each block includes the previous block's unique hash. Changing an entry here, requires that a new hash must be calculated for that block and every previous block.

The idea of immutable comes from this aspect of that technology. Not only would you have to change all the blocks in the entire chain, but you would also have to do this faster than the other nodes can add new blocks to the chain.

So, then how can a hacker take advantage of this? Nodes on the Blockchain must remain in constant contact in order to compare data and validate transactions. An eclipse attack can happen when an attacker manages to take control of a node's communications and spoofs it where it accepts false data that appears to come from the rest of the miners. This results in confirming fake transactions.

The same types of access control issues for other systems exist for Blockchains. Blockchains will also use software clients and third-party applications that may be insecure. Hackers can break into where the cryptographic keys are stored. This is an issue primarily for online cryptocurrency exchanges. The issue is that most exchanges storage devices are not disconnected from the internet.

Some Blockchains can support smart contracts. A smart contract is a program that facilitates a process flow between multiple parties. It is code based. It is therefore as vulnerable as any other software-based solution.

In the world of smart contracts, a recent Blockchain attack on Ethereum's blockchain resulted in exploiting the code on a blockchain-based investment fund, the Decentralized Autonomous Organization (DAO), resulted in 3.6 million ether, worth around 80 million US$ at the time, being stolen. The fix involved the Ethereum community using a software upgrade called a "hard fork" to get the money back. A hard fork is achieved by a conscious of the DAO community. It was semi-successful in terms of some of the money being returned.

There is much talk about Blockchain's decentralized security model and how real it is. A recent study found that the top four bitcoin-mining operations had more than 53 percent of the system's average mining capacity per week and three Ethereum miners accounted for 61%. This is hardly decentralized. Additionally, there are miner pools that are predominately from China. The West has a fear of a scenario where the Chinese government or a government sponsored organization may take control in this case. At this time, this is more of a perception and not necessarily an issue. The Chinese government does not recognize cryptocurrencies as a medium of exchange as of this writing.

The proof of work consensus model where the 51% rule applies was theoretical and is still theoretical in the bitcoin network, however, the 51% rule was exploited with new cryptocurrencies that had a small number of miners.

What this means for security folks is technology solutions that utilize blockchain as the basis for cryptocurrency or smart contracts have much to think about. Point solutions will be needed for access management, monitoring, event management, and of course risk management.

Blockchains work on a permission-less or permission-based infrastructure. Most corporations that are interested in business-to-business usage are likely to adopt permission based. This allows them to use a proprietary network (similar to segmented network) that is trusted for business partners. This has the same security issues we see with PCI segmented networks. Digital asset risk assessments can be done at the technology and system level to assure appropriate security controls are in place.

AI: the promise of automated risk reduction

Artificial intelligence (AI) is the simulation of human intelligence processes by computers. These processes include learning, reasoning, and self-correction. Learning is the acquisition of information and rules for using that information. Reasoning is using rules to reach information related to that data. Self-correction is the ability to correct without human intervention.

Most solutions involve "supervised learning," which requires users to label data sets that algorithms are trained on. An example would be tagging code that's malware and code that is clean. Access control mechanisms are critical to ensure that hackers do not get access to a security firm's systems. It would be child's play for them to manipulate the machine learning capabilities, impacting data integrity by switching labels so that some malware examples are tagged as clean code.

AI's promise is that it will replace human manual analysis with machines that enable computers to learn and adapt through experience. In a world that is already 5 million workers deficient in cyber this is good news. Use of AI could include anticipating future cyberattacks by using predictive analytics. Innovation in this area is already underway, however, it is immature. Too much reliance on this immature technology could create a false sense of security. This technology is also available to hackers. The downside of AI is that hackers can use it to create automated and sophisticated social engineering cyberattacks. Hackers can use AI to figure out normal user behavior patterns; mimic that behavior and wait patiently until the attacker decides to exploit the AI.

AI learning will evolve and adapt over time. It is nearly impossible to keep up with the newest malware using traditional cybersecurity methods. In order to evolve in cybersecurity, we need to look for technologies that can automate the analysis (just like with cyber risk) required in all aspects of cybersecurity. This includes the ability to identify new malware as quickly and efficiently as possible. AI may be used to automatically identify potentially malicious behavior in near real time, allowing for organizations to adopt a continuously adaptive defense mechanism to identify and quarantine malware faster and easier than ever before. The use of AI may empower security operations analysts to optimize the use of their time and lower the average dwell time from hundreds of days to hours.

In cyber risk management, organizations can start using AI to decrease the amount of manual efforts required to identify system data quality, automatically kick off remediation based on data and the analysis required based on digital asset information. By tying triggers to cyber risk thresholds, AI can be used to preform virtual patching and a host of non-human interactions.

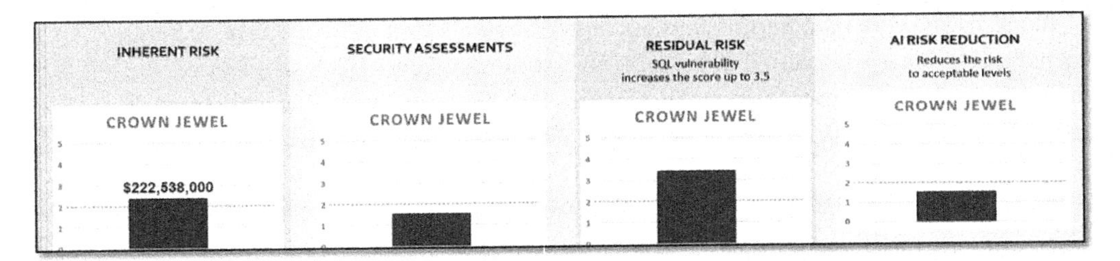

Figure 1 Using AI with Digital Asset Cyber Risk Management[2]

Quantum computing: how cybersecurity needs to change

Today, computers have memories that are made up of bits. A bit is represented by either a one or a zero. A quantum computer uses qubits. Each qubit can represent a one, and a zero at the same time, and can have superposition of those qubit states, meaning that it can calculate and process multiple states in parallel.

Once quantum computing is a reality, legacy encryption solutions will be vulnerable to brute force attacks. This type of technology in the hands of rogue governments will result in challenges to all of our current cyber security programs. The challenges will be primarily in the access control and encryption domains. There is an urgent need to start to design quantum proof or quantum ready cybersecurity solutions before we leap into the quantum era.

Quantum computers can break current public key encryption. The risk of quantum code breaking is so pressing that the US National Institute of Standards and Technology (NIST) has launched a process to develop the next generation of cryptography.[3]

Blockchain and cryptocurrencies are usually built on public key encryption. Quantum computers put these systems at risk. There is a push to work on the next generation of quantum-safe cryptocurrency wallets and blockchains from several vendors.

Mindhunter: the digital asset approach for innovative cyber risk

John Douglas in his book *Mindhunter* reveals how, as an FBI profiler, he understood he had to get into the mind of the serial killer to anticipate how they would pick their prey. It boiled down to what attracted them and how vulnerable they were. We in cyber must get into the mind of the cyber-criminal to understand how an attacker also identifies the most attractive payoff and that weakest link. The biggest loss is the crown jewel assets. Once we know what they are we can look at how weak the links are that protect them and understand their risk.

The digital asset approach allows us to quantify the loss exposures inherently as explained in Chapter 22 and to use the security assessments and residual risk metrics (Chapters 23 and 24) to understand how these innovative technologies will impact cyber risk. Risk assessments at the level of the technology need to be done to understand how well the security controls are in place. The same type of assessments we do that look at access controls, audit, encryption, identification of vulnerabilities, etc., can be used specifically for IoT, Blockchain, and AI technologies.

IoT, Blockchain, and AI cyber risk analytics

To start, one must identify which systems utilize IoT, Blockchain, and AI technology. When we obtain a digital asset inventory this is clearly identified for each organization. IoT is the most used of the innovative technologies we highlight in this chapter. We use IoT devices today in smart metering, smart homes, and other applications. Security assessments for IoT can provide data into how well the security controls of the IoT devices are in place. This data is used to demonstrate when risk will rise above the threshold. Once we understand the IoT risk, we can apply resources to reduce risk down to acceptable levels based on the metrics as we do for any cyber risk.

Critical thought leaders are preparing to and dealing with cyber risk effectively in a manner that puts them in front of the threats and will continue to evolve their programs to do things better. We are just at the beginning of starting to understand how cyber is more of a business issue than simply an IT one. Developments in technology will continue to foster an atmosphere of innovation and new automated cyber risk management solutions will propel us into an era where what was once complex, and overwhelming is now operationally simpler to manage.

May you continue your journey in this unending drama and may this Textbook provide you useful tools, thinking and strategy to tackle this most urgent business need. Sooner than later your organization and partners need to be addressing cyber proactively, not reactively. I hope that this volume provides you the incentive and courage to take steps that demonstrate responsible and effective ways to lead you down this path.

Notes

1. Yoav Intrator, PhD, "The autonomous economy: It's sooner than you think", Managing Director, Head of Israel Innovation and Technology Center, JPMorgan Chase, Dec 2018 and republished in 2020, https://www.jpmorgan.com/global/technology/autonomous-economy?source=cib_os_li_autonecon1218.
2. Evans, Maryellen. Digital Asset Based Cyber Risk Algorithmic Engine, Integrated Cyber Risk Methodology and Automated Cyber Risk Management System. US United States Patent and Trademark Office, 2 Apr. 2020. 2020/0106801 Al
3. The Quantum Threat to Encryption Used Today—Post-Quantum. https://post-quantum.com/the-quantum-threat/

ABBREVIATIONS

2

2FA	Two Factor Authentication

A

ABA	American Bankers Association
AI	Artificial Intelligence
AIA	Aerospace Industries Association
AICPA	American Institute of Certified Public Accountants
AIG	American International Group
AIS	Advanced Info Service
AKA	Also Known As
AMCA	American Medical Collection Agency
AOC	Attestation of Compliance
APT	Advanced Persistent Threat
ARPA	Advanced Research Projects Agency
ARPANET	The Advanced Research Projects Agency Network
ASV	Approved Scanning Vendor
ATM	Automated Teller Machine
ATP	Advanced Threat Prevention
AUAB	Advanced User and Asset Behavioral
AWS	Amazon Web Services

B

BA	British Airways
BAA	Business Associate Agreement
BCM	Business Continuity Management
BIA	Business Impact Analysis
BLS	Bureau of Labor Statistics
BoD	Board of Directors
BPM	Business Process Management

BU	Business Unit
BYOD	Bring your own device

C

CAGR	Compound Annual Growth Rate
CCPA	California Consumer Privacy Act
CD	Compact Disc
CDE	Cardholder Data Environment
CDO	Chief Digital Officer
CE	Covered Entity
CEO	Chief Executive Officer
CERT	Computer Emergency Readiness Team
CFO	Chief Financial Officer
CIA	Confidentiality, Integrity, and Availability Triad
CIO	Chief Information Officer
CIS	Computer Information Systems
CISA	Cybersecurity and Infrastructure Security Agency
CISO	Chief Information Security Officer
CIT	Cyber Innovative Technology
CMF	Content Monitoring and Filtering
CMMC	Content Monitoring and Filtering
CMMI	Capability Maturity Model Integration
COBIT	Control Objectives for Information and Related Technologies
CPA	Colorado Privacy Act
CPNI	Customer Proprietary Network Information
CPO	Chief Privacy Officer for Product
CPU	Central Processing Unit
CRM	Customer Relationship Management
CRO	Chief Risk Officer
CRO	Clinical Research Organization
CSA	Cloud Security Alliance
CSC	Corporation Service Company
CSNET	Computer Science Network
CSO	Chief Security Officer
CSP	Cloud Service Provider
CTI	Cyber Threat Intelligence
CUI	Controlled Unclassified Information
CVE	Common Vulnerability Exposure
CVV	Card Verification Value
CVSS	Common Vulnerability Scoring System

D

D&O	Directors and Officers
DBA	Database Administrator
DBIR	Data Breach Investigations Report
DDoS	Distributed Denial of Service
DEF CON	Defense Readiness Condition
DLP	Data Loss Prevention
DFARS	Defense Federal Acquisition Regulation Supplement
DHS	Department of Homeland Security
DIB	Defense Industrial Base
DLP	Data Loss Prevention
DMZ	Demilitarized Zone
DoD	Department of Defense
DOJ	Department of Justice
DoS	Denial of Service
DPA	Data Protection Authority
DPIA	Data Privacy Impact Assessment
DPO	Data Privacy Officer
DR	Disaster Recovery

E

E&O	Errors and Omissions
ECPA	Electronic Communications Privacy Act
EDPB	European Data Protection Board
EEA	European Economic Area
EHR	Electronic Health Records
EMEA	Europe, Middle East, and Africa
EMR	Electronic Medical Records
EOL	End of Life
ePHI	electronic Protected Health Information
EPS	Extrusion Prevention System
ERM	Enterprise Risk Management
EU	European Union

F

FAIR	Factor Analysis of Information Risk
FBI	United States Federal Bureau of Investigation
FCC	United States Federal Communications Commission
FedRamp	United States Federal Risk and Authorization Management Program
FFRDC	Federally Funded Research and Development Center
FISC	United States Foreign Intelligence Surveillance Act Court

FISMA	United States Federal Information Security Management Act
FTC	United States Federal Trade Commission
FTP	File Transfer Protocol
FTSE 100	Financial Times Stock Exchange 100 Index

G

GC	General Counsel
GDP	Gross Domestic Product
GDPR	General Data Protection Regulation
GL	General Liability
GLBA	Gramm-Leach-Bliley Act
GPS	Global Positioning System
GPU	General Public Use
GRC	Governance, Risk and Compliance
GUI	Graphical User Interface

H

HHS	U.S. Department of Health and Human Services
HIPAA	Health Insurance Portability and Accountability Act
HITECH	Health Information Technology for Economic and Clinical Health
HR	Human Resources
HTML	Hypertext Markup Language
HUMINT	Human Intelligence
HVAC	Heating, Ventilation, and Air Conditioning

I

IaaS	Infrastructure as a Service
IAG	International Consolidated Airlines Group S.A.
IAM	Identify and Access Management
IAPP	International Association of Privacy Professionals
IBM	International Business Machines
ICO	Information Commissioner's Office
IDS	Intrusion Detection System
IEC	International Electrotechnical Commission
IEEE	Institute of Electrical and Electronics Engineers
ILDP	Information Leak Detection and Prevention
ILP	Information Leak Prevention
INCD	Israel National Cyber Directorate
IoT	Internet of Things
IP	Intellectual Property
IPC	Information Protection and Control
IPS	Intrusion Protection Systems

ISA	Internal Security Assessor
ISACA	Information Systems Audit and Control Association
ISC	Internet Systems Consortium
ISMS	Information security management system
ISO	International Organization of Standardization
ISP	Information Security Policy
ISSAF	Information System Security Assessment Framework
IT	Information Technology
ITRM	Information Technology Risk Management

J

JPEG	Joint Photographic Experts Group
JTC	Joint Technical Committee

K

K&R	Kidnap and Ransom
KGB	Russian Committee for State Security
KPI	Key Performance Indicator

L

LAN	Local Area Network
LSE	London Stock Exchange

M

M&A	Mergers & Acquisitions
MFA	Multi-Factor Authorization
MITM	Man in the Middle
MOS	Metal-Oxide-Silicon
MSSP	Managed Security Service Provider

N

NACD	National Association of Corporate Directors
NAIC	National Association of Insurance Commissioners
NAS	National Aerospace Standard
NHS	National Health Service
NIAC	National Infrastructure Advisory Council
NIST	National Institute of Standards and Technology
NIST CSF	National Institute of Standards and Framework's Cybersecurity Framework
NPI	Nonpublic Personal Information

NSA	United States National Security Agency
NSFNET	National Science Foundation Network
NTIA	U.S. Department of Commerce National Telecommunications and Information Administration
NYCRR Part 500	New York Codes, Rules and Regulations Part 500
NYS DFS	New York State Department of Financial Services
NYSE	New York Stock Exchange

O

OCIE	Office of Compliance Inspections and Examinations
OCR	Office of Civil Rights
OFAC	U.S. Treasury Department's Office of Foreign Asset Control
OSINT	Open-Source Intelligence
OSSTMM	Open-Source Security Testing Methodology Manual
OT	Operational Technology
OUSD(A&S)	Office of the Under Secretary of Defense for Acquisition and Sustainment
OWASP	Open Web Application Security Project

P

P&L	Profit and Loss
Paas	Platform as a Service
PCI-DSS	Payment Card Industry Data Security Standard
PCI	Payment Card Industry
PCI SC	Payment Card Industry Security Council
PCI-DSS	Payment Card Industry Data Security Standard
PHI	Protected Health Information
PI	Personal Information
PIA	Privacy Impact Assessment
PII	Personal Identifiable Information
PKI	Public Key Infrastructure
PLA	Peoples Liberation Army
POS	Point of Sale
PR	Public Relations
PSAS	Post Security Assessment Score
PTES	Penetration Testing Execution Standard

Q

QA	Quality Assurance
QSA	Qualified Security Assessor

R

RACI	Responsible, Accountable, Consulted, Informed
RAM	Random Access Memory
RAT	Random Access Trojan
RDP	Remote Desktop Protocol
RMM	Resilience Management Model
ROC	Report on Compliance
ROI	Return on Investment
ROLF	Reputational, Operational, Legal, and Financial Risk
RRTO	Ransomware Recovery Time Objective
RSA	Rivest-Shamir-Adleman
RTO	Recovery Time Objective

S

S&P	Standard & Poor's
SA	Supervisory Authority
SaaS	Software as a Service
SANS Institute	Sysadmin, Audit, Network, and Security Institute
SAP	Systems, Applications, and Products
SAQ	Self-Assessment Questionnaire
SCSP	Server Cache Synchronization Protocol
SEC	Securities and Exchange Commission
SIEM	Security Information and Event Management
SIM	Cyber Simulation
SLA	Service Level Agreement
SMB	Small and Medium Business
SME	Subject Matter Expert
SMS	Short Message Service
SOC	Security Operations Center
SOCMINT	Social Media Intelligence
SoD	Separation of Duties
SQL	Structured Query Language
SSAE	Standards for Attestation Engagements
SSL	Secure Socket Layer
STEM	Science, Technology, Engineering, and Math

T

TCP/IP	Transmission Control Protocol/Internet Protocol
TEU	Twenty-Foot Equivalent Unit

TLS	Transport Layer Security
TBPS	terabit-per-second
TPSP	Third-Party Service Provider
TRIA	Terrorism Risk Insurance Act

U

UARC	University Affiliated Research Center
UMG	Universal Music Group
USB	Universal Serial Bus

V

VCRM	Vendor Cyber Risk Manager
VDI	Virtual Desktop Interface
VM	Virtual Machine
VMS	Vulnerability Management System
VoIP	Voice over Internet Protocol
VPN	Virtual Private Network

W

WAF	Web Application Firewall
WFH	Work From Home
WISP	Written Information Security Program
WLAN	Wireless Local Area Network

GLOSSARY

A

Actuarial Pricing Actuarial pricing is the discipline that applies mathematical and statistical methods to assess risk and price policies in insurance, finance, and other industries and professions.

Advanced Threat Prevention (ATP) Advanced Threat Prevention is a cybersecurity tool that identifies malware, quarantines it, and allow it to be analyzed and identified in and between organizations.

Advanced Persistent Threat An adversary with sophisticated skills and resources that provide it opportunities to achieve its goals using multiple attack vectors (cyber, deception, physical, and malware.)

Alert A notification that detects an incident, vulnerability, or finding.

Annual Revenue Annual Revenue is the amount of yearly income of an organization before taxes.

Antivirus Software A program that monitors the network to detect malicious code and to prevent malware insertion.

Assumption of Breach Assumption of breach is a model that dictates that you have been breached and will be breached again. It was defined by Robert Mueller at the RSA security conference in 2013.

Attack An Attack is an assault perpetrated by a threat source that attempts to exfiltrate data, interruption processes, or alter data or system operations.

Authentication Verifying the identity of a user, process, or device.

Authorization The ability to determine if a user has the right to create, read, update, or delete specific data.

Availability Availability is ability to ensure the data is available to users.

B

Board of Directors Board of Directors in a public company, a board of directors (BoD) is a group of individuals, elected to represent the shareholders. A board's mandate is to establish policies for corporate management and oversight, make decisions on major company issues including cybersecurity. Every public company must have a board of directors.

Botnet A collection of computers compromised by malicious code and controlled across a network.

Bug An unexpected defect in a system or device.

Business Continuity Management (BCM) Business Continuity Management is the process of creating systems of prevention and recovery to deal with potential threats to a company.

Business Interruption Business Interruption is when business as usual is interrupted when the authorized users cannot access an application. In cyber, it is typically a result of a denial-of-service attack.

Business Process Business Process is a set of digital rules that are utilized by one or more systems to take inputs, transform them, and produce outputs that are reported or utilized by other systems.

C

Category Domains In risk modeling, Category Domains are subsets of data that can be allocated into further categorization.

Chief Information Security Officer (CISO) Chief Information Security Officer (CISO) is a senior-level executive within an organization responsible for establishing and maintaining the enterprise vision, strategy, and cybersecurity program to ensure digital assets are adequately protected. There are two types of CISOs: governance and operational. Most companies only have one person who is doing the job of three people. A governance CISO is the individual responsible for the policies, management, and monitoring of cyber risk. The operational CISO is the individual responsible for the day-to-day cybersecurity operations that includes implementation of tools, process and the management of the incident response and security teams. Both work with the board, compliance manager, auditors, etc. Approximately 50% of large organizations have a CISO.

Cloud Computing Cloud Computing provides on-demand work access to a shared pool of computing capabilities or resources that can be provisioned rapidly with minimal management effort.

Capability Maturity Model Integration (CMMI) Capability Maturity Model Integration. Impact and likelihood information can be obtained doing a questionnaire that uses the CMMI as the basis for the answer ratings, which was developed at Carnegie Mellon University (CMU). CMMI is used in terms of process level improvement training and appraisal programs. CMMI defines the following maturity levels for processes: Initial, Managed, Defined, Quantitatively Managed, and Optimizing.

Compliance Manager or Officer A Compliance Manager or Officer is an employee whose responsibilities include ensuring the company complies with its outside regulatory requirements and internal policies. A compliance officer may craft and update internal policies to mitigate the risk of the company breaking laws and regulations and lead internal audits of procedures. In cyber, there are many regulations based on type of data processed, geography, and industry that a compliance manager must be familiar with.

Confidentiality Confidentiality is the ability to ensure that only authorized and approved users have access to the data.

Common Vulnerability Exposure (CVE) Common Vulnerability Exposure (CVE) is a database of vulnerabilities published by NIST. The Common Vulnerability Exposure (CVE) system provides a reference method for publicly known information-security vulnerabilities and exposures. The National Cybersecurity Federally Funded Research and Development Center (FRDC), operated by the Mitre Corporation, maintains the system, with funding from the National Cybersecurity Division of the United States Department of Homeland Security. The Security Content Automation Protocol that uses CVE, and CVE IDs are listed on MITRE's system as well as in the US National Vulnerability Database.

Control Assessment Control Assessment is a security assessment that uses policies, and control tests to ascertain the level of effectiveness of a cybersecurity control both organizationally and technically.

Critical Infrastructure Critical Infrastructure represents the digital assets that are instrumental for society to function without a debilitating impact on the security, economy, health, safety, or environment.

Cybersecurity Cybersecurity is a program of activities that utilize people, process, and tools to protect the information systems of an organization.

Cybersecurity Posture Cybersecurity Posture refers to the maturity and effectiveness of the various cybersecurity control measures.

Cyber Budget Cyber Budgets are a combination of fixed and variable costs and delineated by capital and operational expenses. The cyber budget should be aligned to the fixed operational costs (the security team personnel) and the capital fixed costs (the tools and their licensing costs) and the variable costs. The variable costs are the real-time incidents, findings, and vulnerabilities that need to be fixed.

Cybergeddon A term defined by the author to indicate the worst-case scenario of inherent risks analysis in terms of zero percent effectiveness of controls of an organization.

Cyber Insurance Cyber Insurance is a risk transference mechanism to reduce risk in terms of business interruption, data exfiltration, and regulatory losses due to cyber-attacks.

Cyber Legal Team Cyber Legal Team is the legal team that will be involved in cyber when a breach occurs. Most likely all communications will be run by legal before they are released to the media or a regulator. The communications team usually crafts any breach notifications with the CISO and legal collaborating together.

Cyber Resiliency Cyber Resiliency is a measure of an entity's ability to continuously deliver the intended outcome despite adverse cyber events. It can be used to benchmark and define organizations goals in terms of cybersecurity.

Cyber Risk Cyber Risk is the risk at the digital asset level; system, process, technology, and data that can have reputational, organizational, legal, and/or financial impacts. It is the cornerstone of measuring cyber resiliency.

Cybersecurity Cybersecurity is the body of technologies, processes, and practices designed to protect networks, computers, programs and data from attack, and damage or unauthorized access.

Cyber Simulation (SIM) Cyber Simulation (SIM) is an automated approach to more effectively train Cybersecurity Operations (SOC) teams to adequately respond to evolving threats.

Cyber Threat Cyber Threat is a malicious attempt to damage or disrupt a computer network or system.

Cyber Threat Intelligence (CTI) Cyber Threat Intelligence (CTI) is a cybersecurity tool that works in the deep and dark web to identify hackers and track their malicious activities. CTI provides detailed information about potential or current attacks that threaten an organization.

D

Data Data is the information that is processed and stored. Data can be classified into different types including privacy, credit card, intellectual property, customer data, supply chain data, etc.

Data Breach Data Breach is the unauthorized movement or disclosure of information.

Data Exfiltration Data Exfiltration is when data is stolen by cyber criminals. This can be due to many causes including and not limited to misconfigured systems, poor access controls, from insiders or external actors. Specifically, it is the unauthorized copying, transfer, or retrieval of data from a computer or server. Data exfiltration is a malicious activity performed through various different techniques, typically by cybercriminals over the Internet or other networks.

Data Loss Data Loss can happen due to theft, deletion, or misplacement of data.

Data Loss Prevention (DLP) Data Loss Prevention (DLP) is a cybersecurity tool that provides rules to identify when data is accessed by authorized users and sent outside the organization and add additional rules to prevent unauthorized data leakage. Found mostly in large organizations and those with privacy issues.

Data Privacy Officer (DPO) Data Privacy Officer (DPO) is a senior-level executive within an organization responsible for data privacy. The DPO must ensure that the organization complies with GDPR regulation if it processes EU citizen privacy data regardless of where it is located. The DPO must have a deep knowledge of the GDPR and an awareness where possible regulatory breaches may occur. It is essential that the DPO effectively communicates the company's privacy principles and compliance regulations to employees and reports into the board usually.

Data Type Data Type is the classification of data processed. This can be one or more types including but not limited to privacy, personally identifiable (PII), patent, formula, healthcare, federal, business, credit card, etc.

Detect Detect is the third of the five NIST functions. The Detect Function defines the appropriate activities to identify the occurrence of a cybersecurity event. The Detect Function enables timely discovery of cybersecurity events.

Digital Asset Digital Asset refers to the systems, business processes, technologies, and data type that are used as of basis of automation of work using computer technology.

Disaster Recovery (DR) DR is a discipline to recover from a disaster using a redefined plan that has been tested and is ready to execute.

Distributed Denial of Service (DDOS) Distributed Denial of Service (DDOS) happens when a cyber-offender takes action that prevents legitimate users from accessing targeted computer systems, devices, or other network resources.

Domain In cyber risk modeling, domain is a specific set of data. In this invention, it is related to the cyber risk engine. However, other domains can be created.

E

Encryption Encryption is a process used in cybersecurity that provides scrambling of data in such a way that only authorized parties can access it.

Enterprise Risk Management Enterprise Risk Management is a business program that combines risk management disciplines across several genres, such as operational, credit, cyber, etc.

Event An event is a suspicious occurrence that may be an indication that an incident is occurring.

Exposure Exposure is a condition where the system is unprotected, and an attacker can obtain access to the system or network.

F

Financial Cyber Impacts Financial Cyber Impacts are defined in three categories: data exfiltration, business interruption, and regulatory loss and are aligned to what cyber insurance companies will pay out claims against.

Finding A finding is a result of a control assessment.

Firewalls Firewalls are a cybersecurity tool that that prevents unauthorized access to or from a private network. This a basic cybersecurity tool and most SMEs will also have firewalls.

G

GDPR GDPR is the General Data Protection Regulation that came into effect May 25, 2018 that protects EU citizen privacy data.

H

Hacker A hacker is an unauthorized user who attempts to gain access to a digital asset.

I

Identify Identify is the first of the five NIST functions. The Identify Function assists in developing an organizational understanding to managing cybersecurity risk to systems, people, assets, data, and capabilities. Understanding the business context, the resources that support critical functions, and the related cybersecurity risks enables an organization to focus and prioritize its efforts, consistent with its risk management strategy and business needs.

Identity Access Management (IAM) Identity Access Management (IAM) is a cybersecurity tool that provides authorization and authentication of users to systems.

Impact Impact is the degree to which a cyber-issue may have an adverse outcome on the organization. There are several factors that can influence impact in cybersecurity.

Incident An incident is an occurrence that may result in a loss or adverse consequence to the digital asset.

Incident Response Refers to cybersecurity remediation work where an incident is confirmed, and resources respond to mitigate and repair the damage to the digital assets.

Inherent Cyber Risk Inherent Cyber Risk is the cyber risk without controls in place or as if there was zero percent effectiveness of cybersecurity controls. It is the worst-case scenario and is also called "cybergeddon" risk.

Innovation Innovation is the act or process of introducing new ideas, devices, or methods.

Interconnectivity The term that defines the electronic connections between businesses, systems, processes, vendors, suppliers, governments, and the like.

Insured Insured is a first- or third-party organization that has purchased cybersecurity insurance to transfer risk and increase cyber resiliency.

Integrity Integrity is the ability to ensure that the data is unaltered and is consistent, accurate, and trustworthy over its entire life cycle.

Intrusion Detection System (IDS) Intrusion Detection System (IDS) is a cybersecurity tool that monitors systems for malicious activity or policy violations.

International Standards Organization (ISO) ISO is the International Standards Organization. It publishes the ISO/IEC 27001, which is an information security standard, part of the ISO/IEC 27000 family of standards. ISO/IEC 27001 specifies a management system that is intended to bring information security under management control and gives specific requirements. Organizations that meet the requirements may be certified by an accredited certification body following successful completion of an audit.

IT Auditors IT Auditors are responsible for developing, planning, and executing IT audit programs based on risk assessments in a highly integrated audit environment. This includes documenting and communicating risks, providing counsel on control issues and recommended process changes, and monitoring corrective actions in order to improve the existing practices of the organization reducing cyber risk.

L

Likelihood Likelihood is a probability a cyber-attack will cause damage.

M

Malware Malware is software that is intended to damage or disable computers and computer systems.

Mergers and Acquisitions (M&A) Mergers and Acquisitions (M&A) is the area of corporate finance, management, and strategy that deals with purchasing and/or joining with other companies. In a merger, two organizations join forces to become a new business, usually with a new name. In terms of digital assets, not all digital assets will be acquired or utilized in the merger or acquisition.

Mitigation Mitigation is the use of measures to reduce the likelihood of risk or implementing risk reduction controls based on the impacts.

N

National Institute of Standards and Technology (NIST) NIST is the National Institute of Standards and Technology, a unit of the U.S. Commerce Department. The NIST Cybersecurity Framework (CSF) is a set of 98 control tests that provides a policy framework of computer security guidance for how private sector organizations in the United States can assess and improve their ability to prevent, detect, and respond to cyber-attacks.

New York State (NYS) Part 500 regulation New York State (NYS) Part 500 regulation is a regulation establishing cybersecurity requirements for financial services companies.

O

Operational Risk Operational risk is the prospect of loss resulting from inadequate or failed procedures, systems or policies.

P

Payment Industry Data Security Standard (PCI-DSS) PCI-DSS is the Payment Industry Data Security Standard. It applies to banks, merchants and data processors that process credit card data.

Penetration Testing Penetration testing is a method that searches for vulnerabilities and attempts to circumvent the security features of the system.

Phishing Phishing is the fraudulent practice of sending emails purporting to be from reputable individuals in companies in order to induce users to reveal personal information, such as passwords and credit card numbers.

Physical Security Physical Security are controls for physical access to the organization. These controls are locks, cameras, doors, fire suppression systems, personnel identification (badges), visitor security, etc. All organizations usually have some level of physical security. More mature organizations have electronic means.

Privacy Privacy is related to the confidentiality and integrity of data.

Process Revenue Process Revenue is the amount of revenue based on the use of a particular process.

Protect Protect is the second of the five NIST functions. The Protect Function outlines appropriate safeguards to ensure delivery of critical infrastructure services. The Protect Function supports the ability to limit or contain the impact of a potential cybersecurity event.

Q

Qualitative Qualitative data is information about qualities; information that can't actually be measured from a subjective viewpoint.

Quantitative Quantitative Research is used to quantify the problem by way of generating numerical data or data that can be transformed into usable statistics. It is objective in nature.

R

Recover Recover is the fifth of the five NIST functions. The Recover Function identifies appropriate activities to maintain plans for resilience and to restore any capabilities or services that were impaired due to a cybersecurity incident. The Recover Function supports timely recovery to normal operations to reduce the impact from a cybersecurity incident.

Regulatory Loss Regulatory Loss happens when a regulator fines an organization for a cyber-breach. The costs of the fines are defined by the regulator(s).

Regulatory Risk Regulatory risk is defined as risk of having privileges withdrawn by a regulator, or having conditions applied by a regulator that adversely impact the economic value of an enterprise.

Reputational Risk In cyber, reputational risk is a matter of corporate trust. The loss can be demonstrated in lost revenue; increased operating, capital or regulatory costs, or destruction of shareholder value.

Residual Cyber Risk Residual Cyber Risk is the cyber risk with controls in place. It is the best-case scenario.

Respond Respond is the fourth of the five NIST functions. The Respond Function includes appropriate activities to act regarding a detected cybersecurity incident. The Respond Function supports the ability to contain the impact of a potential cybersecurity incident.

Resources Resources are an operational or capital item. Operational resources are personnel and capital resources are equipment.

Risk Accumulation Risk Accumulation or Amplification is the aggregation of losses from a single event due to the concentration of cyber risk exposed to that single event. In cyber risk, this is based on the digital assets. Some examples are cloud compromise and data exfiltration.

Risk Amplification Risk Amplification is the aggregation of financial losses from a cyber event due to reputational, operational, or legal impacts.

Risk Calculation In risk modeling, Risk Calculation is a mathematical determination of the risk exposures.

Risk Names In risk modeling, Risk Names are measurable exposures that use algorithms to express their value.

Risk Parameters In risk modeling, Risk Parameters are specific numerical or other measurable factors forming one of a set that defines a digital asset risk or sets the conditions of its operation.

Risk Qualifications In risk modeling, Risk Qualifications are calculations that use subjective data from the business.

Risk Quantifications In risk modeling, Risk Quantifications are calculations that use objective financial metrics that are derived metrics of the business and cyber related metrics derived from metric-based organizations.

Risk Questionnaire In risk modeling, is a set of questions that are used for qualitative risk metrics,

S

Security and Exchange Commission (SEC) The Securities and Exchange Commission is a US governmental agency that oversees securities transactions, the activities of financial professionals and mutual fund trading to prevent fraud.

Security Control Measures Security Control Measures refers to the means taken by organizations to identify, protect, detect, recover, or respond to cybersecurity. This includes people, process, and tools.

Security Incident Event Management (SIEM) Security Incident Event Management (SIEM), is a cybersecurity tool that provides real-time analysis of security alerts generated by applications and network hardware to identify brute force, viruses, and firewall attacks. This is a more sophisticated tool and large organizations have SIEM, however, managed security service providers (MSSPs) provide this type of service to smaller companies.

System System is a consolidated set of technologies that provides the basis for collecting, creating, storing, processing, and distributing information.

T

Tabletop Exercise A discussion-based exercise where resources meet and work through a scenario to validate plans, procedures, policies in regard to an incident.

Technology Technology is computer-related components that typically consist of hardware and software, databases, messaging, and devices.

Threat Actor Threat Actor is an entity that is partially or wholly responsible for an incident that impacts—or has the potential to impact—an organization's cybersecurity. In threat intelligence, actors are generally categorized as external, internal, or partners.

V

Vendors Vendors are the third parties that provide goods or services to an organization.

Vendor Cyber Risk The measurement of cyber risk that a third party possesses in relationships to digital assets of the first party.

Vendor Cyber Risk Management Vendor Cyber Risk Management (VCRM) is the measurement and management of cyber risk that deals with third-party products (such as cloud service providers) and services (system integrators, management consultants, and the big 4) and the digital assets they provide or work with.

Verizon Data Breach Report (VRR) The VRR is annual security report from Verizon that provides vast statistics on data breach information.

Vulnerability A vulnerability is a weakness in a system which can be exploited by a threat actor, such as an attacker, to perform unauthorized actions within a computer system. This weakness can be exploited to gain unauthorized access into a computer system leading to data exfiltration or data corruption. Vulnerabilities increase risk. Poor coding practices (i.e. storing passwords in code) can be a large source of vulnerabilities.

Vulnerability Management System (VMS) A Vulnerability Management System is a cybersecurity tool that uses software in a cyclical manner to identify and classify vulnerabilities. VMS vendors include Qualys, Rapid7, Tripwire, Saint, Tenable, Core Security, Critical Watch, Beyond Security, and many others.

W

Weights In cyber risk, Weight refers to the probability weighting that is used for percent complete metrics and maturity weighting and is used to define which parameters are more important than others.

Willful Neglect In cybersecurity, Willful Neglect means conscious, intentional failure, or reckless indifference to the obligation to comply with cybersecurity measures.

INDEX

Note: Locators in *italics* represent figures.